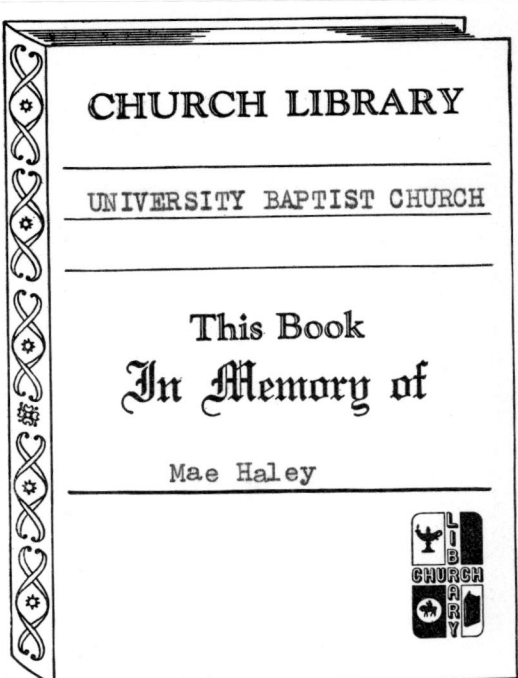

THE NEW TESTAMENT

*A Private Translation
in the Language of the People*

By

CHARLES B. WILLIAMS

CHICAGO

MOODY PRESS

1960

Copyright, 1937, by
BRUCE HUMPHRIES, INC.
COPYRIGHT ASSIGNED, 1949,
to
THE MOODY BIBLE INSTITUTE
of Chicago

Printed in the United States of America

PUBLISHERS' PREFACE

In the minds of many exacting Greek scholars this is the best translation of the New Testament existing in the English language today. Yet, it is not scholarly at the expense of readability. Instead, it will be found to be especially useful for devotional reading in the family circle as well as for private Bible study. This translation is so lucid that anyone can understand the message, and yet it manifests such genuine scholarship that the most exacting scholar can revel in it. It is unique in its copious and illuminating notes on problem passages.

Many evangelical Christians have wished for a modern, easy-reading translation prepared by a scholar who believes, as they do, that the entire Bible is the Word of God. The publishers are happy to be able to present this volume in answer to that long-felt need. Although there is undoubtedly value in any translation by a competent scholar, there is special value in the reader's knowing that the author is thoroughly acquainted both with the text and also with the spirit of the text.

We find two extremes among private translators. Some have been exactingly literal, translating the Greek almost word for word, by-passing the thought that translation is a carrying over of ideas rather than words. As Arthur Way points out in giving his translation of Paul's Epistles and Hebrews, the Authorized and Revised Versions have done just that, thereby serving not one age, but succeeding ages in avoiding paraphrases and explanatory notes that would be limited to a certain time or people. Highest praise is given to both versions for that ageless service. Others have been excessively idiomatic, or unduly free with their use of paraphrase, even to the extent of adding words, phrases, and sentences to aid in clarifying the meaning of the

PUBLISHERS' PREFACE

text. In the present volume the translator seeks to avoid these extremes. He adheres faithfully to the sense of the Greek, as well as rendering it into language easily understood by the average reader.

But the most significant contribution in this translation, and the sphere in which it surpasses the majority of others, is in its bringing out the revealing tense distinctions in the Greek verbs. A good example of this is the translation of the future perfect passive tense in Matthew 16:19 and 18:18. Dr. Williams has rendered these verbs correctly, "Whatever you forbid on earth must be what is already forbidden in heaven."

Attempting to convey accurately the thought of the Greek, rather than to translate its single words, Dr. Williams has added explanatory notes at the beginning of each book, and footnotes, to further clarify the meaning.

Although the publishers do not concur with every rendering in this translation, they are grateful for the opportunity of presenting it to fellow Christians around the world.

FOREWORD

Recently we celebrated the four-hundredth anniversary of the publication of the entire English Bible by Miles Coverdale, the Oxford scholar who first translated the whole Bible into English. The year 1936 was the four-hundredth anniversary of the strangling and burning of William Tyndale, who was condemned to death for translating the New Testament into English and for seeking to put it into the hands of the plain people. In these four centuries scores of other translations have been made. Then why make another? someone asks. A distinguished Bible scholar answers, "Language is a fluid thing. It does not remain fixed for a day. There is therefore constant need of retranslation."

Our aim in publishing this new translation is that of Tyndale, "to cause the plowboy to know the Scriptures." Our aim is to make this greatest book in the world readable and understandable by the plain people. Only three books in the New Testament are written in anything like good literary Greek—Luke, the Acts, and Hebrews. In our translation of these books we have tried to use good, smooth English. Elsewhere we use simple everyday English which reproduces the everyday Greek which the writers used. In accord with this aim we have used practical everyday words to replace many technical religious and theological terms. In other words, we have tried to use the words and phrases that are understandable by the farmer and the fisherman, by the carpenter and the cowboy, by the cobbler and the cab-driver, by the merchant and the miner, by the milkmaid and the housemistress, by the woodcutter and the trucker. If these can understand it, it is certain that the scholar, the teacher, the minister, the lawyer, the doctor, and all others can.

This is not a word-for-word translation, like an interlinear. It

FOREWORD

is rather a translation of the thought of the writers with a reproduction of their diction and style. Greek idioms are not brought over into our translation, but are expressed in corresponding English idioms which express the same thoughts as the Greek idioms. It is the thoughts of our New Testament, not its single words, that we have tried to translate.

Our translation is based on the Westcott and Hort Greek text, recognized as the authoritative text throughout the English speaking world. When there are conflicting variations in the Greek Manuscripts, we have generally followed the Vatican Manuscript, which is the oldest and usually conceded the best.

To introduce the readers to each book we have inserted at the beginning of each a brief statement as to who wrote it, why, and for what purpose. At the foot of the page are added suggestive notes to explain difficult passages and to make clearer many historical, social, and religious references.

May the face of the Christ, who is the Theme of this book and the Light of the world, shine into the heart and upon the life of everyone who reads it!

CHARLES B. WILLIAMS

INTRODUCTION

I think that the translation of the New Testament by Dr. C. B. Williams is one of the best English translations in existence. This translation gives the most accurate rendering of the Greek text of any translation with which I am acquainted. At the same time it maintains a good modern English style and contains many pungent English expressions which fittingly represent the original. I am pleased that the Moody Press has made it possible for Bible readers the world over to possess this most excellent translation which long ago deserved much more recognition and a much wider circulation than it received.

> EDWARD A. MCDOWELL
> *New Testament Interpretation*
> *The Southern Baptist Theological Seminary*
> *Louisville, Kentucky*

Dr. C. B. Williams received his Ph.D. degree from Chicago University, having majored in Greek New Testament, after which he taught ministers Greek for many years. By training and experience he is well equipped to translate the New Testament.

The style of each individual writer is reproduced in the various books. For example, John uses vernacular and Luke literary *koine* Greek, and the rest of the writers come in between.

Dr. Williams has also brought out clearly John's meaning in I John 3:8 and 9 by indicating the progressive action implied in the Greek present tense: "Whoever practices sin belongs to the devil . . . No one born of God makes a practice of sinning."

INTRODUCTION

While teaching a post-graduate Greek class and spending the whole year studying translations of the New Testament, we became convinced that Williams' translation, considering all the factors, is the most accurate and illuminating translation in the English language. Having this conviction, I have no hesitation in commending it to all who desire to penetrate into the depths of the riches of the glorious revelation in the New Testament.

> J. R. MANTEY
> *Department of New Testament Interpretation*
> *Northern Baptist Theological Seminary*
> *Chicago, Illinois*

The work of translating the New Testament from the original Greek into our language is no small task. Not only does it require a detailed knowledge of the vocabulary and grammar of ancient *koine* Greek, but also the faculty of conveying ideas into good, clear English idiom. In his handling of the Greek text the translator must be fair, accurate, and, although in many instances must act in the role of interpreter, he must not permit subjective opinion to have the upper hand.

Williams does what few others have done: he takes some of the finer shades of meaning found in the Greek constructions and fuses them into the English text. This he does, not in a cumbersome, overwrought manner, but in a natural, smooth-flowing style. More than any other translator he brings out the *aktionsart* (kind of action) of the verbs, an element little stressed in standard versions. Besides this there is clear evidence of the results of latest research into the fuller significance of certain words, cases, prepositions, connectives, and other parts of speech.

As with other private translations, this volume is not intended to replace the use of our commonly employed standard versions, but rather to be used as an auxiliary. It will be found to be well adapted to devotional reading in the family circle as well as a valuable aid in private Bible study.

> JOHN MOSTERT
> *Moody Bible Institute*
> *Chicago, Illinois*

TABLE OF CONTENTS

MATTHEW	11
MARK	80
LUKE	125
JOHN	201
THE ACTS OF THE APOSTLES	257
ROMANS	329
FIRST CORINTHIANS	369
SECOND CORINTHIANS	392
GALATIANS	413
EPHESIANS	427
PHILIPPIANS	435
COLOSSIANS	443
FIRST THESSALONIANS	450
SECOND THESSALONIANS	457
FIRST TIMOTHY	461
SECOND TIMOTHY	470
TITUS	476
PHILEMON	480
HEBREWS	482
JAMES	506
FIRST PETER	515
SECOND PETER	525
FIRST JOHN	531
SECOND JOHN	537
THIRD JOHN	539
JUDE	543
THE REVELATION	545

KEY TO FOOTNOTES

abl. ablative; ablatival
ac. action
acc. accusative
acct. account
adj. adjective
adv. adverb; adverbial
advan. advantage
Am. Amos
ans. answer
aor. aorist
art. article
Ara. Aramaic
AV Authorized Version

cf. compare; confer
Chn. Christian
cog. cognate
comp. compare; compound
con. condition; construction
concess. concessive
conclu. conclusion
cond. condition; conditional
conj. conjunction
constr. construction
cont. continued; continue

dat. dative
Dt. Deuteronomy
dif. different

EGT Expositor's Greek Testament
emph. emphatic
Eng. English

fem. feminine
ff. following
fol. following
f.n. footnote
fr. from
fut. future

gen. general; genitive
gov. governor
Grk. Greek

Heb. Hebrew
histor. historical

impf. imperfect
impv. imperative
incep. inceptive
incip. incipient
ind. indicative
inf. infinitive
infin. infinitive
ingress. ingressive

Int. St. Bib. Ency. International Standard Bible Encyclopedia
interrog. interrogative
instru. instrumental

Kg. Kings

Lex. Lexicon
lit. literally

I Mac. I Maccabees
masc. masculine
mid. middle
M. and M. Vocab. Moulton and Milligan Vocabulary
Mod. modern
Ms. (s) manuscript (s)

nec. necessary
neg. negative
neut. neuter
nom. nominative
Nu. Numbers

obj. objective; object
om. omitted
orig. original
O.T. Old Testament

part. participle
pass. passive
pf. perfect
phys. physical
pl. plural
pred. predicate
prep. preposition
pres. present
pro. (s) pronoun (s)
pt. participle

recip. reciprocal
rel. relative
Rom. Roman

sec. second
Sept. Septuagint
sg. singular
Sin. Sinaitic
subj. subjective
subjunc. subjunctive

tr. translation

v. verse
Vat. Vatican
vb. verb
vocab. vocabulary
vs. versus

WH Wescott and Hort Text

MATTHEW

The commonly accepted view is that Matthew the apostle wrote our First Gospel. He especially records the sayings of Jesus—parables, maxims, and addresses; is intensely Jewish, and yet he breathes the spirit of the universal message of Jesus. He wrote to prove that Jesus is the Messiah promised in the Old Testament Scriptures, and that the good news which He brings is for "all the nations."

The readers, likely Jewish Christians in Syria, are suffering persecution and its bitter distresses. It was written about A.D. 67.

1   JESUS' FAMILY TREE, BIRTH, AND NAME

The family tree of Jesus Christ, a descendant of David, a descendant of Abraham.

2 Abraham was the father of [a] Isaac, Isaac the father of Jacob, Jacob the father of Judah and his brothers, 3 Judah the father of Perez and Zerah, whose mother was Tamar; Perez the father of Hezron, Hezron the father of Aram, 4 Aram the father of Aminadab, Aminadab the father of Nahshon, Nahshon the father of Salmon, 5 Salmon the father of Boaz, whose mother was [b] Rahab; Boaz the father of Obed, whose mother was Ruth; Obed the father of Jesse, 6 Jesse the father of King David.

David was the father of Solomon, whose mother had been Uriah's wife; 7 Solomon the father of Rehoboam, Rehoboam the father of Abijah, Abijah the father of Asa, 8 Asa the father of Jehoshaphat, Jehoshaphat the father of Joram, Joram the father of Uzziah, 9 Uzziah the father of Jotham, Jotham the father of Ahaz, Ahaz the father of Hezekiah, 10 Hezekiah the father of Manasseh, Manasseh the father of Amon, Amon the father of Josiah, 11 Josiah the father of Jechoniah and his brothers, at the time of the Babylonian Exile.[c]

---

[a] Lit., *begot*, but *he was the father of* expresses it more elegantly.
[b] Exact meaning in Eng. of the Grk. phrase.
[c] Grk., *the removal to B.*

¹² After the Babylonian Exile Jechoniah became the father of Shealtiel,ᵈ Shealtiel the father of Zerubbabel, ¹³ Zerubbabel the father of Abiud, Abiud the father of Eliakim, Eliakim the father of Azor, ¹⁴ Azor the father of Sadoc, Sadoc the father of Achim, Achim the father of Eliud, ¹⁵ Eliud the father of Eliazar, Eliazar the father of Matthan, Matthan the father of Jacob, ¹⁶ Jacob the father of Joseph, the husband of Mary, who was the mother of Jesus who is called the Christ.

¹⁷ So all the generations from Abraham to David are fourteen, from David to the Babylonian Exile fourteen, from the Babylonian Exile to Christ fourteen.ᵉ

¹⁸ Now the birth of Christ Jesus occurred under these conditions: After His mother, Mary, was engaged to Joseph, but before they had lived together, she was found to be an expectant mother through the influence of the Holy Spirit.ᶠ ¹⁹ But her husband, Joseph, because he was an upright man and did not want to disgrace her, decided to break the engagement by secretly divorcing her.ᵍ

²⁰ But just asʰ this thought occurred to him, an angel of the Lord appeared to him in a dream, and said, "Joseph, descendant of David, do not fear to take Mary as your wife, for it is through the influence of the Holy Spirit that she has become an expectant mother. ²¹ And she will have a son, and you mustⁱ name Him Jesus, for it is He who is to save His people from their sins."

²² Now all this occurred to fulfill what the Lord had said through the prophet:

²³ "The virgin will become pregnant and have a son,
And they will call Him Immanuel"—ʲ

which means "God with us." ²⁴ So when Joseph awoke from his sleep, he did as the angel of the Lord directed him, and tookᵏ her as his wife; ²⁵ but he did not live with her as a husband until she had had a son; and he named Him Jesus.

ᵈ Or, Salathiel.
ᵉ Fol. Ms. B., regarded the best.
ᶠ Lit., *from* or *out of*.
ᵍ According to Jewish law engagement could be properly broken only by divorce.
ʰ Suggested by aor.
ⁱ Impv. fut. indic.
ʲ Isa. 7:14.
ᵏ Grk., *to his side*.

2 — STARGAZERS COME TO WORSHIP THE BABY KING; KING HEROD, DISTURBED, SLAUGHTERS ALL THE BOY BABIES; JOSEPH FLEES TO EGYPT TO SAVE THE BABY JESUS; BACK AT NAZARETH

Now when Jesus was born at Bethlehem in Judea in the days of King Herod, stargazers [a] came from the East to Jerusalem ² and asked, "Where is He that is born King of the Jews? We saw His star when it rose [b] and have come to worship Him."

³ Now when King Herod heard of it, he was disturbed, and all Jerusalem with him. ⁴ So he called together all the high priests and scribes of the people, and anxiously [c] asked them where the Christ was to be born. ⁵ They told him, "At Bethlehem in Judea, for this is what the prophet wrote: [d]

⁶ 'And you, Bethlehem in Judah's land,
You are not at all the least among the leading places of Judah;
For out of you will come a ruler,
Who will shepherd my people Israel.'"

⁷ Then Herod secretly sent for the stargazers, and found out from them exactly the time the star appeared. ⁸ So he sent them to Bethlehem with this order, "Go and carefully search for the child, and when you find Him, bring back word to me, that I too may come and do Him homage."

⁹ After listening to the king, they started on their journey, and the star which they had seen rise led them on until it came and stopped over the place where the child was. ¹⁰ When they saw the star, they were thrilled with ecstatic joy, [e] ¹¹ and went into the house and saw the child with His mother, Mary; and they fell at His feet and worshiped [f] Him. They opened up their treasure sacks and presented Him with gifts of gold, frankincense, and myrrh. ¹² Then, as they had been divinely warned in a dream not to return to Herod, they set out to their own country by another route.

¹³ After they had gone, an angel of the Lord appeared to Joseph in a dream and said, "Wake up! Tenderly take the child and His mother, and escape to Egypt; stay [g] there until I further direct

---

[a] This is, students of stars in relation to events on earth.
[b] Lit., *in rising*.
[c] Impf. of cont. action expressing the King's anxiety.
[d] Mic. 5:2.
[e] Exact meaning of the striking Grk. idiom.
[f] Same word used by Herod above in sense of doing homage; here, *worship*.
[g] Grk., *be there*.

UNIVERSITY BAPTIST LIBRARY

you, for Herod is going to search for the child to destroy Him."

[14] Then he awoke and tenderly took the child and His mother by night and made their escape to Egypt; [15] he stayed there until Herod's death, so as to fulfill what the Lord had said by the prophet,[h] "Out of Egypt I called my Son."

[16] Then Herod, because he saw that a trick had been played on him by the stargazers, was very angry, and sent and slaughtered all the boy babies in Bethlehem and in all that neighborhood, from two years down, in accordance with the time which he had found out from the stargazers. [17] Then the saying was fulfilled which was spoken by the prophet Jeremiah:[i]

[18] "A sob was heard in Ramah,
Weeping and great wailing,
Rachel weeping for her children,
And she refused to be comforted, because they were gone."

[19] But after Herod died, an angel of the Lord in a dream appeared to Joseph in Egypt, [20] and said, "Wake up, tenderly take the child and His mother, and make the trip[j] to the land of Israel, for those who sought the child's life are dead."

[21] Then he awoke, tenderly took the child and His mother, and made the trip to the land of Israel. [22] But because he heard that Archelaus was ruling over Judea in the place of his father, Herod, he was afraid to go there; and because he was divinely warned in a dream, he set out for the region of Galilee. [23] He went to a town called Nazareth and made his home[k] there, so that the saying of the prophet was fulfilled:

"He shall be called a Nazarene."[l]

3 JOHN PREACHES REPENTANCE AND BAPTIZES PEOPLE WHO CONFESS THEIR SINS; JESUS IS BAPTIZED AND HEAVEN ENDORSES HIM AS THE CHRIST

In those days John the Baptist appeared, and kept preaching in the desert of Judea, [2] and saying, "Repent! for the kingdom of heaven is near."

[h] Hos. 11:1.
[i] Jer. 31:15.
[j] Pres. impv. of cont. action gives this meaning.
[k] This vb. means *to dwell permanently;* so, *to make it his home.*
[l] See Isa. 11:1, not for the words but for a suggestion of the thought.

MATTHEW 3

This is he who was mentioned by the prophet Isaiah,[a] when he said:

"Here is a voice of one who shouts in the desert,
'Get the road ready for the Lord;
Make the paths straight for him.'"

4 This very John had his clothing made of camel's hair, and wore a leather belt around his waist; his food was dried locusts and wild honey.

5 Then Jerusalem and all Judea, even the whole Jordan district, continued to go out to him 6 and were baptized by him in the Jordan River, as one by one they continued to confess their sins. 7 But when he saw many of the Pharisees and Sadducees coming for baptism, he said to them, "You brood of vipers, who warned you to escape from the wrath that is coming? 8 Produce, then, fruit [b] that is consistent with the repentance you profess, 9 and do not presume to say to yourselves, 'We have Abraham for our forefather!' for I tell you, God can raise up descendants for Abraham even out of these stones. 10 Now the axe is already lying at the roots of the trees. Every tree then that fails to bear good fruit is to be cut down and thrown into the fire.11 I am baptizing you in water to picture your repentance.[c] But He that is coming after me is stronger than I am, and I am not fit to carry His shoes. He will baptize you in the Holy Spirit and in fire; 12 His winnowing-fork is in His hand, and He will clean out His threshing-floor and store His wheat in His barn, but He will burn up the chaff with fire that never can be put out."

13 Then Jesus came from Galilee to the Jordan to John to be baptized by him. 14 But John tried [d] to prevent Him by saying, "I have need to be baptized by you, and you come to me!"

15 But Jesus answered him, "Let it be so now, for this is the fitting way for both of us to do our full duty to God." [e]

Then he yielded to Him.16 And as soon as Jesus was baptized, He at once went up out of the water, and look! the heavens opened, and John saw the Spirit of God coming down like a dove upon Him,17 and a voice from heaven said, "This is my Son, my Beloved, in whom I am delighted!"

---

[a] 40:3.
[b] That is, *do deeds,* etc.
[c] That is, *to picture your turning from sin to a new life.*
[d] Impf. of attempted action.
[e] Grk., *to fulfill all righteousness.*

4 JESUS TEMPTED BY THE DEVIL; MAKES CAPERNAUM HEADQUARTERS; CALLS FOUR FISHERMEN TO HIS SERVICE

Then Jesus was guided by the Spirit into the desert, to be tempted by the devil. [2] After fasting forty days and forty nights, He at last felt hungry. [3] And the tempter came up and said to Him, "If you are God's Son, order these stones to turn to bread."

[4] But He answered, "The Scripture says,[a] 'Not on bread alone can man live, but on every word that comes from the mouth of God.'"

[5] Then the devil took Him into the holy city, and had Him stand on the tip-top turret [b] of the temple, [6] and said to Him, "If you are God's Son, throw yourself down, for the Scripture says: [c]

"'He will give His angels directions about you,
And they will bear you up on their hands,
So you will never strike your foot against a stone.'"

[7] Jesus said to him, "Again the Scripture says,[d] 'You must not try the Lord your God.'"

[8] Again the devil took Him up on a very high mountain, and showed Him all the kingdoms of the world, and their splendor, [9] and said to Him, "Every bit of this I will give to you, if you will fall on your knees and worship me."

[10] Then Jesus said to him, "Begone, Satan! For the Scripture says,[e] 'You must worship the Lord your God, and serve Him alone.'"

[11] Then the devil left Him, and angels came and continued to wait upon Him.

[12] Now when Jesus heard that John had been arrested, He set out for Galilee. [13] But He left Nazareth and made His home in Capernaum, by the sea, in the district of Zebulon and Naphtali, [14] to fulfill what was spoken by the prophet Isaiah: [f]

[15] "Land of Zebulon and land of Naphtali
On the road to the sea, across the Jordan,
Galilee of the nations;

---

[a] Dt. 8:3.
[b] Grk., *little wing,* the highest point.
[c] Ps. 91:11, 12.
[d] Dt. 6:16.
[e] Dt. 6:13.
[f] Isa. 9:1, 2.

MATTHEW 5

¹⁶ The people that were living in darkness
Have seen a great light,
And on those that were living in the land of the shadow of death
A light has dawned."

¹⁷ From that time Jesus continued to preach and say, "Repent! for the kingdom of heaven is near."

¹⁸ As He was walking by the shore of the sea of Galilee, He saw two brothers, Simon who was surnamed Peter, and his brother Andrew, casting a net into the sea, for they were fishermen. ¹⁹ He said to them, "Come! [g] Follow me, and I will make you fishermen for catching men." [h]

²⁰ And at once they left the nets and followed Him. ²¹ And as He was going on from that point, He saw two others, brothers, James, the son of Zebedee, and his brother John, in the boat with their father Zebedee, getting their nets in order; and He called them. ²² And at once they left the boat and their father, and followed Him.

²³ Then He went all over Galilee, as He continued teaching in their synagogues, preaching the good news [i] of the kingdom, and curing any disease or malady among the people. ²⁴ So the news [j] about Him [k] spread all over Syria, and people brought to Him all who were sick with various diseases, especially those who were suffering with torturing diseases; and he cured them.²⁵ So great crowds followed Him, from Galilee and Decapolis,[l] from Jerusalem and Judea, and from the other side of the Jordan.

5 THE ADDRESS ON THE MOUNT

When He saw the crowds, He went up on the mountain. After He had taken His seat, His disciples came up to Him. ² Then He opened His mouth and continued to teach them as follows: [a]

³ "Blessed are those who feel poor in spiritual things, for the kingdom of heaven belongs to them.

⁴ "Blessed are the mourners, for they will be comforted.

---

[g] Grk., *Here!* etc., an interjection, not an impv.
[h] Obj. gen. vb. implied.
[i] Exact tr. of Greek noun, and impressive in Eng.
[j] Grk., *things heard, report;* so, *news.*
[k] Obj. gen.
[l] Grk., *Ten Cities*—a district east of Jordan comprising ten towns, united for commerce, etc.
[a] Grk., *saying.*

5 "Blessed are the lowly in mind, for they will possess the land.

6 "Blessed are those who hunger and thirst for being and doing right, for they will be completely [b] satisfied.

7 "Blessed are those who show mercy, for they will have mercy shown them.

8 "Blessed are the pure in heart, for they will see God.

9 "Blessed are the peacemakers, for they will be called God's sons.

10 "Blessed are those who suffer persecution for being and doing right, for the kingdom of heaven belongs to them.

11 "Blessed are you when people abuse you, and persecute you, and keep on [c] falsely telling all sorts of evil against you for my sake. 12 Keep on rejoicing and leaping for ecstasy,[d] for your reward will be rich in heaven; for this is the way [e] they persecuted the prophets who lived before you.

13 "You are the salt of the earth. But if salt loses its strength, what can make it salt again? It is good for nothing but to be thrown away and trodden under foot. 14 You are the light of the world. A city that is built upon a hill cannot be hidden. 15 People do not light a lamp and put it under a peck-measure [f] but on a lampstand, and it gives light to all that are in the house. 16 Let your light shine before people in such a way that they may see your good deeds, and praise your Father in heaven.

17 "Do not suppose that I have come to set aside the law or the prophets. 18 I have not come to set them aside but to fill them up to the brim.[g] For I solemnly say to you, heaven and earth would sooner [h] pass away than the dotting of an 'i' [i] or the crossing of a 't' [i] from the law, until it all becomes in force. 19 Whoever, therefore, breaks one of the least of these commands and teaches others so to do, will be ranked as least in the kingdom of heaven; but whoever practices them and teaches others so to do, will be ranked as great in the kingdom of heaven. 20 For I tell you that unless your righteousness far surpasses that of the scribes and Pharisees, you will never get into the kingdom of heaven at all.

[b] Grk., *gorged,* as a calf on clover.
[c] Pres. of cont. action.
[d] Exact meaning of Greek verb.
[e] Grk., *thus, in this way.*
[f] About the size of a grain-measure in Palestine.
[g] Picture of O. T. teaching as an unfilled cup, but filled by Jesus.
[h] Grk., *until heaven,* etc.
[i] In Grk., the smallest letter of the Hebrew alphabet, or horn (curve) of a letter, equivalent to our dotting of an *i* or crossing of a *t.*

MATTHEW 5

²¹ "You have heard that it was said to the men of old, 'You must not murder,' and 'Whoever murders will have to answer to the court.' ²² But I say to you:

"Everyone who harbors malice ʲ against his brother, will have to answer to the court, and whoever speaks contemptuously to his brother, will have to answer to the supreme court; ᵏ and whoever says to his brother, 'You cursed ˡ fool!' will have to pay the penalty in the pit of torture. ²³ So if, in the very act of presenting your gift at the altar, you remember that your brother has something against you, ²⁴ leave your gift right there at the altar, and first go and make peace with your brother, and then come back and present your gift. ²⁵ Be quick to come to terms with your opponent while you are on the road to court with him, so that he may not turn you over to the judge and the judge turn you over to the officer, and you be put in prison. ²⁶ I solemnly say to you, you will never get out at all until you have paid the last penny.ᵐ

²⁷ "You have heard it was said, 'You must not commit adultery.' ²⁸ But I tell you that anyone who looks at a woman so as to have an evil desire ⁿ for her at once has already committed adultery with her in his heart. ²⁹ So if your right eye causes you to do wrong, pluck it out of your way; for it is better to have one part of your body suffer loss than to have your whole body go down ᵒ to the pit.ᵖ ³⁰ And if your right hand causes you to do wrong, cut it off and put it out of your way, for it is better to have one part of your body suffer loss than to have your whole body go down to the pit.

³¹ "It was also said, 'Whoever divorces his wife must ᵍ give her a certificate of divorce.' ³² But I tell you that whoever divorces his wife for any other ground than unfaithfulness,ʳ causes her to commit adultery, and whoever marries a wife who is thus divorced commits adultery.

³³ "Again, you have heard that it was said to the men of old,

---

ʲ Grk., cont. *to be angry*, etc.
ᵏ The Sanhedrin, Supreme Court in Jerusalem.
ˡ Stronger than preceding term of contempt.
ᵐ A very small coin, less than a cent.
ⁿ Exact meaning of Grk.
ᵒ *Be thrown.*
ᵖ Grk., *Gehenna*, a valley or pit where refuse is thrown, here the pit of future punishment.
ᵍ Grk., impv. which expresses obligation.
ʳ Grk., *fornication*, an expression of unfaithfulness: see v. 28—adultery is in the desire, as well as in the act.

'You must not swear falsely, but you must perform your oaths as a religious duty.' [s] 34 But I tell you not to swear at all, either by heaven, for it is God's throne, 35 or by the earth, for it is His footstool, or by Jerusalem, for it is the city of the Great King. 36 Never swear by your own head, for you cannot make a single hair white or black. 37 But your way of speaking must be a simple 'Yes' or 'No.' Anything beyond this comes from the evil one.

38 "You have heard that it was said, 'An eye for an eye and a tooth for a tooth.' 39 But I tell you not to resist the one who injures you; but if anyone slaps you on one cheek, turn him the other, too; 40 and if anyone wants to sue you for your shirt, let him have your coat, too. 41 And if anyone [t] forces you to go one mile, go with him two. 42 If anyone, whoever he may be, keeps on begging you, give to him; if anyone wants to borrow from you, do not turn him away.

43 "You have heard that it was said, 'You must love your neighbor and hate your enemy.' 44 But I tell you, practice loving your enemies and praying [u] for your persecutors, 45 to prove that you are sons of your Father in heaven, for He makes His sun rise on bad as well as good people, and makes the rain come down on doers of right and of wrong alike. 46 For if you practice loving only those who love you, what reward will you get? Do not even the tax-collectors [v] practice that? 47 And if you say 'Good morning' to your brothers only, what more than others are you doing? 48 So you, my followers,[w] ought to be perfect, as your heavenly Father is."

6 THE ADDRESS ON THE MOUNT CONCLUDED

"Take care not to do your good deeds in public, to attract the attention [a] of people; if you do,[b] you will get no reward from your Father in heaven.2 So whenever [c] you do your deeds of charity, never blow your own horn in public, as the hypocrites are in the habit [c] of doing in the synagogues and on the street corners, to be praised by the people. I solemnly say to you, they already have

---

[s] Grk., *for the Lord.*
[t] Relative implying a condition.
[u] Reading of two best Mss.
[v] Outcast grafters of those times.
[w] Grk. pronoun emphatic.
[a] Grk., *to be seen by men.*
[b] Grk., *otherwise.*
[c] Pres. expressing habitual action.

their reward. ³ But whenever you, a follower of mine, do a deed of charity, never let your own left hand know what your right hand is doing, ⁴ so that your deed of charity may be secret, and your Father who sees what is secret will reward you.

⁵ "Also, whenever you pray, you must ᵈ not be like the hypocrites, for they love to pray standing in the synagogues and on the street corners, to attract the attention of people. I solemnly say to you, they already have their reward. ⁶ But whenever you,ᵉ follower of mine, pray, you must go to your most private place, shut the door, and pray to your Father in secret, and your Father who sees what is secret will reward you. ⁷ And whenever you pray, you must not keep on repeating set phrases, as the heathen do, for they suppose that they will be heard in accordance with the length of their prayers. ⁸ So then you must not be like them, for your Father knows what you need before you ask Him. ⁹ So this is the way you must pray:

> Our Father in heaven,
> Your name be revered,
> ¹⁰ Your kingdom come,
> Your will be done on earth as it is done in heaven.
> ¹¹ Give us today our daily bread for the day,
> ¹² And forgive us our debts, as we ᵉ have forgiven our debtors;
> ¹³ And do not let us be subjected ᶠ to temptation,
> But save us from the evil one.

¹⁴ "For if you forgive others their shortcomings,ᵍ your heavenly Father will forgive you, too. ¹⁵ But if you do not forgive others, your heavenly Father will not forgive your shortcomings either.

¹⁶ "Also whenever you fast, you must not look gloomy like the hypocrites, for they put on a gloomy countenance, to let people see them fasting. I solemnly say to you, they already have their reward. ¹⁷ But whenever you, follower of mine, fast, perfume your head and wash your face, ¹⁸ so that your fasting may be seen, not by men but by your Father who is unseen, and your Father who sees what is secret will reward you.

ᵈ Fut. in impv. sense.
ᵉ Doubly emphatic.
ᶠ Greek, *do not bring*, etc.
ᵍ Greek, *failings* or *fallings*, so *shortcomings*.

¹⁹ "Stop [h] storing up your riches on earth where moths and rust make away with them, and where thieves break in and steal them. ²⁰ But keep on storing up your riches in heaven where moths and rust do not make away with them and where thieves do not break in and steal them. ²¹ For wherever your treasure is, there too your heart will be.

²² "The eye is the very lamp of the body. If then your eye is sound, your whole body will be full of light. ²³ But if your eye is unsound, your whole body will be full of darkness.[i] If then the very source of light [j] in you is darkness, how dense is that darkness! ²⁴ No one can be a slave to two masters, for either he will hate one and love the other, or else he will be devoted to one and despise the other. You cannot be slaves of God and money. ²⁵ So I tell you, stop worrying about your life, as to what you will have to eat or drink, or about your body, as to what you will have to wear. Is not life worth more than food and the body worth [k] more than clothes? ²⁶ Take a good look at [l] the wild birds, for they do not sow or reap, or store up food in barns, and yet your heavenly Father keeps on feeding them. Are you not worth [k] more than they? ²⁷ But which of you by worrying can add a single minute [m] to his life? ²⁸ And why should you worry about clothes? Look at the wild lilies and learn [n] how they grow. They do not toil or spin; ²⁹ but I tell you, not even Solomon, in all his gorgeous splendor, was ever dressed up like a single one of these. ³⁰ Now if God so gorgeously dresses the wild grass which today is green but tomorrow is tossed into the furnace, will He not much more surely clothe you, O you with little faith? ³¹ So never worry and say, 'What are we going to have to eat? What are we going to have to drink? What are we going to have to wear?' ³² For the heathen are greedily pursuing all such things; and surely your heavenly Father well knows [o] that you need them all. ³³ But as your first duty keep on [p] looking for His standard of doing right,[q] and for

---

[h] Pres. impv. with negative means *stop*.
[i] So Thayer.
[j] Grk., *the light that is in you*.
[k] Grk., *more than*, but idea of value in it.
[l] Compound verb of perfective action.
[m] The word means *size* or *time;* here *time*.
[n] Compound verb, *to learn by looking*.
[o] Verb is in emphatic position.
[p] Pres. impv. of cont. action.
[q] Following the Vatican Ms. which omits the word *God* and transposes the nouns.

His will,[r] and then all these things will be yours besides. ³⁴ So never worry about tomorrow, for tomorrow will have worries of its own. Each day has evil enough of its own."

7 THE ADDRESS ON THE MOUNT CONCLUDED

"Stop [a] criticizing others, so that you may not be criticized yourselves. ² For exactly as you criticize others, you will be criticized, and in accordance with the measure that you give to others, it will be measured back to you. ³ Why do you keep watching the tiny speck in your brother's eye, but pay no attention to the girder [b] in your own? ⁴ How can you say to your brother, 'Let me get that tiny speck out of your eye,' while all the time there is a girder in your own? ⁵ You hypocrite, first get the girder out of your own eye, and then you can see well enough [c] to get the tiny speck out of your brother's eye.

⁶ "You must never [d] give the things that are sacred to dogs, and you must never throw your pearls before hogs, for fear they might trample them under their feet and turn and tear you in pieces.

⁷ "Keep on [e] asking, and the gift will be given you; keep on seeking, and you will find; keep on knocking, and the door will open to you. ⁸ For everyone who keeps on asking, receives, and everyone who keeps on seeking, finds, and to the one who keeps on knocking, the door will open. ⁹ What human father among you, when his son asks him for bread, will give him a stone? ¹⁰ Or if he asks for a fish, will he give him a snake? ¹¹ So if you, in spite [f] of your being bad, know how to give your children what is good, how much more surely will your heavenly Father give what is good to those who keep on asking Him? ¹² Then you must practice dealing with others as you would like for them to deal with you; for this is the summing up of the law and the prophets.

---

[r] Greek, *His righteousness*—so *His way of doing right; His kingdom*—so *His will.*
[a] Meaning of pres. impv. with neg.
[b] A large piece of lumber on which a house is built.
[c] Prep. denotes completeness.
[d] Force of aor. subjunctive in a prohibition.
[e] Force of pres. impv.
[f] Concessive pt.

[13] "Go in by the narrow gate; for broad and roomy is the road that leads to destruction, and many are going in by it. [14] But narrow is the gate and hard is the road that leads to life, and few are they that find it.

[15] "Look out for false prophets, who come to you under the guise [g] of sheep, but inside they are devouring wolves. [16] You must recognize [h] them by their fruits. People do not pick grapes from thornbushes or figs from thistles, do they? [17] So any healthy tree bears good fruit and a sickly tree bears poor fruit. [18] A healthy tree cannot bear poor fruit, and a sickly tree cannot bear good fruit. [19] Any tree that does not bear good fruit is cut down and burned up. [20] So you must[h] recognize them by their fruits. [21] Not everyone who says to me, 'Lord, Lord,' will get into the kingdom of heaven, but only those who practice [i] doing the will of my Father in heaven. [22] Many will say to me on that day, 'Lord, Lord, was it not in your name that we prophesied, and in your name that we drove out demons, and in your name that we did many wonder-works?' [23] And then I will say to them openly, 'I never knew you at all.[j] Go away from me, you who practiced doing wrong.' "

[24] "So everyone who listens to my words and practices their teaching,[k] will be like a prudent man who built his house on a rocky foundation. [25] And the rain fell, and the rivers rose, and the winds blew and beat against that house, but [l] it did not fall, for its pillars had been laid on a rocky foundation. [26] And anyone who listens to my words and does not practice their teaching, will be like an imprudent man who built his house on sand. [27] And the rain fell, and the rivers rose, and the wind blew and beat against that house, and it collapsed, and the wreck of it was complete."

[28] When Jesus had closed this address,[m] the result was [n] that the crowds were dumfounded at His teaching, [29] for He was teaching them as one who had authority to teach, and not as their scribes did.

[g] Grk., *in the clothes of,* etc.
[h] Fut. indic. in impv. sense; so in v. 16.
[i] Present has this force here.
[j] Strong neg.
[k] Grk., *practices them;* that is, *their teaching.*
[l] Grk., *and,* like Hebrew conjunction, sometimes *but.*
[m] Grk., *these words.*
[n] Grk., *it came to pass that,* etc.

8 A LEPER CURED; A ROMAN CAPTAIN'S GREAT FAITH INCITES JESUS' WONDER; SEVERAL SICK PEOPLE CURED—PETER'S MOTHER-IN-LAW, TWO INSANE MEN, AND OTHERS

When He came down from the mountain, great crowds followed Him. ² And a leper came up to Him, and prostrated himself before Him, and said, "Lord, if you choose to, you can cure me."

³ Then He put out His hand and touched him, and said, "I do choose to; be cured." And at once his leprosy was cured. ⁴ Then Jesus said to him, "See that you tell nobody, but go, show yourself to the priest, and, to testify [a] to the people, make the offering that Moses prescribed."

⁵ When He got back to Capernaum, a Roman military captain came up to Him and kept begging Him, ⁶ "Lord, my servant-boy is at home bed-ridden [b] with paralysis and suffering terrible tortures!"

⁷ He said to him, "I will come and cure him."

⁸ But the captain answered, "I am not fit for you to come under my roof, but simply speak the word, and my servant-boy will be cured. ⁹ For I, too, am under authority of others, and have soldiers under me, and I order this one to go, and he goes, another to come, and he comes, my slave-boy to do this, and he does it."

¹⁰ When Jesus heard it, He was astounded, and said to His followers, "I solemnly say to you, I have not found, in a single case among the Jews,[c] so great faith as this. ¹¹ I tell you, many will come from the east and from the west and take their seats at the feast [d] with Abraham and Isaac and Jacob, in the kingdom of heaven, ¹² while [e] the heirs [f] of the kingdom will be turned out into the darkness outside, where they [g] will be weeping and grinding their teeth."

¹³ Then Jesus said to the captain, "Go; it must [h] be done for you as you have believed." And his servant-boy was cured that very hour.

---

[a] Grk., *for a testimony*.
[b] Grk., pf. has this force.
[c] Grk., *in Israel*.
[d] *Feast* implied in the messianic idea.
[e] Grk., *and*.
[f] Grk., *sons*, so *heirs*.
[g] Grk., *there will be*.
[h] Grk., impv. implies this guaranty.

¹⁴ When He went into Peter's house, He saw his mother-in-law lying in bed sick with fever. ¹⁵ He touched her hand, the fever left her, and she got up and began[i] to wait on Him.

¹⁶ When evening had come, they brought to Him many who were under the power of demons,[j] and at a mere word He drove the spirits out, and cured all who were sick, ¹⁷ and so fulfilled what was spoken by Isaiah the prophet,[k] "He took our sicknesses and bore away our diseases."

¹⁸ Now Jesus, because He saw a crowd about Him, gave orders to cross to the other side. ¹⁹ And a scribe came up and said to Him, "Teacher, I will follow you wherever you may go."

²⁰ And Jesus said to him, "Foxes have holes, even wild birds have roosts, but the Son of Man has nowhere to lay His head."

²¹ Another of His disciples said to Him, "Lord, let me first go back and bury my father."

²² And Jesus said to him, "Follow me, and leave the dead to bury their own dead."

²³ And He got into a boat, and His disciples went with Him.[l] ²⁴ And suddenly a furious storm came up, so that the boat was being covered over by the bursting billows,[m] but He kept on sleeping. ²⁵ So they went to Him and woke Him up, and said, "Lord, save us; we are going down!"[n]

²⁶ And He said to them, "Why are you afraid, O you with little faith?"

Then He got up and rebuked the winds and the sea, and there was a great calm. ²⁷ And the men were dumfounded, and said, "What sort of man is this, for even the winds and the sea obey Him!"

²⁸ When He reached the other side, in the district of Gadara, there faced Him two men, who were under the power of demons, who were just coming out from the tombs. They were such terrors that nobody could pass that way. ²⁹ And they suddenly screamed, "What do you want of us, you Son of God? Have you come here before the appointed time to torture us?"

³⁰ Now there was not far from there a large drove of hogs

---

[i] Impf. of incipient action.
[j] Grk., *demonized.*
[k] Isa. 53:4.
[l] Grk., *followed Him.*
[m] The verb suggests bursting billows.
[n] A boatman's phrase.

feeding. ³¹ And the demons kept begging Him and saying, "If you are going to drive us out, send us into the drove of hogs."

³² And He said to them, "Begone!"

And they went out of the men and got into the hogs, and suddenly the whole drove, in a stampede,º rushed over the cliff into the sea, and died in the water. ³³ And the men who fed them fled, and went off to the town, and told it all, and what occurred to the two men who were under the power of demons. ³⁴ And suddenly all the town turned out ᵖ to meet Jesus, and as soon as they saw Him, they begged Him to move on ᑫ and leave their neighborhood.ʳ

9
A PARALYZED MAN CURED; MATTHEW THE TAX-COLLECTOR, CONVERTED, GIVES JESUS A BANQUET; TWO SHORT STORIES ABOUT FASTING; A WOMAN WITH A HEMORRHAGE CURED; JAIRUS' DAUGHTER RAISED TO LIFE; TWO BLIND MEN CURED

And He got into a boat and crossed to the other side, and went into His home ᵃ town. ² And all at once ᵇ some men were bringing to Him a paralyzed man, lying on a couch. And because ᶜ He saw their faith, Jesus said to the paralyzed man, "Cheer up, my child, your sins are forgiven."

³ Then some of the scribes said to themselves, "He is a blasphemer."

⁴ And Jesus knew their thoughts, and said, "Why do you have such wicked thoughts in your hearts? ⁵ For which is easier, to say 'Your sins are forgiven,' or, to say 'Get up and go to walking'? ⁶ But to show ᵈ you that the Son of Man has authority ᵉ to forgive sins on earth"—turning to the paralyzed man, He said to him—"Get up, pick up your bed, and go home." ᶠ

⁷ And he got up and went home. ⁸ And the crowds saw it, and were stricken with awe, and gave praise to God for giving such power ᵉ to men.

º Implied in the verb *rush*.
ᵖ Grk., *went out*.
ᑫ Implied in verb.
ʳ Grk., *regions*.
ᵃ Grk., *His own town;* i.e., Capernaum.
ᵇ Grk., *behold*.
ᶜ Pt. of cause.
ᵈ Grk., *that you may know*.
ᵉ This word means *power with the right to use it*.
ᶠ Grk., *go into your own house*.

⁹ And as He was passing along from there, He saw a man named Matthew in his seat at the tax-collector's desk, and He said to him, "Follow me." And he got up and followed Him.

¹⁰ While He was at table in the house many tax-collectors and notorious sinners came in and took their seats at table with Jesus and His disciples. ¹¹ And when the Pharisees saw this, they said to His disciples, "Why does your Teacher eat ᵍ with tax-collectors and notorious sinners?"

¹² And when He heard it, He said, "It is not well, but sick people that have to send for a doctor.ʰ ¹³ Go, learn what this means, 'It is mercy and not sacrifice that I want.'ⁱ It is not upright but sinful people that I have come to invite."

¹⁴ Then John's disciples went up to Him, and said, "Why do we and the Pharisees practice ʲ fasting, but your disciples do not?"

¹⁵ Jesus said to them, "The wedding guests cannot mourn, can they,ᵏ as long as they have the bridegroom ˡ with them? But a time ᵐ will come when the bridegroom will be taken away from them, and then they will fast. ¹⁶ Nobody sews a patch of brand-new ⁿ goods on an old coat, for such a patch would tear away from the coat, and the hole would be bigger than ever. ¹⁷ Nobody pours new wine into old wine-bottles; or, if they do, the bottles burst, the wine runs out, and the bottles are ruined.ᵒ But people pour new wine into new wine-bottles, and so both are preserved."

¹⁸ And just as He was saying these things to them, an official came up and fell on his knees before Him, and said, "My daughter has just died, but come and lay your hand upon her and she will come to life."

¹⁹ And Jesus got up and followed him; and His disciples, too. ²⁰ And a woman who had had a hemorrhage for twelve years came up and touched the tassel on His coat.ᵖ ²¹ For she kept saying to herself, "If I can only touch His coat, I will get well."

²² And Jesus, on turning and seeing her, said, "Cheer up, my

ᵍ A social act.
ʰ Grk., *have need of,* etc.
ⁱ Hos. 6:6.
ʲ Pres. of habitual action.
ᵏ Question expects ans., *No.*
ˡ The popular wedding feast He uses to illustrate joy in His service.
ᵐ Grk., *days.*
ⁿ Grk., *unshrunken.*
ᵒ Grk., *are destroyed.*
ᵖ Really *a tunic,* but our word, *coat,* modernizes it.

daughter! Your faith has cured you." And from that moment ᵍ the woman was well.

²³ And Jesus, on coming to the house of the official, and on seeing the flute-players and the wailing crowd, ²⁴ said, "Go away, for the girl is not dead, but is sleeping." And they began to laugh in His face.ʳ ²⁵ But when the crowd had been driven out, He went in and took hold of her hand, and the girl got up. ²⁶ And the news about her ˢ spread all over that country.

²⁷ As Jesus was passing along from there, two blind men followed Him, shouting,ᵗ "Do pity us, O Son of David!"

²⁸ After He had gone into the house, and the blind men had gone up to Him, Jesus said to them, "Do you really believe that I can do this?"

They said to Him, "Yes, Lord."

²⁹ Then He touched their eyes, and said, "In accordance with your faith it must be done for you." ᵘ ³⁰ And their eyes received strength to see.ᵛ Then Jesus sternly charged them, "See that nobody knows it." ³¹ But they went out and spread the news about Him all over that country.

³² But at the very time ʷ they were going out, some people brought to Him a dumb man, who was under the power of a demon, ³³ and after the demon had been driven out, the dumb man could talk.ˣ So the crowds were dumfounded, saying, "Never before among the Jews was anything like this!"

³⁴ But the Pharisees kept on saying, "It is by the help of the prince of the demons that He drives them out."

³⁵ Jesus kept visiting all the towns and villages, teaching in their synagogues, preaching the good news of the kingdom, and curing every sort of sickness and ailment.

³⁶ When He saw the crowds, His heart was moved with pity for them, because they were tired and scattered like sheep without a shepherd. ³⁷ Then He said to His disciples, "The harvest is plentiful,ʸ but the reapers are scarce. ³⁸ So pray the Lord of the harvest to send out reapers to His harvest field."

ᵍ Grk., *hour*, but often equivalent to our *moment*.
ʳ Grk., *laughed Him down*, or *laughed down on Him*.
ˢ Reading the marg. in WH.
ᵗ Grk. adds, *and saying*; not necessary in Eng.
ᵘ Grk., *let it be done for you*.
ᵛ Grk., *were opened*.
ʷ Pt. of time intensified by interjection.
ˣ Grk., *talked*.
ʸ Grk., *great*; so *plentiful*.

10. THE TWELVE APPOINTED AND SENT OUT; WARNED AGAINST PERSECUTORS; REWARDS PROMISED FOR SERVICE TO OTHERS

Then He called His twelve disciples to Him, and gave them authority over foul spirits, so that they could drive them out, and so that they could cure any disease or ailment.

² Here are the names of the twelve apostles: first, Simon, who was named Peter, and his brother Andrew, James the son of Zebedee and his brother John, ³ Philip and Bartholomew, Thomas and Matthew the tax-collector, James the son of Alpheus, and Thaddeus, ⁴ Simon the zealot, and Judas Iscariot, who afterward [a] betrayed Him.

⁵ Jesus sent these twelve out, after giving them the following [b] charge:

"Do not go to the heathen, or to any Samaritan town, ⁶ but rather to the lost sheep of Israel's house. ⁷ And as you go continue to preach, 'The kingdom of heaven is near.' ⁸ Keep on curing the sick, raising the dead, healing lepers, and driving out demons. You received and gave no pay; you must give and take none. ⁹ Do not accept [c] gold or silver or even copper money for your purse,[d] ¹⁰ and do not take a bag for your journey, nor two shirts, nor any shoes, nor a staff, for the workman deserves his support. ¹¹ Into whatever town or village you go, inquire for some deserving person, and stay at his house [e] until you leave the place. ¹² As you go into his house, wish it well,[f] ¹³ and if the house should prove deserving, may your good wish for peace upon it come true; but if not, may your good wish bring peace to yourselves. ¹⁴ And whoever will not welcome you, or listen to your words, on leaving that place shake off from your feet its very dust. ¹⁵ I tell you, the punishment on the day of judgment will be lighter for the land of Sodom and Gomorrah than for that town.

¹⁶ "Listen! I am sending you out as sheep surrounded by wolves.[g] So you must be sensible like serpents and guileless like doves. ¹⁷ Be on your guard against men, for they will turn you

[a] Grk., *also.*
[b] Grk., *charging them, saying.*
[c] Grk., *get* or *acquire.*
[d] Grk., *for your girdles.*
[e] Grk., *stay there.*
[f] Grk., *salute it.*
[g] Grk., *as sheep in the midst of wolves.*

over to the courts and will flog you in their synagogues, 18 and you will be brought before governors and kings for my sake, to bear witness to them and the heathen. 19 But when they turn you over to the courts, you must not worry at all about [h] how or what you ought to speak, for it will be given you at that hour what you ought to speak. 20 For it is not you who are speaking, but the Spirit of your Father that is speaking through [i] you. 21 One brother will turn another over to death, and a father his child, and children will take a stand against their parents, and will have them put to death.[j] 22 And you will be hated [k] by all men, because you bear my name;[l] but whoever bears up to the end will be saved. 23 But whenever they persecute you in one town, flee to a different one.[m] For I solemnly say to you, you will not cover [n] all the towns of Israel before the Son of Man returns. 24 No pupil is better than his teacher, and no slave is better than his master. 25 The pupil should be satisfied to become like his teacher,[o] and the slave should be satisfied to become like his master. If men have called the Head of the house Beelzebub, how much worse names will they heap upon the members of His family! 26 So you must never be afraid of them; for there is nothing covered that will not be uncovered, nor a secret that will not be known. 27 What I speak to you in the dark, tell in the light, and what you hear whispered in your ears, you must proclaim from housetops. 28 You must never be afraid of those who kill the body, but cannot kill the soul. But rather you must keep on fearing Him who can destroy both soul and body in the pit.[p] 29 Do not sparrows sell for a cent apiece? And yet not one of them can [q] fall to the ground without your Father's notice. 30 Even the very hairs on your head have all been counted [r] by God. 31 So stop being afraid; you are [s] worth more than many sparrows. 32 Therefore, everyone

[h] Following aor. subjunc. reading, after two best Mss.
[i] Grk., *in*.
[j] Grk., *will put them to death*.
[k] Pres. part. of cont. action.
[l] Grk., *on account of my name*.
[m] Different in quality.
[n] A modern drummer's term, like the common Grk., *finish the towns*.
[o] Grk., *it is enough*, etc.
[p] Grk., *Gehenna*, almost equivalent to our word *pit*.
[q] Grk., doubly emphatic; so *not one will fall*.
[r] Grk., *have been numbered*.
[s] Grk. vb. very forceful, so emph.

who will own me before men I will own before my Father in heaven, ³³ but anyone who disowns me before men I will disown before my Father in heaven.

³⁴ "Do not suppose that I have come to bring peace to the earth. I have not come to bring peace but a sword. ³⁵ For I have come to set a man against his father, and a daughter against her mother, and a daughter-in-law against her mother-in-law, ³⁶ and a man's enemies will be members of his own family. ³⁷ Anybody who loves father or mother more than he loves me is not worthy of me, ³⁸ and nobody is worthy of me who does not take up his cross and follow me. ³⁹ Anybody who gains his lower life will lose the higher life, and anybody who loses his lower life for my sake will gain the higher life.ᵗ

⁴⁰ "Whoever welcomes you welcomes me, and whoever welcomes me welcomes Him who sent me. ⁴¹ Whoever welcomes a prophet as a prophet ᵘ will receive the same reward as a prophet, and whoever welcomes an upright man as such will receive the same reward as the upright man. ⁴² And I solemnly say to you, no one who gives a cup of cold water to one of the least of my disciples,ᵛ because he is a disciple, will ever fail ʷ to get his reward."

11   JOHN THE BAPTIST, BY A DELEGATION, ASKS JESUS A QUESTION; JOHN PRAISED BY JESUS; CITIES REJECTING JESUS CURSED; BURDEN-BEARERS INVITED TO JESUS FOR REST

When Jesus had closed this charge to His disciples, He left there to teach and preach in their towns.

² Now when John in prison heard of the doings of the Christ, he sent this message by his disciples: ³ "Are you the One who was to come, or should we keep on looking for a different ᵃ one?"

⁴ And Jesus answered them, "Go and tell John what you hear and see: ⁵ the blind are seeing and the crippled are walking, the lepers are being healed and the deaf are hearing, the dead are being raised and the poor are having the good news preached to them. ⁶ And happy is the man who finds no cause for stumbling over me." ᵇ

ᵗ A play on the two-fold use of the word *life* (*psuchee*).
ᵘ Grk., *in the name of a prophet*.
ᵛ Grk., *least of these little ones;* so *disciples*.
ʷ Grk., *lose;* i.e., fail to get.
ᵃ Grk. word means *another of different quality*.
ᵇ Grk., *is not caused to stumble in* or *through me*.

MATTHEW 11

⁷ But as they were leaving, Jesus began to speak to the crowds about John: "What did you go out into the desert to gaze at? A reed that is tossed to and fro by the wind? ⁸ If not, what did you go out there to see? A man dressed in silks and satins?ᵉ No, people who dress in that way are found in the palaces of kings. ⁹ If not, why did you go out there? To see a prophet? ¹⁰ This is the man of whom the Scripture says,ᵈ

"'Attention! I am sending my messenger on before you;
He will prepare the road ahead of you.'

¹¹ "I solemnly say to you, of all men born of women no one greaterᵉ than John the Baptist has ever appeared; and yet the one who is least important in the kingdom of heaven is greater than he. ¹² And from the days of John the Baptist until the present moment the kingdom of heaven has been continuously taken by storm, and those who take it by storm are seizing it as a precious prize.ᶠ ¹³ For up to the days of John all the prophets, and even the law, prophesied about it, ¹⁴ and if you are willing to accept it, Johnᵍ himself is the Elijah who was to come.ʰ ¹⁵ Let him who has ears listen!

¹⁶ "But to what can I compare the leaders of this age? They are like little children sitting in the market places and calling to their fellows in the game,ⁱ

¹⁷ "'We played the wedding march for you, but you did not dance;
We sang the funeral dirge, but you did not beat your breasts.'

¹⁸ For John came neither eating nor drinking with others, and yet they said, 'He has a demon.' ¹⁹ The Son of Man came eating and drinking with others, and they say, 'Just look at Him! A glutton and a wine-drinker, a chum of tax-collectors and notorious sinners!' And yet wisdom is vindicated by her doings!"

²⁰ Then He began to censure the cities in which His many, many wonder-works had been done, because they did not repent. ²¹ "A curse on you, Chorazin! A curse on you, Bethsaida! For if

---

ᶜ Not expressed but strongly implied; Grk., *soft clothing*, Eng., *silks and satins*.
ᵈ Mal. 3:1.
ᵉ Greatness here is measured by his exalted mission in heralding the Messiah.
ᶠ Exact meaning of Grk. vb.
ᵍ Grk., *he himself*. Noun clearer in Eng.
ʰ Cf. Mal. 4:5.
ⁱ A wedding or funeral game often played by little children who sometimes balked in the game. The Pharisees compared to them.

the wonder-works done in you had been done in Tyre and Sidon. long ago they would have repented in sackcloth and ashes. ²² Moreover, I tell you, on the day of judgment the punishment will be lighter^j for Tyre and Sidon than for you! ²³ And you, Capernaum, are you to be exalted to heaven? No, you belong to the regions of the dead!^k For if the wonder-works done in you had been done in Sodom, it would have continued until today. ²⁴ But I tell you, on the day of judgment the punishment will be lighter for the land of Sodom than for you!"

²⁵ At that time Jesus said, "I thank You, Father, Lord of heaven and earth, for concealing these matters from wise and learned men, and for revealing them to little children. ²⁶ Yes, Father, I thank You that Your good pleasure made it so. ²⁷ All things have been entrusted to me by my Father, and no one but the Father perfectly^l knows the Son, and no one but the Son perfectly knows the Father, and the one to whom the Son chooses to make Him known. ²⁸ Come to me, all of you who toil and carry burdens, and I, yes, I, will lead^m you into rest. ²⁹ Put on my yoke, and learn from me, for I am gentle and humble in heart, and you will find rest for your souls, ³⁰ for the yoke I offer is easy to wear, and the load I ask is light to bear."

12 HIS CURING A WITHERED HAND ON THE SABBATH INCITES HIS ENEMIES TO PLOT JESUS' DEATH; THE UNFORGIVABLE SIN DESCRIBED; A SPECTACULAR SIGN REFUSED; REAL KINSMEN OF JESUS

At that time Jesus walked one sabbath through the wheat fields, and His disciples became hungry, and began to pull the heads of wheat and eat them. ² And when the Pharisees saw it, they said to Him, "Just look! Your disciples are doing something that it is against the law to do on the sabbath!"

³ But He said to them, "Did you never read what David did, when he and his soldiers^a became hungry? ⁴ How he went into

---

^j Grk., *it will be more bearable.*
^k Grk., *Hades,* land of the dead.
^l Compound vb. expresses this perfective action.
^m Grk., *cause to rest;* pro. emph., hence tr.
^a Grk., *those about him;* i.e., his soldiers.

the house of God, and they ate the sacred ᵇ loaves, which it was against the law for him or his soldiers to eat, or for anyone except the priests? ⁵ Or, did you never read in the law that the priests in the temple break the sabbath,ᶜ and yet are not guilty? ⁶ But I tell you, there is something greater than the temple here! ⁷ If you only knew what that saying means, 'It is mercy and not sacrifice that I want,'ᵈ you would not have condemned men who are not guilty. ⁸ For the Son of Man is Lord of the sabbath."

⁹ And on leaving there He went into their synagogue. ¹⁰ Now there was a man there with one hand withered. And, to get a charge against Him, they asked Him, "Is it right to cure people on the sabbath?"

¹¹ But He said to them, "What man is there among you, ifᵉ he has only one sheep and it falls into a ditch on the sabbath, will not lay hold on it and lift it out? ¹² And how much more a man is worth than a sheep!ᶠ So it is right to do good on the sabbath." ¹³ Then He said to the man, "Hold out your hand." And he held it out, and it was cured so that it became like the other. ¹⁴ But the Pharisees went out and held a consultation against Him, to put Him to death.

¹⁵ But because Jesus knew it, He left there. And many people followed Him, and He cured them all, ¹⁶ and charged them not to publish Him, ¹⁷ and in this wayᵍ fulfilled the saying spoken by the prophet Isaiah:

¹⁸ "Here is my Servant whom I have chosen,
My Beloved, in whom my soul delights itself.
I will endow Him with my Spirit,
And He will announce a judgment to the heathen.
¹⁹ He will not debate,ʰ nor challenge anyone;
His voice will no one hear in the streets;
²⁰ A broken reed He will not break off;
A flickering wickⁱ He will not put out,

ᵇ The loaves of offering, so *sacred loaves*.
ᶜ They work on the sabbath; so break it.
ᵈ Hos. 6:6.
ᵉ Relative cond. clause.
ᶠ Both nouns in emph. position.
ᵍ The Grk. particle here expresses purpose, but it is close to result.
ʰ Grk., *strive,* so debate.
ⁱ Grk., linen, here used as a wick.

Until He brings His judgment to victory.
21 On His name the heathen will set their hopes."ʲ

22 At that time some people brought to Him a man under the power of demons, who was blind and dumb, and He cured him, so that the dumb man could talk and see. 23 And all the crowds of people were dumfounded, and began to say, "He is by no means ᵏ the Son of David, is He?" 24 But when the Pharisees heard it, they said, "This man is not driving out demons except by the help of Beelzebub, the prince of the demons."

25 But because He knew their thoughts, He said to them, "Any kingdom that is not united is in the process ˡ of destruction, and any city or family that is not united cannot last. 26 Now if Satan is driving out Satan, he has become disunited; how then can his kingdom last? 27 And if I am driving out demons by the help of Beelzebub, by whose help are your sons driving them out? So they must ᵐ be your judges. 28 But if I by the Spirit of God am driving the demons out, then the kingdom of God has come to you. 29 Or, how can anyone get into a giant's house and carry off his goods, unless he first binds the giant? After that he can make a clean sweep ⁿ of his house. 30 Whoever is not in partnership with me is against me, and whoever does not gather in partnership with me scatters. 31 So I tell you, every sin and all abusive speech will be forgiven men, but abuse against the Spirit cannot be forgiven. 32 And whoever speaks a word against the Son of Man will be forgiven for it, but whoever speaks abusively against the Holy Spirit will not be forgiven for it, either in this world or in the world to come.

33 "You must either make the tree healthy and its fruits healthy or make the tree sickly and its fruits sickly, for a tree is judged ᵒ by its fruit. 34 You brood of vipers! How can you, wicked as you are, say anything that is good? For the mouth talks about the things that fill the heart.ᵖ 35 The good man out of his good inner

ʲ Isa. 42:1 ff.
ᵏ Strong negative here used.
ˡ Grk., *is being destroyed.*
ᵐ Fut. indic. in impv. sense.
ⁿ Compound vb. means *to rob to the utmost.*
ᵒ Grk., *known.*
ᵖ Grk., *out of the fullness.* etc

MATTHEW 12

storehouse, brings out good things, the bad man, out of his bad one, bad things. 36 So I tell you, for every worthless word q that men utter they will have to give account on the day of judgment; 37 for it is by your words that you will be acquitted and by your words that you will be condemned."

38 Then some of the scribes and Pharisees answered Him as follows: "Teacher, we would like to see a spectacular sign given by you."

39 But He answered, "Only a wicked and treacherous age is hankering for a spectacular sign,r and no sign will be given it but the sign of the prophet Jonah. 40 For as Jonah was in the whale's stomach for three days and nights, the Son of Man will be three days and nights in the heart of the earth. 41 The men of Nineveh will rise with the leaders of this age at the judgment and condemn them, for they turned to the message preached s by Jonah, and there is more than Jonah here! 42 The queen of the south will rise with the leaders of this age at the judgment and condemn them, for she came from the farthest limits of the earth to listen to Solomon's wisdom, and there is more than Solomon here!

43 "Whenever the foul spirit goes out of a man, it wanders about in deserts t in search of rest, but cannot find it. 44 Then it says, 'I will go back to my house which I left,' and it finds it unoccupied, swept, and ready for use.

45 "Then it goes and gets seven other spirits more wicked than itself, and they go in and make their home there, and so the end of that man is worse than the beginning. This is the way it will be with the wicked leaders of this age."

46 While He was still speaking to the crowds, His mother and His brothers had taken their stand outside, trying hard u to get to speak to Him.v 48 But He answered the man who told Him, "Who is my mother, and who are my brothers?" 49 And with a gesture w toward His disciples He said, "Here are my mother and my brothers. 50 For whoever does the will of my Father in heaven is my mother and sister and brother."

q So Abbott-Smith, Lex.
r Just the kind of sign we know they were looking for; hence tr.
s Exact meaning of vb., prep., and noun.
t Grk., *waterless places—deserts*.
u Expressed by pres. pt.—*continuing to seek*, etc.
v V. 47 om. by best Mss.
w Grk., *stretching out the hand*.

13 TEACHING BY STORIES—THE SOWER, THE WILD WHEAT, THE MUSTARD SEED, THE YEAST, THE BURIED POT OF GOLD, THE COSTLY PEARL, THE DRAGNET

That same day Jesus went out of His house and was sitting on the seashore. ² And the crowds that gathered about Him were so great that He got into a boat and remained sitting in it, while all the crowd stood on the seashore. ³ And in stories,[a] by way of comparison, He told them many things, as He continued to speak:

"A sower went out to sow, ⁴ and as he was sowing, some of the seed fell along the path, and the birds came and ate them up, ⁵ and some fell upon rocky ground where they did not have much soil, and at once they sprang up, because there was no depth of soil, ⁶ and when the sun was up they were scorched and dried up, because they had no root. ⁷ And some fell among the thorns, and the thorns grew up and choked them out. ⁸ And some fell in rich soil, and yielded a crop, some a hundred, some sixty, some thirty-fold. ⁹ Let him who has ears listen."

¹⁰ Then His disciples came up to Him and asked, "Why do you speak to them in stories?"

¹¹ He answered: "It is you [b] and not they who are granted the privilege of knowing the secrets of the kingdom of heaven. ¹² For to anyone who has, more will be given, and his supply will overflow,[c] but from anyone who does not have, even what he has will be taken away. ¹³ This is why I am speaking to them in stories, because they look but do not see, they listen but do not really hear or understand. ¹⁴ So in them the prophecy of the prophet Isaiah is fulfilled,[d] which says:

" 'You will listen and listen [e] and not understand,
And you will look and look and never see at all,
¹⁵ For this people's soul has grown dull,
And with their ears they can scarcely hear,
And they have shut tight their eyes,
So that they will never see with their eyes,
And hear with their ears,

[a] Exact meaning of Grk. word, *parabolee*.
[b] Pro. very emph.; hence our tr.
[c] Exact meaning of vb.
[d] Isa. 6:9,10.
[e] Heb. construction expressing emph.

And understand with their hearts, and turn to me,
So that I may cure them!'

¹⁶ "But blessed are your eyes, for they are beginning to see,ᶠ and your ears, for they are beginning to hear. ¹⁷ For I solemnly say to you, many prophets and upright men yearned to see what you are seeing, and did not see it, and to hear what you are hearing, and did not hear it.

¹⁸ "Now listen closelyᵍ to the story of the sower. ¹⁹ When anyone hears the message ʰ of the kingdom and does not understand it, the wicked one comes and carries off the seed that was sown in his heart. This is what was sown along the path. ²⁰ And what was sown upon the thin rocky soil illustrates the man who hears the message and bubbling over with joy at once accepts it, ²¹ but it takes no real root in him, and he lasts only a little while, and just as soon as suffering and persecution come for the truth's sake, he at once ⁱ yields and falls. ²² And what was sown among the thorns illustrates the man who hears the message, and the worries of the times and the pleasures of being rich choke the truth ʰ out, and he yields no fruit. ²³ And what was sown in rich soil illustrates the man who hears the message and understands it, and yields fruit, one a hundred, one sixty, another thirty-fold."

²⁴ He told them another story, as follows: "The kingdom of heaven is like a man who sowed seed in his field. ²⁵ But while the world was sleeping, his enemy came and sowed wild ʲ wheat seed in the midst of the good seed, and went away. ²⁶ And when the wheat plants grew up and yielded their ripened grain, the wild wheat plants appeared too. ²⁷ And the farmer's slaves came up to him and said, 'Master, did you not sow good seed in your field? Then where did the wild wheat plants come from?' ²⁸ He said to them, 'An enemy has done this.' Then they said to him, 'Do you want us, then, to go and gather them?' ²⁹ And he said, 'No, never, for while you are gathering the wild wheat plants you might root up the good ones with them. ³⁰ Let them both grow together until harvest time, and at the harvest time I will order the reapers,

---

ᶠ Pres. expressing process near its beginning.
ᵍ Suggested by aor. impv.
ʰ Grk., *word*.
ⁱ Grk., *he is caused to stumble*.
ʲ An odious weed, which looks like a stalk of wheat, was often called *wild wheat*.

'Gather first the wild wheat plants and tie them into bundles to be burned up, but get the wheat into my barn.'"

31 He told them this story, as follows: "The kingdom of heaven may be compared to a mustard seed which a man took and sowed in his field. 32 It is the smallest of all seeds, but when it is grown it is the largest of plants; yea, it grows into a tree, so that the wild birds come and roost in its branches."

33 He told another story: "The kingdom of heaven may be compared to yeast which a woman took and worked into a bushel [k] of flour until it all had risen."

34 Jesus told the crowds all this in stories, and without a story He told them nothing, 35 to fulfill what was spoken by the prophet: [l]

"I will open my mouth in stories,
I will utter truths concealed since creation."

36 Then He left the crowds and went into His house. And His disciples came up to Him and said, "Explain to us the story of the wild wheat in the field."

37 And He answered: "The sower of the good seed is the Son of Man; 38 the field is the world; the good seed are the members of the kingdom; the wild wheat seed are the followers of the wicked one. 39 The enemy who sowed them is the devil, the harvest is the close of the age, the reapers are angels. 40 Just as the wild wheat plants are gathered and burned up, so it will be at the close of the age. 41 The Son of Man will send out His angels, and they will gather out of His kingdom all those who cause wrongdoing, and the wrongdoers,[m] 42 and will throw them into the furnace of torturing punishment; [n] there they will wail and grind their teeth. 43 Then the upright will shine out like the sun in the kingdom of their Father. Let him who has ears listen!

44 "The kingdom of heaven is like a pot of gold [o] which was buried in a field, which a man found and buried again; and for joy over it he went and sold all he had and bought that field.

45 "Again, the kingdom of heaven is like a gem-dealer who was

---

[k] A little over a bushel, the usual quantity for a baking.
[l] Ps. 78:2.
[m] Lit., *all that cause others to stumble*, etc.
[n] Grk., *furnace of fire*, fire being a vivid expression for torturing punishment; hence our tr.
[o] Lit., *a treasure*, but referring to an ancient custom of burying pots of gold for safety.

looking for beautiful pearls. ⁴⁶ One day he found a very costly pearl, and he went and sold all he had and bought it.

⁴⁷ "Again, the kingdom of heaven is like a dragnet that was let down into the sea, and gathered fish of every kind, ⁴⁸ which, when it was full, the fishermen drew up on the shore, and sat down and picked out ᵖ the good fish for their baskets and threw the bad away. ⁴⁹ So it will be at the close of the age; the angels will go out and separate the wicked from the upright, ⁵⁰ and will throw them into the furnace of torturing punishment. There they will wail and grind their teeth.

⁵¹ "Do you understand all these stories?" ᵠ

They answered Him, "Yes."

⁵² He said to them, "Every scribe who has become a disciple in the kingdom of heaven is like a householder who can bring out of his storeroom new furnishings as well as old."

⁵³ When Jesus had finished these stories, He left there. ⁵⁴ He went to His own home town, and kept teaching in their synagogue in such a way that they were dumfounded, and said, "Where did He get this wisdom and this power to do such wonder-works? ⁵⁵ Is He not the carpenter's son? Is not His mother's name Mary, are not His brothers James, Joseph, Simon and Judas? ⁵⁶ And are not His sisters all living here with us? Where then did He get all these things?" ⁵⁷ And so they found a cause for stumbling ʳ over Him.

But Jesus said to them, "A prophet never fails to be honored except in his native neighborhood and in his own home." And so ⁵⁸ He did not do many wonder-works there, because of their lack of faith.

14 ANTIPAS, GOVERNOR OF GALILEE, SUPPOSES JESUS IS JOHN THE BAPTIST RISEN FROM THE DEAD; JESUS FEEDS FIVE THOUSAND, WALKS ON THE SEA, AND CURES MANY

At that time Herod the governor heard the reports about Jesus, ² and said to his attendants, "This is John the Baptist. He has risen from the dead, and that is why the powers are at work through him."

³ For Herod had arrested John and bound him and put him out

ᵖ Exact meaning of Grk. vb.
ᵠ Grk., *all these things.*
ʳ Grk., *they were caused to stumble at Him*

of the way[a] by putting him in prison, just to please Herodias,[b] his brother Philip's wife, 4 for John had said to him, "It is not right for you to have her as wife." 5 Although he wanted to have him killed, he was afraid of the people, for they regarded him as a prophet.

6 But when Herod's birthday came, Herodias' daughter danced before the guests.[c] Herod was fascinated by her, 7 and so passionately[d] promised to give her anything she might ask for. 8 And she, prompted by her mother, said, "Give me John the Baptist's head right here on a platter." 9 And the king was sorry, but on account of his oath and his guests, he ordered it to be given her. 10 And he sent and had John beheaded in prison. 11 And his head was brought on a platter and given to the girl, and she took it to her mother. 12 Then John's disciples came and carried off his corpse, and buried him, and went and reported it to Jesus.

13 When Jesus heard it, He left there in a boat for a quiet place, to be alone. And when the crowds heard of it, they followed Him on foot from the towns. 14 So when He got out of the boat and saw a great crowd, His heart was moved with pity for them, and He cured their sick people. 15 But when it was evening, His disciples came to Him and said, "This is a destitute[e] place, and the day is over; send the crowds off to the villages to buy themselves food."

16 But Jesus said to them, "They do not need to leave here; give them something to eat yourselves."

17 They said to Him, "We have nothing here but five loaves and two fish."

18 He said, "Bring them here to me." 19 After ordering the crowds to sit down on the grass, He took the five loaves and two fish and looked up to heaven and blessed them; then He broke the loaves in pieces and gave them to the disciples, and they gave them to the people. 20 And they all ate and had a plenty.[f] Then they took up the pieces left over, which made twelve basketfuls. 21 The people fed numbered[g] about five thousand men, besides women and children.

22 And He at once had the disciples get into the boat and cross

[a] This idea in the prep. *apo*.
[b] Grk., *on account of, for the sake of,* H.
[c] Grk., *in the midst*.
[d] Grk., *with an oath he promised,* Ara. constr. for emph.
[e] Grk., *is desert*.
[f] A popular expression for a full meal.
[g] Grk., *those eating were*.

to the other side ahead of Him, while He dismissed the crowds. ²³ After He had dismissed the crowds, He went up the hill alone to pray. And after the evening came on, He was there alone, ²⁴ but the boat was already a long way from shore,[h] and was being tossed by the waves, for the wind was against them. ²⁵ Just before day[1] He went out to them, walking on the sea. ²⁶ And when the disciples saw Him walking on the sea, they were terrified, and said, "It is a ghost!" And they screamed with fright.

²⁷ Then Jesus at once spoke to them, "Be men of courage! It is I; stop being afraid."

²⁸ Peter answered Him, "Lord, if it is you, let[j] me come to you on the water."

²⁹ And He said, "Come."

And Peter got down out of the boat and walked on the water, and he went toward Jesus. ³⁰ But when he felt[k] the wind, he was frightened, and as he began to go down, he cried out, "Lord, save me!"

³¹ Jesus at once put out His hand and caught hold of him, and said to him, "O you of little faith! Why did you waver so?"

³² And when they got into the boat, the wind lulled. ³³ And the men in the boat worshiped Him, and said, "You are certainly God's Son."

³⁴ And they crossed over to the other side and came to Gennesaret. ³⁵ And the men of that place recognized Him, and sent into all the countryside and brought to Him all who were sick, ³⁶ and they continued to beg Him to let them touch just the tassel on His coat, and all who barely[l] touched it were completely cured.[m]

15 REAL DEFILEMENT DESCRIBED BY JESUS; A HEATHEN MOTHER'S DAUGHTER CURED BECAUSE OF HER WONDERFUL FAITH; JESUS RETURNS TO GALILEE AND FEEDS FOUR THOUSAND

Then some Pharisees and scribes from Jerusalem came to Jesus, and asked Him, ² "Why do your disciples break the rules handed

---

[h] Following WH text and Ms. B.
[1] Grk., *in the fourth watch*, 3-6 A.M.
[j] Grk., *command me*, etc.
[k] Grk., *saw*.
[l] In the aor.
[m] Comp. vb. means exactly this.

down by our forefathers?ᵃ For they do not practice washing their hands when they take their meals."ᵇ

³ But He answered, "Why do you too break God's command for the sake ofᶜ the rules that have been handed down to you? ⁴ For God said, 'Honor your father and mother,' and 'Whoever curses his father or mother must certainlyᵈ be put to death.' ⁵ But you say, 'Whoever tells his father or mother, "Everything I have that might be used for helping you, is devoted to God," ⁶ is under no obligation at all to helpᵉ his parent.' So you have set aside what God has said for the sake of what has been handed down to you. ⁷ You hypocrites! Isaiah prophesied beautifully about you, when he said:ᶠ

⁸ "'This people honor me with their lips,
But their hearts are far, far away from me;
⁹ Their worship of me is an empty show;
The thingsᵍ they teach are only men's precepts.'"

¹⁰ And He called the people to Him and said, "Listen to this and learn it! ¹¹ It is not what goes into a man's mouth that makes him foul; no, it is what comes out of a man's mouth that makes him foul."

¹² Then His disciples came up to Him and asked, "Do you know that the Pharisees were knocked breathlessʰ to hear what you have just said?"

¹³ He answered, "Every plant that my heavenly Father did not plant mustⁱ be rooted up. ¹⁴ Let them alone. They are blind teachers! And if one blind man guides another, they will both fall into the ditch."

¹⁵ Then Peter said to Him, "Explain the maximʲ for us."

¹⁶ And He said, "Are you too, even yet, without understanding? ¹⁷ Do you not understand that whatever goes into the mouth

---

ᵃ Grk., *elders of the past,* so *forefather.*
ᵇ Grk., *take their bread.*
ᶜ Grk., *on account of,* etc.
ᵈ Grk., *die the death,* so emph.
ᵉ Grk., *honor.*
ᶠ 29:13.
ᵍ Grk., *teachings they teach.*
ʰ Grk., *caused to fall.*
ⁱ Fut. indic. in impv. sense.
ʲ *Parabolee* here means *maxim,* not *story* as above.

MATTHEW 15

passes into the stomach and afterwards into the waste? 18 But the things that come out of the mouth come from the heart, and they make the man foul. 19 For out of the heart come evil thoughts, murder, adultery, immorality,[k] stealing, false witnessing, irreverent speech. 20 These are the things that make a man foul, but eating with unwashed hands does not make a man foul."

21 Then Jesus left there and slipped away to the neighborhood of Tyre and Sidon. 22 And a Canaanite woman of that district came out and pleaded,[l] saying, "Do pity me, Lord, Son of David; my daughter is suffering horrors from a demon."

23 But He did not answer her a word. And His disciples came up and kept begging Him, "Send her away, for she keeps on screaming after us."

24 But He answered, "I have been sent only to the lost sheep of Israel's house."

25 But she came and bowed to Him, and kept praying, "Lord, help me!"

26 He answered, "It is not right to take the children's bread and throw it to the house dogs."

27 She said, "Yes, Lord, and yet the house dogs usually[m] eat the crumbs that fall from their master's table."

28 Then Jesus answered her, "O woman, wonderful[n] is your faith! You must have what you want." And her daughter was cured at that very moment.

29 Then Jesus left there and went to the shore of the sea of Galilee. Then He went up the hill and kept sitting there, 30 and great crowds came up to Him bringing with them the lame, the crippled, the blind, the deaf, and many others. They laid them at His feet, and He cured them, 31 so that the crowd was astonished to see the dumb talking, the lame walking, and the blind seeing. So they praised the God of Israel.

32 Then Jesus called His disciples to Him, and said, "My heart is moved with pity for the crowd, for it is now three days they have been staying with me, and they have nothing at all left to eat, and I fear[o] they might give out on the way home."[p]

---

[k] General sex immorality.
[l] *Cried out, saying.*
[m] General pres.
[n] Grk., *great.*
[o] Easily understood with following particle.
[p] Their destination, so readily supplied.

MATTHEW 16

³³ The disciples said to Him, "Where in this destitute place can we get bread enough to satisfy such a crowd?"
³⁴ Then Jesus asked them, "How many loaves have you on hand?"

They answered, "Seven and a few small fish." ³⁵ Then He ordered the crowd q to sit down on the ground, ³⁶ and He took the seven loaves and the fish and gave thanks; then He broke them in pieces, and kept giving the pieces to the disciples, and they to the crowds.q ³⁷ And they all ate and had a plenty, and they took up the pieces left over, which made seven hamper r-basketfuls. ³⁸ Those fed numbered four thousand men, besides women and children.

³⁹ Then He sent the crowds away, got into the boat, and went to the district of Magadan.

16 A SPECTACULAR SIGN NOT TO BE GIVEN; WARNING AGAINST THE TEACHING OF THE PHARISEES AND THE SADDUCEES; JESUS FORETELLS HIS DEATH; THE FOUNDING OF THE CHURCH

The Pharisees and the Sadducees came up, and to test Him asked Him to show them a spectacular sign from heaven. ² He answered,a ⁴ "It is a wicked and immoral b age that is hankering for a spectacular sign, so no sign will be given it but the sign of Jonah." Then He left them and went away.

⁵ When the disciples crossed the sea, they forgot to take any bread. ⁶ And Jesus said to them, "Look out, and keep on guarding yourselves against the yeast of the Pharisees and the Sadducees!"

⁷ Then they began c to discuss it among themselves, and said, It is because we did not take any bread."

⁸ Jesus knew it and said, "Why are you discussing among yourselves the fact that you have no bread? Have you so little faith? ⁹ Do you not understand yet? Do you not remember the five loaves for the five thousand and how many basketfuls you took up? ¹⁰ Nor the seven loaves for the four thousand and how many hamper-basketfuls you took up? ¹¹ How is it that you do not

---
q Following WH text and two best Mss.
r Very large baskets, so our *hampers*.
a Best Mss. om. all from, *He ans.* to close of v. 3.
b Grk., *adulterous*.
c Inceptive impf.

understand that I did not speak to you about bread, when I said, keep on guarding yourselves against the yeast of the Pharisees and the Sadducees?" ¹² Then they understood that He meant, guard yourselves not against yeast for bread,ᵈ but against the teaching of the Pharisees and the Sadducees.

¹³ When Jesus reached the district of Caesarea Philippi, He asked His disciples, "Who do people say that the Son of Man is?" ¹⁴ They answered, "Some say John the Baptist, some Elijah, and others Jeremiah or one of the prophets."

¹⁵ He said to them, "Who do you yourselves ᵉ say that I am?"

¹⁶ Simon Peter answered, "You are the Christ, the Son of the living God."

¹⁷ Then Jesus answered him, "Blessed are you, Simon, son of Jonah, for it is not man ᶠ that made this known to you, but my Father in heaven. ¹⁸ And I, yes I, tell you, your name from now on is to be Peter, Rock, and on a massive rock like this ᵍ I will build my church, and the powers of the underworld ʰ shall never overthrow it. ¹⁹ I will give you the keys ⁱ of the kingdom of heaven, and whatever you forbid on earth must be what is already ʲ forbidden in heaven, and whatever you permit on earth must be what is already permitted in heaven." ᵏ ²⁰ Then He admonished ˡ the disciples not to tell anyone that He was the Christ.

²¹ It was just after ᵐ that that Jesus Christ for the first time clearly ⁿ taught His disciples that He had to go to Jerusalem and submit to many forms ᵒ of suffering at the hands of the elders, high priests, and scribes, and be killed, but be raised to life on the third day. ²² And Peter took Him aside and began to chide Him, as he said, "Heaven shield you, my Lord! This must never be your lot!"

ᵈ Fol. B, the oldest Ms.
ᵉ Doubly emph.
ᶠ Grk., *flesh and blood*, meaning man in his frailty.
ᵍ A different word from the word trans. *Peter;* i. e., πέτρα, a massive rock, meaning *faith in the Christ, the Son of God.*
ʰ Grk., *hades, underworld.*
ⁱ As doorkeeper to open it on Jesus' terms (Bruce, EGT).
ʲ Pf. pass. part., so *things in a state of having been already forbidden.*
ᵏ That is, the church, in the new order, must act in accordance with the will of heaven (God).
ˡ Following WH text based on Ms. B.
ᵐ Grk., *from then,* so *after that.*
ⁿ Grk., *show, make clear.*
ᵒ Grk., *suffer many things.*

²³ But He turned and said to Peter, "Get out of my way, you Satan! You are a hindrance ᵖ to me, for this view of yours is not from God but from men."

²⁴ Then Jesus said to His disciples: "If anyone wants to be my disciple, he must say 'No' to self, put his cross on his shoulders,ᵠ and keep on following me. ²⁵ For whoever wants to save his higher life will have to give up the lower life,ʳ and whoever gives up his lower life for my sake will find the higher life. ²⁶ For what benefit will it be to a man, if he gains the whole world and loses his higher life? What price would a man pay to buy back his life? ²⁷ For the Son of Man is going to come in His Father's splendor, with His angels, and then He will pay back to everyone in accordance with what he has done. ²⁸ I solemnly say to you, some of the people standing here will certainly liveˢ to see the Son of Man coming in His kingdom." ᵗ

17 JESUS TRANSFIGURED; AN EPILEPTIC BOY CURED; FAITH THAT REMOVES MOUNTAINS; TEMPLE TAX PAID BY JESUS

Six days after this, Jesus took Peter and James and his brother John, and led them up on a high mountain, by themselves. ² And in their presence His appearance was changed and His face shone like the sun, and His clothes turned as white as light. ³ Then Moses and Elijah appeared to them and kept talking with Him. ⁴ And Peter interrupted,ᵃ and said to Jesus, "Lord, it is good for us to be here! If you consent, I will put up three tents here, one for you, one for Moses, and one for Elijah."

⁵ While he was still speaking, a bright cloud cast its shadow over them, and a voice from the cloud said, "This is my Son, my Beloved, in whom I am ᵇ delighted. Keep on listening to Him!" ⁶ When the disciples heard it, they fell upon their faces, for ᶜ they were terribly frightened.

ᵖ Grk., *the stick that throws the trap to catch the prey;* so *hindrance.*
ᵠ Grk., *bear,* but usually by putting it on the shoulders.
ʳ A play on double meaning of word *psuchee, life.*
ˢ Grk., *will not at all die,* so *surely live.*
ᵗ Likely His spiritual kingdom, which came through the preaching of the good news.
ᵃ Grk., *answered.*
ᵇ Aor. suggests *the Father had been always delighted,* etc.
ᶜ Grk., *and,* but the clause is causal.

MATTHEW 17

⁷ Then Jesus came and touched them, and said, "Get up and do not be so afraid." ⁸ They looked up and saw no one but Jesus Himself.

⁹ And as they were going down the mountain, Jesus warned [d] them, saying, "Never mention to anyone what you have seen [e] until the Son of Man is raised from the dead."

¹⁰ The disciples asked Him, "Why then do the scribes say that Elijah must come first?"

¹¹ He answered, "Elijah does come and will get everything ready. ¹² But I say to you, Elijah has already come, and they did not recognize him, but treated [f] him as they pleased. Just so the Son of Man is going to suffer at their hands." ¹³ Then the disciples understood that He spoke to them about John the Baptist.

¹⁴ When they reached the crowd, a man came up to Him, kneeling before Him and saying, ¹⁵ "Lord, do pity my son, for he has epilepsy and suffers excruciating pain,[g] and often falls into the fire or into the water. ¹⁶ I brought him to your disciples, and they could not cure him."

¹⁷ And Jesus answered, "O you unbelieving and perverted people of the times! How long can I put up with you? Bring him here to me!" ¹⁸ And Jesus reproved the demon, and it came out of him, and the boy was cured that very moment.[h]

¹⁹ After that the disciples came to Jesus and privately asked, "Why is it we could not drive it out?"

²⁰ He answered them, "Because you have so little faith! [i] For I solemnly say to you, if you have the faith that is living like a grain of mustard, you can say to this mountain, 'Move over from here to yonder,' and it will move over, and nothing will be impossible for you to do." [j]

²² While they were going about in Galilee, Jesus said to them, "The Son of Man is going to be turned over into the hands of men, ²³ and they will kill Him, but on the third day He will be raised again." And they were crushed with grief.[k]

²⁴ When they reached Capernaum, the collectors of the temple

---

[d] Grk., *ordered*.
[e] Grk., *the vision*.
[f] Grk., *acted toward him*.
[g] Either reading has this thought.
[h] Grk., *from that hour*.
[i] Grk., *because of your little faith*.
[j] V. 21 not in the best manuscripts.
[k] Grk., *were greatly grieved*.

tax came to Peter and asked, "Does your Teacher pay the temple tax?"

25 He answered, "Yes."

When Jesus reached home—He got there ahead of Simon—He asked him, "What do you think about it, Simon? From whom do civil rulers collect duties or taxes, from their own citizens or from aliens?"

26 He answered, "From aliens."

Jesus said to him, "So their own citizens are exempt, 27 but still, that we may not influence [1] them to do anything wrong, go down to the sea and throw over a hook. Pull in the first fish that bites,[m] open its mouh and you will find in it a dollar.[n] Take it and pay the tax for both of us."

18 HE TELLS THREE STORIES: BEING LIKE CHILDREN; THE LOST SHEEP FOUND; THE UNFORGIVING SLAVE; HE ALSO TALKS ABOUT UNITED PRAYER, AND HOW TO SETTLE PRIVATE DIFFERENCES

Just at that moment the disciples came up and asked Jesus, "Who then is greatest in the kingdom of heaven?"

2 And He called a little child to Him, and had him stand in the midst of them, 3 and said:

"I solemnly say to you, unless you turn and become like little children,[a] you can [b] never get into the kingdom of heaven at all. 4 So then, whoever becomes as lowly as this little child is the greatest in the kingdom of heaven, 5 and whoever welcomes one little child like this for my sake [c] welcomes me. 6 But whoever leads one of these little ones, who believe in me, to do wrong, had better [d] have a great millstone hung around his neck to sink him to the bottom [e] of the sea. 7 A curse on the world for such influences to do wrong! For they must come, but a curse on the man from whom these influences come!

8 "And if your own hand or your own foot makes you do wrong, cut it off and put it out of your way. It is better for you to get

---

[1] Grk., *lest we should cause them to stumble.*
[m] Grk., *the fish that comes up first.*
[n] Not quite an American dollar.
[a] *Trusting, loving, lowly, forgiving.*
[b] Grk., *will.*
[c] Grk., *in my name.*
[d] Grk., *it would be better.*
[e] Grk., *in the depths,* etc.

into life maimed or crippled than to have both hands or both feet to be thrown into everlasting torture.ᶠ ⁹ And if your own eye makes you do wrong, pluck it out and put it out of your way. It is better for you to go into life with a single eye than to have both eyes to be thrown into the pit of torture.ᶢ

¹⁰ "Be careful not to look with scorn on a single one of these little children, for I tell you that in heaven their angels have uninterrupted ʰ access to my Father in heaven.ⁱ

¹² "What do you think? If a man has a hundred sheep and one of them gets lost, will he not leave the ninety-nine on the hillsides,ʲ and go and search for the one that is lost? ¹³ And if he finds it, I solemnly say to you, he rejoices over it more than he does over the ninety-nine that did not get lost. ¹⁴ Just so it is not the will of my Father in heaven that a single one of these little ones be lost.

¹⁵ "Again, if your brother wrongs you, go and while alone with him show him the wrong. If he listens to you, you have won back your brother. ¹⁶ But if he does not listen to you, take along with you one or two others, so as to have every word confirmed by the testimony of two or three witnesses. If he refuses to listen to them, report it to the church.ᵏ ¹⁷ And if he refuses to listen to the church, treat ˡ him as a heathen and as a tax-collector. ¹⁸ I solemnly say to you, whatever you forbid on earth must ᵐ be already forbidden in heaven, and whatever you permit on earth must be already permitted in heaven.ⁿ

¹⁹ "Again, I tell you, if only two of you on earth agree on what they pray for, they will get ᵒ it from my Father in heaven. ²⁰ For wherever two or three have met as my disciples, I am right there with them."

²¹ Then Peter came up to Him and asked, "Lord, how many times may my brother wrong me and I have to forgive him? As many as seven?" ᵖ

ᶠ Grk., *fire,* symbol of severe punishment.
ᶢ Grk., *Gehenna of fire,* so *pit of torture.*
ʰ Lit., *always cont. to see.*
ⁱ V. 11 omitted in best Mss.
ʲ Grk., *mountain.*
ᵏ Local congregation.
ˡ Grk., *let him be.*
ᵐ Fut. indic. as impv.
ⁿ Mt. 16:19,f.n.
ᵒ Grk., *it will be.*
ᵖ Grk., *up to.*

22 Jesus answered him: "I tell you, not as many as seven, but as many as seventy times seven! **23** So the kingdom of heaven may be compared to a king who decided to settle up his accounts with his slaves. **24** And when he began, a man was brought to him who owed him ten million dollars.q **25** And because he could not pay it, his master ordered him to be sold, yea, even his wife and children and all he had, and payment to be made. **26** So the slave fell down at his feet and pleaded, 'Give me time, and I will pay you every cent of it.' **27** And his master's heart was moved with pity, and he let the slave go free with his debt cancelled.

28 "But that slave went out and found one of his fellow-slaves who owed him twenty dollars, and he caught him by the throat and began to choke him, demanding, 'Pay me what you owe me.'

29 "And his fellow-slave fell down before him and pleaded, 'Give me time, and I will pay you.' **30** But he refused and went out and had him put in jail until he should pay the debt.

31 "When his fellow-slaves saw what had happened, they were greatly troubled, and went and reported all that happened to their master. **32** Then his master called him to him, and said, 'I cancelled all that huge debt of yours, because you pleaded with me to do so. **33** Ought you not to have shown mercy to your fellow-slave, as I too had done for you?' **34** And the master was enraged and turned him over to the official torturers, until he should pay the whole debt. **35** This is the way my heavenly Father too will deal with you, if you do not, each one, heartily forgive your brother."

19 JESUS LEAVES GALILEE; ANSWERS THE QUESTION ABOUT DIVORCE; BLESSES LITTLE CHILDREN; TELLS OF THE PERILS OF RICHES AND THE REWARDS OF SELF-SACRIFICE

When Jesus had finished this discourse, He left Galilee and went into the district of Judea that is on the other side of the Jordan. **2** And great crowds thronged after Him, and He cured them there.

3 And some a Pharisees came up to Him, to try Him out with the question, "Is it right for a man to divorce his wife for any cause?"

4 And He answered, "Have you not read that the Creator at the

q If gold, more.
a No article. so *some*.

MATTHEW 19

beginning made them male and female, ⁵ and said, 'For this reason a man must ᵇ leave his father and mother and be united to his wife, and the two of them must be one'? ⁶ So they are no longer two but one.ᶜ Therefore, what God has joined together man must stop separating." ᵈ

⁷ Then they asked Him, "Why did Moses command us to give a written ᵉ divorce charge, and in this way to divorce a wife?"

⁸ He answered them, "It was because of your moral perversity that Moses allowed you to divorce your wives, but it was not so from the beginning. ⁹ I tell you, whoever divorces his wife for any other cause than her unfaithfulness, and marries another woman, commits adultery."

¹⁰ The disciples said to Him, "If that is a man's relation to his wife, there is no advantage in getting married."

¹¹ He said to them, "It is not every man who has the capacity to carry out this saying, but it is for those to whom the capacity has been given. ¹² For some are born incapable of marriage,ᶠ and some have been made so by men, and some have made themselves so for the sake of the kingdom of heaven. Let him accept it who can."

¹³ After that some little children were brought to Him, for Him to lay His hands on them and pray for them, but His disciples reproved those who brought them.ᵍ ¹⁴ But Jesus said, "Let the little children alone, and stop preventing ʰ them from coming to me, for to such as these the kingdom of heaven belongs." ¹⁵ And He laid His hands on them and left there.

¹⁶ And a man came up to Him and asked, "What is there good that I can do to possess ⁱ eternal life?"

¹⁷ And He answered him, "Why do you ask me about what is good? There is only One who is perfectly good.ʲ But if you want to get into that life, you must practice ᵏ keeping the commandments."

¹⁸ He asked Him, "What sort ˡ of commandments?"

ᵇ Fut. indic. as impv.
ᶜ *One flesh*—one in heart.
ᵈ Pres. impv. so used.
ᵉ Grk., *book of divorce*—so *written charge*.
ᶠ Grk., *some are eunuchs who*, etc.
ᵍ Grk., *them*.
ʰ As note ᵈ above.
ⁱ Aor. means *come into possession*.
ʲ *Agathos, absolutely, perfectly, good*.
ᵏ Pres. impv. means this.
ˡ Interrogative of quality, not identity.

Jesus answered, "You must not murder, You must not commit adultery, You must not steal, You must not lie, ¹⁹ You must practice honoring your father and mother, and you must love your neighbor as you do yourself."

²⁰ The young man said, "I have kept all these commandments; what more do I lack?"

²¹ Jesus said to him, "If you want to be perfect, go and sell everything you have and give the money ᵐ to the poor, and you will have riches in heaven; then come back here and follow me." ²² And when the young man heard that, he went away in deep distress, for he owned a great deal of property.

²³ Jesus said to His disciples, "I solemnly say to you, it will be hard for a rich man to get into the kingdom of heaven. ²⁴ Again, I tell you, it is easier for a camel to go through a needle's eye than for a rich man to get into the kingdom of heaven."

²⁵ But when the disciples heard this, they were dumfounded, and asked, "Who then can be saved!"

²⁶ But Jesus looked at them and said, "This is impossible for men, but anything is possible for God."

²⁷ Then Peter answered Him, "We have left everything we had and followed you. What then are we to get?" ⁿ

²⁸ Jesus said to them: "I solemnly say to you, in the new order of life,º when the Son of Man shall take His seat on His glorious throne, you too, who have followed me, will sit on twelve thrones, and judge the twelve tribes of Israel. ²⁹ And everyone who has given up home or brothers or sisters or father or mother or children or farms, for my sake, will receive many times as much, and in addition will be in possession of eternal life. ³⁰ But many who are first now will be last then, and many who are last now will be first then.

20 THE STORY OF THE LABORERS; HE AGAIN FORETELLS HIS DEATH; HE REBUKES A MOTHER'S AMBITION; CURES TWO BLIND MEN

"For the kingdom of heaven is like an owner of an estate ᵃ who went out early in the morning to hire laborers for his vineyard.

ᵐ Grk., *all your possessions and give to the poor.*
ⁿ Grk., *What will be for us?*
º Grk., *in the regeneration,* etc.
ᵃ Grk., *master of a house,* including estate.

MATTHEW 20

² When he had contracted ᵇ with the laborers at twenty cents a day, he sent them off to his vineyard. ³ He went out again about nine o'clock and found others standing around doing nothing. ⁴ So he said to them, 'You too go out to my vineyard, and I will pay you what is right.' And they went. ⁵ Again he went out about twelve o'clock and three o'clock, and did as before. ⁶ About five he went out again and found still others standing around, and he said to them, 'Why have you been standing here all day doing nothing?' ⁷ They answered him, 'Because nobody has hired us.' He said to them, 'You too go out to my vineyard.'

⁸ "When evening came, the owner of the vineyard said to his manager, 'Call the laborers and pay them their wages, beginning with the last and ending with the first.' ⁹ And they who had been hired ᵉ at five o'clock came and received twenty cents each. ¹⁰ And those who were hired first, when they came, supposed that they would receive more; but they too received twenty cents each. ¹¹ And as they received it, they began to grumble against the owner of the estate, ¹² and say, 'These last worked only one hour, and yet you have put them on the same footing with us who have borne the heavy burdens and scorching heat of the day.' ¹³ But he answered one of them, 'Friend, I am doing you no injustice. Did you not contract with me at twenty cents? ¹⁴ Take what belongs to you and go. I want to give this man hired last as much as I do you. ¹⁵ Have I not the right to do what I please with my own money? ᵈ Or, is your eye causing you to be covetous,ᵉ because I am generous?' ᶠ ¹⁶ So those who are last now will be first then, and those first will be last." ᵍ

¹⁷ And as Jesus was about to go up to Jerusalem, He took the twelve disciples aside, and said to them while on the road, ¹⁸ "Listen! We are going up to Jerusalem, and the Son of Man will be turned over to the high priests and the scribes, and they will sentence ʰ Him to death, ¹⁹ and turn Him over to the heathen to mock and flog and crucify, but on the third day He will rise again."

ᵇ Popular term for it.
ᵉ Implied.
ᵈ Lit., *my own things.*
ᵉ Grk., *wicked.*
ᶠ *Good, generous.*
ᵍ V. 16, core of the story.
ʰ Modern judicial term, but exactly what vb. means.

20 Then the mother of Zebedee's sons came up to Him with her sons, kneeling to Him and asking a favor of Him. **21** And He asked her, "What do you want?"

She answered Him, "Give orders that these two sons of mine may sit one at your right and one at your left in your kingdom."

22 But Jesus answered, "You do not realize[i] what you are asking for. Can you drink the cup that I am about to drink?"

They answered, "Yes, we can."

23 He said to them, "You will drink the cup that I am to drink, but seats at my right and at my left are not mine to give, but they will be given to those for whom they have been prepared by my Father."

24 When the other ten heard of it, they were indignant at the two brothers. **25** But Jesus called them to Him and said, "You know that the rulers of the heathen lord it over them, and their great men rule as despots over them. **26** It is not to be so among you, but whoever wants to be great among you must[j] be your servant, **27** and whoever wants to hold first position among you must be your slave, **28** just as the Son of Man has come, not to be served but to serve, and to give His life a ransom price to set many free."[k]

29 As they were leaving Jericho, a great crowd followed Him. **30** And two blind men sitting by the roadside heard that Jesus was passing and cried out, "Do pity us, Lord, you Son of David!" **31** The crowd reproved them and urged them to keep quiet, but they cried out all the louder, "Do pity us, Lord, you Son of David!"

32 And Jesus stopped and called them, and asked, "What do you want me to do for you?"

33 They answered Him, "Lord, we want our eyes opened!" **34** Then Jesus' heart was moved with pity, and He touched their blinded eyes,[l] and at once they could see again, and followed Him.

21   JESUS RIDES AS KING INTO JERUSALEM; DRIVES THE TRADERS OUT OF THE TEMPLE; TELLS TWO STORIES: THE TWO SONS; THE VILLAINOUS TENANTS

When they were near Jerusalem and had come to Bethphage and the Mount of Olives, Jesus sent two disciples on ahead, **2** and

---

[i] Grk., *know.*
[j] Fut. indic. as impv.
[k] Grk., *a ransom for many;* i.e., *a price paid to set many free.*
[l] Fol. B, rated as best Ms

ordered them, "Go into the village that is ahead of you, and at once you will find a donkey tied there, and a colt with her. Untie her and bring them to me. ³ If anyone says anything to you, you will say, 'The Lord needs them,' and he at once will send them."

⁴ Now this occurred to fulfill what was spoken by the prophet: ᵃ

⁵ "Tell the daughter of Zion
Your King is now comng to you,
Gentle, and riding on a donkey,
Yea, on the colt of a beast of burden." ᵇ

⁶ So the disciples went and did as Jesus had directed them. ⁷ They brought the donkey and the colt and laid their coats upon them, and Jesus took His seat on them. ⁸ And most of the crowd spread their coats along the road, but some were cutting branches from the trees and spreading them along the road. ⁹ And the crowds that went in front of Him and followed Him shouted: ᶜ

"Welcome the Son of David!
Blessed be He who comes in the name of the Lord;
Welcome Him from on high!"

¹⁰ When He came into Jerusalem, the whole city was trembling with excitement,ᵈ and asking, "Who is He?" ¹¹ And the crowds kept saying, "He is the prophet Jesus of Nazareth in Galilee."

¹² And Jesus went into the temple and drove out all the buyers and sellers, and turned the money-changers' tables and the dove-dealers' seats upside down, ¹³ and said to them, "The Scripture says, 'My house must be called a house of prayer,' ᵉ but you have made it a cave for robbers."

¹⁴ Then blind and crippled people came to Him, and He cured them. ¹⁵ But because the high priests and scribes saw the wonders that He did and the children shouting in the temple, "Welcome the Son of David," they were indignant ¹⁶ and asked Him, "Do you hear what they are saying?"

Jesus answered them, "Yes. Did you never read this,ᶠ 'Out of

ᵃ Isa. 62:11; Zech. 9:9.
ᵇ Meaning of Heb. in O. T.
ᶜ Ps. 118:26f.
ᵈ Grk., *shaking as with an earthquake.*
ᵉ Isa. 56:7.
ᶠ Ps. 8:2.

the mouths of little children, yea, of infants, you have perfect praise'?" g

¹⁷ And He left and went out of the city to Bethany, and spent the night there.

¹⁸ Early next morning when He returned to the city, He felt hungry. ¹⁹ As He saw a fig tree by the roadside, He came to it but found on it nothing but leaves, and said to it, "Never again shall a fig ʰ grow on you!" And the fig tree at once withered up.

²⁰ When the disciples saw it, they were dumfounded, and asked, "How is it that the fig tree withered up all at once?"

²¹ And Jesus answered them, "I solemnly say to you, if you have faith and do not doubt at all, you will not only do the sort of wonder done to the fig tree, but even if you say to this mountain, 'Get up and throw yourself into the sea,' it will be done. ²² And whatever you ask for in prayer, if you believe it, you will get it." i

²³ And when He had come into the temple, the high priests and elders of the people came up to Him while He was teaching, and asked, "What sort of authority have you for doing these things, and who gave you this authority?"

²⁴ Jesus answered them, "Let me too ask you just one question, and if you answer it, I will tell you what sort of authority I have for doing as I do. ²⁵ Where did John's baptism come from? From heaven, or from men?" They argued it out among themselves in this way, "If we say, 'From heaven,' He will say to us, 'Then why did you not believe him?' ²⁶ But if we say, 'From men,' we are afraid of the people, for they all consider John a prophet." ²⁷ So they answered Jesus, "We do not know."

He also answered them, "Nor am I going to tell you what sort of authority I have for doing as I do.

²⁸ "But what do you think? There was a man who had two sons. He came to the first ʲ and said, 'Son, go and work in my vineyard today.' ²⁹ And he answered, 'I will, sir,' but he did not go. ³⁰ Then he came to the second and said the same thing. And he answered, 'I will not.' But afterward he changed his mind and went. ³¹ Which of the two did what his father wanted?"

They answered, "The second one."

Jesus said to them, "I solemnly say to you, the tax-collectors and

---

ᵍ Grk., *you made pf. praise*.
ʰ Grk., *fruit*.
ⁱ Grk., *everything you ask in pr., believing*.
ʲ Fol. the order in B.

prostitutes will get into the kingdom of heaven ahead of you.
³² For John came to you walking in the way of uprightness, and yet you did not believe him. The tax-collectors and prostitutes did believe him; but you, even though you saw that, would not change your minds afterward and believe him.

³³ "Listen to another story. There was once an owner of an estate who planted a vineyard and built a fence around it, and hewed out a wine-vat in it, and built a tower, and rented it to tenant farmers,[k] and then went abroad.[l] ³⁴ But when the time for gathering grapes was near, he sent his slaves to the tenants to collect his rent. ³⁵ But the tenants took his slaves and beat the first one, killed the second, and stoned the third. ³⁶ Again he sent other slaves, and more than at first, and they treated them exactly the same way. ³⁷ At last he sent his son to them, for he said to himself, 'They will surely respect my son.' ³⁸ But when the tenants saw the son, they said among themselves, 'This is his heir, come on, let us kill him, and get all that is coming to him!'[m] ³⁹ So they took him and drove him out of the vineyard and murdered him. ⁴⁰ Now when the owner of the estate comes back, what will he do to these tenants?"

⁴¹ They answered, "In vengeance[n] he will put the scoundrels to death, and rent the vineyard to other tenants who will promptly pay him the rent."[o]

⁴² Then Jesus said to them, "Did you never read in the Scriptures:[p]

'That stone which the builders threw away
Has become the cornerstone;
This is the work of the Lord
And seems wonderful to us'?[q]

⁴³ "This, I tell you, is why the kingdom will be taken away from you, and given to a people who will pay a fair rent for it.[r] ⁴⁴ Whoever falls upon that stone will be broken to pieces, but whomever it falls upon will be crushed to powder."

⁴⁵ When the high priests and the Pharisees heard His stories,

[k] Grk., *tillers of the earth.*
[l] So Thayer, Lex.
[m] Lit., *inheritance.*
[n] Grk., *wickedly.*
[o] Grk., *pay him the fruits in season.*
[p] Ps. 118:22,23.
[q] Lit., *in our eyes.*
[r] Grk., *yield fruits for it.*

they knew that He was speaking about them, ⁴⁶ but although they were trying to have Him arrested, they were afraid of the people, for they considered Him a prophet.

22 JESUS TELLS THE STORY OF THE KING'S WEDDING FEAST; ENEMIES TRYING TO TRAP HIM WITH THREE QUESTIONS: IS IT RIGHT TO PAY TAXES TO CAESAR? IS THERE A FUTURE LIFE? WHICH IS THE FIRST COMMANDMENT?

Then Jesus again spoke to them in stories, and said: ² "The kingdom of heaven is like a king,[a] who gave a wedding reception [b] for his son. ³ And he sent his slaves to summon those who had been invited to the wedding reception, but they refused [c] to come. ⁴ A second time he sent other slaves, and said to them, 'Tell the invited guests that I have my reception all ready, my bullocks and fatlings are butchered, and everything is ready. Come to the wedding reception!' ⁵ But they paid no attention [d] to it, but went off, one to his farm, another to his place of business, ⁶ and the rest seized his slaves, treated them with violence, and murdered them. ⁷ Then the king was enraged, and sent his soldiers to put those murderers to death and burned their city. ⁸ After that he said to his slaves, 'My wedding reception is ready, but those invited have proved [e] unworthy. ⁹ So go out to the country crossroads and invite everybody you find to my wedding reception.' ¹⁰ And those slaves went out into the roads and gathered everybody they found, both good and bad, and the bridal-hall was packed [f] with guests. ¹¹ But when the king came in to take a look [g] at the guests, he saw there a man who did not have on a wedding suit.[h] ¹² So he said to him, 'My friend, how is it that you came in here without a wedding suit on?' But his lips were sealed.[i] ¹³ Then the king said to his attendants, 'Tie him hand and foot and throw him out into the darkness on the outside, where he will have to weep and grind his teeth.' ¹⁴ For many are invited, but few are selected."

[a] Grk., *a man, a king.*
[b] A modern term, but exactly expresses Grk.
[c] Grk., *were not willing.*
[d] Grk., *were not concerned.*
[e] Grk., *were.*
[f] Grk., *filled.*
[g] Aorist means this.
[h] Modern term for ancient term, *garment.*
[i] Grk., *muzzled.*

¹⁵ Then the Pharisees went and made a plot to trap Him in argument.ʲ ¹⁶ So they sent to Him their disciples with the Herodians, to say to Him, "Teacher, we know that you are in the habit of telling the truth ᵏ and of teaching the way of God in honesty,ˡ and you do not care what anyone says, for you are not partial.ᵐ ¹⁷ So give us your opinion on the question: Is it right to pay Caesar the poll-tax, or not?"

¹⁸ But Jesus saw their malicious plot, and so asked, "Why are you testing me so, you hypocrites? ¹⁹ Show me a poll-tax coin." ⁿ ²⁰ And He asked them, "Whose likeness and title is this?" ²¹ They answered, "Caesar's."

Then He said to them, "Pay Caesar, therefore, what belongs to Caesar, and pay God what belongs to God." ²² And when they heard it, they were dumfounded; and they left Him and went away.

²³ On the same day some Sadducees, who claim that there is no resurrection, came up to Him, and asked this question: ²⁴ "Teacher, Moses said, 'If a man dies without children, his brother must marry his widow and raise up a family ᵒ for him.' ²⁵ Now there were seven brothers among us. The first married and died without children, and left his widow to his brother. ²⁶ The second also died, and the third, and all down to the seventh. ²⁷ Last of all the woman died, too. ²⁸ Now at the resurrection which one's wife, of the seven, will she be? For they all married ᵖ her."

²⁹ Jesus answered them, "You are wrong in your views, because you do not understand the Scriptures nor the power of God, ³⁰ for after ᑫ the resurrection men do not marry and women are not married, but continue to live together as the angels do in heaven. ³¹ But did you never read, on the resurrection of the dead, what God said to you,ʳ ³² 'I am the God of Abraham and the God of Isaac and the God of Jacob'? Now God is not the God of dead but of living men." ³³ And when the crowds heard this, they were dumfounded at His teaching.

³⁴ Now the Pharisees heard that He had silenced the Sadducees,

ʲ Grk., *word.*
ᵏ Grk., *being true.*
ˡ Grk., *in truth, as He saw it,* so *in honesty.*
ᵐ Grk., *looking on the face.*
ⁿ Not quite twenty cents.
ᵒ Grk., *seed.*
ᵖ Grk., *all had her.*
ᑫ Grk., *in,* but *in the resurrection period,* so *after the resurrection.*
ʳ Grk., *what was said by God to you.*

and so they had a meeting. ³⁵ And one of their number, an expert in the law, to tempt Him, asked, ³⁶ "Teacher, what sort ˢ of command is greatest in the law?"

³⁷ And He answered him, "You must love the Lord your God with your whole heart, your whole soul, and your whole mind.' ³⁸ This is the greatest command, and is first in importance. ³⁹ The second is like it: 'You must love your neighbor as you do yourself.' ⁴⁰ The essence of the whole law and the prophets is packed ᵗ into these two commands."

⁴¹ And when the Pharisees came together, Jesus asked them, ⁴² "What is your opinion of the Christ? Whose son is He?"

They answered Him, "He is David's son."

⁴³ He asked them, "How then does David, under the guidance of the Spirit, call Him Lord, when he says: ᵘ

⁴⁴ " 'The Lord has said to my Lord, Sit at my right hand,
Until I put your enemies under your feet'?
⁴⁵ If David, then, calls Him Lord, how can He be his son?" ⁴⁶ And not one could answer Him a word, and from that day ᵛ on no one ever dared to ask Him any more questions.

23 JESUS EXPOSES THE SINS OF THE PHARISEES; WARNS THE PEOPLE AGAINST THEM; PRONOUNCES SEVEN WOES AGAINST THEM; WEEPS OVER JERUSALEM

Then Jesus said to the crowds and to His disciples:

² "The scribes and Pharisees have taken Moses' seat as teachers.ᵃ ³ So everything they tell you, do and practice,ᵇ but stop doing what they do, for they preach but do not practice.ᶜ ⁴ They tie up heavy burdens and fasten them on men's shoulders, but they refuse to lift a finger to help bear them. ⁵ They do what they do to attract people's attention. They wear on their coats Scripture texts in big letters,ᵈ and they wear large tassels, ⁶ and they like the places of honor at feasts and the front seats in synagogues, ⁷ to be greeted with honor in public places, and to have men call them 'Teacher.'

ˢ Quality emphasized.
ᵗ Grk., *On these hang the weight*, etc.
ᵘ Ps. 110: 1.
ᵛ Grk., *hour*.
ᵃ Implied, since teachers sat.
ᵇ Pres. of cont. action.
ᶜ This our modern maxim exactly trans. what Jesus said.
ᵈ Exact meaning of *phylacteries* (Grk).

MATTHEW 23

8 But as for you, you must not seek * for others to call you 'Teacher,' for you have but one who is 'Teacher,' and you are all brothers. 9 And you must not call anyone on earth 'father,' for the Heavenly One is your Father. 10 And you must not be called 'leaders,' for you have only one Leader, and that is Christ. 11 Whoever is greatest among you must be your servant. 12 Whoever exalts himself will be humbled, and whoever humbles himself will be exalted.[f]

13 "A curse on you, you hypocritical scribes and Pharisees! For you bolt the doors of the kingdom of heaven in men's faces,[g] for you neither go in yourselves, nor do you let those who are trying to do so go in.[h] 15 A curse on you, you hypocritical scribes and Pharisees! For you scour land and sea to win a single convert, and when he is won you make him twice as fit for the pit[i] as you are. 16 A curse on you, you blind leaders who say, 'Whoever swears by the sanctuary is not duty-bound, but whoever swears by the gold of the sanctuary is duty-bound.' 17 You blind fools! which is greater, the gold, or the sanctuary that makes the gold sacred? 18 You say, 'Whoever swears by the altar is not duty-bound, but whoever swears by the offering on the altar is duty-bound!' 19 You blind men! which is greater, the offering, or the altar that makes the offering sacred? 20 So whoever swears by the altar swears by everything on it; 21 whoever swears by the sanctuary swears by it and by Him who dwells in it; 22 whoever swears by heaven swears by the throne of God and by Him who sits on it.

23 "A curse on you, you hypocritical scribes and Pharisees! For you pay tithes on mint and dill and cummin,[j] and yet leave out the more vital [k] matters of the law, justice, love and fidelity. These latter especially [l] you ought to have done, but ought not to have left out the former. 24 You blind leaders, who are straining out the gnat but gulping down the camel! 25 A curse on you, you hypocritical scribes and Pharisees, for you clean the outside of the cup and the dish, but inside they are full of your greed and self-indulgence. 26 You blind Pharisee! You must first clean the inside of the cup and the dish, so that the outside may be clean too.

---

* So EGT.
[f] Some authorities add here the words contained in vs. 14 of K. J. Version.
[g] Grk., *before men,* but our idiom, *bolt the door in the face,* expresses the Grk.
[h] V. 14. Not in best manuscripts.
[i] Grk., *double son of Gehenna.*
[j] Very small garden vegetables; emphasizing punctilious devotion to the law.
[k] Grk., *weightier matters.*
[l] In emph. position, so *these especially.*

⁲⁷ "A curse on you, you hypocritical scribes and Pharisees, for you are like white-washed tombs, which look beautiful on the outside, but inside are full of dead people's bones and everything that is unclean!ᵐ ²⁸ So you, too, on the outside seem to people to be upright, but inside you are full of hypocrisy and lawlessness.

²⁹ "A curse on you, you hypocritical scribes and Pharisees, for you build tombs for the prophets, and decorate monuments for the upright, ³⁰ and say, 'If we had lived in the days of our forefathers, we would not have been sharers with them in shedding the blood of the prophets.' ³¹ So you are witnessing against yourselves that you are the descendants of those who murdered the prophets. ³² Then fill up to the brim the cup of your forefathers' guilt! ⁿ ³³ You serpents! You brood of vipers! How can you escape a sentence to the pit!ᵒ ³⁴ Therefore, I am going to send you prophets, wise men, and scribes, some of whom you will kill—even crucify—ᵖ and some you will flog in your synagogues and chase from city to city, ³⁵ so that on you will come all the righteous blood shed on the earth from the blood of upright Abel to the blood of Zechariah, Barachiah's son, whom you murdered between the sanctuary and the altar. ³⁶ I solemnly say to you, all this will come upon this age!

³⁷ "O Jerusalem, Jerusalem! the city that has kept on murdering the prophets, and stoning those who have been sent to her, how often I have yearned to gather your children around me, as a hen gathers her chickens under her wings, but you refused! ³⁸ Now your house is abandoned by me! ³⁹ For I tell you, you will never see me again until you say, 'Blessed be He who comes in the name of the Lord.' "

24   JESUS TELLS OF THE DOOM OF THE CITY; THE SIGNS OF HIS COMING; THE STORIES OF THE FIG TREE AND OF THE FAITHFUL SERVANTS

And Jesus left the temple, and was going ᵃ away, when ᵇ His disciples came up to Him, to show Him the temple buildings. ² But He answered them, "Do you see all these things? I solemnly say

---

ᵐ Grk., *of all uncleanness.*
ⁿ Grk., *measure,* but cup is a symbol of guilt.
ᵒ Grk., *the judgment to Gehenna.*
ᵖ Most cruel method of capital punishment.
ᵃ Impf. of cont. ac.
ᵇ Grk., *and,* but Ara. influence makes it *when.*

MATTHEW 24

to you, there shall not be left here one stone upon another that shall not be torn down."

³ While He was sitting on the Mount of Olives, the disciples came up to Him by themselves, and said, "Tell us when this is to take place, and what will be the sign of your coming and of the end of the age."

⁴ Jesus answered, "Look out that no one misleads you about it, ⁵ for many will come bearing the name ᵉ of the Messiah, and saying, 'I am the Christ,' and will mislead many people. ⁶ You are going to hear of wars and rumors of wars; take care not to be scared out of your wits. They have to come, but that is not the end yet. ⁷ For nation will go to war ᵈ with nation, and kingdom with kingdom, and there will be famines and earthquakes in many places.ᵉ ⁸ But all this is but the beginning of the agonies. ⁹ At that time they will turn you over to torture, and will murder you, and you will be hated by all the heathen, because you bear my name.ᶠ ¹⁰ Then many will fall by the way,ᵍ and will betray one another and hate one another. ¹¹ Many false prophets will appear and mislead many people; ¹² and because of the increasing crime wave,ʰ most people's love will grow cold. ¹³ But whoever bears up to the end will be saved. ¹⁴ And this good news of the kingdom must be preached all over the inhabited world, for a testimony to all the heathen, and then the end will come.

¹⁵ "So when you see the destructive desecration, mentioned by the prophet Daniel, standing in the Holy Place"—let the reader take notice—ⁱ ¹⁶ "then let those who remain in Judea fly to the hills; ¹⁷ let him who is on the roof of his house not come down to get his household goods out; ¹⁸ let him who is in the field not turn back to get his coat. ¹⁹ Alas for women who are expectant mothers and those who have nursing babies in those days! ²⁰ And pray for your flight not to be in winter or on the sabbath, ²¹ for there will be greater misery at that time than ever has been since the world began,ʲ or ever will be again. ²² And if those days had not been cut

---

ᵉ Grk., *in my name.*
ᵈ Grk., *will rise against nation.*
ᵉ Grk., *from place to place.*
ᶠ Grk., *on account of my name.*
ᵍ Grk., *will be caused to stumble.*
ʰ Grk., *lawlessness.*
ⁱ Grk., *understand.*
ʲ Grk., *from the beginning of the world,* etc.

short, nobody would have escaped, but for the sake of God's chosen people [k] those days will be cut short.

23 "If anyone at that time says to you, 'Here is the Christ!' or 'There He is!' do not believe it, 24 for false Christs and false prophets will announce themselves,[l] and they will show great signs and wonders to mislead, if possible, God's chosen people. 25 Remember,[m] I have told you beforehand. 26 So if they say to you, 'Here He is in the desert,' do not go out to see,[n] or 'Here He is in some secret place,' do not believe it. 27 For just as the lightning starts in the east and flashes clear to the west, so the coming of the Son of Man will be. 28 Wherever there is a carcass,[o] there the vultures will flock.

29 "And immediately after the misery of those days, the sun will turn dark, the moon will not shed its light, the stars will fall from the sky, and the powers of the sky will be shaken. 30 And then the sign of the Son of Man will appear in the sky, and then all the nations of the earth will mourn when [p] they see the Son of Man coming on the clouds of the sky in overwhelming [q] power and splendor. 31 And He will send out His angels with a loud [r] trumpet call, and they will gather His chosen people from the four points of the compass, from one end of the sky to the other.

32 "Now learn what the story of the fig tree means. Just as soon as its branches grow tender, and put forth leaves, you know that summer is near. 33 So when you see all these things, you will know that He is right at your door.[s] 34 I solemnly say to you, the present age will not pass away before all this takes place. 35 Sky and earth will pass away but my words will never pass away. 36 But about that day or hour not a single one knows—not even the angels in heaven or the Son; not a single one but the Father alone. 37 For just as it was in the days of Noah, so it will be at the coming of the Son of Man. 38 For just as in the days before the Flood people went on eating and drinking, marrying and being married, until the very day Noah entered the ark, 39 and knew nothing about it until the Flood came and swept them all away,[t] so it will be at the

---

[k] Grk., *the elect.*
[l] Grk., *rise.*
[m] Grk., *behold,* but *remember* fits the warning given.
[n] Vb. merely implied.
[o] This maxim merely refers to signs of His coming.
[p] Grk., *and* meaning *when,* as footnote B, p. 64.
[q] Grk., *great*—an elastic term; here *overwhelming.*
[r] *Great* in the sense of *loud.*
[s] Grk., *near, at the door.*
[t] Grk., *bore them away,* but the word *flood* suggests, *swept them away.*

coming of the Son of Man. ⁴⁰ Two men will be in the field; one will be taken, one will be left. ⁴¹ Two women will be grinding with the handmill; one will be taken, one will be left. ⁴² So keep on watching, for you do not know on what day your Lord is coming. ⁴³ But be sure of this, that if the master of the house had known in exactly what part of the night the thief would come, he would have been on guard and would not have let his house be broken into. ⁴⁴ So you, too, must continue to be ready, for at an hour you are not expecting Him the Son of Man will come.

⁴⁵ "Who then is the faithful and thoughtful slave, whom his master put in charge of his household, to deal out to the members of it their supplies at the proper time? ⁴⁶ Blessed is that slave if, when his master comes back, he finds him so doing. ⁴⁷ I solemnly say to you, he will put him in charge of all his property. ⁴⁸ But if the slave is bad and says to himself,ᵘ 'My master is going to be gone a long time,' ⁴⁹ and begins to beat his fellow-slaves, and keeps on eating and drinking with those who get drunk, ⁵⁰ the master of that slave will come on the very day he is not expecting him, ⁵¹ and will cut him in two, and give him his share with the hypocrites, where they will weep and grind their teeth."

25 JESUS TELLS THE STORY OF THE TEN BRIDESMAIDS; THE STORY OF THE TALENTS; THE LAST JUDGMENT

"Then the kingdom of heaven will be like ten bridesmaids who took their lamps and went out to meet the bridegroom. ² Now five of them were thoughtless and five were thoughtful. ³ For the thoughtless ones took their lamps but took no oil with them. ⁴ But the thoughtful ones not only took their lamps but also extra oil in their oilcans.ᵃ ⁵ While the bridegroom was delaying, they all got ᵇ drowsy and dropped off ᶜ to sleep. ⁶ But at midnight there was a shout, 'Here comes the bridegroom! Go out to meet him!' ⁷ Then all those bridesmaids awoke and trimmed their lampwicks.ᵈ ⁸ And the thoughtless ones said to the thoughtful ones, 'Give us some of your oil, for our lamps are going out.' ⁹ But the thoughtful ones answered, 'No, no, there may not be enough for

---
ᵘ Grk., *in his heart.*
ᵃ Lit. *vessels,* for oil, so *oilcans.*
ᵇ Aor., so pointed action.
ᶜ Incep. impf.
ᵈ Grk., *lamps,* but really *lampwicks.*

you and us.ᵉ Go to the store ᶠ and buy your own oil.' ¹⁰ And while they were going to buy it, the bridegroom came, and the bridesmaids that were ready went in with him to the wedding reception; and the door was closed. ¹¹ At last the rest of the bridesmaids came, and kept begging,ᵍ 'Master, master, open the door for us!' ¹² But he answered, 'I positively say to you, I do not know you.' ¹³ So you must keep on watching, for you do not know either the day or the hour.

¹⁴ "For it is just like a man who was going on a long journey from his homeland, who called to him his slaves and turned his property over to them. ¹⁵ He gave one five thousand dollars, another two thousand, another one thousand, to each in accordance with his ability. Then he started ʰ on his long journey. ¹⁶ The man who had received the five thousand dollars at once went out and invested it, and made five thousand more. ¹⁷ In the same way the man who had received the two thousand made two thousand more. ¹⁸ But the man who had received the one thousand went off and dug a hole in the ground and buried ⁱ his master's money. ¹⁹ After a long time the master of those slaves came back and settled accounts with them. ²⁰ The man who had received the five thousand dollars came up and brought him five thousand more, saying, 'You turned over to me five thousand dollars; here are five thousand more ʲ I made.' ²¹ His master said to him 'Well done, my good and faithful slave, you have been faithful in the use of a small amount; I will put you in charge of a larger one. Come, share your master's joy!' ²² Then the man who had received the two thousand came up and said, 'Master, you turned over to me two thousand dollars; here are two thousand more I made.' ²³ His master said to him, 'Well done, my good and faithful slave, you have been faithful in the use of a small amount; I will put you in charge of a larger one. Come, share your master's joy!' ²⁴ Then the man who had received the one thousand came up and said, 'Master, I knew you were a hard man, who reaped where you had not sown, who gathered where you had not threshed.ᵏ ²⁵ So I was afraid, and went off and buried your thousand dollars in the ground. Here is your money.' ²⁶ His master answered him, 'You

---

ᵉ This ancient order reversed in modern social life.
ᶠ Grk., *the sellers*.
ᵍ Grk., *saying*, but in begging tone.
ʰ Incep. aor.
ⁱ Grk., *dug in the ground and hid*.
ʲ As in Grk., no relative needed.
ᵏ Grk., *scattered*

wicked, lazy slave, you knew that I reaped where I had not sown and gathered where I had not threshed. ²⁷ So you ought to have deposited my money with the bankers, so that when I came back I could have collected my principal¹ with interest. ²⁸ So take the thousand dollars away from him and give it to him who has ten thousand. ²⁹ For the man who has will have more given to him, even till it overflows,ᵐ but from the man who has nothing even what he has will be taken away. ³⁰ And throw the good-for-nothing slave out into the darkness on the outside, where he will weep and grind his teeth.'

³¹ "When the Son of Man comes in His splendor, and all the angels with Him, He will take His seat on His splendid throne, ³² and all the nations will be gathered before Him, and He will separate them from one another, just as a shepherd separates his sheep from his goats, ³³ and He will put the sheep at His right hand and the goats at his left. ³⁴ Then the King will say to those at His right, 'Come, you who are blessed by my Father, take possession of the kingdom prepared for you from the creation of the world. ³⁵ For when I was hungry, you gave me something to eat, when I was thirsty you gave me something to drink, when I was a stranger you welcomed me to your homes,ⁿ ³⁶ when I needed clothes you put them on me, when I was sick you looked after me, when I was in prison you came to see me.' ³⁷ Then the upright will answer, 'Lord, when did we ever see you hungry and give you something to eat, or thirsty, and give you something to drink? ³⁸ When did we ever see you a stranger and welcome you to our homes, or needing clothes, and put them on you? ³⁹ When did we ever see you sick or in prison, and come to see you?' ⁴⁰ And the King will answer them, 'I solemnly say to you, every time you did a good deed to one of these most insignificantº brothers of mine, you did a good deed to me.'

⁴¹ "Then He will say to those at His left, 'Begone from me, you who are now cursed, to the everlasting fire prepared for the devil and his angels. ⁴² For when I was hungry you gave me nothing to eat, when I was thirsty you gave me nothing to drink, ⁴³ when I was a stranger you did not welcome me to your homes, when I needed clothes you did not put them on me, when I was sick and in prison, you did not look after me.' ⁴⁴ Then they will answer,

¹ Grk., *property*.
ᵐ Exact meaning of vb.
ⁿ Grk., *brought me together with yourselves*.
º Grk., *the least*, so *most insignificant* (in social sense).

'Lord, when did we ever see you hungry, or thirsty, or a stranger, or needing clothes, or sick, or in prison, and did not wait on[p] you?' ⁴⁵Then He will answer, 'I solemnly say to you, every time you failed to do a good deed to one of these most insignificant people, you failed to do a good deed to me.' ⁴⁶Then these will go away to everlasting punishment, but the upright to everlasting life."

26
THEY PLOT TO KILL JESUS; JUDAS POINTED OUT AS THE BETRAYER; JESUS ANOINTED BY MARY; JUDAS BARGAINS TO BETRAY HIM; JESUS INSTITUTES THE MEMORIAL SUPPER; FORETELLS THAT PETER WILL DISOWN HIM; AFTER STRUGGLING IN GETHSEMANE HE IS ARRESTED AS JUDAS BETRAYS HIM; TRIED IN JEWISH COURT; DISOWNED BY PETER

When Jesus had ended this discourse, He said to His disciples, ²"You know that in two days the Passover Feast will take place, and the Son of Man will be turned over to be crucified."

³ Then the high priests and the elders of the people met in the palace of the high priest, whose name was Caiaphas, ⁴ and plotted to arrest Jesus by stratagem and put Him to death. ⁵ But they kept saying, "It must not be at the feast, for [a] a riot may break out among the people."

⁶ When Jesus came back to Bethany, to the home of Simon the leper, ⁷ a woman with an alabaster bottle of very costly perfume came up to Him while He was at table and poured it upon His head. ⁸ When the disciples saw it, they were very indignant, and said, "Why such waste? ⁹ Surely it could have been sold for a large sum and the money given to the poor."

¹⁰ But Jesus, because He understood them, said to them, "Why do you embarrass [b] the woman? She has done a good deed to me, ¹¹ for you always have the poor among you, but you will not always have me. ¹² For in putting this perfume on my body she has done it to prepare me for my burial. ¹³ I solemnly say to you, all over the world wherever this good news is proclaimed, the good deed that she has done will be told, in memory of her."

[p] Grk., *served*, so *waited on*.
[a] Grk., *lest*.
[b] Grk., *trouble*.

MATTHEW 26

¹⁴ Then one of the Twelve, whose name was Judas Iscariot, went to the high priests, ¹⁵ and said, "What will you give me to turn Him over to you?" Then they paid ᵉ him thirty pieces ᵈ of silver. ¹⁶ So from that time he kept looking for a good opportunity to turn Him over to them.

¹⁷ On the first day of the Passover Feast the disciples came to Jesus and said, "Where do you want us to get the Passover supper ready for you to eat?"

¹⁸ And He said, "Go into the city, to a certain man, and say to him, 'The Teacher says, "My time is near. I am going to keep the Passover at your house with my disciples." ' "

¹⁹ So the disciples did as Jesus directed them, and got the Passover supper ready.

²⁰ When evening came, He was sitting at the table with the Twelve. ²¹ And while they were eating, He said, "I solemnly say to you, one of you is going to betray me."

²² They were cut to the bottom of their hearts,ᵉ and began to ask one by one, "It cannot be I, can it, Lord?" ᶠ

²³ He answered, "The man who has just dipped his hand with me in the dish is the man who is going to betray me. ²⁴ The Son of Man is going away as the Scriptures say of Him, but a curse will be on that man by whom He is betrayed. It would have been better for that man, if he had never been born!"

²⁵ Then Judas, who afterward betrayed Him, answered by asking, "It cannot be I, can it, Rabbi?"

Jesus answered him, "Yes, you are the man." ᵍ

²⁶ While they were eating, Jesus took a loaf and blessed it; then He broke it in pieces and gave it to the disciples, and said, "Take this and eat it; this is my body." * ²⁷ He also took the cup of wine ʰ and gave thanks; then He gave it to them, saying, "All of you drink some of it, ²⁸ for this is my blood * which ratifies the covenant, the blood which is to be poured out for many for the forgiveness of their sins. ²⁹ I tell you, I will never again drink the product ⁱ of the vine till the day when I drink the new wine with you in my Father's kingdom."

ᶜ Grk., *stood to him thirty*, etc.
ᵈ About $15.
ᵉ Grk., *exceedingly grieved*.
ᶠ Neg. answer thus expressed.
ᵍ Grk., *you said so*.
ʰ Implied with *cup*.
* Metaphorical language.
ⁱ Exact meaning of Greek.

30 After singing a hymn, they left the city, and went up the Mount of Olives.

31 Then Jesus said to them, "You will all stumble over me to-night, for the Scripture says, 'I will strike the shepherd, and the sheep of the flock will be scattered.' **32** But after I am raised from the dead,[j] I will go back to Galilee to meet you."

33 Peter answered, "Though all the rest of them stumble over you, I will never do so."

34 Jesus said to him, "I solemnly say to you, this very night, before a cock crows, you will disown me three times."

35 Peter answered, "Even if I have to die with you, I will never disown you."

36 Then Jesus came with them to a place called Gethsemane, and He said to the disciples, "Sit down here while I go over yonder and pray." **37** And He took Peter and Zebedee's two sons along with Him and He began to give way[k] to His grief and distress of heart. **38** Then He said to them, "My heart is breaking, it almost kills me! You must stay here and keep watching with me."

39 Then He walked on a few steps and threw Himself upon His face, and in this attitude continued[l] to pray, and say, "My Father, if it is possible, let this cup pass by me; and yet, I pray, not what I want but what you want."

40 Then He came back to the disciples and found them asleep. He said to Peter, "Could you not then watch with me a single hour? **41** You must all[m] keep watching and praying that you may not be exposed[n] to temptation. Man's spirit is willing but human nature[o] is weak."

42 A second time He went away and prayed,

"My Father, if it cannot pass by without my drinking it, your will be done." **43** He came back again and found them still sleeping, for their eyes were so heavy they could hardly hold them open. **44** Then He left them again and prayed the third time, using the same words.[p] **45** After that He came back to the disciples and said to them:

"Still sleeping! Still resting! See! The time has come for the

---

[j] Lit., *after I am raised.*
[k] Grk., *began to be grieved,* etc.; i.e., to show His grief, give way to it.
[l] Pres. pt.
[m] *You* in pl., so *all.*
[n] Grk., *go into.*
[o] Grk., *flesh.*
[p] Grk., *saying the same word.*

Son of Man to be betrayed into the hands of sinful men! ⁴⁶ Get up and let us be going. Look! Here comes my betrayer!"

⁴⁷ Even while He was still speaking, here came Judas, one of the Twelve, and with him a crowd, with swords and clubs, from the high priests and the elders of the people. ⁴⁸ Now His betrayer had given them a signal by saying, "The one I kiss is He. Seize Him!" ⁴⁹ And he went straight up to Jesus and said, "Good evening, Rabbi," and affectionately q kissed Him.

⁵⁰ Jesus said to him, "My friend, do what you came for."

Then they came up, laid hands on Jesus, and arrested Him. ⁵¹ One of the men with Jesus put out his hand and drew his sword, and with a thrust at the high priest's slave cut off his ear. ⁵² Then Jesus said to him, "Put your sword back where it belongs,ʳ for all who wield the sword will die by the sword. ⁵³ Do you suppose that I am unable to appeal to my Father and have Him furnish me on the spot one hundred thousand angels? ˢ ⁵⁴ How then could the Scriptures be fulfilled, for they say this is the way it must be?"

⁵⁵ At that time Jesus said to the crowds: "Have you come out with swords and clubs to arrest me, as though I were a robber? Day after day I used to sit teaching in the temple, and you never laid hands on me. ⁵⁶ But this has all taken place so that the writings of the prophets may be fulfilled." Then the disciples all forsook Him and made their escape.

⁵⁷ The men who had laid hands on Jesus took Him away to Caiaphas, the high priest, at whose home ᵗ the scribes and elders had met. ⁵⁸ And Peter followed Him at a distance as far as the courtyard of the high priest's home; he even went inside and was sitting among the attendants to see how it would end.ᵘ ⁵⁹ Now the high priests and the whole council were trying to get false testimony against Jesus, to have Him put to death; ⁶⁰ but they could not, although many false witnesses came forward to testify.

At last two men came forward ⁶¹ and said, "This man said, 'I can tear down the temple of God, and build it again in three days.'"

⁶² Then the high priest arose and said to Him, "Have you no answer to make? What do you say to the evidence that they bring against you?" ⁶³ But Jesus kept silent. So the high priest said to

---

q In comp. vb.
ʳ Grk., *in its place.*
ˢ Grk., *more than twelve legions,* more than 100,000.
ᵗ Grk., *the high priest, where,* etc.
ᵘ Grk., *to see the end.*

Him, "I charge you, on your oath, in the name of the living God, tell us whether you are the Christ, the Son of God."

⁶⁴ Jesus answered him, "Yes, I am.ᵛ But I tell you, you will all soon see the Son of Man seated at the right hand of the Almighty, and coming on the clouds of the sky."

⁶⁵ Then the high priest tore his clothes, and said, "He has uttered blasphemy. What more evidence do we need? You have just heard His blasphemy. ⁶⁶ What do you think now?"

Then they answered, "He deserves to die." ʷ

⁶⁷ After that they spit in His face and hit Him with their fists, and others boxed His ears, ⁶⁸ saying, "Play the prophet, you Christ, and tell us who struck you."

⁶⁹ Now Peter was sitting outside in the courtyard, and a waiting-girl came up to him, and said, "You, too, were with Jesus the Galilean."

⁷⁰ But he denied it before them all, and said, "I do not understand what you mean."

⁷¹ Then he went out into the gateway, and another waiting-girl saw him, and said to those there, "This fellow was with Jesus the Nazarene."

⁷² Again he denied it, and even swore, "I do not know the man!"

⁷³ A few minutes afterward the bystanders came up to Peter and said, "You are surely one of them, too, for your accentˣ gives you away."

⁷⁴ Then he commenced cursing and swearing, "I do not know the man!" And at once a cock crowed. ⁷⁵ Then Peter remembered Jesus' words, "Before a cock crows, you will disown me three times." And he went outside and wept bitterly.

27 JESUS TURNED OVER TO THE ROMAN COURT; JUDAS COMMITS SUICIDE; JESUS TRIED IN THE ROMAN COURT; MOCKED; CRUCIFIED; BURIED

As soon as day broke, all the high priests and elders held a consultationᵃ against Jesus, to put Him to death. ² So they bound Him, led Him away, and turned Him over to Pilate the governor.ᵇ

³ Then Judas, who had betrayed Him, as he felt condemned, in

ᵛ Grk., *you said so.*
ʷ Grk., *guilty of death.*
ˣ *Even your speech,* etc.
ᵃ The meeting held before day, illegal.
ᵇ Also *judge.*

remorse brought back the thirty pieces to the high priests and elders, ⁴ and said, "I did wrong in turning an innocent ᵉ man over to death."

But they said, "What is that to us? You must see to that yourself."

⁵ Then he tossed the money into the temple and left, and went off and hanged himself.

⁶ The high priests picked up the money and said, "It is not legal to put it into the consecrated treasury,ᵈ for it is blood-money." ⁷ So after consultation they bought with it the Potter's Field as a burying-ground for strangers. ⁸ Now this piece of ground has ever since been called, "The Field of Blood." ⁹ In that way the words spoken by the prophet Jeremiah were fulfilled: "They took the thirty pieces of silver, the price of the one whose price had been fixed by some Israelites,ᵉ ¹⁰ and gave them for the Potter's Field, as the Lord directed me."

¹¹ Now Jesus stood before the governor, and the governor asked Him, "Are you the king of the Jews?"

Jesus answered, "Yes." ¹² And while the charges were being made against Him by the high priests and elders, He made no answer.

¹³ Then Pilate said to Him, "Do you not hear how strongᶠ is the evidence they are bringing against you?" ¹⁴ But He did not answer him a single word, so that the governor was dumfounded beyond expression.

¹⁵ Now at the feast the governor was accustomed to set any prisoner free whom the people wanted. ¹⁶ At that time they had a notorious prisoner named Barabbas. ¹⁷ So when they met for this purpose, Pilate asked them, "Which one do you want me to set free, Barabbas, or Jesus, the so-called Christ?" ¹⁸ For he knew that they had turned Him over to the court out of envy.

¹⁹ Now while he was on the bench, his wife sent him this word, "Do not have anything to do with that righteous man, for I have this morning suffered excruciating pain in a dream causedᵍ by Him."

²⁰ But the high priests and the elders lined up the crowds to ask for Barabbas, and to have Jesus put to death. ²¹ Still the governor

---

ᶜ Grk., *innocent blood.*
ᵈ Grk., *corban, consecrated treasure.*
ᵉ Grk., *sons of Israel.*
ᶠ Grk., *how great things they testify,* etc.
ᵍ Grk., *because of Him.*

answered, "Which of the two do you want me to set free for you?" And they said, "Barabbas." ²² Pilate asked them, "What then shall I do with Jesus, the so-called Christ?"

They all answered, "Have Him crucified!" ²³ He asked, "Why, what has He done that is wrong?"

But they kept on shouting louder and louder, "Have Him crucified!" ²⁴ So Pilate, since he saw that he was making no headway with them, but that a riot was about to break out instead, took some water and washed his hands before the crowd, and said, "I am not responsible for this man's death; you must see to it yourselves." ²⁵ And all the people answered, "His blood be on us and on our children!" ²⁶ Then he set Barabbas free for them, but had Jesus flogged and turned over to be crucified.

²⁷ Then the governor's soldiers took Jesus into the barracks, and gathered about Him the whole battalion.[h] ²⁸ Then they stripped Him, and put a purple cloak on Him, ²⁹ and made a crown of thorns and set it on His head, and they put a stick in His hand, and kneeling before Him they made sport of Him, saying, "All hail, you king of the Jews!" ³⁰ And they spit on Him, and took the stick and kept hitting Him on the head. ³¹ And when they had finished making sport of Him, they took off the cloak, and put His own clothes back on Him, and led Him away to be crucified.

³² As they were going out of the city, they found a Cyrenian named Simon, and they forced him to carry Jesus'[i] cross. ³³ When they came to a place called Golgotha, which means the Place of the Skull, ³⁴ they gave Him some wine mixed with gall, but when He tasted it, He would not drink it. ³⁵ Then they crucified Him and divided among them His clothes by drawing lots, ³⁶ and sitting down they kept watch of Him there. ³⁷ They put above His head the charge against Him, which read:[j]

"THIS IS JESUS, THE KING OF THE JEWS."

³⁸ At the same time two robbers were crucified with Him, one at His right and one at His left. ³⁹ And the passers-by kept hissing at Him, shaking their heads ⁴⁰ and saying, "You who would tear

---

[h] A modern military term, nearly equivalent to Rom. *speira*.
[i] Pronoun in Grk., but noun makes it clearer in Eng.
[j] Grk., *written*.

MATTHEW 27

down the temple and build another in three days, save yourself! If you are really [k] the Son of God, come down from the cross."

⁴¹ And the high priests, too, made sport of Him, with the scribes and elders, and said, ⁴² "He saved others but He cannot save Himself. He is the king of Israel, is He?[l] Well, let Him come down from the cross, and we will believe in Him. ⁴³ He has put His trust in God; let God deliver Him now, if He cares for Him, for He said, 'I am the Son of God.'" ⁴⁴ Even the robbers who were crucified with Him made sport of Him in the same way.

⁴⁵ Now from twelve o'clock till three, darkness covered the whole land. ⁴⁶ About three Jesus cried out with a loud voice, "Eloi, Eloi, lama sabachthani?" [m] which means, "My God! My God! why have you forsaken me?"

⁴⁷ Some of the bystanders, when they heard it, said, "He is calling for Elijah." ⁴⁸ So one of them at once ran off and took a sponge and soaked it in vinegar, put it on a stick and held it up to Him to drink.

⁴⁹ But the others said, "Wait; let us see if Elijah does come to deliver Him."

⁵⁰ But Jesus cried out again with a loud voice, and gave up His spirit. ⁵¹ And at once the curtain of the sanctuary was torn from top to bottom, the earth shook, the rocks were split, ⁵² the tombs were opened, and many bodies of saints then sleeping in death [n] rose ⁵³ and left their tombs, and after His resurrection went into the holy city and appeared to many people.

⁵⁴ And the army captain and his men, who were keeping guard over Jesus, who felt [o] the earthquake and saw all that was taking place, were terribly frightened, and said, "Surely this was God's Son." [p]

⁵⁵ Now several women were there looking on from a distance, who accompanied Jesus from Galilee to care for Him, ⁵⁶ among them Mary of Magdala, Mary the mother of James and Joseph, and the mother of Zebedee's sons.

⁵⁷ Although it was now evening, a rich man named Joseph, from

---

[k] Implied in the form of condition.
[l] Spoken in irony and sarcasm.
[m] His native Ara. better expressing His emotion.
[n] Grk., *sleeping*.
[o] Grk., *saw*.
[p] We use cap. S, for they felt Him to be superhuman.

Arimathea, who was himself a disciple of Jesus, ⁵⁸ came to Pilate and asked for Jesus' body. Then Pilate ordered it to be given to him. ⁵⁹ So Joseph took the body and wrapped it in clean linen, ⁶⁰ and laid it in a tomb of his, which he had cut out of the rock, and he rolled a big boulder over the doorway of the tomb, and went away. ⁶¹ And Mary of Magdala and the other Mary kept sitting there in front of the tomb.

⁶² On the next day, which is the day after the Preparation Day, the high priests and Pharisees met and went in a body to Pilate, ⁶³ and said, "Sir, we remember that that pretender said while He was living, 'After three days I will rise again.' ⁶⁴ Issue an order then to have the tomb closely guarded, so that His disciples cannot come and steal Him and tell the people that He rose from the dead, and the last deception be worse than the first."

⁶⁵ Pilate said to them, "Take the military guard and go and make it as secure as you can." ⁶⁶ So off they went and made the tomb secure by sealing the boulder and setting a guard.

28 THE TWO MARYS SEE THE EMPTY TOMB; THE JEWISH COURT PERSUADES THE GUARD TO DECEIVE THE PEOPLE; JESUS MEETS HIS DISCIPLES AND GIVES THEM HIS LAST DIRECTIONS

After the sabbath, as the first day of the week was dawning, Mary of Magdala and the other Mary went to get [a] a look at the tomb. ² Now there had been a great earthquake. For an angel of the Lord came down from heaven and went and rolled the boulder back and remained [b] sitting upon it. ³ His appearance was as bright [c] as lightning and his clothes as white as snow. ⁴ The men on guard trembled in awe of him, and became like dead men. ⁵ And the angel said to the women, "Do not be afraid,[d] for I know that you are looking for Jesus who was crucified. ⁶ He is not here; He has risen, as He said He would do. Come, get a look at the place where He was lying. ⁷ Then run and tell His disciples, 'He has risen from the dead, and is going back to Galilee ahead of you; you will see Him there.' This is my message to you." ⁸ So off

---
[a] Aor. infin. means this.
[b] Impf. of cont. action.
[c] Grk., *like lightning*.
[d] Pres. impv. with neg.

they hurried from the tomb, frightened and yet in ecstasy, and ran to break the news to His disciples.

⁹ Then Jesus met them Himself, and said, "Good morning!" ᵉ And they went up to Him and clasped His feet, and worshiped Him. ¹⁰ Then Jesus said to them, "Do not be afraid. Go, tell my brothers to go back to Galilee, and there they will see me."

¹¹ While they were on their way, some members of the guard went into the city and told the high priests everything that had taken place. ¹² So they met and held a consultation with the elders, and bribed ᶠ the soldiers with a large sum of money, ¹³ and said to them, "Tell the people that His disciples came by night, while we were sleeping, and stole Him away. ¹⁴ And if news of it gets to the governor's ears, we will make it all right with him, and keep you out of trouble." ¹⁵ So they took the money and did as they were told. And this story has been told among the Jews down to the present time.

¹⁶ The eleven disciples went to Galilee to the mountain to which Jesus had directed them, ¹⁷ and as soon as they saw Him, they fell down and worshiped Him, though some were in doubt about it.

¹⁸ Then Jesus came up to them, and said, "Full ᵍ authority in heaven and on earth has been given to me. ¹⁹ Go then and make disciples of all the nations, baptize them into ʰ the name of the Father, the Son, and the Holy Spirit, ²⁰ and teach them to practice ⁱ all the commands that I have given you. And I myself will surely ʲ be with you all the days, down to the very close of the age."

ᵉ Modern greeting for ancient.
ᶠ Implied in gift.
ᵍ Grk., *all*.
ʰ Expresses transfer of relationship.
ⁱ Grk., *cont. observing*.
ʲ Grk., *behold*, for emphasis; so, *surely*.

MARK

John Mark is generally held to be the writer of our Second Gospel. He was with Paul during part of the first missionary journey, but he was converted under Peter's preaching, then accompanied him on his preaching tours, and so found in Peter's preaching nearly all the materials of his Gospel, which records the wonder-works of Jesus, five of His parables, but only one discourse.

The Christians in Rome requested Mark, since he had all these facts of Jesus' life at his command, to write them down for them. This he did about A.D. 60-65. He wrote to show that Jesus is the Son of God, and so a worker of wonders; also to portray His life of love and service as the example for Christians to follow. He wrote in very poor Greek. We have tried to make the English correspond to it.

1 JOHN THE BAPTIST PREACHING AND BAPTIZING; JESUS IS BAPTIZED; HE IS TEMPTED; HE BEGINS PREACHING IN GALILEE; HE CURES MANY PEOPLE SICK WITH FEVER, LEPROSY, ETC.

The beginning of the good news of Jesus Christ. ² As it is written in the prophet Isaiah:
"Here I send my messenger ahead of you; [a]
He will prepare your way;
³ He is a voice of one who shouts in the desert,
'Get the road ready for the Lord,
Make the paths straight for Him'"; [b]
⁴ John the Baptizer appeared in the desert and was preaching a baptism conditioned [c] on repentance to obtain the forgiveness of sins. ⁵ And people from all over Judea and everybody in Jerusalem kept on going out to him and being baptized by him in the Jordan River, confessing their sins. ⁶ Now John wore clothing [d]

[a] Mal. 3:1.
[b] Isa. 40:3.
[c] Gen. of quality.
[d] Grk., *was clothed*.

made of camel's hair, with a leather belt around his waist, and he used to [e] live on dried locusts and wild honey.

7 He kept [f] preaching the following message, "After me there is coming One who is stronger than I am, whose shoes I am not fit to stoop down and untie. 8 I [g] have baptized you in water, but He [g] will baptize you in the Holy Spirit."

9 Now in those days Jesus came from Nazareth in Galilee, and was baptized by John in the Jordan. 10 And just as soon as He started [h] to come up out of the water, He saw the heavens split [i] open and the Spirit coming down like a dove to enter [j] Him. 11 And out of the heavens came a voice, "You are my Son, my Beloved! In you I am delighted!"

12 Then the Spirit at once drove Him out into the desert. 13 And He stayed in the desert forty days, while He was being tempted by Satan; yea, He was with the wild beasts, but the angels continued to wait upon Him.

14 Now after John was arrested, Jesus went into Galilee, proclaiming the good news of God:

15 "The time is ripe [k] and the kingdom of God is near; repent and believe in the good news."

16 As He was walking along the shore of the sea of Galilee, He saw Simon and his brother Andrew casting their nets in the sea, for they were fishermen. 17 So Jesus said to them, "Come, follow me, and I will make you fishermen for catching men." 18 And at once they forsook their nets and followed Him. 19 He walked on a little farther and saw James, the son of Zebedee, and his brother John; they too were in their boats getting their nets in order. 20 He at once called them. They left their father Zebedee in the boat with the hired men, and went after Him.

21 They went into Capernaum, and as soon as the first sabbath came, He went into the synagogue and began [l] to teach. 22 And they were dumfounded [m] at His teaching, for He was teaching them like one who had authority to teach, and not like the scribes.

[e] Pres. pt. means this.
[f] Impf. of cont. action.
[g] Emph. pronouns.
[h] Adv. and pt. mean this.
[1] Colloquial like the Greek.
[j] In prep., *eis*.
[k] Grk., *fulfilled*.
[l] Incep. impf.
[m] Colloquial to match Mark's Grk.

²³ Just at that moment there was a man in their synagogue who was under the spell of a foul spirit, and so he screamed, ²⁴ "What do you want of us, Jesus, you Nazarene? Have you come to destroy us? I know who you are, God's Holy One!" ²⁵ Jesus reproved him, saying, "Hush up, get out of him!" ²⁶ Then the foul spirit convulsed him and with a deafening ⁿ shriek got out of him. ²⁷ They were all so dumfounded that they kept discussing it among themselves, and asking, "What does this mean? It is a new teaching. He gives orders with authority even to foul spirits, and they obey Him." ²⁸ And His fame at once spread in all directions all over that part of Galilee.

²⁹ As soon as they left the synagogue, they went home with Simon and Andrew, in company with James and John. ³⁰ And Simon's mother-in-law was confined to her bed with a fever. So they at once tell Him about her. ³¹ Then He went up to her, grasped her hand, and had her get up.° The fever left her, and she began to wait upon them.

³² In the evening, when the sun had gone down, they kept on bringing to Him all the people who were sick or under the power of demons, ³³ and the whole town gathered at the door. ³⁴ And He cured many who were sick with various diseases, and drove out many demons, and would not let the demons speak a word, because they knew who ᵖ He was.

³⁵ Early in the morning, long before daybreak, He got up and went out to a lonely spot, and stayed praying there. ³⁶ And Simon and his companions diligently searched for Him ³⁷ and found Him, and said to Him, "Everybody is looking for you."

³⁸ And He said to them, "Let us go somewhere else, to the neighboring towns, to preach in them, too, for that is why I came out here." ³⁹ So He went all over Galilee, preaching in their synagogues and driving out demons.

⁴⁰ There came to Him a leper, begging Him on his knees, saying to Him, "If you want to, you can cure me."

⁴¹ And His heart was moved with pity for him, so He stretched out His hand and touched him, and said, "I do want to! Be cured!" ⁴² And the leprosy at once left him, and he was cured. ⁴³ But Jesus at once drove him out of their presence, and gave him this stringent ᵠ

ⁿ Grk., *with a great voice.*
° Grk., *raised her.*
ᵖ *Intuitively knew Him.*
ᵠ Grk., *sternly charged him.*

charge, ⁴⁴ "See that you tell nobody a single word ʳ about it. Begone; show yourself to the priest, and to prove it to the people, make the offering for your purification which Moses prescribed." ⁴⁵ But he went out and began to publish it so much and to spread the story so far, that Jesus could not any more go into any town openly, but had to stay out in thinly settled ˢ places. But the people kept coming to Him from every quarter.

2 JESUS CURES A PARALYZED MAN; CALLS LEVI; TELLS THREE STORIES ABOUT FASTING; CLAIMS TO BE LORD OF THE SABBATH

After some days He came back to Capernaum, and it was reported that He was at home, ² and so many people gathered there that there was no longer any room even around the door. He was telling them His message. ³ Then four men came bringing to Him a paralyzed man. ⁴ And as they could not get him near to Jesus, on account of the crowd, they dug through the roof over the spot where He was standing and let the pallet down that the paralyzed man was lying on.ᵃ

⁵ When Jesus saw their faith, He said to the paralyzed man, "My son, your sins are forgiven."

⁶ Some scribes were sitting there arguing and saying to themselves, ⁷ "Why is He talking this way? He is blaspheming. Who can forgive sins but God alone?" ⁸ Now Jesus at once felt in His spirit that they were arguing about this, and said, "Why are you arguing to yourselves about this? ⁹ Which is easier, to say to the paralyzed man, 'Your sins are forgiven,' or to say to him, 'Get up, pick up your pallet and start walking'? ¹⁰ But to show ᵇ you that the Son of Man has authority to forgive sins on earth," turning to the paralyzed man He said, ¹¹ "I tell you, get up, pick up your pallet, and go home." ¹² Then he got up and at once picked up his pallet, and went out before them all.

The result ᶜ was that they were all dumfounded and began to praise God and say, "We have never seen anything like this before."

¹³ He went out of the town again and along the seashore, and all

---

ʳ Very emph. neg.
ˢ Grk., *desert places*.
ᵃ Poor Grk., which we try to reproduce in Eng.
ᵇ Grk., *that you may know*—but by being shown.
ᶜ In particle of result.

the people kept coming to Him and He kept teaching[d] them. [14] And as He was passing by, He saw Levi, the son of Alpheus, sitting in the tax-collector's office, and He said to him, "Follow me." Then he got up and followed Him.

[15] Levi was at table in his house, and he had many tax-collectors and notorious sinners as guests, along with Jesus and His disciples, for there were many of them, and they began[e] to follow Him. [16] And when the scribes who belonged to the Pharisees' party saw that He was eating with notorious sinners and tax-collectors, they said to His disciples, "Why does He eat with tax-collectors and notorious sinners?"

[17] Jesus heard it, and said to them, "Not well but sick people have to send for the doctor. It is not upright but sinful people that I have come to invite."

[18] Now John's disciples and the Pharisees were keeping a fast. So some people came and asked Him, "Why do John's disciples and the Pharisees' disciples practice fasting, but yours never do?"

[19] Jesus answered them, "The wedding guests cannot fast, can they, while the bridegroom is with them? As long as they have the bridegroom with them they cannot fast. [20] But a time[f] is coming when the bridegroom will be taken away from them, and then they will fast. [21] No one sews a patch of brand-new goods on an old coat; or, if he does, the patch tears away, the new from the old, and the hole becomes bigger[g] than ever. [22] No one puts new wine into old wine-bottles;[h] or, if he does, the wine will break the bottles, and the wine is lost, and the bottles too. New wine is to be put up in new bottles."

[23] On the sabbath He was passing through the wheat fields, and His disciples started to make a path by pulling off the wheat heads. [24] So the Pharisees were saying to Him, "Just look! Why are they doing on the sabbath what it is against the law to do?"

[25] He answered them, "Have you never read what David did when he and his soldiers were in need and hungry? [26] How is it that he went into the house of God, when Abiathar was high priest, and ate the sacred[i] loaves, which it is against the law for

---

[d] Impf.
[e] Incep. impf.
[f] Grk., *days.*
[g] Grk., *worse,* so bigger hole.
[h] Wine-skins made out of animal hides.
[i] See Mt. 12:3, for explanation.

anyone except the priests to eat, and gave part of them to his soldiers, too?" [27] Then He said to them, "The sabbath was made to serve[j] man and not man to keep the sabbath. [28] So the Son of Man is Lord even of the sabbath."

3 JESUS CURES THE MAN WITH A WITHERED HAND, AND MANY OTHERS; SELECTS THE TWELVE; ANSWERS THE CHARGE THAT HE IS IN LEAGUE WITH DEMONS; TELLS OF THE UNFORGIVABLE SIN

Then He went into a synagogue again, and a man was there who had a withered hand. [2] And they kept closely watching Him, to see whether He would cure him on the sabbath, to get a charge to bring against Him. [3] But He said to the man with the withered hand, "Get up in the crowd." [a]

[4] Then He asked them, "Is it right to do people good on the sabbath, or to do them evil, to save life or to take it?" But they had nothing to say.[b] [5] So Jesus looked around at them in anger, because[c] He was pained over their stubbornness of mind,[d] and said to the man, "Hold out your hand." And he held it out, and his hand was cured.

[6] Then the Pharisees went out and held a consultation with the Herodians[e] against Him, to put Him to death.

[7] So Jesus retired with His disciples to the sea, and a vast throng of people followed Him from Galilee, and from Judea, [8] and from Jerusalem, and from Idumea, and from the other side of the Jordan, and from the neighborhood of Tyre and Sidon—yes, a vast throng of people, as they kept hearing of the great[f] things that He was doing, came to Him. [9] So He told His disciples to keep a little boat ready for Him all the time,[g] to prevent the crowds from crushing Him. [10] For He cured so many people that all who had ailments kept crowding up against Him to touch Him. [11] And whenever the foul spirits saw Him, they fell down

[j] Grk., *for the sake of man.*
[a] Grk., *in the midst.*
[b] Grk., *were silent.*
[c] Causal pt.
[d] Grk., *hardness of heart.*
[e] A political party favoring rule by the Herods.
[f] Or, *many things.*
[g] Pres. of cont. action.

before Him and screamed, "You are the Son of God." ¹² But He charged them time after time ʰ not to tell who He was.ⁱ

¹³ Then He went up on the hillside and summoned to Him those whom He wanted, and they went to Him. ¹⁴ And He appointed the Twelve, to whom He gave the title, apostles,ʲ to be with Him, to send them forth to preach, ¹⁵ and to have the right to drive out the demons. ¹⁶ The Twelve whom He appointed were: Peter, the name which He gave to Simon, ¹⁷ James the son of Zebedee, and John, James's brother (He named them Boanerges, which means, Sons of Thunder), ¹⁸ Andrew, Philip, Bartholomew, Matthew, Thomas, James the son of Alpheus, Thaddeus, Simon the Zealot, ¹⁹ and Judas Iscariot, who betrayed Him.

Then He went home. ²⁰ And again the crowds gathered so that it was not possible for them even to take their meals. ²¹ His kinsmen ᵏ heard of it and came over to get hold of Him, for they kept saying, "He has gone crazy."

²² And the scribes who had come down from Jerusalem kept saying, "He is under the spell of Beelzebub ˡ and by the help of the prince of the demons He drives out the demons."

²³ So He called them to Him, and continued speaking to them in short stories, as follows:

"How can Satan drive out Satan? ²⁴ If a kingdom is disunited, that kingdom cannot last. ²⁵ And if a household is disunited, that household cannot last. ²⁶ And if Satan has made an insurrection against himself and become disunited, he cannot last but is surely ᵐ coming to an end. ²⁷ But no one can get into a giant's house and carry off his goods, unless he first binds the giant; after that he can make a clean sweep of his house. ²⁸ I solemnly say to you, men will be forgiven for all their sins and all the abusive things they say. ²⁹ But whoever speaks abusively against ⁿ the Holy Spirit can never get forgiveness, but is guilty of a sin that has no end." ³⁰ He said so,º because they kept saying, "He is under the spell of a foul spirit."

³¹ Then His mother and His brothers came. They were standing

ʰ Impf. of repeated action.
ⁱ Grk., *make Him known*.
ʲ Grk., *whom He named apostles*.
ᵏ Grk., *those from His side*.
ˡ The pagan god of refuse, identified by the Jews with Satan.
ᵐ Pres. for fut.
ⁿ Grk., *blasphemes against the Holy Spirit*.
º This clause implied.

outside and sent word to call Him. ³² And a crowd was sitting around Him when they told Him, "Your mother and your brothers are outside asking for you."

³³ He answered them, "Who are my mother and my brothers?" ³⁴ Then looking around at the people sitting about Him, He said, "Here are my mother and my brothers. ³⁵ Whoever does the will of God is my brother and sister and mother."

4   TEACHING BY STORIES, AND WHY: THE STORY OF THE SOWER; HE EXPLAINS IT; THE STORY OF THE SECRETLY GROWING SEED; THE STORY OF THE MUSTARD SEED; HE STILLS THE STORM

Then He began again to teach by the seashore. And a crowd gathered around Him so great that He got into a boat and was sitting in it, just off the shore,[a] while all the people were on the land close to the sea. ² He continued teaching them by many stories.[b] In His teaching He spoke to them as follows:

³ "Listen! A sower went out to sow. ⁴ As he was sowing, some of the seed fell along the path, and the birds came and ate them up. ⁵ Some fell upon rocky ground, where they did not have much soil, and they sprang up at once, because the soil was not deep; ⁶ but when the sun came up, they were scorched and withered away, because they had not taken root. ⁷ Some fell among the thorn seed, and the thorns grew up and choked them out, and they yielded no grain. ⁸ Some fell in rich soil, and came up and grew and yielded thirty, sixty, even a hundredfold."

⁹ And He said, "Let him who has ears listen!"

¹⁰ When He was by Himself, those who stayed [c] about Him with the Twelve, began to ask Him about the stories. ¹¹ Then He said to them, "To you the secret of the kingdom of God has been entrusted, but to those who are on the outside everything is presented [d] in stories, so that

¹² 'They may look and look and yet not see,
And listen and listen and yet not understand,
Lest, perchance, they should turn and be forgiven.' "

¹³ Then He said to them:

[a] Grk., *on the sea.*
[b] All these stories taken from the fields or garden.
[c] Grk., *those around Him.*
[d] Grk., *becomes* or *comes.*

"If [e] you do not understand this story, how, indeed, can you understand any of my stories? [14] The message is what the sower sows. [15] The ones along the path are those who have the message sown in their hearts, but as soon as it is sown there, Satan comes and carries off the message that has been sown in their hearts. [16] In like manner these are the ones sown on rocky ground; as soon as they hear the truth, they accept it with ecstasy, [17] but it does not take real root in them, and so they last only a little while; then when trouble or persecution comes on account of the truth, they at once fall by the way. [18] A different class are those people sown among the thorns. They are people who listen to the message, [19] but the worries of the times,[f] the deceiving pleasures of being rich, and evil desires for other things, creep in and choke the truth out, and it yields nothing. [20] And the people sown in rich soil are the people who listen to the message and welcome it and yield thirty, sixty, even a hundredfold."

[21] Then He put a question to them: [g]

"A lamp is not brought to be put under a peck-measure or under a bed, is it? [h] Is it not rather to be put on the lamp-stand? [22] For nothing is ever hidden by people except for the purpose of having it known, and people do not keep secrets except to tell [i] them. [23] If anyone has ears let him listen!"

[24] And He was saying to them:

"Take care what you hear. The measure you give will come back [j] to you, and more besides. [25] For whoever has will have more given to him, but whoever has nothing, even what he has will be taken away."

[26] He also was saying:

"The kingdom of God is like a man who scatters seed on the ground, [27] then continues sleeping by night and getting up by day, while the seed sprouts and comes up without his knowing how. [28] The ground of itself produces, first the stalk, then the head; at last there is [k] the matured grain of wheat in the head. [29] But as soon as the crop will permit it, he puts in the sickle, for the reaping time has come."

---

[e] Cond. not expressed but strongly implied.
[f] Grk., *age*.
[g] Grk., *said to them*.
[h] Expects answer, *No*.
[i] Grk., *come into the open*.
[j] Grk., *be measured*.
[k] Fol. Ms. B.

MARK 5

³⁰ Then He kept on saying:

"How can I further picture¹ the kingdom of God, or by wha story can I illustrate ᵐ it? ³¹ It is like a mustard seed, which, when it is sown in the ground, is the smallest of all seeds, ³² but when it is properly sown, it comes up and grows to be the largest of all the plants, and produces branches so large that the wild birds can roost under its shade."

³³ With many stories like these He kept on telling them the message, as far as they could understand it.ⁿ ³⁴ He did not tell them anything except by stories, but to His own disciples He kept on privately explaining everything.

³⁵ That same day when it was evening, He said to them, "Let us go over to the other side."

³⁶ So they left the crowd and took Him in the boat in which he was sitting. And there were other boats with Him.

³⁷ But a furious squall of wind came up, and the waves were dashing over into the boat, so that it was fast filling. ³⁸ He was in the stern, asleep on the cushion. So they woke Him up and said to Him, "Teacher, is it no concern to you that we are going down?"

³⁹ Then He aroused Himself and reproved the wind, and said to the sea, "Hush! Be still." And the wind lulled, and there was a great calm. ⁴⁰ Then He asked them, "Why are you afraid? Have you no faith yet?"

⁴¹ They were very much frightened, and said to one another, "Who can He be that even the wind and the sea obey Him?"

5   JESUS CURES AN INSANE MAN; CURES A WOMAN WITH A HEMORRHAGE; RAISES JAIRUS' DAUGHTER TO LIFE

So they landed on the other side of the sea in the region of Gerasa. ² As soon as He got out of the boat, a man under the power of a foul spirit and from the tombs met Him. ³ This man lived among the tombs, and no one could any longer subdue ᵃ him even with a chain, ⁴ for he had often been fastened with fetters and chains but had snapped the chains and broken the fetters, and no one was strong enough to overpower ᵇ him. ⁵ All

---

¹ Grk., *liken it.*
ᵐ Grk., *place* or *put it.*
ⁿ Grk., *hear it,* but in above sense.
ᵃ Grk., *bind.*
ᵇ Grk., *tame.*

night and all day he kept screaming among the tombs and on the hills, and kept gashing himself with stones.

⁶ On catching a glimpse of Jesus from a distance, he ran up and fell down on his knees before Him, ⁷ and screamed aloud, "What do you want of me, Jesus, Son of the Most High God? In God's name, I beg you, do not torture me."

⁸ For Jesus ᶜ was saying to him, "You foul spirit, come out of him." ⁹ He asked him, "What is your name?"

He answered, "My name is Legion, for we are many." ¹⁰ And they kept on earnestly begging Him not to send them out of that ᵈ country.

¹¹ Now there was a large drove of hogs grazing on the hillside. ¹² And they ᵉ begged Him, "Send us among the hogs, so that we can get into them." ¹³ So He let them do so. And the foul spirits came out of the man and got into the hogs, and the drove of about two thousand rushed over the cliff and into the sea and were drowned.ᶠ ¹⁴ Then the hog-feeders ᵍ fled and spread the news in the town and in the country around; and the people came to see what had taken place. ¹⁵ When they came to Jesus and saw the man who had once been insane ʰ under the power of many demons, sitting, with his clothes on, and in his right mind, they were frightened. ¹⁶ And those who had seen it told them how it occurred to the man who had been under the power of the demons, and about the hogs. ¹⁷ Then they began to beg Jesus to leave their neighborhood.

¹⁸ And as He was getting into the boat, the once insane ⁱ man kept begging Him to let him go with Him. ¹⁹ However, He did not let him, but said to him, "Go home to your folks,ʲ and tell them how much the Lord has done for you, and has taken pity on you." ²⁰ And so he went away and began to tell everybody in the Ten Cities ᵏ how much Jesus had done for him; and everybody was dumfounded.

²¹ When Jesus again had crossed in the boat to the other side, a great crowd gathered about Him, as ˡ He was standing on the

ᶜ Pronoun in Grk., but noun makes it clear in Eng.
ᵈ Article in sense of demonstrative.
ᵉ The demons.
ᶠ Grk., *choked*.
ᵍ So Thayer, Lex., s.v.
ʰ Implied from context.
ⁱ Grk., *demonized man*.
ʲ Popular term for *kinsmen* (Webster).
ᵏ League of cities, east of Jordan, for commerce and protection.
ˡ Grk., *and He*.

MARK 5

seashore. ²² And a man named Jairus, a leader of a synagogue, came up, and when he saw Jesus ᵐ he flung himself at His feet ²³ and kept earnestly begging Him, saying, "My dear ⁿ little daughter is at the point of death. Come, lay your hands on her, so that she may get well and live." ²⁴ So He went off with him, and a great crowd kept following Him, and jostling Him.

²⁵ Then a woman who had had a hemorrhage for twelve years, ²⁶ and had suffered much at the hands of many doctors, and had spent all she had, and yet was not a whit benefited but rather grew worse, ²⁷ heard the reports about Jesus. So she came up in the crowd behind Him and touched His coat, ²⁸ for she kept saying, "If I can only touch His clothes, I shall get well." ²⁹ Her hemorrhage stopped at once, and she felt in her body that she was cured.

³⁰ Jesus at once perceived ᵒ that power had gone out of Him, and so He turned around in the crowd, and asked, "Who touched my clothes?"

³¹ But the disciples kept saying to Him, "You see the crowd jostling you, and yet you ask, 'Who touched me?'" ³² Still He kept looking around to see her who had done it. ³³ So the woman, as she knew what had taken place for her, though frightened and trembling, came forward and fell on her knees before His feet,ᵖ and told Him the whole truth.

³⁴ And He said to her, "My daughter, your faith has cured you. Go in peace and be free from your disease."

³⁵ Even while He was saying this, people came from the house of the leader of the synagogue and said, "Your daughter is dead; why trouble the Teacher any longer?"

³⁶ But Jesus paid no attention to what was said, but said to the leader of the synagogue, "Do not be afraid; only keep up ᑫ your faith."

³⁷ He let no one go with Him but Peter, James, and James's brother John. ³⁸ They came to the home of the leader of the synagogue, and there He saw confusion, and people weeping and wailing without restraint. ³⁹ And He went into the house and said to them, "Why do you continue all this confusion and crying? The little girl is not dead but is sleeping." ⁴⁰ Then they began to

---

ᵐ Grk., *Him*.
ⁿ Diminutives often mean *dear little*.
ᵒ Grk., *recognized in Him*.
ᵖ Grk., *before Him*.
ᑫ *Keep on believing*.

laugh in His face. But He drove them all out, and took the little girl's father and mother and the men with Him, and went into the room where the little girl was.[r] [41] Then He grasped her hand and said to her, *"Talitha koum,"* which means, "Little girl, I tell you, get up!"

[42] And the little girl at once got up and started walking around, for she was twelve years old. And instantly they were completely dumfounded. [43] But He strictly charged them to let nobody know about it, and told them to give her something to eat.

6 JESUS TEACHES IN HIS HOME TOWN, BUT IS DISOWNED BY HIS FELLOW-TOWNSMEN; SENDS OUT THE TWELVE; SUPPOSED TO BE JOHN THE BAPTIST BY GOVERNOR ANTIPAS; FEEDS FIVE THOUSAND; WALKS ON WATER, ETC.

He left there and went back to His home town,[a] and His disciples followed Him. [2] When the sabbath came, He began to teach in the synagogue. And the people were dumfounded when they heard Him, and said, "Where did He get all these things? What sort of wisdom is it that has been given Him? And such mighty deeds are done by Him! [3] Is He not the carpenter, Mary's son, and the brother of James, Joses, Judas, and Simon? And do not His sisters live here among us?" And so they found a cause for stumbling over him.[b]

[4] But Jesus said to them, "A prophet never fails to be honored except in his native neighborhood, among his kinsmen, and in his own home." [5] He could not do any mighty deeds there, except that He put His hands on a few ailing[c] people and cured them. [6] And He wondered at their lack of faith in Him.

Then He made a circle of the villages and continued teaching. [7] And He called the Twelve to Him and sent[d] them out two by two, and gave them power over the foul spirits. [8] He ordered them not to take anything for the journey except a staff, no bread, no bag, no money in the purse; [9] they were to go with plain sandals on their feet and not to wear two shirts. [10] And He continued to say to them, "Whenever you put up at a house, stay there until

---

[r] Fol. the best Mss.
[a] Grk., *His native place,* so *His home town.*
[b] Grk., *were caused to fall.*
[c] Suffering with minor diseases.
[d] Grk., *began to send.*

you leave that place. ¹¹ And if any ᵉ place refuses to welcome you or to listen to you, when you leave there shake off the very dust from the soles of your feet as a warning ᶠ to them." ¹² So they went out and preached that men should repent, ¹³ and drove out many demons, and cured many sick people by rubbing ᵍ them with oil.

¹⁴ King Herod heard of Him, for His name was now on everybody's lips,ʰ and people were saying that John the Baptizer had risen from the dead, and that this was why such mighty powers were working in Him. ¹⁵ But others were saying that He was Elijah, and still others that He was a prophet like ⁱ the prophets of old. ¹⁶ But when Herod heard of Him, he said, "John, whom I beheaded, has risen from the dead." ¹⁷ For this very Herod had sent and seized John and bound him and put him in prison, just to please Herodias, his brother Philip's wife, because Herod had married her.

¹⁸ For John kept saying to Herod, "It is not right for you to be living ʲ with your brother's wife."

¹⁹ So Herodias had it in for him and wanted to have him killed. But she could not have it done, ²⁰ for Herod stood in awe of John, because he knew that he was an upright and holy man, and so he protected him. When he heard him speak, he was very much disturbed, and yet he liked to hear him.

²¹ When a holiday came and Herod on his birthday gave a banquet to his state officials, his military officers, and other leading men of Galilee, ²² Herodias' daughter ᵏ came in and danced for them, and fascinated Herod and his guests.

So the king said to the girl, "Ask me for anything you want, and I will give it to you." ²³ And he promised her on oath, "I will give you anything you ask for, up to half of my kingdom."

²⁴ She left the room and asked her mother, "What shall I ask him for?"

And she answered, "The head of John the Baptizer."

²⁵ Then she rushed ˡ at once before the king, and made this request, "I want you this very minute ᵐ to give me John the Baptist's head on a platter."

ᵉ Conditional relative.
ᶠ Grk., *for a testimony.*
ᵍ Grk., *anointing.*
ʰ Grk., *His name was known everywhere.*
ⁱ This adv. in Mk. means *like.*
ʲ Grk., *to have her.*
ᵏ Salome; Philip, her father.
ˡ Lit., *went at once with haste.*
ᵐ Strong adv.

²⁶ The king, although exceedingly sorry, yet on account of his oath and his guests, did not like to refuse her, ²⁷ and so at once ordered a soldier of his guard ⁿ to bring his head. The soldier went off and beheaded John in the prison ²⁸ and brought back his head on a platter, and gave it to the girl, and the girl gave it to her mother. ²⁹ When his disciples heard of it, they came and carried off his corpse ᵒ and laid it in a tomb.

³⁰ The apostles returned and met ᵖ Jesus and reported to Him everything, how many things ᑫ they had done and taught. ³¹ And He said to them, "Come with me by yourselves to a quiet place and rest a little while." For there was an endless stream of people coming and going,ʳ and they had no time even to eat. ³² So they got off in their boat to be by themselves in a quiet place. ³³ But many people saw them start and knew of it and ran around the lake ˢ from all the towns and got there ahead of them. ³⁴ So when He got out of the boat, He saw a great crowd waiting, and His heart was moved with pity at the sight of them, for they were like sheep without a shepherd; and so He proceeded to teach them a number of things.

³⁵ When it grew late, His disciples came to Him and said, "This is a destitute place and it is already late. ³⁶ Send the crowds off to the farms and villages to buy themselves something to eat."

³⁷ But He answered them, "Give them something to eat yourselves."

Then they said to Him, "Shall we go and buy forty dollars' worth of bread and give it to them to eat?"

³⁸ Then He asked them, "How many loaves have you? Go and see."

They found out ᵗ and told Him, "Five, and two fish."

³⁹ Then He ordered them all to sit down in rows on the green grass. ⁴⁰ And so they tumbled down ᵘ in groups of hundreds and fifties. ⁴¹ Then He took the five loaves and the two fish and looked up to heaven and blessed the loaves and broke them in pieces and gave the pieces to the disciples to pass on to the people. He also divided the two fish among them all. ⁴² And they all ate and had

---

ⁿ Latin word.
ᵒ Lit., *fallen body.*
ᵖ One vb. with both ideas.
ᑫ Emph.
ʳ Lit. *many cont. coming,* etc.
ˢ Grk., *on foot.*
ᵗ Grk., *knew* (by looking).
ᵘ Grk., *fell up.*

plenty.ᵛ ⁴³ And the pieces they took up from the loaves made twelve basketfuls besides the pieces from the fish. ⁴⁴ There were five thousand men who ate the loaves.

⁴⁵ Then He insisted that the disciples at once get into their boat and cross ahead of Him toward Bethsaida, while He was sending the crowd away. ⁴⁶ After He had told them "Good-by," ʷ He went up the hill to pray. ⁴⁷ Now when evening had come, the boat was in the middle of the sea, while He was alone on land. ⁴⁸ And because He saw that they were struggling at the oars,ˣ for the wind was against them, a while before daybreak He started toward them walking on the sea, and He meant to go right up beside them.ʸ ⁴⁹ But when they saw Him walking on the sea, they thought that it was a ghost and screamed aloud, ⁵⁰ for they all saw Him and were terrified. But He at once spoke to them and said, "Keep up courage!ᶻ It is I; stop being afraid." ⁵¹ Then He went up to them and got into the boat, and the wind lulled. They were completely dumfounded, ⁵² for they did not understand the lesson * of the loaves; their minds were dull.†

⁵³ They crossed over to the other side and came to Gennesaret and anchored the boat. ⁵⁴ As soon as they got out of the boat, the people recognized Him ⁵⁵ and hurried all over the countryside and began to bring the sick to Him on their pallets, wherever they heard He was. ⁵⁶ And whatever villages or towns or country places He came to, they would lay the sick in the market-places and beg Him to let them touch just the tassel of His coat, and everybody that touched it was cured.

7 JESUS TEACHING WHAT REAL UNCLEANNESS IS; CURES A HEATHEN MOTHER'S DAUGHTER AND A DEAF-MUTE

The Pharisees met about Him, and also some scribes who had come from Jerusalem. ² They had noticed that some of His disciples were in the habit of eating their meals without first giving their hands a ceremonial washing to make them clean.ᵃ ³ For the

ᵛ Popular phrase for a full meal.
ʷ Mod. for ancient form.
ˣ Grk., *tortured in rowing*.
ʸ Prep. means this.
ᶻ Emph. character (Thayer).
* Grk., *about the loaves*.
† Grk., *hearts were hardened*.
ᵃ Grk., *with unwashed hands*.

Pharisees and all the Jews practice the customs [b] handed down to them from their forefathers, ⁴ and will never eat until they have carefully [c] washed their hands, and they never eat anything brought from the market until they wash [d] it; and they have many other religious practices which they got from their forefathers, as the washing of cups, pitchers, and pans.

⁵ And so the Pharisees and the scribes asked Him, "Why is it that your disciples do not practice the customs handed down from our forefathers, but eat their meals without purifying their hands?"

⁶ But He answered them, "Isaiah beautifully [e] prophesied about you hypocrites; as the Scripture says: [f]

" 'This people honor me with their lips,
But their hearts are far, far away from me;
⁷ Their worship of me is but an empty show;
The things they teach are but men's precepts.' [g]

⁸ "You give up what God has commanded, ⁹ you cling to what men hand down. You are fine teachers to cancel what God commanded, in order to keep what men have handed down! [h] ¹⁰ For Moses said, 'Honor your father and your mother,' and again, 'Whoever curses his father or mother must certainly be put to death,' ¹¹ but you say, 'If a man tells his father or mother, "Everything I have that may be of use to you is Corban," ' that is, consecrated to God, ¹² you let him off from doing anything more for his father or mother; ¹³ and so you set aside what God has said by what you have handed down. You have many other practices like these."

¹⁴ Again He called the people to Him and said, "Listen to me, all of you, and understand. ¹⁵ Nothing that goes into a man from the outside can make him foul, but the things that come from the inside of a man are the things that make him foul." [i]

¹⁷ Now when He had left the crowd and gone home, His disciples were asking Him the meaning of this story. ¹⁸ And He answered them, "Are you too without understanding yet? Do you not know that nothing from the outside that goes into a man can

---

[b] Grk., *holding the tradition*, etc.
[c] *Wash with fist.*
[d] Either *sprinkle* or *dip it.*
[e] Irony and sarcasm.
[f] Grk., *it stands written.*
[g] Isa. 29:13.
[h] Grk., *you finely cancel God's word*, etc.
[i] V. 16 in A. V. not in best Mss.

MARK 7

make him foul, [19] because it does not reach his heart but only his stomach, and then passes off into the waste?" In thus speaking He made all foods clean.[j]

[20] He kept on saying, "The thing that comes from the inside of a man is the thing that makes him foul, [21] for from the inside, that is, from the hearts of men, designs for doing evil come,[k] sexual immorality,[l] stealing, murder, [22] adultery, greed, malice, deceit, licentiousness, envy,[m] abusiveness, haughtiness, thoughtlessness. [23] All these evils come from the inside of a man and make him foul."

[24] Then He left there and went into the neighborhood of Tyre and Sidon. He went into a house and wanted no one to know that He was there. But He could not escape public notice. [25] On the contrary, a woman, whose little daughter had a foul spirit, at once heard about Him and came and flung herself at His feet. [26] She was a heathen who spoke Greek and had been born in Syro-Phenicia. And she kept begging Him to drive the demon out of her daughter.

[27] But He was saying to her, "Let the children first eat all they want, for it is not right to take the children's bread and throw it out to the house dogs." [28] But she answered Him, "Yes, Lord,[n] and yet the house dogs under the table usually eat the crumbs the children drop."

[29] Then He said to her, "Because you have said this, go home; the demon has gone out of your daughter." [30] She went home and found her daguhter lying in bed, and the demon gone out.

[31] He left the neighborhood of Tyre and went by way of Sidon through the district of the Ten Cities down to the Sea of Galilee. [32] And they brought to Him a man who was deaf and almost dumb, and they begged Him to lay His hand upon him. [33] So He took him off from the crowd by himself and put His fingers in his ears and touched his tongue with saliva.

[34] Then He looked up to heaven and sighed, as He said, "Ephphatha," which means, "Be opened." [35] And his ears were opened and his tongue was untied,[o] and he began to speak distinctly.

[36] Then He charged them not to tell anybody about it; but the

[j] Grk., *making all meats clean.*
[k] Grk., *evil thoughts.*
[l] Gen. term for sex immorality.
[m] Grk., *evil eye.*
[n] Likely expressing some faith in His messiahship.
[o] Grk., *bond of his tongue was loosed.*

more He kept charging them, the more they kept spreading the news. ³⁷ So the people were overwhelmingly dumfounded,ᵖ and kept saying, "How wonderfully He has done everything! He even makes deaf people hear and dumb people talk."

8 JESUS FEEDS FOUR THOUSAND; GIVES NO SPECTACULAR SIGN; WARNS AGAINST THE TEACHING OF THE PHARISEES AND THE POMP OF HEROD; OWNED AS CHRIST BY PETER; CURES A BLIND MAN; FORETELLS HIS DEATH AND RESURRECTION

In those days when a great crowd again had gathered and they had nothing to eat, He called His disciples to Him, and said, ² "My heart goes out in pity for these people, for they have been staying with me three days now, and they have nothing left to eat. ³ And if I send them home hungry, they will give out on the road, for some of them are a long way from home." ᵃ

⁴ But His disciples answered Him, "Where can anyone get bread enough here in this destitute place, to give these people plenty?"

⁵ Then He asked them, "How many loaves have you?"

They answered, "Seven." ⁶ So He ordered the crowd to sit down on the ground. Then He took the seven loaves and gave thanks and broke them in pieces and gave them to His disciples to pass, and they passed them to the people. ⁷ And they had a few small fish, and He blessed them and told them to pass these,ᵇ too, to the people. ⁸ And they ate and had plenty. And they took up the pieces left over, which made seven hamperᶜ-basketfuls. ⁹ About four thousand people were there. Then He sent them away. ¹⁰ And He at once got into the boat and crossed to the district of Dalmanutha.

¹¹ Now the Pharisees came out and began a discussion with Him, and to testᵈ Him asked Him to show them a spectacular sign from heaven. ¹² But He sighed in spirit and said, "Why do the people of these times ask for a spectacular sign? I solemnly say, no sign at all will be given them." ᵉ ¹³ And He left them and again got into the boat and crossed to the other side.

ᵖ Very strong expression in Grk.
ᵃ Grk., *from a great distance.*
ᵇ Fol. WH and Vat. Ms.
ᶜ Very large baskets.
ᵈ Grk., *testing Him.*
ᵉ Heb. constr. for strong neg.

MARK 8

¹⁴Now they had forgotten to bring any bread; that is, they had only one loaf with them in the boat. ¹⁵Then He kept warning them by saying, "Look out! Keep on guarding yourselves against the yeast of the Pharisees and the yeast of Herod."

¹⁶So they were discussing with one another the fact that they had no bread. ¹⁷And as He noticed it He said to them, "Why are you discussing the fact that you have no bread? Do you not yet know nor understand? Are your minds so dull?ᶠ ¹⁸Since you have eyes can you not see with them? Since you have ears can you not hear with them? ¹⁹Do you not remember how many basketfuls of pieces you picked up when I broke the five loaves in pieces for the five thousand?"

They said to Him, "Twelve."

²⁰"And how many hamper-basketfuls of pieces when I broke the seven loaves in pieces for the four thousand?"

They said to Him, "Seven."

²¹He said to them, "How is it that you do not understand?"ᵍ

²²Then they came to Bethsaida. And they brought a blind man to Him and begged Him to touch him. ²³He took himʰ by the hand and led him outside the village, then spit in his eyes, laid His hands upon him, and asked him, "Do you see anything?"

²⁴He looked up and answered, "I see the people, but they look to me like trees moving around."

²⁵Then He laid His hands upon his eyes again, and he looked the best he couldⁱ and was cured, and saw everything distinctly. ²⁶So He sent him home with the warning,ʲ "Do not ever go into the village."

²⁷Then Jesus and His disciples left Galilee and went to the villages around Caesarea Philippi. On the way there He was asking His disciples, "Who do people say that I am?"

²⁸They answered Him, "John the Baptist; others say, Elijah, and others that you are one of the prophets."

²⁹Then He beganᵏ to ask them, "Who do you yourselvesˡ say that I am?"

ᶠ Grk., *heart hardened yet.*
ᵍ Fol. Vat. vs. Sin. Ms.
ʰ Grk., *the blind man;* pro. better in Eng.
ⁱ Grk., *through, thoroughly.*
ʲ Lit., *saying.*
ᵏ Inceptive impf.
ˡ Pro. very emph.

Peter answered Him, "You are the Christ." ³⁰ But He strictly warned them not to tell this about Him to anybody.

³¹ Then He instructed them for the first time that the Son of Man had to endure great suffering and be disowned by the elders and the high priests and the scribes, and be killed but rise again after three days. ³² And without any reserve He was telling them this fact. So Peter took Him aside and began to reprove Him for it. ³³ But He turned and glanced ᵐ at His disciples and reproved Peter by saying, "Get out of my way, Satan! for this view ⁿ of yours is not from God but from men."

³⁴ Then He called the people to Him along with His disciples, and said to them, "If anyone wants to be my disciple,ᵒ he must say, 'No' to self, put the cross on his shoulders, and keep on following me. ³⁵ For whoever wants to save his higher life, will have to give up the lower life, and whoever gives up his lower life for me and for the good news, will save the higher life. ³⁶ For what benefit will it be to a man to gain the whole world and fail ᵖ to gain the higher life? ³⁷ For what price can a man give to buy back life? ³⁸ For whoever is ashamed of me and my teaching in this unfaithful,ᑫ sinful age, then the Son of Man will be ashamed of him, when He comes back in His Father's splendor with the holy angels."

⁹:¹ And He said to them, "I solemnly say to you, some of the people standing here will certainly live ʳ to see the kingdom of God come in its power." ˢ

9 JESUS IS TRANSFIGURED, AND MOSES AND ELIJAH TALK WITH HIM; CURES AN EPILEPTIC BOY; AGAIN FORETELLS HIS DEATH; TEACHES THAT SERVICE IS GREATNESS

² Six days after this, Jesus took Peter, James, and John with Him, and led them up on a high mountain, alone by themselves. And in their presence His appearance was changed, ³ and His clothes were shining as white as white could be,ᵃ yea, whiter than

---

ᵐ Aor. means this.
ⁿ Grk., *you are thinking*, etc.
ᵒ Grk., *come after me*.
ᵖ Grk., *forfeit*.
ᑫ *Adulterous*.
ʳ Grk., *will not die until*, etc.
ˢ The spiritual kingdom.
ᵃ *Shining very brightly*.

any earthly bleacher could bleach them.[b] 4 And Elijah appeared to them, accompanied by Moses, and they were talking with Jesus.

5 Then Peter interrupted [c] and said to Jesus, "Teacher, it is good for us to be here. So let us put up three tents, one for you and one for Moses and one for Elijah." 6 For he did not really know what to say, he was so frightened.

7 Then a cloud came and was circling over them, and a voice came out of the cloud, "This is my Son, my Beloved; keep on listening to Him!" 8 And as quick as a flash, on looking around, they saw no one with them but Jesus by Himself. 9 And while they were going down the mountain, He cautioned them not to tell anyone what they had seen, until the Son of Man should rise from the dead. 10 And they held that caution [d] fast in their minds, as they continued to discuss among themselves what rising from the dead meant.

11 Then they asked Him, "Why do the scribes say that Elijah has to come first?"

12 He answered them, "Elijah does come first and gets everything ready,[e] but how is it that the Scripture says about the Son of Man that He will suffer much and be rejected? 13 But I tell you, Elijah has already come, and people treated him just as they pleased, as the Scripture says about him."

14 When they came to the disciples, they saw a great crowd around them and some scribes arguing with them. 15 And all the people were utterly amazed [f] when they saw Him, and ran up to Him and greeted Him.

16 Then He asked them, "Why are you arguing with them?"

17 A man from the crowd answered Him, "Teacher, I brought my son to you, for he has a dumb spirit. 18 Wherever it seizes him, it convulses him, and he foams at the mouth and grinds his teeth; and is wasting away. So I asked your disciples to drive it out, but they could not do it."

19 He answered them, "Oh, you unbelieving people of the times![g] How long must I be with you! How long must I put up with you! Bring him to me." 20 And they brought the boy [h] to

[b] *No fuller on earth could,* etc.
[c] Grk., *answered.*
[d] Grk., *the word.*
[e] *Restores all things.*
[f] Comp. vb.
[g] *Unbelieving age.*
[h] *Him.*

Him. As soon as the spirit saw Him, it convulsed the boy, and he fell on the ground and kept rolling over and foaming at the mouth.

²¹ Then He asked his father, "How long has he been like this?" He answered, "From his childhood; ²² and many a time it has thrown him into the fire or into the water, to destroy him. But if there is anything you can do for him, do pity us and help us!"

²³ Jesus said to him, "If there is anything I can do! Everything is possible for him who has faith!"

²⁴ The boy's father at once cried out and said, "I do have faith; help my lack of faith!"

²⁵ Then Jesus, because He saw that a crowd was rushing [i] up to Him, reproved the foul spirit and said to it, "You deaf and dumb spirit, get out of him, I charge you, and never get into him again." ²⁶ Then it gave a shriek and violently convulsed the boy, and got out of him. And the boy looked [j] like a corpse, so much so that the people said that he was dead. ²⁷ But Jesus grasped his hand and raised him, and he got up.

²⁸ When Jesus got home and was by Himself, His disciples were asking Him, "Why could not we drive it out?" ²⁹ He answered them, "This sort of thing can be driven out only by prayer." [k]

³⁰ Then they left there and were making a trip through Galilee, and He did not want anybody to know it; ³¹ for He was now teaching His disciples, and saying to them, "The Son of Man is to be turned over into men's hands, and they will kill Him, but three days after that He will rise again." ³² But they did not understand what this statement [l] meant, and they were afraid to ask Him.

³³ Then they reached Capernaum. When He got home, He asked them, "What were you discussing on the way home?" ³⁴ But they had nothing to say, for they had discussed with one another which of them was to be [m] the greatest.

³⁵ So He sat down and called the Twelve to Him and said, "If anyone wants to be the first, he must be the last of all and the servant of all." ³⁶ Then He took a little child and had him stand in the midst of them; then He took him in His arms, and said to them, ³⁷ "Whoever, as a disciple of mine,[n] welcomes one little

---

[i] *Running together.*
[j] Grk., *became a corpse.*
[k] *and fasting,* in A.V., not in best Mss.
[l] Grk., *ignorant of this word.*
[m] Vb. *to be* supplied.
[n] Grk., *in my name;* so, *as a disciple.*

child like this, welcomes me, and whoever welcomes me, welcomes not merely me but Him who sent me."

38 John said to Him, "Teacher, we saw a man using º your name to drive out demons, and we tried to stop him, for he was not one of our followers."

39 Jesus said, "Do not try to stop him, for there is no one who will use my name to do a mighty deed, and then be able soon to abuse me. 40 For whoever is not against us is for us.

41 "For whoever gives you a cup of water to drink, on the ground that you belong to Christ, I solemnly say to you, he will not fail to get his reward. 42 And whoever leads one of these lowly believers to do wrong, might better have a huge millstone hung around his neck and be thrown into the sea. 43 If your hand makes you do wrong, cut it off. You might better go into life maimed than keep both your hands and go down to the pit, to the fire that is never put out.ᵖ 45 And if your foot makes you do wrong, cut it off. You might better go into life crippled than keep both your feet and be thrown into the pit. 47 And if your eye makes you do wrong, tear it out. You might better go into the kingdom of God with only one eye than keep both your eyes and be thrown into the pit, 48 where the worm that feeds upon them ᑫ never dies and the fire is never put out. 49 Everyone must be seasoned with fire. Salt is a good thing, but if salt loses its strength, how can you season it again? 50 You must keep on having salt within you, and keep on living in peace with one another."

10 IN PEREA HE ANSWERS QUESTIONS ABOUT DIVORCE; BLESSES LITTLE CHILDREN; TELLS OF THE PERILS OF RICHES; FORETELLS HIS DEATH AGAIN; REFUSES JAMES'S AND JOHN'S REQUEST; SAYS HE CAME TO SERVE AND SAVE; CURES BARTIMEUS

Then He left there and went through the district of Judea and crossed ᵃ the Jordan, and crowds of people again met around Him, and again He began ᵇ to teach them, as His custom was. 2 Some Pharisees came up, and to test Him they began to ask Him

---

º Grk., *driving out—in your name.*
ᵖ Vv. 44, 46 not in best Mss.
ᑫ Obj. gen.; so, *feeds on them.*
ᵃ Grk., *to the other side.*
ᵇ Incep. impf.

whether a man should be allowed to divorce his wife. ³ And He answered them by asking, "What has Moses commanded you about it?"

⁴ They answered, "Moses allowed a man to divorce his wife, if he wrote out a divorce charge."

⁵ But Jesus said to them, "It was due to your moral perversity ᵉ that Moses wrote that command in your law.ᵈ ⁶ But from the beginning of the creation, 'God made them male and female. ⁷ Therefore, a man must ᵉ leave his father and mother, ⁸ and he and his wife must ᵉ become one,' so they are no longer two but one. ⁹ Therefore, what God has joined together man must stop separating."

¹⁰ On reaching the house the disciples again asked Him about this. ¹¹ So He said to them, "If any man divorces his wife to ᶠ marry another woman, he commits adultery against his former wife, ¹² and if any woman divorces her husband to marry another man, she commits adultery."

¹³ And people were bringing little children ᵍ to Him for Him to touch them, but the disciples reproved them for it. ¹⁴ When Jesus saw it, He was indignant, and said to them, "Let the little children come to me, and stop ʰ keeping them from it, for to such as these the kingdom of God belongs. ¹⁵ I solemnly say to you, whoever does not accept the kingdom of God as a little child does, will never get into it at all." ¹⁶ Then He took the little children into His arms, and as He laid His hands upon them one by one,ⁱ He tenderly ʲ blessed them.

¹⁷ As He was again starting on a journey, a man ran up to Him, and knelt to Him, and was asking Him, "Good Teacher, what must I do to get eternal life?"

¹⁸ And Jesus answered him, "Why do you call me perfectly good? ᵏ No one is perfectly good but God Himself. ¹⁹ You know the commandments: Do not murder, Do not commit adultery, Do not steal, Do not bear false witness, Do not defraud, Practice honoring your father and mother."

ᶜ Grk., *hardness of heart.*
ᵈ Grk., *in your law.*
ᵉ Impv. future indicative.
ᶠ *And* in Heb. often expresses purpose; Mk's Grk. colored with Heb.
ᵍ From three to twelve years (Mk. 5:42).
ʰ Neg. with pres. impv.
ⁱ Pres. pt. means this.
ʲ So comp. vb. Fol. B and Sin. Mss.
ᵏ So this Grk. adj.

²⁰ But he said to Him, "Teacher, I have kept all these commandments ever since I was a child."

²¹ Then Jesus looked at him and loved him, and said to him, "You lack one thing. Go, sell everything you have, and give the money to the poor, and you will have riches in heaven; then come back and follow me." ²² But his countenance fell at that command, and he went away in deep distress, for he owned a great deal of property.

²³ Then Jesus looked around and said to His disciples, "How hard it will be for those who have money to get into the kingdom of God!" ²⁴ His disciples were startled at this statement.[1] But Jesus again said to them as He continued the topic,[m] "My children, how hard it is to get into the kingdom of God! ²⁵ It is easier for a camel to go through a needle's eye than for a rich man to get into the kingdom of God."

²⁶ They were perfectly dumfounded, and said to Him, "Then who can be saved?"

²⁷ But Jesus looked at them and said, "This is impossible for men, but everything is possible for God."

²⁸ Then Peter started to say to Him, "We have left everything we had and followed you."

²⁹ Jesus said, "I solemnly say to you, there is no one who has given up home or brothers or sisters or mother or father or children or farm for me and for the good news, ³⁰ who will not receive now in this life a hundred times as much in houses and brothers and sisters and mothers and children and farms, but along with them persecution, and in the world to come eternal life. ³¹ But many who are first now will be last then, and last now who will be first then."

³² As they were walking along the road up to Jerusalem, Jesus was going on ahead of them, but they[n] were dazed[o] while those who were still following were afraid. Then again He took the Twelve aside and began to tell them what was going to befall Him. ³³ "Listen![p] We are going up to Jerusalem, and the Son of Man will be turned over to the high priests and scribes, and they will sentence Him to death, and will turn Him over to the heathen, ³⁴ and they will make sport of Him, and spit on Him, and flog Him, and kill Him, but three days after He will rise again."

---

[1] Grk., *amazed at these words.*
[m] Pres. of cont. ac. suggests this.
[n] The disciples.
[o] Impf. of vb. *amaze.*
[p] Grk., *behold.*

³⁵ And Zebedee's two sons, James and John, came up to Him and said, "Teacher, we want you to do for us whatever we ask."
³⁶ He asked then, "What do you want me to do for you?"
³⁷ They answered Him, "Grant us to sit, one at your right hand and one at your left, in your splendor."
³⁸ Jesus said to them, "You do not realize q what you are asking for. Can you drink the cup that I am drinking, or endure the baptism of agony that I am to endure?" r
³⁹ They answered Him, "We can."

Jesus said to them, "Yes, the cup that I am drinking you will have to drink, and the baptism of agony s that I am enduring you will have to endure, ⁴⁰ but seats t at my right and at my left are not mine to give, but they will be given to those for whom they have been prepared."

⁴¹ When the other ten heard of it, they were at first u very indignant at James and John. ⁴² Then Jesus called them to Him, and said to them, "You know that those who are supposed to rule the heathen lord it over them, and their great men rule as despots over them; ⁴³ but this is not to be the case among you. Whoever wants to be great among you must be your servant, ⁴⁴ and whoever wants to hold the first positions among you must be everybody's slave. v ⁴⁵ For the Son of Man did not come to be served but to serve, and to give His life a ransom price to set many free." w

⁴⁶ Then they came to Jericho. And as He was leaving Jericho, with His disciples and a great crowd, Timeus' son, Bartimeus, a blind beggar, was sitting on the roadside. ⁴⁷ When he heard that it was Jesus of Nazareth, he began to shout, "Jesus, you son of David, do pity me!"

⁴⁸ Many of the people began to rebuke him and to tell him to keep quiet, but all the louder he kept shouting, "You son of David, do pity me!"

⁴⁹ So Jesus stopped and said, "Tell him to come here."

Then they told the blind man, saying, "Cheer up! Get up! He is calling for you." ⁵⁰ He threw off his coat and jumped up and went to Jesus.

---

q *Do not know.*
r *Be baptized with the baptism, etc.*
s *Expressed in the picture of baptism.*
t *To sit.*
u *Began to be indig.*
v *Slave of all.*
w *Exact meaning of Grk. λύτρον; military term.*

⁵¹ Then Jesus asked him, "What do you want me to do for you?" The blind man answered, "Good Teacher,ˣ I want to see again."

⁵² Then Jesus said to him, "Go; your faith has cured you." And all at once he could see again, and began to follow Jesus along the road.

11
JESUS RIDES AS KING INTO JERUSALEM; CURSES THE FIG TREE; DRIVES THE TRADERS OUT OF THE TEMPLE; TELLS OF FAITH THAT MOVES MOUNTAINS; QUESTIONED BY THE LEADERS HE FLOORS THEM WITH A QUESTION

When they were getting near Jerusalem, that is, were at Bethphage and Bethany in front of the Mount of Olives, He sent two of His disciples on ahead, ² and said to them, "Go into the village in front of you, and as soon as you get into it, you will find a colt tied which has never been ridden by a man. Untie it and bring it here. ³ And if anyone asks you, 'Why are you doing that?' answer, 'The Lord needs it, and will soon send it back here.'"

⁴ So off they went and found a colt tied outside a door at a street corner.ᵃ They untied it, ⁵ but some bystanders said to them, "What are you doing, untying the colt?" ⁶ And they answered as Jesus had directed them, and so they let them bring it. ⁷ They brought the colt to Jesus, and they threw their coats over it, and Jesus mounted it. ⁸ And many of the people spread their coats in the road, while others scattered layers of leaves cut from the fields. ⁹ Then those in front and those behind Him shouted:

"Welcome ᵇ Him!
   Blessed be He who comes in the name of the Lord;
   ¹⁰ Blessed be the coming reign of our father David!
   Welcome Him from on high!"

¹¹ And so He went into Jerusalem and into the temple. After He had looked everything over, as it was already late, He went out with the Twelve to Bethany.

¹² Next day, while they were walking over from Bethany, He felt hungry. ¹³ Now in the distance He saw a fig tree covered with leaves, and He went up to it to see if He might find some figs on

---
ˣ *Rabboni,* a term of endearment.
ᵃ *At two ways.*
ᵇ A title of welcome (so Thayer, Lex.).

it, but when He got to it, He found nothing but leaves, for it was not the time for figs. ¹⁴ So He spoke to it and said, "Never again may anyone eat a fig ᵉ from you!" And His disciples were listening to it.

¹⁵ Then they reached Jerusalem, and He went into the temple and began to drive out of it those who were buying and selling things in it. Then He upset the money-changers' tables and the dove-dealers' counters, ¹⁶ and would not let anybody carry a vessel through the temple. ¹⁷ And He continued teaching them and saying, "Does not the Scripture say, 'My house shall be called a house of prayer for all the nations'? But you have made it a cave for robbers."

¹⁸ Then the high priests and the scribes heard of this, and they kept looking for some way ᵈ to destroy Him, for they were afraid of Him, for everybody was swept off his feet ᵉ at what He said. ¹⁹ So when evening came, He and His disciples used ᶠ to go out of the city.

²⁰ In the morning as they were passing along, they noticed that the fig tree was withered, clear down to its roots.ᵍ ²¹ And Peter remembered about it, and said to Him, "Look, Teacher! The fig tree which you cursed has withered!"

²² Then Jesus answered them, "Have faith in God! ²³ I solemnly say to you, whoever says to this mountain, 'Get up and throw yourself into the sea,' and does not doubt at all in his heart, but has faith that what he says will take place, shall have it. ²⁴ So then I tell you, whenever you pray and ask for anything, have faith that it has been granted you, and you will get it. ²⁵ And whenever you stand and pray, if you have anything against anybody, forgive him, so that your Father in heaven too may forgive you your shortcomings." ʰ

²⁷ Then again they went into Jerusalem. And while Jesus was walking about in the temple, the high priests, scribes, and elders came up to Him ²⁸ and said to Him, "What sort of authority have you for doing as you do? Or, who gave you the authority to do as you do?"

²⁹ Jesus said to them, "Let me ask you just one question, and if

---

ᵉ Grk., *fruit.*
ᵈ Grk., *how.*
ᵉ Grk., *struck out of themselves.*
ᶠ Impf. of customary ac.
ᵍ Grk., *from the roots.*
ʰ Grk., *fallings, failings,* so *shortcomings;* v. 26 om. by best Mss.

MARK 12

you answer me, I will tell you what sort of authority I have for doing as I do. ³⁰ Was John's baptism from heaven or from men? Answer me."

³¹ Then they argued with one another in this way, "If we say, 'It was from heaven,' He will say, 'Then why did you not believe him?' ³² On the other hand, can we say, 'It was from men'?" For they were afraid of the people, because everybody thought that John was really a prophet.

³³ So they said to Jesus, "We do not know."

Jesus also said to them, "Nor am I going to tell you what sort of authority I have for doing as I do."

12
JESUS TELLS THE STORY OF THE VILLAINOUS TENANTS; HIS OPPONENTS ASK HIM "CATCH" QUESTIONS: IS IT RIGHT TO PAY TAXES TO ROME? IS THERE A RESURRECTION? JESUS FLOORS THEM WITH A QUESTION ABOUT DAVID'S SON BEING HIS LORD

Then He began to speak to them in stories. "A man once planted a vineyard and fenced it in and hewed out a wine-vat and built a watchtower; then he rented it to tenant farmers, and went abroad.ᵃ ² At the proper time he sent a slave to the tenants to collect his part of the grape crop.ᵇ ³ But they took him and beat him and sent him back empty-handed.ᶜ ⁴ And again he sent another slave to them, and they beat his head and treated him shamefully. ⁵ Then he sent a third one, and they killed him, and many others, some of whom they beat, some they killed. ⁶ He had one more to send, his dearly loved son; at last he sent him to them, for he said to himself, 'They will surely respect my son.' ⁷ But those tenants said among themselves, 'This is his heir; come on, let us kill him, and all that is coming to himᵈ will be ours.' ⁸ So they took him and killed him, and threw his body outside the vineyard. ⁹ Now what will the owner of the vineyard do? He will come back and destroy those tenants and give the vineyard to others. ¹⁰ Have you never read this passage of Scripture: ᵉ

"'That stone which the builders threw away
Has now become the corner-stone;

ᵃ So Thayer, Lex.
ᵇ Grk., *fruit,* so *grape crop.*
ᶜ Grk., *empty.*
ᵈ Grk., *his inheritance.*
ᵉ Ps. 118:22f.

¹¹ This is the work of the Lord,
And seems wonderful to us' ? ' "

¹² Then they were trying to have Him arrested, but they were afraid of the people, for they knew that He aimed ^f this story at them. And so they left Him and went away.

¹³ Then they sent some Pharisees and Herodians to Him to trap Him in argument.^g ¹⁴ And they came up and said to Him, "We know that you always tell the truth, and pay no personal consideration ^h to anyone, but teach the way of God honestly. Is it right to pay the poll-tax to Caesar, or not? ¹⁵ Should we pay it, or should we not?"

Now because He saw their pretense, He said to them, "Why are you testing me so? Bring me a twenty-cent coin ⁱ to look at." ¹⁶ And they brought Him one.

Then He asked them, "Whose picture ^j and title is this?"

They answered Him, "Caesar's."

¹⁷ So He said, "Pay Caesar what belongs to Caesar, and pay God what belongs to God." And they were utterly dumbfounded ^k at Him.

¹⁸ Then some Sadducees, who claim that there is no resurrection, came up to Him and asked Him this question, ¹⁹ "Teacher, Moses gave ^l us a law that if a man's brother died leaving a wife but no child, the man must marry ^m the widow and raise up a family for his brother. ²⁰ There were once seven brothers. The eldest married a wife and on dying left no child, ²¹ and the second married her and died leaving no child; and so did the third. ²² And not one of the seven left a child. At last the woman died too. ²³ Now at the resurrection, which one's wife will she be? For all seven of them married her."

²⁴ Jesus said to them, "Does not this prove that you are wrong in your views,ⁿ because you do not understand either the Scriptures or the power of God? ²⁵ For when people rise from the dead, men do not marry and women are not married, but continue to live together as the angels in heaven do. ²⁶ But as to the rising

---

^f Grk., *spoke.*
^g Grk., *word* or *speech.*
^h Grk., *you have no personal bias for anyone.*
ⁱ *Denarius,* a coin worth nearly twenty cents.
^j Grk., *image.*
^k Strong vb. for expressing this emotion.
^l Grk., *wrote.*
^m Grk., *take.*
ⁿ Grk., *is it not on acct. of this, because you do not.*

of the dead,º did you never read in the book of Moses, in the passage about the bush, how God said to him, 'I am the God of Abraham, the God of Isaac, and the God of Jacob'? ²⁷ He is not the God of dead but of living people! You are entirely wrong in your views."

²⁸ Then one of the scribes, on hearing them arguing, came up, and since he saw that Jesus ᵖ had answered them properly, he asked Him, "What sort of command is the first of all commands?" ᵠ
²⁹ Jesus answered, "The first one is, 'Hear, O Israel, the Lord our God is one Lord, ³⁰ and you must love the Lord your God with your whole heart, your whole soul, your whole mind, and your whole strength.' ³¹ And this is the second, 'You must love your neighbor as you do yourself.' No other command is greater than these."

³² Then the scribe said to Him, "Indeed, Teacher, you have properly said that He ʳ is one by Himself, and there is no other but Him, ³³ and to love Him with one's whole heart, one's whole understanding, and one's whole strength, and to love one's neighbor as one loves himself is far more than all the burnt-offerings and sacrifices."

³⁴ So Jesus said to him, as He saw that he had answered thoughtfully, "You are not far from the kingdom of God." And no one ventured to ask Him any more questions.

³⁵ While He was teaching in the temple, He answered them and said, "How can the scribes say that the Christ is the son of David? ³⁶ David himself, under the guidance of the Holy Spirit,ˢ said: ᵗ
'The Lord has said to my Lord, "Sit at my right hand
Until I make your enemies the footstool of your feet."'
³⁷ David himself called him Lord, so how can He be his son?"

Most ᵘ of the people liked to hear Him. ³⁸ And in His teaching He continued to say: "Beware of the scribes who like to go about in long robes, to be saluted with honor in public places, ³⁹ to be seated in the front seats in the synagogues, to occupy the places of honor at banquets—⁴⁰ men who eat up widows' houses and to cover it up ᵛ make long prayers. They will get a much heavier sentence!"

  º *Grk., about the dead, that they rise.*
  ᵖ *Grk., He, but noun better in Eng.*
  ᵠ *Grk., first of all.*
  ʳ *Best Mss. om. the word, God.*
  ˢ *Grk., in or by the Holy Spirit.*
  ᵗ Ps. 110:1.
  ᵘ *Grk., the much of the people.*
  ᵛ *Lit., for a pretense.*

⁴¹ Then He sat down in front of the collection-box and was watching the people as they dropped their money into it. And many rich people were dropping in large sums.ʷ ⁴² Then a poor widow came and dropped in two little copper coins, which make scarcely a cent. ⁴³ And He called His disciples to Him and said, "I solemnly say to you, this poor widow has put in more than all these others who have been putting money into the collection-box. ⁴⁴ For all of them put in out of their surplus, but she in her want put in all she had, yes, all she had to live on."

13 JESUS TELLS OF THE DESTRUCTION OF JERUSALEM; THE FINAL COMING OF CHRIST; THE STORIES OF THE FIG TREE AND THE DOORKEEPER, TO URGE HIS FOLLOWERS TO WATCH

As He was leaving the temple, one of His disciples said to Him, "Look, Teacher! What stupendous stones, what beautiful buildings!" ᵃ

² Jesus said to him, "Are you looking in wonder ᵇ at these great buildings? Not one stone will be left here upon another that will not be torn down."

³ As He was sitting on the Mount of Olives opposite the temple, Peter, James, John, and Andrew, in a private group,ᶜ were asking Him, ⁴ "When will all this take place? Tell us. And what will be the sign that it is about to be put into effect?"

⁵ Jesus began to say to them:

"Look out that no one misleads you about it. ⁶ Many will come bearing the name of Messiah,ᵈ and saying, 'I am He,' and they will mislead many. ⁷ But when you hear of wars and rumors of war, stop getting alarmed. They have to come, but the end is not yet. ⁸ For one nation will go to war ᵉ with another, and one kingdom with another. There will be earthquakes in many places; ᶠ there will be famines. But this is only the beginning of the agonies.ᵍ ⁹ So you must be on the lookout for yourselves;

ʷ Grk., *much or many things*.
ᵃ Grk., *what stones*, etc.!
ᵇ In context.
ᶜ Grk., *alone*.
ᵈ Grk., *in my name*.
ᵉ *Nation will rise*, etc.
ᶠ Grk., *from place to place*.
ᵍ Lit., *birth pangs*.

MARK 13

they will turn you over to courts, and to synagogues where you will be beaten, and you must appear before governors and kings for my sake, to testify to them. 10 But before the end comes, the good news must be proclaimed [h] to all the heathen. 11 Now when they take you to court for trial,[i] do not be worrying beforehand about what you should say, but say whatever is given you at that time, for it is not you that will be speaking, but the Holy Spirit. 12 One brother will turn another over to death, and a father his child, and children will take a stand against their parents and have them put to death. 13 You will be hated by everybody, because you bear my name.[j] But whoever bears up to the end will be saved.

14 "So when you see the destructive desecration standing where he has no right to stand"—let the reader take notice—"then let those who remain in Judea fly to the hills; 15 let him who is on the roof of his house not go down and go into the house to get anything out of it; 16 let him who is in the field not turn back to get his coat. 17 Alas for the women who are expectant mothers and those who have nursing babies, in those days! 18 And pray that it may not be in winter, 19 for there will be such misery at that time as has never been since the beginning of God's creation, and never will be again. 20 If the Lord [k] had not cut those days short, nobody would have escaped, but for the sake of the people chosen as His own [l] He has cut them short.

21 "If anyone says to you at that time, 'Look! Here is the Christ,' or, 'Look! There He is,' do not believe it. 22 For false Christs and false prophets will announce themselves,[m] and they will do signs and wonders to mislead, if possible, even God's chosen people. 23 So you must be on your guard. I have warned [n] you about it all beforehand.

24 "But in those days, after that misery, the sun will turn dark, the moon will not shed its light, 25 the stars will be falling from the sky, and the powers of the sky will be shaken. 26 And then they will see the Son of Man coming on the clouds in overwhelming power and splendor. 27 Then He will send out His angels, and

[h] *Must first be preached.*
[i] Implied in word *court.*
[j] *On acct. of my name.*
[k] Implied.
[l] Grk., *the elect whom He elected.*
[m] Grk., *arise.*
[n] Grk., *told.*

gather His chosen people º from the four points of the compass,ᵖ from one end of the sky to the other. ²⁸ "Now learn what the story of the fig tree means. Just as soon as its branches grow tender, and put forth leaves, you know that summer is near. ²⁹ So when you see all these things taking place, you will know that He is right at the door. ³⁰ I solemnly say to you, the present generation will not pass away before all this takes place. ³¹ Earth and sky will pass away, but my words will never pass away. ³² But about that day or hour not a single one knows— not even the angels in heaven, nor the Son; not a single one but the Father. ³³ Keep looking, keep alert, for you do not know when the time will be. ³⁴ It will be like a man who leaves his home and goes on a journey, after he has given orders to his slaves, to each his particular task, and has given orders to the watchman to keep watch.ᑫ ³⁵ So you must keep alert, for you do not know when the master of the house is coming—in the evening or at midnight or at daybreak or early in the morning—³⁶ so that he may not come unexpectedly and find you asleep. ³⁷ And so what I say to you, I say to everybody, keep alert."

14   JESUS ANOINTED WITH COSTLY PERFUME; JUDAS DRIVES A BARGAIN TO BETRAY HIM; PASSOVER SUPPER EATEN AND MEMORIAL SUPPER INSTITUTED BY JESUS; SUFFERING IN GETHSEMANE, BETRAYED, ARRESTED, AND TRIED IN JEWISH COURT

Now the feast of the Passover and of Unleavened Bread was two days later. So the high priests and scribes kept looking for some way to arrest Him by stratagem and have Him put to death, ² for they kept saying, "It must not be at the feast, for there might be a riot."

³ While He was in Bethany, He was a guest in the home of Simon the leper, and as He was sitting at table, a woman came in with an alabaster bottle ᵃ of pure nard perfume, very costly; she broke the bottle and poured the perfume on His head. ⁴ But some of the guests were indignantly saying to themselves, "Why was such a waste of the perfume made? ⁵ It might have been sold for

---

º Grk., *the elect.*
ᵖ Grk., *from the four winds.*
ᑫ Grk., *the doorkeeper to keep watch.*
ᵃ A sort of flask, but *bottle* in modern Eng.

MARK 14

more than sixty dollars, and the money have been given to the poor." So they kept on grumbling at her.

⁶ But Jesus said, "Let her alone; why do you embarrass ᵇ her? She has done a good deed to me. ⁷ For you always have the poor among you, and whenever you please you can do them good, but you will not always have me. ⁸ She has done all she could; she has beforehand ᶜ perfumed my body for my burial. ⁹ I solemnly say to you, all over the world wherever this good news is proclaimed, the deed that she has done will also be told, in memory of her."

¹⁰ Then Judas Iscariot, one of the Twelve, went to the high priests to betray Him to them. ¹¹ They were delighted to hear it, and promised to pay ᵈ him for it. So he kept looking for a good opportunity to betray Him to them.

¹² On the first day of the feast of Unleavened Bread, the usual time for killing the Passover lamb, Jesus' disciples asked Him, "Where do you want us to go and get the Passover supper ready for you to eat?"

¹³ So He sent off two of His disciples, and said to them, "Go into the city and you will meet a man ᵉ carrying a pitcher of water. Follow him, ¹⁴ and whatever house he goes into, tell the owner that the Teacher asks, 'Where is my room where ᶠ I may eat the Passover supper with my disciples?' ¹⁵ Then he will show you a large upstairs room, furnished and ready; get everything ready for us there." ¹⁶ So off the disciples went; they reached ᵍ the city, found everything just as He had told them, and they got the Passover supper ready.ʰ

¹⁷ When evening came, He went with the Twelve. ¹⁸ And while they were sitting at table and eating, Jesus said, "I solemnly say to you, one of you, one who is now ⁱ eating with me, is going to betray me."

¹⁹ And they began to show that they were hurt ʲ and to ask Him one by one, "It cannot be I, can it?"

²⁰ He answered them, "It is one of the Twelve, the one who is

---

ᵇ Grk., *trouble.*
ᶜ *She has taken on her beforehand,* etc.
ᵈ Grk., *gave him money.*
ᵉ Grk., *a man will meet you,* etc.
ᶠ Rel. adv. in Grk., colloquial as in Eng.
ᵍ Two vbs., *went off* and *went into* (reached).
ʰ Colloquial in Eng. and Grk.
ⁱ Pres. pt. expresses process.
ʲ Grk., *to be grieved* or *pained.*

dipping his bread in the dish with me. ²¹ For the Son of Man is going away, as the Scriptures say of Him, but a curse will be on that man by whom He is betrayed. It would have been better for that man, if he had never been born."

²² While they were eating, He took a loaf and blessed it and broke it in pieces and gave it to them, saying, "Take this; it is my body." [k]

²³ He also took the cup of wine [1] and gave thanks and gave it to them, and they all drank some of it. ²⁴ Then He said to them, "This is my blood [k] which ratifies the covenant, the blood which is to be poured out for many. ²⁵ I solemnly say to you, I will never again drink the product [m] of the vine till the day when I drink the new wine in the kingdom of God."

²⁶ After singing a hymn they went out of the city and up the Mount of Olives. ²⁷ Then Jesus said to them, "You will all stumble over me, [n] for the Scripture says, 'I will strike the shepherd, and the sheep will be scattered.' ²⁸ But after I am raised from the dead, [o] I will go back to Galilee to meet you." [p]

²⁹ Then Peter said to Him, "Although all the rest of them stumble over you, yet I will never do so myself."

³⁰ Then Jesus said to him, "I solemnly say to you, this very night, before the cock crows twice, you, yes, you, will disown me three times."

³¹ But Peter kept on emphatically saying, "Even if I have to die with you, I will never disown you." And they all kept saying the same thing.

³² Then they came to the place called Gethsemane, and He said to His disciples, "Sit down here while I pray."

³³ And He took Peter, James, and John along with Him, and He began to feel completely dazed [q] and to realize His anguish of heart, ³⁴ and so He said to them, "My heart is breaking, it almost kills me! You must stay here and keep watching."

³⁵ Then He walked on a few steps and threw Himself upon the ground, and kept praying that if it were possible He might escape

---

[k] Metaphorical language.
[1] Implied.
[m] *Fruit.*
[n] Grk., *will be caused to fall.*
[o] Implied in vb. *rise.*
[p] Grk., *before you.*
[q] Comp. vb. means *to be intensely amazed, dazed.*

the hour of agony,^r ^36 and He was saying, "Abba," which means, "Father," "anything is possible for you! Take this cup away from me! Yet, I pray,^s not what I want but what you want!"

^37 And He went back and found them asleep, and He said to Peter, "Simon, are you asleep? Could you not watch a single hour? ^38 You must all ^t keep watching and praying that you may not be exposed ^u to temptation. Man's spirit is willing but human nature is weak."

^39 He went away again and prayed in the same words. ^40 When He went back again, He found them asleep again, for their eyes were so heavy they could hardly hold them open; ^v and they did not know what answer to make Him.

^41 He came back the third time and said to them, "Are you still sleeping and resting? No more of that! The hour has come. See! The Son of Man is betrayed into the hands of sinful men. ^42 Get up, let us be going. Look! here comes my betrayer!"

^43 At that very moment, while He was still speaking, Judas, one of the Twelve, came up, and with him a crowd of men with swords and clubs, from the high priests, scribes, and elders. ^44 Now His betrayer had given them a signal, saying, "The one I kiss is He; seize Him and lead Him safely away." ^45 So when he came he went straight up to Jesus, and said, "Rabbi," and with much affection ^w kissed Him.

^46 Then they laid hands on Him and arrested Him. ^47 But one of the bystanders drew his sword and struck at the high priest's slave and cut his ear off. ^48 And Jesus spoke and said to them, "Have you come out with swords and clubs to arrest me, as though I were a robber? ^49 Day after day I used to be with you teaching in the temple, and you never laid hands on me. But this is so to fulfill the Scriptures."

^50 Then all His disciples ^x forsook Him and made their escape. ^51 And a young man was following Him, with only a linen sheet thrown about his body; and they seized him, ^52 but he left the linen sheet behind and fled away naked.

---

^r Grk., *that the hour might pass*, etc.
^s Implied.
^t *You* in pl., so *all*.
^u Grk., *led into*.
^v Grk., *eyes weighed down*.
^w Comp. vb. means this.
^x *His disciples* implied from context.

⁵³ They took Jesus away to the high priest, and all the high priests, elders, and scribes met there. ⁵⁴ And Peter followed Him at a distance, as far as the courtyard of the high priest; he was sitting with the attendants and warming himself before the fire.

⁵⁵ The high priests and the whole council were trying to get evidence against Jesus to put Him to death, but they could find none, ⁵⁶ for although many men gave false testimony against Him, their testimonies did not agree. ⁵⁷ Some took the witness stand and gave this false testimony against Him: ⁵⁸ "We ourselves have heard Him say, 'I will tear down this temple built by men's hands, and in three days I will build another, made without hands.' " ⁵⁹ But even in this matter their testimony did not agree.

⁶⁰ Then the high priest arose in the midst and asked Jesus, "Have you no answer to make? What about this testimony they are giving against you?" ⁶¹ But He kept silent and made no answer at all.

So the high priest again questioned Him in these words, "Are you the Christ, the Son of the Blessed One?"

⁶² Jesus said, "Yes, I am,[y] and you will all see the Son of Man seated at the right hand of the Almighty and coming in the clouds of the sky!"

⁶³ Then the high priest tore his clothes and said, "What more evidence do we need now? ⁶⁴ Did you hear His own blasphemy? What do you think now?"[z] And they all condemned Him as deserving to die. ⁶⁵ And some of them started to spit on Him and to blindfold Him and to hit Him with their fists, and say to Him, "Now play the prophet!" Even the attendants took charge of Him with slaps at Him.

⁶⁶ While Peter was down in the courtyard, one of the high priest's waiting-girls came up, ⁶⁷ and when she saw that Peter was warming himself, she looked at him and said, "You were with Jesus of Nazareth too!"

⁶⁸ But he denied it, saying, "I do not know or understand what you mean."[*] Then he went out of the courtyard and was in the gateway to it.

⁶⁹ And the waiting-girl saw him there and began again to tell the bystanders, "This fellow is one of them!" ⁷⁰ But he denied it again.

And again a few minutes later [†] the bystanders began to say to

---

[y] Grk., *I am.*
[z] Grk., *what appears to you?*
[*] Grk., *say.*
[†] Grk., *a little later.*

Peter, "You are surely one of them, for you are a Galilean too."

⁷¹ Then he commenced cursing and swearing, "I do not know this man that you are talking about."

⁷² At that moment ‡ for the second time a cock crowed. Then Peter remembered how Jesus had said to him, "Before the cock crows twice, you will disown me three times!" And when he remembered that, he burst into tears. §

15 JESUS TRIED IN THE ROMAN COURT; BARABBAS SET FREE; THE SOLDIERS MAKING SPORT OF JESUS; CRUCIFIED ON GOLGOTHA; SUFFERING SIX HOURS; BURIED BY JOSEPH IN HIS NEW TOMB

As soon as it was daylight, the high priests held a consultation with the elders and scribes; and the whole council, after binding Jesus, took Him away and turned Him over to Pilate.

² Then Pilate asked Him, "Are you the king of the Jews?"
He answered, "Yes."

³ And the high priests kept piling up ᵃ accusations against Him.
⁴ Then again Pilate asked Him, "Have you no answer to make? Just see how many charges they are making against you!" ⁵ But Jesus made no further answer at all, so that Pilate was astonished.

⁶ Now at the time of the feast Pilate usually set a prisoner free whom the people requested. ⁷ There was in prison a man named Barabbas, among some revolutionaries who in their uprising had committed murder. ⁸ So a crowd of people came up and started to request of the governor the usual favor.ᵇ

⁹ Then Pilate answered them by asking, "Do you want me to set the king of the Jews free for you?" ¹⁰ For he knew that the high priests out of envy had turned Him over to him. ¹¹ But the high priests stirred up the crowd to get him to set Barabbas free for them instead.

¹² Then Pilate again said to them, "What then do you want me to do to the man whom you call king of the Jews?"

¹³ They shouted back,ᶜ "Crucify Him!"

¹⁴ Then Pilate again asked, "Why, what has He done that is wrong?"

‡ Grk., *at once.*
§ Incip. impf.
ᵃ *Were making many accusations.*
ᵇ Grk., *just as he usually did.*
ᶜ Grk., *again.*

But they shouted at the top of their voices,[d] "Crucify Him!" ¹⁵ So, as Pilate wanted to satisfy the crowd,[e] he set Barabbas free for them, but after having Jesus flogged, he turned Him over to be crucified.

¹⁶ Then the soldiers led Him away to a place inside the court yard, that is, of the governor's palace,[f] and they called the whole battalion together. ¹⁷ And they dressed Him in a purple robe and made a crown of thorns and crowned Him with it, ¹⁸ and they began to shout at Him, "All hail, you king of the Jews!" ¹⁹ And they kept hitting Him on the head with a stick, and kept spitting on Him, and on bending knees they kept doing Him homage. ²⁰ When they had finished [g] making sport of Him, they took off the purple robe and put His own clothes on Him.

Then they led Him out of the city to crucify Him. ²¹ They forced a certain passer-by, who was coming in from the country, to carry His cross—Simon, a Cyrenian, the father of Alexander and Rufus. ²² And they led Him to Golgotha, which means, the Place of the Skull. ²³ They offered Him wine flavored with myrrh, but He would not take it. ²⁴ Then they crucified Him and divided among them His clothes, by drawing lots for them to see which piece each of them should have. ²⁵ It was nine o'clock in the morning when [h] they crucified Him. ²⁶ And the notice of the charge against Him read,[i] "The king of the Jews." ²⁷ They crucified two robbers along with Him, one at His right and one at His left.[j]

²⁹ And the passers-by kept hissing at Him, shaking their heads and saying, "Aha! You are the man who would tear down the temple and build another in three days! ³⁰ Now save yourself by coming down from the cross."

³¹ The high priests too made sport of Him to one another with the scribes, and kept saying, "He saved others but He cannot save Himself! ³² Let the Christ, the king of Israel, come down now from the cross, so that we may see it and believe!" Even the men who were crucified with Him made sport of Him.

³³ At twelve o'clock darkness covered the whole land and lasted until three in the afternoon. ³⁴ And at three o'clock Jesus cried

---

[d] Grk., *exceedingly*.
[e] Grk., *make it satisfactory to*.
[f] Grk., *praetorium*.
[g] Effective aor.
[h] Grk., *and*.
[i] Grk., *written*.
[j] V. 28 om. from best Mss.

with a loud voice, *"Eloi! Eloi! lama sabachthani?"* which means, "My God! my God! why have you forsaken me?"

35 Some of the bystanders when they heard it said, "Listen! k He is calling for Elijah!"

36 So one man ran and soaked a sponge in vinegar and put it on a stick and held it up to Him to drink, saying, "Wait, let us see whether Elijah does come to take Him down!"

37 Then Jesus gave a loud cry, and expired. 38 And the curtain of the sanctuary was torn in two, from top to bottom. 39 And when the captain who stood facing him saw that He expired in this way, he said, "This man was surely God's Son."

40 Now several ¹ women were there looking on from a distance, among them Mary of Magdala, Mary the mother of the younger James and of Joses, and Salome, 41 who used to accompany Him when He was in Galilee, besides several other women who had come up to Jerusalem with Him.

42 Although it was now evening, yet since it was the Preparation Day, that is, the day before the sabbath, 43 Joseph of Arimathea, a highly honored member of the council, who was himself looking for the kingdom of God, ventured to go to Pilate and ask for Jesus' body. 44 Pilate wondered whether He was dead yet, and calling the captain to him asked whether He was already dead; 45 but when he found out from the captain that He was, he gave him permission to take His body. 46 So he bought a linen sheet, he took Him down from the cross, wrapped Him in the linen sheet, and laid Him in a tomb that had been hewn out of the rock, and rolled a boulder ᵐ up to the doorway of the tomb. 47 And Mary of Magdala and Mary, Joses' mother, were looking on to see where He was put.

16 SOME WOMEN SEE THE EMPTY TOMB; THE ANGEL ORDERS THEM TO TELL HIS DISCIPLES; JESUS APPEARS TO MARY OF MAGDALA; TO TWO MORE WALKING INTO THE COUNTRY; TO THE ELEVEN; GIVES THEM HIS LAST ORDER; GOES UP TO HEAVEN

When the sabbath had ended, Mary of Magdala, Mary, James's mother, and Salome bought spices to go and anoint Him. ² It was very early, just after the sun had risen, on the first day of the

---
ᵏ Grk., *behold!*
¹ Implied from v. 41.
ᵐ *A very large stone;* so *boulder* expresses it.

week, when they went to the tomb. ³ And they kept saying to one another, "Who will roll the boulder back from the doorway of the tomb for us?"

⁴ Then they looked up and saw that the boulder had already been rolled to one side,ᵃ for it was a very large one. ⁵ And when they went into the tomb, they saw a young man dressed in a white robe sitting at the right; and they were utterly astounded.

⁶ But he said to them, "You must not be so astounded; you are looking for Jesus of Nazareth who was crucified. He has risen; He is not here. See! here is the spot ᵇ where they laid Him. ⁷ But you go and tell His disciples and Peter, 'He is going back to Galilee to meet you; ᶜ you will see Him there, just as He told you.'"

⁸ Then they left the tomb and fled, for they were trembling and bewildered,ᵈ and they did not tell anybody a single thing ᵉ about it, for they were afraid to do so.ᶠ

⁹ Now after He had risen, early on the first day of the week, He appeared first to Mary of Magdala, out of whom He had driven seven demons. ¹⁰ She went out and told it to His disciples,ᵍ while they were mourning and weeping. ¹¹ But although they had heard that He was alive and had been seen by her, they would not believe it. ¹² After this He showed Himself in a different form to two of them as they were walking along, on their way into the country. ¹³ Then they went back and told the rest, but they would not believe them either. ¹⁴ Later on He appeared to the Eleven themselves while they were at table, and reproved them for their lack of faith and their stubbornness,ʰ because they had not believed those who had seen Him after He had been raised from the dead.

¹⁵ Then He said to them, "You must go all over the world ⁱ and preach the good news to all the creation. ¹⁶ He who believes it and is baptized will be saved, but he who does not believe it will be condemned. ¹⁷ And the following ʲ signs will attend those who

---

ᵃ A different vb.
ᵇ Grk., *place*, but *spot* means *the very place*.
ᶜ Grk., *before you*.
ᵈ Grk., *trembling and bewilderment held them*.
ᵉ Strong Grk. neg.
ᶠ End of Mk. in two best **Mss.** Later Mss. add vv. 9-20.
ᵍ Implied.
ʰ Grk., *hardness of heart*.
ⁱ Greek uses the strongest word for *all;* hence our tr. *all over*, etc.
ʲ Grk., *these*.

MARK 16

believe: By using [k] my name they will drive out demons; they will speak in foreign [1] languages; [18] they will take snakes in their hands; even if they drink anything poisonous, it will not hurt them; they will lay their hands on the sick, and they will get well."

[19] So the Lord Jesus, after He had spoken to them, was caught up into heaven and took His seat at God's right hand. [20] Then they went out and preached everywhere, while the Lord kept on working with them and confirming their message by the signs that attended it.

[k] Grk., *in my name.*
[1] Grk., *speak in tongues.*

LUKE

The writer is Luke, the physician, who accompanied Paul in his missionary labors. He was a cultured Greek who accepted Christianity for himself and felt that it was the religion for everybody. He wrote in a charming Greek style. So we shall try to make our English translation correspond to it.

The occasion which moved him to write it was that he possessed some valuable facts about Jesus' life, works, and teachings, which had not as yet been included in the earlier Gospels. The most of these were found in scrolls which he had discovered in his travels with Paul. The date of his writing was about 68.

The purpose of writing was to give a full narrative of Jesus' life, works, and teachings, and by means of these facts to prove to his pagan patron, Theophilus, that Christianity is the true religion, and is for all classes and all races of mankind.

1   THE WRITER'S FOREWORD; THE BAPTIST'S BIRTH FORETOLD; MARY'S VISIT TO ELIZABETH; MARY'S SONG OF PRAISE; ZECHARIAH'S SONG OF PRAISE

Since many writers have undertaken to compose narratives about the facts [a] established among us, ² just as the original [b] eyewitnesses who became ministers of the message ³ have handed them down to us, I too, most excellent Theophilus, because I have carefully investigated them all from the start, have felt impressed [c] to write them out in order for you, ⁴ that you may better [d] know the certainty of those things that you have been taught.

⁵ In the days when Herod was king of Judea, there was a priest whose name was Zechariah, who belonged to the division of Abijah. His wife was also a descendant of Aaron,[e] and her name was Elizabeth. ⁶ Now they were both upright in the sight of God, walking without reproach in all the Lord's commands and re-

---
[a] Easily implied from the word, *established*.
[b] Grk., *from the beginning*.
[c] Grk., *it seemed good to me*.
[d] Grk., *fully know*.
[e] The family of priests.

LUKE 1

quirements. [7] And they had no child, because Elizabeth was barren, and both of them were far advanced in years.[f]

[8] Once when he was acting as priest before God, when his division was on duty,[g] it fell to his lot, [9] in accordance with the priests' custom, to go into the sanctuary of the Lord to burn the incense, [10] while all the throng of people were praying outside at the hour of the incense burning. [11] In the meantime, an angel of the Lord appeared to him, standing at the right of the altar of incense. [12] When Zechariah saw him, he was agitated, even overwhelmed with fear.[h]

[13] But the angel said to him, "Do not be afraid, Zechariah, because your prayer has been heard, and your wife Elizabeth will bear you a son, and you must[i] name him John. [14] This will bring[j] you gladness and delight, and many will rejoice over his birth. [15] For he will be great in the sight of the Lord. He must[i] drink no wine nor strong drink, and so he will be filled with the Holy Spirit even from his birth. [16] And he will turn many of Israel's descendants to the Lord their God. [17] He will go before Him in the spirit and the power of Elijah to turn the hearts of fathers to their children and the disobedient to the wisdom of the upright, to make ready for the Lord a people perfectly prepared."

[18] Then Zechariah said to the angel, "How shall I know that this is so?[k] For I am an old man, and my wife is far advanced in years."

[19] The angel answered him, "I am Gabriel; I stand in the very presence of God. I have been sent to talk with you and to tell you this good news. [20] Now you will keep silent and be unable to talk until the day when this takes place, because you did not believe what I told you,[l] for it will be fulfilled at the proper time."

[21] Meanwhile the people kept waiting for Zechariah and wondering why[m] he stayed so long in the sanctuary. [22] But when he came out, he could not speak to them, and so they knew that he had seen a vision in the sanctuary. Meanwhile he kept on making signs to them, and remained dumb. [23] But when the period of his service was over, he went back to his home.

---

[f] Grk., *in their days;* we say, *years.*
[g] Grk., *in the order of his division.*
[h] Grk., *fear fell upon him.*
[i] Impv. fut. indic.
[j] Grk., *be to* or *for you.*
[k] Grk., *know this.*
[l] Grk., *my words.*
[m] Grk., *wondering at his delaying.*

²⁴ So after this his wife Elizabeth became pregnant,ⁿ and she kept herself in seclusion for five months, saying, ²⁵ "This is what the Lord has done for me when He smiled ᵒ upon me to take away my disgrace among men."

²⁶ Now in the sixth month the angel Gabriel was sent by God to a town in Galilee called Nazareth, ²⁷ to a maiden there engaged to be married to a man named Joseph, a descendant of David; and the maiden's name was Mary. ²⁸ So the angel came to her home ᵖ and said, "Congratulations, you highly favored woman! The Lord be with you!"

²⁹ But she was agitated ᑫ at what he said, and began to ponder what this greeting meant. ³⁰ Then the angel said, "Stop being afraid, Mary, for you have found favor with God. ³¹ Listen! You will become pregnant and bear a son, and you must name Him Jesus. ³² He will be great and will be called the Son of the Most High. The Lord God will give Him the throne of His forefather David, ³³ and He will reign over the house of Jacob forever; His reign will have no end."

³⁴ But Mary said to the angel, "How can this be, since I have no husband?"

³⁵ Then the angel answered her, "The Holy Spirit will come upon you, and the power of the Most High will overshadow you, and so your child ʳ will be called holy, the Son of God. ³⁶ And listen! your relative, Elizabeth, has herself too become pregnant, although she is old,ˢ and this is the sixth month with her who was called barren. ³⁷ For nothing is ever impossible for God." ³⁸ Then Mary said, "I am the Lord's slave. May what ᵗ you say take place with me." Then the angel left her.

³⁹ Now in those days Mary got up and hurried off to the hill country, to a town in Judah, ⁴⁰ and she went to Zechariah's home and greeted Elizabeth. ⁴¹ When Elizabeth heard Mary's greeting, the baby leaped within ᵘ her. And Elizabeth was filled with the Holy Spirit, ⁴² and with a loud shout she said:

ⁿ Grk., *conceived.*
ᵒ Grk., *looked upon me to.*
ᵖ Grk. has pro.; noun better in Eng.
ᑫ Implied in the two preps.
ʳ Grk., *that which is born.*
ˢ Grk., *in her old age.*
ᵗ Grk., *let it be to me according to your word.*
ᵘ Grk., *in her womb.*

"Blessed are you among women,
And blessed is your child!
⁴³ Why is this privilege mine,ᵛ
To have the mother of my Lord come to me?

⁴⁴ "For as soon as your greeting reached my ears,
The baby leaped for joy within me!
⁴⁵ Blessed is she who has believed,
For what is promised to her by the Lord will be fulfilled."

⁴⁶ Then Mary said:

"My soul extols the Lord;
⁴⁷ My spirit exults in God my Saviour;
⁴⁸ For He has smiled upon His slave in her lowly station,
For from this day all ages will count me happy!

⁴⁹ "For the Almighty has done wondersʷ for me,
And holy is His name!
⁵⁰ He shows His mercy from age to age
To those who fear him.

⁵¹ "He has done mighty deeds with His arm,
He has scattered those that are proud in the purpose of their hearts,
⁵² He has dethroned monarchs and exalted the poor,
⁵³ He has satisfied the hungry with good things and sent the rich away with empty hands.

⁵⁴ "He has helped His servant Israel,
So as to remember mercy,
⁵⁵ As He promised our forefathers,
Abraham and his descendants forever."

⁵⁶ Now Mary stayed with her about three months, and then returned home.

⁵⁷ So it was timeˣ for Elizabeth to bear a child, and she bore a son. ⁵⁸ And her neighbors and relatives heard that the Lord had shown her great mercy,ʸ and so they were rejoicing with her. ⁵⁹ On

---

ᵛ Lit., *Whence this to me?*
ʷ Grk., *great things.*
ˣ Grk., *the time was fulfilled.*
ʸ Grk., *has magnified.*

the eighth day they came to circumcise the child, and they tried to name him Zechariah, after his father.* ⁶⁰ But his mother said, "Never! But he must be named John."

⁶¹ Then they said to her, "There is no one among your relatives that bears that name." ⁶² So they began to make signs to his father to find out what he might wish him to be named.

⁶³ Then he asked for a writing-tablet, and wrote, "His name is John."

And they were all astonished. ⁶⁴ Then the use of his voice and tongue was at once restored,* and he began to speak, and continued to praise God. ⁶⁵ And all the neighbors were overwhelmed with awe,† and all over the hill country of Judea these things were being talked, ⁶⁶ and all who heard them kept them in their hearts, and said, "What then is this child to be?" For the hand of the Lord was with him.

⁶⁷ Now his father Zechariah was filled with the Holy Spirit, and he uttered the following prophecy: ‡

⁶⁸ "Blessed be the Lord, the God of Israel,
For He has come and brought His people deliverance; §
⁶⁹ And He has made a mighty Saviour for us ∥
In the house of His servant David,

⁷⁰ "As He promised ¶ by the lips of His ancient prophets
⁷¹ Deliverance from our foes and from the hands of all who hate us,
⁷² To show mercy to our forefathers,
And carry out His sacred covenant,

⁷³ "The oath which He swore to our forefather Abraham,
⁷⁴ To grant us deliverance from the dreaded hand of our foes,
So that we could serve Him ⁷⁵ in holiness and uprightness
In His own presence all our days.

⁷⁶ "And you, my child, will be called a prophet of the Most High,
For you will go before the Lord to make ready His ways,

* Grk., *After the name of.*
* Grk., *his mouth and tongue were opened.*
† Grk., *awe fell,* etc.
‡ Grk., *prophesied, saying.*
§ Grk., *redemption,* but in general sense.
∥ Grk., *raise up a horn of salvation.*
¶ Grk., *spoke.*

77 To give His people the knowledge of salvation
Through the forgiveness of their sins.

78 "Because the heart of our God is merciful,**
And so the day will dawn upon us from on high,
79 To shine on those who sit in darkness and the shadow of death,
To guide our feet into the way of peace."

80 Now the child continued to grow and to gain strength in the Spirit, and he lived †† in the desert until the day when he announced himself ‡‡ to Israel.

2   THE BIRTH OF JESUS; THE SONG OF THE ANGELS AND THE VISIT OF THE SHEPHERDS; THE BABY CIRCUMCISED AND NAMED JESUS; SYMEON AND HANNAH PRAISE GOD FOR HIS BIRTH; THE BOY JESUS WORSHIPS

Now in those days an edict was issued by the Emperor Augustus that a census[a] of the whole world[b] should be taken. 2 This, the first census, was taken while Quirinius was governor of Syria. 3 So everyone was going to his own town to register. 4 And Joseph too went up from Nazareth, a town in Galilee, to the town of David in Judea called Bethlehem, because he was a descendant of the house and family of David, 5 to register with Mary who was engaged to be married to him and who was an expectant mother. 6 While they were there, the time came for her to give birth, 7 and she bore her firstborn son; and she wrapped Him up and laid Him in a manger, for there was no room for them at the inn.

8 Now there were some shepherds in the same neighborhood, living in the open fields and keeping watch over their flock by night. 9 Then an angel of the Lord stood by them, and the glory of the Lord shone around them, so that they were fearfully[c] frightened. 10 But the angel said to them:

"Stop being afraid, for now I bring you good tidings of great joy which is to be for all the people; for today, in the town of

---
** Lit., *because of the heart of mercy of*, etc.
†† Grk., *was*.
‡‡ Grk., *the day of his showing forth*.
[a] To register for being taxed.
[b] The Rom. Empire.
[c] Cog. acc. used as adv.

David, a Saviour for you has been born, who is to be your Messiah [d] and Lord. [12] And this is proof for you: You will find a baby wrapped up and lying in a manger." [13] Then suddenly there appeared with the angel a throng of the heavenly host, praising God and saying:

[14] "Glory to God in highest heaven!
And peace on earth to men who please him." [e]

[15] Then when the angel left them and returned to heaven, the shepherds said to one another,

"Let us now go over to Bethlehem and see this thing that has taken place, which the Lord has told us." [16] So they hurried [f] to the place [g] and found Joseph and Mary; also the baby lying in the manger. [17] When they saw this, they informed them of the story [h] that had been told about this child. [18] And all who heard it were astounded at what was told them by the shepherds, [19] but Mary continued to treasure it all up and to ponder it in her heart. [20] Then the shepherds went back continuing to give glory and praise to God for all that they had heard and seen, just as it had been told them.

[21] When He was eight days old and it was time to circumcise Him, He was named Jesus, the name given by the angel before Mary [i] had conceived Him.

[22] Now when the period of their purification ended, in accordance with the law of Moses, they took Him up to Jerusalem to present Him to the Lord, to do as it is written in the law of the Lord, [23] "Every first-born male [j] shall be counted [k] consecrated to the Lord," [l] [24] and to offer the sacrifice in accordance with what is specified in the law of the Lord, [m] A pair of turtle-doves or two young pigeons."

[25] Now there was in Jerusalem a man named Symeon, an upright, devout man; he was expecting to see [n] the consolation of

[d] *The Anointed One.*
[e] Grk., *the men of His good pleasure.*
[f] *Went hastening.*
[g] Implied.
[h] Lit., *the word.*
[i] Pro. referring to Mary.
[j] Grk., *every male that opens the matrix.*
[k] Grk., *called.*
[l] Ex. 13:2.
[m] Lev. 12:8.
[n] Implied.

Israel, and he was under the guidance of the Holy Spirit.º ²⁶ It had been revealed to him by the Holy Spirit that he should not die without seeing the Lord's Messiah.ᵖ ²⁷ So under the Spirit's guidance he went into the temple, and when the parents brought the child Jesus there to do for Him as the custom of the law required, ²⁸ Symeon also took Him in his arms and blessed God, and said:

²⁹ "Now, Master, you will let your slave go free
In peace, as you have promised; ᑫ
³⁰ For my eyes have seen your Salvation,
³¹ Which you prepared before all peoples,
³² A light of revelation to the heathen,
And a glory to your people Israel."

³³ And His father and mother kept wondering at the things spoken by Symeon about Him. ³⁴ Then Symeon gave them his blessing,ʳ and said to Mary, the child's ˢ mother, "This child is destined to bring the falling and the rising of many in Israel, and to be a sign continuously disputed—³⁵ yea, a sword will pierce your heart—so that the secret purposes of many hearts will be revealed."

³⁶ There was also a prophetess there, Hannah, a daughter of Phanuel, who belonged to the tribe of Asher. ³⁷ She was very old; ᵗ from girlhood she had lived seven years with a husband, and now had been a widow eighty years. She never left the temple, but continued to worship all day and all night with fastings and prayers. ³⁸ Just at that time she came up and began to give thanks to God and to speak about the child to all who were expecting the deliverance of Jerusalem.

³⁹ Now when they had completed everything that was in accordance with the law of the Lord, they returned to Galilee, to their own town of Nazareth. ⁴⁰ And the child continued to grow and gain in strength; He continued to increase in wisdom, and the spiritual blessing ᵘ of God was on Him.

⁴¹ His parents were in the habit of going to Jerusalem every

º Grk., *the Holy Spirit was upon him.*
ᵖ Grk., *he should not see death before,* etc.
ᑫ Grk., *according to your word.*
ʳ Grk., *blessed them.*
ˢ Implied from pro.
ᵗ Grk., *far advanced in days.*
ᵘ Grk., *grace;* but in sense of spir. blessing.

year at the feast of the Passover. ⁴² And when He was twelve years old, they went up as usual to the feast ⁴³ and stayed the usual time.ᵛ When they returned, the boy Jesus stayed behind in Jerusalem, but His parents were not aware of it. ⁴⁴ They supposed that He was somewhere in the caravan, and so they traveled a whole day before ʷ they began to make an anxious search for Him among His relatives and acquaintances. ⁴⁵ As they did not find Him, they returned to Jerusalem in anxious search for Him. ⁴⁶ And after three days they finally ˣ found Him in the temple sitting among the teachers, listening to them and asking them questions. ⁴⁷ Now everyone who was listening to Him was showing ʸ astonishment at His intelligence and at His answers. ⁴⁸ When His parents saw Him, they were utterly amazed,ᶻ and yet His mother said to Him, "My child, why did you treat us so? Just see how your father and I, in agony * of mind, have been searching for you!"

⁴⁹ Then He said to them, "Why is it that you were searching for me? Did you not know that I must be in my Father's house?" ⁵⁰ But they did not understand what He said to them. ⁵¹ So He went back to Nazareth with them and continued to obey them. But His mother continued to treasure up all these sayings in her heart. ⁵² Meanwhile Jesus grew constantly in wisdom and in body,† and in favor with God and man.

3 JOHN PREACHES REPENTANCE AND BAPTIZES THOSE WHO CONFESS THEIR SINS; JESUS IS BAPTIZED AND ENDORSED BY HEAVEN; HIS LEGAL PEDIGREE

In the fifteenth year of the reign of the Emperor Tiberius, when Pontius Pilate was governor of Judea, and Herod ᵃ was governor of Galilee, and his brother Philip was governor of the territory of Iturea and Trachonitis, and Lysanias was governor of Abilene, ² in the high priesthood of Annas and Caiaphas, the message of God came to John, the son of Zechariah, in the desert. ³ And he went all over the Jordan valley, preaching a baptism

---

ᵛ Grk., *acc. to the custom of the feast,* etc.
ʷ Grk., *and.*
ˣ Effective aor.
ʸ Impf. of cont. action.
ᶻ Very strong comp. vb. expressing overwhelming emotion.
* Adv. pt. of manner.
† Our popular term for stature.
ᵃ Antipos.

conditioned on repentance [b] to obtain the forgiveness of sins, 4 as it is written in the sermon-book [e] of the prophet Isaiah:

"Here is a voice of one shouting in the desert,
'Get the road ready for the Lord,
Make the paths straight for Him.
5 Every ravine must be filled up,
And every mountain and hill leveled down;
The crooked places must become straight roads,
And the rough roads must be made smooth,
6 And all mankind must see the salvation of God.'"

7 So he used to say to the crowds that continued to come out there to be baptized by him:
"You brood of vipers! Who warned you to escape from the wrath that is coming? 8 Produce, then, fruit that is consistent [d] with the repentance that you profess, and do not even [e] begin to say within yourselves, 'We have Abraham for our forefather,' for I tell you, God can raise up descendants for Abraham even out of these stones. 9 Now the axe is already lying at the roots of the trees. Every tree, then, that fails to bear good fruit is to be cut down and thrown into the fire."

10 So the crowds were asking him this question, "What then ought we to do?"

11 He answered them, "The man who has two shirts must share with him who has none, and the man who has food must do the same."

12 Then even the tax-collectors came to be baptized, and said to him, "Teacher, what ought we to do?"

13 So he said to them, "Stop collecting any more than is prescribed for you."

14 Then some soldiers too were asking him, "What ought we too to do?"

So he said to them, "Never [f] extort money from anyone, never [f] make a false accusation, and always [f] be satisfied with your wages."

[b] Descriptive gen. setting forth the quality of the baptism.
[e] Grk., *book of words* (sermons).
[d] Grk., *worthy*.
[e] Force of aor. subjunc.
[f] Exact force of tenses.

¹⁵ Now while the people were on tiptoe ᵍ in their expectations, and they were all arguing in their hearts about John whether he was himself the Christ, ¹⁶ John expressly answered them all,

"I am baptizing you in water only, but there is coming the One who is stronger than I am, whose shoestrings I am not fit to untie. He will baptize you in the Holy Spirit and in fire; ¹⁷ His winnowing-fork is in His hand, and He will clean out His threshing-floor, and store His wheat in His barn; but He will burn up the chaff with fire inextinguishable.ʰ "

¹⁸ So with many and varied exhortations John continued to proclaim the good news to the people. ¹⁹ But Herod the governor, because he was repeatedly reproved by him for Herodias his brother's wife, and for all the wicked deeds that Herod had done, ²⁰ added this on top of it all, that he put John in prison.

²¹ Now when all the people had been baptized, and when Jesus had been baptized and was still praying, heaven opened ²² and the Holy Spirit came down upon Him in bodily form as a dove, and a voice came out of heaven,

"You are my Son, my Beloved! In you I am delighted!"

²³ Now Jesus Himself was about thirty years old when He began His work; He was the son, as was supposed, of Joseph, the son of Eli, ²⁴ the son of Matthat, the son of Levi, the son of Melchi, the son of Jannai, the son of Joseph, ²⁵ the son of Mattathias, the son of Amos, the son of Nahum, the son of Esli, the son of Naggai, ²⁶ the son of Maath, the son of Mattathias, the son of Semein, the son of Josech, the son of Joda, ²⁷ the son of Johanan, the son of Resa, the son of Zerubbabel, the son of Salathiel, the son of Neri, ²⁸ the son of Melchi, the son of Addi, the son of Cosam, the son of Elmadam, the son of Er, ²⁹ the son of Jesus, the son of Eliezer, the son of Jorim, the son of Matthat, the son of Levi, ³⁰ the son of Symeon, the son of Judah, the son of Joseph, the son of Jonam, the son of Eliakim, ³¹ the son of Melea, the son of Menna, the son of Mattatha, the son of Nathan, the son of David, ³² the son of Jesse, the son of Obed, the son of Boaz, the son of Sala, the son of Nahshon, ³³ the son of Admin,ⁱ the son of Arni, the son of Hezron, the son of Perez, the son of Judah, ³⁴ the son of Jacob, the son of Isaac, the son of Abraham, the son of Terah,

ᵍ Implied in pres. pt. and context.
ʰ We use this literary term to harmonize with Luke's style.
ⁱ Or, *Aminadab*.

the son of Nahor, ³⁵ the son of Serug, the son of Ragau,ʲ the son of Peleg, the son of Heber, the son of Shelah, ³⁶ the son of Cainan, the son of Arphaxad, the son of Shem, the son of Noah, the son of Lamech, ³⁷ the son of Methuselah, the son of Enoch, the son of Jared, the son of Maleleel, the son of Cainan, ³⁸ the son of Enosh, the son of Seth, the son of Adam, the son of God.

4 JESUS TEMPTED BY THE DEVIL; HE BEGINS HIS WORK IN GALILEE, CURES THE SICK, TEACHES AND PREACHES THE MESSAGE OF THE KINGDOM

Then Jesus, full of the Holy Spirit, returned from the Jordan, and for forty days He was led about in the desert under the Spirit's guidance, ² while He was being tempted by the devil. During that time ᵃ He ate nothing, and so at the end of it He felt hungry. ³ Then the devil said to Him, "If you are God's Son, order this stone to turn to a loaf of bread."

⁴ But Jesus answered him, "The Scripture says,ᵇ 'Not on bread alone does man live.'"

⁵ Then he took Him up and in a second of time he showed Him all the kingdoms of the world. ⁶ And the devil said to Him, "I will give you all this power and all their splendor, for it has been turned over to me, and I give it to anyone I please. ⁷ So if you will worship before me just once,ᶜ it shall all be yours."

⁸ But Jesus answered him, "The Scripture says,ᵈ 'You must worship the Lord your God, and serve Him alone.'"

⁹ Then he took Him to Jerusalem, and had Him stand on the tip-top turret of the temple, and said to Him, "If you are God's Son, throw yourself down from here, ¹⁰ for the Scripture says,ᵉ 'He will give His angels directions about you, to protectᶠ you,' ¹¹ and, 'They will bear you up on their hands, so that you will never strike your foot against a stone.'"

¹² And Jesus answered him, "It has been said, 'You must not try the Lord your God.'"

¹³ After the devil had finished every sort of temptation, he left Him till another time.

ʲ Or, *Reu.*
ᵃ Grk., *in those days.*
ᵇ Dt. 8:3.
ᶜ Expressed by aor.
ᵈ Dt. 6:13.
ᵉ Ps. 91:11, 12.
ᶠ Grk., *thoroughly to guard you.*

14 Then Jesus in the power of the Spirit returned to Galilee, and news of Him spread all over the surrounding country. **15** Meanwhile He began to teach in their synagogues, and was continuously [g] receiving praise from all.

16 So He came to Nazareth where He had been brought up, and as His habit was on the sabbath, He went to the synagogue and stood up to read. **17** The roll of the prophet Isaiah was handed to Him, and He unrolled it and found the place where it was written: [h]

18 "The Spirit of the Lord is upon me,
For He has consecrated me to preach the good news to the poor; [i]
He has sent me to announce release to captives and recovery of sight to the blind;
To send the downtrodden away in liberty and
19 To announce the year of favor from the Lord." [j]

20 Then He rolled up the roll and gave it back to the attendant and took His seat. Now the eyes of everyone in the synagogue were gazing at Him. **21** Then He began to speak to them, "Today this Scripture has been fulfilled here in your hearing." [k]

22 So they all began to speak well [l] of Him and to wonder at the gracious words that fell from His lips, [m] and yet they continued to say, "Is He not Joseph's son?"

23 He said to them, "Doubtless you will quote this proverb to me, 'Doctor, cure yourself! Do the things here in your home town that we hear you did in Capernaum.'" **24** He added, [n] "I solemnly say to you, no prophet is welcome in his native neighborhood. **25** But in truth I tell you, there were many widows in Israel in Elijah's time, when the heaven was closed for three years and a half, and there was a great famine over all the land, **26** and yet Elijah was not sent to a single one of them except to a widow at Zarephath in Sidon. **27** And there were many lepers in Israel in Elisha's time, and yet not one of them was cured except Naaman the Syrian."

---

[g] Pres. pt.
[h] Isa. 61:1, 2.
[i] Grk., *anointed me to,* etc.
[j] *The acceptable year of the Lord.*
[k] Grk., *ears.*
[l] *Bear witness to Him.*
[m] Grk., *mouth.*
[n] Grk., *He said.*

LUKE 4

²⁸ Then all the people in the synagogue, on hearing these things, were filled with fury, ²⁹ and they rose up and drove Him out of town and took Him to the brow of the hill on which their town was built, to hurl ᵒ Him down the cliff. ³⁰ But He Himself passed through the midst of them and went on His way.

³¹ So He came down to Capernaum, a city in Galilee. And He continued to teach them on the sabbath, ³² and they were completely astounded, because His message was spoken ᵖ with authority.

³³ Now there was a man in the synagogue who was under the power ᑫ of the spirit of a foul demon, and he screamed with a loud voice, ³⁴ "Ha! What do you want of us,ʳ Jesus, you Nazarene? Have you come to destroy us? I know who you are. You are God's Holy One."

³⁵ But Jesus reproved him, saying, "Be quiet! Get out of him at once!" ˢ

So the demon threw the man down in the midst of them and came out of him without doing him any harm. ³⁶ Amazement then seized them all and they continued to talk it over among themselves, and to say, "What does this message mean? For with authority and power He gives orders to foul spirits, and they come out." ³⁷ And so news of Him continued to spread to every place in the surrounding region.

³⁸ Then He rose to leave the synagogue, and He went to Simon's house. And Simon's mother-in-law was in the grip of a burning fever; so they asked Him about her. ³⁹ Then He took His stand by her and reproved the fever, and it left her. She got up at once and began to wait on them.

⁴⁰ As the sun was setting, all who had friends sick with various diseases brought them to Him. Then He continued to lay His hands upon them one by one ᵗ and cured them. ⁴¹ Even demons came out of many people, shrieking and saying, "You are the Son of God!" But He reproved them and would not let them speak, because they knew that He was the Christ.

⁴² As day broke He left the house and went to a lonely spot, **and**

ᵒ Or, *throw.*
ᵖ *His word was with authority.*
ᑫ *Had the spirit of a foul demon.*
ʳ Grk., *what have we for you?*
ˢ In the aor.
ᵗ Grk., *upon each one.*

the crowds continued to look for Him; they overtook Him, and tried to keep Him from leaving them. ⁴³ But He said to them, "To other towns also I must preach the good news of the kingdom of God, for that is what I was sent to do." ᵘ

⁴⁴ So He continued to preach in the synagogues of Judea.

5   SIMON CALLED TO SERVICE; A LEPER AND A PARALYTIC CURED; LEVI, CONVERTED, GIVES JESUS A BANQUET; STORIES ABOUT FASTING

Once as the crowd was pressing against Him to hear the message of God, He found ᵃ Himself standing on the shore of Lake Gennesaret. ² Then He saw two boats lying up ᵇ on the shore of the lake, but the fishermen had left ᶜ them and were washing their nets. ³ So He got into one of the boats, which belonged to Simon, and asked him to push out a little from the shore. Then He sat down and continued to teach the crowds from the boat. ⁴ When He stopped speaking, He said to Simon, "Push out into deep water, and set ᵈ your nets for a haul."

⁵ Simon answered, "We have toiled all night and caught ᵉ nothing, but since ᶠ you tell me to do so, I will set the nets again." ⁶ They did so and caught so vast a shoal of fish that their nets began to break. ⁷ So they beckoned to their partners in the other boat to come and help them. And they came and filled both boats so full that they began to sink. ⁸ When Simon Peter saw it, he fell down at Jesus' feet and said, "Leave me, Lord, because I am a sinful man." ⁹ For at the haul of fish that they had made, bewildering amazement had seized him and all his men, ¹⁰ as well as James and John, Zebedee's sons, who were Simon's partners.

Then Jesus said to Simon, "Stop being afraid; from now on you will be ᵍ catching men." ¹¹ So after they had brought the boats to land, they left everything and followed Him.

¹² Now while He was in one of the towns, a man covered with

ᵘ Grk., *for this purpose I was sent.*
ᵃ Grk., *it came to pass,* etc.
ᵇ Grk., *standing by.*
ᶜ Grk., *gone off.*
ᵈ Grk., *let down,* but *set* is the fisherman's term.
ᵉ Grk., *enclosed.*
ᶠ Grk., *at your word.*
ᵍ In pres. pt.

leprosy saw Jesus and fell on his face and begged Him, saying, "Lord, if you choose to, you can cure me." ¹³ So He reached out His hand and touched him, saying, "I do choose to; be cured." And at once the leprosy left him. ¹⁴ Then He warned him not to tell anybody, but rather He said, "Go, show yourself to the priest, and, to prove ʰ it to the people, make the offering for your purification, just as Moses prescribed."

¹⁵ But the news about Him continued to spread, and great crowds were gathering to hear Him and to be cured of their diseases. ¹⁶ But Jesus Himself continued His habit ⁱ of retiring to lonely spots and praying.

¹⁷ One day as He was teaching, there were some Pharisees and teachers of the law sitting by who had come from every village of Galilee and Judea and from Jerusalem. And the power of the Lord was with Him to cure people. ¹⁸ Now some men were carrying on a bed a man who was paralyzed, and they were trying to get him in and lay him before Jesus.ʲ ¹⁹ And as they could not find a way because of the crowd, they went up on the roof and let him down with his pallet through the tiles, among ᵏ the people right in front of Jesus. ²⁰ When He saw their faith, He said, "Friend,ˡ your sins are forgiven."

²¹ But the scribes and the Pharisees began to argue,ᵐ saying, "Who is this fellow who speaks blasphemy? Who can forgive sins but God alone?"

²² Jesus saw that they were arguing, and answered them: "Why are you arguing so in your hearts? ²³ Which is easier, to say 'Your sins are forgiven,' or to say 'Get up and start walking'? ²⁴ But to show you that the Son of Man has authority to forgive sins on earth"—turning to the man who was paralyzed, He said to him, "Get up, pick up your pallet, and go home."

²⁵ Then at once he got up before them all, picked up the pallet ⁿ on which he had been lying, and went off home, giving praise to God. ²⁶ Then an overwhelming wonder ᵒ seized them all and they

---

ʰ *For witness to them.*
ⁱ In impf.
ʲ Noun better in Eng., though pro. in Grk.
ᵏ Grk., *in the midst.*
ˡ Grk. has *man,* in sense of *friend.*
ᵐ Reasoning.
ⁿ Grk., *that on which he lay,* called by Lk. *bed* or *little bed;* so *pallet.*
ᵒ Grk., *ecstasy.*

began to give praise to God. They were filled with awe and continued to say, "We have seen unthinkable wonders today!" [p]

27 After this He went out and saw a tax-collector named Levi in his seat at the tax-collector's desk,[q] and He said to him, "Follow me." 28 So he left everything behind, got up and followed Him.

29 Then Levi gave a great reception [r] for Him in his house, and there was a large crowd of tax-collectors and others who were at table with them. 30 Now the Pharisees and their scribes were grumbling at His disciples, and were saying, "Why are you eating and drinking with tax-collectors and notorious sinners?"

31 But Jesus answered them, "Not well but sick people have to send for the doctor. 32 It is not upright but sinful people that I have come to invite to repentance."

33 After that they said to Him, "John's disciples rigidly practice fasting and offering up prayers; so do the Pharisees, but your disciples keep right on eating and drinking."

34 But Jesus said to them, "You cannot make the wedding-guests fast while the bridegroom is with them, can you? 35 But a time [s] will come when the bridegroom is taken away from them; at that time [s] they will fast."

36 Then He told them a short story:

"No one tears a piece [t] from a new coat and puts it on an old one; or if he does, he will tear the new one too, and the patch from the new coat will not match the old one. 37 So no one puts fresh wine into old wine bottles; or, if he does, the fresh wine will burst the bottles, the wine will run out, and the bottles will be ruined. 38 But fresh wine must be put into new bottles. 39 No one after drinking old wine wants new, for he says, 'The old is good enough.'"

6   JESUS AND HIS DISCIPLES BREAKING THE SABBATH LAWS OF THE PHARISEES; THE TWELVE CHOSEN AND SENT OUT; THE ADDRESS ON THE PLAIN

One sabbath He happened to be passing through the wheatfields, and His disciples were pulling and eating the heads of wheat, rubbing them in their hands. 2 And some of the Pharisees

---

[p] Grk., *paradoxes, things unthinkable.*
[q] *At the tax-collector's place.*
[r] Exact meaning of Grk. word.
[s] Grk., *days;* repeated second time for emph.
[t] Grk., *patch;* i.e., piece for a patch.

said, "Why are you doing what is against the law to do on the sabbath?"

³ Jesus answered them, "Did you never read what David did, when he and his soldiers [a] became hungry? ⁴ How he went into the house of God and took and ate the sacred [b] loaves, which it was against the law for anyone to eat except the priests, and gave some to his soldiers?" ⁵ Then He said to them, "The Son of Man is Lord of the sabbath."

⁶ On another sabbath He found Himself in the synagogue teaching; and there was there a man whose right hand was withered. ⁷ And the scribes and the Pharisees were closely watching Him to see whether He would cure him on the sabbath, in order to get a charge against Him. ⁸ But He knew what they were thinking, and He said to the man with the withered hand, "Get up and stand at the front." So he got up and stood there.

⁹ Then Jesus said to them, "Is it right on the sabbath to do people good, or to do them evil, to save life or to take it?" ¹⁰ Then He glanced around at them all and said to him, "Put out your hand." And he did so, and his hand was at once [c] completely restored. ¹¹ But they were filled with fury [d] and began to discuss what they could do to Jesus.

¹² Now it was in those days that He went up on the mountain to pray, and He spent the whole night in prayer to God. ¹³ When day came, He called His disciples to Him, and selected from them twelve whom He also named apostles: ¹⁴ Simon whom He named Peter, his brother Andrew, James, John, Philip, Bartholomew, ¹⁵ Matthew, Thomas, James the son of Alpheus, Simon who was called the Zealot, ¹⁶ Judas the son of James, and Judas Iscariot, who afterward turned traitor.

¹⁷ Then He came down with them and took His stand on a level place where [e] there was a great throng of His disciples and a vast crowd of people from all over Judea and from Jerusalem and the seacoast district of Tyre and Sidon, who had come to hear Him and to be cured of their diseases. ¹⁸ Even those who were troubled by foul spirits were being cured.[f] ¹⁹ So all the people were trying

---

[a] Grk., *the men about him.*
[b] The loaves of presentation.
[c] In aor.; action once for all.
[d] Grk., *anger, rage.*
[e] Grk., *and, but* in Ara. sense.
[f] Impf. of repeated action.

to touch Him, because power continued to go forth from Him and to cure them all.

²⁰ Then He fixed His eyes upon His disciples, and began to speak. "Blessed are you who are poor, for the kingdom of God is yours!

²¹ "Blessed are you who are hungry now, for you will be completely satisfied!

"Blessed are you who are weeping now, for you will laugh!

²² "Blessed are you when people hate you and exclude you and denounce you, and spurn your name as evil, for the sake of the Son of Man. ²³ Burst ᵍ into joy on that day and leap ᵍ for ecstasy, for your reward will be rich ʰ in heaven; for this is the way your forefathers used to treat the prophets.

²⁴ "But a curse on you who are rich, for you are now receiving your comforts in full.

²⁵ A curse on you who live in luxury ⁱ now, for you will be hungry.

"A curse on you who laugh now, for you will mourn and weep.

²⁶ "A curse on you when everyone speaks well of you, for this is the way their forefathers used to treat the false prophets.

²⁷ "But I say to you who listen now to me, practice loving your enemies, practice doing good to those who hate you,²⁸ continue to bless those who curse you, and continue ʲ to pray for those who abuse you. ²⁹ To the man who strikes you on one cheek, offer him the other too; and from the man who takes away your coat,ᵏ do not keep back your shirt ˡ either. ³⁰ Practice giving to everyone who asks of you, and stop demanding back your goods from him who takes them away. ³¹ Yes,ᵐ you must practice dealing ⁿ with others as you would like them to deal with you. ³² Now if you practice loving only those who love you, what credit ᵒ do you get for that? Why, even notorious sinners practice loving those who love them. ³³ And if you practice doing good only to those who do good to you, what credit do you get for that? Even notorious

---

ᵍ Aor. gives this sense.
ʰ Grk., *great*.
ⁱ Grk., *perfectly full*.
ʲ All these impvs. pres. of cont. ac.
ᵏ An upper garment.
ˡ *Undergarment*.
ᵐ Grk., *and*.
ⁿ Grk., *doing to*.
ᵒ Lit., *thanks*.

sinners practice the same. ³⁴ And if you ever ᵖ lend to people expecting ᵍ to get it back, what credit do you get for that? Even notorious sinners practice lending to one another,ʳ expecting to get it back in full. ³⁵ But you must practice loving your enemies, doing good to them, and lending to them, despairing of nothing; so that your reward will be great, and you will be sons of the Most High, because He is kind to the ungrateful and wicked. ³⁶ Continue to be ˢ merciful, just as your Father is merciful. ³⁷ Then stop criticizing others, and you will never be criticized; stop condemning others, and you will never be condemned ³⁸ Practice forgiving others, and you will be forgiven. Practice giving to others, and they will give ᵗ to you, good measure, pressed down, shaken together, and running over, people will pour into your lap. For the measure you use with others they in turn will use with you."

³⁹ Then He told them a story:

"Can one blind man lead another? Will they not both fall into the ditch? ⁴⁰ A pupil is not better than his teacher, but everyone when fully trained will be like his teacher. ⁴¹ Why do you continue to look at the tiny speck in your brother's eye, but pay no attention to the heavy girder ᵘ in your own eye? ⁴² How can you say to your brother, 'Brother, let me get that tiny speck out of your eye,' when you cannot see the girder in your own eye? You hypocrite! First get the girder out of your own eye, and then you will see clearly how to get out the tiny speck in your brother's eye.

⁴³ "For there never is a healthy tree that bears poor fruit, nor a sickly tree that bears good fruit. ⁴⁴ For every tree is known by its fruit. People do not pick figs from thornbushes, or gather grapes from a bramble-bush. ⁴⁵ The good man, out of his good inner storehouse,ᵛ brings forth what is good, the bad man, out of his bad one, what is bad. For a man's mouth usually speaks the things that fill his heart.ʷ

⁴⁶ "So why do you call me 'Lord, Lord,' but do not practice what I tell you? ⁴⁷ Everyone who comes to me and continues to listen to

ᵖ Force of aor.
ᵍ Grk., *from whom.*
ʳ Grk., *notorious sinners.*
ˢ Grk., *continue to become,* etc.
ᵗ Grk., *it will be given to you.*
ᵘ A heavy piece of lumber on which a house is built; a sill
ᵛ Grk., *out of the treasury of his heart.*
ʷ Grk., *out of the overflow of the heart one's mouth speaks.*

my words and practices their teaching,ˣ I will show you whom he is like. ⁴⁸ He is like a man who was building a house, who dug deep, and laid its foundation upon the rock; and when a flood came, the torrent burst upon that house but it could not shake it, because it was well built.ʸ ⁴⁹ But the man who merely hears them and does not practice them is like a man who built a house upon the ground without a foundation. The torrent burst upon it, and at once it collapsed, and the wreck of that house was complete." ᶻ

7 A ROMAN CAPTAIN'S SLAVE CURED; A WIDOW'S SON AT NAIN BROUGHT TO LIFE; THE BAPTIST IN DOUBT, BUT JESUS PAYS HIM A HIGH TRIBUTE; JESUS ANOINTED BY THE SCARLET WOMAN WHOSE SINS HE FORGIVES

When He had finished all these sayings in the hearing of the people, He went into Capernaum.

² There was a Roman captain ᵃ who had a slave that was very dear to him, and he was sick and at the point of death. ³ When the captain heard about Jesus, he sent some Jewish elders to Him, to ask Him to come and bring his slave safe through the illness.ᵇ ⁴ So they went to Jesus and continued to urge Him earnestly, saying, "He deserves that you do this for him, ⁵ for he loves our nation, and he is the man who built us our synagogue."

⁶ Then Jesus started ᶜ to go with them. But when He was not far from the house, the captain sent friends to say to Him, "My Lord, stop troubling yourself, for I am not worthy to have ᵈ you come under my roof. ⁷ And so I did not deem myself worthy even to come to you. But simply speak the word, and let my servant-boy ᵉ be cured. ⁸ For I too am under authority of others, and have soldiers under me, and I order one to go, and he goes, another to come, and he comes, my slave to do this, and he does it."

⁹ When Jesus heard this, He was astounded at him, and turning to the crowd that was following Him He said, "I tell you, I have

ˣ Grk., *practices them.*
ʸ Fol. best Mss.
ᶻ Grk., *great.*
ᵃ Grk., *centurion; captain,* modern.
ᵇ Comp. vb. means this (so Robertson).
ᶜ Incep. impf.
ᵈ Grk., *not worthy that,* etc.
ᵉ Different words.

not found, in a single case among the Jews,[f] so great faith as this!" [10] Then the messengers returned to the house and found the slave well.

[11] Soon afterwards He chanced to go to a town called Nain, and His disciples and a great throng of people were going along with Him. [12] As He approached the gate of the town, look! there was being carried out a dead man, his mother's only son, and she was a widow. A considerable crowd of townspeople were with her.

[13] Now when the Lord saw her, His heart was moved with pity for her, and so He said to her, "Stop weeping." [14] Then He went up and touched the hearse,[g] and the bearers stopped; and He said, "Young man, I tell you, arise."

[15] Then the dead man sat up and began to speak, and Jesus[h] gave him back to his mother. [16] So awe seized them all, and they began to praise God, saying, "A great prophet has appeared among us!" and, "God has visited His people!" [17] This story about Him spread all over Judea and all the surrounding country.

[18] Now John's disciples told him about all these things. [19] So John called two of them to him and sent them to the Lord, to ask, "Are you the One who was to come, or should we continue to look for someone else?"

[20] So the men went to Him and said, "John the Baptist sent us to you to ask, 'Are you the One who was to come, or should we continue to look for someone else?'"

[21] At that very hour He cured many people of diseases and scourges and evil spirits, and graciously granted sight to many blind persons. [22] And so He answered them, "Go and report to John what you have seen and heard: The blind are seeing and the crippled are walking, the lepers are being healed and the deaf are hearing, the dead are being raised and the poor are having the good news preached to them. [23] And happy is the man who finds no cause for stumbling over me."[i]

[24] But when John's messengers had gone, He began to speak to the crowds about John: "What did you go out into the desert to gaze at?[j] A reed that is tossed to and fro by the wind? [25] If not,[k] what did you go out there to see? A man dressed in silks and

---

[f] Grk., *in Israel.*
[g] Modern term; so we use it rather than *bier.*
[h] Grk., *He,* referring to Jesus.
[i] Grk., *is not caused to stumble at me.*
[j] From this Grk. vb. comes our word, *theatre,* a place for gazing at scenes.
[k] Grk., *but.*

satins?[1] No.[m] People who dress gorgeously and live luxuriously are found in royal palaces. [26] If not, then what did you go out there to see? A prophet? Yes, I tell you, and one who is far more than a prophet. [27] This is the man of whom the Scripture says:

"'Attention! I send my messenger on before you,
He will prepare the road ahead of you.'

[28] "I tell you, of all men born of women there is not one greater[n] than John; and yet the one who is of least importance in the kingdom of God[o] is greater than he. [29] And all the people, even the tax-collectors, when they heard him, vindicated the righteous requirements[p] of God by submitting to John's baptism, [30] but the Pharisees and experts in the law thwarted God's purpose for themselves by refusing to be baptized by him. [31] So to what can I compare the men of this age, and what are they like? [32] They are like little children sitting in the market-place and calling to their fellows in the game:[q]

"'We played the wedding march for you, but you did not dance;
We sang the funeral dirge, but you did not mourn.'

[33] "For John the Baptist came eating no bread and drinking no wine, and yet you say, 'He has a demon!' [34] The Son of Man has come eating and drinking with others, and yet you say, 'Just look at Him! A glutton and a wine-drinker, an intimate friend[r] of tax-collectors and notorious sinners!' [35] But wisdom is vindicated by all who are truly wise."[s]

[36] Now one of the Pharisees invited Him to take dinner[t] with him. So He came to the Pharisee's house and took His place at the table. [37] There was a woman in the town who was a social outcast,[u] and when she learned that He was taking dinner at the Pharisee's house, she brought an alabaster bottle of perfume [38] and took her stand behind Him at His feet, continually weeping. Then she began to wet His feet with her tears, but she continued to wipe them off with the hair of her head, and she kept right on

---

[1] Lit., *soft clothes.*
[m] Grk., *behold; no* implied.
[n] In mission.
[o] Messiah's kingdom.
[p] *Vindicated God.*
[q] *Game* implied.
[r] In strong sense.
[s] Grk., *sons;* i.e., like wisdom; truly wise.
[t] Likely 5 o'clock dinner.
[u] *Sinner;* i.e., a scarlet woman; prostitute.

kissing His feet with affection ᵛ and anointing them with the perfume. ³⁹ So when the Pharisee who invited Him saw it, he said to himself, "If He were really a prophet, He would know who and of what character the woman is who is clinging to Him—that she is a social outcast."

⁴⁰ Then Jesus answered him, "Simon, I have something to say to you."

"Teacher," says he, "go on and say it."

⁴¹ "Two men were in debt to a money-lender. One owed him a hundred dollars, the other ten.ʷ ⁴² Since they could not ˣ pay him, he graciously canceled the debts for both of them. Now which one of them will love him more?"

⁴³ Simon answered, "The one, I suppose, for whom he canceled most."

Then He said, "You are correct in your judgment." ⁴⁴ And turning face to face with the woman He said to Simon, "Do you see this woman? I came to your house; you did not give me any water for my feet, but she has wet my feet with tears and wiped them with her hair. ⁴⁵ You did not give me a kiss, but she, from the moment I came in, has not ceased to kiss my feet with affection. ⁴⁶ You did not anoint my head with oil, but she anointed my feet with perfume. ⁴⁷ Therefore, I tell you, her sins, as many as they are, are forgiven,ʸ for she has loved me so much. But the one who has little to be forgiven loves me little."

⁴⁸ And He said to her, "Your sins are forgiven!"

⁴⁹ The men at the table began to say to themselves, "Who is this man, who even forgives sins?"

⁵⁰ But He said to the woman, "It is your faith that has saved you; go on in peace."

8 TOURING IN GALILEE; THE STORY OF THE SOWER; STILLING THE STORM; CURING AN INSANE MAN; CURING A WOMAN WITH A HEMORRHAGE; RAISING JAIRUS' DAUGHTER

Soon afterwards He chanced to be making a tour of Galilee from town to town and from village to village preaching and

---

ᵛ Comp. vb. has this meaning.
ʷ Grk., *five hundred denaries*, etc.
ˣ Grk., *had nothing with which to pay*.
ʸ Pf. tense, but it means *in a state of forgiveness;* so pres. better in Eng.

telling the good news of the kingdom of God. The Twelve went with Him, ² and some women who had been cured of evil spirits and diseases: Mary, who was called Mary of Magdala, out of whom seven demons had gone, ³ and Joanna, the wife of Chuza, Herod's household manager, and Susanna, and many other women, who continued to contribute to their needs out of their personal means.[a]

⁴ Now as a great crowd was coming together and people were coming to Him from one town after another, He said by way of a story: [b]

⁵ "A sower went out to sow his seed. As he was sowing, some of the seed fell along the path, and were trodden down, and the wild birds ate them[c] up. ⁶ Another portion of them fell upon the rock, and as soon as they sprang up, they withered, because they had no moisture. ⁷ Still another portion fell among the thorns, and the thorns grew up with them and choked them out. ⁸ And another portion fell in rich soil and grew and yielded a crop of a hundredfold."

As He said this, He exclaimed, "Let him who has ears to hear with, listen!"

⁹ His disciples were asking Him what this story meant. ¹⁰ So He said, "You are granted the privilege of knowing the secrets of the kingdom of God, but to others they are told in stories, so that they may look and not see, may hear and not understand. ¹¹ This is what the story means: The seed is God's message. ¹² Those along the path illustrate those who hear it, but then the devil comes and carries off the message from their hearts, so that they may not believe it and be saved. ¹³ The portion of them on the rock illustrates those who accept the message, bubbling over with joy when they first hear it, but it takes no real root. They believe for awhile, but in the time of testing they fall away. ¹⁴ And the portion of them falling among the thorns illustrates those who hear it, but as soon as they pass on they are choked out by the worries and wealth and pleasures of life, and thus yield no mature fruit. ¹⁵ But the portion in rich soil illustrates those who listen to the message, keep it in good and honest hearts, and in patience yield fruit.

¹⁶ "Nobody lights a lamp and then covers it with a pot [d] or puts

---

[a] These women helped with the expenses of Jesus and His apostles.
[b] Grk., *parable;* here a story from the fields.
[c] Collective noun: so pl. pro.
[d] Grk., *vessel;* likely a pot or a pan.

it under a bed, but puts it on a lampstand, so that those who come in may see the light. [17] For there is nothing hidden which shall not come out into the open, and nothing kept secret which shall not be known and come to light.[e] [18] So take care how you listen; for whoever gets more [f] will have more given to him, and whoever does not get more will have even what he thinks he has taken away from him."

[19] His mother and His brothers came to see Him, but they could not get in touch with Him, on account of the crowd. [20] So it was reported to Him, "Your mother and your brothers are standing outside; they want to see you."

[21] Then He answered them, "My mother and my brothers are those who listen to God's message and practice it."

[22] One day He got into a boat with His disciples, and He said to them, "Let us cross to the other side of the lake."

So they set sail. [23] Now as they were sailing along, He fell off [g] to sleep. But a furious squall of wind rushed down upon the lake, and they were filling up [h] and were in impending [i] peril. [24] So they came to Him and woke Him up, and said, "Master, Master, we are perishing!" Then He aroused Himself and reproved the wind and the surge of the water, and they stopped at once,[j] and instantly [j] there came a calm.

[25] Then He said to them, "Where is your faith?"

But they were frightened and astounded, and continued to say to one another, "Who can He be? For He gives orders even to the winds and the water, and they obey Him."

[26] They landed in the neighborhood of Gerasa, which is just across the lake from Galilee. [27] As soon as He stepped out upon the shore, there met Him a man from town, who was under the power of demons; and for a long time he had worn no clothes, and did not stay in a house but in tombs. [28] When he saw Jesus, he screamed and flung himself down before Him, and said in a loud voice, "What do you want of me, Jesus, Son of the Most High God? I beg you not to torture me!" [29] For He was commanding the foul spirit to get out of the man. For on many occasions

[e] Same vb. as *come out into the open;* changed it for variety's sake.
[f] In spiritual sense.
[g] Exact meaning of prep. and aor.
[h] That is, the boat was filling.
[i] Impf. of cont. action; so *in impending peril.*
[j] Implied in aor.

it had seized him, and repeatedly he had been fastened with chains and fetters under constant guard,[k] and yet he would snap his bonds, and the demon would drive[1] him into desert places.

[30] So Jesus asked him, "What is your name?"

And he answered, "Legion!" For many demons had gone into him. [31] Then they continued to beg Him not to order them to go off to the bottomless pit.[m] [32] Now there was a large drove of hogs feeding there on the hillside. So they begged Him to let them go into those hogs. And He let them do so. [33] Then the demons came out of the man and went into the hogs, and the drove rushed over the cliff into the lake and were drowned. [34] When the men who fed them saw what had taken place, they fled and spread the news in the town and in the country around. [35] So the people went out to see what had taken place, and they went to Jesus and found the man out of whom the demons had gone sitting at the feet of Jesus, with his clothes on and in his right mind; and they were frightened. [36] Then they who had seen it told them how the man who had been under the power of demons was cured. [37] Then all the inhabitants[n] of the country around Gerasa asked Him to go away from them, because they were terribly frightened. So He got into a boat and went back.

[38] The man out of whom the demons had gone begged Him to let him go[o] with Him, but Jesus sent him away and said, [39] "Go back to your home, and continue to tell what great things God has done for you." But he went off and told all over the town what great things Jesus had done for him.

[40] Now as Jesus was returning, the crowd welcomed Him, for they were all expecting Him. [41] Just then a man named Jairus came up, who had long[p] been leader of the synagogue. He fell down at Jesus' feet and persisted in begging Him to come to his house, [42] because his only daughter, about twelve years old, was dying. While He was going, the crowds of people continued to press upon Him. [43] Then a woman who had had a hemorrhage for twelve years, who could not be cured by anybody, [44] came up behind Him and touched the tassel on His coat, and the hemor-

---

[k] Pres. pt. of *guard, so under constant guard.*
[1] Passive in Grk., but active smoother in Eng.
[m] *Abyss* in Grk.
[n] Grk., *the whole multitude of the country.*
[o] Grk., *to be.*
[p] Impf. expresses this idea of duration.

rhage stopped at once. ⁴⁵ Then Jesus said, "Who was it that touched me?"

But as all were denying that they had done so, Peter said, "Master, the crowds are jamming you and jostling you."

⁴⁶ Still Jesus said, "Somebody touched me, for I felt it when the power passed from me." ᵍ

⁴⁷ When the woman saw that she had not escaped His notice, she came forward trembling, and falling down before Him she told in the presence of all the people why she had touched Him and how she had been cured at once. ⁴⁸ So He said to her, "My daughter, it is your faith that has cured you; go on in peace."

⁴⁹ While He was still speaking, someone came from the house of the leader of the synagogue and said, "Your daughter is dead; stop troubling the Teacher any more." ʳ

⁵⁰ But Jesus heard it and said to him, "Do not be afraid; just have faith, and she will get well."

⁵¹ When He reached the house, He let no one go in with Him but Peter, James, and John, and the child's father and mother. ⁵² Now they were all weeping and wailing over her. But He said, "Stop weeping! For she is not dead but asleep." ⁵³ Then they began to laugh in His face, for they knew that she was dead. ⁵⁴ But He grasped her hand and called out, "My child, get up!" ⁵⁵ So her spirit returned and she got up at once, and He directed that something be given her to eat. ⁵⁶ And her parents were astounded, but He ordered them not to tell anyone what had taken place.

9 THE TWELVE TOURING GALILEE; GOVERNOR ANTIPAS IN DREAD OF JESUS; PETER CONFESSES JESUS AS THE CHRIST; HOW TO SAVE THE HIGHER LIFE; JESUS TRANSFIGURED; AN EPILEPTIC BOY CURED, ETC.

Then He called the Twelve together and gave them power and authority over all the demons, and to cure diseases, ² and then He sent them out to preach the kingdom of God and to cure the sick. ³ So He said to them, "Take nothing with you for your journey, no staff, no bag, no bread, no money, nor even have two shirts. ⁴ Into whatever house you go, stay there and continue to go out from it as headquarters.ᵃ ⁵ And when you leave that city, shake off

ᵍ Grk., *I knew that power had passed from me.*
ʳ Pres. impv. with neg. means, stop, etc. Fol. WH text and Vat., Sin. Mss.
ᵃImplied in linear ac. expressed by impv.

the very dust from your feet as a protest [b] against all [c] the people who do not welcome you." ⁶ And so they set out and went from village to village, telling the good news and curing people everywhere.

⁷ Now Herod the governor [d] heard of all that was taking place, and he continued to be puzzled over the reports—by some that John had risen from the dead, ⁸ by others that Elijah had appeared, and by still others that one of the ancient prophets had come back to life.[e] ⁹ So Herod said, "John I beheaded, but who can this be about whom I hear such reports?" So he was trying to see Him.

¹⁰ Now the apostles returned and told Jesus all that they had done. Then He took them and privately retired to a town called Bethsaida. ¹¹ But the crowds learned of it, and followed Him; and He welcomed them and began [f] to speak to them about the kingdom of God and to cure the people who needed to be cured.[g] ¹² As the day began to decline, the Twelve came up and said to Him, "Send the crowd off to the villages and farms around, to get lodging and to find food there, for we are in a destitute place here." [h]

¹³ But He said to them, "Give them something to eat yourselves." [h]

Then they said, "We have only five loaves and two fish, unless we go ourselves and buy food for all these people." ¹⁴ For there were about five thousand men.

So He said to His disciples, "Have them sit down in reclining groups of about fifty each." ¹⁵ And they did so, and made all the people sit down and recline. ¹⁶ Then He took the five loaves and two fish and looked up to heaven and blessed them, and He broke them in pieces and gave them to the disciples to pass on to the people. ¹⁷ And they all ate and had a plenty, and what they had left over was taken up, twelve baskets of broken pieces.

¹⁸ One day while He was praying in solitude, His disciples were near by, and He asked them, "Who do people say that I am?"

¹⁹ They answered, "John the Baptist; though others say Elijah, and still others that one of the ancient prophets has come back to life."

²⁰ So He said to them, "But who do you, yourselves,[h] say that I am?"

[b] Lit. *testimony*.
[c] Grk., *as many as*.
[d] Of Galilee and Perea.
[e] Lit., *risen from the dead*.
[f] Incep. impf.
[g] Noun in Grk.
[h] Very emph.

Peter answered, "The Christ of God!"

21 But He particularly warned, yea, even commanded, them not to tell this to anybody, 22 as He said, "The Son of Man has to endure great suffering and be disowned by the elders, the high priests, and the scribes, and be put to death but be raised to life on the third day."

23 Then He said to them all, "If anyone chooses to be my disciple, he must say 'No' to self, put the cross on his shoulders daily, and continue to follow me. 24 For whoever chooses to save his lower life will lose his higher life, but whoever gives up his lower [i] life for my sake will save his higher [i] life. 25 For what benefit will it be to a man to gain the whole world and lose or forfeit himself? 26 For whoever is ashamed of me and my teaching,[j] the Son of Man will be ashamed of him, when He comes back in all the splendor of His Father and of the holy angels. 27 I solemnly say to you, some of you who stand here will certainly live [k] to see the kingdom of God."

28 Now about eight days after Jesus said this, He took Peter, John, and James, and went up on the mountain to pray. 29 And while He was praying, the look on His face changed,[l] and His clothes turned [m] dazzling white. 30 And two men were talking with Him. They were Moses and Elijah, 31 who appeared in splendor and were speaking of His departure which He was about to accomplish at Jerusalem.

32 Now Peter and his companions had been overcome by sleep, but all at once they became wide awake [n] and saw His splendor and the two men who were standing with Him. 33 And just as they were starting to leave Him, Peter said to Jesus, "Master, it is good for us to be here. Let us put up three tents, one for you, one for Moses, and one for Elijah"—although he did not know what he was saying. 34 But as he was saying this, a cloud came and was circling over them, and they were frightened as the two visitors entered into the cloud.

35 Then a voice came out of the cloud and said, "This is my Son, my Chosen One; continue to listen to Him!"

36 When the voice had ceased, Jesus was found to be alone. And

---

[i] A play on the two meanings of the word *life*.
[j] Grk., *words*.
[k] Grk., *will not taste of death, until,* etc.
[l] Grk., *was different*.
[m] Grk., *were dazzling white*.
[n] Expressed by prep. and aor.

they kept silence and told no one anything that they had seen at that time.º

37 The next day, when they had come down from the mountain, a great crowd met Him. 38 Then a man in the crowd at once ᵖ shouted, "Teacher, I beg you to look at my son, because he is my only child; 39 all at once a spirit seizes him, and he suddenly screams, and it convulses him until he foams ᵠ at the mouth, and in a struggle ʳ it bruises him and then leaves him. 40 I begged your disciples to drive it out, but they could not."

41 Then Jesus answered, "O you unbelieving, stubborn people of the times! ˢ How long must I be with you and put up with you? Bring him here to me." 42 Even while the boy was coming to Him, the demon dashed him down and convulsed him, but Jesus reproved the foul spirit and cured the boy and gave him back to his father. 43 So they all continued to be utterly astounded ᵗ at the greatness of God.

Now while everybody was wondering at all that He was doing, He said to His disciples, 44 "You must store away in your memories ᵘ these words, for the Son of Man is going to be turned over ᵛ to the hands of men!" 45 But they remained ignorant of what this meant; indeed, it had been hidden from them, so that they did not grasp it, and they were afraid to ask Him about this statement.

46 Now a controversy sprang up among them as to which of them might be the greatest. 47 But Jesus, as He knew that the controversy was going on ʷ in their hearts, took a little child and had it stand by His side. 48 Then He said to them, "Whoever welcomes this little child on my account is welcoming me, and whoever welcomes me is welcoming Him who sent me; for the one who is lowliest among you all is really great."

49 Then John answered, "Master, we saw a man driving out demons by the use ˣ of your name, and we tried to stop him, because he does not belong to our followers." ʸ

º *In those days.*
ᵖ Suggested by aorist.
ᵠ *Disturbs him with foaming.*
ʳ Grk., *with difficulty it departs.*
ˢ Grk., *age.*
ᵗ This vb. was translated *dumfounded* in Mt. and Mk., but *utterly astounded* accords with Lk.'s style.
ᵘ *Ears.*
ᵛ Or, *betrayed.*
ʷ Grk., has gen. (of).
ˣ Lit., *in or on your name.*
ʸ Grk., *did not follow with us.*

LUKE 10

⁵⁰ Jesus said to him, "Stop hindering him, for the man who is not against you is for you."

⁵¹ Now as the time was coming to a head ᵃ when He should be taken up to heaven, He firmly set His face to continue His journey to Jerusalem; ⁵² so He sent messengers before Him. Then they went on and entered into a Samaritan town, to make preparations for Him. ⁵³ But they would not receive Him, because He was facing in the direction * of Jerusalem.† ⁵⁴ When the disciples, James and John, saw this, they said, "Lord, do you want us to bid fire come down from heaven and consume them?" ⁵⁵ But He turned at once ‡ and reproved them. ⁵⁶ Then they went on to a different village.

⁵⁷ While they were going along the road, a man said to Him, "I will follow you wherever you go."

⁵⁸ But Jesus said to him, "Foxes have holes, even wild birds have roosts, but the Son of Man has nowhere to lay His head." ⁵⁹ He said to another man, "Follow me."

But he said, "Let me first go back and bury my father."

⁶⁰ Then He answered him, "Leave the dead to bury their own dead; but you go on and continue to spread the good news of the kingdom of God."

⁶¹ Still another man said, "I will follow you, Lord, but let me first say 'Good-by' to the homefolks."

⁶² Jesus said to him, "No one who puts his hand to the plough, and then continues to look back, is fitted for service § in the kingdom of God."

10
THE SEVENTY SENT OUT; JESUS REJOICES OVER THEIR REPORT AND THE FATHER'S GRACIOUS PLAN; TO SHOW WHO IS A GOOD NEIGHBOR HE TELLS THE STORY OF THE GOOD SAMARITAN; HE STAYS IN THE BETHANY HOME

After this the Lord appointed seventy ᵃ others and sent them on before Him, two by two, to every town or place which He was going to visit. ² So He was saying to them:

ᵃ Grk., *the days were being completed,* etc.
* Grk., *His face was going to.*
† The Samaritans hated the Jews because of racial and religious prejudice.
‡ Implied in aor.
§ Lit., *well-placed;* so *fitted for service in,* etc.
ᵃ Against Vat. Ms. which has seventy-two.

"The harvest is plentiful, but the reapers are scarce.[b] So pray the Lord of the harvest to send out reapers to His harvest-field. [3] Go on. Listen! I am sending you out as lambs surrounded [c] by wolves. [4] Do not carry a purse, a bag, or shoes, and do not stop [d] to say 'Good morning' to anybody on the road. [5] Whenever you go to a house for headquarters,[e] first say, 'Peace to this household.' [6] And if anyone there loves peace,[f] your peace will come upon him; but if not, it will come back to you. [7] Stay on at the same house, eating and drinking what they provide, for the workman deserves his support.[g] Do not keep moving about from house to house. [8] And if you go into any town and they welcome you, continue to eat what is offered you, [9] to cure the sick there, and to say, 'The kingdom of God is close upon you.' [10] But if you go into any town and they do not welcome you, go out into the streets and say, [11] 'We are wiping off against you the very dust from your town that has stuck to our feet. But understand this, the kingdom of God is close by.' [12] I tell you, on that day the punishment will be lighter [h] for Sodom than for that town. [13] A curse on you, Chorazin! A curse on you, Bethsaida! For if the wonder-works done in you had been done in Tyre and Sidon, long ago they would have repented, sitting in sackcloth and ashes. [14] But at the judgment the punishment will be lighter for Tyre and Sidon than for you. [15] And you, Capernaum, are you to be exalted to heaven? No, you are to go down to the regions of the dead.[i] [16] Whoever listens to you listens to me, and whoever pays no attention to you pays no attention to me, and whoever pays no attention to me pays no attention to Him who sent me."

[17] Now the seventy returned and joyously reported,[j] "Lord, even the demons are submitting to us in your name."

[18] He said to them, "I was looking at Satan falling like a flash [k] of lightning from heaven. [19] Listen! [l] I have given you power to tread on snakes and scorpions, and to trample on all the power

[b] Grk., *harvest is great, workers few.*
[c] Lit., *in the midst of wolves.*
[d] *Only* implied.
[e] Implied.
[f] Grk., *son of peace; one like peace,* so *loves peace.*
[g] Grk., *worthy of his wages.*
[h] Lit., *it will be more bearable,* etc.
[i] That is, to Hades.
[j] Grk., *saying with joy.*
[k] Expressed in aor.
[l] Grk., *behold!*

LUKE 10

of the enemy, and **nothing at all**[m] will ever harm you. [20] However, you must stop **rejoicing** over the fact that the spirits are submitting to you, but continue to rejoice that your names are enrolled in heaven."

[21] At that very moment, by the power of the Holy Spirit,[n] He exulted and said, "I thank you, Father, Lord of heaven and earth, for concealing these matters from wise and learned men, and for revealing them to little children. Yes, Father, I thank you[o] that your good pleasure made it so. [22] All things have been entrusted to me by my Father, and no one knows who the Son is but the Father, and who the Father is but the Son, and anyone to whom the Son chooses to make Him known."

[23] Then He turned to His disciples when they were alone, and said, "Blessed are the eyes that see what you are seeing. [24] For I tell you, many prophets and kings have wished to see what you are seeing, but they did not, and to hear what you are hearing, but they did not."[p]

[25] Just then an expert in the law got up to test Him by asking, "Teacher, what shall I do to get possession of eternal life?"

[26] And He answered him, "What is written in the law? How does it read?"[q]

[27] Then he answered, "You must love the Lord your God with your whole heart, your whole soul, your whole strength, and your whole mind, and your neighbor as you do yourself."

[28] He said to him, "You have answered correctly. Continue to do this, and you will live."

[29] But he, as he wished to justify his question,[r] said, "But who is my neighbor?"

[30] Jesus answered:[s]

"A man was on his way down from Jerusalem to Jericho, and he fell into the hands of robbers, who both stripped him and beat him till he was half dead, and then went off and left him. [31] Now a priest happened to be going that way, but[t] when he saw him, he

---

[m] Double neg. emph.
[n] Lit., *in the Holy Spirit*.
[o] Vb. implied.
[p] Vbs., repeated in Grk., but Eng. better without them.
[q] Grk., *How do you read it?*
[r] Grk., *to justify himself*.
[s] Lit., *took him up*.
[t] Grk., *and;* in adversative sense.

went by on the other side of the road. ³² So a Levite likewise came down to the place, but when he saw him, he went by on the other side. ³³ But a Samaritan, while on a journey, came down to him, and when he saw him, his heart was moved with pity for him. ³⁴ So he went to him and dressed his wounds by pouring oil and wine upon them, and then he put him on his donkey and brought him to an inn and took care of him. ³⁵ The next day he took out a half dollar ᵘ and handed it to the inn-keeper, and said, 'Take care of him, and on my way back I will repay you.' ³⁶ Which one of these three do you think proved himself a real neighbor to the man who fell into the robbers' hands?"

³⁷ He said, "The one who took pity on him."

Jesus said to him, "Go and practice it yourself."

³⁸ Now as they were journeying on, He came to a certain village where a woman named Martha welcomed Him to her house. ³⁹ She had a sister named Mary who took her seat at the Lord's feet, and remained listening to His message. ⁴⁰ But Martha was getting worried about having to wait on them so much,ᵛ so she came up suddenly and said, "Lord, do you not care that my sister has left me to do all the housework alone? ʷ Then tell her to take hold and help me."

⁴¹ The Lord answered her, "Martha, Martha, you are worried and vexed about many things. ⁴² But there is actual need of few things, really of only one thing. For Mary has chosen the good portion which must not be taken away from her."

11 THE MODEL PRAYER AND A STORY ON PRAYER; JESUS ACCUSED OF BEING IN LEAGUE WITH DEMONS; HIS DEFENSE; DENOUNCES THE WICKEDNESS OF THOSE TIMES, ESPECIALLY THE HYPOCRISY OF THE PHARISEES

Once He was praying in a certain place, and when He ceased, one of His disciples said to Him, "Lord, teach us to pray, as John taught his disciples."

² So He said to them, "Whenever you pray, say:

ᵘ *Two denaries,* not quite a half dollar.
ᵛ Lit., *much serving.*
ʷ Grk., *to serve alone.*

Father,
Your name be revered,
Your kingdom come;
³ Continue giving us day by day our daily bread,ᵃ
⁴ And forgive us our sins, for we ourselves forgive everyone who does us wrong,
And do not let us be subjected to temptation."

⁵ Then He said to them: "Suppose one of you has a friend, and you go to him in the middle of the night and say to him, 'Friend, lend me three loaves; ⁶ for a friend of mine has just come to my house on a journey, and I have nothing to set before him to eat.' ⁷ And suppose he answers from inside, 'Stop bothering me; the door is now locked, and my children are packed about me in bed; I cannot get up and give you any.' ⁸ I tell you, although he will not get up and give you any because he is your friend, yet because of your persistence he will get up and give you all your needs. ⁹ So I tell you, keep on asking, and the gift will be given you; keep on seeking, and you will find; keep on knocking, and the door will open to you. ¹⁰ For everyone who keeps on asking, receives; and the one who keeps on seeking, finds; and to the one who keeps on knocking, the door will open.ᵇ ¹¹ Now is there a fatherᶜ among you who, if his son asks him for a fish, will give him a snake instead? ¹² Or, if he asks for an egg, will give him a scorpion? ¹³ So if you, in spiteᵈ of your being bad, know how to give your children what is good, how much more surely will your Father in heaven give the Holy Spirit to those who continue to ask Him?"

¹⁴ Now He was driving a dumb demon out of a man, and when the demon went out of him, the dumb man spoke. The crowds were astonished. ¹⁵ But some of them said, "It is with the help of Beelzebub, the prince of demons, that He is driving the demons out." ¹⁶ But others, to test Him, were demanding from Him a spectacularᵉ sign from heaven.

¹⁷ But He knew what they were thinking, and so said to them, "Any kingdom that is not united is in the process of destruction, and one house falls after another. ¹⁸ And if Satan is really disunited,

ᵃ Lk. has pres. impv., so we tr. *Continue giving us,* etc.
ᵇ This continuance in prayer is in the pres. impvs. and pres. pts., often repeated.
ᶜ Lit., *What father is there,* etc.
ᵈ Concessive pt.
ᵉ Implied from the facts in their history.

how can his kingdom last? Yet you say that I am driving the demons out with Beelzebub's help. ¹⁹ Now if I with Beelzebub's help am driving the demons out, with whose help do your sons drive them out? ²⁰ But if I by the finger of God am driving the demons out, then the kingdom of God has come to you. ²¹ When a strong man well armed keeps guard over his dwelling, his property is secure.ᶠ ²² But when a man stronger than he attacks him and overcomes him, he strips him of all his arms on which he relied, and distributes his goods as spoils.ᵍ ²³ Whoever is not in partnership with me is against me, and whoever does not gather in partnership with me, scatters.

²⁴ "When the foul spirit goes out of a man, it wanders about in deserts in search for rest, and since it finds none, it says, 'I will go back to my house which I left.' ²⁵ And it goes and finds it unoccupied, swept, and ready for use. ²⁶ Then it goes and gets seven other spirits more wicked than itself, and they go in and make their home there, and so the end of that man is worse than the beginning."

²⁷ Just as He was saying this, a woman in the crowd lifted her voice and said, "Blessed is the mother who bore you and nursed you!"

²⁸ But He said, "Yes, but better still, blessed are those who listen to God's message and practice it!" ʰ

²⁹ Now as the crowds continued to throng upon Him, He began to say: "This is a wicked age. It is looking for a spectacular sign, but none will be given it but the sign of Jonah. ³⁰ For just as Jonah became a sign to the people of Nineveh, so the Son of Man will be a sign to this age. ³¹ The queen of the south will rise at the judgment with the men of this age and will condemn them; for she came from the very ends of the earth to listen to Solomon's wisdom; and yet, One who is more than Solomon is here. ³² The men of Nineveh will rise at the judgment with the men ⁱ of this age and will condemn them, for they turned to the message preached ʲ by Jonah, and yet One who is more than Jonah is here. ³³ No one lights a lamp and puts it in a cellar or under a peckmeasure, but he puts it on the lampstand, that the people who come in may enjoy ᵏ the light. ³⁴ Your eye is the very lamp of your

---

ᶠ *Is in peace;* so *secure.*
ᵍ Grk., *distributes his goods.*
ʰ Grk., *continue to observe,* so *practice.*
ⁱ Implied.
ʲ Noun means *message preached;* prep., *to,* not *at; repent, turn.*
ᵏ Grk., *see,* in sense of *enjoy.*

body. When your eye is sound, your whole body is full of light. But if your eye is unsound, your body is full of darkness. ³⁵ So be on your guard that the very source of light in you is not darkness. ³⁶ If then your whole body is full of light with no part of it in darkness, it will all be as light for you as it is when a lamp makes it light for you by its shining."

³⁷ When He had said this, a Pharisee asked Him to lunch at his house, and He went in and took His place at table. ³⁸ The Pharisee noticed that He did not first wash before lunch, and was surprised. ³⁹ But the Lord said to him, "Now you Pharisees have the habit of cleaning the outside of your cups and dishes,¹ but inside you yourselves are full of greed and wickedness. ⁴⁰ You fools! Did not the One who made the outside make the inside too? ⁴¹ But dedicate once for all your inner self,ᵐ and at once you will have everything clean. ⁴² But a curse on you Pharisees, because you pay tithes on mint, rue, and every tiny garden herb, but neglect justice and the love of God! These latter especially ⁿ you ought to have done, but ought not to have neglected the former. ⁴³ A curse on you Pharisees, because you like to have the front seats in synagogues, and to be greeted with honor in public places! ⁴⁴ A curse on you, because you are like unmarked graves which men walk over without knowing it!"

⁴⁵ Then an expertᵒ in the law interrupted Him and said, "Teacher, in saying this you are insulting us, too."

⁴⁶ He said, "Yes, a curse on you experts in the law, too, because you load people down with loads too heavy to carry, and yet you do not touch the loads yourselves with one of your fingers! ⁴⁷ A curse on you, because you build monuments for the prophets, whom your forefathers killed! ⁴⁸ So you testify to what your forefathers did ᵖ and approve it, because they killed them and you build monuments for them. ⁴⁹ This is why the Wisdom of God said, 'I will send to them prophets and apostles, and some of them they will kill, and some they will persecute'; ⁵⁰ so that the blood of all the prophets that has been shed from the creation of the world may be charged against the men of this age—⁵¹ from the blood of Abel to the blood of Zechariah who perished between the altar and the sancutary. Yes, I tell you, it will be charged against the men of this age. ⁵² A curse on you experts in the law,

---

¹ Lit., *outside of cup and dish.*
ᵐ Grk., *give the things inside of you.*
ⁿ Emph. position.
ᵒ Grk., *a certain one of the experts,* etc.
ᵖ Lit., *you testify to the deeds of your fathers.*

because you have taken away the key to the door of knowledge! You did not go in yourselves, and you kept out those who tried to get in."

⁵³ After He left the house, the scribes and the Pharisees began to be violently enraged against Him and to try to draw Him out on many subjects,ᵠ ⁵⁴ plotting, as if in ambush, to entrap Him in something that might fall from His lips.ʳ

12 JESUS WARNS AGAINST HYPOCRISY; TELLS THE STORY OF THE FOOLISH FARMER TO WARN AGAINST COVETOUSNESS; COMMENDS TRUSTFULNESS AND ALERTNESS; TELLS THE STORY OF THE GOOD MANAGER TO ILLUSTRATE ALERTNESS

Meanwhile as the people had gathered in tens of thousands, so that they were trampling upon one another, He began to say, first of all, to His disciples:

"Beware of the yeast of the Pharisees, that is, hypocrisy. ² There is nothing covered up that will not be uncovered, nor secret that will not be made known; ³ because what you have spoken in darkness will be heard in the light, and what you have whispered in people's ears, behind closed doors,ᵃ will be proclaimed from the housetops. ⁴ So I tell you, my friends, never be afraid of those who kill the body but after that have nothing more that they can do. ⁵ But I will show you whom to fear. Fear Him who, after killing you, has power to hurl you down to the pit; ᵇ yes, I tell you, fear Him. ⁶ Are not sparrows sold five for two cents? ᶜ And yet not one of them is forgotten by God.ᵈ ⁷ Yes, the very hairs on your heads have all been counted by God! ᵉ Stop being afraid; you are worth more than many sparrows. ⁸ I tell you, everyone who owns me before men the Son of Man will own before the angels of God; ⁹ but anyone who disowns me before men will be disowned before the angels of God. ¹⁰ And anyone who speaks a word against the Son of Man will be forgiven; but no one who speaks abusively about the Holy Spirit will be forgiven. ¹¹ Now when they are bringing you before the synagogues or the magistrates or the authorities,

---

ᵠ Grk., *on many things.*
ʳ Grk., *stealthily to catch something from His mouth.*
ᵃ Lit., *in secret places.*
ᵇ *Gehenna.*
ᶜ As near as we can say it in our money.
ᵈ Grk., *forgotten before God.*
ᵉ Implied.

LUKE 12

never worry about how to defend yourselves, or what to say, ¹² for at that very moment the Holy Spirit will teach you what you ought to say."

¹³ Just then a man in the crowd said to Him, "Tell my brother to share with me our inheritance."

¹⁴ But He said to him, "Man, who made me a judge or umpire in your affairs?" ¹⁵ And then He said to them, "Be ever [f] on the alert and always [f] on your guard against every form of greed, because a man's life does not consist in his possessions, even though they are abundant."

¹⁶ Then He told them a story, as follows:

"A certain rich man's lands yielded bountifully. ¹⁷ So he began to argue with himself, What am I to do, because I have nowhere to store my crops? ¹⁸ Then he said, This is what I will do: I will tear down my barns and build larger ones, and in them I will store all my grains and my goods. ¹⁹ Then I will say to my soul, 'Soul, you have plenty of good things laid up for many years. Go on taking your ease; continue to eat, drink, and enjoy yourself.' ²⁰ But God said to him, 'You fool! This very night your soul is to be demanded [g] of you. Then who will have all that you have prepared?' ²¹ So it is with the man who continues to pile up possessions for himself, and is not rich in God."

²² Then He said to His disciples:

"Stop worrying, then, about life, as to what you will have to eat, or about your body, as to what you will have to wear. ²³ Your life is worth more than food, and your body more than clothes. ²⁴ Just think of the ravens! [h] For they neither sow nor reap, they have no storehouses nor barns, and yet God continues to feed them. How much more are you worth than the birds! ²⁵ Which of you by worrying can add a single minute [i] to his life? ²⁶ So if you cannot do this very little thing, why should you worry about the rest? ²⁷ Just think of how the lilies grow! They do not toil nor spin. But, I tell you, not even Solomon, in all his splendor, was ever dressed like one of them. ²⁸ Now if God so gorgeously dresses the wild grass which today is green but tomorrow is tossed into the furnace, how much more surely will He clothe you, O you with little faith? ²⁹ So you must stop seeking what to eat and what to

---

[f] Pres. impvs.
[g] Lit., *they demand* (passive better in Eng.).
[h] A large black bird of prey, resembling our crow.
[i] Means *size* or *time;* latter here.

drink, and must stop being in suspense [j] about these things. [30] For all these are the very things the nations of the world are greedily trying to get, and surely your Father well [k] knows that you need them. [31] But continue to seek His will,[l] and these things will be yours besides. [32] Stop being afraid, my little flock, for your Father has gladly chosen to give you the kingdom. [33] Sell your property and give to charity. Provide for yourselves purses that will never wear out, riches that never fail in heaven, where a thief cannot come near nor a moth destroy. [34] For wherever your treasure is, there too your heart will be.

[35] "You must keep your belts tight [m] and your lamps burning, [36] and be like men waiting for their master when he comes home from the wedding, that when he comes and knocks, they at once may open the door for him. [37] Happy are those slaves whom the master, when he comes, will find on the watch for him. I solemnly say to you, he will tighten his belt and have them sit at table, and he will go around and wait on them. [38] Whether he comes before or after [n] midnight, if he finds them so, happy are they. [39] But be sure of this, that if the master of the house had known what time the thief was coming, he would not have let his house be broken into. [40] So you, too, must always be ready, for at an hour that you are not expecting, the Son of Man will come."

[41] Peter said to Him. "Lord, do you mean this story for us, or is it for everybody?"

[42] And the Lord said, "Who then is the faithful, thoughtful manager whom his master will put in charge of his household, to give out the supplies at the proper time? [43] Happy is that slave whom his master, when he comes, will find so doing. [44] I tell you truly, he will put him in charge of all his property. [45] But if that slave says to himself, my Master is not coming back for a long time,[o] and begins to beat the men and women slaves, and to eat and drink and get drunk, [46] his master will come back some day when he is not expecting him, and at an hour of which he is not aware, and will cut him in two, and give him his share with the unfaithful. [47] That slave who knows his master's wishes and does not get

---

[j] Dif. word in Lk.; *suspense*, the core of its meaning.
[k] Vb. in emph. position.
[l] Grk., *seek His kingdom;* so *will.*
[m] Grk., *gird up your loins*—equivalent to our, *tighten your belt.*
[n] *In the second or third watch.*
[o] Lit., *delays to come.*

ready or act upon them will be severely punished.ᵖ ⁴⁸ But the one who does wrong without knowing it ᑫ will be lightly punished. Much will be demanded from anyone to whom much has been given; yea, people will demand much more from anyone to whom they have entrusted much.

⁴⁹ "It is fire that I have come to bring upon the earth, and how I wish it were already kindled! ⁵⁰ I have a baptism to be baptized with, and how I am pressed with anguish till it is accomplished! ⁵¹ Do you think that I came to give peace on earth? I tell you, not so at all, but rather discord. ⁵² For from now on, five in a house will be divided, three against two, and two against three. ⁵³ Father will be against son and son against father, mother against daughter and daughter against mother, mother-in-law against daughter-in-law and daughter-in-law against mother-in-law."

⁵⁴ And He said to the crowds, "When you see a cloud rising in the west, at once you say, 'It is going to rain,' ʳ and it does. ⁵⁵ And when you see a south wind blowing, you say, 'It is going to be very hot,' and so it is. ⁵⁶ You hypocrites! You know how to interpret day by day the look of earth and sky. Then how is it that you do not know how to interpret the present crisis? ˢ ⁵⁷ Why do you not of yourselves decide what is right? ⁵⁸ For instance, when you are on the way to court with your opponent, take the utmost pains on the way to get entirely rid of him, so that he may not rush ᵗ you before the judge, and the judge turn you over to the sheriff,ᵘ and the sheriff put you in prison. ⁵⁹ I tell you, you will never get out of it until you have paid the last penny!" ᵛ

13 REPENTANCE EMPHASIZED BY EXAMPLES AND STORY; A WOMAN BENT DOUBLE BY RHEUMATISM CURED ON THE SABBATH; THE STORIES OF THE MUSTARD SEED AND YEAST; GOVERNOR ANTIPAS REPROVED; JERUSALEM LAMENTED

Just at that time some people came up to tell Him about the Galileans whose blood Pilate mingled with that of their sacrifices.

ᵖ Grk., *beaten with many lashes.*
ᑫ Grk., *does not know,* etc.
ʳ Grk., *rain is coming.*
ˢ Grk., *this time.*
ᵗ Lit., *drag.*
ᵘ Modern term almost equivalent to the ancient officer.
ᵛ Value only a small fraction of a cent.

² Then He answered them, "Do you think, because these **Galileans** suffered like this, that they were worse sinners than all the rest of the Galileans? ³ By no means, I tell you; but unless you repent, you will all perish as they did. ⁴ Or those eighteen people at Siloam on whom the tower fell and whom it crushed to death,ᵃ do you think that they were offenders worse than all the rest of the people who live in Jerusalem? ⁵ By no means, I tell you; but unless you repent, you will all perish as they did."

⁶ Then He told them this story:

"A man had a fig tree planted by ᵇ his vineyard, and he kept going and looking for figs ᶜ on it, but did not find any. ⁷ So he said to the vine-dresser, 'Look here! for three years I have been coming to look for figs on this fig tree, and have not found any. Cut it down. Why waste the ground with it?' ᵈ ⁸ But he answered, 'Leave it, sir, just one more year, till I dig around it and manure it. ⁹ If it bears figs in the future, well; ᵉ but if not, you will have to cut it down.'"

¹⁰ One sabbath He was teaching in one of the synagogues, ¹¹ and there was a woman there who for eighteen years had had a disease caused by a spirit.ᶠ She was bent double and could not straighten herself up at all. ¹² As soon as Jesus saw her, He called her to Him and said to her, "Woman, you are freed from your disease!" ¹³ Then He laid His hands on her, and at once she straightened herself up and burst into praising God.

¹⁴ But the leader of the synagogue, indignant because Jesus had cured her on the sabbath, answered the crowd, "There are six days on which people must work; so come on these and be cured, but not on the sabbath."

¹⁵ Then the Lord answered him, "You hypocrites! Does not everyone of you on the sabbath untie his ox or donkey and lead him out of the stable to water him? ¹⁶ And so was it not right for this woman, a descendant of Abraham, whom Satan has for eighteen years kept bound, to be freed from this bond on the sabbath?"

¹⁷ Even while He was saying this, His opponents were blushing with shame, but all the people were rejoicing over all the glorious things that were being done by Him.

ᵃ Grk., *and it killed them.*
ᵇ Lit., *in.*
ᶜ Grk., *fruit;* so *figs.*
ᵈ Grk., *why does it waste,* etc.
ᵉ Implied, as conclu. of cond.
ᶠ Grk., *a spirit of a disease* (obj. gen.).

¹⁸ So He went on to say, "What is the kingdom of God like? To what may I compare it? ¹⁹ It is like a mustard seed which a man took and dropped in his garden, and it grew and became a tree, and the wild birds roosted in its branches."

²⁰ And again He said, "To what may I compare the kingdom of God? ²¹ It is like yeast which a woman took and hid ᵍ in a bushel ʰ of flour until it all had risen."

²² Then He was traveling from town to town and from village to village, teaching and making His way toward Jerusalem. ²³ And someone asked Him, "Lord, are only a few to be saved?"

And He said to them, ²⁴ "You must struggle on to get in through the narrow door, for I tell you, many will try to get in, but will not succeed,ⁱ ²⁵ when once the master of the house gets up and shuts the door, and you begin to stand on the outside and to knock on the door again and again,ʲ and say, 'Lord, open it for us'; but He will answer, 'I do not know where you come from.' ²⁶ Then you will begin to say, 'We ate and drank with you, and you taught in our streets.' ²⁷ But He will say to you, 'I do not know where you come from. Go away from me, all you wrongdoers!' ²⁸ There you will weep and grind your teeth, when you see Abraham and Isaac and Jacob and all the prophets in the kingdom of God, and you yourselves being driven away on the outside. ²⁹ People will come from east and west, from north and south, and take their seats at the feast ᵏ in the kingdom of God. ³⁰ And so there are those now last who will be first then, and there are those now first who will then be last."

³¹ Just at that time some Pharisees came up and said to Him, "Get out at once! Get away from here, for Herod wants to kill you!"

³² But He said to them: "Go and tell that fox, 'Here I am, driving out demons and performing cures, today and tomorrow, and on the third day I will finish these tasks.ˡ ³³ But I must continue on my way, for it is not possible for a prophet to perish outside Jerusalem.' ᵐ

³⁴ "O Jerusalem! Jerusalem! the city that continues to murder the prophets, and to stone those who are sent to her, how often I

ᵍ In connection with kneading
ʰ A little over a bushel—a regular baking.
ⁱ Grk., *be able*.
ʲ Pres. infin. of repeated ac.
ᵏ Central idea.
ˡ Supplied from context; Grk., *I will finish* (them).
ᵐ A thrust with keenest sarcasm.

have yearned to gather your children around me, as a hen gathers her brood under her wings. But you refused! ³⁵ Now your house is abandoned to its fate!ⁿ And I tell you, you will never see me again until you say, 'Blessed be He who comes in the name of the Lord!' "

14
JESUS DINES WITH A PHARISEE; CURES A MAN WITH DROPSY; TELLS THREE STORIES ABOUT BANQUETS; TELLS TWO MORE STORIES ABOUT COUNTING THE COST

One sabbath, when He went to take a meal at the house of a Pharisee who was a member of the council,ᵃ they continued to watch Him closely. ² Just in front of Him was a man who was suffering from dropsy. ³ So He answered the experts in the law and the Pharisees by asking, "Is it right to cure people on the sabbath or not?" ⁴ But they made no answer. So He took hold of the man and cured him and sent him away. ⁵ Then He said to them, "Which of you, if his son or ox falls into a well, will not at once pull him out on the sabbath?" ⁶ But they could make no reply to this.

⁷ When He noticed how the guests were picking out the best places, He told them the following story:

⁸ "When you are invited by anyone to a wedding supper, never take the best place, forᵇ someone of greater distinction than you may have been invited, ⁹ so that your host may not come and say to you, 'Make room for this man'; and then in embarrassmentᶜ you will proceed to take and keep the lowest place.ᵈ ¹⁰ But when you are invited anywhere, go and take the lowest place, so that when your host comes in, he may say to you, 'My friend, come up to a better place.' Then you will be honored in the presence of all your fellow-guests. ¹¹ For everyone who exalts himself will be humbled, but whoever humbles himself will be exalted."

¹² Then He proceeded to say to the man who invited Him: "When you give a luncheon or a dinner, stop the social customᵉ of inviting your friends or your brothers or your relatives or your

---

ⁿ Lit., *Behold! your house is left to you.*
ᵃ Grk., *one of the ruling Pharisees.*
ᵇ Lit., *lest.*
ᶜ Grk., *with shame.*
ᵈ Lit., *the last place.*
ᵉ Expressed by neg. with pres. impv.

rich neighbors, for ᶠ they may invite you in return and so you will be repaid. ¹³ But when you give a reception, make it your habit to invite people that are poor, maimed, crippled, or blind.ᵍ ¹⁴ Then you will be happy, because they cannot repay you; you will be repaid at the resurrection of the upright."

¹⁵ But one of the fellow-guests heard this, and said to Him, "Happy will be the man who is fortunate ʰ enough to be at the feast in the kingdom of God."

¹⁶ Then Jesus said to him:

"Once a man was giving a great dinner and invited many people to it. ¹⁷ And at the dinner hour he sent his slave to say to the invited guests, 'Come, for it is now ready.' ¹⁸ But they all in the same attitude ⁱ began to excuse themselves. The first one said, 'I have just bought a piece of land and I must go and look it over. Please excuse me.' ʲ ¹⁹ Another said, 'I have just bought five yoke of oxen, and I am on my way to try them. Please excuse me.' ²⁰ Another said, 'I have just gotten married, and so I cannot come.' ²¹ So the slave returned and reported these answers to his master. Then the master of the house became angry and said to his slave, 'Hurry out into the streets and lanes of the city and bring in here the poor, the maimed, the crippled, and the blind.' ²² Then the slave said, 'Sir, what you ordered has been done, and still there is room.'

²³ "Then the master said to his slave, 'Go out on the roads and by the hedges and make ᵏ the people come in, so that my house may be filled. ²⁴ For I tell you, not one of those people who were invited shall get a taste ˡ of my dinner!'"

²⁵ Now great crowds were going along with Him, and all at once ᵐ He turned and said to them:

²⁶ "If anyone comes to me and does not hate his own father and mother and wife and children and brothers and sisters, and still more, his own life too, he cannot be a disciple of mine. ²⁷ Whoever does not persevere in carrying his own cross and thus ⁿ follow after me, cannot be a disciple of mine.

ᶠ Lit., *lest*.
ᵍ No article, so quality emphasized; hence our tr.
ʰ Grk., *who will eat*, etc.
ⁱ Expressed in adj. *one*.
ʲ Grk., *I beg you, hold me excused*.
ᵏ Strong vb.; *urge, constrain*, probably not *to use phys. force*.
ˡ Punctiliar action in fut. tense.
ᵐ In aor.
ⁿ Implied; to follow Him is conditioned on carrying the cross.

28 "What man among you, if he wishes to build a tower, does not first sit down and calculate the cost, to see whether he has money enough to complete it? 29 Lest, perchance, after he has laid the foundation but cannot complete the building, all who see it begin to make sport of him, 30 and say, 'This fellow started to erect a building but could not complete it!'

31 "Or what king, when he is going to make an attack on another king, does not first sit down and deliberate whether he is able with ten thousand soldiers to meet the other king who is coming against him with twenty thousand? 32 And if he cannot, while the other is still far away, he sends envoys and asks for terms º of peace.

33 "Just so,ᴾ no one of you who does not forsake everything that he has, can be a disciple of mine. 34 Salt is good; but if salt itself loses its strength, how can that strength be restored? 35 It is fit for neither soil nor manure. People throw it away. Let him who has ears to hear with give heed!"

15 JESUS TELLS THREE STORIES TO DEFEND HIS FRIENDSHIP TO NOTORIOUS SINNERS: THE LOST SHEEP, THE LOST COIN, THE LOST BOY

Now all the tax-collectors and notorious sinners were crowding around Him to listen to Him. 2 And so the Pharisees and scribes continually grumbled, and said, "This fellow ᵃ is welcoming notorious sinners, and even eating with them."

3 So He told them the following story:

4 "What man among you, if he has a hundred sheep, and if he loses one of them, does not leave the ninety-nine in the desert and continue to look for the lost one until he finds it? 5 And when he finds it, with joy he puts it on his shoulders, 6 and when he reaches home he calls in his friends and neighbors, and says to them, 'Rejoice with me, because I have found my lost sheep!' 7 Just so, I tell you, there will be more joy in heaven over one sinful person who repents than over ninety-nine upright people who do not need any repentance.

8 "Or what woman, if ᵇ she has ten silver coins and loses one of them, does not light a lamp and sweep the house, and look care-

---

º Lit., *pertaining to peace.*
ᴾ The logical conclu. of what He has said in the last three paragraphs.
ᵃ Spoken in contempt; hence our tr.
ᵇ Adv. pt. implying Con.

fully until she finds it? ⁹ And when she finds it, she calls in her friends and neighbors, and says, 'Rejoice with me, because I have found the coin which I lost!' ¹⁰ Just so, I tell you, there is joy among the angels of God over one sinful person who repents!"

¹¹ Then He said:

"There was a man who had two sons. ¹² The younger of them said to his father, 'Father, give me the share of the property that falls to me.' So he divided his property between them. ¹³ Not many days after that, the younger son got together all he had and went away to a distant country, and there he squandered all his property by living in dissipation. ¹⁴ After he had spent it all, a severe famine struck ᵉ that country, and he began to suffer want. ¹⁵ So he went and hired himself out ᵈ to a citizen of that country, and he sent him to his fields to feed hogs. ¹⁶ And often ᵉ he craved to fill himself with the carob-pods which the hogs were eating, and nobody gave him a bite. ¹⁷ Then he came to himself and said, 'How many of my father's hired men have more to eat than they need, and here I am dying of hunger! ¹⁸ I will get up and go to my father, and say to him, "Father, I have sinned against heaven and in your opinion; ᶠ ¹⁹ I no longer deserve to be called your son; just treat me like one of your hired men."' ²⁰ So he got up and went to his father. But, while he was still a long way off, his father saw him, and his heart was moved with pity for him, and he ran and fell on his neck, and kissed him affectionately.ᵍ ²¹ His son said to him, 'Father, I have sinned against heaven and in your opinion; I no longer deserve to be called your son; just treat me like one of your hired men.' ²² But his father said to his slaves, 'Bring out at once ʰ a robe, yes, the finest one,ⁱ and put it on him, and put a ring on his hand and shoes on his feet; ²³ take the fattening ʲ calf and kill it, and let us feast and celebrate, ²⁴ because this son of mine was dead and has come to life, was lost and has been found!' So they began to celebrate.

²⁵ "Now his elder son was in the field. So, on coming in, as he came near the house, he heard music and dancing. ²⁶ Then he called

---

ᵉ Grk., *came upon.*
ᵈ Grk., *glued himself to.*
ᵉ Impf. of repeated action.
ᶠ Lit., *before you.*
ᵍ In comp. vb.
ʰ Grk., *quickly.*
ⁱ Fol. two best Mss.
ʲ Grk., *wheat-fed.*

one of the servant-boys ᵏ and asked him what this meant. ²⁷ He said to him, 'Your brother has come back, and your father has killed the fattening calf, because he has gotten him back safe and sound.' ²⁸ So he became angry and would not go into the house. Then his father came out and began to plead with him. ²⁹ But he answered his father, 'See! I have served you all these years and have never disobeyed a command of yours, but you have never given me even a kid, so that I could celebrate with my friends. ³⁰ But when this son of yours arrives, who has eaten up your property with immoral women,ˡ you have killed for him the fattening calf.' ³¹ Then he said to him, 'My child, you have been with me all the time, and all I have is yours. ³² But we just had to celebrate and rejoice, because this brother of yours was dead and has come to life, was lost and has been found.'"

16 THE STORY OF THE DISHONEST MANAGER; THE PHARISEES REPROVED FOR BEING LOVERS OF MONEY; THE STORY OF THE RICH MAN AND LAZARUS

Now He was saying to the disciples:

"Once there was a rich man who had a household manager,ᵃ and he was accused to his master of squandering the latter's ᵇ property. ² So he called the manager to him and said, 'What is this that I am hearing about you? Balance your accounts and show how you are conducting my affairs, for you cannot be manager any longer.' ³ Then the manager said to himself, What shall I do, because my master is going to take my position away from me? I am not strong enough to dig; I am ashamed to beg. ⁴ I know what I will do—I will ask ᵉ them * to take me into their homes when I am removed from my position. ⁵ So he called in each of his master's debtors, and asked the first one, 'How much do you owe my master?' ⁶ He answered, 'Nine hundred gallons of oil.' ᵈ Then he said to him, 'Take your bill and sit right down and write four hundred and fifty.' ⁷ Then he asked another, 'And how much do you owe?' He answered, 'Twelve hundred bushels of wheat.' He

---

ᵏ Exact meaning of term.
ˡ Lit., *harlots.*
ᵃ Grk., *steward;* one who manages for another; so *manager.*
ᵇ Grk., *his.*
ᵉ Implied before the conj. *that.* * "My master's debtors," implied.
ᵈ Grk., *one hundred baths;* a bath is about nine gals.

said to him, 'Take your bill and write nine hundred and sixty.' [8] And his master praised the dishonest manager, because he acted with shrewd business sense.[e] For the men of the world act with more business sense toward their fellows than the men who enjoy spiritual light.[f] [9] So I tell you, make friends by the right use of your money, which so easily tends to wrongdoing, so that when it fails, your friends may welcome you to the eternal dwellings.[g] [10] The man who is dependable in a very small matter is dependable also in a large deal, the man who is dishonest in a very small matter is dishonest also in a large deal. [11] So if you have not proved dependable in handling your ill-gotten riches, who will trust you with the true riches? [12] And if you have not proved dependable in what belongs to someone else, who will trust you with what belongs to you? [13] No house-servant can be a slave to two masters, for either he will hate one and love the other, or he will be devoted to one and despise the other. You cannot serve God and money.[h]

[14] Now the Pharisees, who were lovers of money, had been listening to all this, and they began to ridicule Him. [15] Then He said to them, "You are the men who exhibit[i] your uprightness before the public, but God knows your hearts. For what stands high in the sight of men is detestable in the sight of God. [16] It was the law and the prophets until John, but ever since that time the good news of the kingdom of God has been proclaimed, and everybody has been taking it by storm.[j] [17] It is easier for heaven and earth to pass away than for one dotting of an 'i' in the law to fail. [18] Any man who divorces his wife to[k] marry another woman commits adultery, and the man who marries the woman divorced from her husband commits adultery.

[19] "Once there was a rich man who used to dress in purple and fine linen and live in dazzling luxury[l] every day. [20] And a beggar named Lazarus, covered with sores, had been laid at his gate, [21] and he was always craving to get a square meal[m] from the scraps that fell from the rich man's table. Yes, the very dogs used to come

[e] Grk., *shrewdly.*
[f] Lit., *sons of light.*
[g] *Tents* in orig.
[h] Grk., *Mammon,* the god of money.
[i] Pres. pt. of cont. ac.
[j] I.e., rushing into it.
[k] *And,* in Aramaic source, expressing purpose.
[l] In vb. and adv.
[m] Lit., *be gorged.*

and lick his sores. ²² One day the beggar died and was carried away by the angels to be Abraham's bosom companion,ⁿ and the rich man too died and was buried. ²³ And in hades ᵒ he looked up, in constant tortures as he was, and saw Abraham far away and Lazarus his bosom companion. ²⁴ So he called and said, 'Father Abraham, take pity on me and send Lazarus to dip the tip of his finger in water to cool off my tongue, because I am ceaselessly ᵖ tortured in this flame.' ²⁵ But Abraham said, 'My child, remember that you received in full your blessings in your lifetime, and Lazarus his hardships in his; but now he is continuously comforted here, while you are continuously tortured there. ²⁶ Besides all this, between you and us there stands fixed a great chasm, so that those who want to cross from this side to you cannot, nor can they cross from your side to us.' ²⁷ Then he said, 'For this reason, I beg you, father, to send him to my father's house ²⁸ (for I have five brothers) to warn them, that they too may not come to this place of torture.' ²⁹ But Abraham said, 'They have Moses and the prophets; let them listen to them.' ³⁰ But he pleaded, 'No, father Abraham, but if someone went to them from the dead, they would repent.' ³¹ Then he answered, 'If they do not listen to Moses and the prophets, they will not be convinced, even if someone rises from the dead.'"

17 FOUR GREAT SAYINGS ON LAYING SNARES FOR OTHERS, FORGIVING OTHERS, TRIUMPHANT FAITH, AND THE STORY OF AN UNPROFITABLE SLAVE; TEN LEPERS CURED; THE COMING OF THE KINGDOM AND OF THE SON OF MAN

Now He said to His disciples: "It is inevitable that snares ᵃ to evil will come, but a curse be on the man through whom they come! ² It would be better for him to have a millstone hung around his neck, and he be hurled into the sea, than for him to ensnare ᵇ one of these lowly ones.

³ "Be always looking out for one another. If your brother ever ᶜ sins, reprove him, and if he repents, forgive him. ⁴ Even if he sins

---

ⁿ Grk., *to Abraham's bosom.*
ᵒ *Underworld,* not *Gehenna.*
ᵖ Pres. of cont. ac.
ᵃ Grk., *things which trip up;* so *snares.*
ᵇ Grk., *cause to trip up.*
ᶜ In the aor.

against you seven times in a day and seven times turns to you and says, 'I am sorry,' you must forgive him."

⁵ Then the apostles said to the Lord, "Give us more faith."

⁶ Then the Lord said to them, "If you had faith that grows ᵈ like a mustard seed, you might have been saying to this mulberry tree, 'Pull yourself up by the roots and plant yourself in the sea,' and it would have obeyed you!

⁷ "What man among you, if he has a slave ploughing or tending sheep, will say to him when he comes in from the field, 'Come at once and take your seat at the table,' ⁸ but will not rather say to him, 'Get my supper ready, and dress yourself and wait on me until I eat and drink, and you yourself can eat and drink afterward'? ⁹ Does he praise the slave for doing what he was ordered to do? ¹⁰ So you too, when you do all that you are ordered to do, say, 'We are worthless slaves; we have done only what we ought to have done.'"

¹¹ As He was going on to Jerusalem, He chanced to pass through Samaria and Galilee. ¹² And as He was going into one village, ten lepers met Him, who got up ᵉ at some distance from Him, ¹³ and raised their voices and said, "Jesus, Master, do take pity on us!"

¹⁴ So as soon as He saw them, He said to them, "Go at once ᶠ and show yourselves to the priests." And while they were going they were cured. ¹⁵ But one of them, when he saw that he was cured, came back, praising God with a loud voice, ¹⁶ and fell on his face at Jesus' feet, and continued to thank Him. Now he was a Samaritan.

¹⁷ And Jesus said, "Were not ten cured? Where are the other nine? ¹⁸ Were none found to return and give praise to God except this foreigner?" ¹⁹ Then He said to him, "Get up and go on your way. Your faith has cured you."

²⁰ Now, when He was asked by the Pharisees when the kingdom of God would come, He answered them, "The kingdom of God is not coming with visible display, ²¹ and so people will not say, 'Look! Here it is,' nor, 'There it is,' for the kingdom of God is within you."

²² Then He said to His disciples, "The time ᵍ will come when

ᵈ Implied in the character of the seed to grow.
ᵉ Fol. WH.
ᶠ In aor.
ᵍ No article, so quality of the time emphasized.

you will long to see one of the days of the Son of Man, but you will not see it. 23 And men will say to you, 'Look! There he is!' or, 'Look! Here He is!' Do not start ʰ in pursuit of Him, 24 for just as when the lightning flashes, it shines from one end of the sky to the other, so will the Son of Man be when He comes.ⁱ 25 But first He has to endure much suffering, and be disowned by this age. 26 And just as it was in the time ᵍ of Noah, so it will be in the time ᵍ of the Son of Man. 27 People continued to eat, drink, marry, and be married, right up to the day when Noah went into the ark, and the Flood came and destroyed them all. 28 It was so in the time of Lot; people continued to eat, drink, buy, sell, plant, and build; 29 and the very day Lot went out of Sodom, it rained fire and brimstone from heaven and destroyed them all. 30 It will be so on the day when the Son of Man appears.ʲ 31 The man who is on the roof of his house that day, and his goods in the house, must not come down to carry them out; and the man in the field, too, must not turn back. 32 Remember Lot's wife! 33 Whoever tries to preserve ᵏ his life will lose it, but whoever loses it will preserve ᵏ it. 34 I tell you, two men will be in the same ˡ bed that night; one will be taken, the other left. 35 Two women will be grinding together; one will be taken, the other left." ᵐ

37 Then they asked Him, "Where, Lord, will this be?"

And He said to them, "Wherever there is carrion ⁿ the vultures will flock."

18 THE STORY OF THE GODLESS JUDGE; OF THE PHARISEE AND THE TAX-COLLECTOR; LITTLE CHILDREN TO BE ALLOWED TO COME TO JESUS; THE RICH YOUNG RULER'S REFUSAL SHOWS IT IS HARD FOR THE RICH TO BE SAVED; BLIND BARTIMEUS CURED

Now He told them the following story to show how necessary it is for people always to pray and never to give up:

2 "Once there was in a city a judge who had no reverence for

ʰ Fol. WH; ingress. aor.
ⁱ Lit., *in His day*.
ʲ Lit., *is revealed*.
ᵏ Different Grk. vbs. but same meaning.
ˡ *In one bed*.
ᵐ V. 36 om. by best Mss.
ⁿ Lk. fol. Homer in use of *soma* for *carcass*.

God nor respect for men. ³ And in that city there was a widow who continued to come to him and say, 'Give me justice and protection from my opponent.' ⁴ And he would not for a time, but afterward he said to himself, Though I have no reverence for God nor respect for men, ⁵ yet because this widow continues to bother me, I will give her justice and protection,ᵃ so that she may not finally wear me out by her continual coming."

⁶ Then the Lord added, "Listen to what the unrighteous judge says! ⁷ And will not God give justice and protection to His chosen people who continue to cry to Him day and night, since ᵇ He is so patient with them? ⁸ I tell you, He will give them justice and protection, and that without delay. But when the Son of Man comes, will He find faith on earth?"

⁹ To some people who were confident that they themselves were upright, but who scorned everybody else, He told the following story:

¹⁰ "Two men went up to the temple to pray, one a Pharisee, the other a tax-collector. ¹¹ The Pharisee stood and said this self-centered ᶜ prayer, 'O God, I thank you that I am not like the rest of men, robbers, rogues, adulterers, or even like this tax-collector. ¹² I fast two days in the week. I pay a tithe on everything I get.' ¹³ But the tax-collector stood at a distance and would not even lift his eyes to heaven, but continued to beat his breast,ᵈ and say, 'O God, have mercy on me, a sinner!' ¹⁴ I tell you, this man, and not the other, went back home forgiven and accepted ᵉ by God. For everyone who exalts himself will be humbled, but whoever humbles himself will be exalted."

¹⁵ Now some people were bringing even their babies ᶠ to Him to have Him touch them, but the disciples, when they saw it, reproved them for it.

¹⁶ But Jesus called them to Him and said, "Let the little children ᶠ come to me, and stop preventing them from it, for to such as these the kingdom of God belongs. ¹⁷ I solemnly say to you, whoever does not accept the kingdom of God as a little child does, will never get into it at all."

ᵃ Protection in idea of prep.
ᵇ Adv. pt.
ᶜ Lit., *to* or *before himself;* so his prayer was self-centered.
ᵈ Expressing penitence.
ᵉ Grk., *justified;* i.e., forgiven and accepted.
ᶠ Dif. words.

¹⁸ Then a certain member of the council ᵍ asked Him, "Good Teacher, what must I do to get possession of eternal life?"

¹⁹ Jesus said to him, "Why do you call me perfectly good?ʰ No one is perfectly good but God Himself.ⁱ ²⁰ You know the commandments: 'Do not commit adultery, Do not murder, Do not steal, Do not bear false witness, Practice honoring your father and mother.'"

²¹ But he said, "I have kept all these commandments ever since I was a child." ʲ

²² When Jesus heard this, He said to him, "One thing you still lack. Sell everything you have, and distribute the money among the poor, and you will have riches in heaven; then come back and follow me." ²³ But when he heard that, he was very sad, for he was surpassingly ᵏ rich.

²⁴ So when Jesus saw it, He said, "How hard it is for those who have money to get into the kingdom of God! ²⁵ For it is easier for a camel to go through a needle's eye ˡ than for a rich man to get into the kingdom of God."

²⁶ But those who heard it said, "Then who can be saved?"

²⁷ So He said, "The things impossible for men are possible for God."

²⁸ Then Peter said to Him, "We ᵐ have left our very own,ⁿ homes and all, and have followed you."

²⁹ So He said to them, "I solemnly say to you, there is no one who has given up home or wife or brothers or parents or children for the kingdom of God, ³⁰ who will not receive in return ᵒ many times more in this world, and in the next ᵖ eternal life."

³¹ Now He took the Twelve aside and said to them, "Listen! We are going up to Jerusalem, and everything written by the prophets about the Son of Man will be fulfilled. ³² For He will be turned over to the heathen and sport made of Him, He will be insulted and spit upon, ³³ and then they will flog Him and kill

---

ᵍ Lit., *leader*.
ʰ ἀγαθός means this.
ⁱ Lit., *but One, God*.
ʲ Grk., *from childhood*.
ᵏ Very strong comp. adv.
ˡ Dif. word in Lk.
ᵐ Emph.—*we Twelve*.
ⁿ Fol. WH.
ᵒ In comp. vb.
ᵖ Grk., *in this time, in next age*.

Him, but on the third day He will rise again." ³⁴ But they did not understand about these things, and this statement was an insoluble riddle ᵠ to them; they did not even begin to grasp what He meant.ʳ

³⁵ As He was approaching Jericho, a blind man chanced to be sitting by the roadside begging. ³⁶ As he heard a crowd going by, he asked what it meant. ³⁷ They told him that Jesus of Nazareth was coming by. ³⁸ Then he cried out, "Jesus, you Son of David, do pity me!" ³⁹ But those who were marching in front reproved him and told him to keep quiet, but he cried out all the louder, "O Son of David, do pity me!"

⁴⁰ Then Jesus stopped and ordered him to be brought to Him. And when he approached Jesus, He said to him, ⁴¹ "What do you want me to do for you?"

He answered, "Lord, I want to see again!"

⁴² Then Jesus said to him, "See again! Your faith has cured you." ⁴³ So at once he saw again, and began to follow Him, giving thanks to God. And all the people saw it and gave praise to God.

19 RICH ZACCHEUS ENTERTAINS JESUS; JESUS BLESSES HIM AND HIS HOME; JESUS TELLS THE STORY OF THE POUNDS; HE RIDES INTO JERUSALEM AS KING; WEEPS OVER THE CITY; DRIVES THE TRADERS OUT

Then He went into Jericho and was passing through it. ² Here there was a man named Zaccheus, who was tax-commissioner ᵃ of the district, and he was a rich man too. ³ Now he was trying to see Jesus to find out ᵇ who He was, but he could not because of the crowd, as he was so small in stature. ⁴ So he ran on ahead and climbed up in a mulberry tree, just to get a glimpse of Him, for Jesus was coming through on that street.ᶜ

⁵ And as Jesus came to the place, He looked up and said to him, "Zaccheus, come down quickly! for today I must stop ᵈ at your house." ⁶ So in haste he came down, and with gladness welcomed Him.

ᵠ Grk., *hidden from* (them).
ʳ Grk., *the things said.*
ᵃ Lit., *head* or *chief tax-collector.*
ᵇ *Only* implied.
ᶜ Last phrase implied.
ᵈ Expressed by aor. infin.

⁷ And when they all saw it, they began to grumble and say, "He has gone in to lodge with a notorious sinner!"

⁸ Then Zaccheus got up and said to the Lord, "Listen, Lord! I now give to the poor half of my property, and if I have defrauded anyone of anything, I will pay him back four times as much."

⁹ Then Jesus said to him, "Today salvation has come to this home, for he too is a real ᵉ descendant of Abraham. ¹⁰ For the Son of Man has come to seek and to save the people that are lost."

¹¹ As they were listening to these things, He told them another story, because He was near Jerusalem and because they supposed that the kingdom of God was going to appear at once. ¹² So He said:

"Once upon a time a man of noble birth went off to a distant country to get for himself a kingdom and then return. ¹³ He called in ten of his slaves and gave them twenty dollars apiece ᶠ and told them to do business with his money while he was gone. ¹⁴ But his citizens continued to hate him, and sent a delegation after him to say, 'We do not want this man to become king over us.' ¹⁵ Then after he had gotten the appointment as king, he returned and ordered those slaves to whom he had given his money to be called in, that he might find out what business they had done. ¹⁶ Now the first one came in and said, "Your twenty dollars, sir, has made two hundred more.' ¹⁷ So he said to him, 'Well done, my good slave! Because you have proven dependable in a very small business, be governor of ten cities!' ¹⁸ The second one came in and said, 'Your twenty dollars, sir, has made a hundred!' ¹⁹ So he said to him too, 'Be governor of five cities!' ²⁰ But another one came in and said, 'Here is your twenty dollars, sir, which I kept laid away in a handkerchief. ²¹ For I lived in constant ᵍ dread of you, because you are a stern man, you pick up what you did not put down, you reap what you did not sow.' ²² He said to him, 'On the ground of what you say ʰ I will sentence you, you wicked slave! You knew that I was a stern man, that I picked up what I did not put down, and reaped what I did not sow. ²³ So why did you not put my money into the bank? In that case, when I came

---

ᵉ I.e., a spiritual son.
ᶠ Grk., *a pound;* nearly twenty dollars.
ᵍ Grk., *I continued to fear you.*
ʰ Lit., *out of your mouth.*

back I could have gotten interest[i] on my principal.' ²⁴ So he said to the bystanders, 'Take the twenty dollars away from him and give it to the man who has the two hundred.' ²⁵ And they said, 'Sir, he has two hundred already.' ²⁶ 'I tell you, the man who gets will have more given to him, but the man who does not get will have even what he has taken away from him! ²⁷ But bring those enemies of mine here who did not want me to become king over them and slay them in my presence!'"

²⁸ After saying these things, He went on ahead of them, on His way to Jerusalem.

²⁹ When He approached Bethphage and Bethany by the hill called the Mount of Olives, He sent on two of His disciples, and ³⁰ said, "Go on to the village in front of you, in which, just as you enter, you will find a colt tied, which no man has ever yet ridden. Untie it and bring it here to me. ³¹ And if anyone asks you why you are untying it, you are to answer, 'The Lord needs it.'"

³² So off the two messengers went and found it just as He had told them. ³³ And while they were untying the colt, its owners said to them, "Why are you untying the colt?"

³⁴ And they answered, "The Lord needs it." ³⁵ So they brought it to Jesus. ³⁶ Then they threw their coats upon it and mounted Jesus upon it. As He was going on, the people continued to spread their coats under Him on the road. ³⁷ Just as He was approaching the city, going down the Mount of Olives, the whole throng of the disciples began to praise God exultantly and loudly for all the wonder-works that they had seen, ³⁸ and said:

"Blessed is the King who comes in the name of the Lord;
Peace in heaven and praise on high!"

³⁹ Then some Pharisees in the crowd said to Him, "Teacher, reprove your disciples."

⁴⁰ But He answered, "I tell you, if they keep silent, the stones will cry out!"

⁴¹ As He approached it, just as soon as He saw the city, He burst[j] into tears over it, ⁴² and said: "If today you yourself had only known the conditions[k] of peace! But now they are hidden from you.[l] ⁴³ For a time is coming upon you when your enemies

---

[i] Grk., *gotten it with interest.*
[j] Ingress. aor.
[k] *Things pertaining to peace.*
[l] Lit., *from your eyes.*

will throw up earthworks around you and surround you and hem you in on all sides, ⁴⁴ and they will throw you and your children within you to the ground, and they will not leave one stone upon another in you, because you did not know when [m] God visited you."

⁴⁵ Then He went into the temple and began to drive out those who were selling things in it, ⁴⁶ and He said to them, "The Scripture says, 'And my house shall be a house of prayer,' but you have made it a cave for robbers."

⁴⁷ So He was teaching daily in the temple, and the high priests and the scribes and the leading men of the people were trying to destroy Him, ⁴⁸ but they could not find, as hard as they tried,[n] what to do with Him, for all the people continued to hang on His words.

20 JESUS' AUTHORITY CHALLENGED; HE AIMS AT HIS CHALLENGERS THE STORY OF THE VILLAINOUS TENANTS; THEY ASK HIM TWO "CATCH" QUESTIONS: IS IT RIGHT TO PAY TAXES TO ROME? IS THERE A RESURRECTION? HE ROUTS THEM WITH A QUESTION

One day while He was teaching the people in the temple and preaching the good news, the high priests and the scribes, together with the elders,[a] took a stand against Him, ² and said to Him, "Tell us what sort [b] of authority you have for doing as you do, or who is it that gave you such authority?"

³ Then He answered them, "I will ask you a question too. Tell me, ⁴ was John's baptism from heaven or from men?"

⁵ And they argued with one another, and said, "If we say, 'From heaven,' He will say, 'Why did you not believe him?' ⁶ But if we say, 'From men,' all the people will stone us to death,[c] for they are convinced that John was a prophet." ⁷ So they answered and said that they did not know where it was from.

⁸ Then Jesus said to them, "Nor am I going to tell you what sort of authority I have for doing as I do."

[m] Grk., *the time of your visitation* (by God).
[n] Impf. of both vbs. gives this idea.
[a] All members of the supreme court.
[b] Interrog. of quality.
[c] Lit., *stone us down*.

LUKE 20

⁹ Then He went on ᵈ to tell the people the following story:

"Once upon a time a man planted a vineyard and leased it to tenant farmers, and then went abroad for a long stay. ¹⁰ So at the proper time He sent a slave to the tenants, that they might pay him his part of the grape-crop,ᵉ but the tenants beat him and sent him back empty-handed. ¹¹ Then again he sent another slave, and they beat him and insulted him, and sent him back empty-handed. ¹² And again he sent a third slave, and they wounded him and threw him out of the vineyard. ¹³ Then the owner of the vineyard said, 'What shall I do? I will send my dearly loved son. They will, I should think, respect him.' ¹⁴ But when the tenants saw him, they argued among themselves, 'This is the heir; let us kill him, so that what he inherits ᶠ may be ours.' ¹⁵ So they drove him out of the vineyard and killed him. What then will the owner of the vineyard do to them? ¹⁶ He will come and put those tenants to death and give the vineyard to others."

When they heard this, they said, "May it never be so!"

¹⁷ But He glanced at them and said, "Then what does this Scripture ᵍ mean:

'That stone which the builders threw away
Has now become the cornerstone'?

¹⁸ Everyone who falls upon that stone will be shattered, and he on whom it falls will be crushed to dust."

¹⁹ Then the scribes and the high priests tried to arrest Him at that very hour, but they were afraid of the people; for they knew that He meant this story for them. ²⁰ So they closely watched and sent spies who pretended to be upright men, to catch Him in His conversation, so as to turn Him over to the power and authority of the governor. ²¹ They asked Him, "Teacher, we know that you speak and teach what is right, and show no favors to anyone, but teach the way of God honestly. ²² Is it right for us to pay taxes to Caesar, or not?"

²³ But He detected their cunning, and said to them, ²⁴ "Show me a twenty-cent coin.ʰ Whose picture and title does it bear?"

They answered, "Caesar's."

ᵈ Grk., *He began.*
ᵉ Grk., *from the fruits of the vine.*
ᶠ Lit., *the inheritance.*
ᵍ Ps. 118: 22.
ʰ *A denarius;* worth a little less than twenty cents.

LUKE 20

²⁵ He said to them, "Then pay Caesar what belongs to Caesar, and pay God what belongs to God!" ²⁶ So they could not use[i] what he said before the people, and in astonishment at His answer they said no more.

²⁷ Then some of the Sadducees, who say that there is no resurrection, came up and asked Him, ²⁸ "Teacher, Moses wrote for us a law that, if a man's brother dies and leaves a wife but no child, the man should take the widow and raise up a family for his brother. ²⁹ Now there were seven brothers. And the first brother married a wife and died childless. ³⁰ Then the second, ³¹ and the third, married her; as also the seven did who died but left no child. ³² Last of all, the woman died. ³³ Now at the resurrection which one's wife will the woman be? For the seven married her."

³⁴ Jesus said to them, "The people of this world marry and are married, ³⁵ but those who are considered worthy to attain that other world and the resurrection from the dead, neither marry nor are married. ³⁶ For they cannot die again. They are like the angels, and since they are reborn in the resurrection,[j] are children of God. ³⁷ But that the dead are raised, even Moses at the bush has demonstrated, when he calls the Lord 'the God of Abraham, the God of Isaac, and the God of Jacob.'[k] ³⁸ He is not the God of dead but of living[l] people, for all live to Him."

³⁹ Then some of the scribes answered Him, "Teacher, you have given a fine answer."[m] ⁴⁰ For they did not dare to ask Him any more questions.

⁴¹ Then He said to them, "How do people say that the Christ is David's Son? ⁴² For David himself in the Book of Psalms says:

'The Lord has said to my Lord, "Sit at my right hand,
⁴³ Until I make your enemies the footstool of your feet."'

⁴⁴ So David calls Him Lord, then how can He be his Son?"

⁴⁵ While all the people were listening, He said to His disciples, ⁴⁶ "Beware of the scribes who like to go about in long robes and love to be saluted with honor in public places, to be seated in the front seats in the synagogues, and to occupy the places of honor

---

[i] Grk., *take hold of His saying*—to twist it.
[j] Grk., *being sons of the resurrection*.
[k] Ex. 3:6.
[l] Lack of art. Emph. their character as living.
[m] Lit. *you spoke finely*.

at banquets—⁴⁷ men who eat up widows' houses and to cover it up ⁿ make long prayers! They will receive a much heavier ᵒ sentence."

21 THE WIDOW'S ONE-CENT CONTRIBUTION COMMENDED BY JESUS; THE DESTRUCTION OF JERUSALEM AND HIS SECOND COMING FORETOLD; HIS WARNING AGAINST PERSECUTION AND SUFFERING

Now He looked up and saw the rich people dropping their gifts into the treasury. ² Then He saw a poor widow drop in two little coins which make scarcely a cent. ³ And He said, "I tell you the truth, this poor widow has dropped in more than all of them; ⁴ for all the rest of them made their contributions ᵃ out of their surplus, but she out of her want dropped in all that she had to live on."

⁵ Now while some people were talking about the temple, how it was decorated with beautiful stones and votive-offerings, He said,

⁶ "As for all this that you are admiring, the time is coming when not one stone will be left upon another, that will not be torn down."

⁷ Then they asked Him, "Teacher, when will this be? And what is the sign that ᵇ it is about to take place?"

⁸ So He said, "You must take care not to be misled about it! For many will come bearing the name of Messiah,ᶜ and saying, 'I am He,' and, 'The time is near.' Do not go after them. ⁹ And when you hear of wars and tumults, never be panic-stricken. For this has to take place first, but the end will not come all at once."

¹⁰ Then He continued to say to them, "One nation will go to war with another, and one kingdom with another. ¹¹ There will be great earthquakes and pestilences and famines in various places, and there will be dreadful portents and awful signs in the sky.ᵈ ¹² But before all this takes place, people will arrest you and persecute you, and turn you over to synagogues and prisons, and you will be brought before kings and governors for my name's sake. ¹³ It will furnish you an opportunity ᵉ to testify. ¹⁴ So you must purpose

---

ⁿ Lit., *for a pretense.*
ᵒ Strong adj. in comparative.
ᵃ Grk., *dropped into the gifts,* etc.
ᵇ Grk., *when.*
ᶜ Grk., *in my name;* i.e., as Messiah.
ᵈ Grk., *dreadful things,* etc
ᵉ In dat. of advan.

in your hearts not to prepare beforehand how to make your defense, ¹⁵ for I will give you such wisdom of speech ᶠ as all your opponents combined will not be able to resist and refute. ¹⁶ Yes, you will be betrayed even by parents and brothers and kinsmen and friends, and they will put some of you to death, ¹⁷ and you will be continuously hated by everyone, because you bear my name.ᵍ ¹⁸ And yet not a single ʰ hair on your head will perish. ¹⁹ By your endurance you will win your souls.

²⁰ "When you see Jerusalem being surrounded by armies, then understand that her devastation is near. ²¹ Then let those in Judea begin to fly to the mountains, and those within the city begin to get out of it, ²² for these are the days of vengeance when all that is written in the Scriptures will be fulfilled. ²³ Alas for the women who are pregnant and those who have nursing babies in those days! For there will be great misery in the land and wrath on this people. ²⁴ They will fall by the edge of the sword and will be carried off as captives among all the nations, and Jerusalem will be trampled under the feet of the heathen, until the times of the heathen come to full measure.ⁱ ²⁵ And there will be signs in sun and moon and stars, and on earth despair of nations in bewilderment at the roaring of the sea and its waves, ²⁶ men fainting with fear and apprehension of the things that are to come upon the world, for the powers of the sky will be shaken. ²⁷ Then they will see the Son of Man coming on a cloud in overwhelming power and splendor. ²⁸ When these things begin to take place, look up and lift your heads, for your deliverance is drawing near."

²⁹ Then He told them a story. "Look at the fig tree and all the trees. ³⁰ When you see ʲ them shooting forth their buds, you know of yourselves that summer now is near. ³¹ So when you see these things taking place, you must ᵏ understand that the kingdom of God is near.

³² "I solemnly say to you, this generation will not pass away before all this takes place. ³³ Sky and earth will pass away, but my words will never pass away. ³⁴ But ever be on your guard, so that your hearts may not be loaded down with self-indulgence, drunk-

---

ᶠ Lit., *speech and wisdom*.
ᵍ Grk., *because of my name*.
ʰ Implied in the strong neg.
ⁱ Grk., *fulfilled*.
ʲ Lit., *when they shoot, etc., and you see it*.
ᵏ Impv. of obligation.

enness, and worldly worries, and that day, like a trap, catch you unawares. ³⁵ For it will come upon all who are living anywhere on the face of the earth. ³⁶ But ever be watching and always praying, so that you may have strength to escape all this that is going to take place, and so you may take[1] your stand in the presence of the Son of Man."

³⁷ Now during the days He continued to teach in the temple, but He would go out and spend the nights on the hill called the Mount of Olives; ³⁸ while [m] all the people would rise early in the mornings and come to listen to Him in the temple.

22
JUDAS BARGAINS TO BETRAY HIM; JESUS INSTITUTES THE MEMORIAL SUPPER; DEFINES TRUE GREATNESS; WARNS PETER THAT SATAN WILL SIFT HIM; WARNS ALL OF APPROACHING PERILS; IN GETHSEMANE SUFFERING, BETRAYED, ARRESTED; TRIED IN THE JEWISH COURT

Now the feast of Unleavened Bread, which is called the Passover, was drawing near. ² So the high priests and the scribes continued to seek how they might put Him to death, for they were afraid of the people. ³ But Satan entered into Judas, who is called Iscariot, who belonged to the circle [a] of the Twelve. ⁴ So he went off and discussed with the high priests and captains [b] of the temple how he could betray Him to them. ⁵ They were delighted and made a bargain to pay him for it. ⁶ He in turn accepted their offer [c] and began to seek a favorable opportunity to betray Him to them without exciting an uprising.[d]

⁷ Then the day of Unleavened Bread came, on which the Passover lamb had to be sacrificed. ⁸ So He sent Peter and John, saying to them, "Go and make preparations for us to eat the Passover meal."

⁹ They asked Him, "Where do you wish us to prepare it?"

¹⁰ He answered them, "Just after you enter the city, a man with a pitcher of water will meet you. Follow him into the house which he enters ¹¹ and say to the owner of the house, 'Our Teacher

---
[1] Aor. infin.
[m] Greek, *and* (from Ara. source).
[a] Lit., *being one of the Twelve.*
[b] *Military,* or *police, officers.*
[c] Grk., *confessed* or *agreed to it.*
[d] Lit , *apart from an uprising.*

says to you, "Where is the room in which I am to eat the Passover supper with my disciples?"' ¹² Then he will show you a large room upstairs already furnished. There make the preparations." ¹³ So they went off and found it just as He had said, and they prepared the Passover supper.

¹⁴ Now when the hour came, He took His place at the table, with the apostles about [e] Him. ¹⁵ And He said to them, "I have heartily [f] desired to eat this Passover supper with you before I suffer. ¹⁶ For I tell you, I shall never again eat one until it finds its full fruition [g] in the kingdom of God."

¹⁷ Then He received a cup of wine, gave thanks, and said, "Take this and share it among you, ¹⁸ for I tell you, I shall not after today drink the product of the vine until the kingdom of God comes."

¹⁹ Then He took a loaf, gave thanks, and broke it in pieces, and gave it to them, and said, "This is my body [h] which is to be given [i] for you. Do this as a memorial to me."

²⁰ In like manner after supper He took a cup of wine, and said, "This cup of wine is the new covenant to be ratified by my blood,[hj] which is to be poured out for you. ²¹ Yet look! The hand of the man who is betraying me is with me on the table! ²² For the Son of Man is going away, as it has been divinely decreed, but a curse will be on that man by whom He is betrayed!"

²³ Then they began to discuss among themselves which one it was who was going to do this. ²⁴ There arose also among them a contention as to which one of them should rank [k] as greatest. ²⁵ But He said to them, "The kings of the heathen lord it over them and those who exercise authority over them are given the title of 'Benefactor.' ²⁶ But you are not to do so. On the contrary, the greatest among you must be like the youngest [l] and the leader as the servant. ²⁷ Which one, indeed, is the greater, the guest at the table or the servant who waits on him? Is it not the guest at the table? But I am among you as the servant who waits on you. ²⁸ Yet you have continued to stand by me in my trials; ²⁹ and as my

[e] Grk., *with Him.*
[f] Cog. instr. for emphasis.
[g] Lit., *is filled full.*
[h] Metaphorical language.
[i] Pres. for fut.
[j] Grk., *in my blood;* however, the whole passage about the cup is bracketed by WH.
[k] Grk., *seems to be greatest.*
[l] I.e., do menial services, as is custom in the Orient.

Father has conferred on me a kingdom, ³⁰ so I confer on you the privilege of eating and drinking at my table in my kingdom and of sitting on thrones and judging the twelve tribes of Israel.

³¹ "Simon, Simon, listen! Satan has asked permission to sift all ᵐ of you like wheat, ³² but I have prayed especially for you that your own faith may not utterly fail. And you yourself, after you have turned, must strengthen your brothers."

³³ But Peter said to Him, "Lord, I am ready to go even to prison and to death with you!" ³⁴ But He said, "I tell you, Peter, the cock will not crow today before you deny three times that you know me!"

³⁵ Then He said to them, "When I sent you out without purse or bag or shoes, you did not need anything, did you?"

They answered, "Nothing at all."

³⁶ Then He said to them, "But now the man who has a purse must take it, and a bag too. And the man who does not have a sword must sell his coat and buy one. ³⁷ For I tell you, what has been written about me must be fulfilled: 'He was classed ⁿ with the outlaws.' Yes, that saying about me has its fulfillment." ᵒ

³⁸ So they said, "Lord, look! here are two swords!"

And He answered them, "Enough!"

³⁹ Then He went out of the city and up the Mount of Olives, as He was in the habit of doing; and His disciples, too, followed Him there. ⁴⁰ Now when He reached the spot, He said to them, "Continue to pray that you may not be subjected ᵖ to temptation."

⁴¹ And He Himself withdrew about a stone's throw from them, and after kneeling down He continued to pray, ⁴² "Father, if you are willing, take this cup away from me. Yet, not my will but always ᵠ yours be done!" ʳ

⁴⁵ When He rose from His prayer, He went to the disciples and found them asleep from sorrow. ⁴⁶ Then He said to them, "Why are you sleeping? Get up and keep praying that you may not be subjected ᵖ to temptation."

⁴⁷ While He was still speaking, look! a crowd had come up, and Judas, one of the Twelve, was their guide;ˢ and he stepped up to

---

ᵐ Pl. of *you*; so *all of you.*
ⁿ Grk., *reckoned, counted.*
ᵒ Grk., *has its end;* so *fulfillment.*
ᵖ Grk., *not to enter at all into.*
ᵠ In pres. impv.
ʳ Vv. 43 and 44 om. in best Mss.
ˢ Lit., *was coming before them.*

Jesus to kiss Him. ⁴⁸ Then Jesus said to him, "Judas, will you betray the Son of Man with a kiss?"

⁴⁹ Those who were about Him saw what was about to take place, and said, "Lord, shall we use our swords now?" ᵗ ⁵⁰ Then one of them struck the high priest's slave and cut off his right ear.

⁵¹ But Jesus said, "Permit me to go as far as this!" So He touched his ear and healed him. ⁵² Then Jesus said to the high priests, captains of the temple, and elders, who had come to take Him, "Have you come out with swords and clubs as though I were a robber? ⁵³ While I was among you day after day in the temple, you never laid a hand on me! But this is your opportunity, even the power which darkness ᵘ gives you!"

⁵⁴ Then they arrested Him and led Him away and brought Him to the house of the high priest. Peter was following at a distance. ⁵⁵ And when they had kindled a fire in the middle of the courtyard and had taken their seats together, Peter, too, was sitting among them. ⁵⁶ A servant-girl saw him sitting by the fire and fixed her eyes ᵛ on him and said, "This fellow was with Him too."

⁵⁷ But he denied it and said, "I do not know Him, woman."

⁵⁸ A little later a man looked at ʷ him and said, "You are one of them too."

But Peter said, "Man, I am not." ⁵⁹ About an hour later another man emphatically asserted, "He certainly was with Him, for he is a Galilean!"

⁶⁰ But Peter said, "Man, I do not know what you mean." And all at once, while he was still speaking, a cock crowed. ⁶¹ Then the Lord turned and looked at Peter, and Peter was reminded of the word that the Lord had spoken to him, "Before a cock crows today, you will disown me three times." ⁶² And he went outside and burst ˣ into bitter tears.

⁶³ Then the men who held Him in custody flogged Him and made sport of Him, ⁶⁴ and after blindfolding Him they asked Him, "Play the prophet and tell us who it is that struck you!" ⁶⁵ And they continued to say many other abusive ʸ things to Him.

⁶⁶ As soon as day came, the elders of the people, the high priests,

---

ᵗ Grk., *shall we smite,* etc.
ᵘ Subj. gen.
ᵛ Strong vb. in aor.; hence our tr.
ʷ Aor.
ˣ Ingress aor.
ʸ Grk., *in blaspheming they were saying many other things,* etc.

and the scribes assembled, and brought Him back before their council, and said,⁶⁷ "Tell us, if you are the Christ."

But He said to them, "If I tell you, you will not believe me, ⁶⁸ and if I ask you a question, you will not answer me. ⁶⁹ But from today the Son of Man will be seated at the right hand of the mighty God."

⁷⁰ Then they all asked, "Are you then the Son of God?"

And He answered, "Yes, I am." ᵃ

⁷¹ Then they said, "What more evidence do we need? For we have heard it ourselves from His own mouth!"

23 JESUS STANDS AT THE ROMAN BAR; ANTIPAS MAKES SPORT OF HIM; PILATE DECLARES HIM INNOCENT, BUT LETS THEM CRUCIFY HIM; SIX HOURS OF SUFFERING ON CALVARY; A PENITENT ROBBER PROMISED PARADISE; JOSEPH BURIES JESUS

Then the whole body of them arose and brought Him to Pilate.ᵃ ² Here they began to make the following charges against Him:

"We have found this fellow corrupting our nation and forbidding to pay taxes to Caesar and claiming to be a king himself."

³ Then Pilate asked Him, "Are you the king of the Jews?"

And He answered him, "Yes, I am."

⁴ Then Pilate said to the high priests and crowds, "I do not find anything blameworthy in this man."

⁵ But they continued emphatically insisting, "He is exciting the people by teaching all over Judea. He started in Galilee and now He is here."

⁶ When Pilate heard this, He asked if the man were a Galilean. ⁷ So when he learned with certainty ᵇ that he belonged to Herod's jurisdiction, He sent Him up to Herod, for he was in Jerusalem at that time. ⁸ Now Herod was very glad to see Jesus, for he had been wanting to see Him for a long time on account of what he had heard about Him; also he was hoping to see some spectacular performance ᶜ done by Him. ⁹ So he continued to question Him for a long ᵈ time, but Jesus gave him no answer at all. ¹⁰ Mean-

---
ᵃ Grk., *you say that I am.*
ᵃ Rom. gov. and judge.
ᵇ Comp. vb. means this.
ᶜ Grk., *sign.*
ᵈ Lit., *with many words.*

while the high priests and the scribes stood by and continued vehemently to accuse Him. [11] Then Herod and his body-guard [e] treated Him with contempt and made sport of Him and put a gorgeous robe on Him and sent Him back to Pilate. [12] So Herod and Pilate became personal [f] friends that very day; they had been at enmity before.

[13] Then Pilate called a meeting of the high priests, the leaders of the council, and the people, [14] and said to them, "You brought this man to me on a charge of turning the people from allegiance, and here in your presence I have examined Him and do not find Him guilty of the charges you make against Him. [15] No; nor does Herod, for he has sent Him back to us. Indeed, He has done nothing to deserve the death penalty.[g] [16] So I will flog Him and let Him go." [h]

[18] But they all together began to shout, "Away with this fellow, but let us have Barabbas released! [19] (He was a man who had been put in prison for a riot that had occurred in the city and for murder.) [20] Then Pilate again appealed to them, for He wanted to let Jesus go. [21] But they continued to shout at him, "Crucify Him, crucify Him!"

[22] Then a third time he spoke to them, "Why, what wrong has He done? I have found nothing in Him deserving the death penalty. So I will flog Him and let Him go."

[23] But they continued to press him with loud voices in their ceaseless demands that He be crucified, and their shouts [i] began to prevail. [24] Then Pilate pronounced his sentence that their demand be carried out. [25] So he released the man who had been put in prison for riot and murder, whom they continued to demand, but turned Jesus over to their will.

[26] Now as they led Him away, they seized a man named Simon, from Cyrene,[j] as he was coming in from the country, and put the cross on his shoulders, for him to carry as he walked [k] behind Jesus. [27] There was following Him also a vast throng of the people and of women who were beating their breasts and lamenting Him.

[28] But Jesus turned to the women and said, "Women of Jerusalem, stop weeping for me, but continue to weep for yourselves

---

[e] Grk., *his soldiers*.
[f] Lit., *friends with one another*.
[g] Lit., *worthy of death*.
[h] V. 17 om. by most ancient Mss.
[i] Grk., *voices*.
[j] In N. Africa, but he is not a Negro.
[k] Implied.

and for your children. ²⁹ For a time is coming when people will say, 'Happy are the women who are childless, and the women who have never borne and nursed babies!' ³⁰ Then people will begin to say to the mountains, 'Fall upon us!' and to the hills, 'Cover us up!' ³¹ For if they do this when the wood is green, what will they do when it is dry?"

³² Two others, criminals, were also led out to be executed with Him.

³³ When they reached the place called "The Skull," they crucified Him there; also the criminals, one at His right and one at His left. ³⁴ *They drew lots¹ to divide His clothes among them. ³⁵ Meanwhile the people stood looking on. Even the members of the council ᵐ were scoffing at Him and saying, "He saved others, let Him now save Himself, if He really is the Christ of God, His Chosen One!"

³⁶ The soldiers also made sport of Him as they continued to come up and offer Him vinegar, ³⁷ and to say, "If you are the king of the Jews, save yourself!" ³⁸ Yes, there was a placard above His head: "THIS IS THE KING OF THE JEWS."

³⁹ Now one of the criminals who were hanging from their crosses kept abusing Him, saying, "Are you not the Christ? Then save yourself and us too!"

⁴⁰ But the other one reproved him and said, "Do you not fear even God when you are suffering the same penalty? ⁴¹ And we are suffering it justly, for we are getting our deserts for what we have done, but this man has done nothing wrong." ⁿ ⁴²Then he went on to say, "Jesus, remember me when you come in your kingdom!"

⁴³ So He said to him, "I solemnly say to you, this very day you will be in paradise with me."

⁴⁴ It was already about noon, and darkness covered ᵒ the whole country, and lasted until three o'clock, ⁴⁵ for the sun had failed to shine.ᵖ And the curtain before the sanctuary was torn in two.ᑫ

⁴⁶ Then Jesus uttered a loud cry, and said, "Father, I now commit my spirit to your care." As He said this He breathed His last.ʳ

* Oldest and best Mss. omit "And Jesus said ... what they do."
¹ Grk., *cast lots.*
ᵐ Grk., *rulers, leaders.*
ⁿ Lit., *nothing out of the way.*
ᵒ Grk., *came over.*
ᵖ Grk., *was darkened.*
ᑫ Lit., *split in the middle.*
ʳ Lit., *breathed out.*

⁴⁷ When the captain saw what had taken place, he praised God and said, "He certainly was an innocent ˢ man!"

⁴⁸ And all the crowds who had come together for this sight, when they had seen what took place, returned to the city ᵗ but continued to beat their breasts in grief.ᵘ ⁴⁹ But all His acquaintances, and the women who used to follow Him from Galilee in a group,ᵛ were standing at a distance looking on.

⁵⁰ Now there was a man named Joseph, a member of the council, a good and upright man, ⁵¹ who had not voted ʷ for the plan and action of the council. He came from a Jewish town, Arimathea, and he was waiting for the kingdom of God. ⁵² He went to Pilate and asked for Jesus' body. ⁵³ Then he took it down from the cross and wrapped it in a linen sheet and laid it in a tomb hewn out of rock, where no one had yet been laid. ⁵⁴ It was the Preparation Day, and the sabbath was just beginning. ⁵⁵ So the women, who had come with Jesus ˣ from Galilee, followed closely after Joseph ˣ and saw the tomb and how His body was laid there. ⁵⁶ Then they went back home,ʸ and prepared spices and perfumes.

24 THE TOMB FOUND EMPTY BY THE WOMEN; THE STORY OF JESUS' MAKING HIMSELF KNOWN TO TWO DISCIPLES AT EMMAUS; HE APPEARS TO PETER, THEN TO A GROUP OF DISCIPLES IN JERUSALEM; HE GIVES HIS FAREWELL MESSAGE; ASCENDS TO HEAVEN

Now on the sabbath they rested, in accordance with the commandment, but on the first day of the week at early dawn they went to the tomb, taking the spices which they had prepared. ² But they found the boulder rolled back from the tomb, ³ and yet on going inside they did not find the body.ᵃ

⁴ And as they were being perplexed about this, two men in dazzling robes suddenly took their stand beside them. ⁵ Because the

---

ˢ Grk., *righteous.*
ᵗ Implied.
ᵘ Meaning of beating the breast.
ᵛ Grk., *together.*
ʷ Grk., *had not put himself down with.*
ˣ Grk. has pros.; nouns nec. in Eng.
ʸ Implied.
ᵃ Phrase, *of the Lord Jesus,* om. by WH.

women were so frightened and were turning their faces to the ground, they said to them, "Why are you looking among the dead for Him who is alive? 6 [He is not here but has risen.]b Remember what He told you while He was still in Galilee, when 7 He said that the Son of Man had to be turned over to wicked men and crucified, but was to rise again on the third day."

8 Then they recalled His words 9 and returned from the tomb and reported all these things to the Eleven and all the rest. 10 They were Mary of Magdala and Joanna, and Mary, James's mother, who, with the other women, reported these things to the apostles. 11 But the report seemed to them to be nonsense, and so they continued to disbelieve the women.c 12 [Peter, however, got up and ran to the tomb, and stooped down and saw the linen clothes but nothing else. Then he went home d wondering at what had taken place.]e

13 On that very day, strange to say, two of them were on their way to a village called Emmaus, about seven miles from Jerusalem, 14 and were talking together about all these things that had taken place. 15 And as they were talking, and discussing these things, Jesus Himself came up near to them and continued to walk with them, 16 but their eyes were in suchf a state as to keep them from recognizing Him.

17 Then He said to them, "What is this that you are discussing together as you walk?"

So they stopped and stood stillg with puzzled countenances. 18 Finally one of them, whose name was Cleopas, answered Him, "Are you the only visitorh to Jerusalem who has not heardi of the things that have taken place there in these last days?"

19 And He said to them, "What sortj of things?"

They answered Him, "The things about Jesus of Nazareth, who in the sight of God and of all the people became a prophet mighty in deed and word, 20 and how the high priests and leading men turned Him over to be sentenced to death, and had Him crucified. 21 But we kept hoping that He was the One who was coming to set

---

b This sentence bracketed by WH.
c Fem. pro. in Grk.
d Implied.
e Bracketed by WH, though in many old Mss.
f Grk., *eyes held so as not to recog. Him.*
g Suggested by aor.
h Vb. means *to sojourn.*
i Lit., *has not come to know.*
j Interrog. of quality.

Israel free.ᵏ Moreover, besides all this, it is now the third day since these things occurred. ²² Yes, indeed, some women of our number have astounded us! They went to the tomb early this morning ²³ and could not find His body, but came and told us that they had actually had a vision of angels who said He was alive. ²⁴ Then some of our company went to the tomb and found it just as the women had said, but they did not see Him."

²⁵ Then He said to them, "O men sluggish in mind and slow in heart to believe all that the prophets have said! ²⁶ Did not the Christ have to suffer these things and thus to enter into His glory?" ²⁷ Then He began with Moses and went through all the prophets and explained to them all the passages¹ in the Scriptures about Himself.

²⁸ Then they approached the village to which they were going, and He acted as though He were going on farther, ²⁹ but they earnestly urged Him, and said, "Stop and stay ᵐ with us, for it is getting toward evening and the day is nearly spent."

So He went in to stay with them. ³⁰ And after He had taken His place at table with them, He took the loaf and blessed it and broke it in pieces and handed it to them. ³¹ Then their eyes were instantly opened and they recognized Him, and at once He vanished from them.

³² Then they said to each other, "Did not our hearts keep burning in our bosoms ⁿ as He was talking to us on the road, as He went on explaining the Scriptures to us?" ³³ So at once ᵒ they got up and went back to Jerusalem and found the Eleven and their company ᵖ all together, ³⁴ who told them that the Lord had really risen and had been seen by Simon. ³⁵ Then they themselves began to tell what had occurred ᑫ on the road, and how He was recognized by them when He broke the loaf in pieces.

³⁶ Even while they were talking about these things, He took ʳ His stand among them Himself, [and said to them, "Peace to you!"]ˢ

ᵏ Grk., *ransom.*
¹ Lit., *the things in all the Scriptures.*
ᵐ *Stop* in aor., *stay* in vb.
ⁿ Grk., *in us.*
ᵒ Lit., *at that very hour.*
ᵖ Lit., *those with them.*
ᑫ Grk., *the things on the road.*
ʳ Aor. means this.
ˢ So in WH, though found in some ancient Mss.

LUKE 24

³⁷ and they were so startled and terror-stricken that they were beginning to think that they saw a ghost.

³⁸ But He said to them, "Why are you so disturbed and why are doubts arising in your hearts? ³⁹ Look at my hands and my feet, for it is I, myself. Feel of me and see for yourselves, for a ghost does not have flesh and bones, as you see I have." ⁴⁰[After He had said this He showed them His hands and His feet.]ˢ

⁴¹ So while they were still disbelieving for sheer joy and still wondering about it, He asked them, "Have you anything here to eat?" ⁴² Then they gave Him a piece of broiled fish, ⁴³ and He took it and ate it before their eyes.ᵗ

⁴⁴ Then He said to them, "This is what I told you while I was still with you, that everything which is written about me in the law of Moses, in the prophets, and in the Psalms, had to be fulfilled."

⁴⁵ Then He opened their minds so that they might continue to understand the Scriptures, ⁴⁶ and said to them, "The Scriptures said that the Christ should suffer as He has suffered,ᵘ should rise from the dead on the third day, ⁴⁷ and that in His name repentance as the condition ᵛ for the forgiveness of sins should be preached to all the nations. Beginning at Jerusalem ⁴⁸ you are to continue as witnesses to these things. ⁴⁹ And I will send down upon you what my Father has promised. But you, on your part, must stay right here in the city until you are clothed with power from on high."

⁵⁰ Then He led them out as far as Bethany, and lifted up His hands and blessed them. ⁵¹ And while He was blessing them, He parted from them, and was taken up to heaven.ʷ ⁵² And with great joy they went back to Jerusalem; ⁵³ and they were continually in the temple, praising God.

ᵗ Grk., *before them.*
ˢ Lit., *in this way.*
ᵛ Grk., *repentance with a view to forgiveness,* etc.
ʷ Fol. B, the best Ms., though WH text brackets last clause.

JOHN

The writer is likely John the apostle, a view supported by the statements made by early Christian writers, Polycarp, Irenaeus, and others, and also by evidence furnished by the Gospel itself, suggesting that he was a Palestinian Jew who was an eyewitness of most of the events discussed. However, some scholars think another John wrote it.

It was occasioned by the presence, in the province of Asia, of Gnosticism, a blend of Greek philosophy, oriental religions, and Christianity, which was undermining faith in Jesus' divinity and power to save men. It was written about A. D. 90 to 95.

The purpose was to counteract the influence of Gnosticism, to prove that Jesus is the eternal Son of God, but as a real human being is the photograph of God to men, and only through Him, by faith that conditions the renewing power of the Spirit, can men be saved.

This Gospel is written in the simplest everyday Greek of that period, and we have sought to put the translation in the simplest English.

1 THE ETERNAL WORD BECAME HUMAN, TO MAKE GOD KNOWN TO MEN, TO MAKE MEN GOD'S CHILDREN; THE BAPTIST'S TESTIMONY TO JESUS; JESUS' FIRST DISCIPLES

In the beginning the Word existed; and the Word was face to face with God; yea, the Word was God Himself.[a] 2 He is the One who was face to face with God in the beginning. 3 It was through Him that everything came into existence,[b] and apart from Him not a single thing came into existence. 4 It was by[c] Him that life began to exist, and that life was the light of mankind. 5 So the light continues to shine in the darkness, for[d] the darkness has never overpowered it.

6 There appeared a man named John, sent from God. 7 He came for the purpose of testifying, to testify to the light, so that every-

[a] Prep. for *face to face;* exact meaning; word, *God,* emphatic, so *God Himself.*
[b] Grk., *became.*
[c] Instr. use of prep. *en.*
[d] *And* in Ara. sense, so, *for.*

JOHN 1

one through him might come to believe. [8] He was not the light; he came to testify to the light. [9] The real light, which sheds light upon everyone, was just coming into the world.[e] [10] He came into the world, and though [f] the world through Him began to exist, it did not recognize Him. [11] He came into His own world, but His own people did not welcome Him. [12] But to all who did accept Him, and trust in His name, He gave the right to become the children of God, [13] who were born of God and not of natural blood [g] nor of physical or human impulse.[h]

[14] So the Word became human [i] and lived a little while [j] among us, and we actually saw [k] His glory, the glory of One who is an only Son from His Father, and He was full of spiritual blessing and truth. [15] John testified to Him and cried out, for this was the one who said, "The One who is coming after me has been put before me, because He existed before me."

[16] For from His bounty we have all received spiritual blessing after spiritual blessing.[l] [17] For while the law was given through Moses, spiritual blessing and truth have come through Jesus Christ. [18] No one has ever seen God; the only son, Deity Himself,[m] who lies upon His Father's breast, has made him known.[n]

[19] Now this is the testimony which John gave when the Jews sent priests and Levites to him from Jerusalem, to ask him, "Who are you?"

[20] He frankly admitted, and did not try at all to deny it; yes, he frankly admitted, "I am not the Christ."

[21] So they asked him again, "What are you then? Elijah?"

And he answered, "Of course, I am not."

"Are you the prophet?"

He answered, "No."

[22] Then they said to him, "Who are you? Tell us, so that we can have an answer to give to those who sent us. What have you to say for yourself?"

---

[e] Fol. WH.
[f] Implied.
[g] Grk., *from bloods.*
[h] Lit., *nor of the will of flesh or man.*
[i] Grk., *became flesh.*
[j] Grk., *tented.*
[k] Histor. aor. of strong vb.
[l] Lit., *grace for grace.*
[m] Fol. WH and ancient Mss.
[n] Grk., *interpreted Him.*

JOHN 1

²³ He said, "I am a voice of one shouting in the desert, 'Make the road straight for the Lord,' as the prophet Isaiah said." °

²⁴ Now the messengers belonged to the party ᵖ of the Pharisees; ²⁵ so they asked him, "Why are you baptizing then, if you are not the Christ, nor Elijah, nor the prophet?"

²⁶ John answered them, "I am baptizing only in water. There is standing among you One with whom you are not acquainted. ²⁷ He is to become my successor,ᑫ because He has been put before me, and I am not fit to untie His shoestrings." ²⁸ This took place at Bethany on the farther side of the Jordan, where John was baptizing.

²⁹ The next day John saw Jesus coming toward him, and he said, "Look! He is the Lamb of God who is to take away the world's sin. ³⁰ This is the One about whom I said, 'After me there is coming a man who has already been put before me, because He existed before me.' ³¹ I did not know Him myself, but I came baptizing in water, that He might be made known to Israel."

³² Then John gave this testimony:

"I saw the Spirit coming down from heaven like a dove, and it remained on Him. ³³ I did not know Him myself, but the very One who sent me to baptize in water said to me, 'The One on whom you see the Spirit coming down and remaining, is the One who is to baptize in the Holy Spirit.' ³⁴ I did see ʳ it, and my testimony is ʳ that He is the Son of God."

³⁵ Again the next day John was standing with two of his disciples, ³⁶ and as he saw Jesus passing by he said, "Look! He is the Lamb of God!"

³⁷ The two disciples heard him say this, and so they followed Jesus. ³⁸ Now Jesus turned, and as He saw them following Him, He said, "What are you looking for?"

They said to Him, "Rabbi," (which means Teacher), "where are you staying?"

³⁹ He said to them, "Come and you will see." So they went and saw where He was staying, and they spent the rest ˢ of the day with Him; it was about four in the afternoon.

⁴⁰ Andrew, Simon Peter's brother, was one of the two who heard

---

° Isa. 40:3.
ᵖ Grk., *were of the Pharisees.*
ᑫ Grk., *He is to come after me.*
ʳ Both vbs. in pf., emphasizing the results as still present; hence our tr.
ˢ Lit., *that is, from four on.*

John and followed Jesus.[t] [41] He first found his brother Simon and said to him, "We have found the Messiah" (which means, the Christ). [42] Then he took him to Jesus.

Jesus looked him over and said, "You are Simon, son of John. From now on your name [u] shall be Cephas" (which means Peter, or Rock).

[43] The next day Jesus decided to leave for Galilee. So He sought out Philip and said to him, "Follow me."

[44] Now Philip was from Bethsaida, the town of Andrew and Peter. [45] Philip sought out Nathaniel and said to him, "We have found the One about whom Moses wrote in the law and the One about whom the prophets wrote; it is Jesus, the son of Joseph, who comes from Nazareth."

[46] Then Nathaniel said to him, "Can anything good come out of Nazareth?"

Philip said to him, "Come and see."

[47] Jesus saw Nathaniel coming toward Him, and said of him, "Here is a genuine [v] Israelite with no deceit in him!"

[48] Nathaniel said to Him, "How do you know me?"

Jesus answered him, "While you were still under the fig tree, before Philip called you, I saw you."

[49] Nathaniel answered Him, "Teacher,[w] you are the Son of God, you are the king of Israel!"

[50] Jesus answered him, "Do you believe in me because I told you that I saw you under the fig tree? You will see greater things than this." [51] Then He said to him, "I most solemnly[x] say to you all, you[y] will see heaven opened and the angels of God going up, and coming down upon the Son of Man!"

2 JESUS PERFORMING HIS FIRST WONDER-WORK, TURNING WATER INTO WINE; DRIVING THE TRADERS OUT OF THE TEMPLE COURT

Two days later [a] there was a wedding at Cana in Galilee, and Jesus' mother was there. [2] Jesus and His disciples, too, were in-

---

[t] Pro. in Grk.
[u] Lit., *you shall be called.*
[v] Grk., *truly.*
[w] *Rabbi;* means *Teacher.*
[x] *Verily, verily.*
[y] *You* in pl.
[a] Grk., *on the third day.*

vited to the wedding. ³ When the wine was all gone, Jesus' mother said to Him, "They have no wine!"

⁴ Jesus said to her, "Woman, what have you to do with me? My time to act [b] has not yet come."

⁵ His mother said to the servants, "Do whatever He tells you."

⁶ Now in accordance with the custom [c] of purification [d] practiced by the Jews, six stone water jars were standing there, each holding from twenty to thirty gallons. ⁷ Jesus said to them, "Fill these jars with water." So they filled them up to the brim. ⁸ Then He said to them, "Now draw some [e] out and take it to the manager [f] of the feast." So they took him some.

⁹ As soon as the manager tasted the water just turned into wine, without knowing where it came from, although the servants who had drawn the water did know, He called the bridegroom ¹⁰ and said to him, "Everybody, as a rule,[g] serves his good wine first, and his poorer wine after people have drunk freely; you have kept the good wine till now."

¹¹ Jesus performed this, the first of His wonder-works,[h] at Cana in Galilee. By it He showed His glorious power,[i] and so His disciples believed in Him.

¹² After this Jesus went home to Capernaum, with His mother and brothers and disciples, and stayed there for a few days.

¹³ Now the Jewish Passover was approaching; so Jesus went up to Jerusalem. ¹⁴ And in the temple court He found the dealers [j] in cattle, sheep, and pigeons; the money-changers, too, seated at their tables. ¹⁵ So He made a lash out of cords, and drove them all, together with the sheep and cattle, out of the temple court, scattered the money-changers' coins and upset their tables. ¹⁶ Then He said to the pigeon-dealers, "Take these things out of here! Stop using my Father's house as a market place!"

¹⁷ His disciples recalled that the Scriptures say, "My zeal for your house will consume me!" [k]

[b] Implied.
[c] Implied.
[d] *Washing hands, vessels,* etc. as a religious duty.
[e] Grk., *out of.*
[f] Lit., *ruler;* our *manager,* or *toastmaster.*
[g] Gen. pres.
[h] Grk., *sign,* the usual term for *miracle* in Jno.
[i] Grk., *showed His glory.*
[j] Lit., *those who sell.*
[k] Ps. 69:9.

¹⁸ Then the Jews addressed Him and asked,¹ "What sign can you show us that you have authority ᵐ to act in this way?"

¹⁹ Jesus answered them, "Destroy this sanctuary, and I will raise it in three days."

²⁰ Then the Jews retorted,ⁿ "It took forty-six years to build ᵒ this sanctuary, and you are going to raise it in three days!" ²¹ But He meant the sanctuary of His body. ²² So after He had risen from the dead, His disciples recalled that He had said this, and so believed the Scripture ᵖ and the statement that He had made.

²³ Now while He was in Jerusalem at the Passover Feast, many people, because they saw the wonder-works which He was performing, trusted in Him as the Christ.ᑫ ²⁴ But He would not trust Himself to them, because He knew all men ²⁵ and needed no testimony from anyone about them, for He well knew what was in human nature.ʳ

3 JESUS TELLS NICODEMUS ABOUT THE NEW BIRTH; GOD'S LOVE AND HIS SON'S MISSION TO THE WORLD; JOHN FURTHER TESTIFIES TO JESUS

Now there was a man named Nicodemus, who belonged to the party of the Pharisees and was a leader among the Jews. ² He came to Jesus one night and said to Him, "Teacher, we know that you have come from God, for no one can perform the wonder-works that you are doing, unless God is with him."

³ Jesus answered him, "I most solemnly say to you, no one can ever see the kingdom of God, unless he is born from above."

⁴ Nicodemus said to Him, "How can a man be born when he is old? He cannot again enter his mother's womb and be born, can he?"

⁵ Jesus answered, "I most solemnly say to you, no one can ever get into the kingdom of God, unless he is born of water and the Spirit.ᵃ ⁶ Whatever is born of the physical ᵇ is physical, and whatever is born of the Spirit is spiritual. ⁷ Never wonder at my telling

---

¹ Lit., *answered and said.*
ᵐ Implied.
ⁿ Grk., *said.*
ᵒ Grk. has passive; active smoother in Eng.
ᵖ That is, the passage just quoted.
ᑫ Lit., *trusted in His name.*
ʳ Lit., *about man*—He knew what was in man.
ᵃ Water the symbol, the Spirit, the agent, of renewal.
ᵇ Grk., *flesh.*

you that you must all be born from above. ⁸ The wind blows where it pleases, and you hear the sound of it, but you do not know where it comes from or where it goes. That is just the way ᵉ it is with everyone who is born of the Spirit."

⁹ Then Nicodemus answered by asking, "How can this be?"

¹⁰ Jesus answered him, "Are you a teacher of Israel and do not know this? ¹¹ I most solemnly say to you, we know what we are talking about and we have seen what we are testifying to, yet you are all ᵈ rejecting our testimony. ¹² If you do not believe the earthly ᵉ things I tell you, how can you believe the heavenly things, if I tell you about them? ¹³ And yet no one has gone up into heaven except the Son of Man who came down out of heaven.ᶠ ¹⁴ And just as Moses in the desert lifted the serpent on the pole,ᵍ the Son of Man must be lifted up,ʰ ¹⁵ so that everyone who trusts in Him may have eternal life.

¹⁶ "For God loved the world so much that He gave His Only Son,ⁱ so that anyone who trusts in Him may never perish but have eternal life. ¹⁷ For God sent His Son into the world, not to pass sentence on it,ʲ but that the world through Him might be saved. ¹⁸ Whoever trusts in Him is never to come up for judgment; but whoever does not trust in Him has already received his sentence, because he has not trusted in the name of God's only Son. ¹⁹ And the ground ᵏ for the sentence is this, that the light has come into the world, and yet, because their actions were evil, men have loved darkness more than the light. ²⁰ For anyone who is in the habit of doing wrong hates the light, and to keep his actions from being reproved, he does not come out into the daylight. ²¹ But whoever is in the habit of living ˡ the truth will come out in the daylight, that his actions may be shown to be performed with God's help."

²² After this, Jesus and His disciples went into Judea,ᵐ and for some time He stayed there with them and kept baptizing people. ²³ But John too was baptizing people at Aenon, near Salim, for

---

ᶜ I.e., as mysterious as the wind's blowing.
ᵈ *You,* in pl.
ᵉ Necessity of new birth.
ᶠ Only Jesus can reveal them.
ᵍ Implied.
ʰ On the cross.
ⁱ *Only begotten* in Grk.
ʲ *World* repeated.
ᵏ Grk., *this is the judgment.*
ˡ Grk., *doing.*
ᵐ Lit., *Judean land.*

there was plenty of water there, and so the people were coming and being baptized. ²⁴ (For John had not yet been put in prison.) ²⁵ Then a discussion came up between John's disciples and a Jew about purification. ²⁶ And they went to John and said to him, "Teacher, the man who was with you on the other side of the Jordan, to whom you bore testimony yourself, is baptizing people and everybody is going to Him."

²⁷ John answered, "A man cannot get anything, unless it is given to him from heaven. ²⁸ You can bear testimony to me yourselves that I said, 'I am not the Christ, but I have been sent as His announcer.'ⁿ ²⁹ It is the bridegroom who has the bride, but the bridegroom's friend, who stands outside and listens to him, is very happy to hear the bridegroom's voice.º So this happiness of mine is running over. ³⁰ He must grow greater and greater,ᵖ but I less and less."ᵖ

³¹ He who comes from above is far above all others. He who springs from earth belongs to the earth and speaks of earth. He who comes from heaven is far above all others. ³² He continues to bear testimony to what He has actually seen and heard, and yet no one accepts His testimony. ³³ Whoever does accept His testimony has certified ᑫ with a seal that God is true. ³⁴ For He whom God has sent continues to speak the words of God, for God continues to give Him the Spirit without measure. ³⁵ The Father loves His Son and has put everything in His hands. ³⁶ Whoever trusts in the Son possesses eternal life, but whoever refuses to trust ʳ in the Son will not see life, but the wrath of God continues to remain on him.

4 JESUS LEAVES JUDEA FOR GALILEE; TALKS WITH THE WOMAN OF SAMARIA AND TELLS HER HE IS THE TEACHING MESSIAH; THE MEN OF SYCHAR HEAR HIM AND PROCLAIM HIM THE SAVIOUR OF THE WORLD

Now when the Lord learned that the Pharisees had heard that He was winning ᵃ and baptizing more disciples than John—² though

---

ⁿ Grk., *before Him, to introduce Him.*
º Grk., *on account of his voice.*
ᵖ In impf.
ᑫ Lit., *sealed;* certified with a seal.
ʳ Grk., *is without trust, does not trust.*
ᵃ Grk., *gaining.*

Jesus Himself was not baptizing, it was His disciples—³ He left Judea and went back again to Galilee. ⁴ And He had to go through Samaria. ⁵ So He came to a town in Samaria called Sychar, near the field which Jacob gave to his son Joseph; ⁶ and Jacob's spring was there. So Jesus, tired from His journey, was sitting by the spring just as He was.[b] It was about noon. ⁷ A woman of Samaria came to draw water. Jesus said to her, "Give me a drink." ⁸ For His disciples had gone into the town to buy some food.

⁹ So the Samaritan woman said to Him, "How is it that a Jew like you asks a Samaritan woman like me for a drink?" For Jews have nothing to do with Samaritans.

¹⁰ Jesus answered her, "If you just knew what God has to give[c] and who it is that said to you, 'Give me a drink,' you would have been the one[d] to ask Him, and He would have given you living water."

¹¹ She said to Him, "You have nothing to draw with, sir, and the well is deep. Where do you get your living water? ¹² You are not greater than our forefather Jacob, are you, who gave us this well, and drank from it himself, with all his sons and flocks?"

¹³ Jesus answered her, "Anyone who drinks this water will get thirsty again; ¹⁴ but whoever drinks the water that I will give him will never, no never, be thirsty again, for the water that I will give him will become a spring of water that keeps on bubbling[e] up within him for eternal life."

¹⁵ The woman said to Him, "Give me this water at once, sir, so I may never get thirsty again, nor have to come so far[f] to draw water."

¹⁶ He said to her, "Go and call your husband and come back here."

¹⁷ The woman answered, "I have no husband."

Jesus said to her, "You were right in saying, 'I have no husband,' ¹⁸ for you have had five husbands, and the man you now have is not your husband. What you have said is true."

¹⁹ The woman said to Him, "I see that you are a prophet. ²⁰ Our forefathers worshiped on this mountain, but you Jews say that

---

[b] Lit., *thus* or *so*, emph.; without washing, etc.
[c] Grk., *the gift of God*.
[d] *You*, very emph.; hence this tr.
[e] Grk., *leaping*.
[f] Lit., *hither, to this place*.

Jerusalem ᵍ is the place where people ought to worship Him."

²¹ Jesus said to her, "Believe me, woman, the time is coming when you will worship the Father neither on this mountain nor in Jerusalem. ²² You Samaritans do not know what you are worshiping; we Jews do know what we are worshiping, for salvation comes from the Jews. ²³ But a time is coming—indeed, it is already here—when the real worshipers will worship the Father in spirit and reality,ʰ for the Father is looking for just such worshipers. ²⁴ God is a spiritual Being,ⁱ and his worshipers must worship Him in spirit and reality."

²⁵ The woman said to Him, "I know that the Messiah is coming, the One who is called the Christ. When He comes, He will tell us everything."

²⁶ Jesus said to her, "I, the very one who is talking to you, am He!"

²⁷ Just then His disciples came up, and they were surprised to find Him talking with a woman, yet not one of them asked Him, "What do you want?" or "Why are you talking with her?"

²⁸ The woman then left her pitcher and went back to town and said to the people, ²⁹ "Come, see a man who has told me everything I ever did. He is not the Christ, is He?" ³⁰ So the people left town and rushed out to see ʲ Him.

³¹ Meanwhile the disciples were asking Him, and saying, "Teacher, eat something."

³² But He said to them, "I have food to eat of which you do not know."

³³ So the disciples began to say to one another, "Nobody has brought Him anything to eat, has he?"

³⁴ Jesus said to them, "My food is to do the will of Him who sent me, and to finish His work. ³⁵ Are you not saying, 'In four months more the harvest comes'? Look! I tell you, lift up your eyes and scan the fields, for they are already white for harvesting. ³⁶ Now the reaper is already getting pay, for ᵏ he is gathering a crop for eternal life, so that the sower and the reaper may rejoice together. ³⁷ For in this matter the adage is true, 'One sows, another

---

ᵍ Grk., *in Jerusalem is the place*.
ʰ Grk., *in spirit and truth;* i.e., sincerely, which is really to worship.
ⁱ Lit., *God is Spirit;* no art. emphasizes His spiritual being.
ʲ Lit., *were coming to Him; to see,* implied.
ᵏ Heb. use of *and*.

reaps.' ³⁸ I have sent you to reap a harvest which you have not labored to make. Other men have labored, but you have reaped the results of their labors."¹

³⁹ Many of the Samaritans in that town believed in Him because of the woman's testimony, when she said, "He has told me everything I ever did." ⁴⁰ So when the Samaritans came to Jesus, they kept on urging ᵐ Him to stay with them; so He did stay there two days. ⁴¹ Then a much larger number believed in Him because of what He said Himself, ⁴² and they were saying to the woman, "It is not merely because of what you said that we now believe, for we have heard Him ourselves, and we know that He is really the Saviour of the world."

⁴³ After the two days were over, Jesus left there and went on to Galilee, ⁴⁴ for He Himself declared ⁿ that a prophet had no honor in his own country. ⁴⁵ So when He reached Galilee, the Galileans welcomed Him, for they had seen everything that He had done at the feast in Jerusalem, for they too had attended the feast.

⁴⁶ So He came back to Cana in Galilee where He had turned the water into wine. Now there was at Capernaum an officer of the king's court ᵒ whose son was sick. ⁴⁷ When he heard that Jesus had come back from Judea to Galilee, he went to Him and began to beg Him to come down and cure his son, for he was at the point of death. ⁴⁸ Then Jesus said to him, "Unless you see signs and wonders, you will never believe."

⁴⁹ The king's officer pleaded with Him, "Sir, come down at once ᵖ before my child is dead!"

⁵⁰ Jesus said to him, "You may go; your son is going to live."

The man believed what ᑫ Jesus said to him and started home. ⁵¹ While he was still coming down, his slaves met him and told him, "Your boy is going to live." ⁵² So he asked them at what hour he began ʳ to get better, and they said to him, "Yesterday at one ˢ o'clock the fever left him."

⁵³ Then the father knew that that was the very hour when Jesus had said to him, "Your son is going to live." So he and his whole

---

¹ Grk., *have entered into their labors.*
ᵐ Lit., *asking.*
ⁿ Grk., *testified.*
ᵒ Likely an attendant of one of the Herods.
ᵖ In aor. impv.
ᑫ Grk., *the word that Jesus spoke.*
ʳ Ingress. aor.
ˢ Lit., *at the seventh hr.* As Rom. day started at 6 A.M., this is 1 P.M.

household believed in Jesus.[t] ⁵⁴ This is the second wonder-work that Jesus performed after He had come back from Judea to Galilee.

5   A CRIPPLED MAN CURED; THE PHARISEES RAISE A CONTROVERSY BECAUSE HE WAS CURED ON THE SABBATH; JESUS ANNOUNCES HE IS THE RESURRECTION LIFE

After this there was a feast of the Jews, and so Jesus went up to Jerusalem. ² Now in Jerusalem near the sheep-gate there is a pool called in Hebrew Bethzatha,[a] which has five porticoes,[b] ³ and in these there used to lie a great crowd of sick people, blind, crippled, paralyzed.[c] ⁵ And there was one man there who had been an invalid for thirty-eight years. ⁶ Jesus saw him lying there, and when He found out that he had been in that condition for a long time, He asked him, "Do you want to get well?"

⁷ The sick man answered, "Sir, I have no one to put me into the pool when the water is moved, but while I am trying to get down, somebody else steps down ahead of me."

⁸ Jesus said to him, "Get up, pick up your pallet, and go to walking." ⁹ And at once the man was well, and picked up his pallet, and went to walking.

Now it was the sabbath.[d] ¹⁰ So the Jews began to say to the man who had been cured, "It is the sabbath, and it is against the law for you to carry your pallet."

¹¹ He answered them, "The man who cured me said to me, 'Pick up your pallet and go to walking.'"

¹² They asked him, "Who is the man that said to you, 'Pick up your pallet and go to walking'?" ¹³ The man who had been cured did not know who He was, for since there was a crowd at the place, Jesus had slipped away.

¹⁴ Afterward Jesus found him in the temple court, and said to him, "See! You are now [e] well. Stop sinning or something worse may [f] befall you." ¹⁵ The man went back and told the Jews that it

[t] Pro. in Grk.
[a] Means *House of Olives*.
[b] Almost like wards.
[c] V. 4 not in best Mss.
[d] Grk., *sabbath on that day.*
[e] Pf., *have become well.*
[f] Lit., *lest,* etc

was Jesus who had cured him. ¹⁶ This is why the Jews were persecuting Jesus, because He persisted [g] in doing such things on the sabbath.

¹⁷ Then He answered them, "My Father is still working, and so am I." ¹⁸ It was on account of this that the Jews tried all the harder [h] to put Him to death, because He not only persisted in breaking the sabbath, but also kept on saying that God was His Father, and so was making Himself equal to God.

¹⁹ So Jesus answered them:

"I most solemnly say to you, the Son can do nothing by Himself, except as He sees the Father doing it, for whatever the Father is in the habit of doing the Son also persists in doing. ²⁰ For the Father loves the Son and shows Him everything that He Himself is doing, and He will show Him greater deeds than these, so that you will keep on wondering. ²¹ For just as the Father raises the dead and makes them live on, so the Son too makes alive any whom He chooses to. ²² For the Father passes sentence on no one, but He has committed all judgment to the Son, ²³ that all men may honor the Son as they do the Father. Whoever does not honor the Son does not honor the Father who sent Him.

²⁴ "I most solemnly say to you, whoever listens to me and believes Him who has sent me possesses eternal life, and will never come under [i] condemnation, but has already passed out of death into life. ²⁵ I most solemnly say to you, a time is coming—indeed, it is already here—when the dead will listen to the voice of the Son of God, and those who listen to it will live. ²⁶ For just as the Father has life in Himself, so He has granted to the Son to have life in Himself. ²⁷ He has also granted to Him authority to act as Judge,[j] because He is the Son of Man. ²⁸ Stop being surprised at this, for the time is coming when all that are in the graves will listen to His voice, ²⁹ and those who have done good will come out for a resurrection [k] to life,[l] but those who have done evil for a resurrection to condemnation.[l] ³⁰ I cannot do anything by myself. As I get orders,[m] so I judge, and my judgment is a just one,

[g] Impf. of cont. action.
[h] Grk., *were trying the more.*
[i] Grk., *into.*
[j] Lit., *do justice,* judgment.
[k] Quality here emphasized.
[l] Obj. gen.
[m] Grk., *as I hear.*

JOHN 5

for I am not trying[n] to do my own will but the will of Him who has sent me.

[31] "If I bear witness to myself, my testimony is of no force.[o] [32] There is someone else who testifies to me, and I know that the testimony which He gives to me is of force. [33] You yourselves sent to John, and he has testified to the truth. [34] However, I do not accept mere human[p] testimony, but I am saying this that you may be saved. [35] John[q] was the lamp that kept on burning and shining, and you decided for a time to delight yourselves in his light. [36] But I have testimony that is higher[r] than John's, for the works which my Father has committed to me to finish, the very works that I am doing, testify to me that the Father has sent me; [37] yes, the Father who has sent me has testified to me Himself. You have never heard His voice nor seen His form; [38] and you do not keep His message living[s] in you, because you do not believe in the messenger[t] whom He has sent.

[39] "You keep on searching the Scriptures, for you yourselves suppose that you will get possession of[u] eternal life through them; and yet they are witnesses that testify to me, [40] but you refuse to come to me to get possession of life. [41] I do not accept any honor from men, [42] but I am sure that you do not have the love of God in your hearts.[v] [43] I have come in my Father's name, but you refuse to accept me. If anyone else should come in his own name, you would accept him. [44] How can you believe, you who are always accepting honor from one another, but never seek the honor that comes from the one God? [45] Do not be thinking that I am going to accuse you to the Father. You have your accuser; it is Moses on whom you have set your hopes! [46] For if you really believed Moses, you would believe me, for he wrote about me. [47] But if you do not believe what he wrote,[w] how will you ever believe what I say?"[w]

[n] Lit., *seeking*.
[o] Grk., *not true*.
[p] Lit., *tes. of a man*.
[q] Pro. in Grk.
[r] Grk., *greater* (in quality).
[s] Grk., *abiding*.
[t] Lit., *the one whom He sent*.
[u] Grk., *have*.
[v] Lit., *in you*.
[w] Grk., *his writings—my words*.

6
JESUS FEEDS THE FIVE THOUSAND; THEY TRY TO CROWN HIM KING, BUT HE RETIRES TO PRAY; WALKING ON THE WATER OF THE SEA OF GALILEE; HE TELLS THEM HE IS THE BREAD FROM HEAVEN; MANY FORSAKE HIM; THE TWELVE STAND BY HIM

After this Jesus went to the other side of the sea of Galilee, or Tiberias. [2] And a vast crowd continued to follow Him, for they pressed on to view the wonder-works which He performed for the sick people. [3] And so Jesus went up on the hill and was sitting there with His disciples. [4] Now the Passover, the Jewish feast, was approaching. [5] So Jesus looked up [a] and saw that a vast crowd was coming toward Him, and said to Philip, "Where can we buy bread for these people to eat?" [6] He was saying this to test him, for He knew Himself what He was going to do.

[7] Philip answered Him, "Forty dollars' worth of bread is not enough to give them all even a scanty meal apiece." [b]

[8] Another of His disciples, Andrew, Simon Peter's brother, said to Him, [9] "There is a little boy here who has five barley loaves and a couple of fish, but what are they among so many?"

[10] Jesus said, "Make the people sit down." Now there was plenty of grass at the spot; so the men, about five thousand, threw themselves down. [11] Then Jesus took the loaves and gave thanks, and distributed them among the people who were sitting on the ground; so too with the fish as much as they wanted. [12] When they had a plenty, He said to His disciples, "Pick up the pieces that are left, that nothing be wasted." [13] So they picked them up and filled twelve baskets with the pieces that were left from the five barley loaves, which were more than the eaters wanted.

[14] When the people, therefore, saw the wonder-works that He performed, they began to say, "This is surely the prophet who was to come into the world." [15] So when Jesus learned that they were going to come and carry Him off by force to crown Him king, He again retired to the hill by Himself.

[16] When evening came, His disciples went down to the sea [17] and got into a boat and started across the sea to Capernaum. Now it was already dark, and Jesus had not come to them. [18] The sea was getting rough, because a strong wind was blowing. [19] When they

---

[a] Grk., *lifted His eyes.*
[b] Lit., *that each may take a little.*

JOHN 6

had rowed about three or four miles, they saw Jesus walking on the sea and coming near the boat, and they were terror-stricken. ²⁰ But He said to them, "It is I; stop being afraid!" ²¹ Then they were willing to take Him on board, and at once the boat came to the shore it was making for.

²² Next day the people who had stayed on the other side of the sea saw that there was only one boat there, and that Jesus had not gotten into it with His disciples, but that His disciples had gone away by themselves. ²³ Other boats from Tiberias had landed near the place where the people ate the bread after the Lord had given thanks. ²⁴ So when the crowd saw that neither Jesus nor His disciples were there, they got into boats themselves and went to Capernaum to look for Jesus.

²⁵ So when they had crossed the sea and found Him, they asked Him, "Teacher, when did you get here?"

²⁶ Jesus answered them, "I most solemnly say to you, you are looking for me, not because of the wonder-works you saw, but because you ate the loaves and had plenty. ²⁷ Stop toiling for the food that perishes, but toil for the food that lasts for eternal life, which the Son of Man will give you, for God the Father has given Him authority[c] to do so."

²⁸ Then they asked Him, "What must we do to perform the works that God[d] demands?"

²⁹ Jesus answered them, "The work that God demands of you is this, to believe in the messenger whom He has sent."

³⁰ So they asked Him, "What wonder-work then are you going to perform for us to see and so believe in you? What work are you going to do? ³¹ Our forefathers in the desert ate the manna, as the Scripture says, 'He gave them out of heaven bread to eat.'"

³² Then Jesus said to them, "I most solemnly say to you, it was not Moses who gave you the real bread out of heaven, but it is my Father who gives you the real bread out of heaven, ³³ for the bread that God gives is what comes down out of heaven and gives life to the world."

³⁴ Then they said to Him, "Give us that bread always, sir!"

³⁵ Jesus said to them, "I am the bread that gives life. Whoever comes to me will never[e] get hungry, and whoever believes in me will never[e] get thirsty. ³⁶ But I have told you that, although[f] you

---

c Grk., *sealed,* so *certified with authority.*
d Lit., *works of God.*
e Double emph. neg.
f Hebraistic use of *and* (concessive).

have seen me, yet [f] you do not believe in me. ³⁷ All that my Father gives to me will come to me, and I will never, no, never reject anyone who comes to me, ³⁸ because I have come down from heaven, not to do my own will but the will of Him who sent me. ³⁹ Now the will of Him who sent me is this, that I should lose none of all that [g] He has given me, but should raise them [g] to life [h] on the last day. ⁴⁰ For it is my Father's will that everyone who sees the Son and believes in Him shall have eternal life, and that I shall raise him to life on the last day."

⁴¹ Then the Jews began to grumble about His saying, "I am the bread that came down out of heaven." ⁴² And they said, "Is He not Jesus, Joseph's son, whose father and mother we know? So how can He say, 'I have come down out of heaven'?"

⁴³ Jesus answered them, "Stop grumbling to one another. ⁴⁴ No one can come to me unless the Father who sent me draws him to me; then I myself will raise him to life on the last day. ⁴⁵ In the prophets it is written, 'And all men will be taught by God.' Everyone who ever [i] listens to the Father and learns from Him will [j] come to me. ⁴⁶ Not that anyone has ever seen the Father, except Him who is from God; of course,[h] He has seen the Father. ⁴⁷ I most solemnly say to you, whoever believes in me possesses eternal life. ⁴⁸ I am the bread that gives life. ⁴⁹ Your forefathers in the desert ate the manna, and yet they died. ⁵⁰ But here [k] is the bread that comes down out of heaven, so that anyone may eat it and never die. ⁵¹ I am this [l] living bread that has come down out of heaven. If anyone eats this bread, he will live forever, and the bread that I will give for the life of the world is my own flesh." [m]

⁵² But the Jews kept on wrangling with one another and saying, "How can He give us His flesh to eat?"

⁵³ Then Jesus said to them, "I most solemnly say to you, unless you eat the flesh of the Son of Man and drink His blood, you do not have life in you. ⁵⁴ Whoever continues to eat my flesh and drink my blood already [n] possesses eternal life, and I will raise

---

[f] Hebraistic use of *and* (concessive).
[g] Neut. but *persons* meant.
[h] Implied.
[i] Aor.
[j] General pres.
[k] Grk., *this*.
[l] Expressed by article.
[m] Fol. WH.
[n] Implied in pres.

him to life on the last day. ⁵⁵ For my flesh is real food and my blood is real drink. ⁵⁶ Whoever continues ᵒ to eat my flesh and drink my blood continues to live ᵖ in union ᑫ with me and I in union with him. ⁵⁷ Just as the living Father has sent me and I live because of the Father, so whoever keeps on eating me will live because of me. ⁵⁸ This is the bread that has come down out of heaven; not as your forefathers ate the manna, and yet died. Whoever continues to eat this bread will live forever."

⁵⁹ He said this as He taught in the synagogue at Capernaum.

⁶⁰ So many of His disciples, when they heard it, said, "This teaching ʳ is hard to take in. Who can listen to it?"

⁶¹ But as Jesus naturally ˢ knew that His disciples were grumbling about this, He said to them, "Is this shocking to you? ⁶² Suppose ᵗ you were to see the Son of Man going back where He was before? ⁶³ The Spirit is what gives life; the flesh does not help at all. The truths ᵘ that I have told you are spirit and life. ᵛ ⁶⁴ But there are some of you who do not trust in me." For Jesus knew from the start who they were that did not trust in Him, and who it was that was going to betray Him. ⁶⁵ So He continued, "This is why I told you that no one can come to me, unless it is granted ʷ to him by my Father."

⁶⁶ As a result of this many of His disciples turned their backs ˣ on Him and stopped ʸ accompanying Him. ⁶⁷ So Jesus said to the Twelve, "You too do not want to go back, do you?" ᶻ

⁶⁸ Simon Peter answered Him, "To whom can * we go, Lord? You have the message that gives eternal life, ⁶⁹ and we have come to believe, yes more, we know by experience, † that you are the Holy One of God."

⁷⁰ Jesus answered them, "Did I not myself select you as the

ᵒ Pres. pt.
ᵖ Lit., *abide*.
ᑫ Grk., *in me*.
ʳ Lit., *this word*.
ˢ Grk., *in Himself*.
ᵗ Incomplete con.
ᵘ Grk., *the things* or *words*.
ᵛ He means, then, that we must eat and digest His teachings.
ʷ Implying divine help and divine decree.
ˣ Lit., *went to the things behind Him*.
ʸ Neg. of cont. ac.
ᶻ Neg. ans. expected.
* Lit., *shall*.
† *Experimental knowledge.*

Twelve? And yet one of you is a devil." ⁷¹ He was referring to Judas, Simon Iscariot's son, for he was going to betray Him, although he was one of the Twelve.

7   JESUS' BROTHERS DO NOT ACCEPT HIM AS THE CHRIST; HE CLAIMS TO HAVE COME FROM GOD; THE PEOPLE AND LEADERS ARE STARTLED; AT THE FEAST OF TENTS HE OFFERS RIVERS OF LIVING WATER

After this, Jesus went on moving about in Galilee; He would not do so in Judea, because the Jews were trying to kill Him. ² Now the Jewish feast of Dwelling in Tents was approaching. ³ So His brothers said to Him, "You must leave here and go to Judea, to let your disciples also see the works that you are doing; ⁴ for no one does anything in secret when ᵃ he is trying to be known to the public.ᵇ If you are going to do this, show yourself publicly to the world." ⁵ For even His brothers did not believe in Him.

⁶ Then Jesus said to them, "It is not yet time for me to do so, ᶜ but any time is suitable for you. ⁷ It is impossible for the world to hate you; it is I whom it hates, because I continue to testify that its works are wicked. ⁸ Go up to the feast yourselves; I am not going up to it yet, for it is not quite time for me to go." ⁹ He told them this and stayed on in Galilee.

¹⁰ But after His brothers had gone up to the feast, then He went up too, not publicly but, as it were, privately. ¹¹ Now the Jews at the feast were looking for Him and kept asking, "Where is He?" ¹² And there was a great deal of grumbling about Him among the crowds, some saying that He was a good man, and others that He was not, but was misleading the masses. ¹³ And yet, for fear of the Jews, nobody daredᵈ to speak in public about Him.

¹⁴ Now when the feast was already half over, Jesus went up to the temple and began to teach. ¹⁵ The Jews were dumfounded and said, "How can this uneducatedᵉ man know the Scriptures?"

¹⁶ Jesus answered them, "My teaching is not my own, but it comes from Him who sent me. ¹⁷ If anyone is willingᶠ to keep on

---

ᵃ Grk., *and*.
ᵇ Lit., *be in the public*.
ᶜ Implied.
ᵈ Ingressive impf.
ᵉ Lit., *not having learned*.
ᶠ General pres.

JOHN 7

doing God's will, he will know whether my teaching comes from God, or merely expresses my own ideas. ᵍ ¹⁸ Whoever utters merely his own ideas is seeking his own honor, but whoever seeks the honor of him who sent him is sincere,ʰ and there is no dishonesty ⁱ in him. ¹⁹ Did not Moses give you the law? And yet not one of you is keeping that law. If so, why are you trying to kill me?"

²⁰ The crowd answered, "You are certainly under the power of a demon! ʲ Who is trying to kill you?"

²¹ Jesus answered them, "I have done just one deed, and yet you are all dumfounded! ²² Then Moses gave you the rite of circumcision—not that it had its origin with Moses but with your earlier forefathers—and you circumcise a male ᵏ child even on the sabbath. ²³ Well, if a male child undergoes ˡ circumcision on the sabbath, to keep the law of Moses from being broken, are you angry with me for making a man perfectly well on the sabbath? ²⁴ Stop judging superficially; ᵐ you must judge fairly." ⁿ

²⁵ Then some of the people of Jerusalem said, "Is not this the man they are trying to kill? ²⁶ Just look! He is talking in public, and yet they do not say a word to Him! It cannot be that the authorities have really learned that He is the Christ, can it? ²⁷ But we know where this man is from; when the Christ comes, however, no one will know where He is from."

²⁸ So Jesus, as He was teaching in the temple, cried out, "Yes, you do know me and you do know where I come from, and I have not come on my own authority, but the One who has sent me exists as the Real One, ᵒ whom you do not know. ²⁹ I know Him myself, because I have come from Him, and He has sent me."

³⁰ Then they kept on trying to arrest Him, and yet no one laid a hand on Him, for the time had not yet come. ³¹ But many of the crowd believed in Him, and said, "When the Christ comes, He will not perform greater wonder-works than ᵖ He did, will He?"

³² The Pharisees heard the people whispering ᑫ this about Him,

---

ᵍ Grk., *speak from myself.*
ʰ Lit., *true.*
ⁱ Grk., *no unrighteousness.*
ʲ Lit., *you have a demon!*
ᵏ Grk., *a man* (child).
ˡ Lit., *receives.*
ᵐ Grk., *by external appearances.*
ⁿ Lit., *judge righteous judgment.*
ᵒ Lit., *True* (One or God).
ᵖ Grk. has *than what.*
ᑫ Lit., *grumbling* or *muttering.*

and so the high priests and Pharisees sent some officers to arrest Him. ³³ Then Jesus said to them, "Just a little while longer I am to be with you, and then I am going back to Him who has sent me. ³⁴ You will then look for me, but you will not find me, and you cannot come where I am going."

³⁵ The Jews then said to one another, "Where is He about to go that we shall not find him? He is not going to our people scattered ʳ among the Greeks, and going to teach the Greeks, is He? ³⁶ What does He mean ˢ by saying, 'You will look for me and will not find me, and you cannot come where I am going'?"

³⁷ On the last day, the great day, of the feast, Jesus stood and cried aloud, "If anyone is thirsty, let him come to me and drink. ³⁸ Whoever continues ᵗ to believe in me will have, as the Scripture says, rivers of living water continuously ᵗ flowing from within him." ᵘ ³⁹ By this He referred to the Spirit that those believing in Him were going to receive—for the Spirit had not yet come, because Jesus had not yet been glorified.

⁴⁰ So some of the people, when they heard this, said, "This is surely the prophet."

⁴¹ Others said, "This is the Christ."

But still others said, "The Christ does not come from Galilee, does He? ⁴² Do not the Scriptures say that the Christ is to spring ᵛ from David and to come from the village of Bethlehem where David lived?"

⁴³ So the people were divided because of Him, ⁴⁴ and some of them wanted to arrest Him, but no one ventured ʷ to lay a hand upon Him.

⁴⁵ So the officers went back to the high priests and Pharisees. The latter asked the officers, "Why have you not brought Him?"

⁴⁶ The officers answered, "No man ever talked as He does!"

⁴⁷ Then the Pharisees answered, "You are not swept off your feet ˣ too, are you? ⁴⁸ None of the authorities or of the Pharisees have believed in Him, have they? ⁴⁹ But this mob, which knows nothing about the law, is bound to be accursed!"

ʳ Lit., *the dispersion;* i.e., Jews scattered among the heathen.
ˢ Grk., *what is this saying?*
ᵗ Pres. pt. and fut. indic. in linear sense.
ᵘ Lit., *out of his belly.*
ᵛ Grk., *is from David's seed.*
ʷ Ingressive aor.
ˣ Lit., *deceived.*

JOHN 8

⁵⁰ One of them, Nicodemus, who had formerly gone to Jesus,ʸ said to them, ⁵¹ "Our law does not condemn a man before it hears what he has to say and finds out what he is doing, does it?"

⁵² Then they answered him, "You are not from Galilee, too, are you? Search the record and see that no prophet has ever come from Galilee." ᶻ

8 THE FATHER TESTIFIES TO JESUS AS SON; ᵃ JESUS TELLS THE JEWS HE IS SOON TO GO AWAY; THAT THEY ARE NOT GOD'S CHILDREN BUT ARE SLAVES OF SIN; THEY ACCUSE HIM OF BEING UNDER THE POWER OF A DEMON

¹² ᵃ Then Jesus again addressed them and said, "I am the light of the world. Whoever continues to follow me need ᵇ never walk in darkness, but he will enjoy ᶜ the light that means life." ᵈ

¹³ The Pharisees then said to Him, "You are testifying to ᵉ yourself; your testimony is not true."

¹⁴ Jesus answered them, "Even if I do testify to myself, my testimony is true, because I know where I have come from and where I am going. But you do not know where I come from or where I am going. ¹⁵ You are judging in accordance with external ᶠ standards, but I judge nobody. ¹⁶ Even if I should judge, my decision is fair, because I am not alone, but there are two ᵍ of us, I and the Father who has sent me. ¹⁷ Even in your own law it is written, 'The testimony of two persons is true.' ¹⁸ I do testify to myself, and the Father who has sent me testifies to me."

¹⁹ Then they began to say to Him, "Where is your Father?"

Jesus answered, "You do not know either me or my Father. If you knew me, you would know my Father too."

²⁰ He said these things in the treasury as He was teaching in the temple, and yet no one ventured to arrest Him, because the time had not yet come for Him.

ʸ Pro. in Grk.
ᶻ V. 53 not in best Mss.
ᵃ Vv. 1-11 not in best Mss.
ᵇ This translates subjunc. after best Mss.
ᶜ Lit., *have*.
ᵈ Obj. gen.
ᵉ Lit., *about*.
ᶠ Grk., *according to the flesh*.
ᵍ Implied.

JOHN 8

²¹ Then Jesus again said to them, "I am going away, and you will look for me, but you will die under the curse of your sins;^h for where I am going you can never come."

²² Then the Jews began to say, "He is not going to kill Himself, is He? Is that why He said, 'Where I am going you can never come'?"

²³ He continued, "You are from below; I am from above. You belong to this present world; I do not belong to this present world. ²⁴ So I have told you that you would die under the curse of your sins, for unless you believe that I am the Christ,ⁱ you will die under the curse of your sins."

²⁵ Then they asked Him, "Who are you anyway?"^j

Jesus answered them, "Why do I even talk to you at all?^k ²⁶ I have much to say about you and much to condemn in you; but He who sent me is truthful, and I am telling the world only what I have learned^l from Him." ²⁷ They did not understand that He was speaking to them about the Father. ²⁸ So Jesus said to them, "When you lift the Son of Man [on the cross],^m you will know that I am the Christ,ⁱ and that I do nothing on my own authority, but that I say exactly what my Father has instructed me to say. ²⁹ Yes, He who sent me is ever with me; I am not alone, because I always practice what pleases Him." ³⁰ Even while He was saying this, many believed in Him.

³¹ So Jesus said to the Jews who believed in Him, "If you liveⁿ in accordance with what I teach, you are really my disciples, ³² and you will know the truth and the truth will set you free."

³³ They answered Him, "We are Abraham's descendants and we never have been anybody's slaves. How can you say to us, 'You will be set free'?"

³⁴ Jesus answered them, "I most solemnly say to you, everyone who lives in sin^o is a slave of sin. ³⁵ Now a slave does not live permanently^p in a household, but a son does.^q ³⁶ So if the Son sets

---

^h Lit., *die in your sins;* i.e., in their power, under their curse.
ⁱ Grk., *I am He.*
^j Emph. *you.*
^k Fol. Grk., *fathers* (see EGT).
^l Lit., *heard from Him.*
^m Last phrase to be supplied.
ⁿ Lit., *abide in my word.*
^o Lit., *practices sin.*
^p Grk., *forever.*
^q Grk., repeats vb. and modifier.

you free, you will be really free. ³⁷ I know that you are Abraham's descendants, and yet you are trying to kill me, because there is no room ʳ in you for my teaching. ³⁸ I am telling you what I have seen in my Father's presence, and you are practicing what you have learned from your ˢ father."

³⁹ They answered Him, "Our father is Abraham."

Jesus said to them, "If you are Abraham's children, you must be practicing what Abraham did.ᵗ ⁴⁰ But right now you are trying to kill me, a man who has told you the truth that He has learned from God. Abraham never did that. ⁴¹ You are practicing what your real father does."

They said to Him, "We are not illegitimate children; we have one Father, even God."

⁴² Then Jesus said to them, "If God were your Father, you would love me, for I came from God and now am here. No, indeed, I have not come on my own authority, but He has sent me. ⁴³ Why is it that you misunderstand ᵘ what I say? It is because you cannot listen to what I teach.ᵛ ⁴⁴ You sprang from the devil, your real father, and you want to practice your father's wishes. He was a murderer from the very start, and he does not stand by the truth, because there is no truth in him. When he tells a lie, he speaks out of his own nature,ʷ because he is a liar and the father of lies.ˣ ⁴⁵ But because I tell you the truth, you do not believe me. ⁴⁶ Who of you can prove ʸ me guilty of sin? But if I do tell you the truth, why do you not believe me? ⁴⁷ Whoever is sprung from God listens to what God says. This is why you do not listen to me: you are not sprung from God."

⁴⁸ Then the Jews answered Him, "Are we not right in saying ᶻ that you are a Samaritan and are under the power of a demon?"

⁴⁹ Jesus answered: "I am not under the power of a demon; on the other hand, I am honoring my Father, but you are dishonoring me. ⁵⁰ However, I am not seeking honor for myself; there is One who is seeking it for me, and He is judge. ⁵¹ I most solemnly

---

ʳ Lit., *my word has no place in you.*
ˢ Om. by WH and best Mss., but implied.
ᵗ Lit., *the works of A.*
ᵘ Lit., *do not understand.*
ᵛ Grk., *my word.*
ʷ Lit., *his own things.*
ˣ Grk., *of it.*
ʸ Lit., *convict,* etc.
ᶻ Lit., *rightly say.*

say to you, if anyone follows* my teaching, he will never experience† death."

⁵² Then the Jews said to Him, "Now we know that you are under the power of a demon. Abraham is dead; the prophets too, and yet you say, 'If anyone follows my teaching, he will never experience death.' ⁵³ You are not greater than our forefather Abraham, are you? He is dead and the prophets are dead. Who do you claim to be?"

⁵⁴ Jesus answered, "If I glorify myself, such glory amounts to nothing. It is the Father who glorifies me; and you claim that He is your God. ⁵⁵ And yet you have not learned to know Him; but I know Him, and if I say I do not know Him, I will be a liar like you. On the other hand, I do know Him and I do follow His teaching. ⁵⁶ Your forefather Abraham exulted in the hope‡ of seeing my day. He has seen it and is glad of it."

⁵⁷ The Jews then said to Him, "You are not yet fifty years old, and have you seen Abraham?" §

⁵⁸ Then Jesus said to them, "I most solemnly say to you, I existed before Abraham was born." ⁵⁹ At this the Jews took up stones to stone Him, but Jesus made His way out of the temple unperceived.‖

9 A MAN BORN BLIND IS MADE TO SEE; BECAUSE IT OCCURRED ON THE SABBATH, THE PHARISEES PUT THE MAN OUT OF THE SYNAGOGUE; JESUS LEADS THE MAN TO BELIEVE IN HIM, BUT CONDEMNS THE PHARISEES FOR BEING BLIND

As He passed along, He saw a man who had been blind from his birth. ² So His disciples asked Him, "Teacher,[a] for whose sin was this man born blind, his own [b] or that of his parents?"

³ Jesus answered, "It was neither for his own sin nor for that of his parents, but to show what God could do [c] in his case. ⁴ We

---

* Grk., *keeps.*
† Lit., *see.*
‡ Grk., *A. exulted to see.*
§ Some old Mss. read, *Has A. seen you?*
‖ Lit., *Jesus hid Himself and.*
[a] *Rabbi;* means *Teacher.*
[b] Referring to the belief that he might have lived in a previous state.
[c] Lit., *that the works of God might be shown.*

must continue to do the **works of Him** who sent me while it is daylight. Night is coming when no one can do any work. ⁵ While [d] I am in the world, I am the light of the world."

⁶ On saying this He spit on the ground and made clay with the saliva, and put it on the man's eyes, ⁷ and said, "Go and wash them in the pool of Siloam" (which means One who has been sent). So he went and washed them and went home [e] seeing.

⁸ Now his neighbors and those who saw that he was formerly blind, kept saying, "Is not this the man who used to sit and beg?"

⁹ Some said, "Yes, it is he." Others said, "No, but it surely does look like him." [f]

He himself said, "I am the man."

¹⁰ So they kept on asking him, "How in the world did you come to see?" [g]

¹¹ He answered, "The man called Jesus made some clay and rubbed [h] it on my eyes, and said to me, 'Go to Siloam and wash them.' So when I had gone and washed them I could see."

¹² Then they asked him, "Where is He?"

He answered, "I do not know."

¹³ They took the man who had been blind to the Pharisees. ¹⁴ Now it was on the sabbath when Jesus had made the clay and caused the man's eyes to see.[i] ¹⁵ So the Pharisees again asked him how he had come to see. He answered them: "He put some clay on my eyes, and I washed them, and so now I can see."

¹⁶ Then some of the Pharisees said, "This man does not come from God, for He does not keep the sabbath."

Others said, "How can a sinful man perform such wonderworks?" So there was a difference [j] of opinion among them.

¹⁷ Then again they asked the blind man, "What do you say about Him yourself, since He has made your eyes to see?"

He answered, "He is a prophet."

¹⁸ But the Jews did not believe that he had really been blind and that he had come to see again, until they called the parents of the man who saw again, ¹⁹ and asked them, "Is this your son,

---

[d] Grk., *whenever.*
[e] Implied.
[f] Lit., *he is like him.*
[g] Grk., *how were your eyes opened?*
[h] Lit., *anointed,* etc.
[i] Lit., *opened his eyes.*
[j] Grk., *there was a division among them.*

and do you affirm that he was born blind? If so,[k] how is it then that he now can see?"

20 His parents answered, "We know that this is our son, and that he was born blind. 21 But we do not know how it is that he now can see, or who it was that made his eyes to see. Ask him; he is of age; he can speak for himself." 22 His parents said this, because they were afraid of the Jews, for the Jews had already agreed that if anyone owned Jesus [1] as the Christ, he should be shut out of the synagogues. 23 This is why his parents said, "He is of age, ask him."

24 So a second time they called the man who had been blind, and said to him, "Give God the praise; we know this man is a sinner."

25 Then he answered, "I do not know whether He is a sinner. I do know one thing, that once I was blind but now I can see."

26 Again they said to him, "What did He do to you? How did He make your eyes to see again?"

27 He answered them, "I have already told you and you would not listen to me. Why do you want to hear it again? You do not want to become His disciples, do you?"

28 Then they jeered him, and said, "You are a disciple of His yourself,[m] but we are disciples of Moses. 29 We do know that God spoke to Moses, but we do not know where this fellow comes from."

30 The man answered them, "Well, there is something strange about this! You do not know where He comes from! And yet He has made my eyes to see! 31 We know that God does not listen to sinful men; but He does listen to anyone who worships God and lives to do His will.[n] 32 It has never been heard of in this world that anyone ever made the eyes of a man who was born blind to see. 33 If this man had not come from God, He could not have done anything like this."[o]

34 Then they retorted, "You were born in total depravity,[p] and yet you are trying to teach us!" And so they turned [q] him out of the synagogue.

35 Jesus heard that they had turned the man out of the synagogue:

[k] Cond. implied.
[1] Pro. in Grk.
[m] Pros. very emph.
[n] Lit., *Keeps on doing His will.*
[o] Last two words implied.
[p] Grk., *wholly in sins.*
[q] Lit., *threw him out.*

so He found him and said to him, "Do you believe in the Son of Man yourself?"

³⁶ He answered, "Who is He, sir? Tell me, so that I may believe in Him."

³⁷ Jesus answered him, "You have seen Him; you are talking to Him right now!"

³⁸ So he said, "Lord, I believe!" Then he worshiped Him.

³⁹ Then Jesus said, "I have come into this world to judge people,ʳ so that those who do not may see, and those who do see may become blind."

⁴⁰ Some of the Pharisees who were with Him heard this, and asked Him, "We are not blind, are we?"

⁴¹ Jesus answered them, "If you were blind, you would not be guilty; ˢ but now you keep on claiming, 'We canᵗ see'; so your sin remains."

10
JESUS THE DOOR TO THE SHEEPFOLD; THE GOOD SHEPHERD TOO; HE GUARANTEES THAT HE AND HIS FATHER WILL PROTECT HIS SHEEP; THE JEWS TRIED TO ARREST HIM FOR CLAIMING TO BE ONE WITH THE FATHER

"I most solemnly say to you, whoever does not enter the sheepfold by the door, but climbs over at some other place is a thief and a robber. ² But the one who enters by the door is the shepherd of the sheep. ³ The doorkeeper opens the door to him, and the sheep obey ᵃ his voice; and he calls his own sheep by name, and leads them out. ⁴ So when he gets his sheep all out, he goes on before them, and the sheep come on behind him, because they know his voice. ⁵ But they will never come on behind a stranger, but will run away from him, because they do not know the voice of strangers."

⁶ Jesus told them this allegory,ᵇ but they did not understand what He meant by it. ⁷ So Jesus said to them again:

"I most solemnly say to you, I am the door to the sheepfold myself.ᶜ ⁸ All who came as such before me are thieves and robbers.ᵈ

ʳ Grk., *for judgment*.
ˢ Lit., *would not have sin*.
ᵗ Gen. pres.
ᵃ Lit., *hear;* sense of heed, obey.
ᵇ *Proverb, parable,* or *allegory;* last here.
ᶜ Pro. emph.
ᵈ Means false Messiahs.

but the true sheep would not listen to them. ⁹ I am the door myself. Whoever enters through me will be saved, and will go in and out and find pasture. ¹⁰ A thief does not come for any purpose but to steal and kill and destroy; I have come for people to have life and have it till it overflows.ᵉ ¹¹ I am the good shepherd myself. The good shepherd gives ᶠ his own life for his sheep. ¹² The hired man, who is not a shepherd and does not own the sheep, sees the wolf coming and leaves the sheep and runs away, and the wolf carries off some of the sheep and scatters the flock. ¹³ This is because he is a hired man and does not care a straw for the sheep. ¹⁴ I am the good shepherd myself. I know my sheep and my sheep know me, ¹⁵ just as the Father knows me and I know the Father, and I am giving my own life for my sheep. ¹⁶ I have other sheep too that do not belong to this fold. I must lead them too, and they will listen to my voice, and all my sheep will become one flock with one shepherd. ¹⁷ This is why the Father loves me, because I am giving my own life to take it back again. ¹⁸ No one has taken it from me, but I am giving it as a free gift.ᵍ I have the right to give it and I have the right to take it back. I have gotten this order from my Father."

¹⁹ These words ʰ again led to difference of opinion among the Jews. ²⁰ Many of them said, "He is under the power of a demon and is going crazy. Why are you listening to Him?"

²¹ Others said, "These are not the words of a man who is under the power of a demon. A demon cannot make the eyes of the blind see, can he?"

²² At that time came the feast of Rededication ⁱ at Jerusalem. It was winter ²³ and Jesus was walking in Solomon's portico. ²⁴ So the Jews surrounded Him and kept asking Him, "How much longer are you going to keep us in suspense?ʲ If you are really the Christ, tell us so plainly."

²⁵ Jesus answered them, "I have already told you so, but you do not believe me. The works which I am doing on my Father's authority ᵏ are my credentials,ˡ ²⁶ but still you do not believe in me,ᵐ

ᵉ Lit. *meaning.*
ᶠ Lit., *lays down.*
ᵍ Lit., *of myself.*
ʰ *On acct. of—a division,* etc.
ⁱ Celebrates the dedication of the temple by Judas Maccabeus, 165 B. C.
ʲ Lit., *take away our breath.*
ᵏ Grk., *in my Father's name.*
ˡ Lit., *testify to me.*
ᵐ Implied.

for you do not belong to my sheep. ²⁷ My sheep listen to my voice, and I know them and they follow me, ²⁸ and I give to them eternal life, and they shall never get ⁿ lost, and no one shall snatch them out of my hand. ²⁹ My Father who gave them to me is stronger ᵒ than all, and no one can snatch them out of my Father's hand. ³⁰ The Father and I are one."

³¹ The Jews again picked up stones to stone Him. ³² Jesus answered them, "I have shown you many good deeds from my Father. For which of them are you going to stone me?"

³³ The Jews retorted, "It is not for a good deed but for blasphemy we are going to stone you; namely, because you, although a mere man, claim to be God."

³⁴ Jesus answered them, "Is it not written in your law, 'I said, "You are gods"'? ³⁵ If men to whom God's message came are called gods—and the Scriptures cannot be made null and void—³⁶ do you now say to me whom my Father has set apart to it and sent into the world, 'You are a blasphemer,' because I said, 'I am the Son of God'? ³⁷ If I am not doing the things that my Father is doing, do not believe me. ³⁸ But if I am doing so, even if you will not believe me, believe the deeds, that you may come ᵖ to know and continue ᑫ to know that the Father is in union with me and I am in union with the Father."

³⁹ Once more they were trying to arrest Him, but He escaped from their hands. ⁴⁰ He again crossed the Jordan at the place where John at first used to baptize, and there He stayed. ⁴¹ And many people came to Him and kept on saying, "John did not perform any wonder-works, but everything he ever said about this man was true." ⁴² And so many of them at that place believed in Him.

11 LAZARUS IS SICK; MARTHA AND MARY, HIS SISTERS, SEND FOR JESUS; HE WAITS FOR HIM TO DIE, THEN COMES AND BRINGS HIM BACK TO LIFE; THE COUNCIL PLOTS TO KILL HIM

Now a man was sick; it was Lazarus who lived in Bethany, the village of Mary and her sister Martha. ² It was the Mary who poured the perfume upon the Lord and wiped His feet with her

---

ⁿ Aor.
ᵒ Lit., *greater*.
ᵖ Aor. of pointed action.
ᑫ Pres. of linear action.

hair, whose brother **Lazarus** was sick. ³ So the sisters sent this message to Jesus, "Lord, listen!ᵃ the one you love so well is sick."

⁴ When Jesus received the message, He said, "This sickness is not to end in death but is to honor God, that the Son of God through it may be honored."

⁵ Now Jesus held ᵇ in loving esteem ᶜ Martha and her sister and Lazarus. ⁶ But when He heard that Lazarus was sick, He stayed over for two days in the place where He was. ⁷ After that He said to His disciples, "Let us go back to Judea."

⁸ The disciples said to Him, "Teacher, the Jews just now were trying to stone you, and are you going back there again?"

⁹ Jesus answered, "Does not the day have twelve hours? If a man travels in the daytime, he does not stumble, for he can see the light of this world; ¹⁰ but if he travels in the nighttime, he does stumble, because he has no light." ¹¹ He said this, and after that He added, "Our friend Lazarus has fallen asleep, but I am going there to wake him."

¹² The disciples said to Him, "Lord, if he has merely fallen asleep, he will recover." ¹³ But Jesus had spoken about his death. However, they supposed that He was referring to falling into a natural sleep.ᵈ

¹⁴ So Jesus then told them plainly: "Lazarus is dead, ¹⁵ and I am glad for your sake that I was not there so that you may come to have real faith in me. But let us go to him."

¹⁶ Then Thomas the Twin said to his fellow-disciples, "Let us go too, and die with Him."

¹⁷ When Jesus reached there, He found that Lazarus had been buried for four days. ¹⁸ Now Bethany is only about two miles from Jerusalem, ¹⁹ and a goodly number of Jews had come out to see Martha and Mary,ᵉ to sympathize with them over their brother. ²⁰ When Martha heard that Jesus was coming, she went out to meet Him,ᶠ but Mary stayed at home.ᵍ ²¹ Then Martha said to Jesus, "Lord, if you had been here, my brother would not have died.

ᵃ Lit., *behold!*
ᵇ Impf. of cont. ac. gives this idea.
ᶜ *Phileo* used in v. 3, for *emotional love;* here *agapao, loving esteem.*
ᵈ Context makes this clear.
ᵉ Fol. WH and best Mss.
ᶠ Ingress. aor.
ᵍ *Sitting in the house.*

JOHN 11

²² But even now I know that whatever you ask God for He ʰ will give you."

²³ Jesus said to her, "Your brother will rise again."

²⁴ Martha said to Him, "I know that he will rise at the resurrection, on the last day."

²⁵ Jesus said to her, "I am the resurrection and the life myself.ⁱ Whoever continues to believe in me will live right on,ʲ even though he dies, ²⁶ and no person who continues to live and believe in me will ever die at all.ᵏ Do you believe this?"

²⁷ She said to Him, "Yes, Lord, I believe that you are the Christ, the Son of God, who was to come into the world."

²⁸ On saying this she went back and called her sister Mary, whispering to her, "The Teacher is here and is asking for you."

²⁹ As soon as she heard it, she jumped¹ up and started to Jesus,ᵐ ³⁰ for Heᵐ had not yet come into the village, but He was still at the place where Martha had met Him. ³¹ So the Jews who were with her in the house sympathizing with her, when they saw Mary jump up and go out, followed her, because they supposed that she was going to the grave to pour out her griefⁿ there. ³² When Mary came where Jesus was and saw Him, she threw herself at His feet, and said, "Lord, if you had been here, my brother would not have died."

³³ So when Jesus saw her weeping and the Jews who had come with her weeping too, He sighed in sympathyº and shook with emotion,ᵖ ³⁴ and asked, "Where have you laid him?"

They answered, "Lord, come and see." ³⁵ Jesus burst ᑫ into tears.

³⁶ So the Jews said, "See how tenderlyʳ He loved him!" ³⁷ But some of them said, "Could not this man, who made that blind man see, have kept Lazarus from dying?"

³⁸ Now Jesus sighed again and continued ˢ to sigh as He went to

---

ʰ *God* in Grk.
¹ Pro. emphatic.
ʲ Linear fut.
ᵏ Strongest neg.
¹ Expressed in adv. and vb.
ᵐ Noun and pro. reversed in Grk.
ⁿ Lit., *to wail*.
º Grk., *sighed in spirit*.
ᵖ Lit., *was agitated,* or *disturbed Himself*.
ᑫ Ingress. aor.
ʳ Expressed by adv. and vb. of emotional love *(phileo)*.
ˢ Pres. pt. means it.

the grave. It was a cave with a stone lying over the mouth of it.

³⁹ Jesus said, "Slip the stone aside."

The dead man's sister, Martha, said to Him, "Lord, by this time he is offensive, for he has been dead four days."

⁴⁰ Jesus said to her, "Did I not promise you that if you would believe in me, you should see the glory of God?" ⁴¹ So they slipped the stone aside.

And Jesus looked up and said, "Father, I thank you for listening to me; ⁴² yes, I knew that you always listen to me. But I have said this for the sake of the crowd that is standing by, that they may come to believe that you have sent me." ⁴³ On saying this, He shouted aloud, "Lazarus, come out!"

⁴⁴ Then out came the dead man, his feet and hands tied with wrappings, and his face tied up with a handkerchief. Jesus said to them, "Untie him and let him go."

⁴⁵ Thus many of the Jews, who came to see Mary and who saw what Jesus had done, believed in Him; ⁴⁶ but some of them went back to the Pharisees and told them what He had done.

⁴⁷ So the high priests and the Pharisees called a meeting of the council, and began to say, "What are we to do? For this man is certainly performing many wonder-works. ⁴⁸ If we let Him go on this way, everybody will believe in Him, and the Romans will come and blot out [t] both our city [u] and nation."

⁴⁹ But one of them, Caiaphas, who was high priest that year, said to them, "You know nothing about this; ⁵⁰ you do not take into account that it is for your own welfare that one man should die for the people, and not that the whole nation should be destroyed." ⁵¹ Now he did not say this on his own authority, but because he was high priest that year he uttered this prophecy from God,[v] that Jesus was to die for the nation, ⁵² and not only for the nation, but also to unite the scattered children of God. ⁵³ So from that day they plotted to kill Jesus.

⁵⁴ It was for this reason that Jesus no more appeared [w] in public among the Jews, but He left that part of the country and went to the district near the desert, to a town called Ephraim, and stayed there with His disciples. ⁵⁵ Now the Jewish Passover was approach-

---

[t] Lit., *take up and carry away.*
[u] Grk., *our place.*
[v] Implied from denial just made.
[w] Lit., *walked about.*

ing, and many people from the country went up to Jerusalem, to purify themselves before the Passover. ⁵⁶ So they kept looking for Jesus and saying to one another, as they stood in the temple, "What do you think? Do you think He will not come to the feast at all?"

⁵⁷ Now the high priests and the Pharisees had given orders that if anyone should learn ˣ where He was, he should let it be known so that they might arrest Him.

12
MARY POURS HER COSTLY PERFUME ON JESUS; JESUS RIDES AS KING INTO JERUSALEM; GREEKS INTERVIEW JESUS; HE TEACHES THAT LIFE COMES FROM SACRIFICIAL DEATH; OPPOSITION INCREASES AS HE CONTINUES TO CLAIM GOD AS FATHER

Now six days before the Passover, Jesus came to Bethany where Lazarus lived, whom He had raised from the dead. ² So they gave a dinner there in honor of Jesus,ᵃ and Martha was waiting on them, but Lazarus was one of the guests with Jesus.ᵇ ³ Then Mary took a pound of expensive perfume, made of the purest oil,ᶜ and poured it on Jesus' feet, and wiped them with her hair; and the whole house was filled with the fragrance of the perfume.

⁴ But Judas Iscariot, one of His disciples, who was going to betray Him, said, ⁵ "Why was this perfume not sold for sixty dollars and the money given to the poor?" ⁶ He said this, not because he cared for the poor, but because he was a thief and as the carrier of the purse for the Twelve ᵈ he was in the habit of taking what was put into it.

⁷ Then Jesus said, "Let her alone; let her keep ᵉ it for the day of my funeral,ᶠ ⁸ for you always have the poor among you, but you will not always have me."

⁹ A goodly number of the Jews learned that He was at Bethany, and so they came there, not only to see Jesus but also to see Lazarus, whom He had raised from the dead. ¹⁰ But the high priests

---

ˣ Aor. of vb. *to know,* so *come to know.*
ᵃ Lit., *for Him.*
ᵇ Grk., *with Him.*
ᶜ Lit., *pure nard,* a fragrant oil made from the nard plant.
ᵈ The Twelve implied.
ᵉ Fol. WH.
ᶠ Lit., *burial.*

planned [g] to kill Lazarus, [11] for on account of him many of the Jews were leaving them and believing in Jesus.

[12] The next day the vast crowd that had come to the feast, on hearing that Jesus was coming into Jerusalem, [13] took palm-branches and went out to meet Him, and kept on shouting:

> "Blessings on Him! [h]
> Blessed be He who comes in the name of the Lord;
> Blessings on the King of Israel!" [i]

[14] Then Jesus found a young donkey and mounted it, doing as the Scripture says: [j]

> [15] "Cease from fearing, Daughter of Zion;
> See, your King is coming mounted on an ass's colt!"

[16] His disciples at the time [k] did not understand this, but after Jesus was glorified, they remembered that this had been written about Him and that they had fulfilled [l] it in His case. [17] The crowd that had been with Him when He called Lazarus out of the grave and raised him from the dead, kept on talking [m] about it. [18] This is why the crowd went out to meet Him, because they had heard that He had performed this wonder-work. [19] So the Pharisees said to one another, "You see, you cannot help it at all; the whole world has gone off after Him!"

[20] There were some Greeks among those who were coming up to worship at the feast, [21] and they went to Philip who was from Bethsaida in Galilee, and kept making this request of him, "Sir, we want to see Jesus."

[22] Philip went and told Andrew; Andrew and Philip both went and told Jesus. [23] Jesus answered them, "The time has come for [n] the Son of Man to be glorified. [24] I most solemnly say to you, unless a grain of wheat falls into the ground and dies, it remains a single grain. But if it does die, it yields a great harvest. [25] Whoever loves his lower life will lose the higher; but whoever hates his lower

---

[g] Grk., *held a consultation.*
[h] Lit., *Hosanna.*
[i] Cf. Ps. 118:26.
[j] Zech. 9:9.
[k] Lit., *at first.*
[l] Grk., *they did this to Him.*
[m] Lit., *testifying.*
[n] Grk., *that,* etc.

life in this world preserves the higher ⁰ for eternal life. ²⁶ If anyone serves me, he must ᴾ continue to follow me, and my servant also must go wherever I go.ᑫ If anyone serves me, my Father will show him honor. ²⁷ Now my soul is troubled; what shall I say? Father, save me from this hour of agony! ʳ And yet it was for this very purpose that I came to this hour of agony. ²⁸ Father, glorify your name."

Then a voice came out of heaven, "I have already glorified it and I will again glorify it."

²⁹ The crowd of bystanders on hearing it said that it was thunder; others, however, said, "An angel has spoken to Him!"

³⁰ Jesus answered, "This voice did not come for my sake, but for yours. ³¹ This world is now in process ˢ of judgment; the prince of this world is now to be expelled. ³² And if I am lifted up from the earth, I will draw all men to me." ³³ He said this to show the kind ᵗ of death He was going to die.

³⁴ The crowd answered Him, "We have learned from the law that the Christ is to remain here forever, and so how can you say that the Son of Man must be lifted up? Who is this Son of Man?"

³⁵ Jesus said to them, "Only a little while longer you will have the light. Keep on living by it while you have the light, so that darkness may not overtake you, for whoever walks about in the dark does not know where he is going. ³⁶ While you have the light believe in the light, that you may become sons of light." ᵘ On saying this Jesus went away ᵛ and hid Himself.

³⁷ Although He had performed so many wonder-works right before their eyes, they did not believe in Him, ³⁸ so that the utterance of the prophet Isaiah was fulfilled: ʷ

"Lord, who has believed what they heard from us? ˣ

And to whom has the mighty arm of the Lord been shown?" ʸ

³⁹ So they could not believe, for Isaiah again has said:

⁰ A play on the double meaning of word *life (psuchee)*.
ᴾ Impv. of obligation.
ᑫ Lit., *wherever I am*.
ʳ Lit., *this hour*, but agony (of the cross) is meant; so *this hour of agony*.
ˢ Lit., *now is the judgment*.
ᵗ Interrog. of quality.
ᵘ I.e., *filled with light*.
ᵛ Clauses reversed, but exact meaning.
ʷ *Which he spoke*, om.
ˣ Lit. meaning.
ʸ Isa. 53:1.

⁴⁰ "He has blinded their eyes and benumbed their hearts,
So that they cannot see with their eyes and understand with their hearts,
And turn to me to cure them."ᵃ

⁴¹ Isaiah said this, because he saw His glory; yes, he spoke about Him. ⁴² And yet in spite of all this, even among the leading men many came to believe in Him, but because of the Pharisees they did not own it, for fear of being turned out of the synagogue; ⁴³ for they loved the praise of men instead of the praise of God.

⁴⁴ But Jesus cried aloud, "Whoever believes in me believes not merely in me but in Him who has sent me; ⁴⁵ and whoever sees me sees Him who has sent me. ⁴⁶ I have come as light into the world, so that no one who continues to believe in me can* remain in darkness. ⁴⁷ If anyone hears my words and fails to keep them, it is not I that judge him, for I have not come to judge but to save the world. ⁴⁸ Whoever persistently rejects me and refuses to accept my teachings† has something to judge him; the very message I have spoken will judge him on the last day. ⁴⁹ This is because I have not spoken on my own authority, but the Father who has sent me has given me orders Himself what to say and what to tell. ⁵⁰ And I know that His orders mean‡ eternal life. So whatever I speak I am speaking as the Father has told me."

13 JESUS WASHES THE DISCIPLES' FEET AND BY EXAMPLE TEACHES THEM THAT HUMILITY AND SERVICE PAVE THE WAY TO HAPPINESS; JUDAS ISCARIOT POINTED OUT; PETER WARNED THAT HE IS GOING TO DISOWN CHRIST

Before the Passover feast started, Jesus knew that His time had come for Him to leaveᵃ the world and goᵃ to the Father, and as He had loved His own in the world He loved them to the last. ² So Jesus, while supper was on—although He knew that the devil had suggestedᵇ to Judas Iscariot, Simon's son, to betray Him—³ because He was sureᶜ that the Father had put everything into His hands,

---

ᵃ Lit., *and I will cure them.*
* Lit., *may remain.*
† Lit., *my spoken words.*
‡ Grk., *are.*
ᵃ Both ideas in one vb.
ᵇ Grk., *put into the heart.*
ᶜ Lit., *knew.*

JOHN 13

and that He had come from God and was going back to God, ⁴ got up from the table, took off His outer clothes, and took a towel and tied it around His waist. ⁵ Then He poured water into a basin and began to wash the disciples' feet and to wipe them with the towel which was around His waist. ⁶ Thus He came to Simon Peter. Peter said to Him, "Lord, are you going to wash my feet?"

⁷ Jesus answered him, "You do not now understand what I am doing, but by-and-by ᵈ you will learn."

⁸ Peter said to Him, "You must ᵉ never wash my feet!"

Jesus answered, "Unless I do wash you, you can ᶠ have no share with me."

⁹ Simon Peter said to Him, "Lord, do not stop with my feet, then; but wash my hands and face ᵍ too!"

¹⁰ Jesus said to him, "Anyone who has just taken a bath has no need of washing anything but his feet, but he is clean all over.ʰ And you are now clean, though not all of you are." ¹¹ For He knew who was going to betray Him; this is why He said, "You are not all clean."

¹² So when He had washed their feet and had put on His clothes and taken His place at the table, He said to them again: "Do you understand what I have done to you? ¹³ You call me Teacher and Lord, and you are right in calling me so, for that is what I am. ¹⁴ If I then, your Lord and Teacher, have washed your feet, you too ought to wash one another's feet. ¹⁵ For I have set you an example, in order that you too may practice what I have done to you. ¹⁶ I most solemnly say to you, no slave is superior to his master, and no messenger is greater than the man who sends him. ¹⁷ If you know all this, happy are you if you practice it. ¹⁸ I do not mean all of you. I know whom I have chosen; but I know that the Scriptures must be fulfilled:

> 'The man who is eating my bread
> Has lifted his heel against me.' ⁱ

¹⁹ From now on I will tell you things before they take place, so that when they do take place, you may believe that I am the Christ.ʲ

ᵈ Lit., *after this.*
ᵉ Grk., *shall.*
ᶠ Grk., *you have.*
ᵍ Lit., *head.*
ʰ Lit., *the whole of him is clean.*
ⁱ Ps. 41:9.
ʲ Grk., *that I am He.*

²⁰ I most solemnly say to you, whoever welcomes any messenger [k] I send welcomes me, and whoever welcomes me welcomes Him who has sent me."

²¹ After saying this Jesus was deeply moved in spirit and solemnly said, "I most solemnly say to you, one of you is going to betray me."

²² The disciples kept looking at one another, but were at a loss to know which one He meant.[1] ²³ One of the disciples, whom Jesus specially loved, was sitting very close to Jesus at His right.[m] ²⁴ So Simon Peter nodded to him to ask Him which one it was that He meant. ²⁵ He leaned back on Jesus' breast and said to Him, "Lord, who is it?"

²⁶ Jesus answered, "It is that one to whom I give the piece of bread when I dip it in the dish." So He dipped it into the dish and took it and gave it to Judas, Simon Iscariot's son. ²⁷ As soon as [n] he took the bread, Satan took possession of Judas.[o]

Then Jesus said to him, "Make quick work of what you are to do." ²⁸ But no one else at the table knew what He meant by this,[p] ²⁹ for some of them were thinking, as Judas had the purse, that Jesus meant to say to him, "Buy what we need for the feast," or to give something to the poor. ³⁰ So as soon as he took the piece of bread, he left the room.[q] It was then night.

³¹ When he had left,[r] Jesus said, "Now the Son of Man has been glorified, and God has been glorified in Him, ³² and God will through Himself glorify Him, and He will glorify Him at once. ³³ Dear children,[s] I am to be with you only a little while longer. You will look for me, but, as I told the Jews, so I now tell you, you cannot just now go where I am going. ³⁴ I give you a new command, to love one another. Just as I have loved you, you too must love one another. ³⁵ By this everybody will know that you are my disciples, if you keep on showing [t] love for one another."

³⁶ Simon Peter said to Him, "Lord, where are you going?"

---

[k] Lit., *if I shall send anyone,* etc.
[1] Grk., *at a loss about whom He spoke.*
[m] Lit., *reclining on His bosom,* the place of first honor; hence our trans.
[n] Lit., *after the bread.*
[o] Grk., *Satan entered into him.*
[p] Lit., *on account of what He,* etc.
[q] Grk., *went out.*
[r] Fol. WH and best Mss.
[s] Lit., *little children;* term of endearment.
[t] Grk., *if you keep on having love,* etc.

Jesus answered, "I am going where you cannot follow me just now, but you will later follow me."

³⁷ Peter said to Him, "Lord, why can I not follow you right now? I will lay down my life for you."

³⁸ Jesus answered, "You will lay down your life for me! I most solemnly say to you, before a cock crows, you will three times disown me!"

14
JESUS COMFORTS HIS TROUBLED DISCIPLES BY TELLING THEM HE IS GOING TO PREPARE FOR THEM DWELLING PLACES IN HEAVEN; THAT HE WILL COME BACK TO TAKE THEM THERE; PROMISES THE SPIRIT TO HELP AND GUIDE THEM TILL THEN

"Stop letting your hearts be troubled; keep on believing in God, and also in me. ² In my Father's house there are many dwelling places;ᵃ if there were not, I would have told you, for I am going away to make ready a place for you. ³ And if I go and make it ready for you, I will come back and take you to be face to faceᵇ with me, so that you may alwaysᶜ be right where I am. ⁴ And you know the way to the place whereᵈ I am going."

⁵ Thomas said to Him, "Lord, we do not know where you are going, and so how can we know the way?"

⁶ Jesus answered him, "I am the way and the truth and the life. No one canᵉ come to the Father except through me. ⁷ If you knew me, you would know my Father too. From now on you do know Him and you have seen Him."

⁸ Philip said to Him, "Lord, let us seeᶠ the Father, and that will satisfy us."

⁹ Jesus said to him, "Have I been with you disciplesᵍ so long, and yet you, Philip, have not recognized me? Whoever has seen me has seen the Father. How can you say, 'Let us see the Father'? ¹⁰ Do you not believe that I am in union with the Father and that the Father is in union with me? I am not saying these things

ᵃ Exact meaning of Grk. word.
ᵇ Real meaning of prep. (Robertson).
ᶜ Vb. expresses linear ac.
ᵈ Poor Eng., but reproduces the poor Grk.
ᵉ *Ability* implied.
ᶠ Lit., *show us the F.*
ᵍ Implied in pl. pro.

on my own authority, but the Father who always remains in union with me is doing these things Himself. ¹¹ You must believe me, that I am in union with the Father and that the Father is in union with me, or else you must do so because of the very things that I am doing. ¹² I most solemnly say to you, whoever perseveres in believing in me can [h] himself [i] do the things that I am doing; yes, he can do even greater things than I am doing, because I am going to the Father. ¹³ And anything you ask for as bearers of my name [j] I will do for you, so that the Father may be glorified through the Son. ¹⁴ Yes, I repeat it,[k] anything you ask for as bearers of my name I will do it for you.

¹⁵ "If you really love me, you will keep my commands. ¹⁶ And I will ask the Father and He will give you another Helper, to remain with you to the end of the age;[l] ¹⁷ even the Spirit of truth, whom the world cannot accept, because it does not see Him or recognize Him, because He is going to remain with you, and will be within you. ¹⁸ I will not leave you helpless orphans.[m] I am coming back to you. ¹⁹ In just a little while the world will not see me any more, but you will be seeing me. Because I am to live on,[n] you too will live on. ²⁰ At that time [o] you will know that I am in union with my Father and you are in union with me and I am in union with you. ²¹ Whoever continues to hold and keep my commands is the one who really loves me, and whoever really loves me will be loved by my Father; yes, I will love him myself and will make myself real [p] to him."

²² Judas (not Judas Iscariot) said to Him, "Why is it, Lord, that you are going to make yourself real to us and not to the world?" ²³ Jesus answered him, "If anyone really loves me, he will observe my teaching,[q] and my Father will love him, and both of us will come in face-to-face [r] fellowship with him; yes, we will make our special [s] dwelling place with him. ²⁴ Whoever does not really love

[h] Implied.
[i] Pro. emph.
[j] Grk., *in my name.*
[k] Supplied from context.
[l] Lit., *into the age, forever.*
[m] Exact meaning of Grk. word (ours from it).
[n] Pres. of cont. ac.
[o] Lit., *on that day;* i.e., *after the resurrection.*
[p] Lit., *will appear* or *show Myself.*
[q] Grk., *my word.*
[r] *Pros* again; strongest prep.
[s] Fol. WH and best Mss., reading mid. voice.

me does not observe my teaching; and yet the teaching which you are listening to is not mine but comes from the Father who has sent me.

25 "I have told you this while I am still staying with you. 26 But the Helper, the Holy Spirit, whom the Father will send to represent[t] me, will teach you everything Himself, and cause you to remember everything that I have told you. 27 I now leave you the blessing[u] of peace, I give you the blessing[u] of my own peace. I myself do not give it in the way the world gives it. Stop letting your hearts be troubled or timid. 28 You have heard me say that I am going away and coming back to you; if you really loved me, you would rejoice over my telling you that I am going to the Father, because my Father is greater than I. 29 And now I have told you this before it takes place, that when it does take place you may believe in me.

30 "I shall not talk much more with you, for the evil ruler[v] of this world is coming and he has nothing in common with me, 31 but he is coming that the world may know that I love the Father and am doing what the Father has ordered me to do. Get up and let us go away."

15 THE ALLEGORY OF THE VINE AND ITS BRANCHES; THE JOY OF UNION WITH CHRIST; THE WORLD TO HATE THE DISCIPLES; THE GUILT OF SINNING AGAINST THE LIGHT; THE SPIRIT, THE HELPER, WILL TESTIFY TO JESUS

"I am the real vine, and my Father is the cultivator.[a] 2 He cuts away any branch on me that stops bearing fruit, and He repeatedly prunes every branch that continues to bear fruit, to make it bear more.[b] 3 You are already pruned because of the teaching that I have given[c] you. 4 You must remain in union with me and I will remain in union with you. Just as no branch by itself can bear fruit unless it remains united to the vine, so you cannot unless you remain in union with me. 5 I am the vine, you are the branches. Whoever remains in union with me and I in union with him will

---

[t] Lit., *in my name;* so *to represent me.*
[u] Implied from context.
[v] Refers to Satan; hence evil ruler.
[a] Lit., *worker of the soil.*
[b] Grk., *more fruit.*
[c] Lit., *words that I have spoken.*

bear abundant fruit,[d] because you cannot do anything cut off[e] from union with me. 6 If anyone does not remain in union with me, he is thrown away as a mere branch and is dried up; then it is picked up and thrown into the fire and burned up.[f] 7 If you remain in union with me and my words remain in you, you may[g] ask whatever you please and you shall have it. 8 By your continuously bearing abundant fruit and in this way[h] proving yourselves to be real disciples of mine, my Father is glorified. 9 I have loved you just as the Father has loved me. You must remain in my love.[i] 10 If you continue to keep my commands, you will remain in my love, just as I have kept my Father's commands and remain in His love.

11 "I have told you these things, that the joy which I have had[j] may remain in you and that your joy may be complete. 12 This is my command to you, to keep on loving one another as I have loved you. 13 No one can show[k] greater love than this, the giving of his life for his friends. 14 You are my friends, if you keep on doing what I command you to do. 15 I no longer call you slaves, because the slave does not know what his master is doing; I now call[l] you friends, because I have told you everything that I have learned from my Father. 16 You have not chosen me; I have chosen you, and appointed you to go and bear fruit, that your fruit may remain too, so that the Father may grant you, as bearers of my name, whatever you ask Him for.

17 "What I command you to do is, to keep on loving one another. 18 If the world continues to hate you, remember[m] that it has first hated me. 19 If you belonged to the world, the world would love what is its own. But it is because you do not belong to the world, but I have chosen you out of the world, that the world hates you. 20 Remember what I once told you: No slave is greater than his master. If they have persecuted me, they will persecute you too. If they have observed my teaching, they will observe

[d] Grk., *much fruit.*
[e] Lit., *apart from me.*
[f] Grk. changes voice many times in v. We use passive to make it smoother.
[g] Impv. of permission.
[h] Phrase implied.
[i] Fut. indic. of obligation.
[j] Lit., *my own joy.*
[k] Grk., *no one has.*
[l] Pf. but result persists to present; so *I now call.*
[m] Lit., *know.*

yours too. 21 They will do all this to you on account of me, because they do not know Him who has sent me.

22 "If I had not come and spoken to them, they would not be guilty ⁿ of sin. But now the fact ᵒ is, they have no excuse for their sin. 23 Whoever continues to hate me continues to hate my Father too. 24 If I had not done things among them that no one else has ever done, they would not be guilty of sin. But now the fact is, they have seen and even hated both my Father and me. 25 But this is so that the saying written in their law may be fulfilled, 'They hated me without a cause.' ᵖ

26 "When the Helper comes whom I will send from the Father to you, the Spirit of truth that comes from the Father, He will testify to me. 27 And you too are to bear testimony to me, because you have been with me from the start."

16 JESUS WARNS OF FUTURE HARDSHIPS; IF HE LEAVES, THE HELPER WILL COME TO CONVINCE THE WORLD; HE WILL LEAD THE DISCIPLES TO KNOW SPIRITUAL TRUTHS; JESUS CHEERS THEIR SORROWING HEARTS

"I have told you these things to keep you from falling over stumbling blocks.ᵃ 2 Men will turn you out of their synagogues. Yes, indeed, the time is coming when anyone who kills you will think that he is rendering a religious service to God. 3 They will do this, because they have never come to know ᵇ God nor me. 4 But I have told you these things that when the time does come, you may remember that I told you. I did not tell you these things at the start, because I was with you. 5 But now I am going away to Him who has sent me, and not one of you is asking me where I am going, 6 but sorrow has taken complete ᶜ possession of your hearts, because I have told you these things. 7 Yet it is nothing but the truth I now tell you, that it is better for you that I should go away. For if I do not go away, the Helper will not come into close fellowship ᵈ with you, but if I do go away, I will send Him to be in close fellowship with you.

ⁿ Lit., *would not have sin;* i.e., *would not be guilty.*
ᵒ Lit., *but now it is.*
ᵖ Pss. 35:19; 69:4.
ᵃ Grk., *lest you be caused to stumble.*
ᵇ Ingressive aor. with *ouk (not).*
ᶜ Lit., *has filled your hearts.*
ᵈ *Pros* again, so close *fellowship.*

8 "And when He comes, He will bring conviction to worldly people e about sin and uprightness and judgment; 9 about sin, because they do not believe in me; 10 about uprightness, because I go away to the Father so that f you can no longer see me; 11 about judgment, because the evil ruler of this world has been condemned.

12 "I have much more to tell you, but you cannot grasp it now. 13 But when the Spirit of truth comes, He will guide you into the whole truth; for He will not speak on His own authority but will tell what is told Him,g and will announce to you the things that are to come. 14 He will glorify me, because He will take the things that belong to me and tell them to you. 15 Everything that the Father has is mine; this is why I have told you, 'He will take the things that are mine and tell them to you.'

16 "In just a little while you will not see me any longer; and yet, in just a little while after you will see me again."

17 So some of His disciples said to one another, "What does He mean by telling us, 'In just a little while you will not see me, and yet in just a little while after you will see me again,' and 'Because I am going away to the Father'?" 18 So they kept saying, "What does He mean by saying, 'a little while'? We do not know what He is talking about."

19 Jesus knew that they wanted to ask Him a question, and so He said to them, "Are you inquiring of one another about this saying of mine, 'In just a little while you will not see me, and yet in just a little while after you will see me again'? 20 I most solemnly say to you, you will weep and wail, but the world will be glad; you will grieve but your grief will be turned into gladness. 21 When a woman is in labor, she is in pain, for her time has come, but when the baby is born,h she forgets her pain because of her joy that a human being has been born into the world. 22 So you too are now in sorrow; but I am going to see you again, and then your hearts will be happy, and no one can i rob you of your happiness. 23 At that time you will ask me no more questions. I most solemnly say to you, the Father will give you, as bearers of my name, whatever you ask Him for. 24 Up to this time you have not asked for anything as bearers of my name, but now you must keep on asking, and you

---

e Grk., *the world.*
f Lit., *and you.*
g Grk., *what He hears.*
h Active in Grk., passive better in Eng.
i Implied in context.

will receive, that your cup of joy may be full to the brim.ʲ

²⁵ "I have told you these things in allegories, but a time is coming when I shall not do so any longer, but will plainly tell you about the Father. ²⁶ At that time you will ask, as bearers of my name, and I do not say that I will ask the Father for you, ²⁷ for the Father tenderlyᵏ loves you Himself, because you nowˡ tenderly love me and now believe that I have come from the Father. ²⁸ I did come from the Father and I have come into the world. Now I am leaving the world and going back to the Father."

²⁹ His disciples said to Him, "Now you are talking plainly and not in allegory at all. ³⁰ Now we know that you know everything and do not need that anyone should ask you questions. For this reason we believe that you have come from God."

³¹ Jesus answered them, "Do you now really believe? ³² Listen! A time is coming, yea, it is right here, when you will all be scattered to your own homes and will leave me alone. And yet, I am not alone, because the Father is with me. ³³ I have told you these things, that you through unionᵐ with me may have peace. In the world you have trouble; but be courageous! I have conquered the world."

17 JESUS PRAYS FOR HIMSELF, FOR HIS DISCIPLES, AND ALL HIS FUTURE FOLLOWERS; HE ASKS THAT THEY BE PRESERVED, CONSECRATED, UNIFIED, AND GLORIFIED

When Jesus had said all these things, He lifted His eyes to heaven and said: "Father, the time has come. Glorify your Son, that He may glorify you, ² just as you have given Him authority over all mankindᵃ to give eternal life to all whom you have given Him. ³ Now eternal life means knowing you as the only true God and knowing Jesus your messengerᵇ as Christ. ⁴ I have glorified you down here upon the earth by completing the work which you have given me to do. ⁵ So now, Father, glorify me up there in your presence just as you didᶜ before the world existed.

ʲ Lit., *that your joy may be full.*
ᵏ *Phileo, love tenderly.*
ˡ Pf. but result pres.
ᵐ Lit., *in me,* but really meaning *union with Christ.*
ᵃ Grk., *all flesh,* that is, *mankind.*
ᵇ Lit., *the one whom you sent.*
ᶜ Grk., *with the glory which I had.*

⁶ "I have made your very self ᵈ known to the men whom you have given me out of the world. At first they were yours, but now you have given them to me, and they have obeyed your message. ⁷ Now they have come to know that everything you have given me really comes ᵉ from you; ⁸ for I have given them the teachings ᶠ that you gave me, and they have accepted them, and they have come to know in reality that I did come from you, and so they are convinced ᵍ that you did send me. ⁹ I am praying ʰ for them. I am not praying for the world now, but only for those whom you have given me, because they are yours—¹⁰ really, all that is mine is yours, and all that is yours is mine—and I have been glorified through them. ¹¹ And now I am no longer to be in the world, but they are to stay on ⁱ in the world, while I am going to be ʲ with you. Holy Father, keep them by the power which ᵏ you have given me, so that they may be one just as we are. ¹² As long as I was with them, I kept them by your power which you gave me, and I protected them, and not one of them was lost, except the one who is now doomed ˡ to be lost, so that the Scripture might be fulfilled. ¹³ And now I am going to be with you, and I am saying these things while still in the world, that the joy which I experience may be fully experienced in their own souls.ᵐ ¹⁴ I have given them your message, and the world has hated them, because they do not belong to the world, just as I do not belong to it.ⁿ ¹⁵ I am not asking you to take them out of the world, but to keep them from the evil in it. ¹⁶ They do not belong to the world just as I do not belong to it. ¹⁷ Consecrate them by your truth; your message is truth. ¹⁸ Just as you have sent me into the world, I have sent them into the world, too. ¹⁹ And so for their sake I am consecrating ᵒ myself, that they too may be consecrated ᵒ by truth.

²⁰ "I make this petition, not for them only, but for all who ever come to believe in me through their message, ²¹ for them all to be

---

ᵈ Lit., *your name* (meaning *self* to a Heb.)
ᵉ Grk., *is*.
ᶠ Lit., *the uttered words*.
ᵍ Grk., *have come to believe*.
ʰ Lit., *asking, making a petition*.
ⁱ Lit., *are*.
ʲ Grk., *going to you*.
ᵏ Lit., *by the name which* (WH).
ˡ Grk., *the son of perdition*.
ᵐ Lit., *completed in them*.
ⁿ Grk., repeats *now*.
ᵒ I.e., set apart.

one, just as **you, Father,** are in union with me and I in union with you, for them to be in union with us, so that the world may be convinced p that you have sent me. ²² I have given them the glory which you gave me, so that they may be one, just as we are, ²³ I in union with them and you in union with me, so that they may be perfectly united,q and the world may be surer that you sent me and that you have loved them just as you have loved me. ²⁴ **Father,** I want to have those whom you have given me right where I am, in order that they may see the glory which you have given me, because you loved me before the creation s of the world. ²⁵ Righteous Father, although the world did not know you, I didt know you, and these men have come to know that you sent me, ²⁶ and I made known to them your very self,d and I will make you known still further, so that the love which you have shown to me may be felt in them, and I in union with them."

18   JUDAS GUIDES THE OFFICERS TO ARREST JESUS; THEN THEY TAKE HIM BEFORE ANNAS AND CAIAPHAS; PETER DISOWNS JESUS WHILE HE IS BEING TRIED IN THE ROMAN COURT

On saying these things He went out with His disciples across the Ravine of Cedars to a place where there was a garden, and He went into it witha His disciples. ² Now Judas, too, who betrayed Him, knew the spot, because Jesus had often met with His disciples there. ³ So Judas got togetherb the Roman garrisonc and some attendants from the high priests and Pharisees, and went there with lanterns and torches and weapons.

⁴ Then Jesus, as He knew everything that was going to befall Him, came forward and asked them, "Who is it that you are looking for?"

⁵ They answered Him, "Jesus of Nazareth."

He said to them, "I am He." And Judas who betrayed Him was standing among them. ⁶ So when He said to them, "I am He,"

---

p Lit., *come to believe.*
q *Perfected into one.*
r Lit., *know.*
s *Foundation.*
t Pro. and vb. emph.
a Lit., *and His disciples.*
b Grk., *took.*
c The cohort stationed at Antonia castle for keeping peace.

they took a lurch ᵈ backward and fell to the ground. ⁷ So once more He asked them, "Who is it that you are looking for?"

They said, "Jesus of Nazareth."

⁸ Jesus answered, "I have already told you that I am He; so if you are really looking for me, let these men go." ⁹ He said this that the statement He had just made might be fulfilled, "I have not lost one of those whom you have given me." ¹⁰ So Simon Peter, who had a sword, drew it and struck the high priest's slave and cut off his right ear. The slave's name was Malchus.

¹¹ Then Jesus said to Peter, "Put your sword back into the sheath. Must ᵉ I not drink the cup which the Father has handed ᶠ me?"

¹² So the garrison and its commander ᵍ and the attendants of the Jews arrested Jesus and put handcuffs ʰ on Him, ¹³ and took Him first to Annas. For he was father-in-law of Caiaphas who was high priest that year. ¹⁴ Now it was Caiaphas who had advised the Jews that it was for their welfare that one should die for the people.

¹⁵ Simon Peter and another disciple followed on after Jesus. And that other disciple was acquainted with the high priest, and so went on with Jesus into the high priest's courtyard, ¹⁶ but Peter stood outside before the door. So this other disciple, who was acquainted with the high priest, stepped out and spoke to the woman doorkeeper and brought Peter in. ¹⁷ Then the servant-girl at the door said to Peter, "You too are not one of this man's disciples, are you?"

He answered, "No, I am not." ¹⁸ Because it was cold, the slaves and attendants had made a charcoal fire and were standing about it warming ⁱ themselves; so Peter too was standing among them warming himself.

¹⁹ Then the high priest questioned Jesus about His disciples and His teaching. ²⁰ Jesus answered him, "I have spoken publicly to the world; I have always taught in the synagogues and in the temple where all the Jews are in the habit of meeting, and I have not spoken anything in secret. ²¹ So why are you questioning me? Ask those who heard what I told them. Of course,ʲ they know what I said."

ᵈ All at once (aor.) etc.
ᵉ Impv. fut. indic.
ᶠ Lit., *has given me.*
ᵍ Lit., *chiliarch.*
ʰ Grk., *bound.*
ⁱ Lit., *and were warming.*
ʲ Grk., *behold.*

JOHN 18

²² After He had said this, one of the attendants standing by slapped Jesus in the face,ᵏ and said, "Is this the way you answer the high priest?"

²³ Jesus answered him, "If I have said anything wrong, on oath¹ tell what it is; but if what I have said is true, why do you slap me?" ²⁴ So Annas sent Him over, still in handcuffs, to Caiaphas the high priest.

²⁵ But Simon Peter still stood warming himself. So they said to him, "You too are not one of His disciples, are you?"

He denied it and said, "No, I am not."

²⁶ One of the high priest's slaves, who was a kinsman of the one whose ear Peter had cut off, said, "Did I not see you in the garden with Him?"

²⁷ Then Peter again denied it, and at that moment a cock crowed.

²⁸ Then they took Jesus from Caiaphas to the governor's palace.ᵐ It was early in the morning, and they would not go into the governor's palace themselves, in order not to be defiled,ⁿ so as to be unfit to eat the Passover supper. ²⁹ So Pilate came outside and asked, "What is the charge you bring against this man?"

³⁰ They retorted, "If He were not a criminal, we would not have turned Him over to you."

³¹ Pilate said to them, "Take Him yourselves, and try Him in accordance with your own law."

Then the Jews said to him, "It is not lawful for us to execute the death penalty ᵒ on anyone." ³² This made it possible ᵖ for the word of Jesus to be fulfilled which He spoke to indicate what sort ᑫ of death He was to die.

³³ So Pilate went back into the governor's palace and called Jesus and asked Him, "Are you the king of the Jews?"

³⁴ Jesus answered him, "Do you ask me this on your own initiative,ʳ or have others suggested ˢ it to you about me?"

³⁵ Pilate answered, "I am not a Jew, am I? Your own people and their high priests have turned you over to me. What have you done?"

ᵏ Lit., *gave J. a slap.*
¹ Lit., *testify.*
ᵐ Lit., *the pretorium,* which was the governor's palace.
ⁿ I.e., ceremonially.
ᵒ Grk., *to kill anyone,* the aim which moved them in this trial.
ᵖ Implied.
ᑫ Interrog. of quality.
ʳ Lit., *from yourself.*
ˢ Grk., *said.*

³⁶ Jesus answered, "My kingdom does not belong to this world. If my kingdom did belong to this world, my attendants would have been fighting ᵗ to keep me from being turned over to the Jews. But as a matter of fact, my kingdom does not come from such a source." ᵘ

³⁷ Then Pilate said to Him, "So you are a king then?"

Jesus answered, "Certainly I am a king. For this very purpose I was born, for this very purpose I have come into the world, to testify for truth. Everybody who is a friend of truth listens to my voice."

³⁸ Pilate asked Him, "What is truth?"

On saying this he went outside again to the Jews, and said to them, "As far as I can see,ᵛ I can find no ground for a charge against Him. ³⁹ Now you have a custom to have me set one man free at your Passover time. So do you wish me to set the king of the Jews free?"

⁴⁰ Then they all shouted back, "No! Not Him, but Barabbas!" Now Barabbas was a robber.

19 PILATE ORDERS JESUS FLOGGED; THEN SENTENCES HIM TO DEATH; THE SOLDIERS CRUCIFY HIM AND TAKE HIS CLOTHES; HE COMMITS HIS MOTHER TO JOHN; HE EXPIRES; HIS SIDE IS PIERCED BY A SOLDIER'S LANCE; BURIED BY JOSEPH AND NICODEMUS

So then Pilate took Jesus and had Him flogged. ² And the soldiers made a crown out of thorns and put it on His head, and put a purple ᵃ coat on Him, ³ and kept marching up to Him and saying, "All hail, you king of the Jews!" each one slapping Him on the face.

⁴ And Pilate went outside again and said to the Jews, "Listen! I am going to bring Him out to you, for you to see ᵇ that I can find no ground for a charge against Him." ⁵ So Jesus came outside still wearing the crown of thorns and the purple coat. Then Pilate said to them, "Here is the man!"

ᵗ Past linear cond.
ᵘ Lit., *is not from here*.
ᵛ Pronoun very emph.
ᵃ A sign of royalty, to mock His claim as king.
ᵇ Grk., *know*.

JOHN 19

⁶ When the high priests and attendants saw Him, they shouted, "Crucify Him! Crucify Him!"

Pilate said to them, "Take Him yourselves and crucify Him, for I can find no ground for a charge against Him."

⁷ The Jews answered him, "We have a law, and in accordance with that law He deserves to die, for claiming ᶜ to be God's Son."

⁸ As soon as Pilate heard that, he was more awe-stricken ᵈ than before ⁹ and went back into the governor's palace and asked Jesus, "Where do you come from?" But Jesus made no answer. ¹⁰ Then Pilate said to Him, "Do you refuse to speak to me? Do you not know that I have it in my power to set you free or to crucify you?"

¹¹ Jesus answered him, "You would have no power at all over me, if it had not been given to you from above.ᵉ So the man who betrayed me to you is more guilty than you." ᶠ

¹² Because of this Pilate kept on trying to set Him free, but the Jews shouted, "If you set Him free, you are no friend to the emperor.ᵍ Anyone who claims to be a king is uttering treason against the emperor!" ¹³ On hearing this Pilate had Jesus brought out and had Him sit on the judge's bench at the place called the Stone Platform, or in Hebrew, Gabbatha. ¹⁴ It was the day of Preparation for the Passover, and it was about noon. Then Pilate said to the Jews, "There is your king!"

¹⁵ But they shouted, "Kill Him! Kill Him! Crucify Him!"

Pilate said to them, "Must I crucify your king?"

The high priests answered, "We have no king but the emperor!"

¹⁶ So Pilate then turned Him over to them to be crucified.

Then they took Jesus, ¹⁷ and He went out carrying the cross by Himself ʰ to a spot called The Place of the Skull, or in Hebrew, Golgotha. ¹⁸ There they crucified Him, with two others, one on each side, and Jesus in the middle. ¹⁹ Pilate had a placard ⁱ written and had it put over the cross: "JESUS OF NAZARETH, THE KING OF THE JEWS."

²⁰ Many of the Jews read this placard, because the place where Jesus was crucified was near the city, and it was written in He-

---

ᶜ Lit., *because He said,* etc.
ᵈ He feared because he felt He was divine.
ᵉ That is, His death is to be by God's purpose and permission.
ᶠ Either Judas or Caiaphas meant.
ᵍ Tiberius at that time.
ʰ Fol. the Vat. Ms., the most ancient.
ⁱ Lit., *title, inscription.*

brew, Latin, and Greek. ²¹ So the high priests of the Jews said to Pilate, "You must not write, 'The king of the Jews,' but write, 'He said, I am the king of the Jews.'"

²² Pilate answered, "What I have written, I have written!"

²³ When the soldiers had crucified Jesus, they took His clothes and divided them into four parts, one for each soldier, except j the coat, which was without a seam, woven in one piece from top to bottom. ²⁴ So they said to one another, "Let us not tear it, but let us draw k for it to see who gets it." This was to fulfill the Scripture which says,

> "They divided my clothes among them,
> And for my clothing they cast lots." l

Now this was what the soldiers did.

²⁵ Near Jesus' cross were standing His mother and her sister Mary, the wife m of Clopas, and Mary of Magdala. ²⁶ So Jesus, on seeing His mother and the disciple whom He loved standing near, said to His mother, "There is your son."

²⁷ Then He said to His disciple, "There is your mother." And from that very hour His disciple took her to his own home.

²⁸ After this, as Jesus knew that everything was now finished, that the Scripture might be fulfilled, n He said, "I am thirsty."

²⁹ A bowl full of sour wine was sitting there. So they put a sponge soaked in sour wine on a stick o and put it to His lips. p

³⁰ As soon as Jesus took the sour wine, He said, "It is finished!" Then He bowed His head and gave up His spirit.

³¹ As it was the day of Preparation for the Passover, that the bodies might not remain on the crosses during the sabbath, for that sabbath was a very important one, the Jews requested Pilate to have their legs broken and their bodies taken down. ³² So the soldiers went and broke the legs of the first man and of the other one who had been crucified with Him. ³³ But when they came to Jesus, as they saw that He was already dead, they did not break His legs, ³⁴ but one of the soldiers thrust a lance into His side and blood and water at once flowed out. ³⁵ The man who saw it has testified to it—and his testimony is true, and he knows that he is

---

j Lit., *and the coat,* but next clause shows it is excepted.
k Lit., *cast lots.*
l Ps. 22:18.
m So EGT; but may be daughter or sister.
n Grk., *brought to an end.*
o Lit., *hyssop;* stick of hyssop plant.
p Lit., *mouth.*

telling the truth—in order that you too may come to believe it.
³⁶ For this took place that this Scripture might be fulfilled, "Not a bone of His will be broken." ᵠ ³⁷ And again another Scripture says, "They shall look at Him whom they pierced." ʳ

³⁸ After this, Joseph of Arimathea, who was a disciple of Jesus, but a secret one because of his fear of the Jews, asked permission ˢ of Pilate to remove the body of Jesus, and Pilate granted it. So he went and removed His body. ³⁹ Now Nicodemus also, who had formerly come to Jesus at night, went and took a mixture of myrrh and aloes that weighed ᵗ about one hundred pounds. ⁴⁰ So they took the body of Jesus and wrapped it in bandages with the spices, in accordance ᵘ with the Jewish custom of preparing a body for burial. ⁴¹ There was a garden at the place where Jesus had been crucified, and in the garden there was a new tomb in which no one had yet been laid. ⁴² So, because it was the Jewish Preparation day and because the tomb was near by, they laid Him there.

20 THE TOMB FOUND EMPTY BY MARY, PETER, AND JOHN; JESUS APPEARS TO MARY, THE TEN, AND THE ELEVEN (ESPECIALLY TO THOMAS); JOHN'S AIM IN WRITING

On the first day of the week, very early in the morning while it was still dark, Mary of Magdala went to the tomb, and she saw that the stone had been removed from the tomb. ² So she ran away and went to Simon Peter and the other disciple whom Jesus tenderly ᵃ loved, and said to them, "They have taken away the Lord from the tomb, and we do not know where they have put Him."

³ So Peter and the other disciple left the city and started ᵇ for the tomb. ⁴ And they both kept running, but the other disciple outran Peter and got to the tomb first. ⁵ And he stooped down and peered in ᶜ and saw the bandages lying on the ground, but he did not go in. ⁶ Then Simon Peter came running up behind him, and he went inside, and saw the bandages lying on the ground, ⁷ but

ᵠ Ex. 12:46; Ps. 34:20.
ʳ Zech. 12:10.
ˢ Expressed in next clause.
ᵗ Implied.
ᵘ Grk., *as is the custom.*
ᵃ *Phileo, tenderly love.*
ᵇ Lit., *went out,* etc.
ᶜ Vb. has both ideas.

the handkerchief which had been over His face was not lying with the bandages, but was folded up by itself in another place. ⁸ So then the other disciple, who had reached the tomb first, went inside and saw, and he came to believe it.ᵈ ⁹ For they had not previously understood the Scripture which saidᵉ that He must rise from the dead. ¹⁰ So the disciples went home again.

¹¹ But Mary stood just outside the tomb and kept weeping. So, as she was weeping, she stooped down and peered into the tomb ¹² and saw seated there two angels in white robes, one at the head, one at the feet, where Jesus' body had lain. ¹³ And they said to her, "Woman, why are you weeping?"

She said to them, "They have taken away my Lord, and I do not know where they have put him." ¹⁴ On saying this she turned around and saw Jesus standing there, but she did not know that it was Jesus.

¹⁵ Jesus said to her, "Woman, why are you weeping? Whom are you looking for?"ᶠ

Because she supposed it was the gardener, she said to Him, "If it was you, sir, who carried Him away, tell me where you put Him, and I will remove Him."

¹⁶ Jesus said to her, "Mary!"

At onceᵍ she turned and said to Him in Hebrew, "Rabboni!" which means Teacher.

¹⁷ Jesus said to her, "Stop clinging to me so,ʰ for I have not yet gone up to my Father; but go to my brothers and tell them that I am going up to my Father and your Father, to my God and your God."

¹⁸ Mary of Magdala went and announced to the disciples that she had seen the Lord and that He had told her this.

¹⁹ In the evening of that same first day of the week, even with the doors of the roomⁱ bolted where the disciples had met for fear of the Jews, Jesus went in and stood among them and said to them, "Peace be with you!" ²⁰ On saying this, He showed them His hands and His side, and the disciples were thrilledʲ with joy over seeing their Lord.

ᵈ Aor. means here, *he came to believe it* (the resurrection of J.).
ᵉ Lit., *the Scripture that He,* etc.
ᶠ Poor Eng. but it accords with the Grk.
ᵍ In aor.
ʰ As if I had come to remain permanently.
ⁱ Implied.
ʲ In the context.

²¹ Jesus again said to them, "Peace be with you! Just as my Father has sent me forth, so I am now sending you."

²² On saying this, He breathed upon them, and said, "Receive the Holy Spirit! ²³ If you get [k] forgiveness for people's sins, they are forgiven them; if you let people's sins fasten upon them, they will remain fastened upon them."

²⁴ Now Thomas, one of the Twelve, who was called the Twin, was not with them when Jesus came in. ²⁵ So the rest of the disciples kept saying to him, "We have seen the Lord!"

But he said to them, "Unless I see the nailprints in His hands, and put my finger into them, and put my hand into His side, I will never believe it!"

²⁶ Just a week later [1] the disciples were in the room again and Thomas was with them. Although the doors were bolted, Jesus came in and stood among them, and said, "Peace be with you!"

²⁷ Then He said to Thomas, "Put your finger here and look at my hands, and take your hand and put it in my side, and stop being an unbeliever, but be a believer!"

²⁸ Thomas answered Him, "My Lord and my God!"

²⁹ Jesus said to him, "Is it because you have seen me, Thomas, that you believe? [m] Blessed be those who believe, even though they have not seen me!" [n]

³⁰ Now there are many other wonder-works which Jesus performed in the disciples' presence which are not recorded in this book. ³¹ But these have been recorded, in order that you may believe that Jesus is the Christ, the Son of God, and that through believing you may have life, as bearers of His name.[o]

21   JESUS APPEARS TO SEVEN DISCIPLES IN A GREAT CATCH OF FISH; HE PREPARES AND EATS BREAKFAST WITH THEM; TESTS PETER'S LOVE

After this Jesus again showed Himself to the disciples at the sea of Tiberias,[a] and this is the way He showed Himself.

---

[k] Lit., *if you forgive;* but He is emphasizing their winning others; hence our tr. inserting *get.*

[1] Grk., *eight days after;* one week in the clear, as they counted first and last days.

[m] Pf., *have believed,* but result cont. to pres., so *now believe.*

[n] Lit., *Blessed be those who have not seen, and yet,* etc. Concess. pt.

[o] Grk., *in His name.*

[a] Another name for sea of Galilee.

JOHN 21

[2] Simon Peter, Thomas called the Twin, Nathaniel of Cana in Galilee, the sons of Zebedee, and two other disciples of Jesus, were all together. [3] Simon Peter said to them, "I am going fishing."

They said to him, "We are going with you too." They went out and got into the boat, but that night they caught nothing.

[4] Now just as day was breaking, Jesus took His stand on the shore, though the disciples did not know that it was Jesus. [5] So Jesus said to them, "Lads,[b] you have no fish,[b] have you?"

They answered, "No."

[6] Then He said to them, "Set your net on the right side of the boat, and you will catch them."

They did so, and they could not drag it in for the big catch[c] of fish. [7] So that disciple whom Jesus used to love tenderly[d] said to Peter, "It is the Lord!"

When Simon Peter heard that it was the Lord, he belted on his fisherman's coat,[e] for he had taken it off,[f] and plunged into the sea. [8] The rest of the disciples followed in the little boat, for they were not far from shore—only about a hundred yards—dragging in the net full[g] of fish.

[9] When they landed, they saw a charcoal fire all made and a fish lying on it; also some bread. [10] Jesus said to them, "Fetch[h] some of the fish you have just caught." [11] So Simon Peter got into the boat, and pulled the net ashore, full of big fish, a hundred and fifty-three; and though there were so many, the net was not torn. [12] Jesus said to them, "Come and have breakfast."

None of the disciples dared to ask Him, "Who are you?" because they knew it was the Lord. [13] Jesus went and took the bread and gave it to them, and the fish too. [14] This was now the third time that Jesus showed Himself to His disciples, after He had risen from the dead.

[15] After they had finished breakfast,[i] Jesus said to Simon Peter, "Simon, son of John, are you more devoted[j] to me than you are to these things?"[k]

[b] Lit. *children—nothing to eat*; context and usage confirm tr. (so EGT).
[c] Common fishermen's term.
[d] Impf. so.
[e] So EGT and fathers.
[f] Lit., *naked*.
[g] Lit., *net of fish*
[h] Good word in Eng. lit. Exact meaning for this case.
[i] Effective aor.
[j] *Agapao, to love intelligently, with devotion.*
[k] That is, *more devoted to me than you are to boats, nets,* etc.

Peter answered Him, "Yes, Lord, you know that I tenderly[1] love you."

Jesus said to him, "Then feed my lambs."

[16] Jesus again said to him a second time, "Simon, son of John, are you really devoted to me?"

He said to Him, "Yes, Lord, you know that I tenderly love you."

Jesus said to him, "Then be a shepherd to my sheep."

[17] For the third time Jesus asked him, "Simon, son of John, do you really tenderly love me?"

Peter was hurt because Jesus the third time asked him, "Do you really tenderly love me?" So he answered Him, "Lord, you know everything; you know that I do tenderly love you."

Jesus said to him, "Then feed my sheep. [18] I most solemnly say to you, when you were young, you used to put on your own belt and go where you pleased, but when you grow old, you will stretch out your hands and someone else will put a belt on you and you will go where you do not please to go." [19] He said this to point out the sort[m] of death by which Peter was to glorify God. So after He had said this, He said to Peter, "Keep on following me!"

[20] Peter turned and saw following them the disciple whom Jesus specially loved, who at the supper leaned back upon Jesus' breast and asked, "Lord, who is it that is going to betray you?" [21] So when Peter saw him, he said to Jesus, "But, Lord, what about him?"

[22] Jesus answered him, "If I wish him to wait until I come, what is that to you? You must keep on following me."

[23] So the report[n] got out among the brothers that this disciple was not going to die. But Jesus did not tell him that he was not going to die; He said only, "If I wish him to wait until I come, what is that to you?"

[24] This is the disciple who testifies to these things and who wrote them down, and we know that his testimony is true.

[25] There are many other things that Jesus did, which, if they were all[o] written down in detail,[p] I do not suppose that the world itself could hold the books that would have to be written.

---

[1] *Phileo, to love tenderly, with personal affection.*
[m] Interrog. of quality.
[n] Lit., *the word.*
[o] Implied in the relative and context.
[p] Grk., *one by one.*

THE ACTS OF THE APOSTLES

The writer is generally thought to be Luke the beloved physician, who also wrote the Gospel that bears his name. Nearly all the writers of the Early Church ascribe both books to Luke. The evidence furnished by the books themselves confirms this view—the vocabulary, especially rich in medical terms, the excellent style of Greek, and the attitude of the author toward Jesus and Paul.

The purpose of the writer was to supplement his early story of Jesus' life and works on earth with a historical account of the works done by the ascended Christ, through the Holy Spirit who endued the disciples with power from on high. It is really the first history of the Church.

As the writer was not an eyewitness of the events recorded, he must have had trustworthy sources, namely, a Jewish Christian account of the church in Jerusalem by an eyewitness. He also picked up many of the facts from personal contact with those Christians, while he was in Palestine with Paul at his arrest, and during Paul's imprisonment at Caesarea. For the events in Paul's life he had his own account as an eyewitness. So the historical accuracy of this book cannot be questioned. The date was about A. D. 70 to 75.

1   THE RISEN JESUS GIVES CONVINCING PROOFS THAT HE IS ALIVE, GIVES FINAL ORDERS; GOES BACK TO HEAVEN; THE APOSTLES AND OTHERS MEET TO PRAY; PETER SUGGESTS THE CHOOSING OF JUDAS' SUCCESSOR; MATTHIAS CHOSEN

I wrote[a] my first[b] volume, Theophilus, about all that Jesus did and taught from the beginning ² up to the day when through the Holy Spirit He gave the apostles whom He had chosen their orders, and then was taken up to heaven. ³ After He had suffered, He had shown Himself alive to them, by many convincing proofs,[c] appearing to them through a period of forty days, and telling them the things about the kingdom of God. ⁴ And once while He

---
[a] Lit., *I made.*
[b] Referring to the Gospel of Lk.
[c] Word so used by Plato and other writers.

THE ACTS OF THE APOSTLES 1

was eating [d] with them, He charged them not to leave Jerusalem but to wait for what the Father had promised.

"You have heard me speak of it," He said,[e] 5 "for John baptized people in water, but in a few days [f] you will be baptized in the Holy Spirit."

6 So those who were present began to ask Him, "Lord, is this the time when you are going to set up the kingdom again for Israel?"

7 He answered them, "It is not your business to learn times and dates which the Father has a right to fix,[g] 8 but you are going to receive power when the Holy Spirit comes upon you, and you must be [h] witnesses for me in Jerusalem and all over Judea and Samaria, and to the very ends of the earth."

9 After saying this, He was taken up while they were looking at Him, and a cloud swept under [i] Him and carried Him out of their sight. 10 And while they were gazing after Him into heaven, two men dressed in white suddenly stood beside them, 11 and said to them, "Men of Galilee, why do you stand looking up into heaven? This very Jesus who has been taken up from you into heaven will come back in just the way you have seen Him go up into heaven."

12 Then they returned to Jerusalem from the hill called The Mount of Olives, which is near Jerusalem, only half a mile away. 13 When they reached the city, they went to the room upstairs where they had been staying; they were Peter and John, James and Andrew, Philip and Thomas, Bartholomew and Matthew, James the son of Alpheus, Simon the Zealot, and Judas the son of James. 14 With one mind they were all continuing to devote themselves to prayer, with the women and Mary and His brothers.

15 At that time Peter got up among the brothers [j] (there were about a hundred and twenty present) [k] and said, 16 "Brothers, that Scripture had to be fulfilled which the Holy Spirit uttered by the mouth of David in the former times about Judas who became the guide to those who arrested Jesus; 17 for he was one of our number,[l] and he received a share in this ministry of ours. 18 (This

---

[d] Lit., *taking salt,* so eating.
[e] Implied in change to direct discourse.
[f] Lit., *not many days after this.*
[g] Grk., *fix by His right.*
[h] Fut. indic. in impv. sense.
[i] Lit., *got under and took.*
[j] Fol. two best Mss.
[k] *Crowd of names,* etc.
[l] *Numbered with us.*

man bought a piece of land with the money which he took for his treachery,[m] and he fell there face downward and his body broke in two,[n] and all his intestines poured out. 19 It became known to all the residents of Jerusalem, so that this piece of land was called in their language Akeldamach, that is, The Field of Blood.) 20 For in the Book of Psalms it is written:

> 'Let his estate be desolate,
> And let no one live on it,'

and

> 'Let someone else take his position.'

21 "So one of these men who have been associated [o] with us all the time the Lord Jesus came and went among us, 22 from the time of His baptism by John down to the day when He was taken up from us, must be added [p] to our number as a witness to His resurrection."

23 Then they nominated two men, Joseph called Barsabbas, who was also called Justus, and Matthias. 24 And they prayed, saying, "Lord, you who know the hearts of all, show us which one of these two men you have chosen 25 to take a share in this service as an apostle,[q] from which Judas fell away to go to his own place."

26 They then drew lots for them, and the lot fell on Matthias, and he was added [r] to the eleven apostles.

2

THE SPIRIT COMES AT PENTECOST; PETER EXPLAINS THE STARTLING EFFECTS OF THE SPIRIT ON THE DISCIPLES; SHOWS THAT JESUS IS THE MESSIAH, HIS DEATH BEING A PART OF GOD'S PROGRAM TO SAVE THE WORLD; THREE THOUSAND REPENT AND ARE BAPTIZED; THE CHURCH AN INFLUENTIAL BROTHERHOOD

When the day of Pentecost [a] had now come, they were all meeting in one mind, 2 when suddenly there came from heaven a sound

---

[m] Lit., *iniquity.*
[n] Lit., *his middle broke.*
[o] Grk., *those who come with us.*
[p] Lit., *become in fellowship with us.*
[q] Grk., *service and apostleship.*
[r] Lit., *he was voted in fellowship with the eleven apostles.*
[a] Means *Fifty*—fifty days from the Passover; with thanksgiving it celebrated the harvest in-gathering.

like a terrific blast [b] of wind, and it filled the whole house where they were sitting. ³ And they saw tongues like flames of fire [c] separating and resting on their heads, one to each of them, ⁴ and they were all filled with the Holy Spirit, and began to speak in foreign languages as the Spirit granted them to utter divine things.[d]

⁵ Now there were devout Jews from every part [e] of the world living in Jerusalem. ⁶ And when this sound was heard, the crowd rushed together in great excitement,[f] because each one heard them speaking in his own language. ⁷ They were perfectly astounded, and in bewilderment they continued to say, "Are not all these men who are speaking Galileans? ⁸ So how is it that each of us hears them speaking [g] in his own native tongue? [h] ⁹ Parthians, Medes, Elamites, residents of Mesopotamia, of Judea and Cappadocia, of Pontus and Asia, ¹⁰ of Phrygia and Pamphylia, of Egypt and the district of Lybia around Cyrene, transient dwellers from Rome, Jews and proselytes,[i] ¹¹ Cretans and Arabs—we hear them all alike telling in our own tongues the great wonders of God." ¹² And thus they all continued to be astounded and bewildered, and continued to say to each other, "What can [j] this mean?"

¹³ But others in derision were saying, "They are running over with new wine."

¹⁴ Then Peter stood with the Eleven around him, and raising his voice he addressed them, "Men of Judea and all you residents of Jerusalem, let me explain [k] this to you, and give close attention to my words. ¹⁵ These men are not drunk as you suppose, for it is only nine o'clock in the morning.[l] ¹⁶ But this is what was spoken by the prophet Joel:

> ¹⁷ 'It will occur in the last days, says God,
> That I will pour out my Spirit upon all mankind;
> Your sons and daughters will prophesy,
> Your young men will have visions,

[b] Lit., *a violent wind rushing on*.
[c] Grk., *like fire*.
[d] Noun implied in comp. vb. (so EGT).
[e] Lit., *every nation under heaven*.
[f] Grk., *poured together*.
[g] Implied.
[h] Grk., *dialect in which we were born*.
[i] *Heathen converts to Judaism*.
[j] Lit., *what might this wish to be?*
[k] Lit., *let this be known to you*.
[l] Grk., *third hour of the day*.

Your old men will have dreams.
¹⁸ Even on my slaves, both men and women,
I will pour out my Spirit in those days,
And they will become prophets.
¹⁹ I will show wonders in the sky above
And signs upon the earth below,
Yes, blood and fire and smoky mist.
²⁰ The sun will turn to darkness,
And the moon to blood,
Before the coming of the great and glorious day of the Lord.
²¹ Then everyone who calls upon the name of the Lord will be saved.' [m]

²² "Fellow Israelites, listen to what I say. Jesus of Nazareth, as you yourselves well know, a man accredited to you by God through mighty deeds and wonders and wonder-works [n] which God performed through Him right here among you, ²³ this very Jesus, I say, after He was betrayed, in accordance with the predetermined plan and foreknowledge of God, you had wicked men kill by nailing Him to a cross; ²⁴ but God raised Him up by loosing [o] Him from the pangs of death, since it was impossible for Him to be held by the power of death. ²⁵ For David says of Him:
'I always kept my eyes upon the Lord,
For He is at my right hand, so that I may not be removed.
²⁶ So my heart is glad and my tongue exults
And my body still lives in hope.
²⁷ For you will not forsake my soul to hades,[p]
Nor will you let your Holy One experience decay.[q]
²⁸ You have made known to me the ways of life,
And you will fill me with delight in your presence.' [r]

²⁹ "Brothers, I may confidently say to you about the patriarch David, that he died and was buried, and that his grave is here among us to this very day. ³⁰ So, as he was a prophet and knew that God with an oath had promised to put one of his descendants on his throne, ³¹ he foresaw the resurrection of the Christ and told of it, for He was not forsaken to Hades, and His body did not

---

[m] Joel 2:28-32.
[n] Lit., *signs*.
[o] Adv. pt. used instrumentally.
[p] The underworld to which all the dead go.
[q] Lit., *see*.
[r] Ps. 16:8-11.

undergo decay. ³² I mean ˢ Jesus whom God raised from the dead, to which fact we are all witnesses. ³³ So He has been exalted to God's right hand and has received from His Father, as promised, and poured out upon us the Holy Spirit, as you see and hear. ³⁴ For David did not go up to heaven, but he himself ᵗ says:

'The Lord said to my Lord, "Sit at my right hand,
³⁵ Until I make your enemies the footstool of your feet." '

³⁶ "Therefore, let all the descendants of Israel understand beyond a doubt that God has made this Jesus whom you crucified both Lord and Christ."

³⁷ When they heard this, they were stabbed to the heart, and said to Peter and the rest of the apostles, "Brothers, what shall we do?"

³⁸ Peter said to them, "You must repent—and, as an expression of it,ᵘ let every one of you be baptized in the name of Jesus Christ—that you may have your sins forgiven; and then you will receive the gift of the Holy Spirit, ³⁹ for the promise belongs to you and your children, as well as to all those who are far away whom the Lord our God may call to Him."

⁴⁰ With many more words he continued to testify and to plead with them to save themselves from that crooked age. ⁴¹ So they accepted his message and were baptized, and about three thousand persons ᵛ united with them on that day. ⁴² And they devoted themselves to the teaching of the apostles and to fellowship with one another, to the breaking of bread and to prayer.

⁴³ A sense of reverence seized everyone, and many wonders and wonder-works were done by the apostles. ⁴⁴ And all the believers lived together and ʷ held all they had as common goods to be shared by one another. ⁴⁵ And so they continued to sell their property and goods and to distribute the money to all, as anyone had special need. ⁴⁶ Day after day they regularly attended the temple; they practiced breaking their bread together in their homes, and eating their food with glad and simple hearts, ⁴⁷ constantly praising God and always having the favor of all the people. And every day the Lord continued to add to them the people who were being saved.ˣ

ˢ Implied.
ᵗ Ps. 110:1.
ᵘ These five words implied from context and usage in the Early Church.
ᵛ *Souls* here means *persons*.
ʷ Fol. WH and best Mss.
ˣ That is, different people each day.

3 A CRIPPLED BEGGAR CURED BY PETER AND JOHN; THE CURE IS CREDITED TO JESUS; THE PEOPLE URGED TO REPENT AND BELIEVE IN JESUS

Peter and John were on their way up to the temple at the three o'clock hour of prayer, ² when a man crippled from his birth was being carried by, who used to be laid every day at what was called The Beautiful Gate of the temple, to beg from people on their way into the temple. ³ So when he saw Peter and John about to go into the temple, he asked them to give him something. ⁴ Peter looked him straight in the eye, and so did John, and said, "Look at us."

⁵ The beggar looked at them, supposing that he was going to get something from them. ⁶ But Peter said, "No silver or gold have I, but what I do have I will give you. In the name of Jesus of Nazareth start walking." ⁷ Then he took him by the right hand and lifted him, and his feet and ankles instantly grew strong, ⁸ and at once he leaped to his feet and started walking; then he went into the temple with them, walking, leaping, and praising God. ⁹ When all the people saw him walking about and praising God, ¹⁰ and recognized him as the very man who used to sit at The Beautiful Gate of the temple to beg, they were completely astounded and bewildered [a] at what occurred to him.

¹¹ While he was still clinging to Peter and John, all the people in utter amazement crowded around them in what was called Solomon's portico. ¹² When Peter saw this, he said to the people, "Fellow Israelites, why are you so surprised at this? Why do you keep staring at us, as though we had by our own power or piety made this man walk? ¹³ The God of Abraham, Isaac, and Jacob, the God of our forefathers, has glorified His Servant Jesus, whom you yourselves betrayed and disowned before Pilate, although he had decided to set Him free. ¹⁴ Yes, you disowned the Holy and Righteous One and asked a murderer to be pardoned as a favor to you, ¹⁵ and you killed the Prince of life; but God raised Him from the dead, to which fact we are witnesses. ¹⁶ It is His name, that is, on condition of faith in His name, that has made strong again this man whom you see and recognize—yes, faith inspired [b] by Him has given this man the perfect health you all see.[c]

[a] Lit., *filled with amazement and astonishment.*
[b] Obj. gen., so vb. implied.
[c] Grk., *in your presence.*

17 "And yet, I know, brothers, that you did not realize what you were doing, any more than your leaders did. 18 But in this way God fulfilled what He by the lips of all the prophets foretold, that the Christ should suffer. 19 So now repent and turn to Him,[d] to have your sins wiped out, that times of revival may come from the presence of the Lord, 20 and He may send back Jesus, the Christ who long ago was appointed [e] for you. 21 Yet heaven must retain [f] Him till the time for the universal restoration of which God in the early ages spoke through the lips of His holy prophets. 22 Moses, indeed, said:

'The Lord God will raise up a prophet for you from among your brothers, as He did me.[g] You must attentively [h] listen to everything that He tells you. 23 The result will be, that any person who will not listen to that prophet will be utterly destroyed from among the people.' 24 Yes, all the prophets who have spoken, from Samuel down, have also foretold these days. 25 And you are the descendants of the prophets and the heirs of the sacred compact [i] which God made with your forefathers, when He said to Abraham: 'All the families of the earth are to be blessed through your posterity.' [j] 26 It was to you first that He sent His Servant, after raising Him from the dead, to bless you by causing every one of you to turn from his wicked ways." [k]

4 PETER AND JOHN ARRESTED AND PUT INTO PRISON; TRIED AND SET FREE; THE CHURCH PRAYS FOR COURAGE TO BE LOYAL UNDER PERSECUTION; THEY PRACTICE BROTHERLY LOVE BY HOLDING THEIR GOODS IN COMMON

While they were talking to the people, the high priests, the military commander of the temple, and the Sadducees came down upon them, 2 because they were very much disturbed over their

---

[d] Pro. implied; means *God* or *Christ*.
[e] Lit., *formerly appointed Christ* (WH).
[f] Grk., *receive—retain* implied.
[g] Dt. 18:15.
[h] Linear fut. indic.
[i] Lit., *covenant,* a sacred compact.
[j] Gr., *seed.*
[k] Lit., *wicked things.*

continuing to teach the people and to declare in the case of Jesus the resurrection from the dead. ³ So they arrested them and put them into prison until next morning, for it was already evening. ⁴ But many of those who heard their message believed, and the number of the men grew to about five thousand.

⁵ On the next day the leading members of the council, the elders, and the scribes, ⁶ met in Jerusalem, including [a] Annas the high priest, Caiaphas, John, Alexander, and all that were members of the high priest's family.

⁷ They had the men stand before them and repeatedly inquired of them, "By what sort of power and authority [b] have you done this?"

⁸ Then Peter, because he was filled with the Holy Spirit, said to them, "Leaders and elders of the people, ⁹ if it is for a good deed to a helpless man, or to learn how he was cured, that we are today being tried, ¹⁰ you and all the people of Israel must know that it is by the authority of Jesus Christ of Nazareth, whom you crucified but whom God raised from the dead—yes, I repeat it, it is by His authority that this man stands here before you well. ¹¹ He is the stone that was thrown away by you builders, which has become the cornerstone.[c] ¹² There is no salvation by [d] anyone else, for no one else in all the wide world [e] has been appointed among men as our only medium [f] by which to be saved."

¹³ They were surprised to see the courage shown by Peter and John and to find that they were uneducated men, and especially untrained in the schools; [g] but they recognized the fact that they had been companions of Jesus, ¹⁴ and since they saw the man who had been cured standing with them, they had nothing to say in reply. ¹⁵ But they ordered the prisoners to step [h] outside the council, and they conferred together ¹⁶ and repeated, "What shall we do with these men? For it is evident to everybody living in Jerusalem that an unmistakable [i] wonder-work has been done by them; and we cannot deny it. ¹⁷ But to keep it from spreading

[a] Grk., *and Annas,* et al.
[b] *By what sort of name?*
[c] See Ps. 118:22.
[d] Grk., instr. prep. ἐν·
[e] Lit., *under heaven.*
[f] Grk., *as the medium by which.*
[g] Trained only in public school.
[h] Lit., *go away outside.*
[i] Grk., *knowable.*

farther among the people, let us severely threaten them not to say anything at all to anyone else about this person." j

¹⁸ So they called them in and ordered them not to speak or teach at all about the name of Jesus. ¹⁹ But Peter and John answered them, "You must decide whether it is right in the sight of God to obey you instead of Him, ²⁰ for we cannot keep from k telling what we have seen and heard."

²¹ So, after further threatening them, they turned them loose, because they could not find any way to punish them, on account of the people, because they all continued to praise God for what had taken place; ²² for the man on whom the wonderful l cure had been performed was more than forty years old.

²³ When they were turned loose, the apostles went back to their companions and told them what the high priests and elders m had said to them. ²⁴ When they heard this, with one united prayer n to God they said:

"O Lord, you are the Maker of heaven, earth, and sea, and everything that is in them, and the One ²⁵ who spoke thus through the Holy Spirit by the lips of our forefather David, your servant: o

'Why did the heathen rage,
And the peoples make vain designs?
²⁶ The kings of the earth took their stand,
The rulers met
Against the Lord, and too, against His Christ.' p

²⁷ For in this city they actually met against your holy Servant Jesus, whom you had consecrated—Herod and Pontius Pilate, with the heathen and the peoples of Israel, ²⁸ to do all that your hand and will had predetermined to take place. ²⁹ And now, Lord, give attention to their threats and help your slaves with perfect courage to continue to speak your message, ³⁰ by stretching out your hand to cure people and to perform signs and wonders by the authority q of your holy Servant Jesus."

³¹ When they had prayed, the place where they were meeting

---

j Lit., *name.*
k Lit., *cannot stop,* etc.
l Lit., *this sign of curing.*
m Two of the three classes constituting the council.
n Grk., *with one accord they lifted their voices to God.*
o Text involved but this is the sense.
p Ps. 2:1,2.
q Lit., *in or by the name,* etc.

was shaken, and they were all filled with the Holy Spirit, and continued courageously to speak God's message.

³² Now there was but one heart and soul in the vast number of those who had become believers, and not one of them claimed that anything that he had was his own, but they shared everything that they had as common property. ³³ So with great power the apostles continued to give their testimony to the resurrection of the Lord Jesus, and God's favor rested richly on them all. ³⁴ For none of them was in want, for as many of them as were owners of farms or houses proceeded to sell them, one by one,ʳ and continued to bring the money received for the things sold ³⁵ and to put it at the disposal of the apostles; then distribution was continuously made to everyone in proportion to his need.

³⁶ Now Joseph, a Levite, a native of Cyprus, who by the apostles was named Barnabas, which means Son of Encouragement, ³⁷ sold the farm he had and brought the money and put it at the disposal of the apostles.

5   ANANIAS AND SAPPHIRA, HYPOCRITES, PUNISHED WITH DEATH; THE APOSTLES PERFORM MANY WONDERS BUT ARE PUT INTO PRISON; DELIVERED BY THE LORD, THEY CONTINUE TO PREACH AS BEFORE; GAMALIEL, COUNCIL MEMBER, PLEADS FOR CAUTION

But a man named Ananias, in partnership ᵃ with his wife Sapphira, sold a piece of property, ² and with his wife's full knowledge ᵇ of it kept back for themselves a part of the money and brought only a part of it and put it at the disposal of the apostles.

³ And Peter said, "Ananias, why has Satan so completely possessed your heart ᶜ that you have lied to the Holy Spirit and kept back for yourselves a part of the money received for the land? ⁴ As long as it was unsold, was it not yours, and when it was sold, was not the money at your disposal? ᵈ How could you have the heart ᵉ to do such a thing! You did not lie to men but to God!"

ʳ Implied in impf.
ᵃ Lit., *with*.
ᵇ Grk., *his wife also knowing it with him*.
ᶜ Lit., *filled your heart*.
ᵈ Grk., *in your authority*.
ᵉ Lit., *Why did you put it in your heart to*, etc.

THE ACTS OF THE APOSTLES 5

⁵ When Ananias heard these words, he fell dead,[f] and a strange awe seized [g] everybody who heard it. ⁶ The younger men, however, got up, wrapped up his body, carried it out, and buried it.

⁷ About three hours later, his wife came in, without having learned what had taken place. ⁸ Peter said to her, "Tell me, did you sell the land for such and such a sum?"

She answered, "Yes, that is it."

⁹ Peter said to her, "How could both of you agree in such a way [h] to test the Spirit of the Lord? Listen! The feet of the men who buried your husband are at the door; they will carry you out, too."

¹⁰ She instantly fell dead at his feet. When the young men came in, they found her dead, and they carried her out and buried her beside her husband. ¹¹ So a strange awe seized the whole church and everybody who heard it.

¹² Many signs and wonders were continuously performed by the apostles among the people. And by common consent they all used to meet in Solomon's portico. ¹³ Not one of those on the outside dared to associate with them, although the people continued to hold them in high regard; ¹⁴ but still a vast number of people, both men and women, who believed in the Lord, continued to join them, ¹⁵ so that they kept bringing out into the streets their sick ones and putting them on little couches or pallets, that at least the shadow of Peter, as he went by, might fall on some of them. ¹⁶ Even from the towns around Jerusalem crowds continued coming in to bring their sick ones and those troubled with foul spirits, and they were all cured.[i]

¹⁷ Now the high priest took a stand, and all his friends, the party of the Sadducees; and being filled with jealousy, ¹⁸ they had the apostles arrested and put into the common jail.

¹⁹ But in the night the angel of the Lord threw open the jail doors and let them out, and said to them, ²⁰ "Go and take your stand in the temple square and continue to tell the people the message of this new life." [j] ²¹ So they obeyed, and about the break of day they went into the temple square and began to teach.

The high priest and his party arrived and called a meeting of the council and the whole senate of the sons of Israel, and sent to

---

[f] Grk., *falling he died.*
[g] Lit., *great awe came upon all.*
[h] Implied.
[i] Lit., *who were,* etc.
[j] Grk., *of this life.*

the prison to have the men brought in. ²² But the attendants who went for them could not find them in the jail, and so came back and ²³ reported, "We found the prison safely locked and the keepers on duty at the doors,ᵏ but on opening the doors we found no one on the inside." ²⁴ When the military commander of the temple square and the high priest heard this, they were utterly at a loss to know¹ how this might turn out.

²⁵ But somebody came by and reported to them, "The men that you put in jail are standing right here in the temple square, teaching the people." ²⁶ Then the military commander went with his attendants and brought them back, but without any violence, for they were afraid of being pelted with stones by the people. ²⁷ So they brought them and had them stand before the council.

And the high priest asked them, ²⁸ "Did we not positively ᵐ forbid you to teach any more on this authority, and yet you have filled Jerusalem with your teaching, and now want to bring on us the people's vengeance for this man's death!" ⁿ

²⁹ Peter and the apostles answered, "We must obey God rather than men. ³⁰ The God of our forefathers raised Jesus to life after you had hanged Him on a cross and killed Him. ³¹ God has exalted to His right hand this very One as our Leader and Saviour, in order to give repentance and forgiveness of sins to Israel. ³² We and the Holy Spirit that God has given to those who practice obedience to Him are witnesses to these things."

³³ When they heard this, they were furious,º and wanted to kill them. ³⁴ But a Pharisee named Gamaliel, a teacher of the law, highly respected by all the people, got up in the council and gave orders to put the men out of the council a little while; ³⁵ then he said to them:

"Fellow Israelites, take care as to what you are about to do to these men. ³⁶ For in the days gone by Theudas appeared, claiming that he was a man of importance,ᵖ and a considerable number of men, about four hundred, espoused his cause, but he was slain and all his followers were dispersed and as a party annihilated.ᑫ ³⁷ After

ᵏ Lit., *standing at the doors.*
¹ Implied to complete the sense of preceding phrase.
ᵐ Hebraism for emphasis.
ⁿ Lit., *this man's blood.*
º Grk., *sawn asunder* (in heart).
ᵖ Lit., *somebody.*
ᑫ Grk., *came to nothing.*

him, at the time of the enrollment for the Roman tax,[r] Judas the Galilean appeared and influenced people to desert and follow him; but he too perished and all his followers were scattered. ³⁸ So in the present case, I warn you, stay away from these men, let them alone. For, if this program or movement has its origin in men, it will go to pieces, ³⁹ but if it has its origin in God, you can never stop it. It is to be feared [s] that you may find yourselves fighting God."

⁴⁰ They were convinced by him, and after calling the apostles in and having them flogged, they charged them to stop speaking on the authority of Jesus, and then turned them loose. ⁴¹ So they went out from the presence of the council, rejoicing that they had been considered worthy to suffer disgrace for Jesus'[t] name; ⁴² and not for a single day did they stop teaching in the temple square and in private houses the good news of Jesus the Christ.

6 SEVEN NEW OFFICERS SELECTED BY THE CHURCH TO SERVE THE NEEDY; STEPHEN ARRESTED FOR CHAMPIONING THE NEW FAITH

In those days, as the number of the disciples was increasing, complaint [a] was made by the Greek-speaking Jews against the native Jews [b] that their widows were being neglected in the daily distribution of food. ² So the Twelve called together the whole body [c] of the disciples, and said, "It is not desirable that we should leave off preaching the word of God to wait on tables. ³ So, brothers, you must select from your number seven men of good standing, full of the Spirit, and of good practical sense,[d] and we will assign them to this business, ⁴ while we will go on devoting ourselves to prayer and the word of God."

⁵ This suggestion [e] was approved by the whole body, and so they selected Stephen, a man full of faith and of the Holy Spirit, Philip, Procorus, Nikanor, Timon, Parmenas, and Nicholas of Antioch, who was a convert [f] to Judaism. ⁶ They presented these men to the

[r] Rom. census, A.D. 6-8.
[s] Implied.
[t] Lit., *for the name* (WH); *Jesus* understood.
[a] *Secret grumbling.*
[b] That is, by Hellenists against Hebrews.
[c] Grk., *the whole multitude.*
[d] Lit., *wisdom.*
[e] Grk., *word.*
[f] Grk., *a proselyte.*

apostles, and after they had prayed they laid their hands upon them.

⁷ So God's message continued to spread, and the number of the disciples in Jerusalem continued to grow rapidly; a large number even of priests continued to surrender ᵍ to the faith.

⁸ Now Stephen, full of grace and power, went on performing great signs and wonders among the people. ⁹ But members of the synagogue known as that of the Libyans, Cyreneans, and Alexandrians, and men from Cilicia and Asia, got to debating with Stephen, ¹⁰ but they could not cope ʰ with his good practical sense and the spiritual power ⁱ with which he usually spoke. ¹¹ So they instigated men to say, "We have heard him speaking abusive words against Moses and God."

¹² By this means they excited the people, the elders, and the scribes, and so they rushed upon him, seized him, and brought him before the council. ¹³ Then they put up false witnesses who said, "This man never stops saying things against this holy place and against the law, ¹⁴ for we have heard him say that Jesus of Nazareth will tear this place down, and change the customs which Moses handed down to us."

¹⁵ Then all who were seated in the council fixed their eyes upon him and saw that his face was like that of an angel.

7 STEPHEN SPEAKS IN HIS OWN DEFENSE BUT STILL IS STONED TO DEATH; HE PRAYS FOR HIS ENEMIES WHILE HEAVEN OPENS TO GIVE HIM A VISION OF JESUS EXALTED IN GLORY

The high priest asked, "Are these statements true?"
² He answered:

"Listen, brothers and fathers. The glorious God appeared to our forefather Abraham while he was in Mesopotamia before he ever made his home ᵃ in Haran, ³ and said to him, 'Leave your country and your kinsmen and come to whatever country I may show you.' ᵇ ⁴ So he left the country of the Chaldeans and for a time made his home in Haran. Then after the death of his father,

---

ᵍ Lit., *obey*.
ʰ Lit., *stand against*.
ⁱ Grk., *his spirit*.
ᵃ Aor. of vb. *to dwell permanently*.
ᵇ Gen. 12:1.

God had him move to this country in which you now live. ⁵ He gave him no property in it, not even a foot of land, and yet He promised to give it to him and his descendants after him, as a permanent possession, although he had no child at that time. ⁶ This is what God promised: 'His descendants will be strangers living in a foreign land, and its people ᵉ will enslave and oppress them for four hundred years.' ⁷ But God further promised: 'I will pass sentence on the nation that enslaves them, and after that they will leave that country and worship me on this very spot.' ⁸ And with Abraham ᵈ He made the sacred compact of circumcision, and he became the father of Isaac and circumcised him on the eighth day, and Isaac became the father of Jacob, and Jacob of the twelve patriarchs. ⁹ And the patriarchs became jealous of Joseph and sold him as a slave into ᵉ Egypt. But God was with him ¹⁰ and delivered him from all his troubles, and allowed him to win favor and to show wisdom before Pharaoh, king of Egypt, and so he appointed Joseph governor of Egypt and of his whole household. ¹¹ Then a famine spread all over Egypt and Canaan, and with it great suffering, and our forefathers could not find the simplest food.ᶠ ¹² But Jacob heard that there was food in Egypt and sent our forefathers on their first visit down there. ¹³ On their second visit Joseph made himself known to his brothers, and thus Joseph's race ᵍ was revealed to Pharaoh. ¹⁴ Then Joseph sent and invited his father Jacob and all his kinsmen, seventy-five in all; ¹⁵ and Jacob came down to Egypt. There he and our forefathers died ¹⁶ and were carried back to Shechem and laid in the tomb which Abraham had bought with a sum of money from the sons of Hamor in Shechem. ¹⁷ As the time approached for realizing ʰ the promise which God had made to Abraham, the people multiplied and became more numerous in Egypt, ¹⁸ until another king, who knew nothing about Joseph, ascended the throne. ¹⁹ By taking a cunning advantage of our race he oppressed our forefathers by forcing them to expose their infants so that they should not live. ²⁰ At this time Moses was born. He was a divinely ⁱ beautiful child. For three months he was cared for in his

ᶜ Implied from previous statement.
ᵈ Implied from next clause.
ᵉ Implied in vb. *sold*.
ᶠ Lit., *grass, herbs,* etc.
ᵍ Word means *origin, family, race*.
ʰ Lit., *time of the promise*.
ⁱ *Beautiful to God*.

father's house. ²¹ When he was exposed,ʲ Pharaoh's daughter adopted him and brought him up as her own son. Thus ²² Moses was educated in all the culture of the Egyptians, and was a mighty man in speech and action.ᵏ ²³ As he was rounding out his fortieth year, it occurred to him to visit his brothers, the descendants of Israel. ²⁴ Because he saw one of them being mistreated, he defended and avenged the man who was suffering ill-treatment by striking down the Egyptian. ²⁵ He supposed that his brothers would understand that God through his instrumentality was going to deliver them, but they did not. ²⁶ The next day he showed himself to two of them engaged in a fight, and he tried¹ to get them to make friends, saying, 'You are brothers, why should you harm each other?' ²⁷ But the man who was harming his brother pushed him aside, saying, 'Who made you our ruler and referee? ²⁸ Do you want to kill me as you did the Egyptian yesterday?' ²⁹ At this statement Moses fled, and went and lived in the land of Midian, and became the father of two sons. ³⁰ When forty years had passed, an angel appeared to him in the desert of Mount Sinai, in the flame of a burning bush. ³¹ When Moses saw it, he wondered at the sight, and when he went up to look at it, the voice of the Lord said to him, ³² 'I am the God of your forefathers, the God of Abraham, Isaac, and Jacob.' Moses was so terrified that he did not dare to look at the bush.ᵐ ³³ Then the Lord said to him, 'Take your shoes off your feet, for the place where you are standing is sacred ground. ³⁴ Because I have seen the oppression of my people in Egypt and heard their groans, I have come down to deliver them. So come! I will send you back to Egypt as my messenger.'ⁿ ³⁵ That very Moses whom they refused, saying, 'Who made you our ruler and referee?' was the man whom God sent to be both their ruler and deliverer, by the helpº of the angel who had appeared to him in the bush. ³⁶ It was he who brought them out of Egypt by performing wonders and signs there and at the Red Sea— as he did also in the desert for forty years. ³⁷ It was this Moses who said to the descendants of Israel, 'God will raise up a prophet for you from among you, just as He did me.' ³⁸ This is the one who

ʲ *Put out to die.*
ᵏ Word and work.
¹ Inceptive impf. of vb. *reconcile.*
ᵐ Only implied.
ⁿ Noun implied in vb.
º Lit., *by the hand.*

in the congregation in the desert went between the angel, who spoke to him on Mount Sinai, and our forefathers, who also received, to be handed down to you, utterances that still live. ³⁹ But our forefathers would not listen to him, but pushed him aside, and in their hearts they hankered [p] after Egypt; ⁴⁰ and they said to Aaron, 'Make us gods to march in front of us, for as for this Moses, who brought us out of the land of Egypt, we do not know what has become of him!' ⁴¹ In those days they even made a calf, and offered sacrifice to their idol, and held a celebration over the works of their own hands. ⁴² So God turned away from them and gave them over to worship the starry host,[q] as it is written in the Book of the Prophets:

'Did you really offer me victims and sacrifices
Those forty years in the desert, O house of Israel?
⁴³ No, you offered me the tent of Moloch
And the star of your god Rompha,
The images you had made to worship!
So I will now remove you beyond Babylon.' [r]

⁴⁴ "In the desert our forefathers had the tent of the testimony, like the model Moses had seen, as God who spoke to him ordered him to make it. ⁴⁵ This tent our forefathers brought in and passed on when under Joshua they dispossessed the nations which God drove out before them, and it remained until the time of David. ⁴⁶ He found favor with God and begged to design a dwelling [s] for the God of Jacob, ⁴⁷ but it was Solomon who came to build a house for Him. ⁴⁸ But the Most High does not live in buildings built by human hands. As the prophet says:

⁴⁹ ' "Heaven is my throne,
And earth a footstool for my feet.
What house can you build for me?" says the Lord;
"Or what place is there in which I can rest?"
⁵⁰ Was it not my hand that made them all?" ' [t]

⁵¹ "You people, stubborn in will, heathenish in hearts and ears,[u] you are always resisting the Holy Spirit, as your forefathers did, too. ⁵² Which of the prophets did your forefathers fail to persecute?

---

[p] Grk., *turned toward.*
[q] Lit., *host of heaven.*
[r] Am. 5:25-27.
[s] Grk., *find a dwelling* (tent).
[t] Isa. 66:1, 2.
[u] Lit., *stiff in neck, uncircumcised in hearts and ears.*

They killed the prophets who foretold the coming of the Righteous One, and now you have betrayed and murdered Him,ᵛ ⁵³ you who received the law by order of the angels, and yet you did not obey it!"

⁵⁴ As they continued to listen to this address, they were becoming infuriated and began to grind their teeth at him. ⁵⁵ But since he was full of the Holy Spirit, he looked right into heaven and saw the glory of God and Jesus standing at God's right hand. ⁵⁶ So he said, "Look! I see heaven open, and the Son of Man standing at God's right hand."

⁵⁷ But they raised a great shout and held their ears, and all together rushed upon him, ⁵⁸ and dragged him out of the city and continued stoning him. The witnesses, in the meantime, laid their clothes at the feet of a young man named Saul. ⁵⁹ They continued stoning Stephen as he continued praying, "Lord Jesus, receive my spirit!"

⁶⁰ Then he fell on his knees and cried out, "Lord, do not charge this sin on the book against them!" ʷ On saying this he fell asleep in death.

8 STEPHEN IS BURIED; CHRISTIANS PERSECUTED BUT PREACHING THE GOOD NEWS WHEREVER THEY FLEE; PHILIP PREACHES IT IN SAMARIA; BELIEVERS THERE RECEIVE THE SPIRIT; PHILIP PREACHES TO AN ETHIOPIAN STATE TREASURER

Saul heartily approved of his being put to death. So on that day a severe persecution broke out against the church in Jerusalem, and all of them, except the apostles, were scattered over Judea and Samaria. ² Some devout men ᵃ buried Stephen and made loud lamentation for him. ³ But Saul continued ᵇ to harass the church, and by going from house to house and dragging off men and women he continued ᵇ to put them into prison.

⁴ Now those who were scattered went from place to place preaching the good news of the message. ⁵ So Philip went down to the city of Samaria and began to preach the Christ to the Samaritans. ⁶ As the crowds continued to listen to his message

---

ᵛ Grk., *whose traitors and murderers you are.*
ʷ Technical accounting term; so *charge on book.*
ᵃ Likely Christians.
ᵇ Impf.

and continued to see his wonder-works which he was performing, as with one mind they became interested in what was said by Philip. ⁷ For many of those under the power of foul spirits cried out and the spirits came out of them, and many paralyzed and crippled people were cured. ⁸ So there was great rejoicing in that city.

⁹ There was a man named Simon in the city, who had kept the Samaritan people thrilled ᶜ by practicing magic there and by claiming to be a great man. ¹⁰ Everybody, high and low,ᵈ kept running after him,ᵉ saying, "He is certainly what is known as the Great Power of God!" ¹¹ They kept running after him, because for a long time he had thrilled them with his magical performances. ¹² But when the people came to believe ᶠ the good news proclaimed by Philip about the kingdom of God and the name of Jesus Christ, both men and women were constantly baptized. ¹³ So Simon himself came to believe too, and after he was baptized he continued to be devoted to Philip, and he was always thrilled at seeing such great signs and wonder-works continuously performed.

¹⁴ When the apostles at Jerusalem heard that Samaria had accepted God's message, they sent Peter and John there. ¹⁵ They came and prayed for them that they might receive the Holy Spirit, ¹⁶ for as yet He had not come upon any of them, but they had been baptized merely in the name of the Lord Jesus. ¹⁷ Then they laid their hands upon them, and one by one ᵍ they received the Holy Spirit. ¹⁸ So when Simon saw that the Holy Spirit was conferred by the laying on of the apostles' hands, he offered them money, ¹⁹ and said, "Give me this power too, that when I lay my hands on anyone he may receive the Holy Spirit."

²⁰ But Peter said to him, "Your money go to perdition with you for even dreaming you could buy the gift of God with money! ²¹ You have no share or part in this matter, for your heart is not sincere ʰ in the sight of God. ²² So repent of this wickedness of yours, and pray to the Lord, to see if this thought of your heart may be forgiven you. ²³ For I see that you are a bitter weed ⁱ and a bundle of crookedness!"

ᶜ Lit., *astound;* so *thrill.*
ᵈ *Small and great.*
ᵉ Lit., *paying mind to.*
ᶠ Aor. expresses pointed ac. Hence tr.
ᵍ Impf. of repeated action.
ʰ Lit., *straight, right.*
ⁱ Prep. in Heb. idiom used as pred. noun

²⁴ So Simon answered, "Both of you ʲ beg the Lord for me that none of the things you have said may befall me!"

²⁵ So after they had given their testimony and spoken the Lord's message, they started ᵏ back to Jerusalem, and on the way ˡ continued to tell the good news in many Samaritan villages.

²⁶ Now an angel of the Lord said to Philip, "Get up and go south by the road that leads from Jerusalem to Gaza; this is the desert road." ²⁷ So he got up and went.

Now there was an Ethiopian official,ᵐ a member of the court of Candace, queen of the Ethiopians, her chief treasurer, who had come to Jerusalem to worship, ²⁸ and now was on his way home. He was seated in his chariot, reading the prophet Isaiah. ²⁹ So the Spirit said to Philip, "Go up and join him in his chariot."

³⁰ Then Philip ran up and listened to him reading the prophet Isaiah, and he asked, "Do you understand what you are reading?" ³¹ He answered, "How in the world ⁿ could I, unless someone teaches me?" And he begged him to get up and sit with him. ³² Now this was the passage of Scripture that he was reading:

"Like a sheep He was led away to be slaughtered,
And just as a lamb is dumb before its shearer,
So He does not open His mouth.
³³ Justice was denied Him in His humiliation.º
Who can tell of His times? ᵖ
For His life is removed from the earth." ᵍ

³⁴ "Tell me, I pray, of whom is the prophet speaking," asked the official of Philip, "of himself or of someone else?" ³⁵ Then Philip opened his mouth, and starting from this passage, he told him the good news about Jesus.

³⁶ As they continued down the road, they came to some water, and the official said, "Look! here is some water! What is there to keep me from being baptized?" ʳ ³⁸ So he ordered the chariot to stop, and Philip and the official both went down into the water,

---

ʲ Pl., so *you both*.
ᵏ Incep. impf.
ˡ Implied.
ᵐ Lit., *eunuch*, but he was an official; most attendants at court were made eunuchs in those days.
ⁿ The particle, *gar*, has this force.
º Lit., *justice was taken away*, etc.
ᵖ Grk., *generation*.
ᵍ Isa. 53:7, 8.
ʳ V. 37 not in best Mss.

and Philip baptized him. ³⁹ When they came up out of the water, the Spirit of the Lord suddenly took Philip away; the official saw him no more, for he went on home rejoicing; ⁴⁰ but Philip was found at Ashdod, and he went on telling the good news in all the towns until he reached Caesarea.

9 SAUL CONVERTED; PREACHES AT DAMASCUS THAT JESUS IS THE CHRIST; JEWS PLOT TO KILL HIM; CHRISTIANS RESCUE HIM IN A BASKET; AT JERUSALEM JEWS TRY TO KILL HIM; ESCAPES TO TARSUS; PETER PREACHES; RAISES DORCAS TO LIFE

Now Saul, as he was still breathing threats of murder [a] against the disciples of the Lord, went to the high priest ² and asked him for letters to the synagogues in Damascus, that if he found any men or [b] women belonging to The Way [c] he might bring them in chains to Jerusalem. ³ As he traveled on he finally approached Damascus, and suddenly a light from heaven flashed around him.

⁴ He dropped to the ground; then he heard a voice saying to him, "Saul, Saul, why are you persecuting me?"

⁵ He asked, "Who are you, sir?"

And He said, "I am Jesus whom you are persecuting. ⁶ But get up and go into the city, and there it will be told you what you ought to do." [d]

⁷ His fellow-travelers stood speechless, for they heard the voice but could not see anyone. ⁸ Then Saul got up off the ground, but he could not see anything, although his eyes were wide open. So they took him by the hand and led him into Damascus, ⁹ and for three days he could not see, and he did not eat or drink anything.

¹⁰ Now there was in Damascus a disciple named Ananias, and the Lord said to him in a vision, "Ananias!"

And he answered, "Yes, Lord, I am here."

¹¹ And the Lord said to him, "Get up and go to the street called 'The Straight Street,' and ask at the house of Judas for one named Saul, from Tarsus, for he is now praying there. ¹² He has seen in a vision a man named Ananias come in and lay his hands on him, to restore his sight."

[a] Lit., *threat and murder*.
[b] Grk., *any, both men and women*.
[c] A popular term for the life led by Jesus' followers.
[d] The rest of vv. 5 and 6 not in best Mss.

¹³ But Ananias answered, "Lord, I have heard many people tell of this man, especially the great sufferings [e] he has brought on your people [f] in Jerusalem. ¹⁴ Now he is here and has authority from the high priests to put in chains all who call upon your name."

¹⁵ But the Lord said to him, "Go, for he is a chosen instrument [g] of mine to carry my name to the heathen and their kings, and to the descendants of Israel. ¹⁶ For I am going to show him how great are the sufferings he must endure for my name's sake."

¹⁷ So Ananias left and went to that house, and there he laid his hands upon Saul, and said, "Saul, my brother, the Lord Jesus, who appeared to you on the road on which you were coming here, has sent me that you may regain your sight and be filled with the Holy Spirit." ¹⁸ And all at once [h] something like scales fell from his eyes, he regained his sight, got up and was baptized, ¹⁹ and after taking some food he felt strong again.[i]

For several days he stayed with the disciples at Damascus, ²⁰ and at once he began to preach in their synagogues that Jesus is the Son of God. ²¹ And all who heard him were astounded and said, "Is not this the man who harassed those who called upon this name in Jerusalem, and has come here expressly for the purpose of putting them in chains and taking them back to the high priests?" ²² But Saul grew stronger and stronger and continued to put to utter [j] confusion the Jews who lived in Damascus, by proving that Jesus is the Christ.

²³ After several days had gone by, the Jews laid a plot to murder him, ²⁴ but their plot was found out [k] by Saul. Day and night they kept guarding the city gates, to murder him, ²⁵ but his disciples took him one night and let him down through the city-wall, by lowering him in a hamper-basket.

²⁶ Now when Saul arrived at Jerusalem, he tried to join the disciples there, but they were all afraid of him, because they did not believe that he was really a disciple. ²⁷ Barnabas, however, took him up and presented him to the apostles, and he told them how on the road he had seen the Lord, and how the Lord [l] had spoken

---

[e] Lit., *what great evils he has done.*
[f] Grk., *your saints.*
[g] Lit., *vessel.*
[h] Adv. in emph. position.
[i] Ingress. aor.
[j] Comp. vb. has this idea; impf. of cont. ac.
[k] Lit., *became known.*
[l] Pro. in Grk., noun clearer in Eng.

to him, and how courageously he had spoken in the name of Jesus at Damascus. ²⁸ So he was one of them,ᵐ going in and out constantly at Jerusalem, ²⁹ and he continued to speak courageously in the name of the Lord, and to speak and debate with the Greek-speaking Jews. But they kept ⁿ trying to murder him. ³⁰ So when the brothers found this out, they took him down to Caesarea, and from there sent him back to Tarsus.

³¹ So the church ᵒ all over Judea, Galilee, and Samaria enjoyed peace, and as it continued to be built up spiritually ᵖ and to live in reverence for the Lord, it continued to increase in numbers through the encouragement that the Holy Spirit gave.ᑫ

³² Now, as Peter was going here and there among them all, he finally went down to God's people who lived at Lydda. ³³ There he found a man named Aeneas, who had been bedridden ʳ for eight years as a paralytic. ³⁴ So Peter said to him, "Aeneas, Jesus Christ now cures you! Get up and make your bed!" And at once he got up. ³⁵ Then all the people who lived at Lydda and Sharon saw him, and so they turned to the Lord.

³⁶ At Joppa there was a woman, a disciple, whose name was Tabitha, which in Greek means Dorcas, that is, Gazelle. She had filled her life with good deeds and works of charity, which she was always doing. ³⁷ Just at that time it happened that she had been taken ill and had died. They washed her body and laid her out in a room upstairs. ³⁸ As Joppa was near Lydda, the disciples heard that Peter was there, and sent two men to him, begging him to come to them without delay. ³⁹ So Peter at once ˢ got up and went with them. When he reached there, they took him to the room upstairs, and all the widows took their stand around him, crying and showing him the shirts and coats that Dorcas had made while she was still with them.

⁴⁰ Then Peter put them all out of the room, knelt down and prayed, and, turning to the body, said, "Tabitha, get up!" Then she opened her eyes, and when she saw Peter, she sat up. ⁴¹ He gave her his hand and lifted her to her feet, and calling in the Lord's people and the widows, he gave her back to them alive. ⁴² This be-

---

ᵐ Grk., *was with them.*
ⁿ Impf. of cont. ac. See EGT for use of vb. in this sense.
ᵒ Fol. WH.
ᵖ Adv. implied from context.
ᑫ Lit., *through the encouragement of H.S.*
ʳ Exactly expresses the periphrastic constr.
ˢ Implied in aor.

came known all over Joppa, and many came to believe in the Lord. ⁴³ So it came about that Peter stayed in Joppa several days, at the house of a tanner named Simon.

10 COLONEL CORNELIUS AND FRIENDS IN CAESAREA CONVERTED AS PETER PREACHES TO THEM, PREPARED BY A VISION THUS TO DO; THESE HEATHEN BELIEVERS RECEIVE THE HOLY SPIRIT AS THE CHURCH IN JERUSALEM DID AT PENTECOST

Now at Caesarea there was a man named Cornelius, a colonel in what was known as the Italian regiment,[a] ² a religious man, too, who revered God with all his household, who was always liberal [b] in his many deeds of charity to the people, and who had the habit [c] of praying to God. ³ One afternoon about three o'clock [d] he had a vision and clearly saw an angel of God come to him and say, "Cornelius!"

⁴ He stared at him and in terror asked, "What is it, sir?"

The angel [e] answered him, "Your prayers and your deeds of charity have gone up and been remembered [f] before God. ⁵ So now send men to Joppa and invite over a man named Simon, who is also called Peter. ⁶ He is a guest of a tanner named Simon, whose house is close by the sea."

⁷ After the angel who had spoken to him had gone, Cornelius called two of his household servants, and a religious soldier who was one of his devoted attendants,[g] ⁸ and after telling them the whole story, sent them to Joppa.

⁹ The next day, while those men were traveling on and not far from the town, Peter went up on the housetop about noon to pray. ¹⁰ But he got very hungry and wanted something to eat. While they were getting it ready, he fell into a trance ¹¹ and saw the sky opened, and something like a great sheet coming down, lowered to the earth by the four corners, ¹² which contained all kinds of four-footed animals, reptiles, and wild birds. ¹³ A voice came to him, "Get up, Peter, kill something and eat it."

[a] Corresponds exactly with Grk. word, *band*.
[b] Lit., *always doing*, etc.
[c] Pres. pt. of habitual ac.
[d] Grk., *ninth hour*; nine from 6 A.M., so 3 P.M.
[e] Grk. has pro.; noun clearer in Eng.
[f] Lit., *to be remembered*.
[g] Pres. pt. of cont. ac. gives idea of devotion.

THE ACTS OF THE APOSTLES 10

¹⁴ But Peter said, "Never by any means, sir, for I have never eaten anything common, or not ceremonially cleansed."

¹⁵ A second time the voice came to him, "The things that God has cleansed you must not call unclean." ¹⁶ This took place three times; then all at once the thing was taken up into the sky.

¹⁷ Now while Peter was still at a loss to know what the vision he had seen could mean, the men who had been sent by Cornelius had asked for the way to Simon's house and had stopped at the gate; ¹⁸ and they called and inquired if Simon who was called Peter was staying there. ¹⁹ While Peter was meditating on the vision, the Spirit said to him, "There are two men looking for you. ²⁰ Get up and go down, and without hesitation go on with them, for I have sent them."

²¹ So Peter went down and said to the men, "I am the man you are looking for. What is the purpose of your coming?" [h]

²² They answered, "Cornelius, a colonel in the army, an upright man and one who reveres God, and a man of high reputation [i] with the whole Jewish nation, was instructed by a holy angel to send for you to come to his house and to listen to a message you would bring." [j] ²³ So Peter invited them in and entertained them.

²⁴ The next day he started off with them, and some of the brothers in Joppa went along with him. The day after that they reached Caesarea. Cornelius was waiting for him, as he had invited in his kinsmen and close friends. ²⁵ When Peter went into the house, Cornelius met him and fell at his feet and did homage [k] to him. ²⁶ But Peter lifted him to his feet, saying, "Get up, I too am just a man myself."

²⁷ As he continued to talk with him he went into the house and found a great crowd [l] had gathered, ²⁸ and he said to him, "You know that it is against the law for a Jew to associate with a foreigner or to visit one; but God has taught me not to call any man vulgar [m] or ceremonially unclean; ²⁹ so I have come, since I was sent for, without any hesitation."

³⁰ Then Cornelius said, "Four days ago, about this hour, three o'clock in the afternoon, I was praying in my house, and all at

[h] Lit., *for what have you come?*
[i] Grk., *attested to.*
[j] Lit., *words from you.*
[k] Not as God but as God's representative.
[l] Grk., *many.*
[m] Lit., *common; vulgar* more appropriate of a person.

once a man in dazzling clothing stood before me, ³¹ and said, 'Cornelius, your prayer has been heard and your deeds of charity have been remembered by God. ³² So send to Joppa and invite Simon, who is called Peter, to come over. He is being entertained at the house of a tanner named Simon, by the seashore.' ³³ So at once I sent for you, and you have been kind enough to come.ⁿ So now we are all here in God's presence to listen to anything that the Lord has commanded you to say."

³⁴ Then Peter opened his mouth and said, "Now I really see° that God shows no partiality, ³⁵ but in every nation the man who reveres God and practices doing right is acceptable to Him. ³⁶ He has sent His message to the descendants of Israel, by telling them the good news of peace through Jesus Christ. He is Lord of all. ³⁷ You know the story yourselves that spread all over Judea, beginning from Galilee after the baptism that John preached, ³⁸ how God consecrated Jesus of Nazareth with the Holy Spirit and power, and then He went about doing good and curing all who were overpowered by the devil, because God was with Him. ³⁹ We are witnesses of everything that He did in the country of the Jews and in Jerusalem. Yet they murdered Him by hanging Him upon a tree. ⁴⁰ But God raised Him to life on the third day, and permitted Him to be clearly seen, ⁴¹ not by all the people but by witnesses whom God had beforehand appointed, namely, by us who ate and drank with Him after His resurrection from the dead. ⁴² He also ordered us to proclaim to the people and solemnly ᵖ to testify that this is the One whom God has appointed to be the Judge of the living and the dead. ⁴³ To this very One all the prophets bear witness that everyone who believes in Him is to receive the forgiveness of sins through His name."

⁴⁴ While Peter was still speaking these truths,ᑫ the Holy Spirit fell upon all who were listening to the message. ⁴⁵ Then the Jewish believers who had gone along with Peter were astounded because the gift of the Holy Spirit had been showered ʳ upon the heathen too, ⁴⁶ for they heard them speaking in foreign languages and telling of the greatness of God. Then Peter asked, ⁴⁷ "No one

---

ⁿ Grk., *you have kindly come.*
° Grk. vb. means *apprehend, see with mind.*
ᵖ Comp. vb. means this.
ᑫ Lit., *these words.*
ʳ Lit., *poured out.*

can refuse the use of water, can he,[g] for these to be baptized, since they have received the Holy Spirit just as we did ourselves?" ⁴⁸ So he ordered them to be baptized in the name of Jesus Christ. Then they begged him to stay on there a few days.

11   PETER DEFENDS HIMSELF BEFORE THE CHURCH IN JERUSALEM FOR EATING WITH THE HEATHEN; THE FIRST CHURCH ON HEATHEN SOIL ORGANIZED AT ANTIOCH; BARNABAS AND SAUL CONDUCT A GREAT REVIVAL THERE; THEY TAKE A CONTRIBUTION FROM ANTIOCH CHRISTIANS TO SUFFERING JEWISH CHRISTIANS

Now the apostles and the brothers all over Judea heard that the heathen too had accepted God's message. ² So when Peter returned[a] to Jerusalem, the champions of circumcision began to bring charges against him ³ for having visited and eaten[b] with men who were not Jews.[c]

⁴ Then Peter explained the whole matter to them from beginning to end.[d] He said, ⁵ "I was praying in the town of Joppa, and while I was praying I fell[e] in a trance and had a vision. I saw something like a great sheet coming down out of the sky, lowered by the four corners; and it came right down to me. ⁶ With fixed eyes I kept looking at it and saw all kinds of four-footed animals, wild beasts, reptiles, and wild birds. ⁷ And I heard a voice say to me, 'Get up, Peter, kill something and eat it!' ⁸ But I answered, 'Never by any means, sir, for nothing common or not ceremonially cleansed has ever passed my lips.'[f] ⁹ Then the voice from heaven answered again, 'The things that God has cleansed you must not call unclean.' ¹⁰ This took place three times; then all at once the whole thing was drawn back into the sky. ¹¹ Just at that moment three men, who had been sent from Caesarea for me, stopped at the house where we were staying. ¹² And the Spirit told me to go with them without any hesitation at all. These six brothers, too, went

[g] Strong neg. answer.
[a] Prep. here means *back*, not *up*.
[b] Fol. WH and Ms. B.
[c] Lit., *not circumcised*.
[d] Grk., *beginning he set forth in detail*.
[e] Implied.
[f] Lit., *entered my mouth*.

with me, and we all went into the man's house. [13] Then he told us how he had seen the angel stand in his house and say to him, 'Send to Joppa and invite Simon, who is called Peter, to come over; [14] he will tell you truths [g] through which you and your whole household will be saved.' [15] When I began to speak, the Holy Spirit fell upon them as He did upon us at the beginning, [16] and I remembered the saying of the Lord, 'John baptized in water, but you will be baptized in the Holy Spirit.' [17] So if God had given them the same gift that He gave us when we believed upon the Lord Jesus Christ, who was I to try [h]—and how could I if I tried—to thwart God?"

[18] When they heard this, they had no answer to make, but gave God the glory, saying, "So God has given even the heathen the repentance that leads [i] to life."

[19] Now the fugitives from the persecution [j] that started over Stephen went all the way to Phoenicia, Cyprus, and Antioch, telling the message to none but Jews. [20] But there were some of them, men from Cyprus and Cyrene, who on reaching Antioch began to speak to the Greeks [k] too, and proceeded to tell them the good news about the Lord Jesus. [21] And the hand of the Lord was with them, and a large number of people believed and turned to the Lord. [22] Now the news [l] about them came to the ears of the church at Jerusalem, and so they sent Barnabas all the way to Antioch. [23] When he reached there and saw the spiritual blessing God had given them,[m] he was delighted, and continuously encouraged them all with hearty purpose [n] to continue to be devoted to the Lord; [24] for he was a good man, and full of the Holy Spirit and faith. So a large number of people were united to the Lord. [25] Then Barnabas went over to Tarsus to search out Saul, [26] and after he had found him, he brought him to Antioch.

Now for a whole year their meeting with the church lasted,[o] and they taught large numbers of people. It was at Antioch too that the disciples first came to be known as "Christians."

[27] At that time some prophets from Jerusalem came down to

[g] Grk., *things uttered*.
[h] Ingress. aor.
[i] Lit., *with a view to life*.
[j] Grk., *distress*.
[k] Fol. Sinaitic Ms. vs. WH.
[l] Lit., *the word*.
[m] Grk., *the grace or favor of God*.
[n] Lit., *purpose of heart*.
[o] Implied in the time word.

Antioch, ²⁸ and one of them named Agabus got up and, through the Holy Spirit, foretold ᵖ that there was going to be a great famine all over the world, which occurred in the reign of Claudius. ²⁹ So the disciples decided to send a contribution, each in proportion to his prosperity,ᑫ to help ʳ the brothers who lived in Judea. ³⁰ And this they did and sent it to the elders by Barnabas and Saul.

12 JAMES BEHEADED, PETER PUT INTO PRISON; THE CHURCH PRAYS FOR PETER'S RELEASE; AN ANGEL RELEASES HIM; THE GUARDSMEN KILLED FOR LETTING HIM GET OUT; HEROD AGRIPPA MEETS A TRAGIC DEATH FOR ACCEPTING PRAISE AS A GOD

About that time Herod ᵃ arrested some who belonged to the church, in order to do them violence. ² He had James the brother of John murdered with a sword, ³ and when he saw that this was agreeable to the Jews, he proceeded to arrest Peter too—it was at the time of the feast of Unleavened Bread. ⁴ He had him seized and put into prison, and turned him over to four squads ᵇ of soldiers to guard him, planning after the Passover to bring him out again to the people. ⁵ So Peter was being kept in prison, but earnest prayer to God for him was persistently ᶜ made by the church.

⁶ Now just as Herod was going to bring him out, that is, the very night before, Peter was fastened with two chains and was sleeping between two soldiers, and the guards were at the door guarding the prison. ⁷ And suddenly an angel of the Lord stood by him, and a light shone in his cell,ᵈ and by striking Peter on the side the angel woke him, and said, "Get up quickly!" At once the chains fell off his hands.

⁸ Then the angel said to him, "Tighten your belt and put on your shoes!" He did so.

Then the angel said to him, "Put on your coat and follow me!"

⁹ So he kept following him out, but he was not conscious that what was being done by the angel was real; he thought he was dreaming it.ᵉ ¹⁰ They passed the first guard, then the second, and

ᵖ Lit., *showed.*
ᑫ Grk., *as they prospered.*
ʳ Lit., *for service to.*
ᵃ Agrippa I, grandson of Herod the Great.
ᵇ To make his escape impossible.
ᶜ Expressed by the pres. pt. of cont. action.
ᵈ Lit., *the place where he dwelt.*
ᵉ Grk., *that he was seeing a vision.*

at last came to the iron gate which led into the city. The gate[f] of itself opened to them, and they passed out and proceeded one block,[g] when all at once the angel left him.

[11] Then Peter came to himself and said, "Now I really know that the Lord has sent His angel and rescued me from the power of Herod and from all that the Jewish people were expecting to do to me."

[12] When he became conscious of his situation,[h] he went to the house of Mary, the mother of John who was also called Mark, where a large number of people had met and were praying. [13] When he knocked at the outer door, a servant-girl named Rhoda came to answer it, [14] and on recognizing Peter's voice, in her joy she failed to open the door but ran and told them that Peter was standing at the door.[i]

[15] They said to her, "You are crazy!" But she persistently[j] insisted that it was so. Then they said, "It is his guardian angel!"[k]

[16] But Peter, meanwhile, kept on knocking. So they opened the door, and when they saw him, they were astounded. [17] With his hand he motioned to them to be quiet, and then he told them how the Lord had brought him out of the prison. He added, "Tell all these things to James[l] and the brothers." Then he left them and went somewhere else.

[18] When morning came, there was no little commotion among the soldiers as to what had become of Peter. [19] Herod had search made for him, and when he could not find him, he examined the guards and ordered them to be put to death. Then he left Judea for Caesarea, and stayed there.

[20] Now Herod cherished a bitter grudge[m] against the people of Tyre and Sidon. So in a united body they came to meet him, and after winning the favor of Blastus, the king's chamberlain, they asked for peace, because their country depended for its food-supply upon the king's country. [21] So, on a day appointed, Herod, dressed in his royal robes, took his seat on his throne, and made

---

[f] Grk. has pro.; noun more forceful in Eng.
[g] Lit., *one street*.
[h] Last word implied.
[i] That is, at the outer door.
[j] Impf. of a vb. of strong action.
[k] Lit., *his angel,* guardian implied, in accordance with Jewish belief.
[l] Half brother of Jesus, now pastor of the church at Jerusalem.
[m] Lit., a *battle or fight in his heart*.

them a popular address, ²² and the people shouted, "It is a god's voice, not a man's!"

²³ But the angel of the Lord at once struck him down, because he did not give the glory to God; he was eaten by worms, and so died.ⁿ ²⁴ But the message of the Lord continued to grow and spread.

²⁵ When Barnabas and Saul had finished their helpful service, they returned from Jerusalem, and took along with them John who was called Mark.

13 BARNABAS AND SAUL THE WORLD'S FIRST FOREIGN MISSIONARIES; SENT OUT BY THE SPIRIT THROUGH THE CHURCH AT ANTIOCH; VISIT CYPRUS, PISIDIAN ANTIOCH, ICONIUM, LYSTRA, AND DERBE, MAKING MANY CONVERTS AND FOUNDING CHURCHES

Now in the church at Antioch there were prophets and teachers, Barnabas, Simeon who is called Niger, Lucius the Cyrenian, Manaen who was an intimate friend ᵃ of the governor, and Saul. ² While they were worshiping the Lord and fasting, the Holy Spirit said, "Set apart for me Barnabas and Saul, for the work to which I have called them." ³ So after fasting and praying, they laid their hands upon them and let them go.

⁴ So, as they were sent out by the Holy Spirit, they went down to Seleucia,ᵇ and from that port sailed away to Cyprus. ⁵ When they reached Salamis,ᶜ they began to preach God's message in the Jewish synagogues. They had John with them as their assistant.ᵈ

⁶ Then they went through the whole island as far as Paphos, and there they found a Jewish magician and false prophet whose name was Barjesus. ⁷ He was an intimate friend ᵉ of the governor, Sergius Paulus, who was an intelligent man. The governor sent for Barnabas and Saul and in this way tried to hear God's message. ⁸ But Elymas the magician—for this is the meaning of his name ᶠ—

ⁿ Josephus tells of his death, B.J. vii. 7, 8.
ᵃ So in inscriptions (Deissmann).
ᵇ Seaport to Antioch.
ᶜ Town in E. Cyprus.
ᵈ Lit., *attendant*.
ᵉ Lit., *closely associated with*.
ᶠ *Barjesus* his Jewish, *Elymas* his Grk., name.

continued to oppose them by trying to keep the governor from accepting the faith.[g]

[9] Then Saul, who was also called Paul,[h] because he was full of the Holy Spirit, looked him straight in the eye [i] [10] and said, "You expert [j] in every form of deception and sleight-of-hand, you son of the devil, you enemy of all that is right, will you never stop trying to make the Lord's straight paths crooked! [11] Right now the hand of the Lord is upon you, and you will be so blind that you cannot see the sun for a time." And suddenly a dark mist fell upon him, and he kept groping about begging people to lead him by the hand. [12] Then the governor, because he saw what had occurred, was thunderstruck [k] at the Lord's teaching, and so came to believe.

[13] Then Paul and his party set sail from Paphos and crossed over to Perga in Pamphylia. Here John quit [l] them and returned to Jerusalem, [14] but they went on from Perga and arrived at Antioch in Pisidia. On the sabbath they went to the synagogue and took seats. [15] After the reading of the law and the prophets, the leaders of the synagogue worship sent to them and said, "Brothers, if you have any message of encouragement for the people, you may speak."

[16] Then Paul got up and motioned with his hand and said:

"Fellow Israelites, and you who reverence God,[m] listen! [17] The God of this people Israel chose our forefathers, and made this people important [n] during their stay in Egypt, and then with an uplifted arm He led them out of it. [18] Then after He had fed them forty years in the desert, [19] He destroyed seven nations in Canaan [20] and gave them their land as an inheritance for about four hundred and fifty years. And after that He gave them judges until the time of Samuel the prophet. [21] Then they demanded a king, and for forty years God gave them Saul, the son of Kish, a man of the tribe of Benjamin. [22] Then He deposed him and raised up for them David to be king, to whom He bore this testimony, 'I have found in David, the son of Jesse, a man after my own heart, who will do all that my will requires.' [o] [23] It is from this man's

[g] Grk., *turn him from the faith.*
[h] *Saul,* his Jewish, *Paul* his Rom. name.
[i] Lit., *gazed at him.*
[j] Grk., *full of all deception.*
[k] Lit., *struck out* (of himself).
[l] Grk., *separated from.*
[m] Title for converts to Judaism.
[n] Lit., *high.*
[o] Lit., *my willings.*

descendants that God, as He promised, has brought to Israel a Saviour in the person of Jesus, ²⁴ as John, before His coming, had already preached baptism as an expression ᵖ of repentance, for all the people of Israel. ²⁵ As John was closing his career, he said, 'What do you take me to be? I am not the Christ; ᑫ no, but He is coming after me, and I am not fit to untie the shoes on His feet.' ²⁶ Brothers, descendants of the race of Abraham, and all among you who reverence God, it is to us that the message of this salvation has been sent. ²⁷ For the people of Jerusalem and their leaders, because they were ignorant of Him, by condemning Him have actually fulfilled the utterances of the prophets which are read every sabbath, ²⁸ and although they could not find Him guilty of a capital offense,ʳ they begged Pilate to have Him put to death. ²⁹ When they had carried out everything that had been written in the Scriptures about Him, they took Him down from the cross and laid Him in a tomb. ³⁰ But God raised Him from the dead, ³¹ and for many days He appeared to those who had come up with Him from Galilee to Jerusalem, and they are now witnesses for Him to the people. ³² So now we are bringing you the good news about the promise that was made to our forefathers, ³³ that God has fulfilled it to us their children, by raising Jesus to life, just as the Scripture says in the Second Psalm, 'You are my Son, today I have become your Father.' ˢ ³⁴ Now as a proof that He has raised Him from the dead, no more to return to decay, He has spoken this, 'I will fulfill to you the holy promises made to David.' ᵗ ³⁵ Because in another psalm he says, 'You will not let your Holy One experience decay.' ᵘ ³⁶ For David, after having served God's purpose in his own generation, fell asleep and was laid among his forefathers, and so he did experience decay, ³⁷ but He whom God raised to life did not experience it. ³⁸ So, my brothers, you must understand that through Him the forgiveness of your sins is now proclaimed to you, ³⁹ and that through union with Him every one of you who believes is given right standing with God ᵛ and freed ʷ from every charge from which you could

ᵖ Implied in obj. gen.
ᑫ Grk., *I am not He.*
ʳ Lit., *no cause of death, not worthy of death.*
ˢ Grk., *I have begotten you.*
ᵗ Isa. 55:3.
ᵘ Ps. 16:10.
ᵛ Lit., *is justified from.*
ʷ Implied in prep.

not be freed by the law of Moses. ⁴⁰ So take care that what is said in the prophets does not come upon you:

⁴¹ 'Look, you scoffers! Then wonder and vanish away,
For I am doing a work in your times
Which you will not at all believe though one may tell you in detail.' " ˣ

⁴² As they were leaving the synagogue, ʸ the people kept begging that all this be repeated to them the next sabbath, ⁴³ and after the congregation had broken up, many Jews and devout converts to Judaism ᶻ allied themselves with Paul and Barnabas, and they kept talking to them and urging them to continue to rely on the unmerited favor of God.

⁴⁴ The next sabbath almost the whole town turned out to hear God's message. ⁴⁵ But when the Jews saw the crowds, they were completely overcome * by their jealousy and began to contradict the statements made by Paul, and even to abuse him.

⁴⁶ Then Paul and Barnabas courageously spoke out, "God's message had to be spoken to you Jews first, but since you continue to thrust it from you and since you show yourselves unworthy to receive eternal life, now and here we turn to the heathen. ⁴⁷ For here are the orders that the Lord has given us:

'I have made you a light to the heathen,
To be the means of salvation to the very ends of the earth.' " †

⁴⁸ The heathen kept on listening and rejoicing and giving the glory to God's message, and all who had been destined to eternal life believed, ⁴⁹ and so the message of the Lord spread all over the country.

⁵⁰ But the Jews stirred up the devout women of high rank and the men of first rank in town, and so started a persecution against Paul and Barnabas, and drove them out of their district. ⁵¹ But they shook off the dust from their feet as a protest against them, and went to Iconium; ⁵² and the disciples continued to be full of joy and the Holy Spirit.

ˣ Hab. 1:5.
ʸ Not in best Mss. but implied.
ᶻ Lit., *worshiping proselytes*.
* Lit., *filled*.
† Isa. 49:6.

14
PERSECUTED IN ICONIUM THEY FLEE TO LYSTRA; WORSHIPED BY THE LYSTRANS FOR CURING A CRIPPLED MAN; PAUL STONED ALMOST TO DEATH; ESCAPES TO DERBE; RETRACING THEIR STEPS, THEY ORGANIZE CHURCHES; REPORT TO HOME BASE

At Iconium too they went to the Jewish synagogue and spoke in such a way that a great number of both Jews and Greeks came to believe. 2 But the Jews who refused to accept their message [a] aroused and exasperated the minds of the heathen against the brothers. 3 In spite of this, however, they stayed there a considerable time and continued to speak with courage from [b] the Lord, who continued to bear testimony to His gracious message and kept on granting signs and wonders to be done by them. 4 But the masses of the town were divided; some sided with the Jews and some with the apostles. 5 And so when there was a movement on the part of both the heathen and the Jews, along with their authorities, to insult and stone them, 6 they became aware of it and fled to the Lycaonian towns of Lystra and Derbe, and the surrounding country, 7 and there they continued to tell the good news.

8 Now in the streets of Lystra a man used to sit who had no strength in his feet, who had been crippled from his birth, and had never walked. 9 He continued listening to Paul as he spoke, and as Paul [c] by looking straight at him observed that he had faith that he would be cured, 10 he shouted aloud to him, "Get on your feet and stand erect!" [d] Then up he leaped and began to walk.

11 So the crowds, because they saw what Paul had done, shouted in the Lycaonian language, "The gods in human form [e] have come down to us!" 12 They called Barnabas Zeus [f] and Paul, because he was the principal speaker, Hermes. [g] 13 The priest of the temple of Zeus, which stood at the entrance to the town, came with crowds of people to the gates, bringing bulls and garlands; he meant to offer sacrifices to them.

[a] Lit., *who did not obey*, etc.
[b] Grk., *on the Lord*.
[c] Pro. in Grk.
[d] One vb. expressing both actions.
[e] Lit., *making themselves like men*.
[f] The supreme god of the Greeks.
[g] The god of speech.

¹⁴ But the apostles, Barnabas and Paul, when they heard it, tore their clothes and rushed into the crowd, ¹⁵ and shouted, "Men, why are you doing this? We are merely men with natures ʰ like your own, who are telling you the good news, so that you may turn from these foolish things to the living God, who made heaven and earth and sea and all that they contain. ¹⁶ In ages past He let all the heathen go on in their own ways; ¹⁷ though He did not fail to furnish evidences ⁱ about Himself, in constantly showing His kindness ʲ to you, in sending you rain from heaven and fruit-producing seasons, in giving you food and happiness to your heart's content." ᵏ ¹⁸ Even by saying this it was all that they could do ˡ to keep the crowds from offering sacrifices to them.

¹⁹ But some Jews came from Antioch and Iconium, and won the crowds by persuasion, and they stoned Paul, and dragged him outside the town, supposing he was dead. ²⁰ But the disciples formed a circle about him, and he got up and went back to town. The next day he went on with Barnabas to Derbe. ²¹ They told the good news in that town, and after winning many disciples there, they returned to Lystra, Iconium, and Antioch, ²² strengthening the hearts of the disciples and encouraging them to continue in the faith, and warning them that it is through enduring many hardships ᵐ that we must get into the kingdom of God.

²³ They helped ⁿ them select elders in each church, and after praying and fasting they committed them to the Lord in whom they had believed. ²⁴ Then they passed through Pisidia and went down to Pamphylia, ²⁵ and after telling their message in Perga, they went on to Attalia, ²⁶ and from there they sailed back to Antioch, where they had first been committed to God's favor for the work which they had finished. ²⁷ On arriving there they called the church together, and in detail ᵒ reported to them all that God had done through them as instruments,ᵖ and how He had opened to the heathen the door of faith. ²⁸ And there they stayed a long time with the disciples.

ʰ Lit., *with passions like you.*
ⁱ Grk., *did not leave Himself without witness.*
ʲ Lit., *continuing to do good.*
ᵏ Grk., *filling your hearts with.*
ˡ Grk., *with difficulty they stopped.*
ᵐ Lit., *through distresses.*
ⁿ Implied in dat. of pro.
ᵒ In impf.
ᵖ Lit., *done with them.*

15 JEWISH FANATICS TEACH IN ANTIOCH THAT CIRCUMCISION IS ESSENTIAL TO SALVATION; THE CHURCH SENDS PAUL AND BARNABAS TO CONFER WITH THE APOSTLES ABOUT IT; RESULT, CHRISTIANITY IS FREED FROM JUDAISM

Some people came down from Judea and began to teach the brothers, "Unless you are circumcised in accordance with the custom that Moses handed down, you cannot be saved." ² So, as a dire [a] disturbance and a serious [a] discussion had been created between Paul and Barnabas and them, they decided that Paul and Barnabas and some others from their number should go up to Jerusalem to confer [b] with the apostles and elders about this question. ³ So they were endorsed [c] and sent on by the church, and as they passed through Phoenicia and Samaria, they told of the conversion of the heathen and brought great rejoicing to all the brothers.

⁴ When they arrived at Jerusalem, they were welcomed by the church, the apostles, and the elders, and they reported what God had done through them as instruments. ⁵ But some members of the Pharisaic party, who had become believers, arose and said that such converts [d] must be circumcised and told to keep the law of Moses.

⁶ Now the apostles and elders met to consider [e] this matter. ⁷ After a lengthy discussion Peter got up and said to them, "Brothers, you know that in the early days God chose among you that through me the heathen should hear the message of the good news and believe it. ⁸ And God who knows men's hearts testifies for them by giving them the Holy Spirit, as He did us, ⁹ and in this way He put no difference between us and them, because He cleansed their hearts by faith. ¹⁰ Then why do you now try to test God by putting on these disciples' necks a yoke which neither our forefathers nor we could bear? ¹¹ In fact, we believe that it is through the favor of the Lord Jesus that we are saved, just as they are."

¹² By this he quieted the whole congregation, and they listened to Barnabas and Paul tell of the signs and wonders which God had done through them among the heathen.

[a] Grk., *no little.*
[b] Implied.
[c] In prep. and occasion.
[d] Implied from context.
[e] Lit., *to see about.*

¹³ When they finished,ᶠ James responded as follows: "Brothers, listen to me. ¹⁴ Symeon has told how God at first graciously visitedᵍ the heathen to take from among them a people to bear His name.ʰ ¹⁵ The words of the prophets are in accord with this, as it is written:

¹⁶ ' After this I will return and rebuild David's fallen dwelling; I will rebuild its ruins and set it up again,

¹⁷ So that the rest of mankind may earnestly seek the Lord, Yes, all the heathen who are called by my name,

Says the Lord, ¹⁸ who has been making this known from ages past.' ⁱ

¹⁹ So I give it as my opinion, we ought not to put difficulties in the way of the heathen who turn to God, ²⁰ but we should write them to abstain from everything that is contaminated by idols, from sexual immorality,ʲ from the meat of strangled animals, and from tasting ᵏ blood. ²¹ For Moses from the ancient generations has had his preachers in every town, and on every sabbath has been read aloud in the synagogues."

²² Then the apostles and elders in co-operation with the whole church passed a resolution ˡ to select and send some men of their number with Paul and Barnabas to Antioch. These were Judas, who was called Barsabbas, and Silas, leading men among the brothers. ²³ They sent this letter by them:

"The apostles and elders as brothers ᵐ send greeting to the brothers from among the heathen in Antioch, Syria, and Cilicia. ²⁴ As we have heard that some of our number have disturbed you by their teaching,ⁿ by continuing to unsettle your minds, ²⁵ we have passed a unanimous resolution to select and send messengers ᵒ to you with our beloved brothers Barnabas and Paul, ²⁶ who have risked their lives for the sake of our Lord Jesus Christ. ²⁷ So we send ᵖ Judas and Silas to you, to bring you the same message by word of mouth. ²⁸ For the Holy Spirit and we have decided not to

---

ᶠ Lit., *became silent*.
ᵍ Adv. implied in vb.
ʰ Grk., in His name.
ⁱ Am. 9:11,12.
ʲ Lit., *fornication*, so sexual immorality.
ᵏ Implied.
ˡ Word so used in Herodotus and Thucydides.
ᵐ Fol. WH text.
ⁿ Lit., *by words*.
ᵒ Lit., *men sent*, so *messengers*.
ᵖ Pf., but *sending now*.

lay upon you any burden but these essential requirements, 29 that you abstain from everything that is offered to idols, from tasting blood, from the meat of animals that have been strangled, and from sexual immorality. If you keep yourselves free from these things, you will prosper. Good-by."

30 So the messengers were sent out, and they went down to Antioch, called a meeting of the congregation,q and delivered the letter. 31 When they had read it, they were delighted with the encouragement it brought them. 32 Now Judas and Silas, as they were prophets themselves, in a lengthy talk encouraged and strengthened the brothers. 33 After spending some time there, they were sent back with a greetingr to those who sent them.s 35 But Paul and Barnabas stayed on at Antioch, and with many others continued to teach the Lord's message and to tell the good news.

36 Some days after this Paul said to Barnabas, "Let us go back and visit the brothers in every town where we preached the Lord's message, to see how they are." t 37 But Barnabas persisted in wanting to take along John who was called Mark. 38 Paul, however, did not consider such a man fit to take along with them, the man who deserted them in Pamphylia and did not go on with them to the work. 39 The disagreement was so sharp that they separated, and Barnabas took Mark and sailed for Cyprus. 40 But Paul selected Silas and set out, after the brothers had committed him to the favor of the Lord. 41 He journeyed on through Syria and Cilicia and continued to strengthen the churches.

16
TIMOTHY BECOMES A MISSIONARY PARTNER OF PAUL; THEY GO DOWN TO HISTORIC TROY, THEN CROSS TO EUROPE; PHILIPPI HONORED BY HAVING THE FIRST CHRISTIANS AND THE FIRST CHURCH IN EUROPE; LYDIA THE FIRST CONVERT THERE

Now he went to Derbe and Lystra too. At Lystra there was a disciple named Timothy, whose mother was a Christian Jewess,a but his father was a Greek. 2 He had a high reputation among the brothers in Lystra and Iconium. 3 Paul wanted this man to join

---
q Grk., *multitude*.
r Lit., *with peace*.
s V. 34 not in the best Mss.
t So Abbott-Smith, Lex.
a Lit., *son of a believing Jewess*.

him in his journey; [b] so on account of the Jews in that district he took him and had him circumcised, for everybody knew that his father was a Greek. [4] As they journeyed on from town to town, they delivered to the brothers to keep the decisions reached by the apostles and elders at Jerusalem. [5] So the churches through faith continued to grow in strength and to increase in numbers from day to day.

[6] Then they crossed Phrygia and Galatia. But because they were prevented by the Holy Spirit from speaking the message in Asia, [7] they went on to Mysia and tried to get into Bithynia, but the Spirit of Jesus would not permit them. [8] So they passed by Mysia and went down to Troas.[c] [9] There Paul had a vision one night: a man from Macedonia kept standing and pleading with him in these words, "Come over to Macedonia and help us!"

[10] As soon as he had this vision, we laid our plans to get off to Macedonia, because we confidently[d] concluded that God had called us to tell them the good news.

[11] So we sailed away from Troy and struck a bee line[e] for Samothrace, and the next day on to Neapolis. [12] From there we went on to Philippi, a Roman colony,[f] the leading town in that part of Macedonia.

In this town we stayed some days. [13] On the sabbath we went outside the gate, to the bank of the river, where we supposed there was a place of prayer, and we sat down and began to talk with the women who had met there. [14] Among them was a woman named Lydia, a dealer in purple goods from the town of Thyatira, and she stayed to listen to us. She was already a worshiper of God, and the Lord so moved upon her heart[g] that she accepted[h] the message spoken by Paul. [15] When she and her household were baptized, she begged us by continuing[i] to say, "If you have made up your mind that I am a real believer in the Lord, come and stay at my house." And she continued to insist that we do so.

[16] Once as we were on our way to the place of prayer, a slave-girl

---

[b] Grk., *go out with him.*
[c] Seat of ancient Trojan civilization.
[d] In comp. vb.
[e] Modern nautical term corresponding to Grk. term.
[f] A miniature Rome with special privileges as citizens.
[g] Lit., *opened her heart.*
[h] Lit., *gave heed to.*
[i] Pres. pt. of cont. ac.

THE ACTS OF THE APOSTLES 16

met us who had the gift [j] of magical fortune-telling,[k] and continued to make great profits for her owners by fortune-telling. [17] This girl kept following Paul and the rest of us, shrieking, "These men are slaves of the Most High God, and they are proclaiming to you a way of salvation." [18] She kept this up for a number of days.

Because Paul was so much annoyed by her, he turned and said to the spirit [l] in her, "In the name of Jesus Christ I order you to come out of her." And that very moment [m] it came out.

[19] But as the owners saw that the hope of their profit-making was gone, they seized Paul and Silas and dragged them to the public square,[n] before the authorities, [20] and brought them to the chiefs of the police court.[o] They said, "These men are Jews; they continue to make great disturbance in our town [21] and to advocate practices [p] which it is against the law for us Romans to accept or observe."

[22] The crowd also joined in the attack upon them, and the chiefs of the police court had them stripped and flogged.[q] [23] After flogging them severely, they put them into jail, and gave the jailer orders to keep close watch on them. [24] Because he had such strict orders, he put them into the inner cell and fastened their feet in the stocks.[r]

[25] But about midnight, while Paul and Silas were praying and singing hymns of praise to God, and the prisoners were listening to them, [26] suddenly there was an earthquake so great that it shook [s] the very foundations of the jail, the doors all flew open, and every prisoner's chains were unfastened. [27] When the jailer awoke and saw that the jail-doors were open, he drew his sword and was on the point of killing himself, because he thought that the prisoners had escaped.

[28] But Paul at once shouted out to him, "Do yourself no harm, for we are all here!"

[29] Then the jailer called for lights and rushed in and fell trem-

---

[j] Grk., *had the spirit.*
[k] This meaning proved by the following clause.
[l] Which as an evil spirt caused the magical fortune-telling.
[m] Lit., *hour.*
[n] Grk., *market place,* our public square.
[o] Lit., *rulers or magistrates.*
[p] Lit., *customs.*
[q] *Beaten with rods,* a Rom. form of punishment.
[r] Timbers screwed down tight on the feet.
[s] Lit., *the foundations were shaken.*

bling at the feet of Paul and Silas. ³⁰ After leading them out of the jail, he said, "Sirs, what must I do to be saved?"

³¹ They answered, "Believe on the Lord Jesus,ᵗ and you and your household will be saved." ³² Then they told God's message to him and to all the members of his household. ³³ Even at that time of the night he took them and washed their wounds, and he and all the members of his household at once were baptized. ³⁴ Then he took them up to his house and gave them food, and he and all the members of his household were happy in their faithᵘ in God.

³⁵ When day broke, the chiefs of the police court sent policemen with the message to let the men go. ³⁶ The jailer reported this message to Paul, saying, "The chiefs of the police court have sent orders to let you go. So now you may come out and go in peace."

³⁷ But Paul said to them, "They beat us in public and that without a trial, and put us in jail although we are Roman citizens! Let them come here themselves and take us out!"ᵛ

³⁸ The policemen reported this message to the chiefs of the police court, and they became alarmed when they heard that they were Roman citizens, ³⁹ and came and pleaded with them, and took them out and begged them to leave town. ⁴⁰ After getting out of jail, they went to Lydia's house; they saw the brothers and encouraged them, and then left town.

17 THEY MAKE MANY CONVERTS AT THESSALONICA; RUN OUT OF TOWN BY A RIOT, THEY GO TO BEREA; HERE THE PEOPLE READ THE SCRIPTURES; DRIVEN FROM BEREA, PAUL GOES TO ATHENS; HE PREACHES IN ITS FAMOUS AUDITORIUM BUT IS HECKLED BY THE PHILOSOPHERS

Now they traveled on through Amphipolis and Apollonia until they reached Thessalonica. Here there was a Jewish synagogue. ² So Paul, as he usually did, went to the synagogue,ᵃ and for three sabbaths discussed with them the Scriptures,ᵇ ³ explaining them and

---

ᵗ Fol. WH who omit *Christ*.

ᵘ So all the members of the household, after hearing "God's message," came to have *faith* in God; which means, *faith in the Lord Jesus*.

ᵛ In this way Paul vindicated his innocence and good name; so the church in Philippi became a mighty power in the town.

ᵃ Supplied from the preceding sentence.

ᵇ Lit., *spoke through with them from the Scriptures*.

proving that the Christ had to suffer and rise from the dead, and said, "This very Jesus whom I proclaim to you is the Christ."

4 So some of them were convinced, and they joined Paul and Silas; also quite a number of devout Greeks and not a few women of the first rank. 5 But this enraged the Jews; so they got together some wicked loafers about the public square, formed a mob, and set the town in an uproar. 6 They stopped at Jason's house and tried to bring them out to the people. So, as they could not find them, they dragged Jason and some of the brothers before the town magistrates, shouting, "These fellows, who have turned the world topsy-turvy, have come here too, 7 and Jason has welcomed them. They are all acting contrary to the Emperor's decrees, because they claim there is another king, Jesus."

8 Thus they wrought up to great excitement the crowd and the town magistrates, on their hearing this, 9 and they made Jason and the other brothers give bond,[c] and then turned them loose.

10 That night at once the brothers sent Paul and Silas away to Berea, and on arriving there they went to the Jewish synagogue. 11 The Jews there were better disposed than those in Thessalonica, for they welcomed the message with all eagerness and carried on a daily study of the Scriptures to see if Paul's[d] message was true. 12 Many of them came to believe, and not a few distinguished Greek women and men. 13 But when the Jews at Thessalonica learned that God's message had been proclaimed at Berea by Paul, they came there too to excite the masses and stir up a riot. 14 Then the brothers at once sent Paul off to the coast, while Silas and Timothy stayed on there. 15 The men who acted as Paul's bodyguard[e] took him all the way to Athens, and then went back with orders for Silas and Timothy to come to him as soon as possible.

16 While Paul was waiting for them at Athens, his spirit was stirred to its depths[f] to see the city completely steeped in idolatry.[g] 17 So he kept up his discussions in the synagogue with the Jews and the pagans[h] who were worshiping there, and also day by day in the public square with any who chanced to be there.

18 Some of the Epicurean and the Stoic philosophers[i] began to

[c] Grk., *took security from.*
[d] Grk., *if these things were so.*
[e] Lit., *the men who kept standing Paul down.*
[f] Grk., *his spirit sharpened,* etc.
[g] Lit., *wholly given up to idols.*
[h] Grk., *those worshiping there,* pagan converts to Judaism.
[i] Former emphasize pleasure, latter endurance.

debate with him; and some said, "What is this scraps-of-truth-picker[j] trying to say?"

Others said, "He seems to be a preacher of foreign deities." They said so because he was telling the good news of Jesus and the resurrection.

19 So they took him and brought him to the city auditorium[k] and said, "May we know what this new teaching of yours is? 20 For some of the things you bring sound startling[l] to us; so we want to know just what they mean." 21 (Now all the Athenians and foreign visitors in Athens[m] used to spend their time in nothing else than telling or listening to the latest new thing out.)[n]

22 So Paul stood up in the center of the auditorium and said:

"Men of Athens, at every turn[o] I make I see that you are very religious. 23 For as I was going here and there and looking at the things you worship, I even found an altar with this inscription, 'TO AN UNKNOWN GOD.' So it is about the Being[p] whom you are in ignorance already worshiping that I am telling you. 24 The God who made the world and all that it contains, since He is Lord of heaven and earth, does not dwell in temples made by human hands, 25 nor is He served by human hands as though He were in need of anything, for He Himself gives all men life and breath and everything else. 26 From one forefather He made every nation of mankind, for living all over the face of the earth, fixing their appointed times and the limits of their lands, 27 so that they might search for God, possibly they might grope for Him, and find Him, though He is really not far from any of us. 28 For it is through union with Him that we live and move and exist, as some of your own poets[q] have said,

"'For we are His offspring too.' 29 Since then we are God's offspring, we ought not to suppose that His nature is like gold or silver or stone or anything carved by man's art and thought. 30 Though God overlooked those times of ignorance, He now commands all men everywhere to repent, 31 since He has set a day on which He will justly judge the world through a man whom He

[j] Lit., *seed-picker,* then *scrap-picker.*
[k] *Mars' Hill,* nat. auditorium.
[l] So in *Polybius.*
[m] Implied.
[n] Lit., *something newer.*
[o] Context gives this meaning.
[p] Masc. pronoun suggests this.
[q] Aratus, Cleanthes, possibly others, said so.

has appointed. He has made this credible [r] to all by raising Him from the dead."

[32] But when they heard of the resurrection of the dead, some sneered, but others said, "We will hear you again on this subject." [33] So Paul left the auditorium. [34] Some men, however, joined him and came to believe, among them Dionysius, a member of the city council; also a woman named Damaris, and some others.

18   IN CORINTH PAUL STAYS WITH AQUILA AND PRISCILLA, JEWISH REFUGEES FROM ROME; SILAS AND TIMOTHY COME AND TELL OF THE THESSALONIANS; PAUL BEFORE JUDGE GALLIO WHO DISMISSES THE CASE; APOLLOS TAUGHT BY PRISCILLA

After this he left Athens and went to Corinth.[a] [2] There he found a Jew named Aquila, a native of Pontus, who had recently come from Italy with his wife Priscilla, because Claudius [b] had issued an edict for all Jews to leave Rome. So Paul paid them a visit, [3] and as they all had the same trade, they proceeded to work together. [4] Every sabbath it was Paul's habit to preach in the synagogue and to persuade both Jews and Greeks.

[5] By the time Silas and Timothy arrived from Macedonia, Paul was wholly absorbed in preaching the message [c] and was enthusiastically assuring [d] the Jews that Jesus is the Christ. [6] But as they opposed and abused him, he shook out his clothes in protest and said to them, "Your blood be upon your own heads! I am not to blame for it myself. Hereafter I am going to the heathen."

[7] So he moved into the house of a pagan named Titus Justus, who worshiped the true God; his house was next to the synagogue. [8] But Crispus, the leader of the synagogue, became a believer in the Lord, and so did all his family, and from time to time [e] many of the Corinthians heard, believed, and were baptized.

[9] One night in a vision the Lord said to Paul, "Stop being afraid, go on speaking, never give up; [10] because I am with you, and no

---

[r] Lit., *furnishing faith to all.*
[a] Capital of Rom. province, Greece.
[b] Emperor of Rome, 44-47.
[c] Lit., *wholly absorbed in the word.*
[d] Comp. vb. lit. means, *thoroughly testifying to.*
[e] Expressed by impf.

one is going to attack you so as to injure you, because I have many people in this city." ¹¹ So for a year and a half he settled down among them and went on teaching God's message.

¹² While Gallio ᶠ was governor of Greece, the Jews unanimously attacked Paul and one day brought him before the court, ¹³ and said, "This fellow is inducing people to worship God in ways that violate our laws."

¹⁴ As Paul was about to open his mouth, Gallio said to the Jews, "If it were some misdemeanor or underhanded rascality, O Jews, I would in reason listen to you; ¹⁵ but as it is questions about words and titles ᵍ and your own law, you will have to see to it yourselves. I refuse to act as judge in these matters." ¹⁶ So he drove them away from the court. ¹⁷ Then they all seized Sosthenes, the leader of the synagogue, and kept beating him right in front of the court; but Gallio paid no attention to it.

¹⁸ Now Paul stayed a considerable time longer in Corinth, and then bade the brothers good-by and set sail for Syria, accompanied ʰ by Aquila and Priscilla. At Cenchreae he had his hair cut, for he was under a vow.ⁱ ¹⁹ Then they came to Ephesus, and Paul left them there. He went into the synagogue and had a discussion with the Jews. ²⁰ They asked him to stay longer, but he would not consent. ²¹ But as he bade them good-by, he promised,ʲ "I will come back to you again, if it is God's will." Then he set sail from Ephesus. ²² When he reached Caesarea, he went up to Jerusalem ᵏ and greeted the church there; then he went down to Antioch.

²³ After spending some time there, he started out again, and by a definite schedule ˡ traveled all over Galatia and Phrygia, imparting new strength to all the disciples.

²⁴ Meanwhile, a Jew named Apollos came to Ephesus. He was a native of Alexandria, a learned man, and skillful in the use of the Scriptures. ²⁵ He had been instructed about the way of the Lord, and with spiritual fervor ᵐ he was speaking and was accurately teaching some details about Jesus, although he knew of no bap-

---

ᶠ Half brother of Seneca, the Stoic philosopher.
ᵍ Lit., *names*.
ʰ Grk., *with*.
ⁱ Lit., *had a vow*.
ʲ Grk., *said*.
ᵏ Implied from prep.
ˡ Lit., *in order*.
ᵐ Grk., *boiling in spirit*.

tism but John's. ²⁶ He started speaking courageously in the synagogue, but when Priscilla and Aquila heard him, they took him home with them ⁿ and more accurately explained the way of God to him. ²⁷ Because he wished to cross to Greece, the brothers wrote and urged the disciples there to welcome him. On his arrival he rendered great service to those who through God's favor had believed, ²⁸ for he successfully refuted the Jews in public and proved by the Scriptures that Jesus was the Christ.

19 PAUL IN EPHESUS, HEADQUARTERS FOR HIS WORK IN ROMAN ASIA (PROVINCE); HE WORKS MIRACLES; SCEVA'S SEVEN SONS REPROVED FOR IMITATING HIM; DEMETRIUS SETS THE CITY IN AN UPROAR; PAUL RESCUED BY ROMAN OFFICERS

It was while Apollos was in Corinth that Paul, by passing through the inland districts, came to Ephesus. He found a few disciples there ² and asked them, "Did you receive the Holy Spirit when you believed?"

They answered him, "So far from that,ᵃ we never even heard that there is a Holy Spirit."

³ He then asked, "With what sort of baptism then were you baptized?"

They answered, "With John's baptism."

⁴ Then Paul said, "John baptized with a baptism that was an expression of repentance,ᵇ telling the people to believe in Him who was to come after him; that is, in Jesus." ⁵ On hearing this they were baptized in the name of the Lord Jesus, ⁶ and when Paul laid his hands upon them, the Holy Spirit came upon them, and they began ᶜ to speak in foreign tongues and to prophesy. ⁷ In all there were about twelve men.

⁸ He went to the synagogue there and for three months courageously spoke, keeping up his discussions and continuing to persuade them about the kingdom of God. ⁹ But as some of them grew harder and harder ᵈ and refused to believe, actually criticizing the Way before the people, he left them, withdrew his disciples, and

---

ⁿ Lit., *to them.*
ᵃ Implied in the adversative conjunction, *alla.*
ᵇ Obj. gen. gives this meaning.
ᶜ Inceptive impf.
ᵈ Impf. of cont. ac.

continued his discussions in the lecture-hall of Tyrannus. ¹⁰ This went on for two years, so that everybody living in the province ᵉ of Asia, Greeks as well as Jews, heard the Lord's message.

¹¹ God also continued to do such wonder-works through Paul ¹² as an instrument that the people carried off to the sick, towels or aprons used by him, and at their touch they were cured of their diseases, and the evil spirits went out of them. ¹³ But some wandering Jews who claimed to be driving out the evil spirits ᶠ tried to use the name of the Lord Jesus on those who had evil spirits in them, saying, "I command you by that Jesus whom Paul preaches!"

¹⁴ Sceva, a Jewish high priest, had seven sons who were doing this. ¹⁵ But on one occasion ᵍ the evil spirit answered, "Jesus I know and Paul I know about,ʰ but who are you?"

¹⁶ So the man in whom the evil spirit was, leaped upon them and so violently overpowered two ⁱ of them that they ran out of the house stripped of their clothes and wounded. ¹⁷ This at once became known to everybody living in Ephesus, Greeks as well as Jews, and awe fell upon them all, and the name of the Lord Jesus began to be held in high honor. ¹⁸ And many who became believers kept coming and confessing and uncovering their former practices. ¹⁹ Many people who had practiced magic brought their books together and burned them up before the public gaze.ʲ They estimated the price of them and found it to be ten thousand dollars. ²⁰ In a way of just such power as this the Lord's message kept on spreading and prevailing.

²¹ After these events had been brought to a close, Paul under the guidance of the Spirit decided to pass through Macedonia and Greece on his way to Jerusalem, saying, "After I have gone there I must see Rome too." ²² So he sent off to Macedonia two of his assistants, Timothy and Erastus, while he stayed on for a while in Asia.

²³ Now just about that time a great commotion arose about the Way.ᵏ ²⁴ A silversmith named Demetrius, by manufacturing silver

---

ᵉ Lit., *Asia*, but here the province of which Ephesus is capital.
ᶠ Grk., *exorcists*—those claiming to drive out evil spirits.
ᵍ Implied.
ʰ Different vbs., latter weak.
ⁱ Lit., *both;* may mean *all.*
ʲ Lit., *before all.*
ᵏ The popular expression for the new faith.

shrines of Artemis,[1] was bringing in great profits to his workmen. [25] He called together his workmen, and others engaged in similar trades, and said to them:

"Men, you well know that our prosperity depends on this business of ours, [26] and you see and hear that, not only in Ephesus but all over the province of Asia, this man Paul has led away a vast number of people by persuading them, telling them that gods made by human hands are not gods at all. [27] Now the danger facing us is, not only that our business will lose its reputation but also that the temple of the great goddess Artemis will be brought into contempt and that she whom all Asia and all the world now worship will soon be dethroned from her majestic glory!"

[28] When they heard this, they became furious and kept on shouting, "Great Artemis of Ephesus!" [29] So the whole city was thrown into confusion and with one impulse the people rushed into the theatre and dragged with them two Macedonians, Gaius and Aristarchus, Paul's traveling companions. [30] Paul wanted to go into the assembly and address the people, but the disciples would not let him. [31] Some of the public officials in Asia,[m] who were friendly to him, also sent word to him, begging him not to risk himself in the theatre. [32] So they kept on shouting, some one thing, some another, for the assembly was in confusion, and the majority of them did not know why they had met. [33] Some of the crowd concluded that it was Alexander, since the Jews had pushed him to the front, and since Alexander had made a gesture of the hand as though he would make a defense before the people. [34] But as soon as they saw [n] that he was a Jew, a shout went up from them all as the shout of one man, lasting for two hours:

"Great Artemis of Ephesus!"

[35] At last the city recorder quieted the mob and said:

"Men of Ephesus, who in the world does not know that the city of Ephesus is the guardian of the temple of the great Artemis and of the image that fell down from heaven? [36] So, as this cannot be denied, you must be quiet and do nothing rash. [37] For you have brought these men here, although they are not guilty of sacrilege or of abusive speech against our goddess. [38] So then, if Demetrius

---

[1] An eastern goddess, but often identified with the Greek goddess, whose temple in Ephesus was regarded one of the world's seven wonders.

[m] Lit., *asiarchs*, political or religious officials; likely the former.

[n] Grk., *knew* or *recognized*.

and his fellow-workmen have a charge against anybody, there are the courts and the judges; º let them go to law.ᵖ ³⁹ But if you require anything beyond this, it must be settled in the regular assembly.ᑫ ⁴⁰ For we are in danger of being charged with rioting for today's assembly, as there is not a single reason we can give for it." ⁴¹ With these words he dismissed the assembly.

20 PAUL GOES TO MACEDONIA, GREECE, AND TROY; AT TROY HE SPEAKS TILL MIDNIGHT; YOUTHFUL EUTYCHUS FALLS DEAD FROM A THIRD STORY WINDOW; PAUL RAISES HIM TO LIFE; AT MILETUS HE MAKES A FAREWELL SPEECH TO THE EPHESIAN ELDERS

When the uproar had ceased, Paul sent for the disciples and encouraged them. Then he bade them good-by and started off for Macedonia. ² He passed through those districts and by continuing to talk to them encouraged the people. He then went on to Greece ³ where he stayed three months. Just as he was about to sail for Syria, he changed his mind and returnedᵃ by way of Macedonia, because a plot against him had been laid by the Jews. ⁴ He had as companions Sopater, the son of Pyrrhus, from Berea, Aristarchus and Secundus from Thessalonica, Gaius from Derbe, Timothy, and Tychicus and Trophimus from the province of Asia. ⁵ They went on to Troas and waited there for us, ⁶ while we, after the feast of Unleavened Bread, sailed from Philippi, and five days after joined them at Troas, where we spent a week.

⁷ On the first day of the week when we had met to break bread, Paul addressed them, since he was leaving the next day, and prolonged his speech till midnight. ⁸ There were many lamps in the room upstairs where we met, ⁹ and a young man named Eutychus, who was sitting by the window, was gradually overcome by heavy drowsiness, as Paul kept speaking longer and longer, and at last he went fast asleep and fell from the third story to the ground and was picked up dead.

¹⁰ But Paul went down and fell on him and embraced him, and said, "Stop being alarmed, his life is still in him." ¹¹ So he went

---

º *Governors,* but they acted as judges too.
ᵖ Lit., *make charges against one another.*
ᑫ Same word tr. *church* elsewhere.
ᵃ Grk., *his opinion was to return.*

back upstairs, and broke the bread and ate with them, and after talking with them extendedly, even till daylight, he left them. ¹² Then they took the boy home alive, and were greatly comforted.

¹³ We had already gone on board the ship and set sail for Assos, where we were to take Paul on board; for it had been so arranged by him, as he intended to travel there on foot. ¹⁴ So when he met us at Assos, we took him on board and sailed on to Mitylene. ¹⁵ On the next day we sailed from there and arrived off Chios. On the next day we crossed to Samos, and the next we reached Miletus. ¹⁶ For Paul's plan was to sail past Ephesus, so as not to lose any time in the province of Asia; for he was eager, if possible, to reach Jerusalem by Pentecost.

¹⁷ From Miletus he sent to Ephesus for the elders of the church ¹⁸ When they arrived, he said to them:

"You know how I lived among you all the time from the day I first set foot in the province of Asia, and how I continued ¹⁹ to serve the Lord with all humility and in tears, through the trials that befell me because of the plots of the Jews. ²⁰ I never shrank from telling you anything that was for your good, nor from teaching you in public and in private, ²¹ but constantly and earnestly [b] I urged Greeks as well as Jews to turn with repentance to God and to have faith in our Lord Jesus. ²² And I am here now on my way to Jerusalem, because I am impelled [c] by the Spirit to do so, though I am not aware what will befall me there, ²³ except that in town after town the Holy Spirit emphatically assures me that imprisonment [d] and sufferings are awaiting me. ²⁴ But now I count as nothing the sacrifice of my life, if only I can finish my race and render the service entrusted [e] to me by the Lord Jesus, of faithfully telling the good news of God's favor. ²⁵ And now I know that none of you among whom I went about preaching the kingdom will ever see my face again. ²⁶ I therefore protest to you today that I am not responsible for the blood of any of you, ²⁷ for I never shrank from telling you God's whole plan. ²⁸ Take care of yourselves and of the whole flock, of which the Holy Spirit has made you overseers, so as to continue to be shepherds of the church of God,[f] which He bought with His own blood. ²⁹ Because I know that after I have gone violent wolves will break in among

---

[b] First adv. in the tense, second in prep.
[c] Lit., *bound*.
[d] Grk., *bonds*.
[e] Grk., *service which I rec'd. from the Lord Jesus*.
[f] Some good Mss. read, *the church of the Lord*.

you and will not spare the flock. ³⁰ Even from your own number men will appear who will try, by speaking perversions of truth,[g] to draw away the disciples after them. ³¹ So ever be on your guard and always remember that for three years, night and day, I never ceased warning you one by one, and that with tears. ³² And now I commit you to the Lord, and to the message of His favor, which is able to build you up and to give you your proper possession [h] among all God's consecrated people.[i] ³³ I have never coveted any man's silver or gold or clothes. ³⁴ You know yourselves that these hands of mine provided for my own needs and for my companions. ³⁵ In everything I showed you that by working hard like this we must help those who are weak, and remember the words of the Lord Jesus, that He said, 'It makes one happier to give than to get.'"

³⁶ After he had finished this speech,[j] he fell on his knees with them all and prayed. ³⁷ There was loud weeping by them all, as they threw their arms around Paul's neck and kept on kissing him with affection,[k] because they were especially pained at his saying that they would never see his face again. Then they went down to the ship with him.[l]

21
PAUL GOES ON TO JERUSALEM; STOPS WITH PHILIP AT CAESAREA; WARNED BY PROPHET AGABUS OF IMPRISONMENT BUT NOT DETERRED; REACHES JERUSALEM, INTERVIEWS PASTOR JAMES, TRIES TO WIN THE JEWISH CHRISTIANS; SEIZED BY A MOB BUT RESCUED BY THE ROMAN COLONEL

When we had torn ourselves away from them, we struck a bee line for Cos, and the next day on to Rhodes, and from there to Patara. ² There we found a ship bound for Phoenicia, and so we went aboard and sailed away. ³ After sighting Cyprus and leaving it on our left, we sailed on for Syria, and put in at Tyre, for the ship was to unload her cargo there. ⁴ So we looked up the disciples

---
[g] Lit., *perverted things.*
[h] Grk., *inheritance.*
[i] Lit., *all the consecrated ones.*
[j] Lit., *having said these things.*
[k] Comp. vb. expresses this.
[l] Grk., *sent him forward to the ship.*

there and stayed a week with them. Because of impressions made by the Spirit [a] they kept on warning Paul not to set foot in Jerusalem. ⁵ But when our time was up,[b] we left there and went on, and all of them with their wives and children accompanied us out of town. There we knelt down on the beach and prayed; ⁶ there we bade one another good-by, and we went aboard the ship, while they went back.

⁷ On finishing the sail from Tyre we landed at Ptolemais. Here we greeted the brothers and spent a day with them. ⁸ The next day we left there and went on to Caesarea, where we went to the house of Philip the evangelist, who was one of the Seven,[c] and stayed with him. ⁹ He had four unmarried daughters who were prophetesses. ¹⁰ While we were spending some days here, a prophet named Agabus came down from Judea. ¹¹ He came to see us and took Paul's belt and with it bound his own hands and feet, and said, "This is what the Holy Spirit says, 'The Jews at Jerusalem will bind the man who owns this belt like this, and then will turn him over to the heathen.'"

¹² When we heard this, we and all the people there begged him not to go up to Jerusalem. ¹³ Then Paul answered, "What do you mean [d] by crying and breaking my heart? Why, I am ready not only to be bound at Jerusalem but to die there for the sake of the Lord Jesus."

¹⁴ So, since he would not yield to our appeal,[e] we stopped begging him, and said, "The Lord's will be done!"

¹⁵ After this we got ready and started up to Jerusalem. ¹⁶ Some of the disciples from Caesarea went with us and took us to the house of Mnason, a man from Cyprus, one of the early disciples, to spend the night. ¹⁷ When we reached Jerusalem, the brothers there gave us a hearty welcome.[f] ¹⁸ On the next day we went with Paul to see James, and all the elders of the church came too. ¹⁹ Paul first greeted them and then gave them a detailed account of what God had done among the heathen through his service.

²⁰ They gave the glory to God, when they heard it, and said to him, "You see, brother, how many thousand believers there are

[a] Lit., *through the Spirit.*
[b] Grk., *it came to pass, we finished our days.*
[c] See 6:1-6, acc't. of appointing the Seven.
[d] Lit., *do.*
[e] Grk., *would not be persuaded.*
[f] Lit., *gladly welcomed us.*

among the Jews, all of them zealous champions [g] of the law. 21 They have been repeatedly told [h] about you that you continuously teach the Jews who live among the heathen to turn their backs [i] on Moses, and that you continue to tell them to stop circumcising their children, and to stop observing the cherished [j] customs. 22 What is your duty,[k] then? They will certainly hear that you have come. 23 Now you must do just what we tell you. We have here four men who are under a vow. 24 Take them along with you, purify yourself with them, and bear the expense for them of having their heads shaved. Then everybody will know that none of those things they have been told about you are so, but that you yourself are living as a constant observer of the law. 25 As for the heathen who have become believers, we have sent them our resolution [l] that they must avoid anything that is contaminated by idols, the tasting of blood, the meat of strangled animals, and sexual immorality."

26 Then Paul took the men along with him and on the next day went into the temple with them, purified, and announced the time when the purification would be completed,[m] when the sacrifice for each one of them could be offered.

27 As the seven days were drawing to a close, the Jews from Asia caught a glimpse of him in the temple and began to stir up all the crowd, and seized him, 28 as they kept shouting, "Men of Israel, help! help! [n] This is the man who teaches everybody everywhere against our people and the law and this place; yea, more than that, he has actually brought Greeks into the temple and desecrated this sacred place." 29 For they had previously seen Trophimus of Ephesus in the city with him, and so they supposed that Paul had brought him into the temple.

30 The whole city was stirred with excitement, and all at once the people rushed together, and seized Paul and dragged him out of the temple, and its gates at once were shut. 31 Now while they were trying to kill him, news reached the colonel of the regiment that all Jerusalem was in a ferment. 32 So he at once got together some soldiers and captains and hurried down against them, but as soon

[g] Grk., *zealous for the law.*
[h] Grk., *catechized,* taught repeatedly.
[i] Grk., *turn back from.*
[j] Implied.
[k] Also implied.
[l] Lit., *having decided we sent.*
[m] Lit., *completion of the days,* etc.
[n] Repetition expressed by pt. of cont. ac.

as they saw the colonel and his soldiers, they stopped beating Paul. ³³ Then the colonel came up and seized Paul and ordered him to be bound with two chains; he then asked who he was and what he had done. ³⁴ But they kept shouting in the crowd, some one thing, some another. As he could not with certainty find out about it, because of the tumult, he ordered him to be brought into the barracks. ³⁵ When Paul got to the steps, he was actually borne by the soldiers because of the violence of the mob, ³⁶ for a tremendous crowd of people kept following them and shouting, "Away with him!"

³⁷ As he was about to be taken into the barracks, Paul said to the colonel, "May I say something to you?"

The colonel asked, "Do you know Greek? ³⁸ Are you not the Egyptian who some time ago raised a mob of four thousand cutthroats ᵒ and led them out into the desert?"

³⁹ Paul answered, "I am a Jew from Tarsus, in Cilicia, a citizen of no insignificant city. Please let me speak to the people." ⁴⁰ He granted the request, and Paul, as he was standing on the steps, made a gesture to the people, and after everybody had quieted down, he spoke to them in Hebrew as follows:

22 PAUL IN AN ADDRESS TO THE JEWISH PEOPLE TELLS THE STORY OF HIS CONVERSION; THEN HE IS ARRESTED AND TAKEN BEFORE THE COURT ᵃ

"Brothers and fathers, listen now to what I have to say in my defense." ² When they heard him speaking to them in Hebrew, they became even more quiet, and he continued:

³ "I am a Jew, born in Tarsus in Cilicia, but brought up here in this city, and carefully educated under the teaching of Gamaliel in the law of our forefathers. I was zealous for God, as all of you are today. ⁴ I persecuted this Way even to the death, and kept on binding both men and women and putting them in jail, ⁵ as the high priest and the whole council will bear me witness. Indeed, I had received letters from them to the brothers in Damascus, and I was on the way there to bind those who were there and bring them back to Jerusalem to be punished. ⁶ But on my way, just before ᵇ I

ᵒ Lit., *men of sikarii;* i.e., men who carried concealed daggers, cutthroats.
ᵃ *The Sanhedrin,* the Supreme Court among the Jews.
ᵇ Grk., *as I was approaching.*

reached Damascus, suddenly about noon a blaze of light from heaven flashed [e] around me, [7] and I fell to the ground and heard a voice saying to me, 'Saul! Saul! Why are you persecuting me?' [8] I answered, 'Who are you, Sir?' He said to me, 'I am Jesus of Nazareth whom you are persecuting.' [9] The men who were with me saw the light, but they did not hear the voice of Him who was speaking to me. [10] Then I asked, 'What am I to do, Lord?' [d] And the Lord answered, 'Get up and go into Damascus, and there it will be told you what you are destined to do.' [11] Since I could not see because of the dazzling sheen [e] of that light, I was led by the hand by my companions, and in this way I reached Damascus. [12] There a man named Ananias, a man devout in strict accordance with the law, of good reputation [f] among all the Jews who lived there, [13] came to see me, and standing by my side said to me, 'Saul, my brother, recover your sight!' Then instantly I did recover it and looked at [g] him, [14] and he said, 'The God of our forefathers has appointed you to learn [h] His will and to see the Righteous One and to hear Him speak,[i] [15] because you are to be His witness to all men of what you have seen and heard. [16] And now, why are you waiting? Get up and be baptized and wash your sins away by calling [j] on His name.' [17] After I had come back to Jerusalem, one day while I was praying in the temple, I fell into a trance, [18] and saw Him saying to me, 'Make haste and at once get out of Jerusalem, because they will not accept your testimony about me.' [19] So I said, 'Lord, they know for themselves that from one synagogue to another I used to imprison and flog those who believed in you, [20] and when the blood of your martyr Stephen was being shed, I stood by and approved it, and held the clothes of those who killed him.' [21] Then He said to me, 'Go, because I am to send you out and far away among the heathen.'"

[22] They listened to him until he said this, and then all at once they shouted, "Away with such a fellow from the earth! He is certainly not fit to live!"

[23] While they were shouting and tossing their clothes about and

[c] Force of aor.
[d] Same word as, *sir*, above, but now Paul recognizes Jesus as Lord.
[e] Lit., *glory*.
[f] Grk., *testified to*.
[g] Double use of vb.
[h] Aor. of *know*, so *learn*.
[i] Grk., *hear His voice*.
[j] Adv. pt. of means.

flinging dust into the air, ²⁴ the colonel ordered Paul to be brought into the barracks, and told them to examine him by flogging, in order that he might find out why they were crying out against him in such a way.

²⁵ But when they had tied him for the flogging, Paul asked the captain who was standing by, "Is it lawful for you to flog a Roman, and one who is uncondemned at that?"

²⁶ When the captain heard that, he went to the colonel and reported it. Then he asked him, "What are you going to do? This man is a Roman citizen."

²⁷ So the colonel came to Paul and asked, "Tell me, are you a Roman citizen?"

He answered, "Yes."

²⁸ Then the colonel said, "I paid a large sum for this citizenship of mine."

Paul said, "But I was born a citizen."

²⁹ So the men who were going to examine him left him at once, and the colonel himself was frightened when he learned that he was a Roman citizen and that he had had him bound.

³⁰ The next day, as he wished to learn the exact reason why the Jews accused him, he had him unbound, and ordered the high priest and the whole council to assemble, and took Paul down and brought him before them.ᵏ

23 PAUL INGENIOUSLY DIVIDES THE COURT, PHARISEES AGAINST SADDUCEES; HE PROTESTS HIS INNOCENCE; JESUS COMFORTS HIM; THE JEWS PLOT TO KILL HIM; THE COLONEL FINDS IT OUT AND SENDS HIM TO CAESAREA FOR SAFETY

Paul fixed his eyes upon the council and said, "Brothers, with a clear conscience I have done my duty to God up to this very day."

² At this the high priest Ananias ordered the people standing near him to strike him on the mouth.

³ Then Paul said to him, "You white-washed wall, God will strike you! Do you sit as a judge to try me in accordance with the law and yet in violation of the law you order them to strike me?"

⁴ The people standing near him said, "Do you mean to insult God's high priest?"

ᵏ V. 30 really belongs to the subject-matter of Chap. 23.

5 Paul answered, "I did not know, brothers, that he was high priest, for the Scripture says, 'You must not speak evil against any ruler of your people.' "[a]

6 Because Paul knew that part of them were Sadducees and part of them Pharisees, he began to cry out in the council chamber, "Brothers, I am a Pharisee, a Pharisee's son, and now I am on trial for the hope of the resurrection of the dead."

7 When he said that, an angry dispute arose between the Pharisees and the Sadducees, and the crowded court was divided.[b] 8 For the Sadducees hold that there is no resurrection, and no such thing as an angel or spirit, but the Pharisees believe in all of them.[c]

9 So there was a vociferous yelling until some of the scribes, belonging to the party of the Pharisees, got up and fiercely contended, "We find nothing wrong with this man. Suppose a spirit or angel has really spoken to him!"

10 Since the dispute kept growing hotter and hotter, the colonel became alarmed that Paul might be torn in pieces by them, and so ordered the army to march down and take him out of their hands[d] and bring him back to the barracks.

11 But that same night the Lord stood by Paul's side and said, "Courage! For just as you have testified for me in Jerusalem, you must testify for me in Rome, too."

12 After day had dawned, the Jews formed a conspiracy and took an oath not to eat or drink till they had killed Paul. 13 There were more than forty of them who formed this conspiracy. 14 They went to the high priests and elders and said to them, "We have taken a solemn[e] oath not to taste a morsel till we have killed Paul. 15 So you and the council must now notify the colonel to bring him down to you, as though you were going to look into his case more carefully, but before he gets down we will be ready to kill him."

16 But Paul's nephew heard of the plot and came to the barracks and told Paul. 17 So Paul called one of the captains and said, "Take this young man to the colonel, for he has something to tell him."

18 So he took him and brought him to the colonel and said,

[a] Ex. 22:28.
[b] Lit., *the multitude;* so *the crowded court.*
[c] Or, *both* (likely in sense of all).
[d] Lit., *out of their midst.*
[e] Expressed by cog. instr.

"The prisoner Paul called me to him and asked me to bring this young man to you, because he has something to tell you."

¹⁹ So the colonel took him by the arm, stepped to one side so as to be alone, and asked him, "What is it you have to tell me?" ²⁰ He answered, "The Jews have agreed to ask you to bring Paul down to the council tomorrow, as though you were going to examine his case more carefully.ᶠ ²¹ But do not yield to them, for more than forty of them are lying in wait for him; they have taken an oath not to eat or drink till they have killed him. They are all ready now, just waiting for your promise."

²² So the colonel sent the young man away, with strict directions not to tell anybody that he had notified him of this plot.ᵍ ²³ Then he called in two of his captains and said to them, "Get two hundred men ready to march to Caesarea, with seventy mountedʰ soldiers and two hundred armed with spears, to leave at nine o'clock tonight." ²⁴ He further told them to provide horses for Paul to ride,ⁱ so as to bring him in safety to Felix, the governor, to whom ²⁵ he wrote the following letter: ʲ

²⁶ "Claudius Lysias sends greetings to his Excellency Felix, the governor. ²⁷ This man had been seized by the Jews and they were on the point of killing him when I came upon them with the soldiers and rescued him, because I had learned that he was a Roman citizen. ²⁸ As I wanted to know the exact charge they were making against him, I brought him before their council, ²⁹ and found him to be charged with questions about their law, but having no charge against him involving death or imprisonment. ³⁰ Because a plot against the man has been reported to me as brewing,ᵏ I at once am sending him on to you and have directed his accusers to present their charge against him before you."

³¹ So the soldiers took Paul, as they had been ordered to do, and brought him by night as far as Antipatris. ³² The next day they returned to the barracks, leaving the mounted men to go on with him; ³³ they, on reaching Caesarea, delivered the letter to the governor and turned Paul over to him, too. ³⁴ He read the letter and

---

ᶠ Lit., *diagnose the things about him.*
ᵍ Grk., *these things*—plot and all.
ʰ Lit., *horsemen.*
ⁱ Grk., *for mounting P.*
ʲ Lit., *having this type.*
ᵏ Grk., *about to be.*

asked Paul what province he was from, and on learning that he was from Cilicia, ³⁵ he said, "I will carefully hear your case as soon as your accusers arrive."

Then he ordered him to be kept in custody in Herod's palace.¹

24 PAUL ON TRIAL BEFORE THE ROMAN JUDGE FELIX; TERTULLUS, A BRILLIANT ORATOR, PROSECUTES HIM; PAUL MAINTAINS HIS INNOCENCE; THOUGH UNCONDEMNED, STILL LEFT IN PRISON IN CAESAREA

Five days later, the high priest Ananias came down with some elders and a prosecuting attorney,ᵃ Tertullus, and through him they presented their case against Paul before the governor. ² When Paul was called, Tertullus opened the prosecution by saying:

"Your Excellency, Felix, since we are enjoying perfect ᵇ peace through you and since reforms for this nation are being brought about through your foresight, ³ we always and everywhere acknowledge it with profound ᶜ gratitude. ⁴ But, not to detain you too long, I beg you in your kindness to give us a brief hearing. ⁵ For we have found this man a perfect ᵈ pest and a disturber of the peace among the Jews throughout the world. He is a ringleader in the sect of the Nazarenes; ᵉ ⁶ once he tried to desecrate the temple, but we arrested him,ᶠ* ⁸ and now, by examining him for yourself, you can find out exactly what charges we bring against him."

⁹ The Jews also joined in the charges and maintained that they were true. ¹⁰ At the governor's signal to Paul, he answered:

"Since I know that you for many years have acted as judge for this nation, I cheerfully make my defense, ¹¹ for you can verify ᵍ the fact that not more than twelve days ago I went up to Jerusalem to worship, ¹² and they have never found me debating with anybody in the temple nor making a disturbance in the synagogues or about the city, ¹³ and they cannot prove the charges they have just made against me. ¹⁴ But I certainly admit this as a fact that in accordance

---

¹ This illustrates the Rom. kindness to Paul.
ᵃ Lit., *orator*, but one employed to prosecute.
ᵇ Grk., *much* or *great*.
ᶜ Lit., *much* or *great*.
ᵈ Implied in strong noun.
ᵉ Followers of Jesus of Nazareth.
ᶠ Lit., *seized him*.
ᵍ Grk., *can thoroughly know*.
* V. 7 not in oldest Mss.

with the Way—that they call heresy—I continue to worship the God of my forefathers, and I still believe in everything taught in the law and written in the prophets, ¹⁵ and I have the same hope in God that they cherish for themselves, that there is to be a resurrection of the upright and the wicked. ¹⁶ So I am always striving to have a conscience that is clear before God and men. ¹⁷ After several years' absence I came to bring contributions of charity for my nation, and to offer sacrifices. ¹⁸ While I was performing these duties they found me just as I had completed the rites of my purification in the temple; however, there was no crowd with me and no disturbance at all. ¹⁹ But there were some Jews from Asia [h] who ought to be here before you and to present their charges, if they have any, against me. ²⁰ Or let these men themselves tell what wrong they found in me when I appeared before the council— ²¹ unless it is for one thing that I shouted out as I stood among them, 'It is for the resurrection of the dead that I am here on trial before you today.'"

²² Then Felix, who had a fairly clear conception of the principles [i] involved in the Way, adjourned the trial, saying to the Jews, "When Lysias, the colonel, comes down here, I will carefully look into your case." ²³ He ordered the captain to keep Paul in custody but to let him have freedom and not to prevent his friends from showing him kindness.[j]

²⁴ Some days later, Felix came with his wife Drusilla, who was a Jewess, and sent for Paul and heard him talk [k] about faith in Christ Jesus. ²⁵ But as he continued to talk about uprightness, self-control, and the coming judgment, Felix became alarmed, and said, "For the present you may go, but when I find a good opportunity, I will send for you." ²⁶ At the same time he was hoping to get money from Paul, and so he kept on sending for him and talking with him.

²⁷ But at the close of two whole years Felix was succeeded by Porcius Festus, and as he wanted to gratify the Jews, Felix left Paul still in prison.

[h] The province.
[i] Lit., *the things about the Way*.
[j] Grk., *serving him*.
[k] Lit., *heard him about faith*.

25 BEFORE FESTUS, PAUL AGAIN PLEADS NOT GUILTY; HE APPEALS TO THE EMPEROR; FESTUS TELLS AGRIPPA II ABOUT PAUL; AGRIPPA HEARS PAUL [a]

Now three days after his arrival Festus went up from Caesarea to Jerusalem, [2] and the high priests and the Jewish elders presented their charges against Paul, [3] and begged the governor [b] as a favor to have Paul come to Jerusalem, because they were plotting an ambush to kill him on the way. [4] Festus answered that Paul was being kept in custody in Caesarea, and that he himself was going there soon.

[5] "So have your influential [c] men go down with me," said he, "and present charges against the man, if there is anything wrong with him."

[6] After staying there not more than eight or ten days, he went down to Caesarea, and the next day, after taking his seat on the judge's bench, he ordered Paul brought in. [7] When he arrived, the Jews who had come down from Jerusalem surrounded him, and continued to bring a number of serious charges against him, none of which they could prove. [8] Paul continued to maintain, in his defense, "I have committed no offense against the Jewish law or temple or against the emperor."

[9] Then Festus, as he wanted to ingratiate himself [d] with the Jews, said to Paul, "Will you go up to Jerusalem and be tried on these charges before me there?"

[10] But Paul said, "I now am standing before the emperor's court where I ought to be tried. I have done the Jews no wrong, as you very well know. [11] If I am guilty and have done anything that deserves death, I am not begging to keep from dying; [e] but if there is nothing in the charges which these men make against me, no one can give me up as a favor to them. I appeal to the emperor."

[12] Then Festus, after conferring with the council, answered, "To the emperor you have appealed, to the emperor you shall go!"

[13] After the passing of a few days, King Agrippa and Bernice came to Caesarea to pay official respects to Festus, [14] and as they stayed for several days, Festus laid Paul's case before the king. He

---

[a] This is the son of Herod Agrippa I (Ac. 12).
[b] Implied in pro.
[c] Grk., *powerful*.
[d] Lit., *establish favor with*.
[e] Abl. infin. expresses this.

said, "There is a man here who was left in prison by Felix, 15 and when I was in Jerusalem, the Jewish high priests and elders presented their case against him, and continued to ask for a judgment against him. 16 I answered them that it was not the Roman custom to give up anyone for punishment ᶠ until the accused met his accusers face to face and had an opportunity to defend himself against their accusations. 17 So they came back here with me, and I made no delay to take my seat on the judge's bench, and ordered the man to be brought in. 18 But when his accusers appeared before me, they did not charge him with the crimes of which I had been suspecting him. 19 They merely had a quarrel with him about their own religion and about a certain Jesus who had died, but who Paul kept saying was still alive. 20 I was at a loss how to investigate such matters and so asked Paul if he would go to Jerusalem and there stand trial on these matters. 21 But as Paul appealed to have his case kept for his Majesty's ᵍ decision, I ordered him kept in custody until I could send him up to the emperor."

22 "I should like to hear the man myself," said Agrippa to Festus.

"Tomorrow you shall hear him," said Festus.

23 So the next day, Agrippa and Bernice came with splendid pomp and went into the audience-room, attended by the colonels and the leading citizens of the town, and at the command of Festus, Paul was brought in. 24 Then Festus said:

"King Agrippa and all who are present with us, you now see this man about whom the whole Jewish nation made suit to me, both in Jerusalem and here, continuously clamoring that he ought not to live any longer. 25 But I found that he had not done anything for which he deserved to die; ʰ however, as he has himself appealed to his Majesty, I have decided to send him up. 26 Yet, I have nothing definite to write our Sovereign ⁱ about him. So I have brought him before all of you, especially before you, King Agrippa, to get from your examination something to put in writing. 27 For it seems to me absurd ʲ to send a prisoner up, without specifying ᵏ the charges against him."

ᶠ Implied.
ᵍ Not the title for Caesar; a title of higher dignity.
ʰ Lit., *worthy of death*.
ⁱ *Kurios, Lord*, the same word that is used of Jesus; here in political sense.
ʲ Lit., *out of place, illogical;* so *absurd*.
ᵏ Grk., *signifying*.

26 PAUL'S ADDRESS BEFORE KING AGRIPPA II; HE TELLS THE STORY OF HIS LIFE; FESTUS PRONOUNCES HIM CRAZY; AGRIPPA PRONOUNCES HIM INNOCENT

Then Agrippa said to Paul, "You have permission to speak in defense [a] of yourself."

So Paul with outstretched arm [b] began to make his defense.

2 "I count myself fortunate, King Agrippa," said he, "that it is before you that I can defend myself today against all the charges which the Jews have preferred [c] against me, 3 especially because you are familiar with all the Jewish customs and questions. I beg you, therefore, to hear me with patience.

4 "The kind of life I have lived from my youth up, as spent in my early days among my own nation and in Jerusalem, is well known to all Jews, [d] 5 for they have known all along from the first, if they would but testify to it, that I as a Pharisee have lived by the standard of the strictest sect of our religion. 6 And now it is for the hope of the promise made by God to our forefathers that I stand here on trial, 7 which promise our twelve tribes, by devotedly worshiping day and night, hope to see fulfilled for them. [e] It is for this hope, your Majesty, that I am accused by some Jews. 8 Why is it considered incredible by all of you [f] that God should raise the dead? 9 I myself, indeed, once thought it my duty to take extreme measures [g] in hostility to the name of Jesus of Nazareth. 10 That was what I did at Jerusalem; yes, I received authority from the high priests and shut behind the prison bars [h] many of God's people. Yes, when they were put to death, I cast my vote against them, and often in all the synagogues 11 I had them punished and tried to force them to use abusive language; in my extreme fury against them I continued to pursue them even into distant towns. 12 While in this business I once was on my way to Damascus with authority based on a commission [i] from the high priests, 13 and on the road at noon, your Majesty, I saw a light from heaven, brighter than the sun, flash around me and my

---

[a] Grk., *to make a defense.*
[b] Lit., *hand.*
[c] Grk., *brought.*
[d] Lit., *all the Jews know.*
[e] Grk., *hope to arrive for them.*
[f] Pl. of *you*, so *all of you.*
[g] Lit., *to do many things.*
[h] Lit., *shut down many*, etc.
[i] Lit., *authority and permission.*

fellow-travelers. ¹⁴ We all fell to the ground, and I heard a voice say to me in Hebrew, 'Saul! Saul! Why do you continue to persecute me? It is hurting you to keep on kicking against the goad.' ʲ ¹⁵ 'Who are you, Sir?' said I. 'I am Jesus,' the Lord said, 'whom you are persecuting. ¹⁶ But get up and stand on your feet, for I have appeared to you for the very purpose of appointing you my servant and a witness to me of the things which you have seen and those which I shall yet enable you to see.ᵏ ¹⁷ I will continue to rescue you from the Jewish people and from the heathen to whom I am going to send you, ¹⁸ to open their eyes and turn them from darkness to light and from Satan's power to God, so as to have their sins forgiven ˡ and have a possession among those that are consecrated by faith in me.' ¹⁹ Therefore, King Agrippa, I could not disobey that heavenly vision, ²⁰ but I began to preach first to the people of Damascus and Jerusalem, and all over Judea, and then to the heathen, to repent and turn to God, and to live lives consistent ᵐ with such repentance. ²¹ For these very things the Jews arrested me in the temple and kept on trying to kill me. ²² As I have gotten help from God clear down to this very day, I stand here to testify to high and low alike, without adding a syllable to what Moses and the prophets said should take place, ²³ if the Christ should suffer,ⁿ and by being the first to rise from the dead was to proclaim the light to the Jewish people and to the heathen."

²⁴ As Paul continued to make his defense, Festus shouted aloud, "You are going crazy, Paul! That great learning of yours is driving you crazy!"

²⁵ Paul answered, "I am not going crazy, your Excellency, Festus, but I am telling the straight truth.º ²⁶ The king, indeed, knows about this and I can speak to him with freedom. I do not believe that any of this escaped his notice, for it did not occur in a corner! ²⁷ King Agrippa, do you believe the prophets? I know that you do."

²⁸ Then Agrippa answered Paul, "In brief you are trying to persuade me and make a Christian of me!" ²⁹ Paul answered, "In brief or at length, I would to God that not only you but all my hearers today were what I am—excepting these chains!"

ʲ An adage in Grk. and Lat. lit., possibly.
ᵏ Lit., *as to which I will appear to you.*
ˡ Lit., *receive forgiveness.*
ᵐ Grk., *practice actions worthy of rep.*
ⁿ Involved sentence.
º Lit., *words of sanity and truth.*

30 Then the king rose, with the governor and Bernice and those who had been seated with them, **31** and after leaving the room, as they continued to talk the matter over together, they said, "This man has done nothing to deserve death or imprisonment."

32 Agrippa said to Festus, "He might have been set at liberty, if he had not appealed to the emperor."

27 THE VOYAGE TO ROME; PAUL UNDER ROMAN GUARD; COLONEL JULIUS KIND TO HIM; A FURIOUS STORM THREATENS SHIP AND ALL ON BOARD; PAUL CHEERS THEM BY SAYING NONE SHALL BE LOST; SHIP STRANDED ON MALTA; EVERY LIFE SAVED

When it was decided that we should sail for Italy, they turned over Paul and some other prisoners to a colonel of the imperial regiment, named Julius. **2** After going on board an Adramyttian ship bound for the ports of Asia, we set sail.[a] On board with us was Aristarchus, a Macedonian from Thessalonica. **3** The next day we landed[a] at Sidon, and Julius kindly[b] permitted Paul to visit his friends and enjoy their attentions.[c] **4** After setting sail from there, we sailed under the lee of Cyprus, because the wind was against us, **5** and after sailing the whole length of the sea off Cilicia and Pamphylia, we reached Myra in Lycia. **6** There the colonel found an Alexandrian ship bound for Italy, and put us on board her. **7** For a number of days we sailed on slowly and with difficulty arrived off Cnidus. Then, because the wind did not permit us to go on, we sailed under the lee of Crete off Cape[d] Salmone, **8** and with difficulty coasted along it and finally reached a place called Fair Havens, near the town of Lasea.[e]

9 After considerable time had gone by, and navigation had become dangerous, and the fast[f] was now over, Paul began to warn them **10** by saying, "Men, I see that this voyage is likely to be attended by disaster and heavy loss, not only to the cargo and the ship, but also to our lives."

[a] Technical terms used by sailors.
[b] Lit., *using human kindness*.
[c] Lit., *receive their care*.
[d] Implied, as Salmone is a cape.
[e] Lit., *Lasea near the town*.
[f] Jewish fast of the seventh month.

¹¹ But the colonel was influenced by the pilot and the captain of the ship rather than by what Paul said. ¹² And as the harbor was not fit to winter in, the majority favored the plan to set sail from there and see if they could reach Phoenix and winter there, this being a harbor in Crete facing west-southwest and west-northwest. ¹³ When a light breeze from the south began to blow, thinking their purpose was about to be realized, they weighed anchor and coasted along by Crete, hugging the shore. ¹⁴ But it was not long before a violent wind, which is called a Northeaster, swept down from it. ¹⁵ The ship was snatched along by it and since she could not face the wind, we gave up and let her drive.[g] ¹⁶ As we passed under the lee of a small island called Cauda, with great difficulty we were able to secure the ship's boat. ¹⁷ After hoisting it on board, they used ropes to brace the ship, and since they were afraid of being stranded on the Syrtis quicksands, they lowered the sail and let her drift. ¹⁸ The next day, because we were so violently beaten by the storm, they began to throw the cargo overboard, ¹⁹ and on the next day with their own hands they threw the ship's tackle overboard. ²⁰ For a number of days neither the sun nor the stars were to be seen, and the storm continued to rage, until at last all hope of being saved was now vanishing. ²¹ After they had gone a long time without any food, then Paul got up among them and said:

"Men, you ought to have listened to me and not to have sailed from Crete, and you would have escaped this disaster and loss. ²² Even now I beg you to keep up your courage, for there will be no loss of life, but only of the ship. ²³ For just last night an angel of God, to whom I belong and whom I serve, stood by my side ²⁴ and said, 'Stop being afraid, Paul.[h] You must stand before the Emperor; and listen! God has graciously given to you the lives of all who are sailing with you.' ²⁵ So keep up your courage, men, for I have confidence in my God that it will all come out just as I was told.[i] ²⁶ And yet we must be stranded on some island."

²⁷ It was now the fourteenth night and we were drifting on the Adriatic sea, when at midnight the sailors suspected that land was near. ²⁸ On taking soundings they found a depth of twenty fathoms; and a little later again taking soundings, they found it

[g] Nautical term for letting the ship go with the wind.
[h] Neg. with pres. impv.
[i] Lit., *as it was told me.*

was fifteen. ²⁹ Since they were afraid of our going on the rocks, they dropped four anchors from the stern, and kept wishing for daylight to come. ³⁰ Although the sailors were trying to escape from the ship and had actually lowered the boat into the sea, pretending that they were going to run out anchors from the bow, ³¹ Paul said to the colonel and his soldiers, "Unless these sailors remain on the ship, you cannot be saved." ³² Then the soldiers cut the ropes that held the boat and let it drift away.

³³ Until day was about to break Paul kept begging them all to take something to eat.ʲ He said, "For fourteen days today you have been constantly waiting and going without food, not even taking a bite. ³⁴ So I beg you to eat something, for it is necessary for your safety. For not a hair will be lost from the head of a single ᵏ one of you."

³⁵ After saying this he took some bread and thanked God for it before them all; then he broke it in pieces and began to eat it. ³⁶ Then they all were cheered and took something to eat themselves.ˡ ³⁷ There were about seventy-six of us ᵐ on the ship. ³⁸ When they had eaten enough, they began to lighten the ship by throwing the wheat into the sea. ³⁹ When day broke, they could not recognize the land, but they spied a bay that had a beach, and determined, if possible, to run the ship ashore. ⁴⁰ So they cast off the anchors and left them in the sea; at the same time they undid the ropes of the rudders, and hoisting the foresail to the breeze they headed for the beach. ⁴¹ But they struck a shoal ⁿ and ran the ship aground; the bow stuck and remained unmoved, while the stern began to break to pieces under the beating of the waves.º ⁴² The soldiers planned to kill the prisoners, to keep any of them from swimming ashore and escaping, ⁴³ but the colonel wanted to save Paul, and so he prevented them from carrying out this plan, and ordered all who could swim to jump overboard first and get to land, and the rest to follow, ⁴⁴ some on planks and others on various bits of the ship. And thus they all got safely to land.

ʲ Grk., *take food.*
ᵏ Pro. at head of sentence, so emph.
ˡ Pro. emph. again.
ᵐ Lit., *seventy-six souls.*
ⁿ Lit., *place where two seas meet.*
º Grk., *under the force of.*

28

WINTERING ON THE ISLAND OF MALTA; PAUL NOT POISONED BY A VIPER BITE; CURES THE FATHER OF GOVERNOR PUBLIUS AND OTHERS; LOADED DOWN BY GIFTS OF ISLANDERS, PAUL GOES ON TO ROME; WELCOMED BY CHRISTIANS; TREATED KINDLY BY ROMAN OFFICIALS; AS A PRISONER, ALLOWED TO LIVE IN PRIVATE HOME

After we had been rescued, we learned that the island was called Malta. ² Now the natives [a] showed us remarkable kindness, for they made us a fire and welcomed us to it because of the downpouring rain and the cold. ³ Paul, too, gathered a bundle of sticks, and as he put them on the fire, because of the heat, a viper crawled out of them and fastened itself upon his hand. ⁴ When the natives saw the reptile [b] hanging from his hand, they said to one another, "Beyond a doubt this man is a murderer, for though he has been rescued from the sea, justice will not let him live." [c] ⁵ But he simply shook the reptile off into the fire and suffered no harm. ⁶ The natives kept on looking for him to swell up or suddenly drop dead, but after waiting a long time and seeing nothing unusual take place on him, they changed their minds and said that he was a god.

⁷ The governor [d] of the island, whose name was Publius, owned estates in that part of the island, and he welcomed us and entertained us with hearty hospitality [e] for three days. ⁸ Publius' father chanced to be sick in bed with fever and dysentery, and Paul went to see him and after praying laid his hands upon him and cured him. ⁹ Because this cure was performed,[f] the rest of the sick people on the island kept coming to him and by degrees were cured. ¹⁰ They also honored us with many presents, and when we set sail, they supplied us with everything that we needed.

¹¹ Three months later, we set sail in an Alexandrian ship named The Twin Brothers,[g] which had wintered at the island. ¹² We landed at Syracuse and stayed there three days. ¹³ After weighing anchor and leaving there, we arrived at Rhegium. The next day,

---

[a] Lit., *the barbarians.*
[b] Grk., *the wild beast.*
[c] Showing a fine sense of justice among pagans.
[d] Grk., *the first man.*
[e] Lit., *philanthropically;* a good example of pagan hospitality.
[f] Lit., *this having been done.*
[g] Grk., *Dioscuri,* sons of Zeus, Castor and Pollux.

a south wind began to blow, and the following day we got to Puteoli. ¹⁴ There we found some brothers, and they begged us to spend a week with them. In this way we finally reached Rome. ¹⁵ Because the brothers at Rome ʰ had heard of our coming, they came as far as Appius' Market and the Three Taverns to meet us, and as soon as Paul caught sight ⁱ of them, he thanked God and took courage.

¹⁶ When we did arrive at Rome, Paul was granted permission to live by himself—excepting a soldier to guard him.

¹⁷ Three days later, he invited the leading men of the Jews to come to see him, and when they came, he said to them, "Brothers, I have done nothing against our people or the customs of our forefathers; yet at Jerusalem I was turned over to the Romans as a prisoner. ¹⁸ After examining me the Romans wanted to set me free, because I was innocent of any crime that deserved the death penalty. ¹⁹ But the Jews objected, so ʲ I was forced to appeal to the Emperor; yet it was not because I had any charge to make against my own nation. ²⁰ Now it is for this reason that I invited you to come, namely, to see you and speak with you, for it is on account of Israel's hope ᵏ that I am wearing this chain."

²¹ They answered him, "We have not received any letters from Judea about you, and not one of our Jewish brothers has come and reported or stated anything wicked about you. ²² But we think it fitting to let you tell us what your views ˡ are, for as to this sect it is known by all of us that it is everywhere denounced."

²³ So they set a day for him, and came in large numbers to see him at the place where he was lodging, and from morning till night he continued to explain to them the kingdom of God, at the same time giving them his own testimony and trying from the law of Moses and the prophets to convince them about Jesus. ²⁴ Some of them were convinced by what he said, but others would not believe. ²⁵ Because they could not agree among themselves, they started ᵐ to leave, when Paul had spoken one word more:

"The Holy Spirit beautifully expressed it in speaking to your forefathers through the prophet Isaiah:

ʰ Lit., *from there.*
ⁱ Ingress. aor.
ʲ In the causal pt.
ᵏ The hope for the Messiah.
ˡ Lit., *what you think.*
ᵐ Ingress. impf.

THE ACTS OF THE APOSTLES 28

²⁶ 'Go to this people and say to them,
"You will listen, and listen, and never understand,
And you will look, and look, and never see!
²⁷ For this people's soul has grown dull,
And they scarcely hear with their ears,
And they have shut tight their eyes,
So that they may never see with their eyes,
And understand with their souls,
And turn to me,
That I may cure them." ' ⁿ

²⁸ "So you must understand that this message of God's salvation has been sent to the heathen; and they will listen to it!" ᵒ

³⁰ So Paul for two whole years lived in a rented house of his own; he continued to welcome everybody who came to see him; ³¹ yes, he continued to preach to them the kingdom of God, and to teach them about the Lord Jesus Christ, and that with perfect, unfettered ᵖ freedom of speech.

ⁿ Isa. 6:9,10.
ᵒ V. 29 not in best Mss.
ᵖ Rome now chained Paul's ankles but not his tongue; later she did both.

ROMANS

Paul the apostle is the writer, as is conceded by almost every New Testament scholar. He was once a persecutor of Christians, but near Damascus one day he met the Lord and surrendered to Him as Saviour and Lord. He was called to be an apostle, to preach and teach the good news to the heathen.

Although there was no local occasion in the church at Rome for writing it, he had a good opportunity to send it by deaconess Phoebe, and so under the guidance of the Spirit he wrote to this church, A.D. 57 or 58.

The purpose was to give a somewhat complete statement of the fundamental doctrines of Christianity; to show the universal claims of Christianity, that it was for Greeks, Romans, and all the rest of the nations, as well as for Jews; to enlist the influence of the church at Rome for evangelizing the world, and to show that if one is saved by grace through trust in Christ, his life will fruit in noble moral character and social service.

The letter is characterized by its originality, logical presentation, abundant quotations (74) from the Old Testament, in most eloquent climaxes, and expressions of the sacrificing heart power of the writer.

1 GREETS THE ROMAN CHRISTIANS; TELLS OF HIS RELATIONS TO THEM; STATES HIS THEME, SAVED THROUGH FAITH; LISTS TWENTY-ONE SINS OF THE HEATHEN

Paul, a slave of Jesus Christ, called as an apostle, set apart to preach [a] God's good news, 2 which long ago He promised through His prophets in the holy Scriptures, 3 about His Son, who on the physical [b] side became a descendant of David, and on the holy spiritual side [c] 4 proved to be God's Son in power by the resurrection from the dead—I mean, Jesus Christ our Lord, 5 through whom we have received God's favor and a commission as an apostle in His name to urge [d] upon all the heathen obedience inspired by faith, [e]

---

[a] Implied.
[b] Lit., *according to the flesh.*
[c] Grk., *according to the spirit of holiness.*
[d] Implied.
[e] Subj. gen.

ROMANS 1

⁶ among whom you too as called ones belong to Jesus Christ—⁷ to all those in Rome who are God's loved ones, called to be His people: ᶠ spiritual blessing ᵍ and peace be yours from God our Father and from our Lord Jesus Christ.

⁸ First, through Jesus Christ I thank my God for you all, because the report of your faith is spreading all over the world. ⁹ Indeed, my witness is God, whom I serve in my spirit by telling ʰ the good news about His Son, that I never fail to mention ⁱ you every time I pray, ¹⁰ always entreating God that somehow by His will I may some day at last succeed in getting to see you.ʲ ¹¹ For I am longing to see you, to impart to you some spiritual gift, that you may be strengthened; ¹² in other words, that we may be mutually encouraged, while I am with you, by one another's faith, yours and mine. ¹³ Furthermore, I want you to know, brothers, that I have often planned to come to see you (though until now I have been prevented), in order that I may gather some fruit ᵏ among you too, as I have among the rest of the heathen. ¹⁴ To Greeks and to all the other nations,ˡ to cultured and to uncultured people alike, I owe a duty. ¹⁵ So, as far as I can, I am eager to preach the good news to you at Rome, too.

¹⁶ For I am not ashamed of the good news, for it is God's power for the salvation of everyone who trusts, of the Jew first and then of the Greek. ¹⁷ For in the good news ᵐ God's Way of man's right standing with Him ⁿ is uncovered, the Way of faith that leads to greater faith,º just as the Scripture says, "The upright man must live by faith." ᵖ

¹⁸ For God's anger from heaven is being uncovered against all the impiety and wickedness of the men who in their wickedness are suppressing the truth; ¹⁹ because what can be known of God

---

ᶠ Lit., *separate ones, saints.*
ᵍ Grk., *favor, grace.*
ʰ Implied.
ⁱ Grk., *how ceaselessly I mention you,* etc.
ʲ Lit., *prospered to come to you.*
ᵏ Meaning *spiritual results of his labors.*
ˡ Lit., *the barbarians.*
ᵐ Pro. in Grk.
ⁿ Grk., *God's righteousness,* technical phrase in Paul for *right standing with God,* or *God's way for man to be in right standing with Him*
º Lit., *from faith to faith.*
ᵖ Hab. 2:4.

is clear to their inner moral sense; q for in this way r God Himself has shown it to them. ²⁰ For ever since the creation of the world, His invisible characteristics—s His eternal power and divine nature—have been made intelligible and clearly visible by His works. So they are without excuse, ²¹ because, although they once knew God, they did not honor Him as God, or give Him thanks, but became silly in their senseless speculations, and so their insensible hearts have been shrouded in darkness.ᵗ ²² Though claiming to be wise, they made fools of themselves, ²³ and have transformed the splendor of the immortal God into images in the form of mortal man, birds, beasts, and reptiles.

²⁴ So God has given them up to sexual impurity, in the evil trend of their heart's desires,ᵘ so that they degrade their own bodies with one another, ²⁵ for they had utterly transformed the reality of God into what was unreal,ᵛ and worshiped and served the creature rather than the Creator, who is blessed forever! Amen. ²⁶ This is why God has given them up to degrading passions. For their females ʷ have exchanged their natural function for one that is unnatural, ²⁷ and males too have forsaken the natural function of females and been consumed by flaming ˣ passion for one another, males practicing shameful vice with other males, and continuing to suffer in their persons the inevitable penalty ʸ for doing what is improper. ²⁸ And so, as they did not approve of fully recognizing God any longer, God gave them up to minds that He did not approve,ᶻ to practices that were improper; * ²⁹ because they overflow with every sort of evil-doing, wickedness, greed, and malice; they are full of envy, murder, quarreling, deceit, ill-will; ³⁰ they are secret backbiters, open slanderers, hateful to God, insolent, haughty, boastful; inventors of new forms of evil, undutiful to parents, ³¹ conscienceless,† treacherous, with no human love or pity. ³² Al-

---

q Lit., *within them.*
r Implied.
s Lit., *the invisible things of Him.*
t Lit., *were darkened.*
u Grk., *in their hearts' evil desires.*
v Lit., *the truth of God into what was false* (images).
w Only females, not women.
x Implied in strong term for *passion.*
y Lit., *penalty that was necessary.*
z Preserving Paul's fine play on words.
* *What does not belong to them;* hence *contrary to nature.*
† Lit., *without intelligence* (moral).

though they know full well God's sentence that those who practice such things deserve to die, yet they not only practice them but even applaud others who do them.

2 ALL, JEWS AND HEATHEN, SINNERS; GOD'S JUDGMENT IMPARTIAL; JEWS HAVE GREATER LIGHT, GREATER PUNISHMENT; GENUINE ISRAELITES SUCH IN HEART, NOT BLOOD

Therefore, you have no excuse, whoever you are, who pose as a judge of others, for when you pass judgment on another, you condemn yourself, for you who pose as a judge are practicing the very same sins [a] yourself. ² Now we know that God's judgment justly [b] falls on those who practice such sins as these. ³ And you, who pose as a judge of those who practice such sins and yet continue doing the same yourself, do you for once [c] suppose that you are going to escape the judgment of God? ⁴ Do you think so little of the riches of God's kindness, forbearance, and patience, not conscious that His kindness is meant [d] to lead you to repentance? ⁵ But in your stubbornness and impenitence of heart you are storing up wrath for yourself on the day of wrath, when the justice of God's judgments will be uncovered. [e] ⁶ For when He finally judges, [f] He will pay everyone with exactness for what he has done, ⁷ eternal life to those who patiently continue doing good and striving for glory, honor, and immortality; ⁸ but wrath and fury, crushing suffering and awful anguish, to the self-willed who are always resisting the right and yielding to the wrong, [g] ⁹ to every human soul who practices doing evil, the Jew first and then the Greek. ¹⁰ But glory, honor, and peace will come to everyone who practices doing good, the Jew first and then the Greek; ¹¹ for there is no partiality in God's dealings.

¹² All who sin without having the law will also perish apart from the law, and all who sin under the law will be judged by the

---

[a] Lit., *the same things.*
[b] Grk., *God's judgment is in accordance with truth* (reality).
[c] Aor. pres.
[d] Implied in gen. pres.
[e] Lit., *at the uncovering of God's just judgments.*
[f] Clause implied from context.
[g] *Aleetheia* here means *right,* not *truth.*

law. [13] For merely hearing the law read [h] does not make men upright with God; but men who practice the law will be recognized as upright. [14] Indeed, when heathen people who have no law instinctively do what the law demands,[i] although they have no law they are a law to themselves, [15] for they show that the deeds the law demands are written on their hearts, because their consciences will testify for them, and their inner [j] thoughts will either accuse or defend them, [16] on the day when God through Jesus Christ, in accordance with the good news I preach, will judge the secrets people have kept.

[17] Now if you call yourself a Jew, and rely on law, and boast about God, [18] and understand His will, and by being instructed in the law can know the things that excel,[k] [19] and if you are sure that you are a guide to the blind, a light to those in darkness, [20] a tutor of the foolish, a teacher of the young, since you have a knowledge of the truth as formulated in the law—[l] [21] you who teach others, do you not teach yourself too? You who preach that men should not steal, do you steal yourself? [22] You who warn men to stop committing adultery, do you practice it yourself? You who shrink in horror [m] from idols, do you rob their temples? [23] You who boast about the law, do you by breaking it dishonor God? [24] For, as the Scripture says, the name of God is abused among the heathen because of you.[n]

[25] Now circumcision benefits you only if you practice the law; but if you break the law, your circumcision is no better than uncircumcision.[o] [26] So if the uncircumcised heathen man observes the just demands of the law, will he not be counted as though he were a Jew?[p] [27] And shall not the heathen man who is physically uncircumcised, and yet observes the law, condemn you who have the letter of the law and are physically circumcised, and yet break the law? [28] For the real Jew is not the man who is a Jew on the outside, and real circumcision is not outward physical circumcision. [29] The real Jew is the man who is a Jew on the inside, and real cir-

---

[h] Lit., *hearers.*
[i] Grk., *the things of the law.*
[j] Lit., *thoughts in them.*
[k] This tr. suits context better than *what is right.*
[l] Lit., *form of knowledge and truth.*
[m] Lit., *feel phys. repulsion.*
[n] Isa. 52:5, but not lit. quotation.
[o] Lit., *has become uncircumcision.*
[p] Abstract for concrete terms.

cumcision is heart-circumcision, a spiritual, not a literal, affair. This man's praise q originates, not with men, but with God.

3 HE REPLIES TO JEWISH OBJECTIONS TO HIS CONCLU-
SIONS THAT ALL, JEWS AND HEATHEN ALIKE, ARE
SINNERS; QUOTES THEIR SCRIPTURES TO PROVE IT;
SETS FORTH GOD'S WAY OF FORGIVENESS BY
FAITH IN CHRIST

What special privilege,[a] then, has a Jew?[b] Or, what benefit does circumcision [b] confer? 2 They are great from every point of view. In the first place, the Jews are entrusted with the utterances of God. 3 What then, if some of them have proved unfaithful? Can their unfaithfulness make null and void God's faithfulness? 4 Not at all.[c] Let God prove true, though every man be false! As the Scripture says,

"That you may prove yourself upright in words you speak,
And win your case when you go into court." [d]

5 But if our wrongdoing brings to light the uprightness of God, what shall we infer? Is it wrong (I am using everyday human terms) for God to inflict punishment? 6 Not at all! If that were so, how could He judge the world? 7 But, as you say, if the truthfulness of God has redounded to His glory because of my falsehood, why am I still condemned as a sinner? 8 Why should we not say, as people abusively say of us, and charge us with actually saying, "Let us do evil that good may come from it"? Their condemnation is just.

9 What is our conclusion then? Is it that we Jews are better than they? Not at all! For we have already charged that Jews and Greeks alike are all under the sway of sin, 10 as the Scriptures say:

"Not a single human creature [e] is upright,
11 No one understands, no one is searching for God;

---

q A play on meaning of Heb. word for *Jew, a praised one.*
a Lit., *superfluity.*
b Subj. gen.
c Lit., *let it not be.*
d Ps. 51:4; 116:11.
e Grk., *not any flesh.*

[12] They all have turned aside, all have become corrupt,
No one does good, not even one!
[13] Their throats are just like open graves,
With their tongues they have spoken treachery;
The poison of asps is under their lips.
[14] Their mouths are full of bitter cursing.
[15] Their feet are swift for shedding blood,
[16] Ruin and wretchedness are on their paths,
[17] They do not know the way of peace.
[18] There is no reverence for God before their eyes." [f]

[19] Now we know that everything the law says is spoken to those who are under its authority,[g] that every mouth may be stopped and the whole world be held responsible to God. [20] Because no human creature can be brought into right standing with God [h] by observing the law. For all the law can do is to make men conscious of sin.[i]

[21] But now God's way of giving men right standing with Himself [j] has come to light; a way without connection with the law, and yet a way to which the law and the prophets testify. [22] God's own way of giving men right standing with Himself is through faith in Jesus Christ. It is for everybody who has faith, for no distinction at all is made. [23] For everybody has sinned and everybody continues to come short of God's glory, [24] but anybody may have right standing with God as a free gift of His undeserved favor, through the ransom provided in Christ Jesus. [25] For God once publicly offered Him in His death [k] as a sacrifice of reconciliation through faith, to demonstrate His own justice (for in His forbearance God had passed over men's former sins); [26] yes, to demonstrate His justice at the present time, to prove [l] that He is right Himself, and that He considers right with Himself the man who has faith in Jesus.

[27] So where has human boasting gone? It was completely shut

---

[f] Ps. 14:1-3; 5:9; 140:3; 10:7; 36:1; Isa. 59:7.

[g] Lit., *those in the law*.

[h] Grk., *will be justified*.

[i] *Through the law is the consciousness of sin*.

[j] Lit., *God's righteousness*, but here *God's way of giving men right standing with Himself*.

[k] Lit., *in His blood* (i.e., His death).

[l] Grk., *in order to be right*.

out. On what principle?ᵐ On that of doing something? No, but on the principle of faith. ²⁸ For we hold that a man is brought into right standing with God by faith, that observance of the law has no connection with it. ²⁹ Or is He the God of Jews alone? Is He not the God of heathen peoples too? Of course, He is the God of heathen peoples too, ³⁰ since there is but one God, who will consider the Jews in right standing with Himself, only on condition of their faith, and the heathen peoples on the same condition. ³¹ Do we then through faith make null and void the law? Not at all; instead, we confirm it.

4 ABRAHAM HAD RIGHT STANDING WITH GOD BY FAITH, NOT BY CIRCUMCISION; IT WAS ONLY A SEAL OF HIS RIGHT STANDING; SO HE IS FATHER OF ALL WHO BELIEVE; RESURRECTION FAITH, LIKE ABRAHAM'S, BRINGS RIGHT STANDING WITH GOD

Then what are we to say about our forefather Abraham?ᵃ ² For if he was considered in right standing with God on the condition of what he did, he has something to boast of; but not before God. ³ For what does the Scripture say? "Abraham put his faith in God, and it was credited to him as right standing with God." ᵇ ⁴ Now when a workman gets his pay, it is not considered from the point of view of a favor ᶜ but of an obligation; ⁵ but the man who does no work, but simply puts his faith in Him who brings the ungodly into right standing with Himself, has his faith credited to him as right standing. ⁶ So David, too, describes ᵈ the happiness of the man to whom God credits right standing with Himself, without the things he does having anything to do with it: ᵉ
⁷ "Happy are they whose transgressions have been forgiven, Whose sins were covered up;
⁸ Happy the man whose sin the Lord does not charge against him!" ᶠ
⁹ Now does this happiness come to the Jews alone, or to the heathen peoples too? For we say, "Abraham's faith was credited

---

ᵐ Lit., *through what sort of law* (in sense of principle of operation).
ᵃ Fol. WH and best Mss.
ᵇ Gen. 15:6.
ᶜ Lit., *in accordance with favor*.
ᵈ Lit., *mentions*.
ᵉ Grk., *apart from works*.
ᶠ Ps. 32:1, 2.

to him as right standing." [10] Under what circumstances [g] was it credited to him as right standing? Was it after he was circumcised, or before? Not after but before he was circumcised. [11] Afterward he received the mark of circumcision as God's seal of his right standing with Him on condition of faith [h] which he had before he was circumcised, that he might be the forefather of all who have faith while still uncircumcised,[i] that they might have their faith credited to them as right standing with God; [12] and the forefather of those Jews who not only belong to the circumcision but also follow in the footsteps of our forefather Abraham in the faith he had before he was circumcised.

[13] For the promise made to Abraham and his descendants, that he should own the world, was not conditioned on the law,[j] but on the right standing he had with God through faith. [14] For if the law party is to possess the world, then faith has been nullified and the promise has been made null and void. [15] For the law results [k] in wrath alone; but where there is no law, there can be no violation of it. [16] So it is conditioned on faith,[l] that it might be in accordance with God's unmerited favor, so that the promise might be in force [m] for all the descendants of Abraham, not only for those who belong to the law party but also for those who belong to the faith group of Abraham. He is the father of us all, [17] as the Scripture says, "I have made you the father of many nations."[n] That is, the promise is in force in the sight of God in whom he put his faith, the God who can bring the dead to life and can call to Himself the things that do not exist as though they did. [18] Abraham, building on hope in spite of hopeless circumstances, had faith, and so he actually became the father of many nations, just as it had been told him, "So numberless shall your descendants be." [o] [19] Because he never weakened in faith, he calmly contemplated his own vital powers as worn out (for he was about one hundred years old) and the inability of Sarah to bear a child,

---

[g] Grk., *how* or *when.*
[h] Descriptive gen.
[i] Lit., *during uncircumcision.*
[j] Grk., *through the law.*
[k] Lit., *produces, effects.*
[l] Grk., *out of faith.*
[m] Used in this sense to describe documents that are valid.
[n] Gen. 17:5.

²⁰ and yet he never staggered in doubt at the promise of God but grew powerful in faith, because he gave the glory to God ²¹ in full assurance that He was able to do what He had promised. ²² Therefore, his faith was credited to him as right standing with God.

²³ It was not for his sake alone that it was written, "It was credited to him"; ²⁴ it was for our sakes too, for it is going to be credited to us who put our faith in God who raised from the dead our Lord Jesus, ²⁵ who was given up to death because of our shortcomings and was raised again to give us right standing with God.

5 THE HAPPY STATE OF THE PERSON IN RIGHT STANDING WITH GOD; GOD PROVED HIS LOVE FOR SINFUL MEN BY LETTING HIS SON DIE FOR THEM; SIN AND DEATH THROUGH ADAM, RIGHT STANDING WITH GOD AND LIFE THROUGH CHRIST

Since we have been given right standing with God through faith, then let us continue enjoying [a] peace with God through our Lord Jesus Christ, ² by whom we have an introduction through faith into this state of God's favor, in which we safely stand; [b] and let us continue exulting in the hope of enjoying the glorious presence of God. ³ And not only that, but this too: let us continue exulting in our sufferings,[c] for we know that suffering produces endurance, ⁴ and endurance, tested character, and tested character, hope, ⁵ and hope never disappoints [d] us; for through the Holy Spirit that has been given us, God's love has flooded [e] our hearts.

⁶ For when we were still helpless, Christ at the proper time died for us ungodly men. ⁷ Now a man will scarcely ever give his life for an upright person, though once in a while a man is brave enough to die for a generous friend.[f] ⁸ But God proves His love for us by the fact that Christ died for us while we were still sinners. ⁹ So if we have already been brought into right standing with God by Christ's death, it is much more certain that by Him we shall be saved from God's wrath. ¹⁰ For if while we were God's enemies,

[a] Lit., *holding* or *having*, so *enjoying*
[b] Pf. implies this.
[c] Lit., *pressing burdens.*
[d] Grk., *puts to shame.*
[e] Lit., *poured out into.*
[f] Grk., *a good man,* but qualities of unselfish generosity included.

we were reconciled to Him through the death of His Son, it is much more certain that since we have been reconciled we shall finally ᵍ be saved through His new ʰ life. ¹¹ And not only that, but this too: we shall continue exulting in God through our Lord Jesus Christ, through whom we have obtained our reconciliation.

¹² So here is the comparison: ⁱ As through one man sin came into the world, and death as the consequence of sin, and death spread to all men, because all men sinned. ¹³ Certainly sin was in the world before the law was given, but it is not charged to men's account where there is no law. ¹⁴ And yet death reigned from Adam to Moses, even over those who had not sinned in the way Adam had, against a positive command.ʲ For Adam was a figure of Him who was to come. ¹⁵ But God's free gift is not at all to be compared with the offense. For if by one man's offense the whole race of men have ᵏ died, to a much greater degree God's favor and His gift imparted by His favor through the one man Jesus Christ, has overflowed for the whole race of men. ¹⁶ And the gift is not at all to be compared with the results of that one man's sin. For that sentence resulted from the offense of one man, and it meant condemnation; but the free gift resulted from the offenses of many, and it meant right standing. ¹⁷ For if by one man's offense death reigned through that one, to a much greater degree will those who continue to receive the overflow of His unmerited favor and His gift of right standing with Himself, reign in real life through One, Jesus Christ.

¹⁸ So, as through one offense there resulted condemnation for all men, just so through one act of uprightness there resulted right standing involving life for all men. ¹⁹ For just as by that man's disobedience the whole race of men were constituted sinners, so by this One's obedience the whole race of men may be brought into right standing with God. ²⁰ Then law crept in to multiply the offense. Though sin has multiplied, yet God's favor has surpassed it and overflowed, ²¹ so that just as sin had reigned by death, so His favor too might reign in right standing with God which issues in eternal life through Jesus Christ our Lord.

ᵍ Context shows it is our final salvation at the resurrection.
ʰ I.e., His resurrection life.
ⁱ Lit., *so just as.*
ʲ Grk., *in the likeness of Adam's transgression.*
ᵏ Grk., *the many have died.*

6 RIGHT LIVING RESULTS FROM RIGHT STANDING WITH GOD; UNION WITH CHRIST KILLS SIN; BAPTISM PICTURES OUR UNION WITH CHRIST'S DEATH AND RESURRECTION LIFE; NO LONGER SLAVES TO SIN, BELIEVERS FREED TO SERVE GOD AND RIGHT

What is our conclusion then? Are we to continue to sin for His unmerited favor to multiply? [2] Not at all! Since [a] we have ended our relation [b] to sin, how can we live in it any longer? [3] Or, do you not know that all of us who have been baptized into union with Christ Jesus have been baptized into His death? [4] So through baptism we have been buried with Him in death, so that just as Christ was raised from the dead by the Father's glorious power,[c] so we too should live an entirely new life.[d] [5] For if we have grown into fellowship with Him by sharing [e] a death like His, surely [f] we shall share a resurrection life like His,[g] [6] for we know that our former self was crucified with Him, to make our body that is liable to sin inactive,[h] so that we might not a moment longer continue to be slaves to sin. [7] For when a man is dead, he is freed from the claims of sin. [8] So if we died with Christ, we believe that we shall also live with Him, [9] for we know that Christ, who once was raised from the dead, will never die again; death has no more power over Him. [10] For by the death He died He once for all ended His relation [b] to sin, and by the life He now is living He lives in unbroken [i] relation to God. [11] So you too must consider yourselves as having ended your relation to sin but living in unbroken relation to God.

[12] Accordingly sin must not continue to reign over your mortal bodies, so as to make you continue to obey their evil desires, [13] and you must stop offering to sin the parts of your bodies as instruments for wrongdoing, but you must once for all [j] offer yourselves to God as persons raised from the dead to live on perpetually, and once for all [j] offer the parts of your bodies to God as instruments for right-doing. [14] For sin must not any longer exert its

---

[a] Causal pt.
[b] Lit., *died to sin.*
[c] Grk., *by the Father's glory* (including power).
[d] Lit., *in newness of life.*
[e] Grk., *by the likeness of His death.*
[f] Lit., *on the other hand.*
[g] Lit., *in likeness of His res.*
[h] Lit., *dead.*
[i] Pres. pt. of cont. ac.
[j] Aor., so punctiliar ac. *(once for all).*

mastery over you, for now you are not living as slaves to law but as subjects to God's favor.ᵏ

¹⁵ What are we to conclude? Are we to keep on sinning, because we are not living as slaves to law but as subjects to God's favor? Never! ¹⁶ Do you not know that when you habitually offer yourselves to anyone for obedience to him, you are slaves to that one whom you are in the habit of obeying, whether it is the slavery to sin whose end is death or to obedience whose end is right-doing? ¹⁷ But, thank God! that though you once were slaves of sin, you became obedient from your hearts to that form of teaching in which you have been instructed, ¹⁸ and since you have been freed from sin, you have become the slaves of right-doing. ¹⁹ I am speaking in familiar human terms¹ because of the frailty of your nature.ᵐ For just as you formerly offered the parts of your bodies in slavery to impurity and to ever increasing lawlessness, so now you must once for all offer them in slavery to right-doing, which leads to consecration. ²⁰ For when you were slaves of sin, you were free so far as doing right was concerned. ²¹ What benefit did you then derive from doing the things of which you are now ashamed? None,ⁿ for they end in death. ²² But now, since you have been freed from sin and have become the slaves of God, the immediate result is consecration, and the final destiny is eternal life. ²³ For the wages paid by sin is death, but the gracious gift of God is eternal life through union with Christ Jesus our Lord.

7 BELIEVERS FREED FROM SIN BUT MARRIED TO CHRIST AS IN A SECOND MARRIAGE; THE FUNCTION OF THE LAW TO AWAKEN THE SINNER TO FEEL HIS NEED OF CHRIST; THE LOWER NATURE DOMINATED BY SIN, THE HIGHER STRUGGLES AGAINST IT

Do you not know, brothers—for I speak to those who are acquainted with the law—that the law can press its claim over a man only so long as he lives? ² For a married woman is bound by law to her husband while he lives, but if her husband dies, she is freed from the marriage bond.ᵃ ³ So if she marries another man while

---

ᵏ Lit., *not under law but under unmerited favor.*
¹ Grk., *saying a human thing.*
ᵐ *Flesh* means *human frailty.*
ⁿ Supplied from context.
ᵃ Lit., *from the law of the husband.*

her husband is living, she is called an adulteress; but if he dies, she is free from that marriage bond,[b] so that she will not be an adulteress though later married to another man. [4] So, my brothers, you too in the body of Christ have ended your relation to the law, so that you may be married to another husband, to Him who was raised from the dead, in order that we might bear fruit for God. [5] For when we were living in accordance with our lower nature,[c] the sinful passions that were aroused [d] by the law were operating in the parts of our bodies to make us bear fruit that leads to death. [6] But now we have been freed from our relation to the law; we have ended our relation to that by which we once were held in bonds, so that we may serve in a new spiritual way and not in the old literalistic way.[e]

[7] What are we then to conclude? Is the law sin? Of course not! Yet, if it had not been for [f] the law, I should not have learned what sin was, for I should not have known what an evil desire was, if the law had not said, "You must not have an evil desire."[g] [8] Sin found its rallying point in that command and stirred within me every sort of evil desire, for without law sin is lifeless. [9] I was once alive when I had no connection with the law, but when the command came, sin revived, and then I died; [10] and so, in my case, the command which should have meant life turned out to mean death. [11] For sin found its rallying point [h] in that command and through it deceived me and killed me. [12] So the law itself is holy, and its specific commands are holy, right, and good.

[13] Did that which is good, then, result in death to me? Of course not! It was sin that did it, so that it might show itself as sin, for by means of that good thing it brought about my death, so that through the command sin might appear surpassingly sinful. [14] For we know that the law is spiritual, but I am made of flesh that is frail,[i] sold into slavery to sin. [15] Indeed, I do not understand what I do, for I do not practice what I want to do, but I am always doing what I hate. [16] But if I am always doing what I do not want to do, I agree that the law is right. [17] Now really it is not I that

[b] Grk., *from the* (that) *law.*
[c] Lit., *in the flesh.*
[d] Vb. implied.
[e] Grk., *in newness of spirit* and *not in oldness of letter.*
[f] Lit., *through.*
[g] Ex. 20:14,17; Dt. 5:18,21.
[h] Favorable point of attack.
[i] Word emphasizes the frail material of which our lower nature is made.

am doing these things, but it is sin which has its home[j] within me. [18] For I know that nothing good has its home in me; that is, in my lower self; I have the will but not the power to do what is right. [19] Indeed, I do not do the good things that I want to do, but I do practice the evil things that I do not want to do. [20] But if I do the things that I do not want to do, it is really not I that am doing these things, but it is sin which has its home within me. [21] So I find this law: When I want to do right, the wrong is always in my way. [22] For in accordance with my better inner nature[k] I approve God's law, [23] but I see another power[l] operating in my lower nature in conflict with the power operated by my reason,[m] which makes me a prisoner to the power of sin which is operating in my lower nature. [24] Wretched man that I am! Who can save me from this deadly lower nature? [25] Thank God! it has been done through Jesus Christ our Lord! So in my higher nature[m] I am a slave to the law of God, but in my lower nature, to the law of sin.

8 IN UNION WITH CHRIST THE SPIRIT SETS US FREE; HE HELPS GOD'S CHILDREN LIVE HOLY LIVES; SUFFERINGS STREW THEIR PATH TO GLORY BUT POLISH THEIR CHARACTERS; THE SPIRIT HELPS AND KEEPS THEM THROUGH GOD'S UNCHANGEABLE LOVE

So then there is no condemnation at all for those who are in union with Christ Jesus. [2] For the life-giving power[a] of the Spirit through union with Christ Jesus has set us free from the power of sin and death. [3] For though the law could not do it, because it was made helpless[b] through our lower nature, yet God, by sending His own Son in a body similar to that of our lower nature, and as a sacrifice for sin,[c] passed sentence upon sin through His body, [4] so that the requirement of the law might be fully met in us who do not live by the standard[d] set by our lower nature, but by the standard set by the Spirit. [5] For people who live by the standard set by their lower nature are usually thinking the things suggested

---

[j] Pres. of vb. *to live in,* so *to have its home.*
[k] Lit., *according to the inner man.*
[l] Lit., *another law.*
[m] Grk., *mind, reason, higher nature.*
[a] Lit., *law,* in sense of *force* or *power.*
[b] Grk., *weak.*
[c] Use of phrase in Sept.
[d] In prep. *kata.*

by that nature,[e] and people who live by the standard set by the Spirit are usually thinking the things suggested by the Spirit.[e] [6] For to be thinking the things suggested by the lower nature means death, but to be thinking the things suggested by the Spirit means life and peace. [7] Because one's thinking the things suggested by the lower nature means enmity to God, for it does not subject itself to God's law, nor indeed can it. [8] The people who live on the plane [f] of the lower nature cannot please God. [9] But you are not living on the plane of the lower nature, but on the spiritual plane, if the Spirit of God has His home within you. Unless a man has the Spirit of Christ, he does not belong to Him. [10] But if Christ lives [g] in you, although your bodies must die because of sin, your spirits are now enjoying life because of right standing with God. [11] If the Spirit of Him who raised Jesus from the dead has His home within you, He who raised Christ Jesus from the dead will also give your mortal bodies life through His Spirit that has His home within you.

[12] So, brothers, we are under obligations, but not to our lower nature to live by the standard set by it; [13] for if you live by such a standard,[h] you are going to die, but if by the Spirit you put a stop [i] to the doings of your lower nature, you will live. [14] For all who are guided by God's Spirit are God's sons. [15] For you do not have a sense [j] of servitude to fill you with dread again, but the consciousness of adopted sons by which we cry, "Abba," [k] that is, "Father." [16] The Spirit Himself bears witness with our spirits that we are God's children; [17] and if children, then also heirs, heirs of God and fellow-heirs with Christ—if in reality we share His sufferings, so that we may share His glory too.

[18] For I consider all that we suffer in this present life is nothing to be compared with the glory which by-and-by is to be uncovered for us. [19] For all nature [l] is expectantly waiting for the unveiling of the sons of God. [20] For nature did not of its own accord give up to failure; it was for the sake of Him who let it thus be given up, in the hope [21] that even nature itself might finally be set free

[e] Subj. gen. gives this meaning.
[f] Lit., *are in the flesh, on the plane of the lower nature.*
[g] Grk., *if C. is in you.*
[h] Noun repeated in Grk.
[i] Lit., *put to death.*
[j] Grk., *a spirit of servitude.*
[k] *Father* in Paul's native tongue, Ara.
[l] Lit., *creation.*

from its bondage to decay, so as to share the glorious freedom of God's children. 22 Yes, we know that all nature has gone on groaning in agony together till the present moment. 23 Not only that but this too, we ourselves who enjoy the Spirit as a foretaste of the future,^m even we ourselves, keep up our inner groanings while we wait to enter upon our adoption as God's sons at^n the redemption of our bodies. 24 For we were saved in such^o a hope. 25 But a hope that is seen is not real hope, for who hopes for what he actually sees? But if we hope for something we do not see, we keep on patiently waiting for it.

26 In the same way the Spirit, too, is helping us in our weakness, for we do not know how to pray as we should, but the Spirit Himself pleads for us with unspeakable yearnings, 27 and He who searches our hearts knows what the Spirit thinks, for He pleads for His people in accordance with God's will. 28 Yes, we know that all things go on working together for the good of those who keep on loving God, who are called in accordance with God's purpose. 29 For those on whom He set His heart beforehand^p He marked off^q as His own to be made like His Son, that He might be the eldest of many brothers; 30 and those whom He marked off as His own He also calls; and those whom He calls He brings into right standing with Himself; those whom He brings into right standing with Himself He also glorifies.

31 What are we then to say to facts like these? If God is for us, who can be against us? 32 Since He did not spare His own Son but gave Him up for us all, will He not with Him graciously give us everything else? 33 Who can bring any charge against those whom God has chosen? It is God who declared them in right standing; 34 who can condemn them? Christ Jesus who died, or rather, who was raised from the dead, is now at God's right hand, and is actually pleading for us. 35 Who can separate us from Christ's love? Can suffering or misfortune or persecution or hunger or destitution or danger or the sword? 36 As the Scripture says:

"For your sake we are being put to death the livelong day;
We are treated like sheep to be slaughtered."^r

^m Suggested by *foretaste*.
^n *Redemption* in apposition with *adoption*, but time prominent; hence our trans.
^o Implied from context.
^p Lit., *foreknew*, but in Sept. used as translated.
^q Root meaning of vb.
^r Ps. 44:22.

³⁷ And yet in all these things we keep on gloriously conquering through Him who loved us. ³⁸ For I have full assurance that neither death nor life nor angels nor principalities nor the present nor the future ³⁹ nor evil forces above or beneath, nor anything else in all creation, will be able to separate us from the love of God as shown in Christ Jesus our Lord.

9 PAUL'S GRIEF OVER GOD'S REJECTING ISRAEL FOR THEIR UNBELIEF IN JESUS; GOD IS RIGHT THOUGH HE ACTS AS A SOVEREIGN IN SAVING MEN, AS A POTTER DOES IN MAKING POTS; SO HEATHEN ARE INCLUDED IN GOD'S CHOICE

I am telling the truth as a Christian man,ᵃ I am telling no lie, because my conscience enlightened ᵇ by the Holy Spirit is bearing me witness to this fact, ² that I have deep grief and constant anguish in my heart; ³ for I could wish myself accursed, even cut off ᶜ from Christ, for the sake of my brothers, my natural kinsmen. ⁴ For they are Israelites; to them belong the privileges of sonship, God's glorious presence,ᵈ the special covenants, the giving of the law, the temple service, the promises, ⁵ the patriarchs, and from them by natural descent the Christ has come, who is exalted over all, God blessed forever. Amen!

⁶ But it is not that God's word has failed. For not everybody that is descended from Israel really belongs to Israel, ⁷ nor are they all children of Abraham, because they are his descendants, but the promise was "In the line of Isaac your descendants will be counted." ᵉ ⁸ That is, it is not Abraham's natural descendants who are God's children, but those who are made children by the promise ᶠ are counted his true descendants. ⁹ For this is the language of the promise, "About this time next year I will come back, and Sarah will have a son." ᵍ ¹⁰ Not only that but this too: there was Rebecca who was impregnated by our forefather Isaac. ¹¹ For even before the twin sons ʰ were born, and though they had

ᵃ Lit., *speaking the truth in Christ*.
ᵇ Grk., *by the H.S.*
ᶜ In the prep.
ᵈ Lit., *glory* (shekinah).
ᵉ Gen. 21:12.
ᶠ Subj. gen.
ᵍ Gen. 18:10.
ʰ Implied with pt. from the account in Gen.

done nothing either good or bad, that God's purpose in accordance with His choice might continue to stand, conditioned not on men's actions but on God's calling them, ¹² she was told, "The elder will be a slave to the younger." [i] ¹³ As the Scripture says, "Jacob I have loved, but Esau I have hated." [j]

¹⁴ What are we then to conclude? It is not that there is injustice in God, is it? Of course not! ¹⁵ For He says to Moses, "I will have mercy on any man that I choose to have mercy on, and take pity on any man that I choose to take pity on." [k] ¹⁶ So one's destiny[1] does not depend on his own willing or strenuous actions but on God's having mercy on him. ¹⁷ For the Scripture says to Pharaoh, "I have raised you to your position for this very purpose of displaying my power in dealing with you, of announcing my name all over the earth." [m] ¹⁸ So He has mercy on any man that He chooses to, and He hardens any man that He chooses to harden.

¹⁹ So you will ask me, "Why does He still find fault? For who can resist His will?" ²⁰ On the contrary, friend, who are you anyway that you would answer back to God? Can the clay that is molded ask the man who molds it, "Why did you make me like this?" ²¹ Has not the potter the right with his clay to make of the same lump one vessel for ornamental purposes, another for degrading service? ²² And what if God, though wishing to display His anger and make known His power, yet has most patiently borne with the objects of His anger, already ripe for destruction,[n] ²³ so as to make known the riches of His glory for the objects of His mercy, whom He prepared in ages past to share His glory—²⁴ even us whom He has called, not only from among the Jews but from among the heathen too? ²⁵ Just as He says in Hosea: "I will call a people that was not mine, my people,
And her who was not beloved, my beloved,
²⁶ And in the place where it was said, 'You are no people of mine,' They shall be called sons of the living God." [o]

²⁷ And Isaiah cries out about Israel, "Although the sons of Israel are as numberless as the sands of the sea, only a remnant of them

[i] Gen. 25:23.
[j] Mal. 1:2,3.
[k] Ex. 33:19.
[1] Lit., *it is not of him who wills or runs.*
[m] Ex. 9:16.
[n] Lit., *vessels made ready* (pf. pt.) *for destruction.*
[o] Hos. 2:23.

will be saved, ²⁸ for the Lord will completely and quickly execute His sentence on the earth." ᵖ ²⁹ As Isaiah again has foretold,

"Unless the Lord of hosts had left us some descendants, we would have fared as Sodom did and would have been like Gomorrah." ᵠ

³⁰ What are we then to conclude? That heathen peoples who were not in search for right standing with God have obtained it, and that a right standing conditioned on faith; ³¹ while Israel, though ever in pursuit of a law that would bring right standing, did not attain to it. ³² Why? Because they did not try through faith but through what they could do. They have stumbled over the stone that causes people to stumble, ³³ as the Scripture says:

"See, I put on Zion a stone for causing people to stumble,
a rock to trip them on,
But no one who puts his faith in it will ever be put to shame." ʳ

10 THE FAITH METHOD OF RIGHT STANDING WITH GOD INTENDED FOR ALL; SO THE GOOD NEWS MUST BE PROCLAIMED TO ALL

Brothers, my heart's good will goes out for them, and my prayer to God is that they may be saved. ² For I can testify that they are zealous for God, but they are not intelligently ᵃ so. ³ For they were ignorant of God's way of right standing and were trying to set up one of their own, and so would not surrender to God's way of right standing. ⁴ For Christ has put an end to law ᵇ as a way to right standing for everyone who puts his trust in Him. ⁵ For Moses says of the law-way to right standing with God that whoever can perform the law will live by it. ⁶ But here is what the faith-way to right standing ᶜ says, "Do not say to yourself, 'Who will go up to heaven?'" that is, to bring Christ down; ⁷ or "'Who will go down into the depths?'" that is, to bring Christ up from the dead. ⁸ But what does it say? "God's message is close to you, on your very lips and in your heart"; that is, the message about faith which

ᵖ Isa. 10:22, 23; 28:22.
ᵠ Isa. 1:9.
ʳ Isa. 8:14; 28:16.
ᵃ Lit., *in accordance with knowledge.*
ᵇ Grk., *is the end of the law.*
ᶜ Lit., *the right standing conditioned on faith.*

we preach. ⁹ For if with your lips you acknowledge the fact that Jesus is Lord, and in your hearts you believe that God raised Him from the dead, you will be saved. ¹⁰ For in their hearts people exercise the faith that leads to right standing, and with their lips they make the acknowledgment which means ᵈ salvation. ¹¹ For the Scripture says, "No one who puts his faith in Him will ever be put to shame." ᵉ ¹² But there is no distinction between Jew and Greek, for the same Lord is over them all, because He is infinitely kind ᶠ to all who call upon Him. ¹³ For everyone who calls upon the name of the Lord will be saved.

¹⁴ But how can people call upon One in whom they have not believed? And how can they believe in One about whom they have not heard? And how can people hear without someone to preach to them? ¹⁵ And how can men preach unless they are sent to do so? As the Scripture says, "How beautiful are the feet of men who bring the glad news of His good things!" ᵍ

¹⁶ However, they have not all given heed to the good news, for Isaiah says, "Lord, who has put faith in what we told?" ʰ ¹⁷ So faith comes from hearing what is told, and hearing through the message about Christ. ¹⁸ But may I ask, They had no chance to hear, did they? ⁱ Yes, indeed:

"All over the earth their voices ʲ have gone,
To the ends of the world their words." ᵏ

¹⁹ But again I ask, Israel did not understand, did they? For in the first place Moses says:

"I will make you jealous of a nation that is no nation;
I will provoke you to anger at a senseless nation." ˡ

²⁰ Then Isaiah was bold enough to say:
"I have been found by a people who were not searching for me,
I have made known myself to people who were not asking to know me." ᵐ

ᵈ Grk., *unto salvation.*
ᵉ Isa. 28:16.
ᶠ Lit., *rich* (in kindness).
ᵍ Isa. 52:7.
ʰ Isa. 53:1.
ⁱ Grk. expects ans. *No.*
ʲ Nature's voices.
ᵏ Ps. 19:4.
ˡ Dt. 32:21.
ᵐ Isa. 65:1.

²¹ But of Israel he said:

"All day long I have held out my hands to a people that is disobedient and obstinate." ⁿ

11
ONLY A REMNANT OF JEWS NOW SAVED; AS MOST OF THEM ARE REJECTED, HEATHEN PEOPLES ARE SAVED; GOD'S SEVERITY AND GOODNESS, MAN'S FEAR AND HUMILITY; GOD'S UNIVERSAL MERCY AND INEXHAUSTIBLE RESOURCES IN WISDOM AND KNOWLEDGE

I say then, God has not disowned His people, has He? Of course not! Why, I am an Israelite myself, a descendant of Abraham, a member of the tribe of Benjamin.ᵃ ² No,ᵇ God has not disowned His people, on whom He set His heart beforehand. Do you know what the Scripture says in Elijah's case, how he pleaded with God against Israel? ³ "Lord, they have killed your prophets, they have demolished your altars; I alone have been left, and they are trying to kill me." ᶜ ⁴ But how did God reply to him? ᵈ "I have reserved for myself seven thousand men who have never bent their knees to Baal." ⁵ So it is at the present time; a remnant remains, in accordance with God's unmerited favor. ⁶ But if it is by His unmerited favor, it is not at all conditioned on what they have done.ᵉ If that were so, His favor would not be favor at all. ⁷ What are we then to conclude? Israel has failed to obtain what it is still in search for, but His chosen ones have obtained it. The rest have become insensibleᶠ to it, ⁸ as the Scripture says, "God has given them over to an attitudeᵍ of insensibility, so that their eyes cannot see and their ears cannot hear, down to this very day." ʰ ⁹ And David said:

"Let their food become a snare and a trap to them,
Their pitfall and retribution;

ⁿ Isa. 65:2.
ᵃ Lit., *of the seed of A., of the tribe of B.*
ᵇ Strongly implied.
ᶜ I Kg. 19:10.
ᵈ Lit., *what did the oracle,* etc.
ᵉ Grk., *is not out of works.*
ᶠ Lit., *hardened.*
ᵍ Grk., *spirit.*
ʰ Isa. 29:10; Dt. 29:4.

¹⁰ Let their eyes be darkened, so they cannot see,
And forever bend their backs beneath the load." ⁱ

¹¹ I say then, they did not stumble so as to fall in utter ruin,ʲ did they? Of course not! On the contrary, because of their stumbling, salvation has come to heathen peoples, to make the Israelites ᵏ jealous. ¹² But if their stumbling has resulted in the enrichment of the world, and their overthrow becomes the enrichment of heathen peoples, how much richer the result will be when the full quota of Jews ˡ comes in!

¹³ Yes, I now am speaking to you who are a part of the heathen peoples. As I am an apostle to the heathen peoples, I am making the most ᵐ of my ministry to them, to see ⁿ ¹⁴ if I can make my fellow-countrymen jealous, and so save some of them. ¹⁵ For if the rejection of them has resulted in the reconciling of the world, what will the result be of the final reception of them but life from the dead? ¹⁶ If the first handful of dough is consecrated,ᵒ so is the whole mass; if the tree's root is consecrated, so are the branches.

¹⁷ If some of the branches have been broken off, and yet you, although you were wild olive suckers,ᵖ have been grafted in among the native branches, and been made to share the rich sap of the native olive's root, ¹⁸ you must not be boasting against the natural branches. And if you do, just consider,ᑫ you do not support the root, but the root supports you. ¹⁹ Then you will say, "Branches have been broken off for us to be grafted in." ²⁰ Very well; but it was for lack of faith that they were broken off, and it is through your faith that you now stand where you are. Stop your haughty thinking; rather continue to be reverent, ²¹ for if God did not spare the natural branches, certainly ʳ He will not spare you. ²² So take a look at the goodness and the severity of God; severity to those who have fallen, but goodness to you, on

---

ⁱ Ps. 69:22,23.
ʲ Lit., *so as once for all to fall.*
ᵏ Implied in pro.
ˡ Lit., *their fullness.*
ᵐ Grk., *glorifying, magnifying.*
ⁿ Implied with particle.
ᵒ Lit., *holy.*
ᵖ Grk., uses sg. for pl.
ᑫ Implied.
ʳ Very strong neg. thus trans.

condition that you continue to live by His goodness; otherwise, you too will be pruned away. ²³ And they too, if they do not continue to live by their unbelief, will be grafted in, for God is amply able to graft them in. ²⁴ For if you were cut off from an olive wild by nature, and contrary to nature were grafted on to a fine olive stock, how much easier will it be for the natural branches to be grafted on to their own olive stock?

²⁵ For to keep you from being self-conceited, brothers, I do not want to have a misunderstanding of this uncovered secret, that only temporary insensibility has come upon Israel until the full quota of the heathen peoples comes in, ²⁶ and so in that way all Israel will be saved, just as the Scripture says:

> "From Zion the Deliverer will come;
> He will remove ungodliness from Jacob;
> ²⁷ And this my covenant I make with them,
> When I shall take away their sins." ˢ

²⁸ As measured by the good news the Jews are God's enemies for your sakes, but as measured by God's choice they are His beloved because of their forefathers, ²⁹ for the gracious gifts and call of God are never taken back.ᵗ ³⁰ For just as you once disobeyed God, but now have had mercy shown you because of their disobedience, ³¹ so they too are now disobedient because of the mercy shown you, that they too may now have mercy shown them. ³² For God has locked up all mankind in the prison of disobedience so as to have mercy on them all.

³³ How fathomless the depths of God's resources, wisdom, and knowledge! How unsearchable His decisions, and how mysterious ᵘ His methods! ³⁴ For who has ever understood the thoughts of the Lord, or has ever been His adviser? ³⁵ Or who has ever advanced God anything to have Him pay him back? ³⁶ For from Him everything comes, through Him everything lives, and for Him everything exists. Glory to Him forever! Amen.

ˢ Isa. 59:20,21.
ᵗ Lit., *never regretted because of change of mind.*
ᵘ Grk. literally means *untraceable.*

12 GOD'S MERCY THE GROUND OF SOCIAL SERVICE, WHICH IS ROOTED IN PERSONAL CONSECRATION; THROUGH UNION WITH CHRIST WE ARE HIS BODY EACH WITH FITTING FUNCTIONS; LOVE, SYMPATHY, HUMILITY, KINDNESS, FORGIVENESS, AND SIMILAR SOCIAL GRACES

I beg you, therefore, brothers, through these mercies God has shown you, to make a decisive [a] dedication of your bodies as a living sacrifice, devoted [b] and well-pleasing to God, which is your reasonable service. 2 Stop living in accordance with the customs of this world, but by the new ideals that mold your minds [c] continue to transform yourselves, so as to find and follow [d] God's will; that is, what is good, well-pleasing to Him, and perfect.

3 Now through the unmerited favor God has shown me I would say to every one of you not to estimate himself above his real value,[e] but to make a sober rating of himself, in accordance with the degree of faith which God has apportioned to him. 4 For just as we have many parts united in our physical [f] bodies, and the parts do not all have the same function, 5 so we, though many, are united in one body through union with Christ, and we are individually parts of one another. 6 As we have gifts that differ in accordance with the favor God has shown us, if it is that of preaching, let it be done in proportion to our faith; 7 or of practical service, in the field of service; or of a teacher, in the field of teaching; 8 or of one who encourages others, in the field of encouragement; or one who gives his money, with liberality; or one who leads others, with earnestness; or one who does deeds of charity, with cheerfulness.[g]

9 Your love must be true. You must always turn [h] in horror from what is wrong, but keep on holding to what is right. 10 In brotherly love be affectionate to one another, in personal honors put one

[a] Aor. infin., *once for all offer.*
[b] Lit., *holy,* so devoted.
[c] Lit., *stop conforming to this world, but by renewing of your mind continue,* etc.
[d] Vb. means *test and approve,* so *find and follow.*
[e] Lit., *what he ought to think.*
[f] Implied in contrasting two kinds of bodies.
[g] An involved sentence in both Grk. and Eng.; meaning clear.
[h] In prep. *apo.*

another to the fore,[i] [11] never slack in earnestness, always [j] on fire [k] with the Spirit, always serving the Lord, [12] ever [j] happy in hope, always patient in suffering, ever persistent in prayer, [13] always supplying the needs of God's people, ever practicing hospitality. [14] Keep on blessing your persecutors; keep on blessing and stop cursing them. [15] Practice [j] rejoicing with people who rejoice, and weeping with people who weep. [16] Keep on thinking in harmony [l] with one another. Stop being high-minded but keep on associating with lowly people. Stop being conceited. [17] Stop returning evil for evil to anyone. Always see to it that your affairs are right in the sight of everybody. [18] If possible, so far as it depends on you, live in peace with everybody. [19] Stop taking revenge on one another, beloved, but leave a place for God's [m] anger, for the Scripture says, "Vengeance belongs to me; I will pay them back, says the Lord." [n] [20] Do the opposite.[o] If your enemy is hungry, give him something to eat. If he is thirsty, give him something to drink. For if [p] you act in this way, you will heap burning coals upon his head! [21] Stop being conquered by evil, but keep on conquering evil with good.

13 THE STATE A DIVINE INSTITUTION; DUTIES OF CHRISTIAN CITIZENS; TRUE LOVE OBEYS GOD'S COMMANDS; CHRIST'S SECOND COMING A MOTIVE TO HIGHER LIVING

Everybody must obey the civil [a] authorities that are over him, for no authority exists except by God's permission; the existing authorities have been established by Him, [2] so that anyone who resists the authorities sets himself against what God has established, and those who set themselves against Him will get the penalty due them. [3] For civil authorities are not a terror to the man who does right, but they are to the man who does wrong. Do you want to have no dread of the civil authorities? Then practice doing right

---

[i] Lit. meaning of phrase.
[j] These words exactly tr. Grk. pres. (pt. and impv.).
[k] Lit., *boiling*.
[l] Grk., *the same thing*.
[m] Implied.
[n] Dt. 32:35.
[o] Lit., *on the contrary* (vb. implied).
[p] Cond. adv. pt.
[a] Implied in context.

and you will be commended for it. ⁴ For the civil authorities ᵇ are God's servants to do you good.ᶜ But if you practice doing wrong, you should dread them, for they do not wield the sword for nothing. Indeed, they are God's servants to inflict punishment ᵈ upon people who do wrong. ⁵ Therefore, you must obey them, not only for the sake of escaping punishment,ᵉ but also for conscience' sake; ⁶ for this is the reason why you pay your taxes, for the civil authorities are God's official servants faithfully devoting themselves to this very end. ⁷ Pay all of them what is due them—tribute to the officer ᶠ to receive it, taxes to the officer to receive them, respect to the man entitled to it, and honor to the man entitled to it.

⁸ Stop owing anybody anything, except the obligation to love one another, for whoever practices loving others has perfectly satisfied ᵍ the law. ⁹ For the commandments, "You must not commit adultery, You must not murder, You must not steal, You must not have an evil desire," and any other commandment if there is any, are summed up in this command, "You must love your neighbor as you do yourself." ¹⁰ Love never does a wrong to one's neighbor; so love is the perfect satisfaction of the law.

¹¹ Do ʰ this in particular because you know the present crisis,ⁱ that it is high time for you to wake up out of your sleep, for our salvation is now nearer ʲ to us than when we first believed. ¹² The night has almost passed; the day is at hand. So let us put aside the deeds of darkness, and put on the weapons of light. ¹³ Let us live becomingly for people who are in the light of day, not in carousing and drunkenness, nor in sexual immorality and licentiousness, nor in quarreling and jealousy. ¹⁴ Instead, put on the Lord Jesus Christ, and put a stop to gratifying the evil desires that lurk in your lower nature.

ᵇ To be supplied.
ᶜ Lit., *for good.*
ᵈ Grk., *avengers for wrath.*
ᵉ Lit., *because of wrath.*
ᶠ Only implied.
ᵍ Grk., *has fulfilled or filled to the full.*
ʰ Implied.
ⁱ Lit., *time.*
ʲ Final deliverance at Christ's sec. coming is nearer.

14 AS WE HAVE CONSCIENTIOUS DIFFERENCES OF OPINION ON MINOR MATTERS, WE MUST PUT THE LAW OF BROTHERLY LOVE ABOVE OUR PERSONAL FREEDOM AND REFRAIN FROM DOING MANY THINGS, NOT WRONG IN THEMSELVES, IF THEY HURT OTHERS

Make it your practice to receive into full Christian fellowship [a] people who are overscrupulous,[b] but not to criticize their views. 2 One man believes that he can eat anything, another who is overscrupulous eats nothing but vegetables. 3 The man who eats anything must not look down on the man who does not do so, nor must the man who does not do so condemn the man who does, for God has fully[c] accepted him. 4 Who are you to criticize another man's servant? It is his own master's business [d] whether he stands or falls, and he will stand, for the Lord has power to make him stand. 5 One man rates one day above another, another rates them all alike. Let every man be fully convinced in his own mind. 6 The man who keeps a certain day keeps it for the Lord. The man who eats anything does it for the Lord too, for he gives God thanks. The man who refuses to eat anything does it for the Lord too, and gives God thanks.

7 For none of us can [e] live alone by himself, and none of us can die alone by himself; 8 indeed,[f] if we live, we always live in relation [g] to the Lord, and if we die, we always die in relation to the Lord. So whether we live or die we belong to the Lord. 9 For Christ died and lived again for the very purpose of being Lord of both the dead and the living. 10 Then why should you criticize your brother? Or, why should you look down on your brother? Surely,[f] we shall all stand before God to be judged, 11 for the Scripture says:

" 'As surely as I live,' says the Lord, 'every knee shall bend before me,
And every tongue shall make acknowledgment to God.' " [h]

12 So each of us must give an account of himself to God.

[a] In prep.—perfective ac.
[b] Lit., *weak in faith*.
[c] Expressed by prep.
[d] Dat. of interest.
[e] Implied.
[f] Intensive *gar*.
[g] Dat. of relation.
[h] Isa. 45:23.

¹³ Then let us stop criticizing one another; instead, do this,ᵉ determine to stop putting stumbling blocks or hindrances in your brother's way. ¹⁴ I know, and through my union with the Lord Jesus I have a clear conviction, that nothing is unclean in itself; that a thing is unclean only to the person who thinks it unclean. ¹⁵ For if your brother is hurt because of the food you eat, you are not living by the standard ⁱ of love. Stop ruining, by what you eat, the man for whom Christ died. ¹⁶ Then stop abusing your rights. ¹⁷ For the kingdom of God does not consist in what we eat and drink, but in doing right, in peace and joy through the Holy Spirit; ¹⁸ whoever in this way continues serving Christ is well-pleasing to God and approved by men. ¹⁹ So let us keep on pursuing the things that make for peace and our mutual upbuilding. ²⁰ Stop undoing the work of God just for the sake of food. Everything is clean, but it is wrong for a man to eat anything when it makes another stumble.ʲ ²¹ The right thing to do is not to eat meat, or drink wine, or do anything else, that makes your brother stumble.ʲ ²² On your part, you must exercise your faith by the standard of yourself in the sight of God. Happy is the man who need not condemn himself for doing the thing that he approves. ²³ But the man who has misgivings about eating, if he then eats, has already condemned himself by so doing, because he did not follow his faith, and any action ᵏ that does not follow one's faith is a sin.

15 THE STRONG TO BEAR WITH THE WEAKNESSES OF THE WEAK; TO PLEASE OTHERS AS CHRIST DID; CHRIST WELCOMES HEBREWS AND HEATHEN ALIKE; TO PRAY FOR JOY, PEACE, AND HOPE; PERSONAL MATTERS AND REQUESTS

It is the duty of us who are strong to bear with the weaknesses of those who are not strong, and not merely to please ourselves. ² Each one of us must practice pleasing his neighbor, to help in his immediate ᵃ upbuilding for his eternal ᵃ good. ³ Christ certainly did not please Himself; instead, as the Scripture says, "The re-

---

ⁱ Expressed by prep. *kata* with acc.
ʲ In first clause, lit., *through a cause to stumble;* in second, lit., *by which stumbles.*
ᵏ Lit., *anything not from faith,* etc.
ᵃ Former in *pros,* latter in *eis.*

proaches of those who reproach you have fallen upon me." [b] ⁴ For everything that was written in the earlier times was written for our instruction, so that by our patient endurance and through the encouragement the Scriptures bring we might continuously cherish our hope. ⁵ May God, who gives men patient endurance and encouragement,[c] grant you such harmony with one another, in accordance with the standard which Christ Jesus sets, ⁶ that with united hearts and lips you may praise the God and Father of our Lord Jesus Christ.

⁷ Therefore, practice receiving one another into full Christian fellowship, just as Christ has so received you to Himself. ⁸ Yes, I mean that Christ has become a servant to Israel to prove God's truthfulness,[d] to make valid His promises to our forefathers, ⁹ and for the heathen peoples to praise God for His mercy, as the Scripture says:

"For this I will give thanks to you among the heathen,
And will sing praises to your name." [e]

¹⁰ And again:

"Rejoice, you heathen peoples, with His people!" [f]

¹¹ And again:

"All you heathen peoples, praise the Lord,
Yea, let all peoples sing His praise." [g]

¹² And again Isaiah says:

"The noted Son [h] of Jesse will come,
Even He who rises to rule the heathen;
On Him the heathen will set their hope." [i]

¹³ May the hope-inspiring God [j] so fill you with perfect joy and peace through your continuing faith, that you may bubble over with hope by the power of the Holy Spirit.

¹⁴ As far as I am concerned about you, my brothers, I am convinced that you especially are abounding in the highest goodness,

[b] Ps. 69:9.
[c] Obj. gen.
[d] Lit., *for God's truth.*
[e] Ps. 18:49.
[f] Dt. 32:43.
[g] Ps. 117:1.
[h] Lit., *the* (well-known) *Root of Jesse.*
[i] Isa. 11:1,10.
[j] Obj. or descriptive gen.

richly supplied with perfect knowledge and competent to counsel one another. ¹⁵ And yet, to refresh your memories, I have written you rather freely on some details, because of the unmerited favor shown me by God ¹⁶ in making me a minister of Christ Jesus to the heathen peoples, to have me act as a sacrificing minister of the good news, in order that my offering of the heathen peoples to God may be acceptable, consecrated by the Holy Spirit. ¹⁷ So, as a Christian, I am proud [k] of the things that I have done for God. ¹⁸ For I would venture to mention only what Christ has accomplished through me in bringing the heathen peoples to obedience, by word and by work, ¹⁹ by the power of signs and wonders, by the power of the Holy Spirit. So I have completed the telling of the good news of Christ all the way from Jerusalem around to Illyricum. ²⁰ In this matter it has ever been my ambition to tell the good news where Christ's name had never been mentioned, so as not to build upon foundations laid by other men, ²¹ but, as the Scripture says:

"They will see who were never told of Him,
And they will understand who have not heard." [1]

²² This is the reason why I have so often been prevented from coming to see you. ²³ But now, as there are no more places for me to occupy in this part of the world, and as I have for many years been longing to come to see you, ²⁴ when I make my trip to Spain, I certainly hope to see you on my way there and to be helped forward by you, after I have enjoyed being with you awhile. ²⁵ But just now I am on my way to Jerusalem to help God's people. ²⁶ For Macedonia and Greece were delighted to make a contribution to the poor among God's people in Jerusalem. ²⁷ They certainly were delighted to do it, and they really are under obligation to them, for if the heathen peoples have shared in their spiritual blessings, they ought to serve them in material blessings. ²⁸ So, after I have finished this matter and made sure of the results of this contribution [m] for them, I shall come by you on my way to Spain. ²⁹ And I feel sure that when I do come to you, I shall come with Christ's abundant blessing [n] on me.

³⁰ Now I beg you, brothers, for the sake of our Lord Jesus Christ

---

[k] Lit., *I am boasting in Christ.*
[1] Isa. 52:15.
[m] Lit., *made sure this fruit to them.*
[n] Lit., *in fullness of Christ's blessing.*

and by the love that the Spirit inspires, to wrestle with me in prayers to God on my behalf, ³¹ that I may be delivered from those in Judea who are disobedient, and that the help which I am taking to Jerusalem may be well received by God's people there, ³² so that, if it is God's will, I may come with a happy heart ᵒ to see you and have a refreshing rest while with you. ³³ The peace-giving God be with you all! Amen.

16
PHOEBE THE BEARER OF THE LETTER INTRODUCED; PAUL ASKS TO BE REMEMBERED TO FRIENDS IN ROME; HIS FRIENDS ALSO WISH TO BE REMEMBERED TO THEM; HE WARNS AGAINST TROUBLE-MAKERS IN THE CHURCH, GIVES PRAISE TO GOD

Now I introduce ᵃ to you our sister Phoebe, who is a deaconess in the church at Cenchreae, ² that you may give her a Christian ᵇ welcome in a manner becoming God's people, and give her whatever help she needs from you, for she herself has given protection ᶜ to many, including myself.

³ Remember me ᵈ to Prisca and Aquila, my fellow-workers in the work of Christ Jesus, ⁴ who once risked their very necks for my life. I am so thankful to them; not only I but also all the churches among the heathen thank them. ⁵ Remember me to the church too, that meets at their house. Remember me to my dear Epaenetus, who was the first convert ᵉ to Christ in the province of Asia. ⁶ Remember me to Mary, who has toiled so hard for you. ⁷ Remember me to Andronicus and Junias, my fellow-countrymen, who also served in prison with me; they are held in high esteem among the apostles, and became Christians ᶠ before I did. ⁸ Remember me to Ampliatus, my dear Christian friend.ᵍ ⁹ Remember me to Urbanus, my fellow-worker in the work of Christ, and to my dear friend Stachys. ¹⁰ Remember me to Apelles, that most venerated Christian. Remember me to the members of Aristobulus' family. ¹¹ Remember me to Herodion, my fellow-country-

---

ᵒ Lit., *in joy.*
ᵃ Grk., *commend.*
ᵇ Lit., *welcome in the Lord.*
ᶜ Lit., *been protectress.*
ᵈ Grk., *greet.*
ᵉ Lit., *first fruits.*
ᶠ *Became in Christ before me.*
ᵍ *My beloved in the Lord.*

man. Remember me to the Christian members of Narcissus' family. ¹² Remember me to Tryphaena and Tryphosa, who continued to toil in the work of the Lord. Remember me to my dear friend Persis, who toiled so hard in the work of the Lord. ¹³ Remember me to Rufus, that choicest Christian, and to his mother, who has been a mother to me too. ¹⁴ Remember me to Asyncritus, Phlegon, Hermes, Patrobas, Hermas, and the brothers who are associated with them. ¹⁵ Remember me to Philologus and Julia, to Nereus and his sister, and to Olympas, and all God's people who are associated with them. ¹⁶ Greet one another with a consecrated kiss. All the churches of Christ wish to be remembered to you.

¹⁷ But I beg you, brothers, to keep on the lookout for those who stir up divisions and put hindrances in your way, in opposition to the instruction that you had, and always avoid them. ¹⁸ For such men are really not serving our Lord Christ but their own base appetites,ʰ and by their fair and flattering talk ⁱ they are deceiving the hearts of unsuspecting people. ¹⁹ Yes, your obedience has been told to everybody; so I am delighted about you, but I want you to be wise about what is good and innocent about what is bad. ²⁰ Now the peace-giving God will soon crush Satan under your feet. The spiritual blessing of our Lord Jesus be with you.

²¹ Timothy, my fellow-worker, wishes to be remembered to you; so do Lucius, Jason, and Sosipater too, my fellow-countrymen. ²² I, Tertius, who write this letter, wish to be remembered to you as a fellow-Christian. ²³ Gaius, my host, and host of the whole church here, wishes to be remembered to you. Erastus, the treasurer of the city, wishes to be remembered to you, and so does our brother Quartus.ʲ

²⁵ To Him who can make you strong in accordance with the good news I bring and in accordance with the message preached about Jesus Christ, in accordance with the uncovering of the secret which for ages past had not been told, ²⁶ but now has been fully brought to light by means of the prophetic Scriptures, and in accordance with the command of the eternal God has been made known to all the heathen, to win them to obedience inspired by faith—²⁷ to the one wise God be glory forever through Jesus Christ. Amen.

ʰ Lit., *their own belly.*
ⁱ Grk., *smooth talk and blessing.*
ʲ V. 24 not in best Mss.

FIRST CORINTHIANS

Paul is the writer, as is held by almost every New Testament scholar. The occasion for writing the letter was as follows: While in Ephesus he hears that there are four factions in the church there; three of its members bring a letter which asks him to answer questions about marriage, the status of woman, eating foods offered to idols, and the grading of spiritual gifts. He also learns that immorality and licentiousness, common among pagans, even in their worship in Corinth, were sapping the life out of the church; that some doubted the resurrection of the dead. The date was A. D. 57.

The purpose was to bring about the unity of the church; to correct the moral evils in it, litigation, improper sex relations, misuse of foods offered to idols, etc.; to stimulate their faith in the good news of the cross, and in the resurrection of Christ and the Christian dead; to enlist the church for his world-wide propagation of the good news.

The letter is characterized by its practical wisdom for solving all social problems in accordance with Christianity's moral principles, love, bearing the burdens of the weak, etc.; by many ideas, words, and phrases suggested by its Greek atmosphere, customs, philosophy, and religion; by a style simple and charming, its chapter thirteen being the most beautiful love poem ever written, and chapter fifteen on the resurrection is a brief epic packed with keenest logic, sublime thoughts, and sparkling rhetoric.

1 HE GREETS THEM; THANKS GOD FOR THEIR SPIRITUAL GIFTS; PLEADS FOR UNITY IN THE CHURCH; TELLS HOW THE MESSAGE OF THE CROSS AFFECTS THE PERISHING AND THE SAVED, JEWS AND GREEKS; TELLS OF THEIR LOWLY SOCIAL STATUS

Paul, by the will of God called as an apostle of Jesus Christ, and our brother Sosthenes, [2] to the church of God at Corinth, to those who are consecrated by union with Christ Jesus, and called to be God's people, in fellowship with [a] those who anywhere call upon the name of Jesus Christ, their Lord and ours: [3] spiritual blessing and peace to you from God our Father and from our Lord Jesus Christ.

[4] I am always thanking God for you, for the spiritual blessing given you by God through union with Christ Jesus; [5] because you

---

[a] Prep. *sun* means *fellowship with*.

have in everything been richly blessed [b] through union with Him, with perfect expression and fullness of knowledge.[c] 6 In this way my testimony to Christ has been confirmed in your experience,[d] 7 so that there is no spiritual gift in which you consciously [e] come short, while you are waiting for the unveiling of our Lord Jesus Christ, 8 and to the very end He will guarantee that you are vindicated at the day of our Lord Jesus Christ. 9 God is entirely trustworthy, and it is He through whom you have been called into this fellowship with His Son, Jesus Christ our Lord.

10 Now I beg you all, brothers, for the sake of [f] our Lord Jesus Christ, to be harmonious in what you say and not to have factions among you, but to be perfectly harmonious [g] in your minds and judgments. 11 For I have been informed about you, my brothers, by Chloe's people, that there are wranglings among you. 12 I mean this, that one of you says, "I belong to Paul's party," another, "And I belong to Apollos' party," another, "And I belong to Cephas' party," another, "And I belong to Christ's party." 13 Christ has been parceled out by you! [h] It was not Paul who was crucified for you, was it? You were not baptized in Paul's name, were you? 14 I am thankful that I baptized none of you but Crispus and Gaius, 15 so as to keep anyone from saying that you were baptized in my name. 16 Yes, I did baptize the family of Stephanas, too; I do not now recall that I baptized anyone else. 17 For Christ did not send me to baptize, but to preach the good news—but not by means of wisdom and rhetoric,[i] so that the cross of Christ may not be emptied of its power.

18 For the message of the cross is nonsense to those who are in the process [j] of being destroyed, but it is the power of God to those who are in the process [j] of being saved. 19 For the Scripture says:

"I will destroy the wisdom of the wise,
And I will set aside the learning of the learned." [k]

20 So where is your philosopher? Where is your man of letters?

[b] Lit., *made rich*.
[c] Grk., *all speech and all knowledge*.
[d] Grk., *in you*.
[e] In the vb.; see Lk. 15:14.
[f] Grk., *through the name of*.
[g] Lit., *to say the same thing—in the same mind*, etc.
[h] As a farm divided up.
[i] Lit., *in worldly wisdom*.
[j] Pres. pt. of cont. ac.
[k] Isa. 29:14.

Where is your logician of this age? Has not God shown up the nonsense of the world's wisdom? ²¹ For since in accordance[1] with the wisdom of God the world had never in reality,[m] by means of its wisdom, come to know God, God chose through the nonsense of the message proclaimed, to save the people who put their faith in Him. ²² While Jews are demanding spectacular signs and Greeks are searching for philosophy, ²³ we are preaching the Christ who was crucified—a message that is a trap-stick[n] to the Jews and nonsense to the Greeks, ²⁴ but to those whom God has called, both Jews and Greeks alike, the Christ who is God's power and God's wisdom. ²⁵ It is so, because God's nonsense is wiser than men's wisdom, and God's weakness is mightier than men's might.

²⁶ For consider, brothers, the way God called you;[o] that not many of you, in accordance with human standards,[p] were wise, not many influential, not many of high birth. ²⁷ Just the opposite: God chose what the world calls foolish to put the wise to shame, what the world calls weak to put the strong to shame, ²⁸ what the world calls of low degree, yea, what it counts as nothing and what it thinks does not exist, God chose to put a stop to what it thinks exists, ²⁹ so that no mortal man might ever boast in the presence of God. ³⁰ So you owe it all to Him[q] through union with Christ Jesus, whom God has made our wisdom, our means of right standing, our consecration, and our redemption, ³¹ so that, as the Scripture says, "Let him who boasts boast in the Lord."[r]

2 PAUL'S SIMPLE STYLE OF PREACHING; THE GOOD NEWS, GOD'S WISDOM, NOT MAN'S; ONLY GOD'S SPIRIT CAN UNCOVER THIS SPIRITUAL WISDOM TO MEN

Now when I came to you, brothers, I did not come and tell you God's uncovered secret in rhetorical language or human philosophy,[a] ² for I determined, while among you, to be unconscious of everything but Jesus Christ and Him as crucified. ³ Yes, as for my-

---

[1] Implied in prep. *en.*
[m] Grk., *had never known by experience.*
[n] *The stick that throws the trap to catch the bird;* so the cross has thrown the trap to catch the Jew.
[o] Lit., *your calling* (by God).
[p] Lit., *in accordance with the flesh.*
[q] Lit., *you are out of Him.*
[r] Jer. 9:24.
[a] Lit., *in excellency of speech or wisdom.*

self, it was in weakness and fear and great trembling that I came to you, ⁴ and my language and the message I preached were not adorned with pleasing words of worldly wisdom,ᵇ but they were attended with proof and power given by the Spirit,ᶜ ⁵ so that your faith might not be in men's wisdom, but in God's power.

⁶ Yet, when among mature believers we do set forth a wisdom, but a wisdom that does not belong to this world or to the leaders of this world who are passing away; ⁷ rather, we are setting forth a wisdom that came from God, once a covered secret but now uncovered,ᵈ which God marked off as His plan for bringing us to glory.ᵉ ⁸ Not one of this world's leaders understands it, for if they had, they would never have crucified our glorious ᶠ Lord. ⁹ But, as the Scripture says, they are:

"Things which eye has never seen and ear has never heard,
And never have occurred to human hearts,
Which God prepared for those who love Him." ᵍ

¹⁰ For God unveiled them to us through His Spirit, for the Spirit by searching discovers everything, even the deepest truths about God.ʰ ¹¹ For what man can understand his own inner thoughts except by his own spirit within him? Just so no one but the Spirit of God can understand the thoughts of God. ¹² Now we have not receved the spirit that belongs to the world but the Spirit that comes from God, that we may get an insight into the blessings God has graciously given us. ¹³ These truths we are setting forth, not in words that man's wisdom teaches but in words that the Spirit teaches, in this way fittingⁱ spiritual words to spiritual truths. ¹⁴ An unspiritual ʲ man does not accept the things that the Spirit of God teaches, for they are nonsense to him; and he cannot understand them, because they are appreciated by spiritual insight.ᵏ ¹⁵ But the spiritual man appreciates everything, and yet he himself is not really appreciated by anybody. ¹⁶ For

---

ᵇ Lit., *persuasive words of wisdom.*
ᶜ Grk., *in proof of the Spirit and of power.*
ᵈ Grk., *once a secret but now uncovered.*
ᵉ Lit., *marked off to glory.*
ᶠ Gen. of quality.
ᵍ Isa. 64:4.
ʰ Lit., *deep things of God.*
ⁱ Lit., *judging together.*
ʲ Grk., *a psychical man.*
ᵏ Lit., *spiritually examined.*

who has ever known the Lord's thoughts, so that he can instruct Him? But we now possess Christ's thoughts.

3 FACTIOUS CHRISTIANS UNSPIRITUAL; SPIRITUAL TEACHERS GOD'S FELLOW-WORKERS; SUCH TEACHERS RESPONSIBLE TO BUILD INTO GOD'S TEMPLE ENDURING MATERIALS, AND NOT TO SPOIL IT WITH PERISHING MATERIALS

So I myself, brothers, could not deal [a] with you as spiritual persons, but as creatures of human clay,[b] as merely baby [c] Christians. ² I fed you with milk, not solid food, for you could not take it. Why, you cannot take it even now, ³ for you are still unspiritual.[d] For when there are still jealousy and wrangling among you, are you not still unspiritual and living by a human standard? ⁴ For when one says, "I belong to Paul's party," and another, "I belong to Apollos' party," are you not acting as mere human creatures?

⁵ Then what is Apollos? Or what is Paul? Mere servants through whom you came to believe, as the Lord gave each of us his task. ⁶ I did the planting, Apollos did the watering, but it was God who kept the plants growing.[e] ⁷ So neither the planter nor the waterer counts for much, but God is everything in keeping the plants growing. ⁸ The planter and the waterer are one in aim, and yet each of us will get his own pay in accordance with his own work, ⁹ for we belong to God [f] as His fellow-workers; you belong to God as His field to be tilled, as His building to be built.

¹⁰ As a skilled architect,[g] in accordance with God's unmerited favor given to me, I laid a foundation, and now another is building upon it. But every builder must be careful how he builds upon it; ¹¹ for no one can lay any other foundation than the one that is laid, that is, Jesus Christ Himself. ¹² And whether one puts into the building on the foundation gold or silver or costly stones, or wood or hay or straw, ¹³ the character of each one's work will come to light, for the judgment day will show it up. This is so, because that day will show itself in fire, and the fire will test the

[a] Lit., *say* or *speak*.
[b] Grk. word means *made of flesh* (clay, Eng. equivalent).
[c] Lit., *babies in Christ*.
[d] Grk., *fleshly*, opposite of *spiritual*.
[e] Impf. of cont. ac.
[f] Emph. gen. of possession.
[g] Grk. word anglicized.

character of each one's work. ¹⁴ If the structure ʰ which one builds upon it stands the test,ⁱ he will get his pay. ¹⁵ If the structure which one builds is burned up, he will get no pay; ʲ and yet he himself will be saved; but just as one who goes through a fire.ᵏ

¹⁶ Are you not conscious that you are God's temple, and that the Spirit of God has His permanent home in you?¹ ¹⁷ If anyone destroys God's temple, God will destroy him. For God's temple is sacred to Him, and you are that temple.

¹⁸ Let no one deceive himself. If any one of you supposes that he is wise in this world's wisdom, as compared with the rest of you,ᵐ to become really wise he must become a fool. ¹⁹ For this world's wisdom is mere nonsense to God. For the Scripture says, "He who catches the wise with their own cunning," ²⁰ and again, "The Lord knows that the arguings of the wise are useless." ⁿ ²¹ So let no one boast in men. For everything belongs to you—Paul, Apollos, Cephas, the world, life, death, the present, the future—they all belong to you. ²² Yes, you belong to Christ, and Christ belongs to God.

4 MINISTERS, TRUSTEES OF GOD'S TRUTH; THE APOSTLE CUTS WITH KEENEST IRONY; THEN COUNSELS THEM AS A LOVING FATHER; THOUGH CONSCIOUS OF HIS AUTHORITY, HE PREFERS TO LEAD BY LOVE

As for us apostles,ᵃ men ought to think of us as ministers of Christ and trustees ᵇ to handle God's uncovered truths.ᶜ ² Now in this matter of trustees the first and final ᵈ requirement is that they should prove to be trustworthy. ³ As for me, myself, it is of very little concern to me to be examined by you or any human court; ᵉ in fact, I do not even examine myself. ⁴ For although my conscience does not accuse me, yet I am not entirely vindicated by that. It is the Lord Himself who must examine me. ⁵ So you must

---

ʰ Lit., *work*.
ⁱ Grk., *remains*.
ʲ Lit., *suffer loss* (of pay).
ᵏ Saved without his clothes or valuables.
¹ Pres. of cont. action.
ᵐ Lit., *among you*.
ⁿ Job 5:13; Ps. 94:11.
ᵃ Implied from words, *Paul, Apollos,* and *Cephas*.
ᵇ Lit., *stewards;* modern equivalent, *trustees*.
ᶜ Lit., *mysteries, things once covered, now uncovered*.
ᵈ Grk., *here further*.
ᵉ Lit., *a human day*.

stop forming any premature judgments, but wait until the Lord shall come again; for He will bring to light the secrets hidden in the dark and will make known the motives of men's hearts, and the proper praise will be awarded each of us.

⁶ Now, brothers, for your sakes I have applied all this to Apollos and myself, that from us as illustrations [f] you might learn the lesson, "Never go beyond what is written," so that you might stop boasting in favor of one teacher [f] against another. ⁷ For who makes you superior? [g] And what do you have that you did not get from someone? But if you got it from someone, why do you boast as though you had not? ⁸ Are you satisfied already? Have you grown [h] rich already? Have you ascended [h] your thrones without us to join you? Yes, I could wish that you had ascended your thrones,[i] that we too might join you on them! ⁹ For it seems to me that God has put us apostles on exhibition at the disgraced end of the procession, as they do with men who are doomed to die in the arena.[j] ¹⁰ For we have become a spectacle to the universe, to angels as well as men. For Christ's sake we are held as fools, while you through union with Christ are men of wisdom.[k] We are weak; you are strong. You are held in honor; we in dishonor. ¹¹ To this very hour we have gone hungry, thirsty, poorly clad; we have been roughly knocked around, we have had no home, ¹² we have worked hard with our own hands for a living. When abused by people we bless them, when persecuted we patiently bear it, ¹³ when we are slandered by them we try to conciliate them.[l] To this very hour we have been made the filth of the world, the scum of the universe! [m]

¹⁴ I do not write this to make you blush with shame but to give you counsel as my dear children. ¹⁵ For though you have ten thousand teachers in the Christian life, you certainly could not have many fathers. For it was I myself who became your father through your union with Christ Jesus, which resulted from my telling you the good news. ¹⁶ So I beg you, make it your habit [n] to follow my example. ¹⁷ This is why I have sent Timothy to you. He is a dear

---
[f] Implied.
[g] Lit., *makes you differ?*
[h] Ingress. aor.
[i] Unrealized wish.
[j] Pictures of a triumphal entry into Rome.
[k] Spoken in keenest irony.
[l] Lit., *try to beg.*
[m] Lit., *scum of all things.*
[n] Pres. impv.

child of mine and trustworthy in the Lord's work; he will call to your minds my methods in the work of Christ Jesus, just as I teach them everywhere in every church.

[18]But some of you have become conceited over the thought that I am not coming to see you. [19]But I am coming, and coming soon, if the Lord is willing, and then I will find out, not only what those conceited fellows say but what they can do,[o] [20]for the kingdom of God does not consist in talking but in doing. [21]Which do you prefer? My coming to you with a club, or in a gentle, loving spirit?

5   HE REBUKES THE CHURCH FOR TOLERATING A CASE OF GROSSEST INDECENCY; THE CHURCH HAD DISREGARDED HIS PREVIOUS WARNING

A case[a] of immorality is reported as actually existing among you, an immorality unheard of[a] even among the heathen—that a man co-habits[b] with his father's wife. [2]And yet, you are proud of it,[c] instead of being sorry for it, and seeing[a] to it that the man who has done this be removed from your membership![d] [3]For my part, though I have been absent from you in person, I have been present with you in spirit, and so as really present, by the authority of our Lord Jesus, I have already passed judgment upon the man who has done this—[4]for when you met I too met with you in spirit by the power of our Lord Jesus—[5]to turn such a man as this over to Satan for the destruction of his lower nature,[e] in order that his spirit may be saved on the day of the Lord. [6]Your ground for boasting about such a case is not good. Are you not aware that a little yeast will change the whole lump of dough? [7]You must clean out the old yeast,[f] that you may be a fresh lump, as you are to be free from the old yeast. For our Passover Lamb, Christ, has already been sacrificed. [8]So let us keep our feast, not with old yeast nor with the yeast of vice and wickedness, but with the bread[a] of purity and truth without the yeast.

[9]I wrote you in my letter to stop associating with sexually im-

---

[o] Lit., *not their word but their power* (to do).
[a] Implied.
[b] Grk., *has, holds* (as wife).
[c] Lit., *puffed up.*
[d] Lit., *from your midst.*
[e] Grk., *of his flesh.*
[f] Here a symbol of evil.

moral people—g ¹⁰not that you are to stop all dealings with sexually immoral people of this world, any more than with its greedy graspers,ʰ or its idolaters, for then you would have to get clear out of the world. ¹¹Now what I really meant was for you to stop associating with any so-called brother, if he is sexually immoral, a greedy grasper, an idolater, a slanderer, a drunkard, or a swindler—with such a person you must even stop eating. ¹²For what right have I to judge outsiders? Is it not for you to judge those who are inside the church, ¹³but for God to judge those who are outside? You must expel¹ that wicked person from your membership.

6
CHRISTIANS NOT TO GO TO LAW IN HEATHEN COURTS; URGED NOT TO GO TO LAW WITH ONE ANOTHER; PAGAN VICES INCONSISTENT WITH CHRISTIAN LIVING; OUR FREEDOM NO EXCUSE FOR SENSUALITY; CHRISTIAN REASONS FOR PERSONAL PURITY

When one of you has a grievanceᵃ against his neighbor, does he dare to go to law before a heathen court,ᵇ instead of laying the caseᶜ before God's people? ²Do you not know that God's people are to judge the world? And if the world is to be judged before you, are you unfit to try such petty cases? ³Do you not know that we Christiansᵉ are to sit in judgment on angels, to say nothing of the ordinary cases of life? ⁴So if you have the ordinary cases of life for settlement,ᶜ do you set up as judges the very men in the church who have no standing? ⁵I ask this to make you blush with shame. Has it come to this, that there is not a single wise man among you who could settle a grievance of one brother against another, ⁶but one brother has to go to law with another, and that before unbelieving judges? ⁷To say no more,ᵈ it is a mark of moralᶜ failure among you to have lawsuits at all with one another. Why not rather suffer being wronged? Why not suffer being robbed? ⁸On the contrary, you practice wronging and robbing others, and that your brothers.

ᵍ Lit., *fornicators.*
ʰ Exact meaning of Greek word.
¹ Grk. vb. very forceful, *put out* or *drive out;* so *expel.*
ᵃ Lit., *matter, affair.*
ᵇ Grk., *before the unrighteous.*
ᶜ Implied.
ᵈ Lit., *already.*

⁹ Do you not know that wrongdoers will not have a share ᵉ in the kingdom of God? Stop being misled; people who are sexually immoral or idolaters or adulterers or sensual or guilty of unnatural sexual vice ᶠ ¹⁰ or thieves or greedy graspers for more or drunkards or slanderers or swindlers will not have a share in the kingdom of God. ¹¹ And these are just the characters some of you used to be. But now you have washed yourselves clean, you have been consecrated, you are now in right standing with God, by the name of our Lord Jesus Christ and by the Spirit of God.

¹² Everything is permissible for me, but not everything is good for me. Everything is permissible for me, but I will not become a slave to anything. ¹³ Foods are intended ᵉ for the stomach, and the stomach for foods, but God will finally ᵍ put a stop to both of them. The body is not intended for sexual immorality but for the service ᵉ of the Lord, and the Lord is for the body to serve. ¹⁴ And as God by His power raised the Lord to life, so He will raise us too.

¹⁵ Do you not know that your bodies are parts of Christ Himself? Then may I take away parts of Christ and make them parts of a prostitute? Never! Never! ¹⁶ Or, are you not aware that a man who has to do with ʰ a prostitute makes his body one with hers? For God says, "The two shall be physically one." ⁱ ¹⁷ But the man who is in union with the Lord is spiritually one with Him. ¹⁸ Keep on running from sexual immorality! Any other sin that a man commits is one outside his body, but the man who commits the sexual sin is sinning against his own body. ¹⁹ Or, are you not conscious that your body is a temple of the Holy Spirit that is in you, whom you have as a gift ᵉ from God? Furthermore, you are not your own, ²⁰ for you have been bought and actually paid for.ʲ So you must honor God with your bodies.

ᵉ Grk., *inherit.*
ᶠ Lit., *sodomites.*
ᵍ Aor. fut.
ʰ Lit., *joins with.*
ⁱ Gen. 2:24; lit., *one flesh.*
ʲ Grk., *bought with a price;* i.e., actually paid for.

7 SINGLE OR MARRIED STATE, WHICH? HUSBANDS AND WIVES URGED NOT TO SEPARATE; CHRISTIANS TO REMAIN IN PRESENT SOCIAL CONDITIONS; EARTHLY LIFE FLEETING; A FATHER'S DUTY TO HIS SINGLE DAUGHTER; WIDOWS MAY MARRY AGAIN

Now I take up the matters about which you wrote me. It may be [a] a good thing for a man to remain unmarried; [b] 2 but because of so much sexual immorality [c] every man should have a wife of his own, and every woman a husband of her own. 3 The husband must always give his wife what is due her, and the wife too must do so for her husband.[d] 4 The wife does not have the right to do as she pleases with her own body; the husband has his right to it. In the same way the husband does not have the right to do as he pleases with his own body; the wife has her right to it. 5 You husbands and wives [a] must stop refusing each other what is due, unless you agree to do so just for awhile, so as to have plenty of time for prayer, and then to be together again, so as to keep Satan from tempting you because of your lack of self-control. 6 But I say this by way of concession, not by way of command. 7 However, I should like for everyone to be just as I am myself, yet each of us has his own special gift from God, one for one way, another for another.

8 To unmarried people and to widows I would say this: It would be a fine thing for them to remain single, as I am. 9 But if they do not practice self-control, let them marry. For it is better to marry than to be burning in the fire of passion. 10 To the people already married I give this instruction—no, not I but the Lord—[e] that a wife is not to leave her husband. 11 But if she does leave him, she must remain single, or better,[a] be reconciled to her husband. I instruct the husband too not to divorce his wife.[f]

12 To the rest of the people I myself would say—though the Lord Himself has said nothing about it—if a Christian has a wife that is not a believer and she consents to live with him, he must not divorce her; 13 and a woman who has a husband that is not a believer, but he consents to live with her, must not divorce her

---

[a] Implied.
[b] Grk., *not to touch a woman.*
[c] Lit., *fornication.*
[d] Referring to sexual duties of each to the other.
[e] Referring to what Jesus taught, Mt. 5:32; 19:9.
[f] A general law of Christian teaching, to emphasize the sanctity of marriage; but see exceptions in Mt. 5:32; 19:9; also next verses.

husband. **14** For the unbelieving husband is consecrated by union with his wife and the unbelieving wife by union with her Christian husband; for otherwise your children would be unblessed, but in this way they are consecrated.g **15** But if the unbelieving consort a actually leaves, let the separation stand. In such cases the Christian husband or wife is not morally bound; God has called us to live in peace. **16** For how do you know, wife, whether you will save your husband? Or, how do you know, husband, whether you will save your wife?

17 Only, everybody must continue to live in the station which the Lord assigned to him, in that in which God called him. These are my orders in all the churches. **18** Has a man been called after he was circumcised? He must not try to change it. Has a man been called without being circumcised? He must not be circumcised. **19** Being circumcised or not being circumcised has no value, but keeping God's commands is important. **20** Everybody must remain in the station in which he was called. **21** Were you called while a slave? Stop letting that annoy you. Yet, if you can win your freedom, take advantage of such an opportunity.a **22** For the slave who has been called to union with the Lord is the Lord's freedman; in the same way the freeman who has been called is a slave of Christ. **23** You have been bought and actually paid for; stop becoming slaves to men. **24** Brothers, each one must continue close to God in the very station in which he was called.

25 About unmarried women I have no command from the Lord,h but I will give you my opinion as of one who is trustworthy, since I have had mercy shown me by the Lord. **26** Now this is my opinion in the light of the present distress: i That it is a good thing for a man to remain as he is. **27** Are you married? Stop trying to get a divorce. Are you unmarried? j Stop looking for a wife. **28** But if you do get married, you have not sinned in doing so. And if a girl gets married, she has not sinned in doing so. But those who do will have trouble in their earthly life,k and I am trying to spare you this.

29 I mean this, brothers. The time has been cut short. For the future, men who have wives should live as though they had none,

g That is, one Christian consort is a blessing for the children and the non-Christian consort.
h That is, Jesus said nothing about this topic.
i Lit., *because of*, etc.
j Lit., *bound to a wife . . . loosed from a wife*.
k Grk., *in the flesh*.

³⁰ and those that mourn as though they did not mourn, and those who are glad as though they were not glad, and those who buy as though they did not own a thing, ³¹ and those who are enjoying¹ the world as though they were not entirely absorbed in it. For the outward order of this world is passing away. ³² I want you to be free from worldly * worries. An unmarried man is concerned about the affairs of the Lord. ³³ A married man is concerned about the affairs of the world, and how he can please his wife, and so his devotion* is divided. ³⁴ An unmarried woman or a girl is concerned about the affairs of the Lord, so as to be consecrated in body and spirit, but a married woman is concerned about the affairs of the world, and how she can please her husband. ³⁵ It is for your welfare that I am saying this, not to put restraint on you, but to foster * good order and to help you to an undivided devotion to the Lord.

³⁶ Now if a father * thinks that he is not doing the proper thing regarding his single daughter, if she is past the bloom of her youth, and she ought to do so, let him do what she desires; he commits no sin. Let the daughter and her suitor ᵐ marry. ³⁷ But the father who stands firm in his purpose, without having any necessity for doing so, and he has made the decision in his own heart to keep her single, will do what is right. ³⁸ And so the man who gives his daughter ⁿ in marriage does what is right, and yet the man who does not do so does even better.

³⁹ A wife is bound to her husband as long as he lives. If her husband dies, she is free to marry anyone she pleases, except that he must be a Christian.º ⁴⁰ But in my opinion she will be happier, if she remains as she is, and I think too that I have God's Spirit.

8 MAY CHRISTIANS EAT FOOD ONCE SACRIFICED TO IDOLS? BROTHERLY LOVE SOLVES THIS PROBLEM

Now about the foods ᵃ that have been sacrificed to idols: We know that every one of us has some knowledge of the matter. Knowledge puffs up, but love builds up. ² If a man supposes that he has already gotten some true knowledge, as yet he has not learned it as he ought to know it. ³ But if a man loves God, God ᵇ

* Implied.
¹ Lit., *using the world*—enjoying its life, etc.
ᵐ Lit., *let them*—daughter and suitor—*marry.*
ⁿ Implied in Grk. vb., the key to vv. 36-38.
º Grk., *only in the Lord.*
ᵃ Lit., *things.*
ᵇ Grk., *this one, the latter* (God).

is known by him. ⁴ So, as to eating things that have been sacrificed to idols, we are sure ᵉ that an idol is nothing in the world, and that there is no God but One. ⁵ For even if there are so-called gods in heaven or on earth—as there are, indeed, a vast number ᵈ of gods and lords—⁶ yet for us there is but one God, the Father, who is the source ᵉ of all things and the goal ᵉ of our living, and but one Lord, Jesus Christ, through whom everything was made and through whom we live.

⁷ But it is not in all of you that such knowledge is found. Some, because of their past habits with idols,ᶠ even down to the present moment, still eat such food as was really sacrificed to an idol, and so their consciences, because they are overscrupulous, are contaminated. ⁸ Food will never bring us near to God. We are no worse if we do not eat it; we are no better if we do. ⁹ But you must see to it that this right of yours does not become a stumbling block to overscrupulous people. ¹⁰ For if somebody sees you, who have an intelligent view of this matter, partaking of a meal in an idol's temple, will he not be emboldened,ᵍ with his overscrupulous conscience, to eat the food which has been sacrificed to an idol? ¹¹ Yes, the overscrupulous brother, for whom Christ died, is ruined by your so-called knowledge. ¹² Now if in such a way you sin against your brothers and wound ʰ their overscrupulous consciences, you are actually sinning against Christ. ¹³ So then, if food can make my brother fall, I will never, no, never,ⁱ eat meat again, in order to keep my brother from falling.

9 THE CHURCH IN CORINTH PROOF OF PAUL'S APOSTLESHIP; HIS RIGHT TO MARRY AND HIS RIGHT TO BE SUPPORTED AS A MINISTER; HIS MOTIVES TO WIN OTHERS TO CHRIST; THE WREATH THAT NEVER WITHERS

Am I not free? Am I not an apostle? Have I not seen Jesus our Lord? Are you not the product of my work for the Lord?ᵃ ² If I

ᶜ Intuitional knowledge.
ᵈ *Many* repeated, so *a vast number.*
ᵉ Lit., *out of Him . . . and we for Him* (live).
ᶠ So Abbott-Smith, Lex.
ᵍ Lit., *built up.*
ʰ Lit., *strike.*
ⁱ Treble neg. in Grk.
ᵃ Grk., *my work in the Lord.*

am not an apostle to other people, I certainly am one to you, for you yourselves, by virtue of your union with the Lord, are the proof [b] of my apostleship.

3 My vindication [c] of myself to those who are investigating me is this: 4 It cannot be that we have no right to our food and drink, can it? 5 It cannot be that we have no right to take a Christian wife [d] about with us, can it, as well as the rest of the apostles and the Lord's brothers, and Cephas? [e] 6 Or is it Barnabas and I alone who have no right to refrain from working for a living? 7 What soldier ever goes to war at his own expense? Who plants a vineyard and does not eat any of its grapes? Who shepherds a flock and does not drink any of the milk the flock produces? 8 I am not saying this only by way of human illustrations,[f] am I? Does not the law say so too? 9 For in the law of Moses it is written, "You must not muzzle an ox that is treading out your grain." [g] Is it that God is concerned about oxen only? 10 Is He not really speaking on our behalf? Yes, indeed, this law was written on our behalf, because the plowman ought to plow and the thresher ought to thresh, in the hope of sharing in the crop. 11 If we have sown the spiritual seed for you, is it too great for us to reap a material support [h] from you? 12 If others share this right with you, have we not a stronger claim? Yet, we have never used this right; no, we keep on bearing everything, to keep from hindering the progress of the good news of Christ. 13 Do you not know that those who do the work about the temple get their living from the temple, and those who constantly attend on the altar share its offerings? 14 Just so the Lord has issued orders that those who preach the good news shall get their living out of it.[i] 15 But I myself have never used any of these rights. And I am not writing this just to make it so in my case, for I had rather die than do that.[j] No one shall rob me of this ground of boasting. 16 For if I do preach the good news, I have no ground for boasting of it, for I cannot help doing it.[k] Yes, indeed, I am accursed if I do not preach the good news. 17 For if I

---

[b] Lit., *the seal,* proof of genuineness.
[c] Grk., *defense.*
[d] Lit., *a sister as wife.*
[e] Questions expecting ans. *No.*
[f] Lit., *according to man;* i.e., three illustrations from lite for min. support.
[g] Dt. 25:4—Scriptural proof for same; another in v. 13.
[h] Lit., *fleshly things.*
[i] Grk., *live out of the good news.*
[j] Broken sentence; last phrase implied.
[k] Grk., *necessity lies upon me.*

do it of my own accord, I get my pay; but if I am unwilling to do it, I still am entrusted with trusteeship.¹ ¹⁸ Then what is the pay that I am getting? To be able to preach the good news without expense to anybody, and so never to make full use of my rights in preaching the good news.

¹⁹ Yes, indeed, though I am free from any human power, I have made myself a slave to everybody, to win as many as possible.ᵐ ²⁰ To the Jews I have become like a Jew for the winning of Jews; to men under the law, like one under the law, though I am not under the law myself, to win the men under the law; ²¹ to men who have no written law, like one without any law, though I am not without God's law but specially under Christ's law, to win the men who have no written law. ²² To the overscrupulous I have become overscrupulous, to win the overscrupulous; yes, I have become everything to everybody, in order by all means to save some of them. ²³ And I do it all for the sake of the good news, so as to share with others in its blessings.ⁿ

²⁴ Do you not know that in a race the runners all run, but only one can get the prize? You must run in such a way that you can get the prize. ²⁵ Any man who enters an athletic contest practices rigid self-control in training, only to win a wreath that withers, but we are in to win a wreath that never withers. ²⁶ So that is the way I run, with no uncertainty as to winning. That is the way I box, not like one that punches the air. ²⁷ But I keep on beating and bruising ᵒ my body and making it my slave, so that I, after I have summoned others to the race, may not myself become unfit to run.ᵖ

10 ISRAELITES IN THE DESERT, LACKING SELF-CONTROL, MISSED THE PRIZE; EVERY TEMPTATION MAY BE OVERCOME; WARNS AGAINST IDOLATRY; BROTHERLY LOVE LIMITS PERSONAL FREEDOM

For I would not have you, brothers, to be ignorant of the fact that though our forefathers were all made safe ᵃ by the cloud, and

---

¹ Lit., *stewardship.*
ᵐ Lit., *to win the more.*
ⁿ Lit., *be fellow-sharers of it.*
ᵒ One vb. has both ideas.
ᵖ Lit., *rejected, disqualified.*
ᵃ Implied.

all went securely [a] through the sea, and in the cloud and the sea ² they all allowed [b] themselves to be baptized as followers [a] of Moses, ³ and all ate the same spiritual food, ⁴ and all drank the same spiritual drink—for they continued to drink the water from the spiritual Rock which accompanied them, and that Rock was the Christ— ⁵ still [c] with the most of them God was not at all satisfied, for He allowed [a] them to be laid low in the desert.

⁶ Now all these things occurred as warnings [d] to us, to keep us from hankering after what is evil, in the ways they did. ⁷ Now stop being idolaters, as some of them were, for the Scripture says, "The people sat down to eat and drink and got up to dance." [e] ⁸ Let us stop practicing immorality, as some of them did, and on one day twenty-three thousand fell dead.[f] ⁹ Let us stop trying the Lord's patience, as some of them did, and for it were destroyed by the snakes. ¹⁰ You must stop grumbling, as some of them did, and for it were destroyed by the destroying angel. ¹¹ These things continued to befall them as warnings to others, and they were written down for the purpose of instructing us, in whose lives the climax of the ages has been reached.[g]

¹² So the man who thinks he stands securely must be on the lookout not to fall. ¹³ No temptation has taken hold of you but what is common to human nature.[h] And God is to be trusted not to let you be tempted beyond your strength, but when temptation comes, to make a way out of it, so that you can bear up under it.

¹⁴ So then, my dearly beloved, keep on running from idolatry. ¹⁵ I am speaking to sensible men; decide for yourselves about what I say. ¹⁶ Is not the consecrated cup [i] which we consecrate a sign [a] of our sharing in the blood of Christ? Is not the loaf which we break a sign [a] of our sharing in the body of Christ? ¹⁷ Because there is only one loaf, so we, though many, are only one body, for we all partake of one loaf. ¹⁸ Look at the Israelites in their practices.[j] Are not those who eat the sacrifices in spiritual fellowship with the altar? ¹⁹ Then what do I mean? That the sacrifice to an

[b] Middle voice gives this idea.
[c] Concessive idea implied in conj. *alla*.
[d] Lit., *types;* here in bad sense.
[e] Ex. 32:6.
[f] Last word not in best Mss., but implied.
[g] Lit., *on whom the end of the ages has come.*
[h] Grk., *except a human one.*
[i] Lit., *cup of blessing.*
[j] Grk., *Israel according to the flesh.*

idol is a reality, or that an idol itself is a reality? Of course not! ²⁰ I mean that what the heathen sacrifice they sacrifice to demons, not to God, and I do not want you to be in fellowship with demons.ᵏ ²¹ You cannot drink the cup of the Lord and the cup of demons. You cannot eat at the table of the Lord and at the table of demons. ²² Or, are we trying to incite the Lord to jealousy? We are not stronger than He, are we?

²³ Everything is permissible for people, but not everything is good for them. Everything is permissible for people, but not everything builds up their personality.* ²⁴ No one should always be looking after his own welfare, but also that of his neighbor.

²⁵ As a rule eat anything that is sold in the meat market without raising any question about it for conscience' sake, ²⁶ for the earth and everything that it contains belong to the Lord. ²⁷ If some unbelieving heathen invites you to his house, and you wish to go, eat whatever is set before you without raising any question for conscience' sake. ²⁸ But if someone says to you, "This meat has been offered as a heathen sacrifice," make it your rule not to eat it, for the sake of the man who warned you and for conscience' sake; ²⁹ I mean his conscience, not yours. Why then should my personal* freedom be limited[1] by another's conscience? ³⁰ If I give thanks and thus partake of food, why am I to be blamed for that for which I give thanks?

³¹ So if you eat or drink or do anything else, do everything to honor God. ³² Stop being stumbling blocks to Jews or Greeks or to the church of God, ³³ just as I myself am in the habit of pleasing everybody in everything, not aiming at my own welfare but at that of as many people as possible, in order that they may be saved. 11:1 You must follow my example, just as I myself am following Christ's.

11 WOMAN'S STATUS AND SERVICE IN THE CHURCH; CLIQUES IN CHURCH MEETINGS; DISORDERS IN OBSERVING THE LORD'S SUPPER; ORIGIN AND SACRED SIGNIFICANCE OF THE LORD'S SUPPER

² I prize and praise ᵃ you for always remembering me and for firmly standing by the teachings ᵇ as I passed them on to you. ³ But

---

ᵏ Alluding to Grk. custom; gods called demons.
[1] Lit., *judged* or *criticized*.
ᵃ Grk., *praise,* but the vb. includes the idea of *appreciation.*
ᵇ Lit., *traditions.*
* Implied.

I want you to realize the fact that Christ is the Head of every man, that the husband is the head of the wife, and that God is the Head of Christ. ⁴ Any man who prays or preaches ᵉ with anything on his head dishonors his head, ⁵ and any woman who prays or prophesies bareheaded dishonors her head, for it is one and the same thing with having her head shaved.ᵈ ⁶ For if a woman will not wear a veil, let her have her hair cut off too. Now if it is a dishonor for a woman to have her hair cut off, or her head shaved, let her wear a veil. ⁷ For a man ought not to wear anything on his head, because he is the image and reflected ᵉ glory of God, but woman is man's reflected glory. ⁸ For man did not originate ᶠ from woman, but woman did from man, ⁹ and man was not created for woman's sake, but woman was for man's sake. ¹⁰ This is why woman ought to wear upon her head a symbol of man's ᵍ authority, especially out of respect to the angels.ʰ ¹¹ But from the Lord's point of view woman is not independent of man nor man of woman. ¹² For just as woman originated from man, so man is born ᵍ of woman, and both, with everything else, originated from God. ¹³ You must judge for yourselves in this matter. Is it proper for a woman to pray to God with nothing on her head? ¹⁴ Does not nature itself teach you that it is degrading ⁱ for a man to wear long hair, ¹⁵ but that it is a woman's glory to do so? For her hair is given her for a covering. ¹⁶ But if anyone is inclined to be contentious about it, I for my part prescribe ʲ no other practice than this, and neither do the churches of God.

¹⁷ But as I am giving you these instructions I cannot approve of your meetings, because they do not turn out for the better but for the worse. ¹⁸ For, in the first place, when you meet as a congregation, I hear that there are cliques ᵏ among you, and I partly believe it. ¹⁹ Yes, indeed, there must be parties among you, in order that people of approved fitness may come to the front among you.

²⁰ So when you hold your meetings, it is not to eat the Lord's Supper, ²¹ for each of you is in a rush to eat his own supper, and

ᶜ Lit., *prophesies.*
ᵈ Only lewd women among the Greeks wore short hair or shaved their heads
ᵉ Implied in *doxa* (Abbott-Smith).
ᶠ In prep. *ek.*
ᵍ Implied from context.
ʰ Lit., *for the sake of the angels.*
ⁱ Grk., *dishonoring.*
ʲ Grk., *have* or *hold.*
ᵏ Lit., *schisms*

one goes hungry while another gets drunk. ²² It is not that you have no houses to eat and drink in, is it? Or, are you trying to show your contempt for the church of God and trying to humiliate those who have no houses? What shall I say to you? Shall I praise you? No, I cannot praise you for this. ²³ For the account that I passed on to you I myself received from the Lord Himself,[1] that the Lord Jesus on the night He was betrayed took a loaf of bread ²⁴ and gave thanks for it and broke it and said, "This is my body* which is given for you. Do this in memory of me." ²⁵ In the same way, after supper, He took the cup of wine, saying, "This cup is the new covenant ratified by my blood.* Whenever you drink it, do so in memory of me."

²⁶ For every time you eat this bread and drink from this cup, you proclaim the Lord's death until He comes again. ²⁷ So whoever eats the bread and drinks from the Lord's cup in an unworthy way is guilty of sinning against the Lord's body and blood. ²⁸ A man, then, must examine himself, and only in this way should he eat any of the bread and drink from the cup. ²⁹ For whoever eats and drinks without recognizing [m] His body, eats and drinks a judgment on himself. ³⁰ This is why many of you are sick and feeble, and a considerable number are falling asleep.[n] ³¹ But if we properly saw ourselves, we would not bring down upon us this judgment. ³² But since we do bring down upon us this judgment, we are being disciplined by the Lord, so that finally we may not be condemned along with the world. ³³ So, my brothers, when you meet to eat, wait for one another. ³⁴ If anyone is hungry, let him eat at home, so that your meetings may not bring on you judgment. I will settle in detail the matters that remain, when I come.

12 SPIRITUAL GIFTS; SPIRITUAL INSIGHT NEEDED; THESE GIFTS VARY; CHRISTIANS CONSTITUTE AN ORGANIC UNIT, CHRIST'S BODY; AS IN THE NATURAL BODY, ALL PARTS OF HIS BODY ESSENTIAL FOR STRENGTH AND EFFICIENCY

About spiritual gifts, brothers, I do not want you to be without information.[a] ² You know that when you were heathen you were

---

[1] The word for *Lord* in emphatic position.
[m] Lit., *not discerning, not seeing.*
[n] All these terms in a spiritual sense.
[a] Lit., *be ignorant.*
[*] Metaphorical language.

in the habit of going off, wherever you might be led, after idols that could not speak. ³ So I want to inform you that no one speaking under the power ᵇ of the Spirit of God can say, "Jesus is accursed!" and no one except one under the power of the Holy Spirit can really say, "Jesus is Lord!"

⁴ There are varieties of gifts, but the Spirit is the same in all; ⁵ there are varieties of service, but the Lord to be served ᵇ is the same; ⁶ there are varieties of activities, but it is the same God who does all things by putting energy in us all.ᶜ ⁷ To each of us is given a special ᵇ spiritual illumination ᵈ for the common good. ⁸ To one, wise speech ᵉ is given by the Spirit; to another, by the same Spirit, intelligent speech ᵉ is given; ⁹ to another, through union with the same Spirit, faith; to another, by one and the same Spirit, power to cure the sick; ¹⁰ to another, power for working wonders; to another, prophetic insight; to another, the power to discriminate between the true Spirit and false spirits; to another, various ecstatic utterances; and to another, the power to explain them. ¹¹ But the one and same Spirit accomplishes all these achievements, and apportions power to each of us as He chooses.

¹² For just as the human ᵇ body is one and yet has many parts, and all the parts of the body, many as they are, constitute ᶠ but one body, so it is with Christ. ¹³ For by one Spirit all of us, Jews or Greeks, slaves or free men, have been baptized into one body, and were all imbued ᵍ with one Spirit. ¹⁴ For the body does not consist of one part but of many. ¹⁵ If the foot says, "Since I am not a hand, I am not a part of the body," that does not make it any less a part of the body. ¹⁶ If the ear says, "Since I am not an eye, I am not a part of the body," that does not make it any less a part of the body. ¹⁷ If all the body were an eye, how could we hear? If all the body were an ear, how could we smell? ¹⁸ But as it now is, God has placed the parts, every one of them, in the body just as He wanted them to be. ¹⁹ If they were all one part, how could it be a body? ²⁰ But as it now is, there are many parts, but one body. ²¹ The eye cannot say to the hand, "I do not need you," or the hand to the feet, "I do not need you." ²² No, on the con-

---

ᵇ Implied.
ᶜ Lit., *working in us all.*
ᵈ Grk., *manifestation.*
ᵉ Lit., *speech of wisdom . . . speech of knowledge.*
ᶠ Lit., *are.*
ᵍ Grk., *made to drink.*

trary, even those parts of the body that seem to be most delicate [h] are indispensable, 23 and the parts of it we deem devoid of honor we dress with special honor, and our ill-shaped [i] parts receive more careful attention, 24 while our well-shaped parts do not want for anything. Yes, God has perfectly adjusted the body, giving great honor to its apparently inferior parts, 25 so that there is no disharmony in the body, but all the parts have a common care for one another. 26 If one part suffers, all the parts suffer with it. If one part receives an honor, all the parts can share its joy.

27 So you are Christ's body, and individually parts of it. 28 And God has placed people in the church, first as apostles, second as prophets, third as teachers, then wonder-workers; then people with power to cure the sick, helpers, managers,[j] ecstatic speakers. 29 Not all are apostles, are they? Not all are prophets, are they? Not all are teachers, are they? Not all are wonder-workers, are they? 30 Not all are people with power to cure the sick, are they? Not all are ecstatic speakers, are they? Not all can explain ecstatic speaking, can they? 31 But you must earnestly continue to cultivate your higher spiritual gifts.

13 A POEM ON LOVE; LOVE GIVES QUALITY TO ALL OTHER GIFTS; LOVE ACHIEVES THE GREATEST WONDERS; LOVE ENDURES FOREVER

12:31 And yet I will show you a way that is better by far: [a]

If I could speak the languages of men, of angels too,
And have no love,
I am only a rattling pan [b] or a clashing cymbal.[c]
2 If I should have the gift of prophecy,
And know all secret truths, and knowledge in its every form,[d]
And have such perfect faith that I could move mountains,
But have no love, I am nothing.
3 If I should dole out everything I have for charity,

[h] Lit., *weak* or *fragile*.
[i] See Abbott-Smith, Lex., for this meaning.
[j] Lit., *governments*.
[a] The way of love. I put the poem in blank verse.
[b] Lit., *copper*.
[c] Lit., *clashing cymbal*.
[d] Grk., *all mysteries,* etc.

And give my body up to torture in mere boasting pride,[e]
But have no love, I get from it no good at all.
[4] Love is so patient and so kind;
Love never boils with jealousy; [f]
It never boasts, is never puffed with pride;
[5] It does not act with rudeness, or insist upon its rights; [g]
It never gets provoked, it never harbors evil thoughts; [h]
[6] Is never glad when wrong is done,
But always glad when truth prevails;
[7] It bears up under anything,
It exercises faith in everything,
It keeps up hope in everything,
It gives us power to endure in anything.

[8] Love never fails;
If there are prophecies, they will be set aside;
If now exist ecstatic speakings, they will cease; [i]
If there is knowledge, it will soon be set aside;
[9] For what we know is incomplete and what we prophesy is incomplete.[j]

[10] But when perfection comes, what is imperfect will be set aside.
[11] When I was a child, I talked like a child,
I thought like a child, I reasoned like a child.
When I became a man, I laid aside my childish ways.
[12] For now we see a dim reflection in a looking-glass,[k]
But then we shall see face to face; [l]
Now what I know is imperfect,
But then I shall know perfectly, as God knows me.
[13] And so these three, faith, hope, and love endure,
But the greatest of them is love.

[e] *In order to boast.*
[f] Exact tr.
[g] Lit., *never seeks its own.*
[h] Lit., *never thinks evil.*
[i] Grk., *tongues,* etc.
[j] Lit., *in parts* or *fragments.*
[k] Only a dim reflection could be seen in primitive metallic mirrors.
[l] That is, see the very realities, God Himself, truth itself, etc.

14

PROPHECY SUPERIOR TO ECSTATIC SPEAKING; GOOD ORDER TO BE OBSERVED IN EXERCISING SPIRITUAL GIFTS; WOMAN'S PLACE IN PUBLIC WORSHIP; THE APOSTLE'S AUTHORITY TO SPEAK ON THIS MATTER

Keep on pursuing love, but still keep cultivating your spiritual gifts, especially the gift of prophesying.[a] 2 For whoever speaks in ecstasy is speaking not to men but to God, for no one understands[b] him, and yet by the Spirit he is speaking secret truths.[c] 3 But whoever prophesies is speaking to men for their upbuilding,[d] encouragement, and comfort. 4 Whoever speaks in ecstasy builds up himself alone, but whoever prophesies builds up the congregation too. 5 I would like for all of you to speak in ecstasy, but I would rather that you prophesy. The man who speaks with real prophetic insight renders greater service than the man who speaks in ecstasy, unless the latter explains it, so the congregation may receive an uplift.

6 But as it now is, brothers, if I do come back to you speaking in ecstasy, what good shall I do you, unless my speech contains a revelation or new knowledge or a prophetic message or some teaching? 7 Even inanimate things, like the flute or the harp, may give out sounds, but if there is no difference in the notes, how can the tune that is played on the flute or the harp be told? 8 Again, indeed, if the bugle[e] does not sound a call distinct and clear, who will prepare for battle? 9 So it is with you; unless in your ecstatic speaking you speak a message that is clearly intelligible, how can the message spoken by you be understood? You might just as well[f] be talking to the air! 10 There are, supposedly, ever so many languages in the world, and not one is without its own meaning.[g] 11 So if I do not know the meaning[h] of the language, I should be a foreigner to the man who speaks it, and he would be a foreigner to me. 12 So, as you are ambitious for spiritual gifts, you must keep trying to excel for the upbuilding of the church. 13 Therefore, the man who speaks in ecstasy must pray

[a] Lit., *prophesying;* i.e., speaking new spiritual truths.
[b] Lit., *hears.*
[c] Grk., *mysteries.*
[d] Lit., *speaking upbuilding.*
[e] Grk., *trumpet.*
[f] Lit., *you will be.*
[g] Lit., *without voice* or *sound.*
[h] Grk., *force* or *power.*

for power to explain what he says. ¹⁴ For if I pray in ecstasy, my spirit is praying, but my mind produces no results for anyone. ¹⁵ What is my conclusion then? I will certainly pray with my spirit, but I will pray with my mind in action too. I will certainly sing with my spirit, but I will sing with my mind in action too. For if you give thanks with your spirit only, ¹⁶ how is the man who occupies the place of the illiterate¹ to say "Amen" to your thanksgiving? For he does not know what you are saying. ¹⁷ You are, indeed, doing right to give thanks, but your neighborʲ is not built up. ¹⁸ Thank God, I speak in ecstasy more than any of you. ¹⁹ But in the public congregation I would rather speak five words with my mind in action, in order to instruct the people too,ᵏ than ten thousand words in ecstasy.

²⁰ Brothers, stop being children in intelligence,ˡ but as to evil keep on being babies; and yet as to intelligence be men of maturity. ²¹ In the law it is written, "By men of foreign languages and by the lips of foreigners I will speak to this people, but even then they will not listen to me, says the Lord."ᵐ ²² So speaking in ecstasy is meant as a sign, not for believers but for unbelievers, while prophecy is meant, not for unbelievers but for believers. ²³ Hence, if the whole church has met and everybody speaks in ecstasy, and illiterate people or unbelievers come in, will they not say that you are crazy? ²⁴ But if everybody prophesies, and some unbeliever or illiterate man comes in, he is convinced of his sins by all, he is closely questioned by all, ²⁵ the secrets of his heart are laid bare, he falls upon his face and worships God, declaring, "God is really among you."

²⁶ Then what is our conclusion, brothers? When you meet together, everybody has a song, something to teach, a revelation, an ecstatic utterance, or an explanation of one. It must all be for the upbuilding of all. ²⁷ If anybody speaks in ecstasy, there must be only two, or three at most, and let one speak at a time, and someone explain what he says. ²⁸ But if there is no one to explain it, let him keep quiet in the church and speak to himself and God alone. ²⁹ Let two or three prophets speak, and the rest consider carefully what is said; ³⁰ and if anything is revealed to another

---

ⁱ Lit., *a private, unlearned person.*
ʲ Grk., *the other man.*
ᵏ Lit., *others too.*
ˡ Grk., *in minds.*
ᵐ Isa. 28:11.

who is seated, let the speaker stop. ³¹ For in this way you can all, one after another, speak your prophetic message, so that all may learn and be encouraged, ³² for the spirits of prophets yield to prophets; ³³ for God is not a God of disorder but of order,ⁿ as it is in all the churches of God's people.

³⁴ Women must keep quiet in the churches, for no permission is given them to speak. On the contrary, they must take a subordinate place, just as the law says. ³⁵ If they want to find out about something, they should ask their own husbands at home, for it is disgraceful for a woman to speak in church.º ³⁶ Did the message of God begin with you Corinthians? Or, are you the only people it has reached? ᵖ

³⁷ If anyone claims to have the prophetic spirit, or any other spiritual gift, let him recognize that what I now am writing is the Lord's command. ³⁸ If anyone ignores it, let him ignore it. ³⁹ So, my brothers, cultivate the gift of prophetic speaking, but stop preventing others from speaking in ecstasy. ⁴⁰ Everything must always be done in a proper and orderly way.

15
THE RESURRECTION OF JESUS A FIRST PRINCIPLE IN THE GOOD NEWS; PROVED A FACT BY HIS APPEARANCES; THE GREEKS, DOUBTING ANY RESURRECTION, ANSWERED; BECAUSE JESUS ROSE, CHRISTIANS WILL RISE WITH SPIRITUAL, IMMORTAL BODIES

Now let me remind you, brothers, of the essence ᵃ of the good news which I proclaimed to you, which you accepted, on which you now are standing, ² and through which you are to be saved,ᵇ unless your faith at first was spurious.ᶜ ³ For I passed on to you, among the primary principles of the good news,ᵈ what I had received, that Christ died for our sins, in accordance with the Scriptures, ⁴ that He was buried, that on the third day He was raised from the dead, in accordance with the Scriptures, ⁵ and that He was

---

ⁿ Lit., *peace,* but in the sense of *peaceful order.*
º I.e., for a woman to usurp and exercise authority over men in the church; so EGT. See I Tim. 2:12, for this explanation.
ᵖ A touch of sarcasm, keen but loving.
ᵃ Implied in phrase, *among the primary principles.*
ᵇ At last.
ᶜ Lit., *in vain.*
ᵈ Grk., *among the first things;* good news implied.

seen by Cephas, and then by the Twelve. ⁶ After that, at one time He was seen by more than five hundred brothers, most of whom are still living, though some of them have fallen asleep.ᵉ ⁷ Then He was seen by James, then by all the apostles, and finallyᶠ ⁸ He was seen by me, too, as though I were born out of time. ⁹ For I belong to the lowest ᵍ rank of the apostles, and am not fit to bear the title apostle, because I once persecuted the church of God. ¹⁰ But by God's unmerited favor I have become what I am, and His unmerited favor shown to me was not bestowed for nothing; for I have toiled more extensively than any of them, and yet it was not I but God's unmerited favor working with me. ¹¹ But whether it was I or they, this is ʰ what we preach, and this is what you believed.

¹² Now if we preach that Christ has been raised from the dead, how is it that some of you are saying that there is no such thing as a resurrection of the dead? ¹³ If there is no resurrection of the dead, then Christ has not been raised, ¹⁴ and if Christ was not raised, the message which we preach has nothing in it;ⁱ there is nothing in our faith either, ¹⁵ and we are found guilty of lying about God, for we have testified that He raised Christ, whom He did not raise, if indeed the dead are never raised. ¹⁶ For if the dead are never raised, Christ has not been raised; ¹⁷ and if Christ has not been raised, your faith is a mere delusion; you are still under the penaltyʲ of your sins. ¹⁸ Yes, even those who have fallen asleep, though in union with Christ, have perished. ¹⁹ If for this life only we Christiansʲ have set our hopes on Christ, we are the most pitiable people in the world.

²⁰ But in reality Christ has been raised from the dead, the firstᵏ to be raised of those who have fallen asleep. ²¹ For since it was through a man that death resulted,ʲ it was also through a man that the resurrection of the dead resulted. ²² For just as all men die by virtue of their descentʲ from Adam, so all such as are in union with Christ will be made to live again. ²³ But each in his proper order; Christ first, then at His coming those who belong to Christ. ²⁴ After that comes the end, when He will turn the kingdom over

ᵉ Have died.
ᶠ In aor.
ᵍ Lit., *the least.*
ʰ Grk., *in this way we preach.*
ⁱ False and futile.
ʲ Implied.
ᵏ Lit., *first fruits.*

to God His Father, when He will put an end to all other ʲ government, authority, and power; ²⁵ for He must continue to be king until He puts all His enemies under His feet. ²⁶ Death is the last enemy to be stopped, ²⁷ for He has put everything in subjection under His feet. But when He says that everything has been put in subjection to Him, He Himself is evidently excepted who put it all in subjection to Him. ²⁸ And when everything has been put in subjection to Him, then the Son Himself will also become subject to Him who has put everything in subjection to Him, so that God may be everything to everybody.

²⁹ Otherwise, what do those people mean [1] who submit to being baptized on behalf of their dead? If the dead are never raised at all, why do they submit to being baptized on their behalf? ³⁰ Why too do we ourselves run such risks every hour? ³¹ I protest, by the boasting which I do about you, my brothers, through our union with Christ Jesus our Lord, I myself run the risk ʲ of dying every single day! ³² If from merely human motives ᵐ I have fought wild beasts here in Ephesus, what profit will it be to me? If the dead are never raised at all, "Let us eat and drink, for tomorrow we shall be dead." ⁿ ³³ Do not be so misled: "Evil companionships corrupt good character." ³⁴ Sober up, as is right, and stop sinning, for some of you—to your shame I say so—are without any true knowledge of God.

³⁵ But someone will ask, "How can the dead rise? With what kind of body do they come back?" ³⁶ You foolish man! the seed that you sow never comes to life unless it dies first; ʲ ³⁷ and what you sow does not have the body that it is going to have, but is a naked grain, of wheat (it may be) or something else; ³⁸ but God gives it just the body He sees fit, even each kind of seed its own body. ³⁹ Every kind of flesh is different. One kind ʲ belongs to men, another to cattle, another to birds, another to fish. ⁴⁰ There are heavenly bodies, and earthly bodies, but the splendor of the heavenly bodies is of one kind,ʲ and the splendor of the earthly bodies is of another. ⁴¹ One kind of splendor belongs to the sun, another to the moon, and another to the stars; yes, one star differs from another in splendor. ⁴² It is just like this with the resurrection of the dead.º ⁴³ The body is sown in decay, it is raised without decay; it is sown

---

[1] Grk., *do.*
[m] Lit., *according to a human.*
[n] Motto of the Epicureans.
[o] Lit., *so is the resurrection.*

in humiliation, it is raised in splendor; it is sown in weakness, it is raised in strength; ⁴⁴ it is sown a physical ᵖ body, it is raised a spiritual body. If there is a physical body, there is a spiritual body too. ⁴⁵ This is the way the Scripture puts it too, "The first man Adam became a living creature." ᑫ The last Adam has become a life-giving Spirit. ⁴⁶ But it is not the spiritual that comes first; it is the physical, and then the spiritual. ⁴⁷ The first man was made of the dust of the earth; the second Man is from heaven. ⁴⁸ Now those who are made of the dust are just like him who was first made of dust, and those who are heavenly are like Him who is from heaven, ⁴⁹ and as we have reflected the likeness of him who was made of dust, let us also reflect the likeness of the Man from heaven.

⁵⁰ But this I tell you, brothers: Our physical ʳ bodies cannot take part in the kingdom of God; what is decaying will never take part in what is immortal. ⁵¹ Let me tell you a secret. We shall not all fall asleep, but we ˢ shall all be changed, ⁵² in a moment, in the twinkling of an eye, at the sound of the last trumpet. For the trumpet will sound, and the dead will be raised with bodies not subject to decay, and we shall be changed. ⁵³ For this decaying part of us must put on the body ʲ that can never decay, and this part once capable of dying must put on the body ʲ that can never die. ⁵⁴ And when this part once capable of dying puts on the body that can never die, then what the Scripture says will come true, "Death has been swallowed up in victory. ⁵⁵ O Death, where is your victory now? O Death, where is your sting?" ᵗ ⁵⁶ Now sin gives death its sting, and the law gives sin its power. ⁵⁷ But thank God! He gives us victory through our Lord Jesus Christ. ⁵⁸ So, my dear brothers, continue to be firm, incapable of being moved, always letting the cup run over in the work of the Lord, because you know that your labor in the service ʲ of the Lord is never thrown away.ᵘ

ᵖ Grk., *psychical;* the present body with a soul in it; hence *physical* is best tr.
ᑫ Gen. 2:7.
ʳ Lit., *flesh and blood* (bodies) ; so *physical.*
ˢ Christians living when He comes back.
ᵗ Isa. 25:8; Hos. 13:14.
ᵘ Lit., *in vain,* to no purpose.

16 THE CONTRIBUTION FOR THE FAMINE-STRICKEN IN JUDEA; PRINCIPLES OF GIVING; TIMOTHY AND APOLLOS TO VISIT CORINTH, AS WELL AS PAUL; PAUL CHEERED BY REPORT OF STEPHANAS' COMMITTEE FROM CORINTH; GREETS THEM

Now about the contribution for God's people.[a] I want you to do as I directed the churches of Galatia to do. ²On the first day of every week each of you must put aside and store up something in proportion [b] as he is prospered, so that no contributions need be made when I come back. ³When I get there, I will send on, with credentials,[c] the persons whom you approve, to carry your gift of charity[d] to Jerusalem. ⁴And if it seems proper for me to go too, they shall go as my companions.

⁵I will come to see you after I pass through Macedonia—for I am to pass through Macedonia—⁶and I shall likely stay over with you some time, or may be, spend the winter with you, so that you may help me on to whatever points I may visit.[e] ⁷I do not want to see you right now in a mere stop-over visit, for later I hope to spend some time with you, if the Lord permits me. ⁸But I shall stay on in Ephesus until the time of Harvest Feast.[f] ⁹For I have an opportunity here that is great and calls for work,[g] and it has many opponents.

¹⁰If Timothy gets there, see that he is at ease among you, for he is devotedly [h] doing the work of the Lord, just as I am. ¹¹So no one must slight him at all.[i] But send him on with your good-by, that he may come back to me, for I am expecting him with the other brothers.

¹²As for our brother Apollos, I have earnestly urged him to go to see you, but he is not at all inclined to come just now; yet he is coming when he has a good opportunity.

¹³Be always on your guard; stand firm in your faith; keep on

---

[a] Lit., *the saints;* i.e., the famine-stricken Christians in Judea.
[b] *In respect to what he is prospered.*
[c] Lit., *letters.*
[d] Eng. *charity,* from this word.
[e] Lit., *send me on,* etc.
[f] *Pentecost.*
[g] Lit., *a great door,* etc.
[h] Lit., *continuously doing.*
[i] Expressed by aor. with neg.

acting like men; continue to grow in strength; ¹⁴ let everything be done in love.

¹⁵ Now I beg you, brothers—you know that the family of Stephanas were the first converts ʲ in Greece, and that they have devoted themselves to the service of God's people—¹⁶ I beg you to put yourselves under leaders like these, and under anyone who co-operates with you, and labors hard. ¹⁷ And I am glad that Stephanas, Fortunatus, and Achaicus have come to see me, because they have supplied what you lacked. ¹⁸ Yes, they have cheered my spirit, and yours too. You must deeply ᵏ appreciate such men.

¹⁹ The churches of Asia wish to be remembered to you. Aquila and Prisca, with the church that meets at their house, send you their cordial Christian greetings. ²⁰ All the brothers wish to be remembered to you. Greet one another with a sacred kiss.

²¹ The final greeting is mine—Paul's—with my own hand. ²² A curse upon anyone who does not love the Lord! Our Lord is coming. ²³ The spiritual blessing of the Lord Jesus be with you! ²⁴ My love be with you all in union with Christ Jesus.

ʲ Grk., *first fruits.*
ᵏ Adv. in prep.; lit., *thoroughly know.*

SECOND CORINTHIANS

The writer is generally thought to be Paul the apostle.
The occasion was as follows: Paul was closing his third missionary journey at Ephesus. He learned that his opponents in Corinth were bitterly attacking his message, his authority as an apostle, his speech and its style, and even his character. Titus was sent to put the church in order, but he stayed so long that Paul went down to Troas and crossed to Macedonia, and there they met. Titus reported Paul's triumph in Corinth. The majority had endorsed his message and vindicated him, but a minority, the Judaizing party, were loath to surrender, and threatened to continue their fight on him. So Paul wrote this letter, probably in A. D. 57.
The purpose was to express his joy over the victory of his message in the capital of Greece; to show his interest in the church there; to defend his authority as an apostle and his personal character; if possible, to silence the tongues of his critics; also to urge the church to complete its contribution for the famine-stricken Christians in Judea.
The letter is intensely personal and emotional, with the style of the ordinary common Greek, but marked with boundless variety because of the many topics discussed. His logic is keen, cutting, and convincing. It is one of his four greatest letters.

1 HE GREETS THEM; GIVES THANKS TO GOD FOR COMFORTING HIM; TELLS OF HIS MOTIVES AS PURE, AND WHY HE POSTPONES HIS VISIT TO CORINTH

Paul, by the will of God an apostle of Christ Jesus, and Timothy our brother, to the church of God that is at Corinth, with all God's people all over Greece: 2 spiritual blessing and peace to you from God our Father and the Lord Jesus Christ.

3 Blessed be the God and Father of our Lord Jesus Christ, the merciful[a] Father and the all-comforting[a] God, 4 who comforts me[b] in every sorrow I have, so that I can comfort people who are in sorrow with the comfort with which I am comforted by God. 5 For

---
[a] Lit., *the Father of mercies* (qualitative gen.).
[b] Editorial plural—we.

just as my[e] sufferings for Christ are running over the cup, so through Christ my comfort is running over too. 6 If I am in sorrow, it is on behalf of your comfort and salvation; if I am comforted, it is for the comfort that is experienced[d] by you in your patient endurance of the same sort of sufferings that I am enduring too. 7 My hope for you is well founded; because I know that just as you, brothers, are sharers of my sufferings, so you will be sharers of my comfort too. 8 For I do not want you to be uninformed about the sorrow that I suffered in Asia, because I was so crushed beyond any power to endure that I was in dire despair of life itself. 9 Yes, I felt within my very self the sentence of death, to keep me from depending on myself instead of God who raises the dead. 10 He saved me from a death so horrible, and He will save me again! He it is on whom I have set my hope that He will still save me, 11 because you are helping me by your prayers for me, so that thanks to God will be given by many on my behalf for God's gracious gift[e] to me in answer to the prayers of many.

12 For my boast is this, to which my conscience testifies, that before the world, but especially before you, I have acted from pure motives[f] and in sincerity before God, not depending[g] on worldly wisdom but on God's unmerited favor. 13 For what I am writing you is nothing more than what you can read and understand, and I hope that you will understand it perfectly,[h] just as some of you have come to understand me partially; 14 that is, to understand that you have grounds for boasting of me just as I have for boasting of you, on the day of our Lord Jesus.

15 It was because of this confidence that first I planned to visit you, to give you a double delight; 16 that is, to go by you on my way to Macedonia, and then to come back to you from Macedonia, and have you send me on to Judea. 17 Now I did not resort to fickleness,[i] did I, in planning that? Or, do I make my plans in accordance with worldly notions,[j] to have my "Yes" mean "No," if I want it so? 18 As certainly as God is to be trusted, my message to you has not been a "Yes" that might mean "No." 19 For

[e] Editorial plural—we.
[d] Lit., *operating.*
[e] Grk., *as to the grace-gift.*
[f] Lit., *in purity.*
[g] Implied.
[h] Grk., *to the end.*
[i] Lit., *use lightness.*
[j] Grk., *according to the flesh.*

God's Son, Christ Jesus, who was preached among you by us, Silvanus, Timothy, and me, did not become a "Yes" that might mean "No." 20 But with Him it is always* "Yes," for, as many as the promises of God may be, through Him they are always* "Yes." This is why our "Amen" through Him is for the glory of God when spoken* by us. 21 But it is God who makes us as well as you secure through union with Christ, and has anointed us, 22 and put His seal upon us, and given us His Spirit in our hearts as a first installment of future rewards.[k]

23 But upon my soul I call God to witness that it was to spare you pain that I gave up my visit to Corinth. 24 Not that we are trying to lord it over your faith, but we are workers with you to promote* your joy, for in your faith you are standing firm.

2 HE WRITES IN LOVE; BEGS THE CHURCH TO FORGIVE THE PENITENT OFFENDER; TELLS OF HIS SORROW AND HIS SUCCESS

For I have definitely[a] decided not to pay you another painful visit. 2 For if I make you sad, who is there to make me glad but the very man who has been made sad by me? 3 This is the very thing I wrote you, that when I did come I might not be made sad[b] by the very people who ought to make me glad, for I had confidence in you all that my gladness would be gladness to you all. 4 For out of great sorrow and distress of heart, yes, while shedding many tears,[c] I wrote you, not to make you sad but to make you realize that my love for you continues running over.[d]

5 But if anyone has made anyone sad, it is not I, but you that he has made sad, at least, some of you, not to be severe on all of you. 6 To a man like that, this censure by the majority has been sufficient punishment,[e] 7 so you must do[e] the opposite, freely forgive and comfort him, to keep him from being overwhelmed by his excessive sadness. 8 So I beg you in your love to reinstate him entirely.[f] 9 For this is why I wrote you, to see if you would stand

---

[k] Latent in word for *first installment.*
[a] In emph. pro.
[b] Lit., *not to come again in sadness.*
[c] Grk., *through many tears.*
[d] Lit., *I cont. to have love more overflowingly.*
[e] Implied from context.
[f] Grk., *make love valid to him.*
[*] Implied.

the test, to see if you would be obedient in everything. ¹⁰ The man that you forgive I too forgive. For if I have forgiven him anything, it is what I have forgiven him in the very presence of Christ for your sake, ¹¹ to keep us from being worsted by Satan, for we know what his intentions are.

¹² When I went to Troas to preach the good news of Christ, although I had an opportunity in the service of the Lord, ¹³ I had no rest of spirit, because I did not find my brother Titus there. So I said good-by to them and left for Macedonia. ¹⁴ But thanks be to God, for He always leads me in His triumphal train,ᵍ through union with Christ, and everywhere through me keeps spreading the perfume of the knowledge of Him.ʰ ¹⁵ Indeed, I am the fragrance of Christ to God, alike for those who are being saved and for those who are perishing; ¹⁶ to the one a deadly perfumeⁱ that leads to death, to the other a living perfume that leads to life. ¹⁷ Now who is qualified for such a task? I am,ᵃ for I am not a peddler of God's message, like the most of them, but like a man of sincerity, like a man that is sent from God and living in His presence, in union with Christ I speak His message.

3 HIS CONVERTS AT CORINTH PROOF THAT GOD CALLED HIM TO BE AN APOSTLE; TELLS OF THE SURPASSING GLORY OF THIS SPIRITUAL MINISTRY

Am I beginning to recommend myself again? I do not, like some people, do I, need letters of recommendation to you or from you? ² You are my letter of recommendation,ᵃ written on my heart, read and understood ᵇ by everybody, ³ for you are always showing that you are a letter of Christ, produced by my service, written not in ink but by the Spirit of the living God, not on tablets of stone, but on human hearts.

⁴ Such is the confidence I have through Christ in the presence of God. ⁵ Not that I am myself qualified to consider anything as coming ᵃ from me myself. No; my qualification comes from God, for ᶜ ⁶ He has qualified even me as a minister of the new covenant,ᵈ

ᵍ Picture of a Rom. general marching into Rome in triumph.
ʰ Experimental knowledge of Him diffused like perfume.
ⁱ Lit., *belonging to death.*
ᵃ Implied.
ᵇ Grk. order, *understood and read.*
ᶜ Causal relative.
ᵈ The sacred agreement of God to save those trusting in Jesus.

which is not a written but a spiritual covenant. For the letter kills, but the Spirit gives life.

⁷ Now if the old religious ᵃ service which resulted in death, although its law was carved in letters of stone,ᵉ was introduced with a splendor so great that the Israelites ᶠ could not keep their eyes fixed on Moses' face because of the splendor that was fading from it, ⁸ why should not this spiritual service be attended with much greater splendor? ⁹ For if the service connected with condemnation had such splendor, the service resulting in right standing with God * will surely far surpass it in splendor. ¹⁰ For on account of its surpassing splendor, what was once so splendid has now no splendor at all. ¹¹ For if what passed away was introduced * with splendor, with how much greater splendor must what is permanent be attended? *

¹² So, as I have such a hope, I speak with the greatest boldness, ¹³ not as Moses did, who used to wear a veil over his face, to keep the Israelites from gazing at the end ᵍ of what was passing away. ¹⁴ Besides, their minds were made dull; for to this day that same veil remains unlifted, whenever they read the Old Covenant; because it is only through union with Christ that it is removed. ¹⁵ Indeed, to this very day, whenever Moses is read, a veil hangs over their hearts, ¹⁶ but whenever anybody turns to the Lord, the veil is removed. ¹⁷ Now the Lord means the Spirit, and wherever the Spirit of the Lord is, there is freedom. ¹⁸ And all of us, with faces uncovered, because we continue to reflect like mirrors ʰ the splendor of the Lord, are being transformed into likeness to Him, from one degree * of splendor to another, since it comes from the Lord who is the Spirit.

4 PAUL FAITHFULLY PREACHES THE GOOD NEWS; GOD GIVES HIM STRENGTH TO BEAR HIS SORROWS; HE HOPES FOR HIS BODY TO BE RAISED AND HIS SORROWS TO INCREASE HIS FUTURE GLORIES

So, because I hold a place ᵃ in this ministry and that because I have had God's mercy shown me, I never give up. ² On the other

---

ᵉ Lit., *it was carved* (cut)—law implied.
ᶠ Grk. has *sons of Israel*.
ᵍ The utter collapse of the legal system.
ʰ Vb. means *to reflect like a mirror*.
ᵃ Lit., *I hold or have this ministry*.
* Implied.

hand, I have renounced all underhanded, disgraceful methods; [b] I neither practice cunning nor do I tamper with God's message, but by clear and candid statements of truth [c] I try to commend myself to every human conscience in God's sight. 3 If the meaning of the good news I preach is covered up at all, it is so only in the case of those who are on the way to destruction. 4 In their case, the god of this world has blinded the eyes of the unbelievers, to keep the glorious light of the good news of Christ, who is the likeness of God, from dawning upon them. 5 For I am not proclaiming myself but Christ Jesus as Lord, and myself a slave of yours for Jesus' sake. 6 For God who said, "Let light shine out of darkness," is the One who has shone in my heart, to give me the light of the knowledge of God's glory, reflected [d] on the face of Christ.

7 But I am keeping this jewel [e] in an earthen jar, to prove that its surpassing power [f] is God's, not mine. 8 On every side I am ever hard-pressed, but never hemmed in; always perplexed, but never to the point of despair; 9 always being persecuted, but not deserted; always getting a knockdown, but never a knockout; [g] 10 always being exposed to death as Jesus was, so that in my body the life of Jesus may be clearly shown. 11 For all the time I continue to live I am being given up to death for Jesus' sake, so that in my mortal lower nature the life of Jesus may be clearly shown. 12 So it is death that works in me, but it is life that works in you.

13 Now since I have the same spirit of faith as he who said in the Scriptures, "I believed, and so I spoke," I too believe, and so I speak, 14 because I know that He who raised the Lord Jesus from the dead will raise me too in fellowship with you. 15 For everything is for your sakes, in order that His favor by multiplying the thanksgiving of many may make the cup run over to the praise of God.

16 So I never give up; instead, although my outer nature [h] is wasting away, my inner nature is constantly renewed from day to day. 17 For this slight and momentary sorrow continues to accumulate for me a solid and eternal glory far beyond any comparison,

[b] Grk., *hidden things of disgrace.*
[c] Lit., *by manifestation of the truth.*
[d] Implied.
[e] Lit., *treasure*—the ministry of the good news.
[f] Lit., *that the superiority of,* etc.
[g] Lit., *never destroyed.*
[h] Grk., *outer man.*

¹⁸ because I do not keep my eyes on things that are seen but things that are unseen. For things that are seen are temporary, but things that are unseen are eternal.

5   ON LEAVING HIS PHYSICAL BODY, PAUL HOPES TO MOVE INTO A SPIRITUAL BODY, TO BE THE HOME OF HIS SPIRIT FOREVER; IS INSPIRED BY FEAR, BUT ESPECIALLY BY LOVE, TO LIVE THE HIGHER LIFE OF SERVICE

For I know that if this earthly tent ᵃ in which I live is taken down, I have a building in heaven which comes from God, a house not built by human ᵇ hands but eternal. ² For in this one I am sighing, because I long to put on, like a robe, my heavenly body,ᵇ my future home, ³ and if I do put it on, I shall not find myself to be disembodied.ᶜ ⁴ For I who am still in my tent am sighing beneath my burdens, because I do not want it to be put off but to put on the other over it, so that my dying body ᵇ may be absorbed in life.ᵈ ⁵ Now it is God Himself who has put the finishing touches on me for this change,ᵇ because He has given me the Spirit as the first installment of future bliss.ᵇ

⁶ So I am always cheerful and confident,ᵉ although I know that as long as I am at home in the body I am away from home and the Lord ⁷ (for here I live by what I believe and not by what I see), ⁸ and yet I am cheerful and confident, but really I prefer to be away from home in the body and to be at home with the Lord. ⁹ So whether I am at home or away from home, it is my constant ambition to please Him. ¹⁰ For we must all appear before the judgment-bar of Christ, that each may get his pay for what he has done, whether it be good or bad.

¹¹ So, since I know what the fear of God can do,ᵇ I am trying to win ᶠ men. My inner self is perfectly known to God, and I hope, to your consciences too. ¹² I am not trying to recommend myself to you again. I am giving you ground for speaking well of me, that you may have something to say ᵇ to those who are constantly

    ᵃ His physical body compared with a tent because temporary.
    ᵇ Implied.
    ᶜ Lit., *naked;* word so used by classical writers; referring to disembodied spirits.
    ᵈ Grk., *swallowed up by life.*
    ᵉ Both ideas in one vb.
    ᶠ *Trying to persuade men.*

prating about external privileges and not concerned* about the state* of the heart.g 13 For if I did go crazy,h it was for God's glory;* and if I am keeping my head cool, it is for your good.*
14 For the love of Christ continuously constrains me, because I am convinced that as One died for all, all have died, 15 and He died for all, that those who live might live no longer for themselves, but for Him who died for them and rose again.

16 So from this moment on, I do not estimate anybody by the standard of outward appearances. Although I once did estimate Christ by this standard, I do not do so any longer. 17 For if anybody is in union with Christ, he is the work* of a new creation; the old condition i has passed away, a new condition has come. 18 This has all originated with God, for* He through Christ has reconciled me to Himself and has given me the ministry of reconciliation. 19 For it was through Christ that God was reconciling the world to Himself instead of debiting j men's offenses against them, and He has committed to me the message of this reconciliation.

20 So I am an envoy to represent Christ, because it is through me that God is making His appeal. As one representing Christ I beg you, be reconciled to God. 21 He made Him who personally knew nothing of sin to be a sin-offering k for us, so that through union with Him we might come into right standing with God.

6 AS CHRIST'S ENVOY, PAUL PLEADS WITH THEM TO REALIZE THIS RECONCILIATION; GIVES HIS CREDENTIALS AND AFFECTION; WARNS THEM NOT TO WALK WITH UNBELIEVERS

As God's fellow-worker I beg you too not to accept God's favor and throw it away. 2 For He says:

"At a welcome time I have listened to you,
And on a day of salvation I have helped you." a

Right now the time of welcome is here; right now it is the day of salvation. 3 To keep my ministry from being found fault with, I

g Lit., *boasting of the face and not of the heart.*
h A charge made by opponents.
i *The old things.*
j Accounting term.
k So used in O. T. Grk.
a Isa. 49:8.
* Implied.

am trying not to put a single [b] hindrance in anybody's way. [4] On the contrary, I am trying in everything to prove to people that I am a true servant of God: by my tremendous [c] endurance in sorrows, distresses, difficulties; [5] in floggings, imprisonments, riots, labors, sleepless nights, and hunger; [6] through my personal purity, my knowledge, my patience, my kindness; through the Holy Spirit, my genuine love, [7] my message of truth, and the power of God; with the weapons of right-doing in my right hand and my left; [8] in honor or dishonor, in slander or praise; considered a deceiver and yet true, [9] obscure and yet well-known, on the point of dying and yet I go on living, punished and yet not put to death, [10] sad but always glad, poor but making many people rich, penniless but really possessing everything.[d]

[11] O Corinthians, my tongue is telling you everything; [e] my heart is stretched [f] with love for you. [12] You are not squeezed into a tiny corner in my heart, but you are in your own affections. [13] To pay me back, I tell you, my children, you too must stretch your hearts with love for me.

[14] Stop forming intimate and inconsistent [g] relations with unbelievers. What partnership can right-doing have with law-breaking, or how can light participate with darkness? [15] What harmony exists between Christ and Belial, or what is common between a believer and an unbeliever? [16] And what agreement can a temple of God make with idols? For we are the temple of the living God, just as God said:

"I will live in them and walk in them,
And I will be their God and they will be my people." [h]

[17] Therefore:

"'Come out of company with them,
And separate from them,' the Lord has said,
'And stop touching what is unclean;
Then I will welcome you,
[18] I will be a Father to you,

---

[b] Strong neg. in Grk.
[c] Lit., *great*.
[d] One of the finest sentences in all literature on one's defense.
[e] Grk., *my mouth is open to you*.
[f] Lit., *my heart is broadened* (with love).
[g] First adj. in word, *yoke*; second in *heteros*.
[h] Lev. 26:12; Ezek. 37:27.

And you will be sons and daughters of mine,'
The Lord Almighty said."ⁱ

7:1 So, since we have such promises as these, dearly beloved, let us cleanse ourselves from everything that defiles our bodies and spirits, and in reverence to God carry on our consecration to completeness.ʲ

7 CONTINUES TO TELL OF HIS LOVE FOR THE CORINTHIANS; TITUS REPORTS TRUE REPENTANCE AT CORINTH; PAUL'S HOPE REALIZED, AND HIS CUP OF JOY RUNS OVER

² Make room for me in your hearts.ᵃ I have not wronged or harmed or taken advantage of a single one of you. ³ I do not mean this for your condemnation, because, as I have said before, you have such a place in my heart that I would live with you or die with you. ⁴ I have the greatest confidence in you; I speak most highly of you. I am fully comforted; in the face of all my sorrow my cup is running over with joy.

⁵ For even after I had gotten to Macedonia, my frail, human nature ᵇ could find ᶜ no relief; I was crushed with sorrow at every turn—fightings without and fears within. ⁶ But God, who comforts the downhearted, comforted me by the coming of Titus, ⁷ and not only by his coming but by the comfort he had gotten from you, because he kept on telling me how you were longing to see me, how sorry you were, and how loyal ᵈ you were to me, so that I was gladder still.

⁸ For, although I did cause you sorrow by that letter, I do not now regret it; although I did regret it then. I see that the letter caused you sorrow only for a time. ⁹ I am glad of it now, not because you had such sorrow, but because your sorrow led you to repentance, for you took your sorrow in accordance with the will ᵉ of God, so that you should not suffer any loss at all from me. ¹⁰ For the sorrow that comes in accordance with the will of God results

---

ⁱ Isa. 52:11; Hos. 1:10; Isa. 43:6.
ʲ Really belongs to chap. 6.
ᵃ Implied.
ᵇ Lit., *my flesh.*
ᶜ Grk., *had.*
ᵈ Lit., *your zeal for me.*
ᵉ Grk., *according to God.*

in repentance that leads* to salvation and leaves no regrets; but the sorrow the world f produces results in death. 11 For see what this very sorrow, suffered in accordance with the will of God, has done for you! How earnest g it has made you, how concerned to clear yourselves, how indignant, how alarmed, how much it made you long to see me, how loyal h to me, how determined to punish the offender!* At every point you have cleared yourselves in the matter. 12 So, although I did write to you, it was not for the offender's sake, nor for the offended party's sake, but in the sight of God for the sake of having your enthusiasm for me made perfectly clear to you. This is why I am so comforted.

13 In addition to my own comfort, I was made so glad that my cup ran over at the gladness Titus felt, because his spirit has been set at rest by you. 14 Indeed, if I have been doing some boasting of you to him, I have never been ashamed of it; but just as all I said to him was true, so now my boasting before Titus has been shown to be true.i 15 Yes, his heart is running over toward you, as he continues recalling how you all obeyed him, with what reverence and trembling you welcomed him. 16 I am glad that I have perfect confidence in you now.

8 EXAMPLES OF GENEROUS GIVING; CHURCHES IN MACEDONIA GIVE BEYOND THEIR ABILITY; JESUS GAVE HIMSELF, SO DID THEY; TITUS AND ANOTHER ROUND UP THE CONTRIBUTION

Now I am going to tell you, brothers, of God's spiritual blessing which was given in the churches of Macedonia, 2 because in spite of a terrible test of trouble, the mighty flood a of their gladness mingling with the depths of their poverty b has overflowed and resulted in the abundance of their liberality. 3 For they have given,c I can testify, to the utmost* of their ability, and even beyond their ability. Of their own accord, 4 with earnest entreaty, they kept on begging me for the favor of sharing in this service that is being rendered * to God's people. 5 They did not do as I

---

f Subj. gen.
g Lit., *how great your earnestness.*
h Lit., *your zeal for me.*
i Grk., *became in truth.*
a Grk., *overflow.*
b Lit., *and their deep poverty.*
c To be supplied from context.
* Implied.

expected but even more; ᵈ they first by God's will gave themselves to the Lord, and then to me; ⁶ so that I insisted that Titus, as he had formerly commenced it, should bring to completion this gracious contribution among you too. ⁷ Yes, just as you are growing rich ᵉ in everything else, in faith, expression, knowledge, perfect enthusiasm, and the love inspired in you by us, you must see to it ᵈ that you grow rich in this gracious contribution too.

⁸ I am not saying this in the spirit of a command, but I am simply trying to test the genuineness of your love by the enthusiasm of others. ⁹ For by experience you know the unmerited favor shown by our Lord Jesus Christ; ᶠ that although He was rich, yet for your sakes He became poor, in order that by His poverty you might become rich. ¹⁰ Now I will give you my opinion on this matter. For this is for your interest, because you were not only the first ᵍ to do anything about it, but the first to want to do so; you started it a year ago. ¹¹ Now finish doing it too, so that your readiness to finish it may be just like your readiness to start it, in accordance with what you have. ¹² If a man is ready and willing to give, his gift is acceptable in accordance with what he has, not with what he does not have. ¹³ For I do not want ᵈ it to be a relief for others and a burden on you, ¹⁴ but through an equalizing of matters in the present crisis I do want your abundance to relieve ʰ their need, that some day their abundance may relieve your need, so that equality may exist—¹⁵ just as the Scripture says, "The man who gathered ᵈ much did not have too much, and the man who gathered little did not have too little." ⁱ

¹⁶ But thanks be to God, who kindles in the heart of Titus the same enthusiasm for you that I have; ¹⁷ because he has acceded to my request, or rather,ᵈ because he is so enthusiastic for you, of his own accord he is off to visit you. ¹⁸ I am sending with him the well-known ʲ brother whose praise for spreading the good news is ringing ᵈ through all the churches. ¹⁹ Not only that, but he has been selected by the churches to travel with me for this gracious contribution which is being raised by me, so that it may turn out

---
ᵈ Implied.
ᵉ Grk., *abounding, overflowing*.
ᶠ Subj. gen.
ᵍ In prep. *pro*.
ʰ Lit., *become for*.
ⁱ Ex. 16:18.
ʲ In the art. and context.

for the glory of the Lord and a proof* of my readiness to serve.*
²⁰ I am arranging it so that no one can blame me in the matter of this munificent fund that is being handled by me. ²¹ For I am taking the precaution to do what is right, not only in the sight of the Lord but also in the eyes of men. ²² I send with them another brother of ours, whom I have often in many ways tested and found to be enthusiastic, but now he is more enthusiastic than ever, because of his great confidence in you.

²³ As for Titus, he is my partner and comrade in the work for you, while these brothers of ours, the representatives of the churches, will bring glory to Christ. ²⁴ So you must furnish them, before all the churches, proof of your love and ground for my praising you so highly.

9 THE CONTRIBUTION TO BE READY WHEN PAUL ARRIVES; THE WAY TO GIVE; GRACIOUS BLESSINGS ON GENEROUS GIVING

It is really superfluous for me to write to you about this service which is being rendered to God's people, ² for I know your readiness to help* in it. I am boasting of you about it to the Macedonians, reminding* them that Greece has been ready since last year, and your enthusiasm has stimulated the most of them. ³ But I send the brothers that in this matter my boasting of you may not turn out to be an idle boasting, that you all may be ready, as I have told them you will be, ⁴ to keep me—not to mention you—from being humiliated for having such confidence in you, if some Macedonians come with me and find that you are not ready. ⁵ So I have thought it necessary to urge these brothers to visit you ahead of me and get your promised love-offering ᵃ ready beforehand, so as to have it ready as a real love-offering, not as one grasped and grudgingly given.ᵇ

⁶ Now this is the way it is: Whoever sows sparingly will reap sparingly too, but whoever sows bountifully ᶜ will reap bountifully too. ⁷ Each must give what he has purposed in his heart to give, not sorrowfully or under compulsion, for it is the happy giver that God loves. ⁸ And God is able to make your every spiritual blessing

* Implied.
ᵃ Lit., *blessing*, emphasizing the motive of love.
ᵇ Grk., *grasping for more;* here money gripped and grudgingly given.
ᶜ Lit., *for blessing.*

overflow for you, so that you will always have in every situation an entire sufficiency and so overflow for every good cause; [d] [9] as the Scripture says:

> "He has generously given to the poor,
> His deeds of charity go on forever." [e]

[10] He who always supplies the sower with seed and the eater with bread will supply you with seed and multiply it and enlarge the harvest which your deeds of charity yield. [11] In every way you will grow richer and richer so as to give with perfect liberality, which will through me result in thanksgiving to God for it. [12] Because the service rendered by this sacred offering [f] is not only fully supplying the needs of God's people, but it is also running over with many thanks to God for it. [13] For through the test you get by doing [*] this service you will continue praising God for your fidelity to your confession of the good news of Christ, and for the liberality of your contributions to them and all others; [*] [14] and so in their prayers for you they will continue longing for you, because of God's surpassing favor shown you. [15] Thank God for His unspeakable gift!

10 PAUL PROVES THAT HE IS AN APOSTLE; ANSWERS CHARGES AGAINST HIS PERSONAL APPEARANCE AND SPEECH; CORINTH BELONGS TO HIS APOSTOLIC COMMISSION

Now I appeal to you in person, by the gentleness and fairness of Christ, I, Paul, who am so "condescending when face to face with you, but so courageous toward you when far away!" [a] [2] I beg you not to make me too courageous in that confidence in which I think to take a daring stand against some people who try to think that I am acting from the lowest human motives.[b] [3] For though I do still live the life of a physical human creature, I am not waging this war in accordance with physical human standards,[c] [4] for the weapons used in my warfare are not mere human [d] ones, but

---

[d] Grk., *every good work.*
[e] Ps. 112:9.
[f] Lit., *priestly, official* (so sacred) *service.*
[a] Their actual charge vs. him.
[b] Lit., *according to the flesh,* man's lower nature.
[c] In the prep. *kata.*
[d] Grk., *fleshly.*
[*] Implied.

through my God are mighty for demolishing fortresses. ⁵ For I am demolishing arguments and every barrier that is raised against the genuine ᵉ knowledge of God, taking captive every thought to make it obedient to Christ, ⁶ and am prepared to punish any disobedience, when your obedience is made complete.

⁷ You look at me ᶠ and measure ᶠ me by outward appearances. If anyone is confident in himself that he belongs to Christ, let him have another thought about himself, that just as he belongs to Christ, so do I. ⁸ For if I do boast a little too much about my authority, which the Lord gave me for building you up and not for tearing you down, I shall never have to blush for doing so. ⁹ I do not want to seem to be frightening you with my letters. ¹⁰ For they say, "His letters are impressive ᵍ and forceful, but his physical personality is unimpressive, and his delivery is perfectly contemptible." ʰ ¹¹ Such people should consider this: When I arrive for action I shall do exactly what I said I would in my letters when far away.

¹² Indeed, I do not dare to count or compare myself with certain men who are always recommending themselves. ¹³ But they do not show good sense, because they do continue measuring themselves with one another and comparing themselves with one another. ¹⁴ But I shall never go too far in my boasting; no, I shall stay within the limits of the sphere ⁱ which God apportioned me, so as to reach even you. For I am not overstepping my authority,ʲ as though I should not reach you, for I was the very first to reach as far as you with the good news of Christ. ¹⁵ I am not going too far in my boasting, and actually boasting of other men's labors, but I am cherishing the hope that your faith may so continue to grow that through you my work within my sphere may be so enlarged as to run over,ᵏ ¹⁶ so that I can preach the good news in the regions beyond you, without boasting in another man's sphere of work already done by him. ¹⁷ "But the man who boasts must boast in the Lord." ¹ ¹⁸ For it is not the man who keeps on recommending himself who is really approved, but it is the man whom the Lord recommends.

  ᵉ Which is experimental knowledge.
  ᶠ Implied.
  ᵍ So Abbott-Smith, Lex.
  ʰ Lit., *is weak and his speech is,* etc.
  ⁱ Grk., *boast within the limits of the sphere,* etc.
  ʲ Lit., *overreach myself.*
  ᵏ Lit., *that I may be enlarged so as to run over.*
  ¹ Jer. 9:24.

11

LOVE MOVES PAUL TO DEFEND HIS AUTHORITY; TELLS WHY HE GIVES UP HIS RIGHT TO SUPPORT; CALLS HIS CRITICS SHAM APOSTLES; IRONICALLY DEFENDS HIS SANITY; CLAIMS HIS SUFFERINGS ARE HIS CREDENTIALS TO APOSTLESHIP

I wish you would now listen [a] to a little folly of mine. Please do listen to me! 2 For I feel a divine jealousy for you, as [b] I betrothed you to Christ, to present you as a pure bride to her one husband. 3 But I am apprehensive that, somehow or other, as the serpent by his cunning deceived Eve, your thoughts may be turned aside [c] from single-hearted devotion to Christ. 4 For if anybody comes along and preaches another Jesus than the one I preached, or you receive another spirit different from the one you did receive or a glad message different from the one you did accept, you listen to it all right! [d] 5 For I consider myself not a single bit inferior to those surpassingly superior apostles of yours! [e] 6 Although I am untrained as an orator,[f] yet I am not so in the field of knowledge. Surely, I have always made that perfectly clear to you.

7 Did I do wrong in taking a lowly place to let you have an exalted one, in that I preached the good news about God to you without accepting any pay? 8 I sponged [g] on other churches by taking pay from them to render service to you, 9 and when I was with you and needed money, I never burdened a single one of you for a cent, for the brothers came from Macedonia and supplied what I needed. And so I kept myself, as I shall always do, from being a burden to you in any way. 10 By the truth of Christ in me,[h] this boasting of mine shall never be stopped in the boundaries of Greece. 11 Why? Because I do not love you? God knows I do.

12 And I shall keep on doing as I am, in order to cut the ground from under the feet of those who want an opportunity to show themselves on a level with me in the matters of which they boast.

[a] Lit., *bear,* here *listen* (Abbott-Smith).
[b] Grk., *for.*
[c] Lit., *corrupted.*
[d] Lit., *beautifully, finely*—in sarcasm and irony.
[e] Cutting sarcasm.
[f] Grk., *a private in speech.*
[g] Exact meaning of Grk. vb., *taking money without working for it.*
[h] Lit., *the truth of Christ is in me that,* etc.

¹³ For such men are sham ⁱ apostles, dishonest workmen, masquerading as apostles of Christ. ¹⁴ And no wonder, for even Satan himself masquerades as an angel of light. ¹⁵ So it is no surprise if his servants also masquerade as ministers for doing right, whose doom shall be in accordance with what they do.

¹⁶ Let me say again that no one must think that I am a fool; but if you do, please treat me like a fool and let me do a little boasting too, as other fools do. ¹⁷ But when I talk in this boastful confidence, I am not talking in accordance with the way the Lord talked,ʲ but just as a fool talks. ¹⁸ Since many boast in accordance with their human nature, I will do it too. ¹⁹ For you who are so wise yourselves are glad to listen to fools! ᵏ ²⁰ For you listen to a man, if he makes you his slave, or spends your money for his living, or cheats you, or puts on airs, or slaps you in the face.

²¹ I am ashamed to say that I was, as it were, so weak in the matter.ˡ And yet in whatever respect anyone else is daring to boast—ˡ I am talking like a fool—I too will dare to boast. ²² Are they Hebrews? So am I. Are they Israelites? So am I. Are they descendants of Abraham? So am I. ²³ Are they ministers of Christ? So am I. I am talking like a man that has gone crazy—as suchˡ I am superior!—serving Himˡ with labors greater by far, with far more imprisonments, with floggings vastly worse, and often at the point of death. ²⁴ Five times I have taken thirty-nine lashes from the Jews, ²⁵ three times I have been beaten by the Romans, once I was pelted with stones; three times I have been shipwrecked, and once I have spent a day and a night adrift at sea. ²⁶ I have served Himˡ on frequent journeys, in dangers from rivers, dangers from robbers, dangers from my own people, dangers from the heathen, dangers in the city, dangers in the desert, dangers at sea, dangers from false brothers, ²⁷ through toil and hardship, through many a sleepless night, through hunger and thirst, through many a fasting season, poorly clad and exposed to cold. ²⁸ Besides all other things, there is my concern for all the churches. ²⁹ Who is weak without my being weak too? Who is caused to fall without my being fired with indignation? ³⁰ If I must boast, I will boast of the things that showˡ my weakness! ³¹ The God and Father

---

ⁱ Grk., *false.*
ʲ I.e., not in humility as Jesus did.
ᵏ Lit., *gladly listen to fools*—keenest sarcasm; even more sarcastic in next sentence.
ˡ Implied from context.

of the Lord Jesus,[m] who is blessed forever, knows that I am telling the truth.[n] 32 At Damascus the governor under King Aretas kept guards watching the city gates to capture me, 33 but through a hole in the wall I was lowered in a basket, and so escaped from his clutches.

12 — THOUGH PAUL'S VISIONS ARE SUBLIME, HIS SUFFERINGS ARE MORE VALUABLE AS CREDENTIALS; HE HAS GIVEN THE REAL SIGNS OF A TRUE APOSTLE; ASSERTS HIS MOTIVES ARE UNSELFISH, YET UNEASY AS TO EXPECTED VISIT

I have to keep on boasting. There is no good to be gotten from it, but I will go on to visions and revelations which the Lord has given me. 2 I know a man in union with Christ fourteen years ago—whether in the body or out of it, I do not know, but God knows—who was caught up to the third heaven. 3 Yes, I know that this man—whether in or out of the body, I do not know, but God knows—4 was actually[a] caught up into paradise, and heard things that must not be told, which no man has a right even to mention.[b] 5 On behalf of this man with such an experience[c] I will boast, but on behalf of myself personally I will boast only about my weaknesses. 6 However, if I want to boast, I will not play the fool, for it will be nothing but the truth that I will tell. But I refrain from doing so, to keep anybody, on account of[d] the superiority of the revelations, from giving me a higher rating than my actions and teachings deserve.[e] 7 So, to keep me from being overelated, there was sent upon me a physical disease, sharp as a piercing stake,[f] a messenger of Satan, to continue afflicting me, and so to keep me, I repeat, from being overelated. 8 Three times I begged the Lord about this to make it go away and leave me, 9 but He said to me, "My spiritual strength[g] is sufficient, for it is only by means of conscious weakness that perfect power is developed."[h]

[m] Fol. two best Mss.
[n] Lit., *I do not lie.*
[a] In aor. (historical).
[b] In aor. infin.
[c] Implied in context.
[d] Causal instr.
[e] Lit., *think of me above what you see and hear.*
[f] Grk., *a sharp stake in the flesh,* so *phys. disease.*
[g] Lit., *favor, grace.*
[h] Lit., *in weakness power is made pf.*

¹⁰ So I most happily boast about my weaknesses, so that the strength of Christ may overshadow me. That is why I take such pleasure in weaknesses, insults, distresses, persecution, and difficulties, which I endure* for Christ's sake, for it is when I am consciously weak that I am really strong.

¹¹ I have made a fool of myself, but you have forced me to do it, for I am the man[i] who ought to have been constantly approved by you. For I am not a single bit inferior to your surpassingly superior apostles, though really I am "nobody."[j] ¹² The marks that signify the genuine apostle were exhibited among you in my perfect patience, in signs, wonders, and wonder-works. ¹³ In what respect, then, were you inferior to the rest of the churches, except for the fact that I, and I only, never received from you any financial support? Please forgive me this wrong.[k]

¹⁴ It is now the third time that I have been ready to come to see you, and I will never ask you for financial support, for it is not your money but you yourselves that I want; for children are not by duty bound to lay up money for their parents, but parents for their children. ¹⁵ So in my own case,[l] I will most happily spend my money and myself for your sakes.[m] If I love you much more than I love others,* am I to be loved less by you? ¹⁶ But let it be granted,* you say,* that I never received from you financial support, yet, you say, by being a trickster I cheated you by my cunning. ¹⁷ I did not make any money out of you through anybody that I sent to you, did I? ¹⁸ I actually begged Titus to go, and sent the well-known brother with him. Titus did not make any money out of you, did he? Did not he and I act in the same spirit, and take the very same steps?

¹⁹ Are you thinking all this time that I am defending myself to you? It is in the very presence of God and as one who is in union with Christ that I am speaking. And it is all for building you up, beloved, for I am apprehensive that, somehow or other, when I come I shall find you not as I want to find you, and that you may find me not as you want to find me. ²⁰ I repeat it, I am apprehensive that, somehow or other, there may be quarreling, jealousy, anger, rivalries, slanders, gossiping, haughty pride, and disorders,

---

[i] Doubly emph. pro.
[j] What his foes called him.
[k] Impv. of entreaty, but sarcastic too.
[l] Emph. pro.
[m] Lit., *I will spend my own and be spent myself*; hence tr.
* Implied.

[21] and that when I come back my God may humiliate me before you, and I may have to mourn over some of those who formerly [a] have committed shocking sins, and have not repented for them—their impurity, sexual immorality, and sensuality, which once they practiced.

13   HE ASKS THAT OFFENDERS BE EXAMINED AND, IF GUILTY, PUNISHED; GIVES HIS FAREWELL WARNINGS; SENDS GREETINGS

This is my third visit to you. Any charge preferred must be sustained by the evidence [a] of two or three witnesses. [2] I have already warned those who formerly committed shocking sins,[b] and all the rest, and though so far away I warn them now, as I did on my second visit, that if I come back I will not spare them, [3] since you demand a proof that Christ is speaking through me. For Christ [c] is not exhibiting weakness toward you but power in you. [4] For though He was crucified in weakness, yet by the power of God He goes on living. We too, indeed, show weakness through our union with Him, yet by the power of God we too shall be alive toward you through fellowship with Him. [5] You yourselves must continue testing yourselves to see whether you are continuing in the faith. You must continue standing [d] the test. Do you not know by a growing experience [e] that Jesus Christ is in you?—provided you stand the test.

[6] Now I hope that you will learn that I am standing the test. [7] But I am praying God that you may never do anything wrong, not to show that I am standing the test, but that you should continue doing right, though [f] I should fail to stand the test. [8] For I cannot do anything against the truth, but only for it. [9] I am glad to be consciously weak, if you are really strong. This is my continual prayer, the perfecting of your characters.[g] [10] This is why I am writing this while far away from you, that when I do come, I may not have to deal harshly with you in accordance with the authority which the Lord has given me, for building you up, not for tearing you down.

[a] Lit., *any word at the mouth of . . . must stand.*
[b] Grk., *who sinned formerly,* referring to notorious offenders.
[c] Causal relative referring to Christ.
[d] Stronger word; *stand test.*
[e] In comp. vb.
[f] Implied.
[g] Lit., *yourselves.*

¹¹ Finally, brothers, good-by! Practice the perfecting of your characters, keep listening to my appeals,ʰ continue thinking in harmony and living in peace, and the loving, peace-giving God will be with you. ¹² Greet one another with a sacred kiss. ¹³ All God's people wish to be remembered to you.

¹⁴ The spiritual blessing of the Lord Jesus Christ, the love of God, and the common sharing of the Holy Spirit be with you all.

ʰ Grk., *continue being exhorted.*

GALATIANS

The writer is Paul the apostle. While he was on his second missionary journey, the Judaizers went to Galatia and told the Christians there that Paul was not an apostle and that his message of salvation by trusting Christ was not from God but from men; that it was necessary to be circumcised and keep the law of Moses in order to be saved. When Paul reached Antioch in Syria, he heard of these charges, and this destructive propaganda against him and his work in Galatia. So he wrote this letter about A.D. 54 or 55.

His purpose was to counteract the baneful influence of these false teachers; to defend himself as a divinely appointed apostle; to set forth his elemental message, right standing with God by trusting in Christ, not by circumcision and obedience to the law, to show that this teaching means finer moral living and the bearing of fruit to the Spirit. The letter is characterized by its unity of theme, its merciless severity, its vehement language, and its logical discussion. Although his heart is stirred to its depths, his head keeps cool.

1 IN GREETING THEM HE TELLS OF HIS COMMISSION FROM THE LORD; PROVES THAT HIS APOSTLESHIP AND MESSAGE ARE FROM CHRIST THE LORD; IS ASTONISHED THAT THEY ARE TURNING FROM THIS MESSAGE

Paul, an apostle sent not from men nor by any man, but by Jesus Christ and God the Father who raised Him from the dead— 2 and all the brothers who are here with me—to the churches of Galatia: 3 spiritual blessing and peace to you from God the Father and the Lord Jesus Christ, 4 who gave Himself for our sins, to save us from the present wicked world in accordance with the will of our God and Father; 5 to Him be glory forever and ever. Amen.

6 I am astonished that you are beginning [a] so soon to turn away from Him who called you by the favor of Christ, to a different [b] good news, 7 which is not really another one; only there are certain

---
[a] Incep. pres.
[b] Meaning of pro. *heteros*.

people [e] who are trying to unsettle you and want to turn the good news of Christ upside down. 8 But even if I [d] or an angel from heaven preach a good news that is contrary to the one which I have already preached to you, a curse upon him! 9 As I have said it before, so now I say it again, if anybody is preaching to you a good news that is contrary to the one which you have already received, a curse upon him!

10 Am I now trying to win men's favor, or God's? Or, am I trying to be pleasing [e] to men? If I were still trying to be pleasing to men, I would not be a slave of Christ at all. 11 For I tell you, brothers, the good news which was preached by me is not a human message, 12 for I did not get it from any man; I was not taught it, but I got it through a revelation given by Jesus Christ.[f]

13 You have heard, indeed, of my former conduct as an adherent of the Jewish religion, how I kept on furiously persecuting the church of God, and tried to destroy it, 14 and how I outstripped many of my own age among my people in my devotion to the Jewish religion, because I surpassed all others in my zeal for the traditions handed down by my forefathers. 15 But when God, who had already set me apart from my birth, and had called me by His unmerited favor, 16 chose to unveil [g] His Son in me, so that I might preach the good news about Him among the heathen, at once, before [h] I conferred with any human creatures, 17 and before [h] I went up to Jerusalem to see those who had been apostles before me, I retired to Arabia, and afterwards returned to Damascus.

18 Then three years later I went up to Jerusalem to get acquainted [i] with Cephas, but I spent only two weeks with him; 19 and not another single one of the apostles did I see, except James, the Lord's brother. 20 In writing you this, I swear before God, I am telling you the solemn truth. 21 After that I went into the districts of Syria and Cilicia.[j] 22 But I was personally unknown to the Christian [k] churches in Judea; 23 only they kept hearing people say, "Our former persecutor is now preaching as good news the faith which once he tried to destroy," 24 and they kept on praising God for me.

[e] The Judaizers, who said that circumcision was necessary to salvation.
[d] For editorial we.
[e] First clause, lit., *persuading men or God?*
[f] Subj. gen.
[g] *Uncover*, so *unveil*.
[h] Implied.
[i] So in late Grk. (Abbott-Smith).
[j] His native state.
[k] Lit., *churches of Judea in Christ*.

GALATIANS 2

2 HIS INTERVIEW WITH THE APOSTLES AT JERUSALEM CONFERENCE PROVES HIS POINT; PAUL LATER TEACHES PETER INSTEAD OF PETER TEACHING PAUL; AGAIN EMPHASIZES RIGHT STANDING WITH GOD BY TRUST IN CHRIST

Then, fourteen years later, I again went up to Jerusalem, with Barnabas, and took Titus with me too. ² I went up under the guidance of a divine revelation.[a] Now I laid before them the good news that I was in the habit of preaching among the heathen, but first I did so privately before the leaders, for fear that my course might be or might have been to no purpose. ³ But they did not even try to compel my companion, Titus, although he was a Greek, to be circumcised—⁴ they did not try it even for the sake of the false brothers who had been smuggled in,[b] who stole in to spy out the freedom we enjoy[c] in Christ Jesus, so as to make us slaves again.[d] ⁵ But we did not for a moment yield them submission, in order that the truth of the good news might prevail for you. ⁶ Those who were looked upon as leaders—what they were makes no difference to me—God pays no attention to outward appearances—these leaders added nothing new to me. ⁷ On the contrary, because they saw that I had been entrusted with the good news for the heathen,[e] just as Peter had been entrusted with it for the Jews—[e] ⁸ for He who had been at work in Peter for his apostleship to the Jews had been at work in me too for the apostleship to the heathen—⁹ and because they recognized the favor God had shown me,[f] James, Cephas, and John, the so-called pillar apostles, gave Barnabas and me the right hand of fellowship, with the understanding[e] that we should go to the heathen and they to the Jews. ¹⁰ Only they wanted[c] us to remember the poor, the very thing that I was eager to do.

¹¹ Now when Cephas came to Antioch, I opposed him to his face, because he stood condemned. ¹² For before the coming of certain people from James, he was in the habit of eating with heathen Christians,[c] but after they came, he began to draw back and hold aloof from them, because he was afraid of the circum-

---
[a] Lit., *in accordance with a revelation* (from God).
[b] Grk., *brought in on the side*.
[c] Implied.
[d] I.e., slaves to the legalistic system.
[e] Lit., *uncircumcision . . . circumcision* (abstract for concrete).
[f] Grk. has passive—*favor shown me* (by God).

cision party. ¹³ The rest of the Jewish Christians,ᵉ too, joined him in this pretense,ᵍ so that even Barnabas was influenced to join them in their pretense. ¹⁴ But when I saw that they were not living up to the truth of the good news, I said to Cephas, and that before them all, "If you are living like a heathen and not like a Jew, although you are a Jew yourself, why do you try to make the heathen live like Jews?"

¹⁵ We ourselves are Jews by birth and not heathen sinners,ʰ and yet, ¹⁶ because we know that a man does not come into right standing with God by doing what the law commands,ⁱ but by simple trust in Christ, we too have trusted in Christ Jesus, in order to come into right standing with God by simple trustʲ in Christ and not by doing what the law commands, because by doing what the law commands no man can come into right standing with God. ¹⁷ Now if, in our efforts to come into right standing with God through union with Christ, we have proved ʰ ourselves to be sinners like the heathen themselves, does that make Christ a partyᵏ to our sin? Of course not. ¹⁸ For if I try to build again what I tore down, I really prove myself to be a wrongdoer. ¹⁹ For through the law I myself have become dead to the law, so that I may live for God. ²⁰ I have been crucified with Christ, and I myself no longer live, but Christ is living in me; the life I now live as a mortal man I live by faith in the Son of God who loved me and gave Himself for me. ²¹ I never can nullify the unmerited favor of God. For if right standing with God could come through law, then Christ died for nothing.

3 THE READERS' EXPERIENCE PROVES THAT RIGHT STANDING WITH GOD COMES BY FAITH IN CHRIST; BELIEVERS, GENUINE SONS OF ABRAHAM; CHRIST RANSOMED US FROM THE LAW'S CURSE; LAW NOT AGAINST THE PROMISE BUT LEADS US TO CHRIST

O senseless Galatians! Who has bewitched you, before whose very eyes Jesus Christ was picturedᵃ as the crucified One? ² I

ᵍ I.e., pretending it is not right to eat with heathen.
ʰ See Rom. 1:18—2:16, where Jews and heathen are alike shown to be sinners
ⁱ Through works of law.
ʲ *Trust* is Paul's peculiar use of the word *faith*.
ᵏ Lit., *servant*.
ᵃ Lit., *placarded*.

want to ask you only this one thing: Did you receive the Spirit by doing what the law commands, or by believing the message you heard?[b] ³ Are you so senseless? Did you begin by the Spirit, but are now approaching perfection by fleshly means? ⁴ Have you suffered so much for nothing? If it really is for nothing. ⁵ Now when He supplies you with the Spirit and performs His wonderworks among you, does He do it because you do what the law commands, or because you believe the message that you heard— ⁶ just as "Abraham put his faith in God, and it was credited to him as right standing with God"?[c]

⁷ So you see, it is the men of faith who are the real descendants of Abraham. ⁸ Because the Scripture foresaw that God would bring the heathen into right standing with Himself on condition of faith, He beforehand proclaimed the good news to Abraham in the promise, "It is through you that all the heathen will be blessed."[d] ⁹ So the men of faith are blessed as partners[e] with trusting Abraham.

¹⁰ For those who depend on what the law commands are under a curse, for the Scripture says, "Cursed be everyone who does not continue in all the commands that are written in the book of the law, to do them."[f] ¹¹ Now it is evident that through the law no man is brought into right standing with God, for "The man in right standing with God will live by faith,"[g] ¹² and the law has nothing to do with faith, but it says, "It is the man who does these things that will live by doing them."[h] ¹³ Christ ransomed us from the curse of the law by becoming a curse for us—for the Scripture says, "Cursed be everyone who is hanged on a tree"—[i] ¹⁴ that the blessing promised to Abraham might through Jesus Christ come to the heathen, so that through faith we might receive the promised Spirit.[j]

¹⁵ Brothers, I am going to use a human illustration: Even a human contract, once it has been ratified, no one can annul or change. ¹⁶ Now the promises were made to Abraham and his descendant.

[b] Lit., *by faith from hearing* (the message).
[c] Gen. 15:6.
[d] Gen. 12:3.
[e] Implied in prep. *sun*.
[f] Dt. 27:26.
[g] Hab. 2:4.
[h] Lev. 18:5.
[i] Dt. 21:23.
[j] Lit., *promise of the Spirit,* which means, *the promised Spirit.*

It does not say, "and to your descendants," in the plural, but in the singular, "and to your descendant," that is, Christ. ¹⁷ I mean this: The law which was given four hundred and thirty years later could not annul the contract which had already been ratified by God, so as to cancel the promise. ¹⁸ For if our inheritance depends ᵏ on the law, it can no longer depend on the promise. But it was by promise that God so graciously bestowed it upon Abraham.

¹⁹ Then what about the law? It was added later on to increase transgressions, until the descendant¹ to whom the promise was made should come, enacted through the agency of angels in the person of an intermediary.ᵐ ²⁰ Though an intermediary implies more than one party, yet God is only one. ²¹ Is the law then contrary to God's promises? Of course not. For if a law had been given that was able to impart life, surely, then, right standing would have come through law. ²² But the Scripture pictures all mankind as prisoners of sin, so that the promised blessing through faith in Christ might be given to those who have faith.

²³ But before this faith came, we were kept locked up under the law, in preparation for the faith which was to be unveiled. ²⁴ So the law has been our attendantⁿ to lead us to Christ, so that we might through faith obtain right standing with God. ²⁵ But now that this faith has come, we are no longer in charge of the attendant. ²⁶ For all of you are sons of God through faith in Christ Jesus. ²⁷ For all of you who have been baptized into union with Christ ᵒ have clothed yourselves with Christ. ²⁸ There is no room for Jew or Greek, no room for slave or freeman, no room for male or female, for you are all one through union with Christ Jesus. ²⁹ And if you belong to Christ, then you are real descendants of Abraham, and heirs in accordance with the promise made to him.

ᵏ Vb. supplied.
¹ Christ.
ᵐ Moses.
ⁿ Usually a slave who cared for the Greek child on the way to and from the teacher.
ᵒ Symbolically, as in Rom. 6:4-6.

4 BELIEVERS IN CHRIST, GOD'S SONS; OUTWARD RITES OF NO AVAIL; THE APOSTLE ANXIOUS THOUGH CONSCIOUS OF THE READERS' FORMER AFFECTION FOR HIM; ALLEGORY OF ISHMAEL AND ISAAC ILLUSTRATES THE LAW AND THE FAITH SYSTEMS

I mean this: As long as the heir is under age he is not a whit better off than a slave, although he is heir of all the property, 2 but he is under guardians and trustees until the time fixed by the father. 3 So when we were spiritually under age, we were slaves to the world's crude notions,[a] 4 but when the proper time had come, God sent His Son, born of a woman, born subject to law, 5 to ransom those who were subject to law, so that we might be adopted as sons. 6 And because you are sons, God has sent the Spirit of His Son into your hearts, crying, "Abba," that is, "Father." 7 So you are no longer a slave, but a son; and if a son, then an heir by God's own act.[b]

8 But at that former time, as you did not know the true God, you were slaves to gods that do not really exist, 9 but now, since you have come to know God, or rather have come to be known by Him, how can you turn back to your own crude notions, so weak and worthless, and wish to become slaves to them again? 10 You are observing days, months, seasons, years. 11 I am beginning to fear that I have bestowed my labors on you for nothing.

12 I beg you, brothers, take my point of view, just as I took yours.[c] You did me no injustice then. 13 And yet you know that it was because of an illness [d] of mine that I preached the good news to you the first time, 14 but still you did not scorn the test my illness made of you, nor did you spurn me for it; on the contrary, you welcomed me as an angel of God, as Christ Jesus Himself. 15 Where is your self-congratulation? [e] For I can testify that you would have torn out your very eyes, if you could, and have given them to me. 16 Have I then turned into an enemy to you, because I tell you the truth?

17 These men [f] are paying you special attention, but not sincerely.

[a] Legalism and ritualism as means of being saved.
[b] Lit., *through God.*
[c] Grk., *become,* etc.; i.e., take the view that faith in Christ is the only condition of coming into right standing with God.
[d] Lit., *weakness in the flesh.*
[e] For having the honor of welcoming Paul as a missionary of God.
[f] The Judaizing teachers.

They want to shut you off from me, so that you may keep on paying them special attention. ¹⁸ Now it is a fine thing to have special attention paid you, if it is done sincerely and unceasingly, and not only when I am with you. ¹⁹ O my dear children, I am suffering a mother's birth pangs for you again, until Christ is formed in you.[g] ²⁰ I wish I could be with you right now and change the tone of my speech, for I do not know which way to turn in your case.

²¹ Tell me, you who want to be subject to law, will you not listen to what the law says? ²² For the Scripture says that Abraham had two sons, one by a slave-girl, the other by a free woman. ²³ But the child of the slave-girl was born in the ordinary course of nature, while the child of the free woman was born to fulfill the promise.[h] ²⁴ This is spoken as an allegory. For these women are two covenants, one coming from Mount Sinai, bearing children that are to be slaves; ²⁵ that is, Hagar (and Hagar means Mount Sinai, in Arabia) and corresponds to the present Jerusalem, for Jerusalem is in slavery with her children. ²⁶ But the Jerusalem that is above is free, and she is our mother. ²⁷ For the Scripture says: [i]

> "Rejoice, you childless woman, who never bore a child;
> Break forth into shouting, you who feel no birth pangs;
> For the desolate woman has many children,
> Even more than the married one."

²⁸ Now we, brothers,[j] like Isaac, are children born to fulfill the promise. ²⁹ But just as then the child born in the ordinary course of nature persecuted the one born by the power of the Spirit, so it is today. ³⁰ But what does the Scripture say? "Drive off the slave-girl and her son, for the slave-girl's son shall never share the inheritance with the son of the free woman."[k] ³¹ So, brothers, we are children, not of a slave-girl but of a free woman.

[g] In metaphorical sense; not a second spiritual birth.
[h] Lit., *through a promise.*
[i] Isa. 54:1.
[j] Paul, Galatians, and all Christians.
[k] Gen. 21:10.

5 THE LEGAL WAY SHUTS OUT THE FAITH WAY; THE APOSTLE'S PROTEST; LOVE, THE LAW OF THOSE NOT SUBJECT TO THE LAW; THE STRUGGLE BETWEEN THE LOWER NATURE AND THE SPIRIT OF GOD

This is the freedom with which Christ has made us free. So keep on standing in it, and stop letting your necks be fastened in the yoke of slavery again.

² Here is what I am saying to you: If you let yourselves be circumcised, Christ can do you no good. ³ I again insist that if any man lets himself be circumcised, he is under obligation to obey the whole law. ⁴ You people, whoever you are among you, who try to get into right standing with God through law have cut yourselves off from Christ, you have missed the way of God's favor.[a] ⁵ For we, by the Spirit, are awaiting the hoped-for [b] blessing which our right standing [c] with God will bring us. ⁶ For in union with Christ Jesus neither circumcision nor the lack of it counts for anything; but only faith that is spurred on to action by love.

⁷ You were running beautifully! Who was it that cut [d] into your way and kept you from obeying the truth? ⁸ Such persuasion [e] never came from Him who called you. ⁹ A little yeast will transform the whole dough. ¹⁰ By our union with the Lord I have confidence in you that you will take no other view of the matter. The man who is unsettling you will certainly pay the penalty for it, no matter who it turns out to be. ¹¹ As for me, myself, brothers, if I am still preaching circumcision,[f] why am I still being persecuted? In such a case the hindrance done by the cross has presumably ceased! [g] ¹² I almost wish [h] that these men who are upsetting you would go all the way, and have themselves mutilated.

¹³ For you, brothers, were called to freedom; only you must not let your freedom be an excuse for the gratification of your lower nature, but in love be slaves to one another. ¹⁴ For the whole law is summed up in one saying, "You must love your neighbor as

---

[a] Lit., *fallen out of the grace* (way).
[b] Grk. has, *the hope*.
[c] Subj. gen.
[d] Military term; lit. meaning above.
[e] That by the Judaizers for circumcision.
[f] Paul circumcised Timothy: so they accused him as above.
[g] Irony, sarcasm.
[h] "Impossible wish" (Robertson).

you do yourself." ⁱ ¹⁵ But if you continue to bite and eat one another, beware lest you are destroyed by one another.

¹⁶ I mean this: Practice living by the Spirit and then by no means will you gratify the cravings of your lower nature. ¹⁷ For the cravings of the lower nature are just the opposite to those of the Spirit, and the cravings of the Spirit are just the opposite of those of the lower nature; these two are opposed to each other, so that you cannot do anything you please. ¹⁸ But if you are guided by the Spirit, you are not subject to the law. ¹⁹ Now the practices of the lower nature are clear enough: Sexual immorality, impurity, sensuality, ²⁰ idolatry, sorcery, enmity, quarreling, jealousy, anger, intrigues, dissensions, party-spirit, ²¹ envy, drunkenness, carousing, and the like. I now warn you, as I have done before, that those who practice such things shall not be heirs of the kingdom of God. ²² But the product ʲ of the Spirit is love, joy, peace, patience, kindness, goodness, faithfulness, ²³ gentleness, self-control. There is no law against such things. ²⁴ And those who belong to Jesus the Christ have crucified the lower nature with its passions and evil cravings.

²⁵ If we live by the Spirit, let us also walk where the Spirit leads.ᵏ ²⁶ Let us stop being ambitious for honors, so challenging one another, envying one another.

6 SYMPATHY TO BE SHOWN THE FALLING CHRISTIAN; WE REAP WHAT WE SOW; WRITER'S OWN HANDWRITING; BOASTS IN THE CROSS ALONE; SAYS GOOD-BY

Brothers, if anybody is caught ᵃ in the very act of doing wrong, you who are spiritual, in the spirit of gentleness, must set him right; each ᵇ of you continuing to think of yourself, for you may be tempted too. ² Practice bearing one another's burdens, and in this way carry out the law of Christ. ³ For if anybody thinks he is somebody when really he is nobody, he deceives himself. ⁴ Everyone should test his own work until it stands the test, and then he will have ground for boasting with reference to himself alone, and not with reference to someone else. ⁵ For everyone must carry his own load.ᶜ

ⁱ Lev. 19:18.
ʲ Lit., *fruit.*
ᵏ Vb. suggested by instr. case of the word, *Spirit.*
ᵃ Lit., *surprised; so caught.*
ᵇ Implied in sg. pt.
ᶜ Load of personal responsibility.

GALATIANS 6

⁶ Those who are taught the truth should share all their goods with the man who teaches them. ⁷ Do not be deceived any more; God is not to be scoffed at. A person will reap just what he sows, whatever it is. ⁸ The person who sows to gratify his lower nature will reap destruction ᵈ from that lower nature, and the person who sows to gratify his higher nature will reap ᵈ eternal life from the Spirit. ⁹ Let us stop getting tired of doing good,ᵉ for at the proper time we shall reap if we do not give up. ¹⁰ So then whenever we have an opportunity, let us practice doing good to everybody, but especially to the members of the family of faith.

¹¹ See what large letters I make, when I write to you with my own hand! ᶠ ¹² These men who are trying to force you to let yourselves be circumcised simply want to make a fine outward show, only to keep you from being persecuted for the cross of our Lord Jesus Christ. ¹³ Indeed, the very men who let themselves be circumcised do not themselves observe the law. But they simply want you to let yourselves be circumcised, so that they can boast of you as members of their party. ¹⁴ But may it never be mine to boast of anything but the cross of our Lord Jesus Christ, by which the world has been crucified to me and I to the world! ¹⁵ For neither circumcision nor the lack of it has any value, but only a new creation. ¹⁶ Now peace and mercy be on all who walk by this rule; that is, on the true ᵍ Israel of God.

¹⁷ Let nobody trouble me after this, for I carry on my body the scars ʰ that mark me as Jesus' slave.

¹⁸ The spiritual blessing of our Lord Jesus Christ be with your spirit, brothers. Amen.

ᵈ The wrong and right use of money in supporting the good news.
ᵉ May be tr., *doing right;* probably, *doing good.*
ᶠ He likely dictated to a secretary, but now takes the pen for his autograph.
ᵍ Implied in art. and context.
ʰ Made by the rods and lashes which branded him as Christ's slave. See II Cor., chap. 11.

EPHESIANS

The writer is Paul the apostle; so held by all conservative, and by an increasing number of liberal, scholars. The Gnostics are threatening the whole province of Asia, and so Paul, in A.D. 62 or 63, in the latter part of his first imprisonment in Rome, writes this letter to expand some topics only hinted at in Colossians. So the letter is likely addressed to all the churches of the province of Asia, with Ephesus as the guardian of the letter after it is read by all the other churches.

The purpose is to show that salvation is obtained only in Christ; to emphasize the fellowship of believers with Christ and the oneness of all believers with one another, even suggesting international peace of mankind, and the unification of the whole universe around Christ; to magnify the church as a divine institution; to show that a well-rounded moral and spiritual life flows out of salvation by grace through faith. The letter traces man's salvation back to God's favor, which flows out of His "great love"; it is nonpersonal and general in tone, even cosmopolitan and cosmic; its vocabulary is rich in new words found nowhere else in the New Testament or in Paul, and its style represents his best literary effort, its thoughts being profound and its treatment comprehensive.

1 HE GREETS THEM; TELLS OF GOD'S ETERNAL PURPOSE OF LOVE; UNIVERSAL RANSOM BY CHRIST; TELLS THAT THE SPIRIT STAMPS BELIEVERS AS GOD'S OWN; HE PRAYS HIS FIRST PRAYER FOR THEM TO REALIZE THEIR HOPE AND GOD'S POWER

Paul, by God's will an apostle of Christ Jesus,[a] to God's people [b] who are faithful in Christ Jesus; 2 spiritual blessing and peace to you from God our Father and the Lord Jesus Christ.

3 Blessed be the God and Father of our Lord Jesus Christ, who through Christ has blessed us with every spiritual blessing in the heavenly realm. 4 Through Him He picked us out [c] before the creation of the world, to be consecrated and above reproach in His sight in love. 5 He foreordained us to become His sons by adoption

[a] Order of Vat. Ms.
[b] Om. *In Eph.*, on evidence of best Mss.
[c] Exact meaning of Grk. vb., *to elect*.

through Christ Jesus,[a] to carry out the happy choice of His will, [6] so that we might praise the splendid [d] favor which He has shown us in His beloved Son.[e] [7] It is through union with Him that we have redemption by His blood and the forgiveness of our shortcomings, in accordance with the generosity of His unmerited favor [8] which He lavished upon us. Through perfect wisdom and spiritual insight [9] He has made known to us the secret of His will, which is in accordance with His purpose which He planned in Christ, [10] so that, at the coming of the climax of the ages,[f] everything in heaven and on earth should be unified through Christ, [11] in union with whom we were made God's portion,[g] since we had been foreordained in accordance with the purpose of Him who in everything carries out the plan of His will, [12] that we who had first put our hope in Christ might praise His glory. [13] You too, as you have heard the message of the truth, the good news that means your salvation, and as you have trusted in Him too, have been stamped with the seal of the promised Holy Spirit, [14] who is the first installment of our inheritance, so that we may finally come into full possession of the prize of redemption,[h] and praise His glory for it.

[15] This is why I myself, since I have heard of your faith in the Lord Jesus and in all His people, [16] never cease to thank God for you when I mention you in my prayers, [17] that the God of our Lord Jesus Christ, the glorious Father, may grant you the Spirit to give wisdom and revelation which come through a growing knowledge of Him, [18] by having the eyes of your hearts enlightened, so that you may know what the hope is to which He calls you, how gloriously rich God's portion in His people is, [19] and how surpassingly great is His power for us who believe, measured by His tremendously mighty power [20] when He raised Christ from the dead, and seated Him at His right hand in heaven, [21] far above every other government, authority, power, and dominion, yea, far above every other title that can be conferred, not only in this world but in the world to come. [22] And so He has put all things under His feet and made Him the supreme Head of the church, [23] which is His body, that is being filled [i] by Him who fills everything everywhere.

[d] Lit., *to the praise of the glory of,* etc.
[e] *Son* implied.
[f] *In the dispensation of the fullness of the times.*
[g] So most interpreters.
[h] *Unto the redemption of the possession.*
[i] Lit., *the thing filled by Him.*

2 JEWS AND HEATHEN, LOST IN SIN, SAVED BY GOD'S UNMERITED FAVOR THROUGH FAITH IN CHRIST; CHRIST THE BOND OF INTERNATIONAL PEACE

You too were dead because of the shortcomings and sins ²in which you once lived in accordance with the spirit of this present world,ᵃ and the mighty prince of the air, who is always at work in the disobedient,ᵇ among whom all of us, we Jews as well as you heathen,ᶜ ³once lived while gratifying the cravings of our lower nature, as we continued to carry out the impulses of our lower nature and its thoughts, and by nature we were exposed to God's wrath,ᵇ as the rest of mankind. ⁴But God, who is so rich in mercy on account of the great love He has for us, ⁵has made us, though dead because of our shortcomings, live again in fellowship with Christ—it is by His unmerited favor that you have been saved. ⁶And He raised us with Him and through union with Christ Jesus He made us sit down with Him in the heavenly realm, ⁷to show, throughout the coming ages, the boundless generosity of His unmerited favor shown us in His goodness to us through Christ Jesus. ⁸For it is by His unmerited favor through faith that you have been saved; it is not by anything that you have done,ᵈ it is the gift of God. ⁹It is not the result of what anyone can do, so that no one can boast of it. ¹⁰For He has made us what we are,ᵉ because He has created us through our union with Christ Jesus for doing good deeds which He beforehand planned for us to do.

¹¹So remember that you were once heathen in a physical sense, called the uncircumcised by those who call themselves the circumcised—though only in a physical sense, by human hands.ᶠ ¹²At that time you were without any connection with Christ; you were aliens to the commonwealth of Israel, strangers to the sacred compacts made by God's promise, with no hope, and no God in the world. ¹³But now through your union with Christ Jesus you who were once far away have through the blood of Christ been brought near. ¹⁴For He Himself is our peace, He is the one who has made us both into one body and has broken down the barrier that kept

---

ᵃ *The age of this world.*
ᵇ *Children of disobedience—children of wrath.*
ᶜ *Implied in conjunction.*
ᵈ *Not from* or *out of you.*
ᵉ *We are what He made.*
ᶠ *Handmade.*

us apart; ¹⁵ through His human nature ᵍ He has put a stop to the hostility between us, namely, the law with its commands and decrees, in order to create one new humanity ʰ out of the two parties and so make peace through union with Himself, and in one body ¹⁶ to reconcile them both to God with His cross after He had killed the hostility through it. ¹⁷ When He came, He brought the good news of peace for you who were far away and for you who were near; ¹⁸ for it is by Him through one Spirit that both of us now have an introduction to the Father. ¹⁹ So you are no longer foreigners and strangers, but you are fellow-citizens of God's people and members of His family; ²⁰ for you are built upon the foundation of the apostles and prophets, with Christ Jesus Himself the cornerstone. ²¹ In union with Him the whole building is harmoniously fitted together and continues to grow into a temple, sacred through its union with the Lord, ²² and you yourselves, in union with Him, in fellowship with one another, are being built up into a dwelling for God through the Spirit.

3 PAUL IS ENTRUSTED WITH THE SECRET OF UNIVERSAL PEACE; AGAIN HE PRAYS FOR HIS READERS TO HAVE SPIRITUAL STRENGTH, TO HAVE CHRIST IN THEIR HEARTS, AND TO KNOW CHRIST'S BOUNDLESS LOVE

This is why I, Paul, a prisoner of Christ Jesus for the sake of the heathen—² that is, if you have heard how God's favor has been entrusted ᵃ to me for you, ³ and how by revelation the secret was made known to me, as I have briefly written before. ⁴ By reading this you will be able to understand my insight into the secret about the Christ—⁵ which in the earlier ages, so different from the present,ᵇ was not made known to mankind as fully as now, but through the Spirit it has been revealed to His holy apostles and prophets—⁶ that the heathen through union with Christ Jesus are fellow-heirs with the Jews,ᶜ are members with them of the same body, and sharers with them of the promise through the good news,⁷ for which I was called to serve in accordance with the gift

---

ᵍ Lit., *in His flesh.*
ʰ Grk., *one new man.*
ᵃ Lit., *heard of the trusteeship of God's favor, given,* etc.
ᵇ Lit., *in different ages.*
ᶜ Implied.

of God's unmerited favor which was bestowed on me by the exercise of His power—8 yes, on me, the very least of all His people, this unmerited favor was bestowed—that I might preach as good news to the heathen the boundless riches of Christ,[d] 9 and to make clear how is to be carried out the trusteeship of this secret which has for ages been hidden away in God, the Creator of all things, 10 so that the many phases of God's wisdom may now through the church be made known to the rulers and authorities in heaven, 11 in accordance with the eternal purpose which God executed in the gift of Christ Jesus our Lord. 12 By union with Him and through faith in Him we have a free and confidential introduction to God. 13 So I beg you not to lose heart over the sorrows that I am suffering for your sake, for they bring you honor.

14 For this reason I kneel before the Father, 15 from whom every family in heaven and on earth derives its name, 16 and beg Him to grant you, in accordance with the riches of His perfect character,[e] to be mightily strengthened by His Spirit in your inmost being, 17 and that Christ in His love, through your faith, may make His permanent home[f] in your hearts. You must be deeply rooted, your foundations must be strong, 18 so that you with all God's people may be strong enough to grasp the idea[f] of the breadth and length, the height and depth, 19 yes, to come at last to know the love of Christ, although it far surpasses human understanding, so that you may be filled with the perfect fullness of God. 20 To Him who by His power that is at work within us can do surpassingly more than all we ask or imagine, 21 be glory in the church and through Christ Jesus to all generations for ever and ever. Amen.

4 THE MORAL AND SPIRITUAL LIFE: TO BE FOSTERED THROUGH UNITY AND SERVICE RENDERED BY ALL WITH VARYING GIFTS; VICES TO BE LAID ASIDE, VIRTUES CULTIVATED

So I, a prisoner for the Lord's sake,[a] entreat you to live lives worthy of the call you have received, 2 with perfect humility and

[d] That is, the riches of His love and mercy.
[e] Lit., *riches of His glory;* glory here means the summing up of His perfect character.
[f] So comp. vb.
[a] Lit., *in the Lord.*

gentleness, with patience, lovingly bearing with one another, ³ continuing with eager earnestness to maintain the unity of the Spirit through the tie of peace. ⁴ There is but one body and one Spirit, just as there is but one hope resulting from the call you have received; ⁵ there is but one Lord, one faith, one baptism, ⁶ one God and Father of all, who is over us all, who pervades us all, and who is within us all.

⁷ But in accordance with the measure of Christ's gift, His favor has been bestowed upon each one of us. ⁸ Concerning this the Scripture says:

> "He led a host of captives, when He went up on high,
> And granted gifts to men." ᵇ

⁹ What does "He went up" mean, except that He had first gone down into the lower regions of the earth? ¹⁰ The very One that went down has gone up, too, far above all the heavens, to fill the universe.ᶜ ¹¹ And He has given some men to be apostles, some to be prophets, some to be evangelists, some to be pastors and teachers, ¹² for the immediate ᵈ equipment of God's people for the work of service, for the ultimate ᵈ building up of the body of Christ, ¹³ until we all attain to unity in faith and to perfect knowledge of the Son of God, namely, to a mature manhood and to a perfect measure of Christ's moral stature; ¹⁴ so that we may not be babies any longer, or like sailors tossed about and driven around by every wind of doctrine, by the trickery of men through their cunning in inventing new methods of error. ¹⁵ But, on the other hand, we shall go on holding to the truth and in love growing up into perfect union with Him, that is, Christ Himself who is the Head. ¹⁶ For it is under His direction that the whole body is perfectly adjusted and united by every joint that furnishes its supplies; and by the proper functioning of each particular part there is brought about the growing of the body for its building up in love.

¹⁷ So I mean this and now testify to it in the name of the Lord: You must now stop living as the heathen usually do, in the frivolity of their minds, ¹⁸ with darkened understanding, estranged from the life of God because of the ignorance that exists among them and because of the stubbornness of their hearts; ¹⁹ for in their

---

ᵇ Ps. 68:18.
ᶜ Lit., *the all things,* so universe.
ᵈ In preps. *pros* and *eis.*

recklessness[e] they have abandoned themselves to sensuality which leads to excessive practices of all sorts of immorality. 20 But this is not the way you have learned what Christ means, 21 if, as I take it,[f] you have heard Him and in union with Him have been taught the truth as it is seen [f] in Jesus, 22 to lay aside, with your former way of living, your old self which is on the way to destruction in accordance with its deceptive impulses; 23 and to have a new attitude [g] of mind 24 and put on the new self which has been created in the likeness of God, which fruits in right and holy living inspired by the truth.[h]

25 So you must lay aside falsehood and each of you practice telling the truth to his neighbor, for we are parts of one another. 26 If you do get [i] angry, you must stop sinning in your anger. Do not ever [i] let the sun go down on your anger; 27 stop giving the devil a chance. 28 The man who used to steal must now stop stealing; rather, he must keep on working and toiling with his own hands at some honest vocation,[j] so as to have something to contribute to the needy. 29 You must stop letting any bad word pass your lips, but only words that are good for building up as the occasion demands, so that they will result in spiritual blessing to the hearers. 30 You must stop offending the Holy Spirit of God by whom you have been stamped for the day of redemption. 31 You must remove all bitterness, rage, anger, loud threats, and insults, with all malice. 32 You must practice being kind to one another, tenderhearted, forgiving one another, just as God through Christ has graciously forgiven you.

5 AGAIN WARNS THEM AGAINST LIVING IN VICES; MUST LIVE IN THE LIGHT, BE ALERT, SPIRITUAL, EVER SINGING; TELLS DUTIES OF HUSBANDS AND WIVES

So you must keep on following God's example,[a] as dearly loved children of His, 2 and practice living in love, just as Christ loved you too and gave Himself for you as a fragrant offering and sacrifice to God.

[e] So Moulton and Milligan, Vocab. Grk. N. T.
[f] Implied.
[g] Lit., *spirit*.
[h] Grk., *in uprightness and holiness of truth* (subj. gen.).
[i] In aor.
[j] Lit., *continuing to do the right* (good) *thing*.
[a] In forgiving others.

EPHESIANS 5

³ But sexual vice and any form of immorality or sensual ᵇ greed must not so much as be mentioned among you, as that is the only course becoming in God's people; ⁴ there must be no indecency, silly talk or suggestive jesting, for they are unbecoming. There should be thanksgiving instead. ⁵ For you may be absolutely sure ᶜ that no one who is sexually impure, immoral or greedy for gain (for that is idolatry) can have a part in the kingdom of Christ and God.

⁶ Stop letting anyone deceive you with groundless arguments about these things, for it is because of these very sins that God's anger comes down upon the disobedient. ⁷ So you must stop having anything to do with them.ᵈ ⁸ For at one time you were darkness itself, but now in union with the Lord you are light itself. You must live like children of light, ⁹ for the product of light consists in practicing everything that is good and right and true; ᵉ ¹⁰ you must approve what is pleasing to the Lord. ¹¹ Stop having anything to do with the profitless doings of darkness; instead you must continue to expose them. ¹² For it is disgraceful even to mention the vices practiced in secret by them; ¹³ and yet anything that is exposed by the light is made clear to them, for anything that is made clear is light. ¹⁴ So it is said:

> "Wake up, sleeper,
> Get up from the dead,
> And Christ will make day dawn on you." ᶠ

¹⁵ So you must be very careful how you live, not thoughtlessly but thoughtfully, ¹⁶ and continue to make the most of your opportunities,ᵍ for the times are evil. ¹⁷ So stop becoming senseless, but understand what the Lord's will is. ¹⁸ Stop getting drunk on wine, for that means profligacy, but ever be filled with the Spirit, ¹⁹ and always be speaking to one another in psalms, hymns, and spiritual songs. Keep on praying and praising the Lord with all your heart; ²⁰ continue giving thanks for everything to God our Father; ²¹ keep on living in subordination to one another out of reverence to Christ

---

ᵇ Or *greed for anything.*
ᶜ Two vbs. for emphasis.
ᵈ Lit., *stop becoming sharers with them.*
ᵉ *In all goodness,* etc.
ᶠ Likely from a Christian hymn of that day (EGT).
ᵍ Lit., *buying up the time.*

22 You married women must continue to live in subordination to your husbands, as you do to the Lord, **23** for a husband is the head of his wife, just as Christ is the Head of the church, His body, and Saviour of it. **24** Just as the church is subject to Christ, so the married women in everything must be subject to their husbands. **25** You married men must love your wives, just as Christ loved the church and gave Himself for her, **26** to consecrate her, after cleansing her through His word, as pictured in the water bath,[h] **27** that He might present the church to Himself as a splendid bride[i] without a blot or wrinkle or anything like it, but to be consecrated and faultless. **28** This is the way married men ought to love their wives, as they do their own bodies. The married man who loves his wife is really loving himself, **29** for no one ever hates his own physical person, but he feeds and fosters it, just as Christ does the church; **30** because we are parts of His body. **31** Therefore, a man must leave his father and mother and so perfectly[j] unite himself to his wife that the two shall be one. **32** This is a great secret; I mean this about Christ and the church. **33** But each one of you married men must love his wife as he loves himself, and the married woman, too, must respect her husband.

6
DUTIES OF CHILDREN AND PARENTS; OF SLAVES AND MASTERS; SPIRITUAL WEAPONS FOR MEETING SPIRITUAL FOES; TYCHICUS TO REPORT PAUL'S CONDITION; FAREWELL

Children, obey your parents,[a] for this is right. **2** "You must honor your father and mother"—this is the first commandment, with a promise to make it good—[b] **3** "so that you may prosper and live a long life on earth."[c] **4** You parents,[d] too, must stop exasperating your children, but continue to bring them up with the sort of education and counsel[e] the Lord approves.

[h] Referring to water baptism (so EGT, and most exegetes).
[i] Easily supplied.
[j] Comp. vb. with strong force.
[a] Fol. B and om. phrase, *in the Lord*.
[b] Last phrase implied.
[c] Ex. 20:12.
[d] Lit., *fathers*; often used for both parents.
[e] Oral instruction.

⁵ You slaves must practice obedience to your earthly masters, with reverence and awe, with sincerity of heart, as you would obey Christ, ⁶ not serving them as though they were watching you, but as true slaves of Christ, trying to carry out the will of God. ⁷ Heartily and cheerfully keep on working as slaves, as though it were for the Lord and not for men, ⁸ for you know that everyone, slave or free, will get his reward from the Lord for anything good he has done. ⁹ You slaveowners, too, must maintain the same attitude toward your slaves, and stop threatening them, for you know that their real Lord and yours is in heaven, and that He never shows partiality.

¹⁰ From now on you must grow stronger through union with the Lord and through His mighty power. ¹¹ You must put on God's full armor, so as to be able to stand up against the devil's stratagems. ¹² For our contest ᶠ is not with human ᵍ foes alone, but with the rulers, authorities, and cosmic powers of this dark world; that is, with the spirit-forces of evil challenging us in the heavenly contest.ʰ ¹³ So you must take on God's full armor, so as to be able to take a stand in the day when evil attacks you, and, after having completely finished the contest, to hold your own.ʰ· ¹⁴ Hold your position, then, with your waist encircled with the belt of truth, put on right-doing as a coat of mail, ¹⁵ and put on your feet the preparation the good news of peace supplies. ¹⁶ Besides all these, take on the shield which faith provides, for with it you will be able to put out all the fire-tipped arrows shot by the evil one,ⁱ ¹⁷ take the helmet salvation provides, and take the sword the Spirit ⁱ wields, which is the word of God. ¹⁸ Keep on praying in the Spirit, with every kind of prayer and entreaty, at every opportunity, be ever on the alert with perfect devotion and entreaty for all God's people, ¹⁹ and for me that a message may be given me when I open my lips, so that I may boldly make known the open secret of the good news, ²⁰ for the sake of which I am an envoy in prison; so that, when I tell it, I may speak as courageously as I ought.

²¹ That you may also know how I am,ʲ Tychicus, our dearly loved brother and a faithful minister in the Lord's service, will

---

ᶠ Lit., *wrestling*.
ᵍ Grk., *with flesh and blood*.
ʰ Delicate shades of truth here expressed by preps. and tenses.
ⁱ Subj. gen.
ʲ Lit., *know the affairs as to me*; i.e., how I am.

give you all the information; ²² that is the very reason I am sending him, to let you know how I am and to cheer your hearts.

²³ Peace to the brothers and love with faith, from God our Father and the Lord Jesus Christ. ²⁴ Spiritual blessing be with all who have an undying love for our Lord Jesus Christ.

PHILIPPIANS

The writer is Paul; so held by all New Testament scholars.

Paul was in prison at Rome, and the church at Philippi had sent by Epaphroditus a gift expressive of their love for him. Epaphroditus also told Paul about the danger threatening the church from an attack of the Judaizers and Antinomians. The date was A.D. 62.

The purpose was to pour out his feelings and affections for the Christians there; to warn them against the false teachers named above; to show how his sufferings have contributed to his own Christian development and the progress of the good news in Rome; to show his optimism and joy in spite of imprisonment and impending death.

It is a personal letter; a love letter, a joy letter; it is written in the easy style of the everyday common Greek, though containing a few terms in 2:6-11 that are found in classical and later literary Greek.

1 HE GREETS THEM AND PRAYS FOR THEM; REJOICES OVER THEIR CO-OPERATION AND THAT CHRIST IS BEING PREACHED; WEIGHS WHICH IS BETTER: TO LIVE OR TO DIE; POINTS TO LIFE OF SELF-SACRIFICE

Paul and Timothy, slaves of Christ Jesus, to all God's people in union with Christ Jesus who are at Philippi, with the overseers and assistants: [a] ² spiritual blessing and peace to you from God our Father and the Lord Jesus Christ.

³ Every time I remember you I thank my God, ⁴ and always do it with joy in every entreaty I make for all of you, ⁵ for your co-operation in spreading the good news, from the first day you heard it until now. ⁶ For I am certain [b] of this very thing, that He who began the good work in you will go on until the day of Jesus Christ to complete [c] it. ⁷ And I have a right to think this way about you, because I always have you in my heart, whether shut up in prison or out defending and vindicating the good news, for you are sharers

---

[a] Lit., *servants,* deacons.
[b] Grk., *I am confident,* etc.
[c] Linear fut. demanded by prep. *until.*

with me of God's favor. ⁸ For God is my witness how I never stop yearning for all of you with the affection Christ Jesus inspires.

⁹ And it is my prayer that your love may overflow still more and more, directed by fuller knowledge and keener insight, ¹⁰ so that you may always approve the better things, and be men of transparent character and blameless life,ᵈ ¹¹ men that are abounding in the fruits of right-doing with the help of Jesus Christ, to the honor and praise of God.

¹² Now I want you to rest assured,ᵉ brothers, that those things which have befallen me have actually resulted in the progress of the good news; ¹³ in this way it has become well known throughout the Imperial Guard ᶠ and to all the rest here that I am a prisoner in the service of Christ, ¹⁴ and that most of the Christian brothers have grown confident enough, because of my imprisonment, to dare to tell God's message without being afraid.

¹⁵ Some, indeed, are actually preaching Christ because they are moved by jealousy and partisanship, but others are doing so from the motive of good-will; ¹⁶ the latter, indeed, are doing so from love to me, for they know that I am providentially put here to defend the good news; ¹⁷ the former are preaching Christ from the motive of rivalry, not in sincerity, supposing that this is making it harder for me to bear my imprisonment.

¹⁸ What difference then does it make? In one way or another, whether in pretense or in sincerity,ᵍ Christ is being preached, and that is the thing that makes me glad; yes, more too, I will continue ʰ to be glad of it, ¹⁹ for I know that through your prayers and a bountiful supply of the Spirit of Jesus Christ this will turn out for my spiritual welfare,ⁱ ²⁰ in accordance with my eager expectation and hope that I shall never disgrace myself,ʲ but that now as always hitherto, by my all-conquering courage, whether by living or dying, Christ will be honored in me.

²¹ For to me living means Christ and dying brings gain. ²² But if to keep on living here means fruit from my labor, I cannot tell which to choose. ²³ I am hesitating between two desires, for I long

---

ᵈ Lit., *be wax-like and blameless.*
ᵉ Grk., *to keep on knowing.*
ᶠ The company of Rom. soldiers who guarded the emperor and his palace.
ᵍ Lit., *in truth.*
ʰ Another linear fut.
ⁱ Grk., *salvation* (in general sense).
ʲ By repudiating my faith in Jesus.

to depart and to be with Christ, for that is far, far [k] better. [24] And yet for your sakes it is very necessary for me to stay on here. [25] Now since I am certain of this, I know that I shall stay on and stay by you all to promote the progress of your faith [26] which will result in your joy; so that, through union with Christ Jesus, you may have more than sufficient ground for boasting about me, through my being with you again.

[27] Only you must practice living lives that are worthy of the good news, so that whether I come and see you or stay away, I may hear of you that you are standing firm in one spirit, and that with one purpose you are continuing to co-operate in the fight for faith in the good news. [28] Never in the slightest degree be frightened by your opponents, for such fearlessness will be strong evidence to them of their impending destruction, but to you a sure sign, and that from God, of your salvation. [29] For it has been graciously granted to you for Christ's sake, not only to trust in Him but also to suffer for Him, [30] since you are having the same struggle that you once saw me have and which you hear that I am still having.

2 HE APPEALS FOR BROTHERLY LOVE; URGES CHRIST'S EXAMPLE OF HUMILITY AND SELF-SACRIFICE; TELLS OF SALVATION AS A PROCESS TOWARD A FINISHING POINT; TIMOTHY SENT TO THEM; EPAPHRODITUS TO BE SENT BACK

So, if there is any appeal in our union with Christ, if there is any persuasive power in love,[a] if we have any common share in the Spirit, if you have any tenderheartedness and sympathy, [2] fill up my cup of joy by living in harmony, by fostering the same disposition of love, your hearts beating in unison,[b] your minds set on one purpose. [3] Stop acting from motives of selfish strife or petty ambition, but in humility practice treating one another as your superiors. [4] Stop looking after your own interests only but practice looking out for the interests of others too.

[5] Keep on fostering the same disposition that Christ Jesus had.[c]
[6] Though He was existing in the nature of God,[d] He did not think

---

[k] Double comparative, so emph.
[a] Subj. gen.
[b] Lit., *souls together.*
[c] Grk., *have the mind that was in Christ Jesus.*
[d] *Form*, strong term; so *nature.*

His being on an equality with God a thing to be selfishly grasped, ⁷ but He laid it aside ᵉ as He took on the nature ᵈ of a slave and became like other men. ⁸ Because He was recognized as a man, in reality ᶠ as well as in outward form, He finally humiliated Himself in obedience ᵍ so as to die, even to die on a cross. ⁹ This is why God has highly exalted Him, and given Him the name that is above every other name, ¹⁰ so that in the name of Jesus everyone ʰ should kneel, in heaven, on earth, and in the underworld, ¹¹ and everyone ʰ should confess that Jesus Christ is Lord, to the praise of God the Father.

¹² So, my dearly loved friends, as you have always been obedient, so now with reverence and awe keep on working clear down to the finishing point ⁱ of your salvation,ʲ not only as though I were with you but much more because I am away; ¹³ for it is God Himself who is at work in you to help ʰ you desire it as well as do it. ¹⁴ Practice doing everything without grumbling and disputing, ¹⁵ so that you may prove to be blameless and spotless, faultless children of God in a crooked and perverted age, in which you shine as light-bearers in the world as you continue ¹⁶ to hold up the message of life. That will give me ground for boasting on the day of Christ, because neither my career nor my labor has been a failure.ᵏ ¹⁷ Yes, even if I am pouring out my life as a libation on the sacrifice and service your faith ᵃ is rendering, I am glad to do so and congratulate you upon it; ¹⁸ you too must do likewise, be glad of it, and congratulate me.

¹⁹ I hope, with the approval ʰ of the Lord Jesus, soon to send Timothy to you, so that I too may be cheered on getting the news about you. ²⁰ For I have no one else with a heart like his who would take such genuine interest in you, ²¹ for most people are looking out for their own interests, not for the interests of Jesus Christ. ²² But you know his tested character, how like a son in fellowship with his father he has toiled with me like a slave in preaching the good news. ²³ So I hope to send him to you just as soon as I can

---

ᵉ Lit., *emptied Himself.*
ᶠ Lit., *like a man.*
ᵍ Grk. says, *by becoming obedient,* etc.
ʰ Implied from context.
ⁱ In prep. *kata* (Robertson, Gram. 606).
ʲ The word does not here have its usual sense, including justification, regeneration (Rom. 3:24f; Eph. 2:8) but means the process of character building into the likeness of Christ.
ᵏ Lit., *run nor labored for nothing.*

see how my case is going to turn out. ²⁴ Really, I am trusting that by the help of the Lord I soon shall come myself.

²⁵ But I think it proper now to send back to you Epaphroditus, my brother, fellow-laborer, and fellow-soldier, but your messenger to minister to my needs, ²⁶ for he has been longing to see you and has been homesick because you have heard that he was sick. ²⁷ For he was so sick that he was on the point of dying, but God took pity on him, and not only on him but on me too, to keep me from having one sorrow after another. ²⁸ I very eagerly send him, so that when you see him you may be glad of it, and I may be less sorrowful. ²⁹ So give him a hearty Christian welcome and hold in honor men like him, ³⁰ because he came near dying for the sake of the Lord's work and risked his life to make up for your lack of opportunity to minister to me.

3 OUTWARD PRIVILEGES WORTHLESS AS MEANS OF RIGHT STANDING WITH GOD; PAUL COUNTS HIS PRIVILEGES BUT REFUSE COMPARED WITH PERSONAL EXPERIENCE IN TRUSTING JESUS; ASPIRES TO CHRIST-LIKENESS

Finally, my brothers, continue to be glad that you are in union with the Lord. I am not tired of writing you the same things over and over: it means your safety.

² Look out for those dogs, those mischief-makers, those self-mutilators! [a] ³ For we are the true circumcision, who by the Spirit of God worship Him, who take pride in Christ Jesus only, and do not rely on outward privileges,[b] ⁴ though I too might rely on these. If anyone thinks that he can rely on outward privileges, far more might I do so: ⁵ circumcised when I was a week old; a descendant of Israel; a member of the tribe of Benjamin; a Hebrew, a son of Hebrews. Measured by the standard set by the law, I was a Pharisee; ⁶ by the standard set by zeal, I was a persecutor of the church, and measured by the uprightness reached by keeping the law, I was faultless. ⁷ But for Christ's sake I have counted all that was gain to me as loss. ⁸ Yes, indeed, I certainly do count everything as loss compared with the priceless privilege [c] of knowing Christ Jesus my Lord. For His sake I have lost everything, and value it

---
[a] Lit., *the catacision,* prep. meaning perfective action, so self-mutilators.
[b] Grk., *on the flesh.*
[c] Lit., *the surpassing excellence of the knowledge,* etc.

all as mere refuse, in order to gain Christ 9 and be actually[d] in union with Him, not having a supposed right standing with God which depends on my doing what the law commands, but one that comes through faith in Christ, the real right standing with God which originates[e] from Him and rests[e] on faith. 10 Yes, I long[f] to come to know Him; that is, the power of His resurrection and so to share with Him His sufferings as to be continuously transformed by His death, 11 in the hope of attaining, in some measure, the resurrection that lifts me out from among the dead.[g] 12 It is not a fact that I have already secured it or already reached perfection, but I am pressing on to see if I can capture it, the ideal for which I was captured by Christ Jesus. 13 Brothers, I do not think that I have captured it yet, but here is my one aspiration,[h] so forgetting what is behind me and reaching out for what is ahead of me, 14 I am pressing onward toward the goal, to win the prize to which God through Jesus Christ is calling us upward. 15 So let us all who are mature have this attitude. If you have a different attitude, God will make it clear to you. 16 However, we must continue to live up to that degree of success[i] that we have already reached.

17 Follow my example, brothers, and keep your eyes on those who practice living by the pattern we have set you. 18 For there are many, of whom I have often told you, and now tell you in tears, who practice living as the enemies of the cross of Christ. 19 Their doom is destruction, their stomach is their god, their glory is in their shame, and their minds are feeding on earthly things. 20 But we are citizens of the republic[j] in heaven, from which we are eagerly waiting for our Saviour, the Lord Jesus Christ. 21 He will so change the outward appearance of our lowly bodies that they will be like His glorious body, by the exertion of the power He has to subject everything to Himself.

[d] *Found in Him.*
[e] *In preps.*
[f] *Implied.*
[g] *Double comp. noun, meaning a spiritual, moral resurrection, not the final physical resurrection, which will be the climax of the spiritual, moral one.*
[h] *There is one thing.*
[i] *To what we have reached, etc.*
[j] *So in Plato.*

PHILIPPIANS 4

4 HE CALLS THEM HIS CROWN OF REWARD; BEGS EUODIA AND SYNTYCHE TO AGREE; INSPIRES THEM TO "BEAUTIFUL THOUGHTS AND NOBLE LIVES"; THANKS THEM FOR MANY GIFTS TO HIM; SENDS FAREWELL GREETINGS

So, my dearly loved brothers, whom I long to see, my joy and crown, by the help of the Lord keep on standing firm, dearly loved friends.

2 I beg Euodia and I beg Syntyche to live in harmony by the help of the Lord. 3 And I solemnly beg you, my true comrade, keep on co-operating with those two women, because they shared with me the struggle in spreading the good news, together with Clement and the rest of my fellow-workers, whose names are in the book of life.

4 By the help of the Lord always keep up the glad spirit; yes, I will repeat it, keep up the glad spirit. 5 Let your forbearing spirit[a] be known to everybody. The Lord is near. 6 Stop being worried about anything, but always,[b] in prayer and entreaty, and with thanksgiving, keep on making your wants known to God. 7 Then, through your union with Christ Jesus, the peace of God, that surpasses all human thought, will keep guard over your hearts and thoughts.

8 Now, brothers, practice thinking on what is true, what is honorable, what is right, what is pure, what is lovable, what is high-toned, yes, on everything that is excellent or praiseworthy.[c] 9 Practice the things you learned, received, and heard from me, things that you saw me do, and then the God who gives us peace will be with you.

10 I was made very happy as a Christian[d] to have your interest in my welfare revived again after so long; because you have always had the interest but not the opportunity to show it. 11 Not that I refer to any personal want, for I have learned to be contented in whatever circumstances I am. 12 I know how to live in lowly circumstances and I know how to live in plenty. I have learned the secret, in all circumstances, of either getting a full

---

[a] *Your forbearance.*
[b] Lit., *in everything.*
[c] *If there is any virtue and any praise,* etc.
[d] Lit., *greatly rejoiced in Christ.*

meal or of going hungry, of living in plenty or being in want. ¹³ I can do anything ᵉ through Him who gives me strength. ¹⁴ But you did me a kindness to share my sorrow with me. ¹⁵ And you Philippians yourselves know that immediately after the good news was first preached to you, when I left Macedonia, no church but yours went into partnership with me to open an account of credits and debits.ᶠ ¹⁶ Even while I was at Thessalonica you sent money more than once for my needs. ¹⁷ It is not your gift that I want, but I do want the profits to pile up to your credit.ᶠ ¹⁸ I have received your payment in full, and more too.ᵍ I am amply supplied after getting the things you sent by Epaphroditus; they are like sweet incense, the kind of sacrifice that God accepts and approves. ¹⁹ My God will amply supply your every need, through Christ Jesus, from His riches in glory. ²⁰ Glory to our God and Father forever and ever. Amen.

²¹ Remember me to every one of God's people in union with Christ Jesus. The brothers who are with me wish to be remembered to you. ²² All God's people wish to be remembered to you, but more especially the members of the Emperor's household.

²³ The spiritual blessing of our Lord Jesus Christ be with your spirits.

ᵉ Lit., *I have power for all things through Him who puts a dynamo in me.*
ᶠ Accounting terms, so used in papyri.
ᵍ Used in papyri in receipts in full.

COLOSSIANS

The writer is Paul; so held by scholars, except a very few radicals.
The occasion was the coming of Epaphras to Rome and telling Paul of the love and loyalty of the Colossian Christians to him. But the main information given by Epaphras was that the Gnostics were threatening Christianity in Colossae by teaching the necessity of a long line of intermediaries between God and man, giving some of these the place and work of Christ. It was a direct thrust at the vitals of Pauline Christianity. The date is A.D. 62 or 63.
His purpose was to express his personal interest in the readers; but especially to counteract the Gnostic teachings, and to show that Christ is the core of Christianity, the pre-existent Son, indirect Creator and Upholder of all things, the Redeemer and Head of the church.

1 HE GREETS THEM; TELLS OF HIS GRATITUDE FOR THEM; PRAYS FOR THEIR GROWING KNOWLEDGE OF GOD AND STRENGTH TO BEAR FRUIT; TELLS OF CHRIST'S PERSON AND WORKS, DIVINE AND MAJESTIC; OF HIS SUFFERINGS IN TELLING THE GOOD NEWS

Paul, by God's will an apostle of Christ Jesus, and our brother Timothy, 2 to the consecrated and faithful brothers at Colossae who are in union with Christ: spiritual blessing and peace to you from God our Father.[a]

3 Every time we pray for you we thank God the Father of our Lord Jesus Christ, 4 because we have heard of your faith in Christ Jesus and of your love for all God's people, 5 because[b] of your hope of what[c] is laid up for you in heaven. Long ago you heard of this hope through the message of the good news 6 which reached you, and since it is bearing fruit and growing among you, just as it is all[d] over the world, from the day you first heard of God's favor and in reality came to know it, 7 as you learned it from

[a] Fol. B.
[b] In prep.
[c] Implied.
[1] Hyperbole (Rom. world).

Epaphras, our dearly loved fellow-slave. As a faithful minister of Christ for me [e] [8] he is the very one who told me of the love awakened in you by the Spirit.

[9] This is why, ever since I [e] heard of it, I have never ceased praying for you and asking God to fill you, through full wisdom and spiritual insight, with a clear knowledge of His will, [10] so that you may lead lives worthy of the Lord to His full satisfaction,[f] by perennially bearing fruit in every good enterprise and by a steady growth in fuller knowledge of God; [11] then you will be perfectly empowered by His glorious might for every sort of joyous endurance and forbearance, [12] and you will always be thanking the Father who has qualified you to share the lot of His people in the realm of light.

[13] It is God who has delivered us out of the dominion of darkness and has transferred us into the kingdom of His dearly loved Son,[g] [14] by whom we possess [h] the ransom from captivity,[e] which means the forgiveness of our sins. [15] Yes, He is the exact likeness [i] of the unseen God, His first-born Son who existed before any created thing, [16] for it was through Him that everything was created in heaven and on earth, the seen and the unseen, thrones, dominions, principalities, authorities; all things have been created through Him and for Him. [17] So [j] He existed before all things, and through Him all things are held together. [18] Yes, He is the Head of the church as His body. For He is the beginning, the first-born among the dead, so that He alone should stand first in everything. [19] It is so because it was the divine choice that all the divine fullness should dwell in Him, [20] and that through Him He might reconcile to Himself all things on earth or in heaven, making this peace through the blood He shed on His cross.

[21] So you, who were once estranged from Him, and hostile in disposition as shown [e] by your wrongdoings, He has now reconciled [22] by His death in His human body, so as to present you consecrated, faultless, and blameless in His presence, [23] if indeed you continue well grounded and firm in faith and never shift from the hope inspired by the good news you heard, which has been preached all

---

[e] Editorial we.
[f] Lit., *to all pleasing.*
[g] Grk., *Son of His love* (gen. of quality).
[h] Pres. of permanent possession.
[i] Strong term; so *exact likeness.*
[j] Inferential *and.*

over the world,ᵈ and of which I, Paul, have been made a minister. ²⁴ I am now glad to be suffering for you, and in my own person I am filling in what is lacking in Christ's sufferings for His body, that is, the church. ²⁵ In it I have been made a minister in accordance with the trusteeship God entrusted to me for you, that I might prove among you the universal ᵏ message of God, ²⁶ the open secret, covered up from the people of former ages and generations, but now uncovered to God's people, ²⁷ to whom God has chosen to make known how glorious are the riches of this open secret among the heathen, namely, Christ in you the hope of your glorification. ²⁸ We are proclaiming Him, warning everyone and teaching everyone with ample wisdom, in order to present to God everyone mature through union with Christ. ²⁹ For this I am toiling and struggling by His active energy which is mightily working in me.

2
IN PAIN HE WARNS AGAINST THE GNOSTICS; BEGS THEM TO LIVE IN CONSCIOUS UNION WITH CHRIST; REASSERTS THE FULL DIVINITY OF CHRIST AND HIS RANSOMING US THROUGH HIS DEATH; ANGELS CANNOT MEDIATE; ASCETICISM WORTHLESS

I want you to know what a battle I am fighting for you and for those in Laodicea, yes, for all who have never known me personally, ² that their hearts may be encouraged, by having been knit together in love and by having attained ᵃ to the full assurance of understanding, so that they may finally reach the fullest knowledge of the open secret, Christ Himself, ³ in whom all the treasures of wisdom and knowledge are stored up. ⁴ I am saying this to keep anyone from misleading you by persuasive arguments. ⁵ For though I am far away in person, still I am with you in spirit, and I am glad to note your fine order ᵇ and the firmness of your faith in Christ.

⁶ So, just as you once accepted Christ Jesus as your Lord, you must continue living in vital union with Him, ⁷ with your roots deeply planted ᶜ in Him, being continuously built up in Him, and growing stronger in faith, just as you were taught to do, overflowing through it in your gratitude.

ᵏ Lit., *to fill out the message of God among you;* i.e., show it universal.
ᵃ Implied.
ᵇ Military term for the perfect order of a marching army.
ᶜ Pf. denotes *a state of being rooted.*

⁸ Take care that nobody captures you by the idle fancies ᵈ of his so-called philosophy, following human tradition and the world's crude notions instead of Christ. ⁹ For it is in Him that all the fullness of Deity continues to live embodied, ¹⁰ and through union with Him you too are filled with it. He is the Head of all principalities and dominions. ¹¹ And through your union with Him you once received,ᵉ not a hand-performed circumcision but one performed by Christ, in stripping you of your lower nature, ¹² for you were buried with Him in baptism and raised to life with Him through your faith in the power of God who raised Him from the dead. ¹³ Yes, although you were dead through your shortcomings and were physically uncircumcised, God made you live again through fellowship with Christ. He graciously forgave us all our shortcomings, ¹⁴ canceled the note ᶠ that stood against us, with its requirements, and has put it out of our way by nailing it to the cross. ¹⁵ He thus stripped the principalities and dominions of power ᵃ and made a public display of them, triumphing over them by the cross.ᵍ

¹⁶ Stop letting anyone pass judgment on you in matters of eating and drinking, or in the matter of annual or monthly feasts or sabbaths. ¹⁷ These were but the shadow of what was coming; the reality belongs to Christ.ʰ ¹⁸ Stop letting anyone, in gratuitous humility and worship of angels, defraud you as an umpire, for such a one is taking his stand on the mere visions he has seen, and is groundlessly conceited over his sensuous mind. ¹⁹ Such a person is not continuing in connection with the Head, from which the whole body, when supplied and united through its joints and sinews, grows with a growth that God ⁱ produces.

²⁰ If once through fellowship with Christ you died and were separated from the world's crude notions, why do you live as though you belonged to the world? Why submit to rules such as, ²¹ "You must not handle," "You must not taste," "You must not touch," ʲ ²² which refer to things that perish in the using, in accordance with human rules and teachings? ²³ Such practices have the outward ex-

ᵈ One art. means one idea in two words.
ᵉ At their conversion.
ᶠ Lit., *handwriting*, so note or bond.
ᵍ Pro. in Grk., but the cross is meant (so EGT).
ʰ Lit., *the body is Christ's* (gen. of possession).
ⁱ Subj. gen.
ʲ Ascetic rules practiced by the Gnostics.

pression of wisdom, with their self-imposed devotions, their self-humiliation, their torturings of the body, but they are of no value; they really satisfy the lower nature.

3. RESULTS OF UNION WITH CHRIST: EVIL HABITS GIVEN UP, THE FINER VIRTUES PUT ON LIKE NEW CLOTHES; DUTIES OF HUSBANDS AND WIVES, OF CHILDREN AND PARENTS, OF SLAVES AND THEIR OWNERS

So if you have been raised to life in fellowship with Christ, keep on seeking the things above, where Christ is seated at the right hand of God. ² Practice occupying your minds with the things above, not with the things on earth; ³ for you have died, and your life is now hidden in God through your fellowship with Christ. ⁴ When Christ, who is our life, appears, you too will appear to be glorified [a] in fellowship with Him.

⁵ So once for all put to death your lower, earthly nature with respect to sexual immorality, impurity, passion, evil desire, and greed, which is real idolatry. ⁶ It is on account of these very sins [b] that God's anger is coming. ⁷ You too used to practice these sins, when you used to live that sort of life.[b] ⁸ But now you too must once for all put them all aside—anger, rage, malice, and abusive, filthy talk from your lips. ⁹ Stop lying to one another, for you have stripped off the old self with its practices, ¹⁰ and have put on the new self which is in the process of being made new in the likeness of its Creator, so that you may attain a perfect knowledge [c] of Him. ¹¹ In this new relation there is no Greek and Jew, no circumcised and uncircumcised, no barbarian, Scythian, slave and freeman, but Christ is everything and in us all.

¹² So as God's own chosen people, consecrated and dearly loved, you must once for all clothe yourselves with tenderheartedness, kindness, humility, gentleness, patience; you must keep on ¹³ forbearing one another and freely forgiving one another, if anyone has a complaint against another; just as the Lord has freely forgiven you, so must you also do. ¹⁴ And over all these qualities [b] put on love, which is the tie of perfection that binds us together. ¹⁵ Let the peace that Christ can give keep on acting as umpire [d] in your

---
[a] Lit., *in glory with Him.*
[b] Grk., *these things—lived in these things.*
[c] Lit., *to knowledge upon knowledge.*
[d] Lit. meaning of vb.

hearts, for you were called to this state as members of one body. And practice being thankful. ¹⁶ Let the message of Christ continue to live in you in all its wealth of wisdom;ᵉ keep on teaching it to one another and training one another in it with thankfulness, in your hearts singing praise to God with psalms, hymns, and spiritual songs. ¹⁷ And whatever you say or do, let it all be done with reference to the Lord Jesus, and through Him continue to give thanks to God the Father.

¹⁸ You married women must continue to live in subordination to your husbands, for this is your Christian duty.ᶠ ¹⁹ You husbands must continue to love your wives and stop being harsh with them. ²⁰ Children, practice obedience to your parents in everything, for this is acceptable in Christians. ²¹ Fathers, stop exasperating your children, so as to keep them from losing heart. ²² Slaves, practice obedience to your earthly masters in everything, not as though they were watching you and as though you were merely pleasing men, but with sincerity of heart, because you fear the Lord. ²³ Whatever you do, do it with all your heart,ᵍ as work for the Lord and not for men, ²⁴ for you know that it is from the Lord that you are going to get your pay in the form of an inheritance; so keep on serving Christ the Lord. ²⁵ For the man who wrongs another will be paid back the wrong he has done; and there are no exceptions. ⁴:¹ Masters, you must practice doing the right and square things by your slaves, for you know that you have a Master in heaven.

4 HE URGES THEM TO BE PRAYERFUL AND PRUDENT; SENDS TYCHICUS AND ONESIMUS; SENDS GREETINGS FROM HIS MANY FRIENDS; INSTRUCTIONS CONCERNING HIS LETTERS

² You must persevere in prayer and by this means stay wide awake when you give thanks. ³ At the same time keep on praying for me too, that God may open the door of opportunity for the message, so that I may tell the open secret about Christ, for the sake of which I am held a prisoner, ⁴ in order to make it evident why I have to tell it. ⁵ Practice living prudently in your relations with outsiders, making the most of your opportunities. ⁶ Always

---

ᵉ Grk., *richly in all wisdom.*
ᶠ Lit., *fitting in the Lord.*
ᵍ Grk., *from the soul;* so *with all your heart.*

let your conversation be seasoned with salt, that is, with winsomeness,[a] so that you may know how to make a fitting answer to everyone.

⁷ My dearly loved Tychicus, a faithful minister and my fellow-servant in the Lord's work, will tell you all about me. ⁸ I am sending him to you for the express purpose of letting you know my circumstances, and of cheering your hearts; ⁹ he is accompanied by Onesimus, a faithful and dearly loved brother, who is one of your own number. They will tell you everything that is going on here.

¹⁰ Aristarchus, my fellow-prisoner, wishes to be remembered to you; and so does Mark, the cousin of Barnabas; if he comes to see you, give him a hearty welcome.[b] ¹¹ So does Jesus who is called Justus. These are the only converts from Judaism that are fellow-workers with me here for the kingdom of God, who have proved a real comfort to me. ¹² Epaphras, one of your own number, a slave of Christ Jesus, wishes to be remembered to you. He is always earnestly pleading for you in his prayers that you may stand fast as men mature and of firm convictions in everything required by the will[c] of God. ¹³ For I can testify how great his toiling for you is and for the brothers in Laodicea and Hierapolis. ¹⁴ Our dearly loved Luke, the physician, and Demas, wish to be remembered to you. ¹⁵ Remember me to the brothers in Laodicea and to Nympha and the church that meets at her house. ¹⁶ When this letter has been read to you, have it read to the church at Laodicea too, and see to it that you too read the one that is coming from Laodicea. ¹⁷ And tell Archippus, "See to it that you continue until you fill full your ministry which you received in the Lord's work."

¹⁸ This farewell greeting is in my own hand, from Paul. Remember that I am still a prisoner. Spiritual blessing be with you.

[a] Lit., *with grace;* so used in clas. Grk.
[b] A very strong vb.; so *give him a hearty welcome.*
[c] Lit., *in all the will of God.*

FIRST THESSALONIANS

The writer is Paul; so held by nearly all New Testament scholars.
He is in Corinth; he had sent Timothy back to Thessalonica to help and cheer the persecuted Christians there. Timothy had gone and done his work there, and now he comes to Corinth and reports that the Thessalonians were standing fast by their new faith, were loyal to Paul, but were not clear on the teaching about the Second Coming of Jesus, some fearing that their deceased loved ones would have little or no share in the blessings of His glory. This was the first of Paul's letters, written in A. D. 51.

The purpose was to pour out his heart's affection for them; to cheer them on to endure the persecution of their pagan neighbors; to explain more fully the Second Coming of Jesus; that it would be unexpected; that their deceased Christian loved ones would rise from the dead before those living at that time would meet the Lord.

This is a personal letter, with only one great doctrine, the Second Coming, treated. It is written in the diction and style of the common Greek.

1 HE GREETS THEM; THANKS GOD FOR THEIR FAITH, DEVOTION, AND HOPE; THEY HAD BECOME AN EXAMPLE TO OTHER BELIEVERS EVERYWHERE

Paul, Silvanus, and Timothy to the Thessalonian church in union with God the Father and the Lord Jesus Christ: spiritual blessing and peace be to you.

² We always thank God for you all as we continually mention you in our prayers, ³ for we can never for a moment before our God forget your energizing faith,[a] your toiling love, and your enduring hope in our Lord Jesus Christ. ⁴ For we know, brothers so beloved by God, that He has chosen you,[b] ⁵ for our preaching of the good news came to you not entirely in words but with power

[a] Lit., *your work of faith*, etc.
[b] Grk., *we know your election* (by God).

and with the Holy Spirit and with absolute certainty[c] (for you know the kind of men we were among you for your own sakes). ⁶ And you followed the example set by us and by the Lord, because you welcomed our message with a joy inspired by the Holy Spirit, in spite of the painful persecutions it brought you, ⁷ so that you became examples to all the believers in Macedonia and Greece. For the message of the Lord has rung out from you, not only in Macedonia and Greece, but everywhere the report of your faith in God has been told,[d] so that we need never mention it. ⁸ For the people themselves tell us what a welcome you gave us, and how you turned from idols to the true God,[e] to serve the God who lives on and is real, ⁹ and to wait for the coming from heaven of His Son, whom He raised from the dead, Jesus who delivers us from the wrath to come.

2 REMINDS THEM HOW HE TOLD THEM THE GOOD NEWS; HOW HE LIVED AMONG THEM; THANKS GOD FOR THEIR ENDURANCE IN PERSECUTION; LONGS TO SEE THEM

For you know yourselves, brothers, that our visit to you was by no means a failure. ² But, although we had just suffered and been insulted, as you remember, at Philippi, we again summoned courage by the help of God, in spite of the terrific strain,[a] to tell you God's good news. ³ For our appeal did not originate from a delusion or an impure motive; it was not made in fraud; ⁴ for since we have been so approved by God as to be entrusted with the good news, we are now telling it, not to please men but God, who proves and finds approved our hearts.

⁵ Indeed, we never resorted to flattery, as you are well aware, nor to any pretext for making money; [b] God is our witness. ⁶ We never sought praise from men, either from you or from anyone else; although as apostles we could have stood on our official dignity.[c] ⁷ Instead we were little children among you; we were like a mother nursing her children. ⁸ Because we were yearning for you so tender-

---

[c] Lit., *great and full assurance.*
[d] Lit., *your faith in God has gone out.*
[e] Grk. art. emph. here, so *the true God.*
[a] Lit., *in great agony.*
[b] Grk., *with a pretext of greed.*
[c] Lit., *weight* or *importance* (as apostles)

ly, we were willing, not only to share with you God's good news, but to lay down our very lives too for you, all because you were so dearly loved by us. ⁹ You remember, brothers, our hard labor and toil. We kept up our habit of working night and day, in order not to be a burden to any of you when we preached to you. ¹⁰ You can testify, and God too, with what pure, upright, and irreproachable motives[d] I dealt with you who believed; ¹¹ for you know how, as a father deals with his children, we used to encourage you, cheer you on, and charge each of you ¹² to live lives worthy of God who calls you into His kingdom and His glory.

¹³ For another reason too, we, as far as we are concerned, are constantly giving thanks to God; that is, when you received the message you heard[e] from us, you welcomed it not as the message of men but as the message of God, as it really is, which keeps on working in you who believe. ¹⁴ For you, brothers, followed the example of God's churches in Judea that are in union with Christ Jesus, for you too have suffered the same sort of ill-treatment[f] at the hands of your fellow-countrymen as they did at the hands of the Jews, ¹⁵ who killed the Lord Jesus and persecuted the prophets and us; and who continue to displease God and show themselves in opposition to all mankind, ¹⁶ by trying to keep us from speaking to the heathen, so that they may be saved, so as always to fill to the brim the cup of their sins. But at last God's wrath has come upon them.

¹⁷ Now we, brothers, on our part, when we were separated from you for a little while—in person but not in heart—were extremely eager and intensely longing to see you. ¹⁸ Because we did want to come to see you; I mean, that I myself, Paul, wanted again and again to come, but Satan prevented it. ¹⁹ For what is our hope or happiness or crown of boasting, except you, in the presence of our Lord Jesus Christ when He comes? ²⁰ You, indeed, are our glory and our joy.

3   HE SENDS TIMOTHY TO CHEER THEM; HE IS GRATEFUL FOR THE GOOD TIDINGS THAT TIMOTHY BROUGHT; HE PRAYS FOR THEIR GROWTH IN LOVE AND PURITY

So when I could not bear it any longer, I decided to be left behind in Athens alone, ² and so I sent my brother Timothy, God's

---

[d] Lit., *how holily, uprightly,* etc.
[e] Grk., *message of hearing.*
[f] Lit., *the same things.*

minister in the preaching of the good news of Christ, to strengthen and encourage you in your faith, ³ so that none of you might be deceived amid these difficulties. For you knew yourselves that this is our appointed lot,ᵃ ⁴ for when we were with you, we told you beforehand that we were going to be pressed with difficulties,ᵇ and it took place, as you know. ⁵ That was why, when I could bear it no longer, I sent to learnᶜ about your faith, for I was afraid that the tempter had tempted you and our labor might be lost.

⁶ But now, since Timothy has just come back to me from you, and brought me good tidings of your faith and love, and told me how kindly you remembered me and that you are longing to see me as much as I am to see you, ⁷ this is the very reason, namely, through your faith, brothers, that I have been encouraged about you, in spite of all my distresses and crushing difficulties,ᵇ ⁸ for now I am really living, sinceᵈ you are standing firm in the Lord. ⁹ For how can I render God enough thanks for you, for all the joy I have on account of you in the presence of our God, ¹⁰ as night and day I continue to pray with deepest earnestness and keenest eagernessᵉ that I may see your faces and round out to completeness what is lacking in your faith?

¹¹ Now may our God and Father Himself and our Lord Jesus guide my way to you! ¹² May the Lord make you increase and overflow in love for one another and for all men, as my love for you does, ¹³ so that He may strengthen your hearts to be faultless in purity in the sight of God, when our Lord Jesus comes back with all His consecrated ones.

4   HE URGES THEM TO PERSONAL PURITY, BROTHERLY LOVE, AND HONEST TOIL; ASSURES AND COMFORTS THEM THAT WHEN JESUS COMES BACK THEIR DEAD LOVED ONES WILL RISE TO MEET THE LORD BEFORE THE LIVING SEE HIM

Now, brothers, we ask and beg you, in the face* of our union with the Lord Jesus, as you once received from us how you ought

---

ᵃ Grk., *we are set for this thing.*
ᵇ Picture of a loaded wagon crushed under its heavy load.
ᶜ *Know.*
ᵈ More probable cond., so *since* better than *if.*
ᵉ Grk., *praying surpassingly,* etc.
* *In the Lord Jesus.*

to live so [a] as to please God—as indeed you are living—to continue to live this life better and better.[b] ² For you are aware of the instructions which we gave you by the authority of the Lord Jesus.

³ For it is God's will that you should keep pure in person, that you should practice abstinence from sexual immorality, ⁴ that each man among you should learn to take his own wife [c] out of pure and honorable motives, ⁵ not out of evil passions [d] as the heathen do who do not know God; ⁶ that no one should do wrong and defraud his brother in this matter, because the Lord takes vengeance for all such things, as we told you before and solemnly warned you. ⁷ For God did not call us to a life of immorality, but to one of personal purity. ⁸ So whoever rejects this teaching is rejecting not man but God who continues to put His Spirit in you.

⁹ Now as to brotherly love, you have no need of anyone's writing you, for you have yourselves been taught by God [e] to love one another, ¹⁰ as you are practicing it toward all the brothers all over Macedonia.

We beg you, brothers, to continue to live better and better; [b] ¹¹ also keep up your ambition to live quietly, to practice attending to your own business and to work with your own hands, as we directed you, ¹² so that you may live influentially with the outsiders, and not be dependent on anybody.

¹³ Also we do not want you to have any misunderstanding, brothers, about those who are falling asleep,[f] so as to keep you from grieving over them as others do who have no hope. ¹⁴ For if we believe that Jesus died and rose again, then through Jesus, God will bring back with Him those who have fallen asleep. ¹⁵ For on the Lord's own authority we say that those of us who may be left behind and are still living when the Lord comes back, will have no advantage at all [g] over those who have fallen asleep. ¹⁶ For the Lord Himself, at the summons sounded by the archangel's call and by God's trumpet, will come down from heaven, and first of all the dead in union with Christ will rise, ¹⁷ then those of us who are still living will be caught up along with them on clouds in the

[a] *Live and please God.*
[b] *Keep on overflowing.*
[c] *Vessel;* here *wife.*
[d] Lit., *with personal purity and honor, not in lustful passions* (gen. of quality).
[e] *God-taught;* i.e., in their moral sense.
[f] I.e., are dying.
[g] Emphatic neg.

air to meet the Lord, and so we shall be with the Lord forever. ¹⁸ So continue encouraging one another with this truth.

5   WHEN CHRIST IS TO COME UNKNOWN; SO WATCH AND WAIT; HINTS ON DAILY LIVING; FULL PUBLICITY FOR THIS LETTER

But as to times and dates, brothers, you have no need of anyone's writing you, ² for you yourselves know perfectly well that the day of the Lord is coming like a thief in the night. ³ When people say, "Such peace and security!" then suddenly destruction falls upon them, like birth pains upon a woman who is about to become a mother, but they shall not escape, no, not at all. ⁴ But you, brothers, are not in darkness, so that that day, like a thief, should take you by surprise; ⁵ for you are all sons of the light and sons of the day. We do not belong to the night or the darkness. ⁶ So let us stop sleeping as others do, but let us stay awake and keep sober. ⁷ For those who sleep sleep at night and those who get drunk are drunken at night, ⁸ but let us who belong to the day keep sober, clothed with faith and love for a coat of mail and with the hope of salvation for a helmet. ⁹ For God appointed us not to reap His wrath but to gain salvation through our Lord Jesus Christ, ¹⁰ who died for us, so that whether we still live or sleep [a] we may live in fellowship with Him. ¹¹ So continue encouraging one another and helping [b] one another in character building.

¹² We beg you, brothers, to practice showing respect to those who labor among you, who are your leaders in the Lord's work, and who advise you; ¹³ continue to hold them in the highest esteem for the sake of the work they do. Practice living at peace with one another. ¹⁴ We beg you, brothers, continue to warn the shirkers, to cheer the faint-hearted, to hold up the weak, and to be patient with everybody. ¹⁵ Take care that none of you ever pays back evil for evil, but always keep looking for ways to show kindness to one another and everybody. ¹⁶ Always be joyful. ¹⁷ Never stop praying. ¹⁸ Make it a habit to give thanks for everything, for this is God's will for you through Christ Jesus. ¹⁹ Stop stifling [c] the Spirit. ²⁰ Stop treating the messages of prophecy with contempt, ²¹ but continue to prove all things until you can ap-

[a] Still live or die.
[b] Implied in recip. pro.
[c] Figure of putting out fire by smothering.

prove[d] them, and then hold on to what is good. ²² Continue to abstain from every sort of evil.

²³ May God Himself, who gave you peace, consecrate your whole being. May you be safely kept, spirit, soul, and body, so as to be blameless when our Lord Jesus Christ comes back. ²⁴ He who calls you is trustworthy and He will do this. ²⁵ Brothers, pray for us. ²⁶ Greet all the brothers with a sacred kiss. ²⁷ I solemnly charge you before the Lord to have this letter read to all the brothers.

²⁸ The spiritual blessing of our Lord Jesus Christ be with you.

[d] Double idea in one vb.

SECOND THESSALONIANS

It is usually thought that Paul wrote it, though some deny it.
He was still in Corinth. It was reported to him that the Thessalonians misunderstood what he wrote them in the first letter about the Second Coming of the Lord. Many felt that he meant that He was coming at once, and so they stopped working, went to loafing, but still continued to look for Him to come. Some three to six months elapsed after the first letter before he wrote this one.

The purpose was to correct these misapprehensions; to let them know that Christ is not coming at once, but that other events must first take place; to encourage them to continue to endure their persecutions, but at the same time to bear their part in industry and other social enterprises.

1 HE GREETS THEM; THANKS GOD FOR THEIR FAITH, LOVE, ENDURANCE; TELLS THEM THAT THE LORD WILL VINDICATE THEIR SUFFERINGS WHEN HE COMES; PRAYS CONTINUALLY FOR THEM

Paul, Silvanus, and Timothy to the Thessalonian church in union with God our Father and the Lord Jesus Christ: [2] spiritual blessing and peace be to you.

[3] We always ought to be thanking God for you, brothers, as it is right to do so, because your faith is growing so much and the love of every one of you for one another is increasing [4] so that we are always boasting of you among the churches of God for your patient endurance and faith, in spite of your persecutions and crushing sorrows which you are enduring. [5] This is a proof of God's righteous judgment, His aim [a] being to let you show yourselves worthy of His kingdom, for which you are suffering; since, [6] indeed, it is right for God to repay with crushing sorrows those who cause you these crushing sorrows, [7] and to give rest to you who are being crushed with sorrows, along with us, at the unveiling of our Lord

[a] In pass. infin. of purpose.

Jesus Christ from heaven, with His mighty angels ⁸ in a flame of fire, who will take vengeance on those who do not know God, that is, those who will not listen to the good news of our Lord Jesus. ⁹ These will receive the punishment of eternal destruction as exiles ᵇ from the presence of the Lord and His glorious might, ¹⁰ when on that day He comes to be glorified in His consecrated ones and to be admired by all who believe in Him—because our testimony has been confidently accepted among you.

¹¹ With this in view we are always praying for you too, that our God may make you worthy of His call, and by His power fully satisfy your every desire for goodness, and complete ᶜ every activity of your faith, ¹² so that the name of our Lord Jesus may be glorified in you and you through union with Him, in accordance with the favor of our God and the Lord Jesus Christ.

2 SOME EVENTS TO PRECEDE THE LORD'S RETURN, SO IT IS NOT TO BE AT ONCE; HE AGAIN THANKS GOD FOR THEM, PLEADS WITH THEM, PRAYS FOR THEM

As to the coming of our Lord Jesus Christ and our final muster before Him, we beg you, brothers, ² not to let your minds be easily unsettled ᵃ or even be excited, whether by some message by the Spirit or by some saying or letter that is claimed as coming from me, saying that the day of the Lord is already here. ³ Do not let anybody at all deceive you about this, because that cannot take place ᵇ until the great revolt ᶜ occurs and the representative of lawlessness is uncovered, the one who is doomed to destruction, ⁴ the one who keeps up his opposition and so far exalts himself above every so-called god or object of worship, that he actually takes his seat in the sanctuary of God, proclaiming himself to be God. ⁵ Do you not remember that while I was with you I used to tell you this? ⁶ So now you know the power ᵈ that is holding him back, that he is to be unveiled at His own appointed time. ⁷ For the secret power ᵉ of lawlessness is already at work, but only until he who

---

ᵇ In prep. See Mt. 25:41.
ᶜ Single vb. with double sense and two objects.
ᵃ *Unsettled by* or *because of your mind.*
ᵇ Easily supplied.
ᶜ *Apostasy;* moral revolt.
ᵈ *The thing that,* etc.
ᵉ Lit., *mystery.*

is holding it back has been gotten out of the way. ⁸ Then the representative of lawlessness will be uncovered, and the Lord Jesus will destroy him with the breath of His mouth and put a stop to his operations by His appearance and coming; ⁹ that is, the representative of lawlessness, whose coming is in accordance with the working of Satan, with his plenitude of power and pretended signs and wonders, ¹⁰ and with a completely wicked deception for men who are on the way to destruction, because they refused to love the truth so as to be saved. ¹¹ This is why God sends them a misleading influence till they actually believe what is false, ¹² so that all who have refused to believe the truth but have chosen unrighteousness instead might be condemned.

¹³ We ought always to be thanking God for you, brothers dearly loved by the Lord, because God chose you from the beginning for salvation through the Spirit's consecration of you and through your faith in the truth, ¹⁴ and to this end He called you by our preaching of the good news, so that you may obtain the glory of our Lord Jesus Christ.

¹⁵ So then, brothers, continue to stand firm and keep a tight grip on the teachings you have received from us, whether by word of mouth or by letter. ¹⁶ May our Lord Jesus Christ Himself and God our Father, who has loved us and graciously given us encouragement that is eternal, and a hope that is well-founded, ¹⁷ encourage your hearts and strengthen you in every good thing you do or say.

3   HE ASKS THEM TO PRAY FOR HIM; HE PRAYS FOR THEM;
     URGES THEM TO FOLLOW HIS EXAMPLE IN HONEST
     TOIL, TO HOLD ALOOF FROM SHIRKERS; HOW TO
     IDENTIFY HIS LETTERS; SENDS BLESSING

Finally, brothers, pray for us, that the message of the Lord may continue to spread and prove its glorious power [a] as it did among you, ² and that we may be delivered from unprincipled and wicked men; for not all men have faith.

³ But the Lord is to be trusted, and He will give you strength and guard you from the evil one. ⁴ We have confidence in you through the Lord that you are now practicing the directions which we give you and that you will continue to do so. ⁵ May the Lord

---

[a] Lit., *continue to run and be glorified.*

guide you into a realization [b] of God's love for you and into a patient endurance like Christ's.

⁶ Now we charge you, brothers, on the authority of the Lord Jesus Christ, to hold yourselves aloof from any brother who is living as a shirker [c] instead of following the teachings you received from us. ⁷ You know yourselves how you ought to follow my example; for I was not a shirker when I was with you; ⁸ I did not eat any man's bread without paying for it,[d] but with toil and hard labor I worked night and day, in order not to be a burden to any of you. ⁹ Not that I have no right to be supported,[b] but to make myself an example for you to follow. ¹⁰ For when I was with you, I gave you this direction, "If a person refuses to work, he must not be allowed [b] to eat." ¹¹ But we are informed that some among you are living as shirkers, mere busybodies, instead of busy at work. ¹² Now on the authority of the Lord Jesus Christ we charge and exhort such persons to do their own work with quiet and eat their own bread. ¹³ But you, brothers, must never grow tired of doing right. ¹⁴ If anyone refuses to obey what we have said in this letter, mark that person and stop having anything to do with him, so that he will feel ashamed of it. ¹⁵ You must not regard him as an enemy but warn him as a brother. ¹⁶ And may the Lord who gives us peace [e] give you peace in whatever circumstances you may be. The Lord be with you all.

¹⁷ This greeting is in my own hand, Paul's; it is the mark in every letter of mine. This is my handwriting. ¹⁸ The spiritual blessing of our Lord Jesus Christ be with you all.

[b] Implied from context.
[c] *One who is out of line with daily workers.*
[d] *As a free gift.*
[e] Lit., *the Lord of peace* (obj. gen.).

FIRST TIMOTHY

The author is usually thought to be Paul, although a few New Testament scholars deny it.

He has been released from prison in Rome and is waiting at Philippi before going on to Spain with the good news of Christ. Timothy, a faithful minister and missionary, is stationed at Ephesus, either as pastor of the local church, or, which is more probable, as superintendent of missions for the whole province, and adviser to all the churches in the matter of selecting pastors, deacons, and deaconesses.

The purpose was to encourage Timothy to stand firm as a brave soldier of Christ and as a champion of the truths of the good news as taught by Paul; to instruct him specifically in the proper organization of the churches; to help them secure pastors, deacons, and deaconesses of good Christian character, qualified for their respective offices; to instruct him how to deal with the various classes in the churches and in the relation of Christians to society and government.

1 HE GREETS TIMOTHY; URGES HIM TO WARN THE FALSE TEACHERS; TELLS OF THE PRACTICAL AIM OF THE LAW; THANKS GOD FOR SAVING HIM THOUGH ONCE A PERSECUTOR OF THE CHURCH; URGES TIMOTHY TO CONTINUE THE GOOD FIGHT

Paul, an apostle of Christ Jesus by command of God our Saviour and of Christ Jesus our hope, ² to Timothy my genuine child in faith: spiritual blessing, mercy, and peace be with you from God our Father and Christ Jesus our Lord.

³ As I begged you to do when I was on my way to Macedonia, I still beg you to stay on in Ephesus to warn certain teachers to ⁴ stop devoting themselves to myths and never-ending pedigrees,[a]

[a] Likely referring to the emanations in the Gnostic system.

461

for such things lead [b] to controversies rather than stimulate [b] our trusteeship to God through faith. [5] But the aim of your instruction is to be love that flows out of a pure heart, a good conscience, and a sincere faith. [6] Some people have stepped aside from these things and turned to fruitless talking. [7] They want to be teachers of the law, although they do not understand the words they use or the things about which they make such confident assertions.

[8] Indeed, I know that the law is an excellent thing, if a man makes a lawful use of it; [9] that is, if he understands that law is not enacted for upright people but for the lawless and disorderly, the godless and sinful, the ignorant and profane, people who kill their fathers or mothers, murderers, [10] the immoral, men who practice sodomy,[c] men who make other men their slaves, liars, perjurers, or anything else that is contrary to sound teaching, [11] as measured [d] by the glorious good news of the blessed God, with which I have been entrusted.

[12] I am always thanking Christ Jesus our Lord who has given me strength for it, for thinking me trustworthy and putting me into the ministry, [13] though I once used to abuse, persecute, and insult Him. But mercy was shown me by Him, because I did it in ignorance and unbelief, [14] and the spiritual blessing of our Lord in increasing floods [e] has come upon me, accompanied by faith and love inspired by union with Christ Jesus. [15] It is a saying to be trusted and deserves our fullest acceptance, that Christ Jesus came into the world to save sinners; and I am the foremost of them. [16] Yet, mercy was shown me for the very purpose that in my case as the foremost of sinners Jesus might display His perfect patience, to make me an example to those who in the future might believe on Him to obtain eternal life. [17] To the King eternal, immortal, invisible, the only God, be honor and glory forever and ever! Amen.

[18] This is the instruction which I entrust to you, my son Timothy, which is in accordance with the prophetic utterances formerly made about you, that you may, aided by them, continue [f] to fight the good fight, [19] by keeping your hold on faith and a good conscience; for some have thrust the latter aside and so have made shipwreck of their faith. [20] Among these are Hymenaeus and Alex-

---

[b] One vb. with two senses and two applications.
[c] A common sin among the heathen.
[d] In prep. *kata*.
[e] Lit., *flowed superabundantly*.
[f] Pres. subjunctive fol. WH.

ander, whom I have turned over to Satan to be so disciplined [g] that they will stop their abusive speech.

2 CHRISTIANS MUST PRAY FOR ALL, ESPECIALLY FOR CIVIL OFFICERS; MEN MUST LEAD THE PUBLIC PRAYERS; WOMEN MUST DRESS MODESTLY, BE SUBORDINATE TO MEN

First of all, then, I urge that entreaties, prayers, and thanksgiving be offered for all men, 2 for kings and all who are in authority, so that we may lead peaceful, quiet lives in perfect piety and seriousness. 3 This is the right thing to do and it pleases God our Saviour, 4 who is ever willing for all mankind to be saved and to come to an increasing knowledge of the truth. 5 For there is but one [a] God and one [a] intermediary between God and men, the man Christ Jesus 6 who gave Himself as a ransom for all, a fact that was testified to at the proper time,[b] 7 and for which purpose I was appointed a preacher and an apostle—I am telling the truth, I am not lying,—[c] a teacher of the heathen in the realm of faith and truth.

8 So I want the men everywhere to offer prayer, lifting to heaven holy hands which are kept unstained by anger and dissensions. 9 I want [d] the women, on their part, to dress becomingly, that is, modestly and sensibly, not adorning themselves with braided hair and gold or pearls or expensive dresses, 10 but with good deeds; for this is appropriate for women who profess to be pious.

11 A married [d] woman must learn in quiet and in perfect submission. 12 I do not permit a married woman to practice teaching or domineering over a husband; she must keep quiet. 13 For Adam was formed first, and then Eve; 14 and it was not Adam who was deceived, but it was the woman who was utterly [e] deceived and fell into transgression. 15 But women will be saved through motherhood, if they continue to live in faith, love, and purity, blended [f] with good sense.

[g] So in classical Grk.
[a] Emphatic.
[b] *Testimony at its own time.*
[c] A Heb. way of strongly affirming.
[d] Implied in context.
[e] In comp. vb.
[f] In prep. *meta.*

3 THE QUALIFICATIONS OF PASTORS, DEACONS, AND DEACONESSES; THE CHURCH, THE PILLAR AND FOUNDATION OF TRUTH

This is a saying to be trusted: "Whoever aspires to the office of pastor desires an excellent work." ² So the pastor must be a man above reproach, must have only one wife, must be temperate, sensible, well-behaved, hospitable, skillful in teaching; ³ not addicted to strong drink, not pugnacious, gentle and not contentious, not avaricious, ⁴ managing his own house well, with perfect ᵃ seriousness keeping his children under control ⁵ (if a man does not know how to manage his own house, how can he take care of a church of God?). ⁶ He must not be a new convert, or else becoming conceited he may incur the doom the devil ᵇ met. ⁷ He must also have a good reputation with outsiders, or else he may incur reproach and fall into the devil's trap.

⁸ Deacons, too, must ᶜ be serious, sincere in their talk,ᵈ not addicted to strong drink or dishonest gain, ⁹ but they must continue to hold the open secret of faith with a clear conscience. ¹⁰ They, too, should first be tested till approved, and then, if they are found above reproach, they should serve as deacons. ¹¹ The deaconesses too ᵉ must be serious, not gossips; they must be temperate and perfectly trustworthy. ¹² A deacon too must have only one wife, and manage his children and household well. ¹³ For those who render good service win a good standing for themselves in their faith in Christ Jesus.

¹⁴ Though I hope to come to you soon, I am writing you this, ¹⁵ so that, if I am detained, you may know how people ought to conduct themselves in the house of God, which is the church of the living God, the pillar and foundation of the truth. ¹⁶ Undoubtedly the mystery of our religion is a great wonder:

> "He was made visible in human form,
> He was vindicated by the Spirit,
> He was seen by angels,
> He was proclaimed among the heathen,

ᵃ Grk., *all.*
ᵇ Subj. gen.
ᶜ Implied from v. 7.
ᵈ *Not double-worded.*
ᵉ Women acting as official servants.

He was trusted in throughout the world,
He was taken up to glory." ᶠ

4 TEACHERS TEACH FALSELY ABOUT MARRIAGE AND FOODS; TIMOTHY TO REBUKE THEM AND TRAIN HIMSELF IN PURE LIVING, SPIRITUAL EXERCISES, AND PATIENT TEACHING

Now the Spirit distinctly declares that in later times some will turn away from the faith, because they continuously give their attention to deceiving spirits and the things that demons teach ² through the pretensions of false teachers, men with seared consciences, ³ who forbid people to marry and teach them to abstain from certain sorts of food which God created for the grateful enjoyment ᵃ of those who have faith and a clear knowledge of the truth. ⁴ For everything in God's creation is good, and nothing is to be refused, provided it is accepted with thanksgiving; ⁵ for in this way it is consecrated by the word of God and prayer.

⁶ If you continue to put these things before the brothers, you will be a good minister of Christ Jesus, ever feeding your own soul on the truths ᵇ of the faith and of the fine teaching which you have followed. ⁷ But make it your habit to let worldly and old women's stories alone. Continue training yourself for the religious life. ⁸ Physical training, indeed, is of some service, but religion ᶜ is of service for everything, for it contains a promise for the present life as well as the future. ⁹ This is a saying to be trusted and deserves to be accepted by all. ¹⁰ To this end we are toiling and struggling, because we have fixed our hope on the living God, who is the Saviour of all mankind, especially of believers.

¹¹ Continue to give these orders and to teach these truths. ¹² Let no one think little of you because you are young, but always set an example for believers, in speech, conduct, love, faith, and purity. ¹³ Until I come, devote yourself ᵈ to the public reading of the Scriptures, and to preaching and teaching. ¹⁴ Stop neglecting the gift you received, which was given you through prophetic ut-

---
ᶠ Likely from an early Christian hymn in praise of the person and work of Christ.
ᵃ Lit., *reception with gratitude*.
ᵇ Grk., *nourishing yourself on the words*.
ᶜ Lit., *godliness*, or *worshiping well*.
ᵈ *Give attention to*.

terance when the elders laid their hands upon you. ¹⁵ Continue cultivating these things; be devoted to them, so that everybody will see your progress. ¹⁶ Make it your habit to pay close attention to yourself and your teaching. Persevere in these things, for if you do you will save both yourself and those who listen to you.

5 TELLS TIMOTHY HOW TO TREAT THE OLD AND THE YOUNG, ESPECIALLY WIDOWS; HOW TO SELECT AND TREAT THE OFFICERS OF THE CHURCHES

Never reprove an older man, but always appeal to him as a father. Treat younger men like brothers, ² older women like mothers, younger women like sisters, with perfect purity. ³ Always care for widows who are really dependent.ᵃ ⁴ But if a widow has children or grandchildren, they must first learn to practice piety in the treatment of their own families,ᵇ and to pay the debt they owe their parents or grandparents,ᶜ for this is acceptable to God. ⁵ But a woman who is really a widow and lives alone has fixed her hope on God, and night and day devotes herself to prayers and entreaties, ⁶ while a widow who gives herself up to luxury is really dead though still alive. ⁷ Continue to give these directions so that the people may be without reproach. ⁸ Whoever fails to provide for his own relatives, and especially for those of his immediate family, has disowned the faith and is worse than an unbeliever. ⁹ No widow under sixty years of age should be put on this roll. A widow must have had but one husband,ᵈ ¹⁰ must have a reputation for doing good deeds, as bringing up children, being hospitable to strangers, washing the feet of God's people, helping people in distress, or devoting herself to any sort of doing good. ¹¹ Keep the young widows off this roll, for when they get to indulging their lower nature in opposition to Christ, they want to marry, ¹² and so deserve censure for breaking their previous pledge.ᵉ ¹³ Besides, as they get the habit of gadding about from house to house, they learn to be idle, and not only idle but gossips and busybodies, talking of things they ought not to mention. ¹⁴ So I would have the younger women marry, have children, and keep house, so as not

---

ᵃ Lit., *widows who are really widows.*
ᵇ *Practice piety toward,* etc.
ᶜ One word in both senses, as in classical Grk.
ᵈ One at a time.
ᵉ Religious vow.

to give our opponents any occasion for slander. ¹⁵ For some widows have already turned aside to follow Satan. ¹⁶ If a Christian woman has widowed relatives, she should help them, and let the church be free from the burden, so that it can help the widows who are really dependent.

¹⁷ Elders who do their duties well should be considered as deserving twice the salary they get,[f] especially those who keep on toiling in preaching and teaching. ¹⁸ For the Scripture says, "You must not muzzle an ox when he is treading out the grain,"[g] and, "The workman deserves his pay."[h] ¹⁹ Make it a rule not to consider a charge preferred against an elder, unless it is supported by two or three witnesses. ²⁰ Those who are guilty reprove in public, so that others may be warned. ²¹ I solemnly charge you before God and Christ Jesus and the chosen angels, to carry out these instructions without prejudice and with perfect impartiality. ²² Make it a rule not to ordain anyone in haste, and not to be responsible for the sins of others; keep yourself pure. ²³ Stop drinking water only, but take a little wine to strengthen your stomach and relieve its frequent attacks. ²⁴ Some men's sins are very evident and clearly lead them on to judgment, but the sins of others lag behind. ²⁵ Good deeds, too, are usually very evident, and if they are not, they cannot be completely concealed.

6 SLAVES MUST RENDER WILLING SERVICE; HE WARNS AGAINST FALSE TEACHING AND GREED; TIMOTHY SOLEMNLY CHARGED, ESPECIALLY TO URGE THE RICH TO DO GOOD WITH THEIR MONEY; HE WARNS AGAIN; SAYS FAREWELL

All who are under the yoke of slavery must esteem their masters to be deserving the highest respect, so that the name of God and our teaching may not be abused. ² Those who have Christian masters must not pay them less respect because they are brothers; they must serve them all the better, because those who get the benefit of their service are believers and so are dear to them.

These are the things that you must continue to teach and urge them to do. ³ If anyone teaches different doctrines and refuses to

---

[f] Lit., *double price,* so *double salary.*
[g] Dt. 25:4.
[h] Referring to Jesus' saying, later embodied in the Gospels.

agree with the wholesome messages of our Lord Jesus Christ, the teaching that is in accordance with true religion, ⁴ he is a conceited ignoramus ᵃ with a morbid appetite for discussions and controversies which lead to envy, quarreling, abuse, base suspicions, ⁵ and perpetual friction between people who are depraved in mind and deprived of truth, who imagine that religion is only a means of gain. ⁶ Now the fact is, religion with contentment is a means of great gain. ⁷ For we bring nothing into the world and surely we can take nothing out of it. ⁸ If we have food and clothes we will be satisfied. ⁹ But men who keep planning to get rich fall into temptations and snares and many foolish, hurtful desires which plunge people into destruction and ruin. ¹⁰ For the love of money is the root of all sorts of evil,ᵇ and some men in reaching after riches have wandered from the faith and pierced their hearts with many a pang.

¹¹ But you, as a man of God, must be fleeing always from these things; you must constantly strive for uprightness, godliness, faith, love, steadfastness, gentleness. ¹² Keep up the good fight for the faith. Keep your hold on eternal life, to which God called you, when before many witnesses you made the good profession of faith. ¹³ Before God who preserves the life of all His creatures and before Christ Jesus who in testifying before Pontius Pilate made His good profession, I solemnly charge you ¹⁴ to keep His command stainless and irreproachable until the appearance of our Lord Jesus Christ, ¹⁵ which will be brought about ᶜ in His own time by the blessed, only Sovereign, the King of kings, the Lord of lords, ¹⁶ who alone possesses immortality and dwells in unapproachable light, whom no man has ever seen or can see. To Him be honor and eternal dominion.ᵈ Amen.

¹⁷ Continue charging the rich of this world to stop being haughty and not to fix their hope on a thing so uncertain as riches, but on God who richly and ceaselessly provides us with everything for our enjoyment; ¹⁸ charge them to continue doing good and being rich in good deeds, open-handed and generous-hearted, ¹⁹ in this way amassing for themselves the riches that forever endure in the life to come, so that at last they may grasp the life that is life indeed.

ᵃ Lit., *is puffed up, knowing nothing.*
ᵇ *All evils.*
ᶜ Grk. has active.
ᵈ *Power.*

[20] Timothy, guard what has been entrusted to you; continue to turn away from the worldly, futile phrases and contradictions of what is falsely called "knowledge,"[e] [21] by professing which some individuals have failed[f] in the faith. Spiritual blessing be with you[g] all.

[e] A thrust at the Gnostics.
[f] So in papyri.
[g] Pl., so *you all*

SECOND TIMOTHY

The writer is usually thought to be Paul, though some deny it.
While on the fourth missionary tour he was arrested at Nicopolis (Tit. 3:12) and sent to Rome where he is now a prisoner. He is facing his second trial before Nero (2 Tim. 4:16) and feels sure that he will be sentenced to die, but in peace he is waiting for the heavenly kingdom (4:18). The date is about A.D. 65 or 66.
The purpose is to assert his triumph, through Jesus Christ, over all evil and evil plotters; to encourage Timothy to continue his good fight for the truth and fill his ministry to the brim with service in preaching, teaching, and general directing of the missionary program in the province of Asia.

1 GREETS TIMOTHY; THANKS GOD FOR HIS EARLY RELIGIOUS TRAINING; URGES HIM TO BE COURAGEOUS; TWO TRAITORS EXPOSED; A HERO EXHIBITED

Paul, an apostle of Christ Jesus by the will of God, in accordance with the promise of the life that comes through union with Christ Jesus, [2] to my dearly loved child Timothy: spiritual blessing, mercy, and peace be with you from God our Father and Christ Jesus our Lord.

[3] I thank God, whom I worship, as my forefathers did, with a clear conscience, as I ceaselessly remember you in my prayers. Because I remember the tears you shed for me,[a] I am always longing night and day [4] to see you again, that I may feel the fullest joy [5] on being reminded of your genuine faith, a faith that first found a home [b] in the heart of your grandmother Lois, then in the heart of your mother Eunice, and now in yours too, I am sure.

[6] For this reason I now remind you to rekindle [c] and keep burning the fire of the divine gift which came upon you when I laid my hands upon you. [7] For the Spirit that God has given us does not

[a] Implied.
[b] Vb. means *to dwell permanently;* so *find a home.*
[c] In prep.

impart timidity but power and love and self-control. ⁸ So you must never be ashamed of me His prisoner, but suffer for the good news in fellowship with me and by the power of God. ⁹ For He saved us and called us with a holy call, not in accordance with anything that we had done, but in accordance with His own purpose and unmerited favor which was shown us through union with Christ Jesus eternal ages ago, ¹⁰ but has only recently been made known through the appearance of our Saviour Christ Jesus, who through the good news has put a stop to the power* of death, and brought life and immortality to light. ¹¹ Of this good news I have been appointed a preacher, an apostle, and a teacher. ¹² This is why I am suffering so, but I am not ashamed of it, for I know whom I have trusted and I am absolutely sure that He is able to guard what I have entrusted to Him until that day. ¹³ Continue to be an example in wholesome instructions ᵈ which you learned from me, in the faith and love that come through union with Christ Jesus. ¹⁴ Guard this fine deposit of truth* by the aid of the Holy Spirit who has His home in our hearts.

¹⁵ You know that everyone here who belongs to the Roman province* of Asia has deserted me, including Phygelus and Hermogenes. ¹⁶ May the Lord show mercy to the family of Onesiphorus, because he often cheered me and was not ashamed of the chains I wore. ¹⁷ Yes, when he got to Rome he took pains to look me up and finally found me. ¹⁸ The Lord grant that he may find mercy at His hands on that day. And you very well know yourself how great were the services he rendered me at Ephesus.

2   TIMOTHY URGED TO BE DILIGENT IN TEACHING, PATIENT AND COURAGEOUS IN SUFFERING; TO DISCOURAGE PETTY DEBATING; TELLS OF TWO SORTS OF CHRISTIANS; TIMOTHY WARNED OF SOME PERSONAL PERILS

So you, my son, must keep renewing your strength in the spiritual blessing that comes through union with Christ Jesus. ² The things you learned from me before many witnesses you must commit to trustworthy men who will be competent to teach others too. ³ Take your share of hardships like a good soldier of Christ Jesus. ⁴ No soldier ever allows himself ᵃ to be involved in the busi-

ᵈ Lit., *words.*
ᵃ Grk., *no soldier is ever allowed.*
* Implied.

ness affairs of life, so that he may please the officer [b] who enlisted him. [5] No contestant in the games is crowned, unless he competes according to the rules. [6] The toiling farmer ought to be the first to share the crop.[c] [7] Keep on thinking about what I am saying, for the Lord will grant you understanding of it in all its phases. [8] Continue to remember Jesus Christ as risen from the dead, and descended from David, in accordance with the good news that I preach, [9] for the sake of which I am suffering hardships even to the extent of wearing chains as though I were a criminal. But God's message is not in chains. [10] For this reason I am bearing anything for the sake of His chosen people, so that they too may obtain the salvation [d] that comes through Christ Jesus and with it eternal glory. [11] This message is to be trusted: "If we indeed have died with Him, we will live with Him too. [12] If we patiently endure, we will reign with Him too. If we disown Him, He will disown us too. [13] If we are unfaithful, He remains faithful, for He cannot prove false [e] to Himself."

[14] Keep on reminding men of these things. Solemnly charge them before God to stop petty debating, [f] which does no good at all but brings destruction on those who hear it. [15] Do your best to present yourself to God an approved workman who has nothing to be ashamed of, who properly presents the message of truth. [16] Continue shunning worldly, futile phrases, for they lead on to greater depths of godlessness, [17] and their message will spread like a cancer; men like Hymenaeus and Philetus, [18] who have missed the truth by saying that the resurrection has already taken place, are undermining some people's faith. [19] But God's foundation stands unshaken, with these inscriptions: "The Lord knows the people who belong to Him" [g] and "Everyone who bears the name of the Lord must abstain from evil." [h]

[20] In any great house there are not only gold and silver articles but also wooden utensils, some for honorable [i] uses and some for lowly [j] uses. [21] So if a man will cleanse himself from these things,

[b] Lit., *him who enlists.*
[c] Lit., *fruits.*
[d] The final deliverance at the resurrection.
[e] *Deny himself.*
[f] Lit., *word battles.*
[g] Nu. 16:5.
[h] Isa. 26:13.
[i] As platters and cups for a royal wedding.
[j] As water jars, etc.

he will be an instrument for honorable uses, consecrated, useful for the Master, and ready for any good service.

²² You must keep on fleeing from the evil impulses of youth, but ever strive for uprightness, faith, love, and peace, in association with those who call upon the Lord with pure hearts. ²³ Always avoid foolish discussions with ignorant men, for you know that they breed quarrels, ²⁴ and a slave of the Lord must not quarrel but must be gentle to everybody; he must be a skillful teacher, and not resentful under injuries. ²⁵ With gentleness he must correct his opponents, for God might grant them repentance that would lead them to a full knowledge of the truth, ²⁶ and they might recover their senses and escape from the devil's trap in which they have been caught by him to do his will.

3 LAST DAYS TERRIBLE IN CRIMES AND FALSE TEACHINGS; FALSE TEACHERS LIKE JANNES AND JAMBRES OF OLD; TIMOTHY URGED TO BE FAITHFUL TO HIS TRAINING

Now you must know that in the last days there are going to be hard times. ² For people will be selfish, avaricious, boastful, haughty, abusive, disobedient to parents, ungrateful, irreverent, ³ lacking in love for kinsmen, irreconcilable, slanderers, having no self-control, savage, lacking in love for the good,[a] ⁴ treacherous, reckless, conceited, loving pleasure more than God, ⁵ keeping up the forms of religion but not giving expression to its power. Avoid such people. ⁶ For some of them practice going into people's houses and capturing weak and silly women who are overwhelmed with the weight of their sins, who are easily led about by all sorts of evil impulses, ⁷ who are always trying to learn but never able to come to a full knowledge of the truth. ⁸ Just as Jannes and Jambres resisted Moses, these people resist the truth, for they are depraved in mind and so counterfeits in the faith. ⁹ But they will not make any more progress, for their folly will be evident to everybody, as theirs [b] was. ¹⁰ But you, on your part, have faithfully [c] followed my teaching, my conduct, my aim, my faith, my patience, my love, my steadfastness, ¹¹ my persecutions, my sufferings, such as befell me at Antioch, Iconium, and Lystra, such as I endured—but the Lord delivered me out of them all. ¹² Yes,

[a] So in papyri.
[b] Jannes and Jambres, Egyptian magicians.
[c] In comp. vb.

indeed, everyone who wants to live a godly life as a follower of Christ Jesus will be persecuted. 13 But bad men and impostors will go on from bad to worse, misleading others and misled themselves. 14 But you, on your part, must continue to abide by what you have learned and been led to rely upon, because you know from whom you learned it 15 and that from childhood you have known the sacred Scriptures which can give you wisdom that leads to salvation through the faith that leans on Christ Jesus. 16 All Scripture is inspired by God, and useful for teaching, for reproof, for correction, for training in doing what is right, 17 so that the man of God may be perfectly fit, thoroughly equipped for every good enterprise.d

4 TIMOTHY URGED TO BE ZEALOUS AND TO CONTROL HIMSELF; PAUL OPTIMISTIC AS HE FACES HIS BEHEADING; YET LONELY, SO HE SENDS FOR MARK, HIS COAT, AND HIS BOOKS; STILL ABSOLUTELY TRUSTFUL IN THE LORD, HE SAYS FAREWELL

I solemnly charge you, before God and Christ Jesus who is to judge the living and the dead, and by His appearing and His kingdom, 2 preach the message, stay at it in season and out of season; convince, reprove, exhort people with perfect patience as a teacher.a 3 For a time will come when they will not listen to wholesome teaching, but to gratify their own evil desires will surround themselves with teachers who teach to gratify their own b evil desires, because their ears are itching so to be tickled, 4 and they will cease to listen to the truth and will turn to listen to myths. 5 But you, on your part, must always keep your head cool, suffer hardship, do your work as a herald of the good news, and so fill your ministry to the brim.

6 My life, indeed, is already ebbing out,c and the time has come for me to sail away.d 7 I have fought the fight for the good, I have run my race, I have kept the faith. 8 Now the crown for doing right awaits me, which the Lord, the righteous Judge, will award

---
d Lit., *work*.
a Grk., *with all patience and teaching*.
b Refers to the people, not the teachers.
c Lit., *being poured out*.
d So the Grk. word, a sailor's term.

me on that day, and not only me but also all who have loved His appearing.

⁹ Do your best to come to me soon, ¹⁰ for Demas has forsaken me because he loved the present world, and has gone to Thessalonica; Crescens has gone to Galatia, Titus to Dalmatia; ¹¹ Luke is the only one who is now with me. Pick up Mark and bring him with you, for he is of great service to me, ¹² and I have sent Tychicus off to Ephesus. ¹³ When you come, bring the coat which I left with Carpus at Troas; bring the books, too, especially the parchments.[e] ¹⁴ Alexander, a worker in metal, did me ever so much harm. The Lord will repay him for what he did. ¹⁵ You too must be on your guard against him, for he has vigorously opposed my teaching.

¹⁶ When I first defended myself at court, nobody came to help me, but everybody deserted me. May it never be charged to their account. ¹⁷ But the Lord stood by me and gave me strength, so that the message preached by me might have its full effect and all the heathen might hear it. So I was rescued from the lion's jaws.[f] ¹⁸ The Lord will rescue me from every wicked work and save me to His heavenly kingdom. To Him be glory for ever and ever. Amen.

¹⁹ Remember me to Prisca and Aquila, and to the family of Onesiphorus. ²⁰ Erastus stayed in Corinth; I left Trophimus sick at Miletus. ²¹ Do your best to get here before winter. Eubulus wishes to be remembered to you, and so do Pudens, Linus, Claudia, and all the brothers.

²² The Lord be with your spirit. Spiritual blessing be with you all.

[e] Scrolls of O. T. Scriptures.
[f] Lit., *the lion's mouth*—referring to Nero.

TITUS

The writer is Paul. He had visited the island of Crete and helped Titus, a young minister ever faithful to the apostle and a wise leader among the churches, to begin the organization of the churches there. He had left Titus on the island to continue the work. Date about A.D. 65.

The purpose was to certify to Titus' authority as an apostolic representative; to give further directions to him how to organize the churches; to urge him to encourage sound teaching and pure moral living.

1   HE GREETS TITUS; STATES THE QUALIFICATIONS OF PASTORS; TITUS URGED TO DENOUNCE FALSE TEACHINGS; THE IMMORAL PRACTICES OF THE CRETANS

Paul, a slave [a] of God, and an apostle of Jesus Christ, to stimulate [b] faith in God's chosen people and to lead [b] them on to a full knowledge of religious truth, ² in the hope of eternal life which God, who never lies, promised ages ago ³ but at the proper time made known as His message through the message [c] that I preach with which I have been entrusted by the command of God our Saviour; ⁴ to Titus, my genuine child in our common faith: be spiritual blessing and peace from God our Father and Christ Jesus our Saviour.

⁵ I left you in Crete for this express purpose, to set in order the things that are lacking, and to appoint elders in each town, as I directed you—⁶ each elder [d] must be above reproach, have only one wife, and his children must not be liable to the charge of profligacy or disobedience. ⁷ For as God's trustee a pastor must be above reproach, not stubborn or quick-tempered or addicted to strong drink or pugnacious or addicted to dishonest gain, ⁸ but hospitable, a lover of goodness, sensible, upright, of pure life, self-con-

---

[a] Used in spiritual sense; see I Cor. 6:19, 20.
[b] Implied in *kata* (so EGT).
[c] In ending of noun for *preaching*.
[d] Lit., *if anyone is above reproach* (meaning elders).

trolled, ⁹ and a man who continues to cling to the trustworthy message as he was taught it, so that he may be competent to encourage others with wholesome teaching and to convict those who oppose him.

¹⁰ For there are many insubordinate people, mere talkers with nothing to say, but deceivers of their own minds, especially those of the circumcision party, ¹¹ whose mouths must be stopped, for they upset whole families by teaching things they ought not to think, for the sake of dishonest gain. ¹² One of them, a prophet of their own countrymen, has said, "Cretans are always liars, wicked brutes, lazy bellies." ¹³ Now this tendency is true. So continue correcting them severely, that they may be healthy in faith, ¹⁴ by ceasing to give attention to Jewish myths and to the commands of men who turn their backs on the truth. ¹⁵ To the pure everything is pure, but to the impure and unbelieving nothing is pure, but their very minds and consciences are impure. ¹⁶ They profess to know God, but by their actions they disown Him; they are detestable, disobedient, and useless for anything good.

2   HE STATES THE DUTIES OF THE AGED, OF THE YOUNG, AND OF SLAVES; HE DEMANDS PURE LIVING OF THOSE RANSOMED BY CHRIST

You must continue telling the people what is proper for wholesome teaching: ² the older men to be temperate, serious, and sensible, healthy in faith, in love, and in steadfastness; ³ the older women, too, to be reverent in their deportment, and not to be slanderers or slaves to heavy ᵃ drinking, but to be teachers of what is right, ⁴ so as to train the younger women to be affectionate wives and mothers,ᵇ ⁵ to be serious, pure, homekeepers, kind, and subordinate to their husbands, so as not to cause God's message to suffer reproach.ᶜ ⁶ Keep urging the younger men to be sensible. ⁷ In everything you yourself continue to set them a worthy example of doing good; be sincere and serious in your teaching, ⁸ let your message be wholesome and unobjectionable, so that our opponent may be put to shame at having nothing evil to say about us. ⁹ Continue urging slaves to practice perfect submission to their masters and to give them perfect satisfaction, ¹⁰ to stop resisting

---

ᵃ *Much wine;* women then drank heavily.
ᵇ *Lovers of husbands,* etc.
ᶜ *To be abused.*

them and stealing from them, but to show such perfect fidelity as to adorn, in everything they do, the teaching of God our Saviour.

¹¹ For God's favor has appeared with its offer of salvation to all mankind, ¹² training us to give up godless ways and worldly cravings and live serious, upright, and godly lives in this world, ¹³ while we are waiting for the realization ᵈ of our blessed hope at the glorious appearing of our great God and Saviour Christ Jesus, ¹⁴ who gave Himself for us to ransom us from all iniquity and purify for Himself a people to be His very own, zealous of good works.

¹⁵ You must continue teaching this, and continue exhorting and reproving people, with full authority. Let no one belittle you.

3 CHRISTIANS MUST BE LAW-ABIDING, SOCIAL-MINDED CITIZENS; GOOD EXAMPLES TO BE SET; CONTROVERSIES TO BE AVOIDED; MAKES REQUESTS; SAYS FAREWELL

Constantly remind people to submit to and obey the rulers who have authority over them, so as to be ready for any good enterprise, ² to stop abusing anyone, to be peaceable, fair-minded, showing perfect gentleness to everybody.

³ For once we too were without understanding, disobedient, misled, habitual slaves to all sorts of passions and pleasures, spending our lives in malice and envy. ⁴ But when the goodness and lovingkindness of God our Saviour were brought to light, ⁵ He saved us, not for upright deeds that we had done, but in accordance with His mercy, through the bath of regeneration and renewal of the Holy Spirit,ᵃ ⁶ which He abundantly poured out upon us through Jesus Christ our Saviour, ⁷ so that we might come into right standing with God through His unmerited favor and become heirs of eternal life in accordance with our hope.

⁸ It is a message to be trusted, and I want you to be emphatic about these things, so that those who believe in God may be careful to take the lead in doing good. These things are right and render service to mankind. ⁹ But hold yourself aloof from foolish controversies, pedigrees, strife, and wrangles about the law, for these are fruitless ᵇ and futile. ¹⁰ After one or two warnings to a man who is factious, stop having anything to do with him, ¹¹ for

---

ᵈ Implied.
ᵃ Two phrases express a single idea.
ᵇ Lit., *useless.*

you may be sure that such a man is crooked and sinful, even self-condemned.

¹² When I send Artemas or Tychicus to you, do your best to come to me at Nicopolis, for I have decided to spend the winter there.

¹³ Give a hearty send-off to Zenas the lawyer, and Apollos, so that they may want for nothing. ¹⁴ Our people too must set examples of doing good, so as to meet the necessary demands and not to live unfruitful lives.

¹⁵ All who are with me wish to be remembered to you. Remember me to all who love me as Christians. Spiritual blessing be with you all.

PHILEMON

Paul is the author. He is still in prison in Rome. Onesimus, a slave of Philemon, a personal friend of Paul, had run away from his master and come to Rome. He hears Paul tell the story of the good news about Christ, and is converted. Paul is planning to return him to his master Philemon. The date is about A.D. 62 or 63.

The purpose is to ask Philemon to forgive Onesimus and receive him back as a Christian brother; to engage a room at Philemon's for himself, since he hopes to come back after he is released from prison.

1 HE GREETS PHILEMON; HIS SLAVE, ONESIMUS, CONVERTED UNDER PAUL'S PREACHING, IS NOW BEING RETURNED; PAUL SPEAKS FOR A ROOM AT PHILEMON'S

Paul, a prisoner for Christ Jesus, and my brother Timothy, to our dearly loved fellow-worker Philemon, [2] to our sister Apphia, to our fellow-soldier Archippus, and to the church that meets at your house: [3] spiritual blessing be with you and peace from God our Father and the Lord Jesus Christ.

[4] I always thank my God every time I mention you in my prayers, [5] because I continue to hear of the love and faith you have in the Lord Jesus and all His people, [6] and I pray that their sharing of your faith may result in their recognition in us of everything that is right with reference to Christ. [7] Yes, I have felt great joy and encouragement over your love, because the hearts of God's people have been refreshed by you, my brother.

[8] So, although through union with Christ I have full freedom to order you to do your duty,[a] [9] yet I prefer to appeal to you for love's sake, although I am such as I am, Paul an envoy of Christ Jesus but now a prisoner for Him too; [10] yes, I appeal to you for my child Onesimus, whose father I have become while wearing these

---

[a] Lit., *the fitting thing.*

480

chains.[b] [11] Once he proved to be useless, but now he is useful [c] to you and me; [12] I am sending him back to you, which is all the same as sending my very heart. [13] I would have liked to keep him with me, to wait on me in your stead while I wear these chains for the good news, [14] but I would not do a single thing about it without your consent, so that this kindness of yours to me might not seem to come by compulsion but voluntarily. [15] For perhaps it was for this reason that he was parted from you for a while, that you might have him back forever, [16] not as a slave any longer but more than a slave, a dearly loved brother, especially to me and much more to you, both as a servant and as a Christian. [17] So, if you consider me a comrade, take him to your bosom as you would me. [18] And if he has done you any wrong and owes you anything, charge it to my account. [19] I, Paul, write it with my own hand, I will pay it in full—not to mention the fact that you owe me your very self besides. [20] Yes, brother, I would like some return myself from you in the Lord's work. Through Christ refresh my heart.

[21] I write you in perfect confidence in your compliance with my wish,[d] because I am sure that you will do even more than I ask. [22] And have a guest-room ready for me, too, for I hope that through your prayers I shall have the gracious privilege of coming to you.

[23] Epaphras, my fellow-prisoner in the cause of Christ Jesus, wishes to be remembered to you. [24] So do Mark, Aristarchus, Demas, and Luke, my fellow-workers.

[25] The spiritual blessing of the Lord Jesus Christ be with your spirit.

[b] Grk., *whom I begot in these chains.*
[c] A play on the meaning of his name.
[d] Lit., *trusting in your obedience.*

HEBREWS

Today most scholars feel that Paul is not the author of Hebrews. "God only knows who wrote it," as Origen, the brilliant head of the Alexandrian college, said. Some of us think that Apollos, the brilliant scholar and rhetorician of Alexandria, wrote it; but this is uncertain. Many still hold that Paul wrote it. But the theology of Hebrews is built around the priesthood of Christ, while Paul's is built around justification by faith. Paul's vocabulary is usually that of the simple everyday Greek; his style is rough and rugged, with now and then a smooth and polished sentence; but the vocabulary of Hebrews is more literary, even classical; and its style is beautiful and rhetorical, with well-balanced antitheses and polished sentences.

The readers are suffering persecution, and some are tempted to drift away from Christianity to unbelief. The date is about A.D. 65 to 68. The purpose is to encourage the readers to continue believing in Jesus, since He is superior to angels and prophets, Moses and Aaron, and the Aaronic high priests; yea, He is the very Son of God who aided in creating the worlds and now is upholding them, and as high priest He is eternal, with no successor, and was made a sacrifice for sin (Himself) that is all-sufficient for all the world and for all the ages. He writes to urge them to "go on to perfection"; to convince them that Christianity is the supreme religion. The letter is one of the most beautiful and logical defenses of Christianity ever written.

1 HE SHOWS THE SON TO BE SUPERIOR TO PROPHETS AND ANGELS; CHRIST IS THE SON, BUT ANGELS ONLY SERVANTS WHO WORSHIP HIM

It was bit by bit and in many different ways that God in olden times spoke to our forefathers through the prophets, 2 but in these latter days He has spoken to us through a Son, whom He had appointed lawful owner of everything, and through whom He had made the worlds. 3 He is the reflection of God's glory and the perfect[a] representation of His being, and continues to uphold the universe by His mighty word. After He had procured man's[b] purification from sins, He took His seat at the right hand of God's majesty, 4 thus proving[b] Himself to be as much superior to angels

---

[a] Grk. word means *exact imprint;* so the Son is the perfect representation of God's being.
[b] Implied.

HEBREWS 1

as the title He has inherited is superior to theirs. [5] For to what angel did God [b] ever say, "You are my Son, today I have become your Father"? [c]

[6] Or again, "I will become His Father, and He shall become my Son"? [d]

But when He brings again His first-born Son into the world, He says, "And let all the angels worship Him." [e]

[7] However, regarding the angels He says:

> "He turns His angels into winds
> And His attendants into flames of fire." [f]

[8] But regarding the Son He says:

> "Your throne, O God, will stand [b] forever and ever;
> A righteous scepter is the scepter of His kingdom.
> [9] You loved the right and hated wrong;
> So God, your God, anointed you
> With oil of exultation beyond all [b] your companions." [g]

[10] And:

> "You, Lord, in the beginning founded the earth,
> And the heavens are the works of your hands.
> [11] They will perish, but you always remain;
> They all will grow old like a coat,
> [12] And you will fold them up just like a robe, [b]
> And they will be changed like the changing of one's coat,
> But you are the same, and your years will never cease." [h]

[13] But to what angel did He ever say:

> "Just keep your seat at my right hand,
> Until I make your foes a footstool for your feet"? [i]

[14] Are not the angels all attending spirits sent forth to serve for the sake of those who are going to be unceasing possessors of salvation?

[c] Ps. 2:7.
[d] 2 Sam. 7:14.
[e] Dt. 32:43; Ps. 97:7 (both fr. Sept.).
[f] Ps. 104:4.
[g] Ps. 45:6,7.
[h] Ps. 102:25-27.
[i] Ps. 110:1.

2 DANGEROUS TO DISOBEY THE SON; JESUS THE SON CROWNED WITH GLORY BECAUSE HE DIED FOR ALL; JESUS MADE PERFECT THROUGH SUFFERING

This is why we must pay much closer attention to the message once heard, to keep from drifting to one side. 2 For if the message spoken through angels proved to be valid,[a] and every violation and infraction of it had its adequate penalty, 3 how can we escape, if we pay no attention at all to a salvation that is so great?[b] This is so because it was first proclaimed by the Lord Himself, and then it was proved to us to be valid by the very men who heard Him themselves, 4 while God continued to confirm their testimony with signs, marvels, and various sorts of wonder-works, and with gifts of the Holy Spirit distributed in accordance with His will.

5 For it was not to angels that He gave authority[c] over that world to be, of which we are speaking. 6 For someone somewhere has solemnly said:

> "What is man that you should think of him,
> Or the Son of Man that you should care for Him?
> 7 You made Him inferior to angels for a little while,
> Yet you have crowned Him with glory and honor,
> You have set Him over the works of your hands,
> 8 You have put all things under His feet!"[d]

Now when He gave Him authority over everything, He did not leave a single thing that was not put under His authority. But as yet we do not see everything actually under His authority, 9 but we do see Jesus, who was made inferior to the angels for a little while, crowned with glory and honor because He suffered death, so that by God's favor He might experience[e] death for every human being. 10 For it was appropriate for Him, who is the Final Goal and the First Cause[f] of the universe, in bringing many children to glory, to make the Leader[g] in their salvation perfect through the process of sufferings. 11 For both He who is purifying

---

[a] So used in papyri (M. and M., Vocab.).
[b] Pronoun doubly emph.
[c] *He subjected that world.*
[d] Ps. 8:4-6.
[e] Lit., *taste.*
[f] Grk., *for the sake of—by whom.*
[g] Or, *author.*

them and those who are being purified all spring from one Father; so He is not ashamed to call them brothers, [12] when He says:

"I will announce your name to my brothers;
In the midst of the congregation I will sing your praise"; [h]

[13] and again,

"I too will put my trust in God"; [i]

and again,

"Here I am and the children God has given me." [j]

[14] Since then the children mentioned share our mortal nature, [k] He too took on Himself a full share of the same, in order that He by His death might put a stop to the power of him who has the power of death, that is, the devil, [15] and set at liberty those who all their lifetime had been subject to slavery because of their dread of death. [16] For of course it is not angels but descendants of Abraham that He is to help. [17] Therefore He had to be made like His brothers, so that He could be a sympathetic High Priest, as well as a faithful one, in things relating to God, in order to atone for the people's sins. [18] For inasmuch as He has suffered Himself by being tempted, He is able to give immediate [l] help to any that are tempted.

3 JESUS SUPERIOR TO MOSES; THE WRITER WARNS AGAINST UNBELIEF AND ITS CONSEQUENCES

Therefore, my Christian [a] brothers, fix your thoughts on Jesus, the Messenger and High Priest whom we profess to follow, [b] [2] to see how faithful He was to God who appointed Him, just as Moses was in all the house of God. [3] For just as the man who builds a house has greater glory than the house, by just so much is Jesus judged to be worthy of greater glory than Moses. [4] For every house is built by somebody, but the builder and furnisher [c] of the universe is God. [5] Now Moses was faithful in all the house of God,

[h] Ps. 22:22.
[i] Ps. 18:2.
[j] Isa. 8:18.
[k] Lit., *blood and flesh;* so *our mortal nature.*
[l] In aor. infin.
[a] Grk., *holy brothers; set apart to Christ,* so *Christian brothers.*
[b] Lit., *High Priest of our confession.*
[c] Word means *furnisher* as well as *builder.*

yet only as a servant to bear witness to the message that should be spoken, ⁶ but Christ as a Son set over the house of God was faithful; and we are that house, if we keep up our courage and the joy that hope inspires to the very end. ⁷ Therefore, as the Holy Spirit says:

"If you but hear His voice today,
⁸ You must not harden your hearts as they did in provoking me,
As on the day in the desert they tested me,
⁹ Where your forefathers found I stood their test,
Because they saw my works for forty years.ᵈ
¹⁰ So I was indignant with that generation,
And I said, 'Their hearts are always going astray,
And they have never come to know my ways.'
¹¹ So in my anger I took oath,
'They shall not be admitted to my rest!' " ᵉ

¹² See to it, my brothers, that no wicked, unbelieving heart is found in any of you, as shown by your turning away from the ever-living God, ¹³ but day by day, as long as "Today" shall last,ᶠ continue to encourage one another, so that not one of you may be hardened by sin's deceiving ways.ᵍ ¹⁴ For we have become real sharers in Christ, if we keep firm to the end the faith we had at first, ¹⁵ and yet the warning continues to be spoken:

"If you but hear His voice,
You must not harden your hearts as they did in provoking me."

¹⁶ For who was it that heard and yet provoked Him? Was it not all who came out of Egypt led by Moses? ¹⁷ With whom was He disgusted forty years? Was it not with those who had sinned, whose carcasses fell in the desert? ¹⁸ To whom did He take oath that they should not be admitted to His rest, if it was not to those who disobeyed Him? So we see that it was because of their unbelief ʰ that they could not be admitted to it.

ᵈ *And* in Grk. has Heb. causal idea.
ᵉ Ps. 95:7-11.
ᶠ Lit., *while it is called "Today."*
ᵍ Grk., *deceitfulness of sin.*
ʰ Basic cause of failure.

4 HE CONTINUES WARNING; THEN MAKES AN EARNEST APPEAL; JESUS, THE SON, OUR HIGH PRIEST, SYMPATHIZES WITH US

So let us fear that when the promise for us to be admitted to His rest is still remaining valid some one of you may be found to have missed it. ² For we have had the good news told to us as well as they, but the message heard did them no good, because they were not by faith made one [a] with those who heeded it.[b] ³ For we who have believed are being admitted to that rest, just as He has said:

"As in my anger I took oath,
They shall not be admitted to my rest,"

although God's works had been completed at the creation of the world. ⁴ For somewhere He speaks of the seventh day:

"On the seventh day God rested from all His works"; [c]

⁵ while in this passage again He says:

"They shall not be admitted to my rest."

⁶ Since then it still remains that some are being admitted to it and that those who first had the good news told to them were not admitted because of disobedience, ⁷ He again fixes a definite day, saying long afterward through David, as has been quoted:

"If you but hear His voice,
You must not harden your hearts."

⁸ For if Joshua had really given them rest, He would not afterward have been speaking of another day. ⁹ So a sabbath of rest is still awaiting God's people. ¹⁰ For whoever [d] is admitted into God's rest himself has rested from his works, just as God did.

¹¹ So let us do our best to be admitted to that rest, so that not one of us may fail through the same sort of disobedience. ¹² For God's message is alive and full of power in action,[e] sharper than any double-edged sword, piercing even to the depths of soul and spirit, to the dividing of joints and marrow, and passing judg-

[a] Fol. WH—*mixed by faith*, etc.
[b] *Who heard* (Josh., Caleb).
[c] See Gen. 2:2.
[d] Or, it may mean, *He* (*Christ*) *who*, etc.
[e] *Energetic, full of power, in action.*

ment on the thoughts and purposes of the heart. ¹³ No creature of His can escape God's sight, but everything is bare and exposed to the eyes of Him to whom we have to give account.ᶠ

¹⁴ Since then we have in Jesus, the Son of God, a great High Priest who has gone right up to heaven itself, let us continue to keep a firm hold on our profession of faith in Him. ¹⁵ For we do not have a High Priest who is incapable of sympathizing with us in our weaknesses, but we have One who was tempted in every respect as we are, and yet without committing any sin. ¹⁶ So let us continue coming with courage to the throne of God's unmerited favor to obtain His mercy and to find His spiritual strength to help us when we need it.

5 AS HIGH PRIEST, JESUS, BOTH DIVINE AND HUMAN, MUST HAVE AN APPOINTMENT FROM GOD; ONCE HE AGONIZED IN PRAYER IN THE GARDEN; THE READERS SO DULL IN SPIRITUAL THINGS THEY NEED TO BE WARNED

For every high priest who is taken from men is appointed to officiate ᵃ on behalf of men in matters relating to God, that is, to offer gifts and sin-offerings. ² Such a one ᵃ is capable of dealing tenderly with the ignorant and erring ones, since he himself is subject to weakness, ³ and so is obliged to offer sin-offerings, not only for the people but for himself as well. ⁴ And no one takes this honor upon himself but is called to it by God, as Aaron was. ⁵ So Christ too did not take upon Himself the glory of being appointed High Priest, but it was God who said:

"You are my Son;
I have today become your Father," ᵇ

⁶ as also in another passage He says:

"You are a priest forever,
Belonging to the rank of Melchizedek." ᶜ

⁷ For during His human life ᵈ He offered up prayers and entreat-

---
ᶠ Lit., *no creature is unseen before His face, to whom is our account.*
ᵃ Implied.
ᵇ Ps. 2:7.
ᶜ Ps. 110:4.
ᵈ *In the days of His flesh.*

ies, crying aloud with tears to Him who was always able to save Him out of death, and because of His beautiful spirit of worship His prayer was heard. 8 Although He was a Son, He learned from what He suffered how to obey, 9 and because He was perfectly qualified for it He became the author of endless salvation e for all who obey Him, 10 since He had received from God the title of a High Priest with the rank of Melchizedek.

11 I have much to say to you about Him,f but it is difficult to make it clear to you, since you have become so dull in your spiritual senses. 12 For although you ought to be teachers of others because you have been Christians so long, you actually need someone to teach you over and over again the very elements of the truths that God g has given us, and you have gotten into such a state that you are in constant need of milk instead of solid food. 13 For everyone who uses milk alone is inexperienced in the message of right-doing; he is only an infant. 14 But solid food belongs to full-grown men who on account of constant use have their faculties trained to distinguish good and evil.

6   HE APPEALS TO THEM FOR HEROIC PROGRESS; HE HOPES FOR BETTER THINGS FOR THEM; SUCH HOPE, INSPIRED BY GOD'S PROMISES, IS THE ANCHOR TO THE SOUL

So then let us once for all quit the elementary teaching about Christ and continue progressing toward maturity; let us stop relaying a foundation of repentance from works that mean only death,a and of faith in God, 2 of teaching about ceremonial washings b and the laying on of hands, the resurrection of the dead and final c judgment. 3 And we will progress, if God permits. 4 For it is impossible for those who have once for all been enlightened and have experienced the gift from heaven, who have been made sharers of the Holy Spirit 5 and have experienced how good God's message is and the mighty powers of the age to come, 6 and then have fallen by the wayside—d it is impossible, I say, to keep on

---

e The whole process of deliverance from sin to maturity in heaven, so conditioned on obedience; not in conflict with Paul's teaching, saved by faith.
f Or, *about it* (this topic).
g *Oracles of God*, truths that God gave.
a Lit., *dead works*.
b Jewish washings, John's baptism, and later practices.
c *Eternal*, so *final*.
d Picture of runners falling beside the race track.

restoring them to their first[e] repentance, since they continue to crucify the Son of God to their detriment[f] and hold Him up to contempt. ⁷ For a piece of ground that drinks in the rains so frequently falling on it, and continues yielding vegetation useful to those for whose sakes it is cultivated, receives from God His blessings. ⁸ But if it continues to yield thorns and thistles, it is considered worthless and in danger of being cursed, and its final fate is burning.

⁹ But in your case, my dearly loved friends, even though we speak in such a tone, we are sure of better things, yea, things that point to salvation. ¹⁰ For God is not so unjust as to forget the work you have done and the love you have shown His name in the service you have rendered for your fellow-Christians,[g] and still are doing. ¹¹ And we desire each one of you to continue to show the same earnestness to the very end, that you may enjoy your hope to the fullest,[h] ¹² so that you may not grow careless,[i] but may follow the example of those who through their faith and patient endurance are now possessors of the blessings promised.

¹³ For when God made His promise to Abraham, He took an oath by Himself, since He had no one greater by whom He could take it, ¹⁴ saying:

"I will certainly bless you over and over again, I will extensively increase your numbers."[j] ¹⁵ And so by patiently waiting he obtained what God had promised him. ¹⁶ For it is a custom among men to take oath by something greater than themselves, and an oath taken for confirmation settles any dispute among them. ¹⁷ Therefore, because God wanted to make the strongest demonstration of the unchangeable character of His purpose, He interposed with an oath, ¹⁸ so that by these two unchangeable things[k] in which it is impossible for God to prove false, we who have taken refuge with Him may have encouragement strong enough to make us seize upon the hope that lies ahead of us. ¹⁹ This hope we have as an anchor for our souls, secure and safe, which reaches

[e] Lit., *renew them to repentance* (first step in Chn. life; so EGT).
[f] Dat. of disadvantage.
[g] Grk., *the saints.*
[h] Grk., *for the full assurance of your hope.*
[i] Lit., *dull, sluggish.*
[j] Gen. 22:16, 17.
[k] The promise and the oath.

up behind the heavenly veil, where Jesus has blazed[1] the way for us and became a High Priest with the rank of Melchizedek.

7 MELCHIZEDEK'S HIGH PRIESTHOOD SUGGESTS CHRIST'S PERPETUAL HIGH PRIESTHOOD; HIS SUPERIORITY TO ABRAHAM, SO TO LEVI, AND SO TO LEVITICAL HIGH PRIESTS; THEIR PRIESTHOOD IMPERFECT, SO SUPERSEDED BY CHRIST'S

For this man Melchizedek, king of Salem and priest of the Most High God, who met Abraham as he was coming back from the defeat of the kings, and put his blessing on him, ² to whom Abraham contributed a tenth of all his spoils,[a] who first of all, in accordance with the meaning of his name, is king of righteousness, and then king of Salem, which means king of peace; ³ with no father, no mother, no ancestry; no beginning to his days, no end to his life,[b] but, like the Son of God, as priest continues on and on with no successor.[c]

⁴ Now see how great this man must have been that even the patriarch Abraham gave him a tenth of his spoils. ⁵ And those of the descendants of Levi who accept the priesthood are authorized by the law to collect a tenth from the people; that is, from their own brothers, though they have sprung from Abraham. ⁶ But in this case, the man whose ancestry is not traced from them collected a tenth from Abraham, and put his blessing on the man who had the promises from God.[a] ⁷ Now beyond any contradiction, it is always the inferior that is blessed by the superior. ⁸ In the one case, mortal men collect the tenth, in the other, one who, as the witness states, lives on. ⁹ And I might almost say, Levi too, who now collects the tenth, through Abraham paid the tenth, ¹⁰ for he was a vital part of his forefather though yet unborn,[d] when Melchizedek met him.

¹¹ Now if perfection had been reached through the Levitical priesthood—for on it as a basis even the law was enacted for the people—what further need would there have been of appointing

---
[1] *Has entered as a forerunner for us.*
[a] *Last word (words) implied.*
[b] *That is, no record of these facts.*
[c] *Tense and adv. phrase have this exact meaning.*
[d] *In the loins of, etc.*

a different[e] priest, with the rank of Melchizedek, instead of designating one with the rank of Aaron? 12 For when a change in the priesthood takes place, a change in its law necessarily takes place. 13 For He of whom this is said became a member of a different[e] tribe no member of which ever officiated at the altar. 14 For it is very clear that our Lord sprang from Judah, a tribe about which Moses said nothing as to priests. 15 And it is still more overwhelmingly clear, since[f] a different priest in the likeness of Melchizedek is appointed, 16 who is appointed not on the basis of a physical qualification but on the basis of a power flowing from a life that cannot end. 17 For the Scripture bears witness:

"You are a priest forever, with the rank of Melchizedek."

18 Indeed, the rescinding of a previous regulation takes place, because it was weak and ineffective—19 for the law had never made anything perfect—and so a better hope is brought to us, through which we have approach to God.

20 And by so much as He was not appointed without God's taking an oath—21 for the Levitical priests were appointed without His taking an oath, but He with His oath, when He said to Him:

"The Lord took oath and will not change,
You are a priest forever"—

22 so much the more Jesus has become the guarantee of a better covenant. 23 And the Levitical priests, on the one hand, have become numerous, because they have been prevented by death from continuing in office, 24 but He, on the other hand, because He Himself lives on forever, enjoys the only priesthood that has no successors in office. 25 Therefore, because He Himself lives always to intercede for them always, He is able to save completely any and all who come to God through Him.

26 For we needed such a High Priest, holy, innocent, unstained, far removed from sinful men, and elevated far above the very heavens, 27 who does not need, as did the Levitical priests, to offer sacrifices, first for his own sins and then for those of the people; this latter is just what He did once for all when He offered up Himself. 28 For the law appoints imperfect[g] men as high priests,

[e] Grk. pro. means *another of a different kind.*
[f] Cond. realized, and so equal to our *since,* not *if.*
[g] *Men who had weakness;* so *imperfect.*

but the assertion about the taking of an oath, which was spoken after the time of the law, appoints a Son who is perfectly qualified to be High Priest forever.

8   CHRIST OFFICIATES IN HEAVEN ITSELF; THE EARTHLY SANCTUARY, THE MERE SHADOW OF THE HEAVENLY; THE NEW AND BETTER COVENANT

Now the main point in what I am saying is this: We have such a High Priest as this, one who has taken His seat at the right hand of God's majestic throne in heaven 2 as officiating Priest [a] in that sanctuary, which is also the true tent of worship,[b] which the Lord and not man set up.

3 For every high priest is appointed to offer gifts and sacrifices; so this High Priest too must have some sacrifice to offer. 4 However, if He were still on earth, He would not be a priest at all, because there are those who officiate [b] in accordance with the law in offering the gifts; 5 and yet they officiate in a sanctuary [b] that is a mere copy and shadow of the heavenly one, as Moses, when he was about to make the tent of worship, was warned, for, said He, "See to it that you make it all just like the pattern shown you on the mountain." [c] 6 But, as the case with Him now stands, He has entered upon a priestly service as much superior to theirs as the covenant of which He is the Mediator is superior to theirs, superior because it has been enacted upon superior promises.

7 For if the first covenant had been faultless, there could have been no room for a second one. 8 For, because He was dissatisfied with His people,[d] He said:

> "'See; the time is coming,' says the Lord,
> 'When I will make a new covenant
> With the house of Israel and the house of Judah,
> 9 Unlike the one that I made with their forefathers
> The day I took them by the hand
> To lead them out from the land of Egypt,
> For they did not abide by their covenant with me,
> So I did not care for them,' says the Lord.

[a] *Ministering attendant.*
[b] Implied.
[c] Ex. 25:40.
[d] Pro. in Grk., noun better in Eng.

¹⁰ 'For this is the covenant that I will make with the house of Israel
In those days,' says the Lord;
'I will put my laws into their minds,
And write them on their hearts,
And I will be their God,
And they will be my people.
And nevermore will each one need to teach his fellow-citizen,
¹¹ And each one teach his brother, saying, "Know the Lord,"
For all will know me,
From the lowest to the highest.
¹² For I will be merciful to their deeds of wrong,
And never, never any more will I recall their sins,' " ᵉ
¹³ In speaking of a new covenant He makes the first one obsolete; and whatever is obsolete and antiquated ᶠ is on the verge of vanishing.

9
HE DESCRIBES THE EARTHLY SANCTUARY; ITS EQUIPMENT; THE REAL SANCTUARY OF GOD'S PRESENCE NOT OPENED TILL CHRIST OPENED IT BY OFFERING HIS OWN BLOOD; THE NEW COVENANT VALIDATED BY SACRIFICING HIMSELF, SO TAKING AWAY SIN

So indeed the first covenant had its regulations for worship and its earthly sanctuary. ² For the first or outer part of the tent, which is called the holy place, was equipped with the lamp and table and the presentation bread. ³ But behind the second curtain is the tent that is called the holy of holies, ⁴ with its golden incense-altar and the chest for the covenant, completely covered with gold, and in it ᵃ a golden jar which held the manna, Aaron's staff that budded, and the tablets on which the covenant was written; ⁵ and above the chest were the winged creatures,ᵇ the symbols of God's glorious presence, overshadowing the mercy seat,ᶜ of which I cannot now speak in detail.

⁶ With these arrangements completed in this way, the priests in

* Jer. 31:31-34.
ᶠ *Decaying on account of age.*
ᵃ That is, in the gold-covered chest.
ᵇ *Cherubim,* the symbol of glory.
ᶜ The lid of the chest on which the blood was poured.

conducting their official services regularly go into the outer part of the tent of worship; 7 but into the second or inner [d] part nobody but the high priest may go, and he only once a year, and never without blood which he offers for himself and for the sins committed in ignorance by the people. 8 By this the Holy Spirit was showing that there was as yet no access to the real sanctuary while the outer tent was still in existence, 9 for it is merely a symbol of the present time in connection with which gifts and sacrifices are repeatedly offered though they cannot make the conscience of the worshiper perfect,[e] 10 since they deal only with food and drink and various washings, that is, with mere material regulations which are in force only until the time of setting things straight.[f]

11 But when Christ came as the High Priest of good things that have already taken place,[g] He went by way of that greater and more perfect tent of worship, not made by human hands, that is, not belonging to this material creation, 12 and not with blood of goats and calves, but with His own blood He once for all went into the real sanctuary and secured our eternal redemption. 13 For if the blood of bulls and goats and a heifer's ashes sprinkling those who are ceremonially unclean purifies them with physical cleansing, 14 how much more surely will the blood of Christ, who with an eternal Spirit [h] gave Himself a spotless offering to God, purify your consciences from works that mean mere death, to serve the ever living God?

15 And this is why He is the Mediator of a new covenant, in order that, after He had suffered death for securing redemption from the offenses committed under the first covenant, those who had been invited to share it might obtain the eternal inheritance promised them. 16 For when a will is made, it is necessary that the death of him who makes it be proved.[i] 17 For a will is valid only after a man is dead,[j] since it has no force whatever while the one who made it is alive. 18 So not even the first covenant was ratified without the use of blood. 19 For after every regulation in the law had been spoken by Moses to all the people, he took the blood of

[d] Meaning of second tent.
[e] That is, cannot purify from sin and impart moral perfection.
[f] The age of Messiah—Christian age.
[g] Fol. Vat. Ms.
[h] The Son's pre-existent Spirit.
[i] Lit., *brought in.*
[j] Grk., pl., *men,* so *a universal law.*

calves and goats, with water, crimson wool, and a bunch of hyssop, and sprinkled the book containing the law and all the people, ²⁰ saying, "This is the blood that ratifies the covenant which God commanded me to make with you." [k] ²¹ In the same way he sprinkled with blood the tent and all the utensils of the priestly service. ²² In fact, under the law, almost everything is purified with blood, and without the shedding of blood no forgiveness is granted.

²³ So, on the one hand, the copies of the original things in heaven had to be purified with such sacrifices; but on the other hand, the original things themselves in heaven with better sacrifices than these. ²⁴ For it was not a sanctuary made by human hands, a mere copy of the true one, that Christ entered, but it was into heaven itself that He went, in order now to appear for us in the very presence of God. ²⁵ And He does not enter to offer Himself over and over again, as the high priest enters the sanctuary year after year with blood that is not his own; ²⁶ for, if that had been the case,[l] He would have had to suffer over and over again, ever since the creation of the world. But, as it is, once at the close of the ages He has appeared, to put away sin by His sacrifice. ²⁷ Indeed, just as men must die but once and after that be judged, ²⁸ so Christ was offered once for all to take away the sins of many, but again He will appear, without having anything to do with sin, to save those who are eagerly waiting for Him to bring them final [m] salvation.

10

THE SACRIFICES UNDER THE LAW UNABLE TO TAKE AWAY SINS; CHRIST'S ONE SACRIFICE HAS TAKEN AWAY SINS, BECAUSE IT WAS MADE IN ACCORDANCE WITH GOD'S WILL; TO SHOW THAT IT IS EFFECTIVE HE SITS AT GOD'S RIGHT HAND

For since the law cast only a shadow of the blessings to come and did not possess the reality itself [a] of those blessings, the priests with the same sacrifices that are perpetually offered year after year cannot make perfect those who come to worship. ² Otherwise, would they not have ceased offering them, because those who

---

[k] Ex. 24:8.
[l] Implied with pt.
[m] The prep. expresses this idea.
[a] Grk., *image itself*, suggesting reality.

offered them, having once been purified, would have had no further consciousness [b] of sins? ³ On the other hand, through these sacrifices there is given a real reminder of their sins, ⁴ for the blood of bulls and goats is unable to take away sins. ⁵ So, when Christ was coming into the world, He said:

⁶ "Sacrifice and offering you did not wish,
But a body you have prepared for me;
In burnt-offerings and sin-offerings you never took delight.
⁷ Then I said, 'See, I have come, just as the Scripture writes about me in the book,[c] O God, to do your will.'"

⁸ Although at first He said, "You never wished or took delight in sacrifices and offerings, burnt-offerings and sin-offerings"—all of which are repeatedly offered in accordance with the law—⁹ He afterward said, "See, I have come to do your will." He is taking away the first to let the second take its place. ¹⁰ It is by this will of God [d] that we are consecrated [e] through the offering of Jesus' body once for all. ¹¹ Every other priest stands officiating day after day and over and over again offering the same sacrifices, although they are unable to take away our sins. ¹² But this One offered up once for all and for all time one sacrifice for sins, and once for all took His seat at God's right hand, ¹³ from that time waiting till His enemies should be made the footstool of His feet. ¹⁴ For by that one sacrifice He has made perfect for all time those who are consecrated to Him.[f] ¹⁵ Now the Holy Spirit, too, gives us the testimony, for after saying:

¹⁶ "'This is the covenant that I will make with them
In those last days,' says the Lord:
'I will put my laws into their hearts,
And write them on their minds,'"

¹⁷ He continues to say:

"I will never, never any more recall their sins and deeds of wrong." ¹⁸ For when these are forgiven, there is no more need of an offering for sin.

---

[b] *Conscience* used in sense of *consciousness*.
[c] Ps. 40:6-8.
[d] Lit., *by which will*.
[e] Purified first, then consecrated—vb. has double meaning.
[f] Pro. implied.

¹⁹ Since then, my brothers, we have free access to the real sanctuary ᵍ through the blood of Jesus, ²⁰ the new and living way which He opened for us, through the curtain, that is, His physical nature, ²¹ and since in Him we have a Great Priest over the house of God, ²² let us continue to draw near to God with sincere hearts and perfect faith; ʰ with our hearts cleansed from the sense of sin, and our bodies bathed in clean water; ⁱ ²³ let us, without ever wavering, keep on holding to the hope that we profess, for He is to be trusted who has made the promise. ²⁴ Let us continue so to consider one another as to stimulate one another to love and good deeds. ²⁵ Let us stop neglecting our meeting together, as some do, but let us continue to encourage one another, and all the more because you see that the great day ʲ is drawing near.

²⁶ For if we go willfully sinning after we have received full knowledge of the truth, there is no sacrifice left to be offered for our sins, ²⁷ but only a terrifying prospect of judgment and that fiery indignation which is going to devour God's enemies. ²⁸ Anyone who breaks the law of Moses pays the death penalty without any show of pity, on the evidence of two or three witnesses only. ²⁹ How much severer punishment do you suppose that one deserves who tramples the Son of God underfoot, and counts as a common thing the blood of the covenant by which he was consecrated, and has insulted the Spirit that grants God's unmerited favor? ᵏ ³⁰ For we know who it was that said, "Vengeance belongs to me, I will pay back!" and again, "The Lord will be His people's judge." ˡ ³¹ It is a terrifying thing to fall into the hands of the ever living God!

³² But you must continue to remember those earlier days when first you received the light and then endured so great a struggle with persecution,ᵐ ³³ partly by being exposed as a public spectacle to insults and violent sufferings, and partly by showing yourselves ready to share with those who were living in this condition. ³⁴ For you showed sympathy with those who were in prison and cheerfully submitted to the violent seizure of your property, for you knew that you had in yourselves and in heaven one that was lasting. ³⁵ So you must never give up your confident courage, for it

---

ᵍ The very presence of God in heaven.
ʰ Lit., *full assurance of faith.*
ⁱ Referring to baptism, the symbol of cleansing.
ʲ Christ's return.
ᵏ Obj. gen.; vb. easily supplied.
ˡ Dt. 32:35, 36.
ᵐ Lit., *sufferings.*

holds a rich reward for you. ³⁶ Indeed, to carry out the will of **God** and to receive the blessing He has promised, you need endurance, for:

> ³⁷ "In just a very little while
> The Coming One will come and not delay;
> ³⁸ Meantime my righteous servant will live on by faith.
> But if a man draws back, my soul has no delight in him." ⁿ

³⁹ But we are not of a disposition to draw back so as to perish, but we have faith that leads to the saving of the soul.

11 HE CALLS THE ROLL OF THE HEROES OF FAITH—FROM ABEL, ENOCH, NOAH, ABRAHAM, MOSES, DOWN TO THE PROPHETS AND MACCABEAN CONQUERORS AND SUFFERERS; CHRISTIAN FAITH-CONQUERORS NEEDED TO COMPLETE THE ROLL

Now faith is the assurance of the things we hope for, the proof ᵃ of the reality of the things we cannot see. ² For by it the men of old won God's approval. ³ By faith we understand that the worlds were created, beautifully co-ordinated, and now exist,ᵇ at God's command; so the things that we see did not develop out of mere matter.ᶜ

⁴ By faith Abel offered a sacrifice more acceptable to God than Cain did, for by it he was approved as an upright man, since God approved him for the offering he made; and by it he still continues to speak, though dead. ⁵ By faith Enoch was transplanted from earth,ᵈ so that he did not experience dying; and he could not be found, because God had transplanted him from earth. For before he was transplanted from earth evidence was given him that he pleased God; ⁶ but without faith it is impossible to please Him, for anyone who approaches God must believe that there is a God and that He gives rewards to all who earnestly ᵉ try to find Him. ⁷ By faith Noah, on being divinely warned about things not seen as yet, in reverence prepared an ark for saving his family,

---

ⁿ Hab. 2:3, 4.
ᵃ So used in Plato and other Grk. writers.
ᵇ Grk. vb. means *to create and co-ordinate in symmetry;* pf. means *the result, so they now exist.*
ᶜ *Things that appear.*
ᵈ Last phrase implied in vb.
ᵉ In comp. vb.

and by his faith condemned the world and became possessor of the uprightness that results from faith.ᶠ

⁸ By faith Abraham, on being called, obeyed in starting off for a country which he was to receive as his own, and he did it in spite of the fact that he did not know where he was going. ⁹ By faith he made his temporary home in the land that God had promised him, although a land inhabited by others, living merely in tents with Isaac and Jacob, who were to share the promise with him. ¹⁰ For he was confidently looking forward to that city with the solid foundations, whose architect and builder is God. ¹¹ By faith Sarah received strength to become pregnant, and actually gave birth to a child, although she was past the time of life for it, because she thought that He who made her the promise was to be trusted. ¹² And so there sprang from one man, and that deadᴳ as to any prospects for offspring, a people as numberless as the stars in the sky and as the sands beside the seashore.

¹³ These people all died victoriously as a result of their faith,ᶠ although they did not receive the blessings promised; that is, because they really saw them in the far-off future and welcomed them, and so professed to be only foreigners and strangers here on earth. ¹⁴ For people who make such a profession as this show that they are in search of a country of their own.ʰ ¹⁵ And if they had been cherishing the memory of the country they had left, they would have had an opportunity to go back. ¹⁶ But in reality they were aspiring for a better country, I mean, a heavenly one. This is why God is not ashamed to be called their God, for He has prepared a city for them.

¹⁷ By faith Abraham, when he was put to the test, offered Isaac as a sacrifice; that is, he who had received the promise was starting to offer as a sacrifice his only son, ¹⁸ of whom it had been said, "Through Isaac your offspring must be traced."ⁱ ¹⁹ For he considered the fact that God was able to raise people from the dead; and so from the dead, in a figure, he did receive him back.

²⁰ By faith Isaac put his blessings for the future on Jacob and Esau. ²¹ By faith Jacob, when about to die, put his blessing on each of Joseph's sons, and worshiped, leaning on the top of his staff.

ᶠ So Winer, Gram.
ᴳ Not actually dead, but as to any prospects for offspring.
ʰ That is, their fatherland.
ⁱ Gen. 21:12.

HEBREWS 11

²² By faith Joseph, at the closing of his life, made mention of the future migration of the Israelites, and gave directions what to do with his body.ʲ ²³ By faith, Moses, at his birth was hidden three months by his parents, because they saw that he was a beautiful child, and they were not afraid of the king's decree. ²⁴ By faith Moses, when he had grown up, refused to be known as a son of Pharaoh's daughter, ²⁵ because he preferred to suffer hardships with the people of God than to have the passing enjoyment that results from sin, ²⁶ and thought the reproach endured for the Christ ᵏ was greater wealth than all the treasures in Egypt, for he kept his eye upon the reward. ²⁷ By faith he left Egypt, because he was not afraid of the king's anger, for he persevered as though he were actually seeing Him who is unseen. ²⁸ By faith he instituted the Passover and the pouring of blood upon the doorposts,ˡ so that the destroyer of the first-born might not touch them. ²⁹ By faith they crossed the Red Sea as though it were dry land, while the Egyptians, in attempting it, were drowned. ³⁰ By faith the walls of Jericho collapsed, after being surrounded each of seven days. ³¹ By faith Rahab the prostitute did not perish with those who disobeyed God, because she had welcomed the scouts as friends.ᵐ

³² And why should I continue to mention more? For time would fail me to tell of Gideon, Barak, Samson, Jephthah, David, Samuel, and the prophets, ³³ who by their faith conquered kingdoms, administered justice,ⁿ received new promises, shut the mouths of lions, ³⁴ stopped the force of fire,ᵒ escaped from dying by the sword, out of weakness found great strength, grew mighty in war, put foreign armies to flight.ᵖ ³⁵ Women by a resurrection received their dead again; ᑫ others endured tortures, because they would not accept release, that they might rise to a better life. ³⁶ Still others stood the test of taunts and tortures, and even chains and prisons. ³⁷ They were stoned to death, they were tortured to death, they were sawn in two, they were killed with the sword. With nothing on their bodies but skins of sheep or goats they wandered here and there, destitute, oppressed, mistreated— ³⁸ men of whom

---
ʲ Lit., *about his bones.*
ᵏ Obj. gen.
ˡ Implied.
ᵐ Lit., *with peace,* so *as friends.*
ⁿ So Dods, Moffatt, et al.
ᵒ For last two, see Dan. 6:22; 3:27.
ᵖ See Jdg. 4:15f; I Mac. 3:3, 15, 17f
ᑫ See I Kg. 17:23; 2 Kg. 4:37.

the world was not worthy, though wandering in deserts, mountains, caves, and holes in the ground.

³⁹ Though all these people by their faith won God's approval, yet none of them received what He had promised, ⁴⁰ for God had provided something still better for us, that they, apart from us might not attain perfection.

12
JESUS OUR MODEL HERO OF FAITH; HIS SUFFERINGS FAR GREATER THAN OURS; OUR FATHER LETTING US SUFFER TO DISCIPLINE AND REFINE OUR SOULS; SO BE CHEERFUL, CONSECRATED, CAUTIOUS; SINAI AND MT. ZION CONTRASTED

Therefore, as we have so vast a crowd of spectators in the grandstands,[a] let us throw off every impediment and the sin that easily entangles our feet, and run with endurance the race for which we are entered, ² keeping our eyes on Jesus, the perfect leader and example [b] of faith, who, instead of the joy which lay before Him, endured the cross with no regard for its shame, and since has taken His seat at the right hand of the throne of God.

³ Yes, to keep from growing weary and fainthearted, just think of the examples [c] set by Him who has endured so great opposition aimed at Him by sinful men! ⁴ You have not yet, as you have struggled on against sin, resisted to the point of pouring out your blood, ⁵ and you have forgotten the encouragement which is addressed to you as sons: [d]

"My son, refrain from thinking lightly of the discipline the Lord inflicts,
And giving up when you are corrected by Him.
⁶ For He disciplines everyone He loves,
And chastises every son whom He heartily receives."

⁷ You must submit to discipline. God is dealing with you as His sons. For who is the son that his father never disciplines? ⁸ Now if you are without any discipline, in which all true sons share, you are only illegitimate children and not true sons. ⁹ Furthermore,

---
[a] The ancient arena surrounded by spectators of the sports much like our modern athletic field with spectators in the grandstands; hence our tr.
[b] Lit., *leader and perfecter,* but as our example; hence tr.
[c] Think of Him.
[d] Prov. 3:11, 12; Job 5:17.

we had earthly fathers who disciplined us, and we used to treat them with respect; how much more cheerfully should we submit to the Father of our spirits, and live! ¹⁰ For they disciplined us only a short time, as it seemed proper to them; but He does it for our good, in order that we may share His holy character.ᵉ ¹¹ Now for the time being no discipline seems to be pleasant; it is painful; later on, however, to those who are trained by it, it yields the fruit of peace which grows from upright character. ¹² So tighten the grip of your slipping hands; stiffen the stand of your knocking knees; ᶠ ¹³ and keep your feet in straight paths, so that limbs may not be dislocated,ᵍ but instead be cured.

¹⁴ Continue to live in peace with everybody and strive for that consecration without which no one can see the Lord. ¹⁵ Continue to look after one another, that no one fails to gain God's spiritual blessing; or some evil like a bitter root may spring up and trouble you, and many of you be contaminated by it—¹⁶ some immoral or godless person like Esau, who sold his own birthright for a single meal. ¹⁷ For you know that, when later he wanted to get possession of the blessing, he was rejected, for he could find no opportunity to repent, although with tears he tried to get the blessing.

¹⁸ For you have not come to a blazing fire that can be touched, to gloom and darkness, storm ¹⁹ and trumpet-blast, and a voice whose words made the hearers beg that not a word more should be added; ²⁰ for they did not try ʰ to bear the order, "Even if a wild animal touches the mountain, it must be stoned to death," ⁱ ²¹ and so terrifying was the sight that Moses said, "I am terrified and terror-stricken!" ʲ ²² But you have come to Mount Zion, even to the city of the living God, the heavenly Jerusalem, and to countless hosts of angels, ²³ to the festal gathering and assembly of God's firstborn sons enrolled as citizens in heaven, to a Judge who is the God of all, to the spirits of upright men who have attained perfection, ²⁴ to Jesus the Mediator of the new covenant, and to the sprinkled blood which speaks a better message than even Abel's did.

²⁵ See to it that you do not refuse to listen to Him who is speaking to you. For if they did not escape, because they refused to listen

---

ᵉ Grk., *holiness.*
ᶠ Grk., *restore your hanging hands, your paralyzed knees.*
ᵍ Medical terms in moral sense.
ʰ Ingressive impf.
ⁱ Ex. 19:12, 13.
ʲ Dt. 9:19.

to him who warned them here on earth, how much less can we, if we reject Him who is from heaven? ²⁶ Then His voice shook the earth, ²⁷ but now His promise is, "Once more I will make not only the earth but heaven itself to tremble." ᵏ Now that expression, "Once more," signifies the final removal of the things that can be shaken, to let remain the things that cannot be shaken. ²⁸ Let us, therefore, be thankful for receiving a kingdom that cannot be shaken, and in this way continue to serve God acceptably in reverence and fear; ²⁹ for our God, indeed, is a consuming fire.¹

13 HE URGES THEM TO PRACTICE BROTHERLY LOVE, PURITY, CONTENTMENT; CHRIST AND CHRISTIAN TRUTH UNCHANGEABLE; HE TELLS OF THE CHRISTIAN'S TRUE SACRIFICE AND HOME LAND; GIVES PARTING DIRECTIONS AND GREETINGS

You must let your brotherly love continue. ² Do not remain neglectful of hospitality to strangers, for by it some have entertained angels without knowing it. ³ Continue to remember those who are in prison, as though you were in prison with them, and those who are being ill-treated, since you, too, are liable to similar physical punishment.ᵃ ⁴ Marriage must be held in honor by all, and the marriage relations kept sacred. Persons who are sexually vicious and immoral God will punish. ⁵ You must have a turn of mind that is free from avarice; you must be content with what you have, for God Himself has said, "I will never fail you, I will never forsake you." ᵇ ⁶ So we can confidently say:

"The Lord is my helper; I will not be afraid.
What can men do to me?" ᶜ

⁷ You must not forget your former leaders, for it was they who brought you the message of God. Consider how they closed their lives; ᵈ imitate their faith. ⁸ Jesus Christ is the same yesterday and today, yes, forever. ⁹ You must stop being carried away with varied and strange teachings. For it is a good thing for the heart to be

---

ᵏ Hag. 2:6.
¹ His holiness is the fire that consumes all evil.
ᵃ Lit., *you, too, are in the body;* so *liable to physical punishment.*
ᵇ Gen. 28:15; Dt. 31:6-8; Josh. 1:5.
ᶜ Ps. 118:6.
ᵈ Lit., *their exodus.*

strengthened by God's spiritual strength, not by special kinds of food, from which those adhering to them have gotten no good.

¹⁰ We Christians have an altar at which the ministers of the Jewish tent of worship have no right to eat. ¹¹ For the bodies of those animals, whose blood is taken into the sanctuary by the priest as a sin-offering, are burned outside the camp. ¹² So Jesus, too, in order to purify the people by His own blood, suffered outside the gate. ¹³ Let us, therefore, go to Him outside the camp, enduring the reproach that He endured; ¹⁴ for we have no permanent city here, but we are searching for that city which is to be ours. ¹⁵ So then, through Christ, let us always offer God the sacrifice of praise; that is, the speech ᵉ of lips that glorify the name of God. ¹⁶ And stop neglecting to do good and to be generous, for God is highly pleased with just such sacrifices as these.

¹⁷ Continue to obey and to be submissive to your leaders, for they are ever watching in defense of your souls, as men who will have to give account of their trust. Treat them in this way,ᶠ so that they may work with joy and not with grief.

¹⁸ Pray for me, for I am sure that I have a clear conscience, and in everything I want to live a noble life. ¹⁹ And more especially do I beg you to do so, that I may very soon be brought back to you.

²⁰ May God, who gives us peace, who brought back from the dead our Lord Jesus, who through the blood by which He ratified the everlasting covenant, is now the Great Shepherd of the sheep, ²¹ perfectly fit you to do His will, He Himself, through Jesus Christ, accomplishing through you what is pleasing to Him. To Him be glory forever and ever. Amen.

²² I beg you, brothers, to listen patiently to this message, for I have written you only a short letter. ²³ You must know that our brother Timothy has been released from prison. If he comes soon, he and I will see you together. ²⁴ Remember us to all your leaders and to all the Christians.ᵍ The Christians from Italy wish to be remembered to you.

²⁵ God's spiritual blessings be with you all. Amen.

ᵉ Lit., *fruit of lips that confess,* etc.
ᶠ This clause implied from impvs. in previous sentence.
ᵍ Grk., *to all the saints.*

JAMES

By conservative scholars the author is held to be James, a half brother of Jesus, who was not converted until Jesus was raised from the dead. By the year A.D. 51 we find him the honored pastor of the church at Jerusalem, when he was asked to preside over the conference held there to settle the controversy about circumcision. He also addressed the conference.

The occasion for writing this letter was that the Jewish Christian readers were suffering persecution; laborers were being defrauded of their wages, while their rich employers were piling up gold and silver, and living in luxury. So Christian officials were inclined to be partial to the rich and to slight the poor. The date was about 51.

James wrote to encourage these poor Christians to be patient, to urge officials, and all, not to be partial to the rich; to warn the rich oppressors that they were fattening to be butchered on the day of judgment; in short, to stress the social, practical side of Christianity.

1 HE GREETS THEM; SHOWS THAT TRIALS, THROUGH PRAYER AND PATIENCE, LEAD TO PERFECTION; THAT CHRISTIAN FAITH IS DEMOCRATIC; CONQUERING TEMPTATION BRINGS THE CROWN OF LIFE; GOD GIVES ALL GOOD; TEMPER AND TONGUE MUST BE CONTROLLED; WE ARE TO BE CHARITABLE AND UNSTAINED

James, a slave of God and of the Lord Jesus Christ, sends greetings to the twelve tribes that are scattered over the world.

² You must consider it the purest joy, my brothers, when you are involved in various trials, ³ for you surely know that what is genuine [a] in your faith produces the patient mind that endures; [b] ⁴ but you must let your endurance come to its perfect product, so that you may be fully developed [c] and perfectly equipped, [d] without any defects. ⁵ But if any one of you is deficient in wisdom, let

---

[a] So used in popular Grk. of the day (EGT).
[b] *Endurance*, or *turn of the mind that endures*.
[c] Lit., *perfect, mature*.
[d] *Wholly attaining to one's lot*.

him ask God who generously gives to everyone and never reproaches one with its lack, and it will be given to him. ⁶ But he must ask in faith, without a doubt, for the man who doubts is like a wave of the sea that is whirled and swayed by the wind. ⁷⁻⁸ Such a man, indeed, a person with two minds, unreliable in every step he takes, must not expect to get anything from the Lord.

⁹ Let the poor brother of lowly station rejoice in his exalted station as a Christian,ᵉ ¹⁰ and the rich brother rejoice in his being on a level with the poor, because the rich will fade away like the flower of the grass. ¹¹ For the sun comes up with its scorching heat and dries up the grass, and its flowers wither, and its beauty fades away; so will rich men fade away in their pursuits.

¹² Blessed is the person who endures trial, for when he stands the test, he will receive the crown of life, which God has promised to those who love Him. ¹³ No one must say, when he is tempted to do evil, "I have a temptation from God to do evil," for God cannot be tempted to do evil, and He never tempts anyone to do so. ¹⁴ But anyone is tempted to do evil when he is allured by his own evil desire and enticed by a bait.ᶠ ¹⁵ Then evil desire conceives and gives birth to sin, and when sin is completed, it brings forth death.ᵍ

¹⁶ You must avoid being misled, my dearly loved brothers. ¹⁷ Every good gift and every perfect boon is from above, and comes down from the Father of lights, in whom there is no variation or changing shadow. ¹⁸ In accordance with His will He made us His children by the message of truth, that we might be a kind of first fruits among His creatures.

¹⁹ You must understand this, my dearly loved brothers. Everyone must be quick to hear, slow to speak, slow to get angry; ²⁰ for a man'sʰ anger does not produce the uprightness that God requires. ²¹ So strip yourselves of everything impure and all the evils prevailing around you, and in humble spirit welcome the message which when rooted in your hearts is able to save your souls. ²² Keep on obeying this message; do not merely listen to it, and so deceive yourselves. ²³ Because if anyone merely listens to the message without obeying it, he is like a man who looks in a mirror at his own face, ²⁴ for he looks and then goes off and at once forgets how he

---

ᵉ Implied.

ᶠ Both vbs. fishing or hunting terms.

ᵍ Only a practical, not a philosophical, explanation—of how sinning starts and matures in death.

ʰ A human male's anger, but true also of woman.

looked. ²⁵ But the man who looks at the flawless law¹ that makes men free, and keeps on looking, proving himself to be, not a forgetful hearer but an actual doer of what it requires, will be blessed in what he does. ²⁶ If anyone thinks he is religious, and does not bridle his tongue, but deceives himself, his religious worship¹ is worthless. ²⁷ A religious worship that is pure and stainless in the sight of God the Father is this: To look after orphans and widows in their trouble, and to keep one's own self unstained by the world.

2 CHRISTIANS NOT TO PRACTICE PARTIALITY; DEAD AND LIVING FAITH CONTRASTED; CHRISTIANS URGED TO SHOW THEIR FAITH BY DOING GOOD

My brothers, stop trying to maintain your faith in our Lord Jesus Christ, the glorious presence of God on earth,[a] along with acts of partiality to certain ones.[b] ²For if a man with a gold ring, dressed in fine clothes, comes to your meeting, and at the same time a poor man clad in dirty clothes, ³ and you pay special attention to the man who wears the fine clothes, and say to him, "Sit here in this fine place," and say to the poor man, "Stand up, or sit there on the floor at my feet," ⁴ do you not make improper distinctions among yourselves and prove to be critics with evil motives?[c] ⁵ Listen, my dearly loved brothers. Has not God chosen the poor of the world to be rich in faith and to possess the kingdom which He promised to those who love Him? ⁶ But you, in contrast, have humiliated the poor man. Are not the rich men those who oppress you and drag you to court? ⁷ Are not they the ones who scoff at the beautiful name you bear? ⁸ But if you really observe the law of the King in accordance with the Scripture, "You must love your neighbor as you do yourself," you are doing right; ⁹ but if you show partiality, you are committing sin, because you are convicted by the law as lawbreakers. ¹⁰ For whoever obeys the whole law, except to slip in a single instance, is guilty of breaking it all. ¹¹ For He who said, "You must not commit adultery," also said, "You must not commit murder." Now if you do not commit adultery but you do commit murder, you are just the same a lawbreaker. ¹² You must continue talking and acting like

---

[1] So Hatch and other exegetes.
[a] Lit., *the glory;* i.e., *shekinah,* God's presence.
[b] Implied.
[c] Grk., *critics of evil thoughts.*

people who are to be judged by the law that treats them as free.[d]
¹³ For merciless judgment will be the portion of the merciless man; yet mercy will triumph over judgment.

¹⁴ My brothers, what good is there in a man's saying that he has faith, if he has no good deeds to prove it? Such faith cannot save him, can it? ¹⁵ If some brother or sister is thinly clad and has no food for the day, ¹⁶ and one of you says to him, "Blessings on you, keep warm, eat until you have a plenty," [e] without giving him the things that are needed for the body, what good does it do? ¹⁷ So faith by itself, if it has no deeds to back it up, is dead. ¹⁸ But someone may say, "You have faith, and I have good [b] deeds. Show me your faith without any good deeds, but I will show you mine by my good deeds." ¹⁹ Do you believe in one God? Very well; the demons, too, believe that, and shudder. ²⁰ But, O senseless man, are you willing to learn that faith without good deeds is worthless? ²¹ Was not our forefather Abraham shown to be upright [f] by his good deeds, namely, by offering Isaac his son upon the altar? ²² You see that faith co-operated with his good deeds, and by his good deeds faith was made complete; ²³ and so the Scripture was fulfilled which says, "Abraham put his faith in God, and it was credited to him for uprightness, and he was called God's friend." [g] ²⁴ You see that a man is shown to be upright by his good deeds, and not merely by his faith. ²⁵ Was not even Rahab the prostitute shown to be upright by her good deeds, namely, by entertaining the scouts and sending them off by a different road? ²⁶ Just as the body without the spirit is dead, so faith without good deeds is dead.

3 THE NEED OF BRIDLING THE TONGUE; TRUE WISDOM SHOWS ITSELF IN NOBLE CHARACTER AND LIVING

Many of you, my brothers, should avoid becoming teachers, because you know that we teachers are going to be judged with stricter judgment than other people.[a] ² For we all make many a slip. If anyone never slips in speech, he is a man of maturity; he can control his whole body too. ³ If we put bridles into horses' mouths to make them obey us, we can guide their whole bodies,

---
[d] *By a law of freedom.*
[e] Lit., *be gorged.*
[f] Grk., *justified.*
[g] Gen. 15:6; cf. Rom. 4:3.
[a] Last three words implied.

too. ⁴ Look at ships, too; though great and driven by violent winds, they are steered with a tiny ᵇ rudder wherever the pilot pleases. ⁵ So the tongue, too, is a little organ but can boast of great achievements. See how a spark, ever so tiny can set a vast forest on fire! ⁶ And the tongue is a fire, and takes its place among the parts of our bodies as a world of evil; it soils the whole body and sets on fire the circle ᶜ of man's nature, and itself is set on fire by hell. ⁷ For every kind of beasts and birds, of reptiles and sea animals, can be, or have been, tamed by man; ⁸ but the tongue no human being can tame. It is an evil incapable of being quieted, full of deadly poison. ⁹ With it we bless the Lord and Father, and with it we curse men who are made in God's likeness. ¹⁰ Out of the same mouth flow blessing and cursing! It ought not to be like this, my brothers. ¹¹ A fountain cannot pour from the same opening fresh and brackish water, can it? ¹² A fig tree, my brothers, cannot bear olives, or a grape vine figs, can it? And a salt spring cannot furnish fresh water.

¹³ Who among you is wise and intelligent? Let him show by his noble living that his good ᵃ deeds are done in humility, which wisdom prompts. ¹⁴ But if you cherish bitter jealousy and rivalry in your hearts, stop being proud of it and stop being false to the standard of truth. ¹⁵ This is not the kind ᵃ of wisdom that comes down from above; no, it is earthly, human,ᵈ demoniacal. ¹⁶ For wherever jealousy and rivalry exist, there will be confusion and all sorts of evil practices. ¹⁷ The wisdom that is from above is first pure, then peaceable, gentle, willing to yield, full of compassion and good deeds, free from doubts and insincerity. ¹⁸ The harvest of uprightness is grown from the seed of peace by those who are peacemakers.

4 EVIL DESIRES THE REAL CAUSE OF STRIFE AND WAR; THE FRIENDSHIP OF THE WORLD MEANS ENMITY WITH GOD; EVIL-SPEAKING TO BE STOPPED; LIFE UNCERTAIN

What causes wars and quarrels among you? Is it not your different desires which are ever at war within your bodies? ᵃ You

---

ᵇ In superlative to emphasize the contrast in size of rudder and ship.
ᶜ Grk., *wheel*.
ᵈ Lit., *psychical*, so *human vs. divine*.
ᵃ Lit., *in your members, parts*.

desire things and cannot have them, and so you commit murder.
² You covet things, but cannot acquire them, and so you quarrel and fight. You do not have them, because you do not ask for them. ³ You ask and fail to get them, because you ask with evil, selfish motives,ᵇ to spend them on your pleasures.

⁴ You faithless wives!ᶜ Do you not know that the friendship of the world means enmity with God? So whoever wants to be a friend to the world puts himself down as an enemy to God. ⁵ Or, do you think that the Scripture means nothing when it says, "He jealously yearns for the Spirit that He causes to dwell in your hearts"?ᵈ ⁶ But He gives a greater spiritual blessing. He says, "God opposes haughty people but blesses humble people." ⁷ So then, submit to God. Resist the devil and he will fly from you. ⁸ Draw near to God and He will draw near to you. Get your hands clean, you sinners. Get your hearts purified, you double-minded. ⁹ Be miserable, mourn, and weep aloud. Let your laughter be turned to grief and your joy to gloom. ¹⁰ Humble yourselves before the Lord, and He will lift you high.

¹¹ Stop talking against one another, brothers. Whoever is in the habit of talking against a brother or of criticizing his brother is criticizing and condemning the law. But if you are in the habit of criticizing the law, you are not a practicer but a critic of the law. ¹² There is but one Lawgiver and Judge, the One who has the power to save and to destroy; then who are you that you presumeᵉ to judge your brother?

¹³ Come now, you who say, "Today or tomorrow we are going to such and such a city and stay a year, go into business and make money," ¹⁴ although you do not have the slightest knowledge of tomorrow. What is the natureᶠ of your life? It is really nothing but a mist which appears for a little while and then disappears. ¹⁵ Instead, you ought to say, "If the Lord is willing, we shall live and do this or that." ¹⁶ But, as it is, you boast of your proud pretensions. All such boasting is wicked. ¹⁷ So when a man knows what is right but does not do it, he is guilty of sin.

ᵇ Grk., *ask wickedly for yourselves.*
ᶜ So EGT after best Mss.
ᵈ Not from O. T.; uncertain from what book it comes.
ᵉ Implied.
ᶠ In qualitative interrog.

5 TAINTED MONEY A CURSE; THE LORD'S RETURN SHOULD INSPIRE TO THE PATIENCE OF THE PROPHETS, THE ENDURANCE OF JOB; TELLING THE TRUTH WITHOUT AN OATH; PRAYER, PRAISE, CONFESSION; THE HAPPY SOUL-WINNER

Come now, you rich people, weep aloud and howl over the miseries that are sure to overtake you. ² Your wealth has rotted, your clothes are moth-eaten, ³ your gold and silver have rusted, and their rust will testify against you and devour your flesh like fire. You have stored up these things for the last days. ⁴ See! the wages that you have kept back[a] from the laborers who reaped your fields are crying aloud, and the cries of the reapers have reached the ears of the Lord of hosts. ⁵ Here on earth you have lived in luxury and self-indulgence; you have fattened your hearts for the day of slaughter. ⁶ You have condemned and murdered the upright man; he offers no resistance.[b]

⁷ So be patient, brothers, until the coming of the Lord. See how the farmer keeps on waiting and waiting for the precious crop from his land; how he keeps up his patience over it until he gets the early and the late rains. ⁸ You must be patient, too; you must put iron [c] into your hearts, because the coming of the Lord is close at hand. ⁹ Stop muttering against one another, brothers, so as to keep from being judged yourselves. Look! The Judge is standing at the very door. ¹⁰ As an example of ill-treatment and patience, brothers, take the prophets, who spoke in the name of the Lord. ¹¹ See how we call those who thus endured happy! You have heard how patiently Job endured and have seen how the Lord finally blessed him,[d] because the Lord is tenderhearted and merciful.

¹² Above all, my brothers, stop swearing, either by heaven or by the earth, or by anything else.[e] Let your "Yes" mean Yes, and your "No," No, so as to keep from falling under condemnation.

¹³ Is any one of you suffering ill-treatment? He should keep on praying. Is anyone in a happy mood? He should keep on singing praise to God. ¹⁴ Is anyone sick among you? He should call in the elders of the church, and they should pray over him, and

[a] In passive in Grk., but active better in Eng.
[b] Or, *does he*, etc.?
[c] Lit., *put strength;* above is the Eng. idiom.
[d] Lit., *the end of the Lord* (in blessing him).
[e] Daily swearing then a common sin among the Jews; hence, the exhortation.

anoint him with oil in the name of the Lord, ¹⁵ and the prayer that is offered in faith will save the sick man; the Lord will raise him to health, and if he has committed sins, he will be forgiven. ¹⁶ So practice confessing your sins to one another, and praying for one another, that you may be cured. An upright man's prayer, when it keeps at work,ᶠ is very powerful. ¹⁷ Elijah was a man with feelings just like ours, and yet he earnestly prayed for it not to rain, and it did not rain on the land for three years and six months. ¹⁸ Then again he prayed, and the heavens yielded rain and the earth produced its crops.

¹⁹ My brothers, if any one of you has wandered away from the truth, and someone brings him back, ²⁰ you may be sure that whoever brings a sinner back from his evil ways will save the man'sᵍ soul from death, and cover up a multitude of sins.

ᶠ In pres. pt. of continuous action.
ᵍ Not the worker's soul, but evidently that of the man brought back.

FIRST PETER

The author is usually held to be Peter the apostle, although a few scholars think that the date of the letter must be placed after the execution of the apostle, largely on the grounds of style and close imitation of Ephesians, as they hold. It is written in fairly good Greek, though not so literary that Peter could not have written it.

The Jewish Christians in Pontus, Galatia, Asia (province), Cappadocia, and Bithynia were suffering bitter persecution which incited the sympathy of the apostle. So he wrote this letter to encourage the readers patiently to endure these persecutions in imitation of Christ's example. As He, the Innocent One, gladly suffered for us the unrighteous, so we should congratulate ourselves on having the privilege to suffer for being Christians. Even Christian slaves must suffer "for the Lord's sake," and in this way "silence the ignorant talk of foolish people."

1 HE GREETS THEM; GIVES THANKS FOR THE HOPE OF TOMORROW, REJOICES IN THE TRIALS OF TODAY; PROPHETS AND ANGELS INTERESTED IN THIS SALVATION; AS REDEEMED ONES, WE MUST LIVE PURE, OBEDIENT, CONSECRATED LIVES AND LOVE ONE ANOTHER

Peter, an apostle of Jesus Christ, to the foreign-born [a] Jews who are scattered over Pontus, Galatia, Cappadocia, Asia, and Bithynia, ² the people chosen in accordance with the foreknowledge of God the Father, by the consecration of the Spirit, to obey Jesus Christ and to be sprinkled with His blood: spiritual blessing and peace to you in increasing abundance.[b]

³ Blessed be the God and Father of our Lord Jesus Christ! In accordance with His great mercy He has begotten us anew to an ever living hope through the resurrection of Jesus Christ from the dead; ⁴ yes, to an inheritance that is imperishable, unsullied, and unfading, which is kept in heaven for you ⁵ who are always

[a] *The dispersion*—Jews scattered in other lands.
[b] Lit., *be multiplied*, etc.

guarded by the power of God through faith, in order that you may receive that final [c] salvation which will be ready to be uncovered for you at the last time. 6 In such a hope [d] keep on rejoicing, although for a little while you must be sorrow-stricken with various trials, 7 so that the genuineness [e] of your faith, which is more precious than gold that perishes even after it is shown by the test of fire to be genuine, may result in your praise and glory and honor at the unveiling of Jesus Christ. 8 You must continue to love Him, although you have never [f] seen Him, but because you do believe in Him, although you do not now see Him, you must continue to rejoice with an unutterable and triumphant [g] joy, 9 because you will receive the goal of your faith, the ultimate [h] salvation of your souls.

10 Even the prophets, who prophesied about the spiritual blessing meant for you, made careful investigations and persistent research about this salvation, 11 earnestly trying to find out the time, and the nature of the times, which the Spirit of the Christ within them pointed to, in foretelling the sufferings of the Christ and the glory that should follow them. 12 It was made known to them that they were serving not themselves but you, in their searching for these things that have already been told to you by those who through the Holy Spirit sent from heaven brought you the good news. The angels long to take a peep [i] into these things.

13 Therefore, as a means of spiritual preparation,[h] tighten up the belt about your minds, keep perfectly calm, keep your hope on the spiritual blessing to be conferred upon you at the unveiling of Jesus Christ. 14 As obedient children, stop molding your character by the evil desires you used to cherish when you did not know any better, 15 but in accordance with the Holy Being who has called you, you must prove to be holy too, 16 for the Scripture says:

> "You ought [j] to be holy,
> Because I am holy." [k]

[c] In prep. meaning ultimate end.
[d] Lit., *in which*, but hope implied.
[e] So used in papyri (Deissmann, EGT).
[f] Strong neg.
[g] Lit., *glorified*, so *triumphant*.
[h] Implied from context.
[i] This idea in vb. stem and in aor.
[j] Impv. fut. indic.
[k] Lev. 11:44; 19:2.

[17] And if you address as Father, Him who judges everyone impartially in accordance with what he does, you must live reverently all your fleeting stay on earth, [18] because you know that you have not been ransomed with things that perish as silver or gold, from the futile way of living taught by your fathers, [19] but with the precious blood of Christ, like that of a lamb without a blemish or a blot, [20] who was foreordained[1] for it before the foundation of the world but was brought out to public view at the end of the ages, for the sake of you [21] who through Him trust in God, who raised Him from the dead and gave Him glory; so that your faith and hope may rest in God.

[22] Since you have purified your souls by obeying the truth, in sincere love for the brotherhood you must love one another heartily and fervently, [23] because you have been born anew, not from a germ that perishes but from one that does not perish, by the word of the living and everlasting God. [24] For:

> "All human life is just like grass
> And all its glory like the flower of grass.
> The grass dries up,
> The flowers drop off,
> [25] But the word of the Lord lives on forever"; [m]

that is, the message of the good news which has been brought to you.

2   LOVING CHRISTIANS LIVING STONES IN THE SPIRITUAL TEMPLE BUILT ON CHRIST; LIVING RIGHT SILENCES FOES; CIVIC DUTIES; SERVANTS TO BE FAITHFUL EVEN TO CRUEL MASTERS; CHRIST OUR EXAMPLE OF SUFFERING

So once for all get rid of all malice, deceit, hypocrisy, envy, and all sorts of slander, [2] and like new-born babies thirst for pure spiritual milk, so that by it you may grow up to final salvation, [3] since you have learned by experience that the Lord is kind. [4] Keep on coming to Him, as to a living stone, rejected by men but chosen by God and precious in His sight, [5] and keep on building yourselves up, as living stones, into a spiritual house for a consecrated

---

[1] Lit., *foreknown*.
[m] Isa. 40:6-8.

priesthood,[a] to offer up, through Jesus Christ, spiritual sacrifices that will be acceptable to God. ⁶ It must be so, because the Scriptures say:

> "Here now I lay in Zion a chosen stone, a costly cornerstone,
> And not a single one who puts his trust in Him will ever be put to shame."[b]

⁷ So to you who put your trust in Him the honor belongs, but to those who fail to trust Him:

> "That stone which then the builders threw away
> Has now become the cornerstone,"

⁸ and:

> "A stone for them to stumble over and a rock to trip them up."[c]

They keep on stumbling over the message, because they are disobedient to it, and this is their appointed doom. ⁹ But you are the chosen race, the royal priesthood, the consecrated nation, the people to be His very own, to proclaim the perfections of Him who called you out of darkness into His wonderful light. ¹⁰ Once you were not a people, but now you are the people of God; once His mercy had not been shown you, but now it has.

¹¹ Dearly beloved, I beg you as aliens and exiles to keep on abstaining from the evil desires of your lower nature, because they are always at war with the soul. ¹² Keep on living upright lives among the heathen, so that, when they slander you as evildoers, by what they see of your good deeds they may come to praise God on the judgment day.

¹³ For the Lord's sake submit to all human authority; to the emperor as supreme, ¹⁴ and to governors as sent by Him to punish those who do evil and to reward those who do right. ¹⁵ For it is God's will that by doing right you should silence the ignorant talk[d] of foolish people. ¹⁶ Live like free men, only do not make your freedom a pretext for doing evil, but live like slaves of God. ¹⁷ Show honor to everyone. Practice love for the brotherhood; practice reverence to God and honor to the Emperor.

---

[a] As Peter sees it, all Christians are priests who offer praise, holiness, and service.
[b] Isa. 28:16.
[c] Isa. 8:14.
[d] Lit., the *ignorance,* but the vb. *silence* implies they are talking.

¹⁸ You house-servants must be submissive to your masters and show them perfect respect, not only to those who are kind and fair but also to those who are cruel. ¹⁹ For it is pleasing in the sight of God for one to bear his sorrows though suffering innocently. ²⁰ For what credit is it to bear it patiently, if you do wrong and are beaten for it? But if you do right and patiently suffer for it, it is pleasing in the sight of God. ²¹ Indeed, it was to this kind of living that you were called, because Christ also suffered for you, leaving you an example that you might follow His footsteps. ²² He never committed a sin, and deceit was never found on His lips. ²³ Although He was abused, He never retorted; although He continued to suffer, He never threatened, but committed His case to Him who judges justly. ²⁴ He bore our sins in His own body on the cross,[e] that we might die to sin and live to uprightness. By His wounds you have been healed, ²⁵ for once you were going astray like sheep, but now you have returned to the Shepherd and Overseer of your souls.

3 MARRIED WOMEN TO LIVE IN CHASTITY AND TO DRESS IN SIMPLICITY; MARRIED MEN TO DEFER TO THEIR WIVES; ALL URGED TO LIVE IN BROTHERHOOD; TO WIN THE WICKED BY SUFFERING FOR BEING GOOD; CHRIST OUR EXAMPLE OF SUFFERING

You married women, in the same way, must be submissive to your husbands, so that, if any of them do not believe the message, they may be won over without a word through the living of the wives, ² when they see how chaste and respectful you are. ³ Your adornments must be not of an external nature, with braids of hair or ornaments of gold, or changes of dress, ⁴ but they must be of an internal nature, the character concealed in the heart,[a] in the imperishable quality of a quiet and gentle spirit, which is of great value in the sight of God. ⁵ For this is the way the pious women of olden times, who set their hope on God, used to adorn themselves. ⁶ They were submissive to their husbands, as Sarah, for example, obeyed Abraham and called him master. You have become true daughters[b] of hers, if you practice doing right and cease from every fear.

⁷ You married men, in the same way, must live with your wives

---

[e] Peter used *wood*, or *tree*, for *cross*.
[a] Lit., *the hidden man of the heart*.
[b] Grk., *children*.

in an intelligent consideration^c of them; you must show them deference, too, as the weaker sex, as they share with you the gracious gift of life, so that your prayers may not be hindered.

⁸ Finally, you must all live in harmony, be sympathetic, loving as brothers, tenderhearted, humble, ⁹ never returning evil for evil or abuse for abuse, but blessing instead, because it was for this that you were called, to obtain the blessing of heirs.^d ¹⁰ For:

> "Whoever wants to enjoy life
> And see delightful days
> Must keep his tongue from evil
> And his lips from speaking deceit.
> ¹¹ He must turn, too, away from evil and do right;
> He must seek peace and follow it,
> ¹² Because the eyes of the Lord are on upright men,
> And His ears listen to their pleading cries,
> But His face is against them that do wrong." ^e

¹³ And who is it that will harm you if you are enthusiastic to do right? ¹⁴ Instead, you are happy, even if you should suffer for doing right. Never be afraid of their threats, and never be disturbed, ¹⁵ but in your hearts be consecrated to Christ as Lord, and always be ready to make your defense to anyone who asks a reason for the hope you have. But you must do it in gentleness and reverence, ¹⁶ and keep your conscience clear, so that those who bitterly abuse your excellent conduct as Christians may be ashamed of slandering you.^f

¹⁷ For it is better, if the will of God should plan it so, to suffer for doing right than for doing wrong. ¹⁸ For Christ Himself, once for all, died for our sins, the Innocent for the guilty^g to bring us to God, being put to death in physical form but made alive in the Spirit, ¹⁹ in which He went and preached to the spirits in prison, ²⁰ who had once been disobedient, while God's patience was awaiting in the days when Noah was preparing an ark, in which a few people—eight, to be exact—were brought safely through the water. ²¹ Baptism, which corresponds to this figure,^h now saves

^c Lit., *in accordance with knowledge.*
^d Lit., *inherit a blessing.*
^e Ps. 34:12-16.
^f Grk., *ashamed of that in which you are slandered.*
^g Lit., *the Righteous for the unrighteous.*
^h Grk., *antitype.*

you, too—I do not mean the mere removal of physical stains, but the craving for a clear conscience toward God—through the resurrection of Jesus Christ, ²² who has gone to heaven and is now at God's right hand, with angels, heavenly authorities and powers made subject to Him.

4   INSPIRED BY CHRIST'S EXAMPLE TO BE COURAGEOUS AND PURE; AS TIME IS SHORT, LIVE TO LOVE YOUR FELLOWS, TO GLORIFY GOD, TO SUFFER FOR CHRIST

So then, since Christ has suffered in our physical form, you too must arm yourselves with the same determination. For whoever suffers in his physical form has done with sin, ² so that he no longer can spend the rest of his earthly ᵃ life in harmony ᵇ with human desires but in accordance ᵇ with God's will. ³ For the time that is past is enough for you to have accomplished what the heathen like to do, leading lives that are steeped in sensuality, lustful desires, drunkenness, carousing, revelry, dissipation, and idolatry that leads to lawlessness.ᶜ ⁴ They are astonished that you are not still rushing hand in hand with them into the same excesses of profligate living, and they abuse you for it; ⁵ but they will have to give account for it to Him who is ready to judge living and dead. ⁶ This is why the good news was preached to the dead too, that they may be judged in their physical nature as men are, but live in the Spirit as God does.

⁷ But the end of everything on earth ᵃ is near. So be serious and soberminded, that you may give yourselves ᵃ to prayer. ⁸ Above everything else keep your love for one another fervent, because love covers up a multitude of sins. ⁹ Be ungrudgingly hospitable to one another. ¹⁰ As all of you have received your spiritual talents, you must keep on using them in serving one another, as good trustees of God's many-sided favor. ¹¹ If anyone is preaching, let him do it as one who utters the oracles of God; if anyone is rendering any service to others, let him do it with all the strength that God supplies, so that in everything God may be glorified through Jesus Christ. To Him be glory and dominion forever and ever. Amen.

¹² Dearly beloved, do not be astonished that a test by fire is com-

---

ᵃ Implied.
ᵇ Instr. of measure.
ᶜ Lit., *lawless idolatries.*

ing upon you, as though something strange were happening to you, ¹³ but so far as you are sharing Christ's sufferings, keep on rejoicing, so that at the uncovering of His glory you may rejoice triumphantly. ¹⁴ If you are suffering abuse because you bear the name of Christ, you are happy, because the glorious Spirit of God is resting upon you. ¹⁵ For not one of you should suffer as a murderer or as a thief or any sort of criminal, or as a meddler in other people's business, ¹⁶ but if anyone suffers for being a Christian, he must not be ashamed of it, but should keep on praising God for bearing this name. ¹⁷ Because the time has come for judgment to begin at the household of God, and if it begins with us, what will the end be of those who are rejecting God's good news? ¹⁸ And if it is hard for the upright man to be saved, what will become of the godless and sinful? ¹⁹ Therefore, those who suffer in accordance with God's will must also, in doing right, entrust their souls to the Creator who is faithful.

5 PASTORS TO LIVE AS EXAMPLES TO THEIR FLOCKS; AS THE TEMPTER PROWLS ABOUT LIKE A LION, CHRISTIANS MUST BE ALERT; SENDS FAREWELL GREETING

So, as a joint-elder with them, a witness of the suffering borne by Christ, and a sharer of the glory that is to be uncovered, I beg the elders among you, ² be shepherds of the flock of God that is among you, not as though you had to but of your own free will, not from the motive of personal profit but freely, ³ and not as domineering over those in your charge but proving yourselves models for the flock to imitate; ⁴ and when the Chief Shepherd appears, you will receive the glorious crown that never fades. ⁵ You younger men, on your part, must be submissive to the elders. And you must all put on the servant's apron [a] of humility to one another, because God opposes the haughty but bestows His unmerited favor on the humble. ⁶ Therefore humbly submit to God's strong hand, so that at the proper time He may exalt you. ⁷ Cast every worry you have upon Him, because He cares for you.

⁸ Be calm and alert. Your opponent the devil is always prowling about like a roaring lion, trying to devour you. ⁹ Resist him and be strong in faith, because you know that your brotherhood [b] all

---
[a] Grk. vb. means *to put a waiter's apron on to serve*.
[b] Composed of Christian Jews scattered all over the world.

over the world is experiencing the same sort of sufferings. ¹⁰ And God, the giver of every spiritual blessing, who through your union with Christ has called you to His eternal glory, after you have suffered a little while, will Himself make you perfect, firm, and strong. ¹¹ To Him be dominion forever. Amen.

¹² By Silvanus, our faithful brother, as I regard him, I have written you this short letter, to encourage you and to testify that this is the true, unmerited favor of God. Stand firm in it. ¹³ Your sister-church[c] in Babylon, chosen along with you, and Mark my son, wish to be remembered to you. ¹⁴ Greet one another with a kiss of love. Peace to all of you that are in union with Christ.

[c] Grk. has only feminine art. which might mean, *the lady* or *the church* (implied).

SECOND PETER

The author is usually thought to be the apostle Peter, although many scholars either deny it or doubt it.

The readers are threatened with the destructive teachings of certain greedy, bestial false teachers. The purpose of the writer is to warn them against the evil effects of these false teachings and to describe the base and beastly character of the false teachers—emphasizing the tendencies to immorality of all such false teachers, comparing them to the dog which turns to his own vomit and the pig that wallows in the mire.

1 HE GREETS THEM; RELYING ON GOD'S PROMISES, WE ARE TO KEEP GROWING LIKE CHRIST; THE APOSTLE INSPIRED TO ZEAL BY HIS IMPENDING DEATH; CHRIST'S TRANSFIGURATION SUGGESTS HIS SECOND COMING; OLD TESTAMENT IMPLIES IT

Simon Peter, a slave and apostle of Jesus Christ, to those who through the righteousness of our God and Saviour Jesus Christ have obtained the same precious faith that we have: ² spiritual blessing and peace be to you in increasing abundance through a full knowledge of God and of Jesus our Lord; ³ because His divine power has given us everything that is needful for life and piety, through our full knowledge of Him who through His glory and excellence has called us to Him. ⁴ It is through these that He has given us His precious and glorious promises,[a] so that through them, after you have escaped from the corruption that is in the world because of evil desires, you may come to share in the divine nature. ⁵ Now for this very reason you must do your level best[b] to supplement your faith with moral character,[c] moral character with knowledge, ⁶ knowledge with self-control, self-

[a] Lit., *very great*.
[b] Grk., *furnish all earnestness*.
[c] Lit., *virtue* (in moral sense).

control with patient endurance, patient endurance with piety, ⁷ piety with brotherly affection, brotherly affection with universal ᵈ love. ⁸ For if you have these qualities and they continue to increase in you, they will make you neither idle nor unproductive in attaining a full knowledge of our Lord Jesus Christ. ⁹ For whoever lacks these qualities is blind—or short-sighted—and forgetful of the cleansing that he has received from his former sins. ¹⁰ Therefore, brothers, be all the more in earnest to make certain to yourselves ᵉ God's call and choice of you. For if you cultivate ᶠ these qualities, you will never slip, ¹¹ for it is in this way that to you will be generously granted a triumphant admittance into the eternal kingdom of our Lord and Saviour Jesus Christ.

¹² Therefore, I will always remind you of these things, although you know them and are firmly grounded in the truth that you already have. ¹³ Yet I think it right, as long as I live in this bodily tent,ᵍ to arouse you by a reminder, ¹⁴ because I know that the removal of my bodily tent is to be very soon, as our Lord Jesus Christ has shown me. ¹⁵ Yes, I will be in earnest, so that every time you have occasion, after I have gone away, you may call these things to mind. ¹⁶ For it was not mere stories of fancy ʰ that we followed when we told you of the power and coming of our Lord Jesus Christ, but we had been eyewitnesses of His majesty. ¹⁷ For when He received such honor and glory from God the Father, when from the majestic glory there was borne to Him a voice like this, "This is my Son, my Beloved, in whom I take delight," ¹⁸ we heard this voice ourselves borne from heaven while we were with Him on that sacred mountain. ¹⁹ So we have the message of the prophets more certainly guaranteed. Please pay attention to this message as to a lamp that is shining in a dismal place, until the day dawns and the morning star rises in your hearts; ²⁰ because you recognize this truth above all else, that no prophecy in Scripture is to be interpreted by one's own mind, ²¹ for no prophecy has ever yet originated in man's will, but men who were led by the Holy Spirit spoke from God.

ᵈ Implied in this larger word for *love*.
ᵉ Pronoun trs. mid. voice.
ᶠ Lit., *by doing*, or *putting in practice*.
ᵍ This figure refers to the earthly body as not being the soul's permanent home.
ʰ Grk., *stories invented by cunning*.

2 FALSE TEACHERS FORETOLD AND FOREDOOMED; EXAMPLES OF GOD'S PUNISHING THE WICKED BUT PRESERVING THE RIGHTEOUS; FALSE TEACHERS DESCRIBED; THEIR INFLUENCE IN DEGRADING BACKSLIDERS

Now there were false prophets among the people, just as there will be false teachers among you too, who will insidiously introduce destructive heresies and deny the Master who has bought them, thus bringing on themselves swift destruction. ² Many people will follow their immoral ways, and because of them the true Way will be abused. ³ In their greed they will exploit you with messages manufactured by themselves.[a] From of old their condemnation has not been idle and their destruction has not been slumbering.

⁴ For if God did not spare angels when they sinned, but hurled them down to Tartarus [b] and committed them to dark dungeons to await their doom, ⁵ and if He did not spare the ancient world, but preserved Noah, a preacher of righteousness, and seven others when He brought the flood upon the world of godless people; ⁶ and if He condemned, by burning them to ashes, the cities of Sodom and Gomorrah, making them an example to godless people of what was coming to them, ⁷ and saved the upright Lot who was constantly distressed by the immoral conduct of lawless men—⁸ for as long as that upright man was living among them, his upright soul, day and night, was always being tortured by what he saw and heard in their lawless actions—⁹ surely, then, the Lord knows how to rescue godly people from trial and to keep wrongdoers under punishment for the day of judgment, ¹⁰ especially those who satisfy their lower nature by indulging in its evil passions which defile[c] them, and who despise authority. Daring, headstrong men! They do not tremble when they abuse persons of majesty,[d] ¹¹ whereas angels who are far superior in strength and power to these beings bring no abusive accusation against them before the Lord. ¹² These men, like irrational animals, mere creatures of instinct [e] created to be caught and killed, abuse the things that they do not

---

[a] Last phrase implied.
[b] That is, *hell,* prepared for the devil and his angels (Mt. 25:41).
[c] Grk. has descriptive gen.
[d] Lit., *glories* (**glorious persons, persons of** majesty).
[e] Lit., *created mere physical beings.*

understand, and so by their corruption they will be destroyed, suffering wrong as punishment for their wrongdoing. ¹³ They think their daily luxurious living real pleasure; they are spots and blots, deceitfully living in luxurious pleasure while they continue their religious feasting with you. ¹⁴ They have eyes full of adultery and insatiable by sin. They practice enticing unsteady souls. They have trained their hearts in greed. They are doomed to a curse! ᶠ ¹⁵ They have left the straight road and gone astray. They have followed the road that Balaam, the son of Beor, trod, who fell in love with the profits of wrongdoing ¹⁶ but was reproved for his offense; a dumb animal spoke with a human voice and stopped the prophet's madness.

¹⁷ Such men are dried-up springs, clouds driven by the storm, and they are doomed to densest darkness. ¹⁸ For by uttering arrogant nonsense, through base desires of the lower nature, they entice into immorality men who are just escaping from those who live in error, ¹⁹ promising them freedom, though they are slaves of destruction themselves; for a man is the slave of anything that conquers him.

²⁰ For if, after men have escaped the corrupting ways of the world through a full knowledge of the Lord and Saviour Jesus Christ, they again become entangled in them and are conquered by them, then their last condition is worse than their former one. ²¹ For it would have been better for them never to have known the way of uprightness than to have known it and then to turn their backs on the sacred command committed to their trust. ²² In them is verified the truth of the proverb, "A dog turns back to what he has vomited"; and of that other proverb, "A sow that has washed herself goes back to wallow in the mire." ᵍ

3 WHY THE AUTHOR WRITES; HE WARNS THEM AS TO FALSE TEACHERS WHO RIDICULE THE DELAYED RETURN OF CHRIST; YET THIS RETURN IS CERTAIN THOUGH SUDDEN; IN THE LIGHT OF THAT GREAT DAY HE URGES THEM TO BETTER LIVING

This is the second letter, dearly beloved, that I have already written to you, in both of which I am trying by reminders to stir

---

ᶠ Lit., *children of a curse*.
ᵍ Probably a heathen proverb, but true to the life of the hog.

up your unsullied minds ² to remember the things foretold by the holy prophets, and the command of the Lord and Saviour through your apostles.

³ First of all, you must understand this, that in the last days mockers will come with their mockeries, living in accordance with their evil passions, ⁴ and saying, "Where is His promised coming? For ever since our forefathers fell asleep everything has remained exactly as it was from the beginning of creation!" ⁵ For they willfully ignore the fact that long ago the heavens existed and the earth that had been formed by God's command ᵃ out of water and through water, ⁶ by which ᵇ also the world, through being deluged with water, was destroyed. ⁷ But by the same command the present heavens and earth are stored up for fire and are kept for the day when godless men are to be doomed and destroyed.

⁸ But you must avoid forgetting this one fact, dearly beloved, that with the Lord a single day is like a thousand years and a thousand years are like a single day. ⁹ The Lord is not slow about His promise, in the sense in which some think of slowness, but He is really dealing patiently with you, because He is not willing for any to perish but for all to have an opportunity to repent.ᶜ ¹⁰ The day of the Lord will come like a thief; on that day the heavens will pass away with a roar, the heavenly bodies will be destroyed by being burned up, and the earth with all its works will melt away. ¹¹ If all these things are to be dissolved in this way, what men you ought to be! What holy and pious lives you ought to lead, ¹² since you are awaiting and hastening the coming of the day of God, which will cause the heavens to blaze and dissolve and the heavenly bodies to burn up and melt away! ¹³ In accordance with His promise we are expecting new heavens and a new earth, in which uprightness will have its permanent home.

¹⁴ Therefore, dearly beloved, since you are expecting this, be in earnest to be found by Him without a blot, without reproach, and at peace. ¹⁵ Always think of our Lord's patience as salvation, just as our dearly beloved brother Paul, with the wisdom granted him, wrote you to do, ¹⁶ speaking of it as he does in all his letters. In them are some things hard to understand, which the ignorant and unsteady twist to their ruin, as they do the rest of the Scriptures.

ᵃ Lit., *word.*
ᵇ Pl.; i.e., the earth was formed through His command and through water.
ᶜ Grk., *room for repentance.*

¹⁷ So, dearly beloved, since you have been forewarned, you must always be on your guard against being led astray by the errors of lawless men, and so against falling away from your present firmness; ¹⁸ but instead, you must continue to grow in the spiritual strength and knowledge of our Lord and Saviour Jesus Christ. To Him be glory now and forever!

FIRST JOHN

The author is generally thought to be John the apostle. Some false teachers were teaching in the province of Asia that Jesus was not a real man, that at His baptism a divine element came on Him, making Him the Messiah, but that this element left Him before His death. These teachers, called Docetists, said that Jesus was neither the eternal Son nor a real man. The date was about A. D. 95.

The purpose was to counteract the influence of these teachers. It is said that John would not remain in the public bathhouse with Cerinthus, their leader. On the positive side, he wrote to show that the eternal Son of God was actually made a man in the person of Jesus; to show that the Christian should enjoy personal assurance of his being God's child, and that faith and love, expressing themselves in doing right, obeying God's commands, and in doing good to our suffering fellows, are experimental proofs of such assurance.

1 ETERNAL LIFE HAS BEEN BROUGHT TO US THROUGH JESUS AS A REAL MAN; SINCE GOD IS LIGHT WE ARE TO LIVE PURE LIVES, KEPT SO BY JESUS' BLOOD BUT ARE NOT TO CLAIM TO BE SINLESS

It is what existed from the beginning, what we have heard, what we have seen with our own eyes, what we have beheld, what our own hands have touched, about the very message of life— ² and that life has been unveiled to us, and we have seen it and now testify to it and we now announce it to you, yea, the eternal life that was with the Father and has been unveiled to us. ³ I repeat,[a] it is what we have seen and heard that we now announce to you, so that you too may share this fellowship with us, for [b] this fellowship that we have is with the Father and with His Son Jesus Christ; ⁴ and now we write these things to you to make our joy complete.

⁵ And this is the message that we have heard from Him and now announce to you: God is light, and there is no darkness[c] at all in Him.

[a] Implied.
[b] Aramaic *and,* meaning *for* (context shows).
[c] Light is the symbol of perfect moral character, darkness the symbol of sin.

⁶ If we say "We have fellowship with Him," and yet live in darkness, we are lying and not practicing the truth. ⁷ But if we continue to live in the light, just as He is in the light, we have unbroken ᵈ fellowship with one another, and the blood of Jesus His Son continues ᵈ to cleanse us from every sin. ⁸ If we claim "We are already free from sin," we are deceiving ourselves and the truth is not in our hearts. ᵉ ⁹ If we confess our sins, He is to be depended on, since He is just, to forgive us our sins and to cleanse us from every wrong. ¹⁰ If we claim "We have not sinned," we are making Him a liar, and His message is not in our hearts.

2
TO KEEP HIS COMMANDS GIVES ASSURANCE THAT HE IS OUR SAVIOUR; TO LOVE ONE ANOTHER MEANS TO LIVE IN THE LIGHT; TELLS WHY HE WRITES; WE CANNOT LOVE GOD AND THE WORLD TOO; WARNS AGAINST BACKSLIDING

My dear ᵃ children, I am writing you this so that you may not sin; yet if anyone ever ᵇ sins, we have One who pleads ᶜ our case with the Father, Jesus Christ, One who is righteous. ² And He is Himself the atoning sacrifice for our sins; and not for ours alone, but also for the whole world. ³ By this we can be sure that we know Him—if we practice obedience to His commands. ⁴ Whoever says, "I know Him," but does not practice obedience to His commands is a liar, and there is no truth in his heart; ⁵ but whoever practices obedience to His message really has a perfect love of God in his heart. By this we can be sure that we are in union with Him: ⁶ Whoever claims, "I am always in union with Him," ought to live as He lived.

⁷ Dearly beloved, I am not writing you a new command, but an old one that you have had from the beginning. That old command is the message that you have heard. ⁸ Yet ᵈ it is a new command that I am writing you; it is true in Him and in you, because the darkness is passing away and the true light is already shining.

ᵈ Pres. of cont. ac.
ᵉ Lit., *not in us.*
ᵃ In the diminutive.
ᵇ In aor.
ᶜ Grk., *paraclete, advocate;* our attorney to plead our case.
ᵈ Grk., *again.*

⁹ Whoever claims to be in the light, and yet continues to hate his brother is still in darkness. ¹⁰ Whoever continues to love his brother is always in the light, and he is no hindrance to others. ¹¹ But whoever continues to hate his brother is in darkness and is living in darkness, and he does not know where he is going, because the darkness has blinded his eyes.

¹² I am writing to you, dear children, because for His sake your sins have been forgiven. ¹³ I am writing to you, fathers, because you know Him who has existed from the beginning. I am writing to you, young men, because you have conquered the evil one. I write to you, little children, because you know[e] the Father. ¹⁴ I write to you, fathers, because you know Him who has existed from the beginning. I write to you, young men, because you are strong, and God's message is always in your hearts, and you have conquered the evil one.

¹⁵ Stop loving the world, or the things that are in the world. If anyone persists in loving the world, there is no love for the Father in his heart, ¹⁶ because everything that is in the world, the things that our lower nature and eyes are longing for, and the proud pretensions of life, do not come from the Father, but from the world; ¹⁷ and the world is passing away and with it the evil longings it incites, but whoever perseveres in doing God's will lives on forever.

¹⁸ Little children, it is the last hour, just as you have heard that Antichrist is coming, and already many Antichrists have appeared; so we may be sure that it is the last hour. ¹⁹ They have gone out from our own number, but they did not really belong to us; for if they had, they would have stayed with us. It was to show that none of those who went out really belonged to us. ²⁰ But you have been anointed by the Holy One.[f] You all know the truth; ²¹ I do not write to you because you do not know it, but because you do know it.

²² Who is the notorious[g] liar, if it is not the man[h] who denies that Jesus is the Christ? He is the real Antichrist, the man who disowns the Father and the Son. ²³ No one who disowns the Son can have the Father. Whoever owns the Son has the Father too. ²⁴ Let what you have heard from the beginning continue to live

---

[e] Resultant pf., so equal to pres.
[f] Lit., *the anointing from the Holy One.*
[g] Article in pred. very emph.
[h] Meaning Cerinthus, the leader of the Docetists.

in your hearts; if you do, you will always remain in union with the Son and the Father. ²⁵ And the very thing that He Himself has promised us is eternal life.

²⁶ I write you this with reference to those who are trying to lead you astray. ²⁷ The anointing of the Spirit which you received still remains in your hearts, and so you have no need that anyone should teach you. But just as that anointing of His teaches you about everything, and as it is true and no falsehood, and as it has taught you to do so, you must continue to live in union with Him. ²⁸ And now, dear children, I repeat, you must continue to live in union with Him, so that if He is unveiled, we may have unshaken confidence and not shrink away from Him in shame when He comes. ²⁹ If you know that He is upright, you must know that everyone who practices uprightness is born of Him.

3 GOD'S WONDERFUL LOVE HAS MADE US HIS CHILDREN AND NOW INSPIRES US TO BE PURE, FOR AS SUCH WE CANNOT PRACTICE SINNING; TRUE LOVE A PROOF THAT WE ARE GOD'S CHILDREN; GOD ANSWERS THE PRAYERS OF HIS OBEDIENT CHILDREN

See what wonderful love the Father has bestowed on us in letting us be called God's children, and that is what we are! This is why the world does not know what [a] we are, because it has never come to know Him. ² Dearly beloved, we are now God's children, but what we are going to be has not been unveiled. We know that if it is unveiled, we shall be like Him, because we shall see Him as He is. ³ And everyone who has this hope in him tries to make himself as pure as He is.

⁴ Everyone who commits sin commits lawlessness; sin is lawlessness. ⁵ You know that He appeared [b] to take our [c] sins away, and that there is no sin in Him. ⁶ No one who continues to live in union with Him practices sin. No one who practices sin has ever seen Him or come to know Him. ⁷ Dear children, avoid letting anyone lead you astray. Whoever practices doing right is upright, just as He is upright. ⁸ Whoever practices sin belongs to the devil,

[a] Lit., *know us*.
[b] Same vb. as that translated *unveil* above, but here it refers to the incarnation, Christ becoming human.
[c] Pro. not in Vat. Ms. but implied.

because the devil has practiced sin from the beginning. This is why the Son of God appeared, to undo the devil's works.

⁹ No one who is born of God makes a practice of sinning, because the God-given life-principle ᵈ continues to live in him, and so he cannot practice sinning,ᵉ because he is born of God. ¹⁰ This is the way to distinguish God's children from the devil's children. No one who fails to do right is God's child, and no one who fails to love his brother. ¹¹ It is so because the message that you have heard from the beginning is this: We should love one another. ¹² We must not be like Cain who belonged to the evil one and butchered his brother. And why did he butcher him? Because his own actions were wicked and his brother's upright.

¹³ You must not be surprised, brothers, if the world hates you. ¹⁴ We know that we have passed out of death into life, because we love our brothers. Whoever does not continue to love continues still in death. ¹⁵ Anyone who keeps on hating his brother is a murderer, and you know that no murderer can have eternal life remaining in him.

¹⁶ We know what love is from the fact that He laid down His life for us; and so we ought to lay down our lives for our brothers. ¹⁷ But if anyone has the world's means of supporting life ᶠ and sees his brother in need and closes his heart against him, how can love to God remain in him? ¹⁸ Dear children, let us stop loving with words or lips alone, but let us love with actions and in truth.

¹⁹ In this way we shall know by experience that we are on the side of the truth, and satisfy our consciences ᵍ in God's sight, ²⁰ because if our consciences do condemn us, God is greater than our consciences, and He knows everything. ²¹ Dearly beloved, if our consciences do not condemn us, we come with perfect confidence to God, ²² and we obtain from Him whatever we ask for, because we practice obedience to His commands and do what pleases Him. ²³ His command is this, that we should believe in the name of His Son Jesus Christ and practice loving one another, just as He commanded us to do. ²⁴ Whoever practices obedience to His commands remains in union with Him and He in union with him;

ᵈ Grk., *seed;* so *the life-principle.*
ᵉ Pres. of habitual action. Christians cannot practice sinning, but may sin.
ᶠ Grk. noun has this double meaning.
ᵍ Jno. uses *heart* for *conscience.*

and in this way we know that He remains in union with us, by the Spirit that He has given us.

4 HOW TO DISTINGUISH TRUE TEACHING FROM FALSE; ANOTHER WAY, GOD'S SPIRIT HELPS US TO KNOW THE TRUE; LOVE TO ONE ANOTHER MARKS US AS GOD'S CHILDREN; HIS LOVE TO US INSPIRES US TO TRUST AND LOVE HIM

Dearly beloved, stop believing every so-called spiritual utterance,[a] but keep testing them to see whether they come from God, because many false prophets have gone out into the world. 2 In this way you can recognize the Spirit of God: Every spiritual utterance [a] which owns that Jesus Christ has come in human form comes from God, 3 and no spiritual utterance which disowns Jesus can come from God; it is the utterance of Antichrist. You have heard that it is coming, and right now it is already in the world.

4 You are children of God,[b] dear children, and you have conquered these men, because He who is in our hearts is greater than he who is in the world. 5 They are children of the world; [b] this is why they speak what the world inspires,[c] and why the world listens to them. 6 We are children of God. Whoever knows God by experience listens to us; whoever is not a child of God does not listen to us. This is the way to distinguish a true spiritual utterance from one that is false.

7 Dearly beloved, let us practice loving one another, because love originates with God,[c] and everyone who practices loving is a child of God and knows God by experience. 8 Whoever does not love has never come to know God by experience, because God is love. 9 This is the way God's love for us has been shown, namely, God has sent His only Son into the world that we through Him might have life. 10 In this way is seen the true love, not that we loved God but that He loved us and sent His Son to be the atoning sacrifice for our sins.

11 Dearly beloved, if God has loved us so, we ought to love one another too. 12 No one has ever seen God; yet if we practice loving one another, God remains in union with us, and our love for Him attains perfection in our hearts. 13 By the fact that He has

---

[a] Lit., *every spirit,* but emphasis is on spiritual utterance.
[b] Lit., *out of God*—the world (abl. of source).
[c] Same abl. of source.

given us a portion of His Spirit we can be sure that we remain in union with Him and He in union with us. ¹⁴ We have seen and now testify that the Father has sent His Son to be the Saviour of the world. ¹⁵ Whoever owns that Jesus is the Son of God, God remains in union with him and he in union with God. ¹⁶ So we know by experience and trust the love that God has for [d] us.

God is love, and whoever continues to love continues in union with God and God in union with him. ¹⁷ Our love attains perfection through our having perfect confidence about the day of judgment, because here in this world we are living as He did. ¹⁸ There is no fear in love, and perfect love drives out fear, because fear pertains to punishment, and no one who is subject to fear has attained perfection in love. ¹⁹ We love, because He loved us first. ²⁰ If anyone says, "I love God," and yet habitually hates his brother, he is a liar; for whoever does not love his brother whom he has seen cannot love God whom he has not seen. ²¹ This is the command that we get from Him, that whoever loves God loves his brother too.

5 VICTORIOUS FAITH PROVES THAT WE ARE GOD'S CHILDREN; THREE WITNESSES THAT GOD'S SON CAME IN HUMAN FORM; CERTAIN OF ETERNAL LIFE, OF ANSWERED PRAYER

Everyone who believes that Jesus is the Christ is born of God, and everyone who loves the Father loves His child.[a] ² This is how we can be sure that we love the children of God, by continuing to love God and to obey His commands. ³ For love to God means this, to practice obedience to His commands, and His commands are not burdensome, ⁴ for every child of God continues to conquer the world. Our faith is the victory that has conquered the world. ⁵ Now who is it that continues to conquer the world, if it is not the person who believes that Jesus is the Son of God?

⁶ He is the One who came through water [b] and blood—[c] Jesus Christ; not through water only but through water and blood. The Spirit also testifies to this, because the Spirit is truth.[d] ⁸ Be-

---

[d] Lit., *in us.*
[a] Grk., *whoever loves the Begetter loves the begotten one.*
[b] Refers to His baptism at which the Father expressed His approval.
[c] Means His death.
[d] V. 7 in A. V. not in best Mss.

cause there are three that testify to it, the Spirit, the water, and the blood, and the three agree. [9] If we accept the testimony of men, the testimony of God is stronger still; because this is the testimony that God has borne to His Son. [10] Whoever believes in the Son of God has this testimony in his own heart. Whoever does not believe God has made Him a liar, because he has not believed the testimony that God has borne to His Son. [11] And this testimony is that God has given us eternal life, and this life is given through union with His Son. [12] Whoever has the Son has life; whoever does not have the Son does not have life.

[13] I have written this to you who believe in the person[e] of the Son of God, so that you may know that you already have eternal life. [14] And this is the confidence that we have in Him, that if we ask for anything that is in accordance with His will, He will listen to us. [15] And if we know that He listens to us in whatever we ask Him for, we know that we get from Him the things that we have asked Him for. [16] If anyone sees his brother committing a sin that does not lead[f] to death, he will ask and God[f] will grant him life; yea, He will grant it to any who do not commit a sin that leads to death. There is a sin that leads to death; I do not say that one should pray for that. [17] Any wrongdoing is sin; and there are sins that do not lead to death.

[18] We know that no one who is born of God makes a practice of sinning, but the Son[f] who was born of God continues to keep him, and the evil one cannot touch him. [19] We know that we are children of God, and that the whole world is under the power of the evil one. [20] And we know that the Son of God has come, and has given us insight to recognize the True One; and we are in union with the True One through His Son, Jesus Christ. He is the true God and eternal life.

[21] Dear children, once for all put yourselves beyond the reach[g] of idols.

[e] Lit., *name;* in sense of *person.*
[f] Implied.
[g] In aor.

SECOND JOHN

Most scholars hold that the same John wrote this letter. The same false teaching furnished the occasion for writing it. So the purpose was to commend this faithful woman and her children for their loyalty to the truth and to warn them against the false teaching. Date, about A.D. 96.

> HE GREETS THEM; REJOICES IN THEIR LOYALTY BUT
> WARNS THEM AGAINST THE FALSE TEACHERS; SHOWS
> THE NEED OF SUCH LOYALTY TO THE TRUTH;
> COULD TALK ABOUT MUCH MORE

The Elder to the chosen lady and her children, whom I truly love, and not only I but all who know the truth, because of the truth that lives on in our hearts and will be with us forever: 3 spiritual blessing, mercy, and peace will be with us from God the Father and Jesus Christ, the Father's Son, in truth and love.

4 I am happy to find that some of your children are living by the truth, just as we had been commanded from the Father to do. 5 And now I beg you, my lady, not as though I were writing you a new command, but one which we had from the beginning, that we continue to love one another. 6 Now love means this, that we keep on living in accordance with His commands. The command is this, that we continue to live in love. 7 For many impostors have gone out into the world, men who do not own that Jesus Christ continues[a] to come in human form. A person like this is the impostor and the Antichrist. 8 Look out for yourselves, so as not to lose what we have worked for, but so as to get your full reward. 9 No one has God, who goes too far and fails to stay by the teaching of Christ. Whoever stays by this teaching has the Father and the Son. 10 If anyone continuously comes to see you without bringing this teaching, you must stop welcoming him to your house and

[a] Refers to Christ's showing Himself to believers in continuing experience.

stop bidding him good morning. ¹¹ For whoever keeps on bidding him good morning is sharing in his wicked works.

¹² Though I have much to write you, I do not choose to do so with paper and ink, but I hope to come to see you and talk with you face to face, so that your happiness may be complete. ¹³ The children of your chosen sister wish to be remembered to you.

THIRD JOHN

The same John wrote it. Gaius, a faithful member in his church, was hospitable to some traveling missionaries, but ambitious Diotrephes mistreated them. He wrote to commend Gaius and condemn Diotrephes. Date, A.D. 96.

HE GREETS AND COMMENDS GAIUS; REMINDS THE CHURCH OF DIOTREPHES' AMBITIONS; TELLS OF DEMETRIUS' GOOD REPUTATION; CONCLUDES

The Elder to the dearly beloved Gaius, whom I truly love.

2 Dearly beloved, I am praying for you to continue to prosper in everything, and to keep well, just as your soul is prospering. 3 For I am happy to have some brothers come and testify to the truth that is in you, since you are living by the truth. 4 I have no greater spiritual blessing than this, to hear that my children are living by the truth.

5 Dearly beloved, you are acting faithfully in doing what you can for the brothers, especially as they are strangers. 6 They have testified before the church to your love. You will please [a] send them off on their journey in a way befitting the service of God. 7 For they [b] have started out for His name's sake and so accept nothing from the heathen. 8 So we ought to show hospitality to such men, to prove that we co-operate with them for the truth.

9 I have written briefly to the church, but Diotrephes, who likes to be first among them, refuses to listen to me. 10 So, if I come, I will remind you of what he is doing, how with malicious insinuations [c] he is talking about me. Not content with that, he refuses to welcome the brothers himself, he interferes with those who want to do so, and tries to put them out of the church.

[a] So in papyri.
[b] The traveling missionaries.
[c] Lit., with *wicked words*.

¹¹ Dearly beloved, do not follow bad examples but good ones. Whoever practices doing right is God's child; whoever practices doing wrong has never seen God. ¹² Demetrius has a good testimony from everybody and from truth itself; yea, from me too, and you know that my testimony to him is true.

¹³ I have much to say to you, but I do not want to write it with pen and ink. ¹⁴ I hope to see you very soon and will talk it over face to face. Good-by. Our friends wish to be remembered to you. Remember me to our friends individually.

JUDE

The writer is usually held to be Jude, a half brother of Jesus. The occasion was similar to that calling forth Second Peter—false teachings that were threatening to undermine "the faith once for all entrusted to God's people." Date, about A.D. 70. The letter was written to warn them against these false teachings and to stand firm for the true teaching.

HE GREETS THEM; HE URGES THEM TO DEFEND THE TEACHING OF THE APOSTLES; GIVES EXAMPLES OF JUDGMENT ON THE GODLESS; DESCRIBES THE DISGRACEFUL LIVES OF THE FALSE TEACHERS; TELLS HOW TO LIVE WITH SUCH MEN

Jude, a slave of Jesus Christ, and a brother of James, to those who have been called, who are beloved by God the Father [a] and have been kept through union with Jesus Christ: ² may mercy, peace, and love in abundance be given you.

³ Dearly beloved, while I was doing my best to begin writing [b] you about our common salvation, I found it necessary to write and urge you to carry on [b] a vigorous defense of the faith that was once for all entrusted to God's people. ⁴ For certain persons have sneaked in—their doom was written down long ago—godless persons, who turn the favor of our God into an excuse for licentiousness, and disown our only Master and Lord, Jesus Christ.

⁵ Now I want to remind you, though you know it all already, that although the Lord had saved a people out of the land of Egypt, He afterward destroyed those who did not believe. ⁶ And angels, who did not preserve their original rank but left their proper home, He has kept in everlasting chains under darkness, for the day of judgment, ⁷ just as Sodom and Gomorrah and the neighboring towns which like them indulged in grossest immoral-

[a] Fol. WH.
[b] Pres. infin.

ity ᵉ and **unnatural vice,** stand as a perpetual warning, in suffering the punishment of eternal fire.

⁸ In just the same way these dreamers defile the body, discard authority, and deride the majesties. ⁹ But the archangel Michael himself, when he disputed and argued with the devil about Moses' body, did not dare to bring against him a charge of blasphemy, but merely said, "May the Lord rebuke you!" ¹⁰ But these persons abuse everything they do not understand, and they are going to be destroyed by the very things they know by instinct,ᵈ like the irrational animals. ¹¹ Alas for them, because they have trod the road that Cain did; for gain they have rushed into Balaam's error and have perished in rebellion ᵉ like that of Korah! ¹² They are blots on your love feasts while they feast with you, daringly caring for no one but themselves; rainless clouds swept along by winds; leafless trees that bear no fruit, doubly dead, uprooted; ¹³ wild waves of the sea foaming up their own shame; wandering stars that are forever doomed to utter darkness.

¹⁴ It was about such men also that Enoch, the seventh generation from Adam, prophesied when he said: "See! The Lord comes with myriads of His people ¹⁵ to execute judgment upon all, to convict all the godless of their godless deeds which in their godlessness they have committed, and of all the harsh things that godless sinners have said against Him."

¹⁶ These persons are grumblers, ever complaining about their lot. They live to satisfy their evil passions, their lips boast arrogant things, and they flatter others for personal gain.

¹⁷ But you, dearly beloved, must remember the words that have already been spoken by the apostles of our Lord Jesus Christ, ¹⁸ because they said to you, "In the last times there will be mockers who will live to satisfy their own godless passions." ¹⁹ These are men who cause divisions; mere animals, destitute of any spiritual nature.ᶠ

²⁰ But you, dearly beloved, must continue to build yourselves up on the groundwork ᵍ of your most holy faith and to pray in the Holy Spirit; ²¹ you must keep yourselves in the love of God and continue to wait for the mercy of our Lord Jesus Christ, to

---

ᶜ Comp. pt., lit., *out-fornicated,* indulged in grossest sexual sins.
ᵈ Lit., *by the very things they know physically.*
ᵉ Grk. word means, first, *contradiction,* then, *rebellion.*
ᶠ Lit., *psychical* (in animal sense), not having a spirit.
ᵍ Lit., *build on your most holy faith.*

JUDE

bring you to eternal life. ²² Some people, who continue to waver through doubts, you must pity ²³ and save, snatching them out of the fire; and others you must pity with dread, loathing even the clothes that are soiled by their lower nature.

²⁴ Now to Him who is able to keep you from stumbling and to make you stand in His glorious presence faultless and full [h] of triumphant joy, ²⁵ to the only God our Saviour, through Jesus Christ our Lord, be glory, majesty, might, and authority, as it was before all time, both now and forever and ever. Amen.

[h] Grk. has *in triumphant joy.*

THE REVELATION

The author calls himself the seer, who is generally thought to be John the apostle. The Christians in the province of Asia were being persecuted for refusing to worship the Roman Emperor's statue, which was erected in the leading cities. To be loyal to Jesus they had to refuse to do so. John himself as leader of the Christians was banished to Patmos where he had these visions.

He wrote them down and sent them to the seven churches to encourage suffering Christians with the assurance that Christianity will surely triumph over all evil and all its opponents; that good at last will surely win over evil; that the wicked will be punished by God, and the upright who follow the Lamb and suffer for Him will be welcomed into the New Jerusalem above to be happy forever.

1 WHAT THE BOOK IS; THE WRITER; HE GREETS THE SEVEN CHURCHES; PRAISES THE LAMB WHO LOOSED US FROM SIN; WHERE AND HOW THE MESSAGE CAME; HAS A VISION OF THE GLORIFIED REDEEMER WHO SPEAKS TO ENCOURAGE

A revelation given by Jesus Christ which God gave to Him, to make known to His slaves what must very soon take place. He sent and communicated it through His angel to His slave John, 2 who testifies to what he saw, the message of God and the testimony of Jesus Christ. 3 Blessed be the man who reads [a] them and the people who hear the messages of this prophecy read, and heed what is written in it, for the time is near.

4 John to the seven churches in Asia: spiritual blessing and peace to you from Him who is and was and is to come, and from the seven spirits that are before His throne, 5 and from Jesus Christ the trustworthy witness, the First-born of the dead, and the Sovereign of the kings of the earth. To Him who ever [b] loves us and once [b] for all released us from our sins by His blood, 6 and has made us a kingdom of priests for His God and Father: to Him be glory forever. Amen. 7 See! He is coming on the clouds, and

---

[a] I.e., to the congregations of Christians.
[b] Both words in the tenses, former in pres., latter in aor.

every eye will see Him, even the men who pierced Him, and all the tribes of the earth will lament over Him. Even so. Amen.

⁸ "I am the Alpha and the Omega," says the Lord God, who is and was and is to come, the Almighty.

⁹ I, John, your brother and companion with you in the trouble, the kingdom, and the patient endurance which Jesus gives, found myself on the island called Patmos, for preaching ᵉ God's message and testifying to Jesus. ¹⁰ On the Lord's day I was in the Spirit's power,ᵈ and I heard a voice like a trumpet behind me say:

¹¹ "Write what you see in a book and send it to the seven churches, to Ephesus, Smyrna, Pergamum, Thyatira, Sardis, Philadelphia, and Laodicea."

¹² I turned to see who it was that was speaking to me, and as I turned I saw seven golden lampstands, ¹³ and among the lampstands One resembling the Son of Man, wearing a robe that reached to His feet, and with a belt of gold around His breast. ¹⁴ His head and hair were as white as white wool, as white as snow. His eyes were like coals of fire; ¹⁵ His feet were like bronze refined to white heat in a furnace, and His voice was like the roar ᵉ of many waters. ¹⁶ In His right hand He was holding seven stars, and a sharp, double-edged sword was coming out of His mouth, and His face was shining like the sun at midday. ¹⁷ So ᶠ when I saw Him, I fell at His feet like a dead man. But He laid His right hand upon me and said: "Do not be afraid any more. I am the First and the Last; ¹⁸ yea, the ever-living One. I once was dead, but now I live forever and ever. I carry the keys of death and the underworld.ᵍ ¹⁹ So write what you have seen, what is and what is to take place hereafter. ²⁰ The open secret of the seven stars that you have seen in my right hand, and of the seven golden lampstands, is this: The seven stars are the messengers of the seven churches, and the seven lampstands are the seven churches.

2   THE LETTERS TO THE CHURCHES AT EPHESUS, SMYRNA, PERGAMUM, AND THYATIRA

"To the messenger of the church in Ephesus write:

" 'The One who is holding the seven stars in His right hand and

---

ᵉ Lit., *because of God's message;* i.e., for preaching it.
ᵈ Grk., *in the Spirit.*
ᵉ Lit., *sound.*
ᶠ Ara. *and* of result.
ᵍ *Hades,* the underworld.

is walking among the golden lampstands speaks as follows: ² "I know what you have done; ᵃ your hard work and patient endurance; that you cannot tolerate wicked persons; that you have tested those who claimed to be apostles although they were not, and have found them to be impostors.ᵇ ³ You are showing patient endurance, and you have borne it for my sake, and have not grown weary. ⁴ But I hold it against you that you do not love me as you did at first. ⁵ So remember the heights from which you have fallen, and repent and do as you did at first, or else I will surely come and move your lampstand from its place—if you do not repent. ⁶ But you have it to your credit ᶜ that you hate what the Nicolaitans are doing, as I do too. ⁷ Let everyone who has ears listen to what the Spirit says to the churches. I will give to him who conquers the privilege ᶜ of eating the fruit of the tree of life that stands in the paradise of God." '

⁸ "To the messenger of the church in Smyrna write:

" 'The First and the Last, who once was dead but came to life again, speaks as follows: ⁹ "I know your pressing trouble and poverty, but still you are rich; I know how you are abused by those who claim to be Jews although they are not, but are only a synagogue of Satan.ᵈ ¹⁰ Do not be so afraid of what you are to suffer. See! The devil is going to throw some of you into prison to be tested there and for ten ᵉ days to suffer pressing troubles. Each one of you must prove to be faithful, even if you have to die, and I will give you the crown of life. ¹¹ Let everyone who has ears listen to what the Spirit says to the churches. Whoever conquers will not be hurt at all by the second death." '

¹² "To the messenger of the church in Pergamum write:

" 'The One who is wielding the sharp, double-edged sword speaks as follows: ¹³ "I know where you live, where Satan has his throne. Yet you are clinging to my name and have never renounced your faith in me, even in the days of Antipas, my faithful martyred witness, who was put to death among you, right where Satan lives. ¹⁴ Yet I hold it somewhat against you that you have among you some who are clinging to the teaching of Balaam, who

---

ᵃ Grk., *your works.*
ᵇ Lit., *false.*
ᶜ Implied.
ᵈ See art. Syn. of Satan, Int. St. Bib. Encyc.
ᵉ Symbol of a short time.

taught Balak to set a trap for the children of Israel, to entice ᵉ them to eat the meat that had been sacrificed to idols and to commit immoral practices. ¹⁵ And you also have among you some who are clinging to the teaching of the Nicolaitans. ¹⁶ So repent, or else I will quickly come and make war upon them with the sword that comes from my mouth. ¹⁷ Let everyone who has ears listen to what the Spirit says to the churches. I will give to him who conquers some of the hidden manna, and I will give him a white stone with a new name ᶠ written on it which no one knows except the man who receives it."'

¹⁸ "To the messenger of the church in Thyatira write:

"'The Son of God, whose eyes are like coals of fire, and whose feet are like bronze refined to white heat, speaks as follows: ¹⁹ "I know what you are doing, I know your love and faithfulness, your service and patient endurance, and I know that you are now working harder than you did at first. ²⁰ But I hold it against you that you are tolerating that Jezebel of a woman who claims to be a prophetess, and by her teaching is misleading ᵍ my slaves to practice immorality and to eat meat that has been sacrificed to idols. ²¹ I have given her time to repent, but she refuses to repent of her immorality. ²² See! I am going to lay her on a bed of sickness,ᵉ and bring down to great and pressing sorrow those who practice immorality with her, unless they repent of their ʰ practices; ²³ and I will surely strike her children dead. So all the churches will know that I am He who searches men's inmost hearts,ⁱ and that I will repay each of you for exactly what you have done. ²⁴ But to the rest of you at Thyatira, who do not hold this teaching and have not learned the 'deep things' of Satan—as they speak of them—to you I say, I have no extra burden to lay on you, ²⁵ but keep your hold on what you have until I come. ²⁶ To him who conquers and continues to the very end to do the works that please me, I will give authority over the heathen; ²⁷ he will govern them with a scepter of iron and shatter them like earthen jars—just such authority as I have received from my Father—²⁸ and I will give him the morning star. ²⁹ Let everyone who has ears listen to what the Spirit says to the churches."'

ᶠ Sign of divine approval and protection.
ᵍ Lit., *is teaching and misleading*.
ʰ Fol. marginal reading of WH.
ⁱ Lit., *reins and hearts*.

3 THE LETTERS TO THE CHURCHES AT SARDIS, PHILADELPHIA, AND LAODICEA

"To the messenger of the church at Sardis write: " 'The One who holds the seven spirits of God and the seven stars speaks as follows: "I know what you are doing; you have the reputation of being alive, but in reality [a] you are dead. 2 Wake up, and strengthen what is left, although it is on the very point of dying, for I have not found a thing that you have done complete in the sight of God. 3 So remember what you have received and heard, and continue to obey it, and repent. If you do not wake up, I will come like a thief, and you will never know the hour when I come upon you. 4 Yet you have in Sardis a few who have not soiled their clothes. They will walk with me in white, for they deserve to do so. 5 Whoever conquers will be clothed this way—in white [b] clothes—and I will never blot his name out of the book of life, but I will own him as mine [c] in the presence of my Father and His angels. 6 Let everyone who has ears listen to what the Spirit says to the churches." '

7 "To the messenger of the church in Philadelphia write: " 'The Holy and True One, who carries the keys of David, who opens and no one can [a] shut, who shuts and no one can [a] open, speaks as follows: 8 "I know what you are doing. See! I have put before you an open door that no one can shut. I know [a] that you have but little strength, and yet you have obeyed my message and you have not disowned my name. 9 I will make some, who claim to be Jews although they are not, but are lying—I will make them come and fall at your feet and find out [d] that I have loved you. 10 Because you have kept my message with the patient endurance that I give you, I also will keep you from the time of testing that is about to come upon the whole world, to test the inhabitants of the earth. 11 I am coming soon. Hold on to what you have, so that no one may take away your crown. 12 I will make him who conquers a pillar in the temple of my God, and he shall never again go out of it. I will write on him the name of my God and the name of the city of my God, the new Jerusalem, which is coming down out

---

[a] Implied.
[b] Symbol of purity and perfection.
[c] Grk., *will confess his name*.
[d] Lit., *come to know* (aor.).

of heaven from my God, and my own name. [13] Let everyone who has ears listen to what the Spirit says to the churches." '

[14] "To the messenger of the church in Laodicea write:

" 'The Amen, the true and faithful witness, the origin [e] of God's creation, speaks as follows: [15] "I know what you are doing, and that you are neither cold nor hot. I wish you were cold or hot. [16] As it is, because you are lukewarm and neither hot nor cold, I am going to vomit you out of my mouth. [17] Because you say, 'I am rich, I have already become rich, I need nothing,' and you do not know that you are the very one that is wretched, pitiable, poor, blind, and naked; [18] I advise you to buy of me gold that has been refined in the fire, so that you may become rich, and white clothes to put on, to hide your shameful nakedness, and salve to put on your eyes, to make you see. [19] The people whom I dearly love,[f] I always reprove and discipline. So keep on being earnest and once for all repent. [20] I am now standing at the door and knocking. If anyone listens to my voice and opens the door, I will be his guest and feast with him, and he with me. [21] I will give to him who conquers the privilege [a] of taking his seat with me on my throne, just as I have conquered and taken my seat with my Father on His throne. [22] Let everyone who has ears listen to what the Spirit says to the churches." ' "

4   HE SEES THE MAJESTY OF GOD; THE SPLENDOR AROUND THE THRONE; THE MAJESTY OF GOD HIMSELF

After this I had another vision: A door was standing open in heaven, and the first voice, like a trumpet, that I had heard speaking with me, said, "Come up here, and I will show you what must take place."

[2] Immediately I was under the Spirit's power, and I saw [a] a throne in heaven with One seated on it. [3] The One who was seated on it looked like [b] jasper or sardius, and around the throne there was a rainbow that looked like [b] an emerald. [4] Around the throne there were twenty-four thrones, with twenty-four elders seated on them, clothed in white and with crowns of gold on their heads.

[e] Grk., *beginning*, but in philosophical sense, so *origin*.
[f] *Phileo, to love dearly, tenderly.*
[a] Grk., *I saw, and see!*
[b] Lit., *in appearance like.*

⁵ Out from the throne came flashes of lightning, rumblings ᶜ and peals of thunder, while in front of it seven flaming lamps were burning; they were the seven spirits of God. ⁶ Also in front of the throne there was something like a sea of glass as clear as crystal. Around the throne, at the middle of each side were four living creatures dotted with eyes in front and behind. ⁷ The first living creature was like a lion, the second was like an ox, the third had a face like a man's, and the fourth ᵈ was like an eagle flying. ⁸ And the four living creatures have each of them six wings, and they are dotted with eyes all around and beneath the wings. And day and night they never cease saying:

"Holy, holy, holy is the Lord God, the Almighty, who was and is and is to come."

⁹ And whenever the living creatures offer glory, honor, and thanksgiving to Him who is seated on the throne, to Him who lives forever and ever, ¹⁰ the twenty-four elders fall down before Him who is seated on the throne, and worship Him who lives forever and ever, and they throw their crowns in front of the throne, and say:

¹¹ "You are worthy, our Lord and God,
To have ascribed to you the glory, honor, and power;
For you created everything,
And since you willed it so, they came into existence ᵉ and were created."

5 HE SEES THE BOOK OF THE FUTURE; NONE COULD OPEN IT BUT THE LION OF JUDAH; SEES THE LAMB OF GOD, AND THOUSANDS, ANGELS AND OTHERS, PRAISING HIM

Then I saw in the right hand of Him who was seated on the throne a book with writing on both sides,ᵃ sealed with seven seals.

² And I saw a mighty angel announcing in a loud voice, "Who deserves to open the book and break its seals?" ³ But no one in heaven or on earth or underneath the earth could open the book or look into it. ⁴ Then I began to weep bitterly because no one could be found deserving to open the book or look into it.

ᶜ *Voices, noises, rumblings.*
ᵈ In Grk., noun is repeated each time.
ᵉ *Because of His will,* etc.
ᵃ Lit., *within and without* (behind).

⁵ But one of the elders said to me, "Stop weeping! See! The Lion who sprang from the tribe of Judah, who belongs ᵇ to the line of David, has conquered, so that He can open the book and break ᶜ its seven seals."

⁶ Then I saw, midway between the throne and the four living creatures, standing among the elders, a Lamb that looked as though He had been slaughtered. He had seven horns and seven eyes; the latter are the seven spirits of God which are sent on duty ᶜ to every portion of the earth. ⁷ He came and took the book from the right hand of Him who was seated on the throne. ⁸ When He took it, the four living creatures and the twenty-four elders fell down before the Lamb, each with a harp, and golden bowls that were full of incense, which represent ᵈ the prayers of God's people.

⁹ Then they sang a new song: "You deserve to take the book and break its seals, because you have been slaughtered, and with your blood have bought men from every tribe, tongue, people, and nation, ¹⁰ and have made them a kingdom of priests ᵉ for our God; and they will rule over the earth."

¹¹ Then I looked and heard the voices of many angels surrounding the throne, the living creatures, and the elders. Their number was myriads of myriads and thousands of thousands, ¹² saying in a loud voice:

"The Lamb that was slaughtered deserves to receive power, riches, wisdom, might, honor, glory, and blessing." ¹³ Then I heard every creature in heaven, on earth, underneath the earth, and on the sea, and all that they contain, say:

"Blessing, honor, glory, and power be to Him who is seated on the throne and to the Lamb forever."

¹⁴ Then the four living creatures said, "Amen!" And the elders fell down and worshiped.

6 THE FIRST, SECOND, THIRD, FOURTH, FIFTH, AND SIXTH SEALS BROKEN

And when the Lamb broke the first of the seven seals, I looked and heard one of the four living creatures say with a voice like thunder, "Come!"

ᵇ Grk., *the root of David.*
ᶜ Implied.
ᵈ Grk., *are.*
ᵉ Lit., *a kingdom and priests* (but one idea in two words).

² Then I looked, and a white horse appeared,[a] and his rider[b] was carrying a bow. A crown was given to him, and he rode forth conquering and to conquer.

³ When He broke the second seal, I heard the second living creature say, "Come!"

⁴ And another horse came forth, as red as fire, and power was given to its rider to take peace away from the earth, and to make men slaughter one another; a great sword was given to him.

⁵ When He broke the third seal, I heard the third living creature say, "Come!"

I looked, and a black horse appeared, and its rider was carrying a pair of scales in his hands, ⁶ and I heard what seemed to be a voice from the midst of the four living creatures say:

"Wheat fifty cents a quart, barley fifty cents for three quarts! [c] But you must not injure the oil and wine."

⁷ When He broke the fourth seal, I heard the voice of the fourth living creature say, "Come!"

⁸ I looked, and a pale horse appeared, and its rider's name was Death, and Hades[d] followed him. Power was given to them over one quarter of the earth, to kill the people with sword, famine, death,[e] and the wild animals of the earth.

⁹ When He broke the fifth seal, I saw underneath the altar the souls of those who had been slaughtered for being faithful to God's message and for the testimony they bore to it. ¹⁰ Then in a loud voice they cried out, "Holy and true Master, how long will you refrain from charging and avenging our blood upon the inhabitants of the earth?"

¹¹ Then a white robe was given to each of them, and they were told to keep quiet a little while longer, until the number of their fellow-slaves and brothers, who were killed as they had been, was complete.

¹² When He broke the sixth seal, I looked, and there was a great earthquake, and the sun turned black as sackcloth, and the full moon became like blood, ¹³ and the stars of the sky fell to the earth, just as a fig tree, when shaken by a violent wind, drops its unripe figs. ¹⁴ The sky was swept away just like a scroll that is rolled up; and every mountain and island was moved out of its place. ¹⁵ The

---

[a] *I looked, and see! a white h.*
[b] *He who was seated*, etc.
[c] Exorbitant famine prices.
[d] The underworld which receives all the dead.
[e] Hebrew, *pestilence*.

kings of the earth, the great men, the military leaders, the rich, the mighty—everybody, whether slaves or free—hid themselves in the caves and among the rocks of the mountains. 16 And they said to the mountains and the rocks:

"Fall on us and conceal us from the sight of Him who is seated on the throne, and from the anger of the Lamb, 17 because the great day of their anger has come, and who can stand it?"

7 GOD'S PEOPLE PRESERVED IN DISASTERS; THOUGH HAVING TO SUFFER, SAVED THROUGH THE LAMB; A COUNTLESS THRONG BEFORE THE THRONE

After this I saw four angels standing at the four corners of the earth holding back the four winds of the earth, so that no wind should blow on the earth, the sea, or any tree. 2 Then I saw another angel coming up from the east with the seal of the living God, and he cried out to the four angels who had the power to injure the earth and the sea:

3 "Do not injure the earth, the sea, or the trees, until we mark the slaves of our God with His seal on their foreheads." 4 And I heard the number of those who were marked with the seal, one hundred and forty-four thousand. Those that were marked with the seal were from every tribe of the children of Israel: 5 twelve thousand from the tribe of Judah; twelve thousand from the tribe of Reuben; twelve thousand from the tribe of Gad; 6 twelve thousand from the tribe of Asher; twelve thousand from the tribe of Naphtali; twelve thousand from the tribe of Manasseh; 7 twelve thousand from the tribe of Simeon; twelve thousand from the tribe of Levi; twelve thousand from the tribe of Issachar; 8 twelve thousand from the tribe of Zebulon; twelve thousand from the tribe of Joseph; twelve thousand from the tribe of Benjamin.[a]

9 After this I looked, and there was a vast throng that no one could count from every nation, tribe, people, and tongue, standing before the throne and before the Lamb, clothed in white robes, with palm branches in their hands, 10 and they cried in a loud voice:

"Our salvation is due to our God, who is seated on the throne, and to the Lamb." 11 Then all the angels stood around the throne, the elders, and the four living creatures, and fell on their faces before the throne and worshiped God, 12 saying:

[a] Vb. repeated after *Judah* and *Benjamin*.

"Amen! Blessing, glory, wisdom, thanksgiving, honor, power, and strength be to our God forever and ever. Amen!"

13 Then one of the elders addressed [b] me and said, "Who are these people clothed in white robes, and where did they come from?"

14 I answered him, "You know, my lord."

He said to me: "These are the people who are coming through the great persecution,[c] who have washed their robes and made them white in the blood of the Lamb. 15 This is why they are before the throne of God, and day and night serve Him in His temple, and He who is seated on His throne will shelter them in His tent.[d] 16 They will never again be hungry or thirsty, and never again will the sun strike them, or any scorching heat, 17 because the Lamb who is in the center of the throne will be their Shepherd, and God will wipe every tear from their eyes."

8 THE SEVENTH SEAL IS BROKEN; THE PRAYERS OF GOD'S PEOPLE REPRESENTED BY RISING INCENSE, THE PUNISHMENT OF THEIR ENEMIES BY THE FLINGING OF FIRE TO THE EARTH; FOUR TRUMPETS ARE BLOWN TO SHOW GOD'S CURSES

When He broke the seventh seal, there was silence in heaven for about half an hour. 2 Then I saw the seven angels who stand before God, and seven trumpets were given to them. 3 Then another angel with a censer of gold came and stood at the altar, and a great quantity of incense was given to him to mingle with the prayers of all God's people, on the altar of gold that stood before the throne. 4 So the smoke of the incense went up from the angel's hand to the presence of God for the prayers of His people. 5 Then the angel took the censer, filled it with fire from the altar, and flung it to the earth, and there followed peals of thunder with its rumblings, flashes of lightning, and an earthquake. 6 And the seven angels with the seven trumpets prepared to blow them.

7 The first one blew his trumpet, and there was a shower [a] of hail and fire mixed with blood as it hurled itself upon the earth,

---
[b] Grk., *answered me.*
[c] Lit., *out of the great distress*—the persecution under Domitian.
[d] Lit., *tabernacle over them.*
[a] Implied in vb.

and one-third of the earth was burned up, and all the green grass was burned up.

⁸ Then the second angel blew his trumpet, and what seemed to be a great mountain all ablaze with fire hurled itself into the sea, and one-third of the sea was turned into blood, ⁹ and one-third of all the living creatures in the sea perished, and one-third of the ships were destroyed.

¹⁰ Then the third angel blew his trumpet, and there fell from the sky a great star blazing like a torch, and it fell upon one-third of the rivers and the springs of water. ¹¹ The star is called Absinthus, that is, Wormwood. So one-third of the waters turned to wormwood, and great numbers [b] of people died of the waters, because they had turned bitter.

¹² Then the fourth angel blew his trumpet, and one-third of the sun was cursed with a plague,[c] and one-third of the moon, and one-third of the stars, so that one-third of them were darkened, and there was no light [d] for one-third of the day and for one-third of the night.

¹³ Then I looked, and I heard an eagle flying in mid-air say in a loud voice, "Alas! Alas! Alas for the inhabitants of the earth because of the remaining blasts of the three angels who are going to blow their trumpets!"

9 THE FIFTH TRUMPET IS BLOWN, AND MONSTROUS LOCUSTS TORTURE MANKIND; THE SIXTH IS BLOWN, AND NUMBERLESS HORSEMEN RIDE FORTH TO KILL

Then the fifth angel blew his trumpet, and I saw a star that had fallen from the sky upon the earth. To this angel [a] the key to the pit of the abyss was given, ² and he opened the pit of the abyss, and smoke like the smoke of a huge furnace puffed up out of the pit, and the sun and the air were darkened by the smoke from the pit. ³ Out of the smoke came locusts upon the earth, but the power that was given to them was like the power of earthly scorpions. ⁴ They were told not to injure the grass of the earth or any plant

---

[b] Lit., *many*.
[c] Grk., *was plagued*.
[d] Lit., *day did not appear*.
[a] In Grk., *to him* (the angel).

or tree, but only the people who did not have the mark of God's seal on their foreheads. 5 They were not permitted to kill them, but only to torture them for five months, and the torture they inflicted was like the torture of a scorpion when it stings a man. 6 In those days people will look for death but will not find it, they will long to die but death will flee from them. 7 The locusts look like horses armed for battle; on their heads were what appeared to be crowns of gold; their faces were like human faces; 8 they had hair that looked like women's hair; their teeth were like lions' teeth; 9 they had breastplates that seemed to be made of steel; the noise of their wings was like the noise of vast numbers of chariots and horses rushing into battle; 10 they had tails like scorpions with stings in them, so in their tails their power lay to injure men for five months. 11 They had over them as king the angel of the abyss; in Hebrew he is called Abaddon, in Greek, Apollyon.[b]

12 The first woe is past. See! Two other woes are yet to come.

13 Then the sixth angel blew his trumpet, and I heard a voice from the corners of the altar of gold that was before God 14 say to the sixth angel who had the trumpet:

"Turn loose the four angels that are bound at the river Euphrates." 15 Then the four angels that were kept in readiness for that hour and day and month and year were turned loose to kill one-third of mankind. 16 The number of the armies of the horsemen was two hundred million;[c] I heard their number. 17 In my vision the horses and the horsemen[d] looked like this: Their breastplates were red, blue, and yellow; the horses' heads were like lions' heads, and fire, smoke, and sulphur kept pouring out of their mouths. 18 One-third of mankind was killed by these three plagues: the fire, smoke, and sulphur that kept pouring out of their mouths. 19 For the power of the horses lay in their mouths and their tails; their tails were like snakes, and they had heads with which they injured people. 20 But the rest of mankind, who were not killed by these plagues, did not repent of the works their hands had done, so as to give up worshiping demons and idols of gold, silver, bronze, stone, and wood, which cannot either see or hear or move; 21 and they never did repent of their murders, their practices in magic, their immorality, or their thefts.

[b] Both names mean, *the Destroyer.*
[c] Lit., *twice ten thousand times ten thousand.*
[d] Lit., *the horses and their riders.*

10 THE MIGHTY ANGEL AND THE SEVEN PEALS OF THUNDER; GOD'S PURPOSES SOON TO BE ACCOMPLISHED; THE SEER THEN EATS THE ANGEL'S LITTLE BOOK

Then I saw another mighty angel coming down from heaven. He was clothed in a cloud, with a rainbow over his head; his face was like the sun, his legs were like pillars of fire, 2 and he had a little book open in his hand. He set his right foot on the sea and his left foot on the land, 3 and in a loud voice he shouted like the roaring of a lion; and when he had shouted, the seven thunders rumbled.[a] 4 When the seven thunders had rumbled, I was going to write it down, but I heard a voice from heaven say:

"Seal up what the seven thunders have said, and do not write it down!"

5 Then the angel, whom I had seen standing on the sea and on the land, raised his right hand to heaven, 6 and swore by Him who lives forever and ever, who created the heavens and all that they contain, the earth and all that it contains, and the sea and all that it contains, that there should be no more delay, 7 but in the days when the seventh angel speaks,[b] when he is about to blow his trumpet, then God's mysterious message,[c] in accordance with the good news He gave to His slaves, the prophets, would be accomplished.

8 Then the voice that I heard from heaven spoke to me again, and said, "Go and take the little book that is open in the hand of the angel who is standing on the sea and on the land."

9 So I went up to the angel and asked him to give me the little book. And he said to me, "Take it and eat it; it will make your stomach bitter, but in your mouth it will taste as sweet as honey." 10 So I took the little book from the angel's hand and ate it all,[d] and in my mouth it did taste as sweet as honey, but when I had eaten it all, it made my stomach bitter.[e]

11 Then they said to me, "You must prophesy again about many peoples, nations, languages, and kings."

[a] Lit., *uttered their voices.*
[b] Grk., *days of the seventh angel's voice.*
[c] Grk., *mystery,* but *message* implied.
[d] In comp. vb.
[e] Grk. has passive—*my stomach was made bitter.*

11 HE MEASURES THE TEMPLE—A SIGN OF HOW GOD TAKES CARE OF HIS OWN; THE TWO WITNESSES ARE VESTED WITH PECULIAR POWER BUT FINALLY ARE MURDERED AND ASCEND TO HEAVEN; THE SEVENTH TRUMPET IS BLOWN

Then a measuring rod like a staff was given to me, and I was told:

"Rise and measure the temple of God and the altar, counting those who worship there, [2] but leave off the court outside [a] the temple; do not measure it, because it has been given over to the heathen, and for forty-two months they will trample the city under foot. [3] And I will permit my two witnesses, clothed in sackcloth, to prophesy for one thousand, two hundred and sixty days." [b]

[4] They are the two olive trees and the two lampstands that stand before the Lord of the earth. [5] If anyone wants to injure them, fire comes out of their mouths and consumes their enemies; if anyone wants to injure them, he must himself be killed in that way. [6] They have the power to shut up the sky, so that no rain will fall upon the earth as long as they prophesy, and they have power over the waters to turn them into blood, and to smite the earth with any plague as often as they please. [7] Then, when they have finished testifying, the wild beast that is coming up out of the abyss will make war on them and conquer them and kill them, [8] and their lifeless bodies will lie on the streets of the great city that is figuratively [c] called Sodom and Egypt, where their Lord also was crucified. [9] For three days and a half men of all peoples, tribes, languages, and nations will look upon their lifeless bodies, and will not let them be buried. [10] The inhabitants of the earth will gloat [d] over them and celebrate with feasts and the sending of gifts to one another, because these two prophets had tormented the inhabitants of the earth.

[11] After three days and a half the breath of life from God came into them again, and they stood on their feet, and consternation seized those who saw them.

[12] And they heard a loud voice from heaven say to them, "Come

---

[a] Portion occupied by the heathen.
[b] Corresponding with the forty-two months above.
[c] That is, *spiritually*.
[d] Grk., *rejoice*, but very emph.

up here." And they went up to heaven in a cloud, and their enemies looked on as spectators. ¹³ At that very hour there was a great earthquake, and one-tenth of the city went down. Seven thousand people were killed in the earthquake, and the rest were stricken with awe, and gave glory to the God of heaven.

¹⁴ The second woe is past. See! The third woe is soon to come.

¹⁵ Then the seventh angel blew his trumpet, and loud voices were heard in heaven, saying, "The sovereignty of the world has come into the possession of our Lord* and His Christ, and He will reign forever and ever."

¹⁶ Then the twenty-four elders who were seated on their thrones before God fell on their faces and worshiped God, ¹⁷ saying: "We give you thanks, Lord God Almighty, who are and were, because you have assumed your great power and begun to reign. ¹⁸ The heathen were enraged, but now your anger has come, and the time for the dead to be judged, and for you to reward your slaves the prophets and your people, great and small, who revere your name, and to destroy the destroyers of the earth."

¹⁹ Then the doors of God's temple in heaven were thrown open, and inside the temple was seen the chest containing God's covenant, and there followed flashes of lightning, rumblings, peals of thunder, an earthquake and heavy hail.

12   HE SEES THE SEVEN SYMBOLS: THE SUN-CLAD WOMAN; THE DRAGON WHO IS HURLED DOWN TO EARTH; CHRIST TRIUMPHS THOUGH THE DRAGON PERSECUTES THE WOMAN

Then a great symbol was seen in heaven—a woman clothed in the sun with the moon under her feet, and on her head a crown of twelve stars. ² She was about to become a mother, and she cried out in anguish in giving birth to a child.

³ Another symbol was seen in heaven—there was a huge dragon, red as fire, with seven heads and ten horns, with seven diadems on his heads. ⁴ His tail was dragging after it a third part of the stars of heaven and dashed them down upon the earth. The dragon stood in front of the woman who was about to give birth to a child, in order to devour her child as soon as it was born. ⁵ She gave birth to a son, a male child who is going to rule all the

---

* Lit., *the kingdom of the world became*, etc.

nations with a scepter of iron; and the child was caught up to God, to His throne. ⁶ Then the woman fled into the desert, where she had a place of safety made ready by God, so that she might be cared ᵃ for one thousand, two hundred and sixty days.

⁷ Then war broke out in heaven: Michael and his angels going to war with the dragon. The dragon and his angels fought, ⁸ but they were defeated,ᵇ and there was no room for them in heaven any longer. ⁹ So the huge dragon, the ancient serpent, called the devil and Satan, who deceives the whole world, was hurled down to the earth, and his angels were hurled down with him.

¹⁰ Then I heard a loud voice in heaven say:

"The salvation, power, and kingdom of our God, and the sovereignty of His Christ, have already come, because the accuser of our brothers, who always day and night accuses them before our God, has been hurled down. ¹¹ But they have conquered him because of the blood of the Lamb and because of the message to which they bore testimony, because they did not cling to life but courted death.ᶜ ¹² So celebrate your triumph, you heavens and you who live in them! Alas for the earth and the sea, because the devil has come down to you in a great rage, since he knows that his time is short!"

¹³ When the dragon saw that he had been hurled down to the earth, he started persecuting the woman who had given birth to the male child. ¹⁴ But the two wings of a great eagle were given to the woman, so that she could fly to her place in the desert, where she could be taken care of for a time, times, and a half-time,ᵈ safe from the presence of the serpent. ¹⁵ Then the serpent made water, like a river, spout from his mouth after the woman, to sweep her away with its torrent. ¹⁶ But the earth helped the woman, for it opened its mouth and swallowed the river which the dragon made to spout from his mouth. ¹⁷ So the dragon was enraged against the woman, and he went off to make war with the rest of her descendants, who continue to keep God's commands and to bear testimony to Jesus.

ᵃ Grk. has active; passive better in Eng.
ᵇ Lit., *did not conquer.*
ᶜ Lit., *did not love their life until death.*
ᵈ Same as the forty-two months and 1,260 days above.

13 HE SEES OTHER SYMBOLS: THE FIRST WILD BEAST; CERTAIN RETRIBUTION FOR THE PERSECUTORS; THE SECOND WILD BEAST

Then I stood on the sand of the seashore, and I saw a wild beast coming up out of the sea with ten horns and seven heads, with ten diadems on his horns, and blasphemous titles on his heads. 2 The wild beast which I saw was like a leopard, but his feet were like a bear's, and his mouth was like a lion's mouth. To him the dragon gave his own power and throne with great authority. 3 I saw [a] that one of his heads seemed to have been mortally wounded, but its mortal wound had been healed.

And the whole world was so amazed that they followed the wild beast, 4 and worshiped the dragon for giving the wild beast his authority; they also worshiped the wild beast, and said, "Who is there like the wild beast? Who is there to make war on him?"

5 Then there was given to the wild beast a mouth that uttered boastful, blasphemous words, and permission to wield his authority for forty-two months. 6 Then he opened his mouth to blaspheme against God, His name, and His dwelling place; that is, against those who live in heaven. 7 Permission was given to him to make war on God's people and to conquer them; authority was given to him over every tribe, people, language, and nation. 8 All the inhabitants of the earth whose names, from the foundation of the world, have not been written in the slaughtered Lamb's book of life, will worship him.[b]

9 If anyone has ears let him listen. 10 Whoever leads others [a] into captivity will go into captivity himself. Whoever kills with the sword must be killed with the sword himself. In this way will be shown [a] the patient endurance and the fidelity of God's people.

11 Then I saw another wild beast [c] coming up out of the land. He had two horns like a lamb, but he spoke like a dragon. 12 He exercises the full authority of the first wild beast in his presence; he makes the earth and its inhabitants worship the first wild beast, whose mortal wound had been healed. 13 He performs great wonders; even makes fire come down out of heaven to earth before men's eyes. 14 He leads the inhabitants of the earth astray because of the wonders he is permitted to perform in the presence of the

[a] Implied.
[b] That is, the emperor or Rom. government.
[c] Symbol of Rom. religion.

wild beast, telling the inhabitants of the earth to erect a statue [d] to the wild beast that bears the sword-thrust and yet has lived. 15 Permission has also been given him to impart life to the statue of the wild beast so that it can speak, and to have all who do not worship the statue of the wild beast killed. 16 And he makes all, great and small, rich and poor, freemen and slaves, have a mark stamped on their right hands or on their foreheads, 17 and he permits no one to buy or sell anything unless he bears the mark; that is, the name of the wild beast or the number that represents [e] the name.

18 Here is scope for wisdom! Let anyone who has the mental keenness calculate the number of the wild beast, for it is the number of a certain man; his number is six hundred and sixty-six.

14 HE HEARS THE NEW SONG THE REDEEMED ARE SINGING; HEARS FOUR ANGELS SPEAK; SEES THE JUDGMENT SICKLE IN THE HAND OF THE SON OF MAN

Then I looked, and there the Lamb was standing on Mount Zion, and with Him one hundred and forty-four thousand people who had His name and the name of His Father written on their foreheads. 2 And I heard a sound from heaven like the roar of great waters and the rumbling of loud thunders. The sound that I heard was like that of harpists playing on their harps. 3 They were singing a new song before the throne, the four living creatures, and the elders, and no one could learn the song except the hundred and forty-four thousand who had been redeemed from the earth. 4 These are the men who have not been defiled by relations with women, for they are as pure as virgins.[a] These are the men who follow the Lamb wherever He goes. These have been redeemed from among men as the first fruits for God and the Lamb, 5 and they have never been known to tell a lie with their lips; [b] they are blameless.

6 Then I saw another angel flying in mid-air, with eternal good news to tell to the inhabitants of the earth, to every nation, tribe, language, and people.

7 He cried in a loud voice, "Fear God and give Him glory,

---

[d] Lit., *make an image.*
[e] Referring to the ancient custom of letting numbers represent names.
[a] Lit., *they are virgins* (metaphor).
[b] Grk., *in their mouth a lie was never found.*

THE REVELATION 14

because the hour of His judgment has come. Worship Him who made heaven and earth and sea and the springs of water."

⁸ Then a second angel followed, saying: "She has fallen! Mighty Babylon has fallen, who made all the nations drink the wine of vengeance due her immorality!" ᶜ

⁹ Then a third angel followed them, saying in a loud voice: "Whoever worships the wild beast and his statue and lets his mark be stamped on his forehead or on his hand, ¹⁰ himself will have to drink the wine of God's vengeance,ᵈ poured unmixed into the cup of His wrath,ᵈ and be tortured with fire and brimstone before the eyes of the holy angels and the Lamb. ¹¹ The smoke of their torture will go up forever and ever, and they will have no rest day or night—those who worship the wild beast and his statue, and anyone who bears the mark of his name." ¹² In this way is shown the patient endurance of God's people, who always cling to God's commands and their faith in Jesus.

¹³ Then I heard a voice from heaven say, "Write, 'Blessed are the dead who from this time die as Christians.' " ᵉ

"Yes," says the Spirit, "let them rest from their toils, for the things they have done are going with them." ᶠ

¹⁴ Then I looked, and there was a bright cloud with one seated on it like the Son of man, with a crown of gold on His head and a sharp sickle in His hand.

¹⁵ Then another angel came out of the temple and cried in a loud voice to Him who was seated on the cloud, "Put forth your sickle and reap, for the time to reap has come, because the earth's harvest is ripe." ¹⁶ So He who was seated on the cloud swung His sickle over the earth, and the earth was reaped.

¹⁷ Then another angel came out of the temple in heaven, and he too had a sharp sickle. ¹⁸ And another angel came from the altar, who had power over the fire, and he called in a loud voice to him who had the sharp sickle, "Put forth your sharp sickle, and gather the bunches of grapes from the earth's vine, because its grapes are fully ripe."

¹⁹ So the angel swung his sickle over the earth and gathered the grapes of the earth's vine, and flung them into the wine press of

---

ᶜ Subj. gen.
ᵈ Former word means *the furious outburst*. Latter, *God's fixed anger*.
ᵉ Lit., *die in the Lord*.
ᶠ In increasing their reward.

God's wrath. ²⁰ The grapes in the wine press were trodden outside the city, and blood streamed from the wine press until it reached the horses' bridles for a distance of two hundred miles.

15 HE SEES SEVEN ANGELS BRINGING SEVEN PLAGUES; HEARS THE REDEEMED SING A SONG OF TRIUMPH; THE PLAGUES ARE SENT FROM HEAVEN

Then I saw another symbol in heaven, great and wonderful: seven angels bringing seven plagues which are to be the last, because with them God's wrath is completely expressed.

² Then I saw something that looked like a sea of glass mixed with fire, and standing upon the sea of glass were those who had conquered the wild beast, his statue, and the number representing his name; and they had harps that God had given them. ³ And they were singing the song of Moses, the slave of God, and the song of the Lamb:

"Great and wonderful are your works,
Lord God, Almighty One;
Upright and true your ways,
O King of the ages.
⁴ Who will not fear and glorify your name, O Lord?
For you alone are holy.
All the nations will come and worship you,
Because the justice of your sentences has now been shown." [a]

⁵ After this I looked, and the sanctuary of the tent of testimony [b] was thrown open in heaven, ⁶ and the seven angels bringing the seven plagues came out of the sanctuary. They were clothed in clean, brilliant linen and had belts of gold around their breasts. ⁷ Then one of the four living creatures gave the seven angels seven bowls of gold, full of the wrath of God who lives for ever and ever, ⁸ and the sanctuary was filled with smoke from the glory and power of God, and no one could go into the sanctuary until the seven plagues of the seven angels were at an end.

[a] Lit., *your just judgments have been manifested.*
[b] *The inner temple,* so *sanctuary;* but John blends with it the idea of the early tabernacle (tent of testimony). God approves the plagues.

16 HE SEES THE SEVEN PLAGUES TAKE PLACE: MEN AFFLICTED WITH SORES, SEA TURNED INTO BLOOD, WATERS TOO, SUN SCORCHING MEN, THRONE OF THE WILD BEAST CURSED, EUPHRATES DRIED UP, AND FOUL SPIRITS SEIZE KINGS; THUNDERS, EARTHQUAKES, CURSES

Then I heard a loud voice from the sanctuary say to the seven angels:

"Go and empty [a] the seven bowls of God's wrath upon the earth."

2 So the first angel went and emptied his bowl upon the earth, and horrible, painful [b] sores broke out on the men who bore the mark of the wild beast and worshiped his statue.

3 Then the second angel emptied his bowl into the sea, and it turned into blood like a dead man's, and every living thing that was in the sea died.

4 Then the third angel emptied his bowl into the rivers and the springs of water, and they turned into blood.

5 Then I heard the angel of the waters say: "You are just in passing such a sentence, you who are and were, you the Holy One. 6 Because they have shed the blood of your people and prophets, you have given them blood to drink; they deserve it."

7 And I heard the altar say, "Yes, Lord God Almighty! Your sentences are true and just."

8 Then the fourth angel emptied his bowl upon the sun, and permission was given it to scorch mankind with its fiery heat,[c] 9 so that men were severely scorched, but they only cursed the name of God who had authority over these plagues, and would not repent and give Him glory.

10 Then the fifth angel emptied his bowl upon the throne of the wild beast, and his kingdom was shrouded in darkness, and men in agony gnawed their tongues, 11 and cursed the God of heaven because of their sufferings and sores, but they would not repent of what they had done.

12 Then the sixth angel emptied his bowl upon the great river Euphrates, and its waters were dried up to prepare the way for the kings from the east. 13 Then I saw three foul spirits leap [d] like

---

[a] Lit., *pour out.*
[b] Grk., *bad, evil.*
[c] Lit., *fire.*
[d] Implied.

frogs from the mouth of the dragon, from the mouth of the wild beast, and from the mouth of the false prophet.ᵉ ¹⁴ They are the spirits of demons that perform wonders, and they go forth to the kings of the whole world, to muster them for battle on the great day of the Almighty God. ¹⁵ (See! I am coming like a thief! Blessed is he who stays awake and keeps his clothes ready, so that he may not go naked and people see his shame.) ¹⁶ So they mustered the kings at the place called in Hebrew, Armageddon.

¹⁷ Then the seventh angel emptied his bowl into the air, and a loud voice came out of the sanctuary from the throne, saying, "It is done."

¹⁸ Then there were flashes of lightning, rumblings, and peals of thunder; then there was a great earthquake, an earthquake so great that none like it had ever been since man first existed on the earth. ¹⁹ The great cityᶠ was broken into three parts; the cities of the heathen fell, and God remembered to give mighty Babylon the cup of the wine of His raging wrath. ²⁰ Every island vanished; not a mountain could be seen; ²¹ huge hailstones as heavy as talents fell on men from heaven, and men cursed God for the plague of hail, because the torture of it was severe.

17   HE SEES A WOMAN IN PURPLE AND SCARLET;ᵃ HE HEARS WHAT THE SYMBOL OF THE WOMAN MEANS

Then one of the seven angels with the seven bowls came and spoke to me, saying: "Come, I will show you the doom of the noted prostitute who is seated on many waters, ² in whose prostitution the kings of the earth have joined, and with the wine of whose prostitution the inhabitants of the earth have been intoxicated."

³ So he carried me away in spiritual rapture to a desert, and I saw a woman seated on a scarlet wild beast, covered with blasphemous titles; he had seven heads and ten horns. ⁴ The woman was dressed in purple and scarlet, decorated in gold and precious stones and pearls, and she had in her hand a cup of gold, full of abominations and the impurities of her immorality. ⁵ On her forehead was written a name with a symbolical meaning,ᵇ "Mighty

---

ᵉ That is, one spirit from the mouth of each.
ᶠ Jerusalem.
ᵃ Purple means royalty, scarlet immorality.
ᵇ Lit., *mystery*.

Babylon,[c] the mother of prostitutes and of earth's abominations." [6] I saw the woman drinking herself drunk with the blood of God's people and the blood of the martyred witnesses to Jesus.

When I saw her I was utterly astonished, [7] but the angel said to me: "Why are you astonished? I will tell you the symbolical meaning of the woman, and the wild beast with seven heads and ten horns, that carries her. [8] The wild beast that you saw, once was but now is no more; he is going to come up out of the abyss, but he is going to be destroyed. The inhabitants of the earth, whose names from the foundation of the world have not been written in the book of life, will be astonished when they see that the wild beast once was but now is no more, and yet is to come. [9] Here is scope for a mind that is packed [d] with wisdom. The seven heads are the seven hills on which the woman is seated. [10] There are also seven kings; five have fallen, one is on the throne,[e] the other has not yet come, and when he does he must stay but a little while. [11] So it is with the wild beast that once was but is no more; he is the eighth, and yet is one of the seven, and he is going to be destroyed. [12] The ten horns that you saw are ten kings, who have not yet become kings, but for a single hour they accept authority as kings allied with the wild beast. [13] They have one common policy. They give their power and authority to the wild beast. [14] They will make war upon the Lamb, but the Lamb will conquer them, and His chosen, elect, and faithful followers will conquer [f] with Him, too, because He is Lord of lords and King of kings."

[15] He also said to me: "The waters that you saw, on which the prostitute was seated, are peoples, multitudes, nations, and languages. [16] The ten horns that you saw and the wild beast will be the very ones [g] to hate the prostitute, to make her desolate and naked, to eat up her flesh, and burn her up with fire. [17] For God has put it into their hearts to carry out His purpose by giving up their authority [h] to the wild beast until God's words are carried out. [18] And the woman whom you saw is the great city [e] that has dominion over the kings of the earth."

[c] Rome is meant.
[d] Lit., *Here is the mind that has wisdom.*
[e] Last phrase implied.
[f] So this vb.
[g] Expressed in emph. pro., *these.*
[h] Lit., *kingdom.*

18 HE HEARS THAT MIGHTY BABYLON (ROME) HAS FALLEN; FRIENDS IN GRIEF, GOD'S PEOPLE ESCAPE, HEAVEN REJOICES; A HURLED STONE SYMBOLIZES HER COMPLETE RUIN

After this I saw another angel coming down from heaven. He had great authority and the earth was lighted up with his splendor. ² He shouted with a mighty voice: "She has fallen! Mighty Babylon has fallen! She has become a den ᵃ for demons, a dungeon ᵇ for every foul spirit and every unclean and loathsome bird, ³ because all the nations have fallen by drinking ᶜ the raging wine of her immorality; the kings of the earth have joined her in her immorality, and the businessmen of the earth have grown rich from the wealth ᵈ of her luxury."

⁴ Then I heard another voice from heaven say:

"Come out of her, my people, so that you may not share in her sins and suffer from her plagues. ⁵ For her sins are piled clear up to heaven, and God has remembered the wrongs which she has done. ⁶ Pay her back in her own coin; give her double for what she has done. In the cup that she has mixed, mix twice as much for her. ⁷ To the same degree in which she has lived in splendor and luxury, give her torture and tears. Because she is always boasting in her heart, 'I sit enthroned as queen; I am not a widow, I shall never experience any sorrow'—⁸ for this very reason her plagues will overtake her in a single day, death, grief, and famine, and she will be burned up with fire; because the Lord who has judged her is mighty. ⁹ The kings of the earth who have joined her in her immorality and luxury will weep and lament over her when they see the smoke from her burning. ¹⁰ They will stand a long way off for fear of her torture, saying, 'Alas! alas for the great city, for Babylon the mighty city, because in a single day your judgment has overtaken you!' ¹¹ The businessmen of the earth will weep and mourn over her, because no one can buy their cargoes any more—¹² cargoes of gold, silver, precious stones, fine linen, silk, and scarlet, all kinds of citron wood, all kinds of goods in ivory and costly woods, bronze, iron, and marble, ¹³ cinnamon, spices, **incense**, perfume.

ᵃ Lit., *dwelling place.*
ᵇ Grk., *a prison.*
ᶜ Implied.
ᵈ Lit., *power.*

frankincense, wine, oil, fine flour, wheat, cattle, sheep, horses, carriages, slaves, and the lives of human beings. ¹⁴ The ripe fruit of your soul's desire has gone from you, all your luxury and splendor have perished from your hands, and people will never find them again. ¹⁵ The businessmen who dealt in these things, who had grown rich from their business with her, will stand a long way off for fear of her torture, weeping and mourning, ¹⁶ and saying, 'Alas! alas for the great city that was dressed in fine linen, purple, and scarlet, that was decorated in gold, precious stones, and pearls, ¹⁷ because in a single hour a wealth so vast has been destroyed!' All ship pilots and all who travel by sea, sailors and seafaring men, stood a long way off ¹⁸ and cried out when they saw the smoke from her burning, 'What city was like the great city?' ¹⁹ They threw dust on their heads and wept and mourned, crying out, 'Alas! alas for the great city where all who had ships on the sea grew rich from her great wealth! For in a single hour she has been destroyed.' ²⁰ Celebrate over her, O heaven, you saints, apostles, and prophets too, because God has taken vengeance on her for you."

²¹ Then a mighty angel picked up a stone like a huge millstone and hurled it into the sea, saying: "With violence like this, Babylon the great city will be hurled to ruin, and it will never be found again. ²² The sound of harpists, musicians, flute-players, and trumpeters will never be heard in you again. No craftsmen of any kind will ever be found in you again, and the sound of the grinding mill will never be heard in you again; ²³ the light of the lamp will never shine in you again; the voice of bride and bridegroom will never be heard in you again. For your businessmen were the great men of the earth; by your magic all the nations have been led astray; ²⁴ in her* has been found the blood of prophets, saints, and all who have been slaughtered on the earth."

19   HE HEARS ALL HEAVEN PRAISING THE LORD THAT THE KINGDOM AND FEAST OF THE LORD HAS COME; SEES JESUS RIDING A WHITE HORSE AS KING OF KINGS AND LORD OF LORDS; SEES HIS FOES UTTERLY DESTROYED

After this I heard something like the loud shout of a great multitude in heaven, saying:

* Sudden turn of person from second to third, but it means mighty Rome.

"Praise the Lord! Salvation, glory, and power belong to our God, ² because His judgments are true and just. Because He has passed judgment on the notorious [a] prostitute who corrupted the earth with her immorality,[b] and for the blood of His slaves He has taken vengeance upon her!"

³ A second time they shouted, "Praise the Lord! For [c] the smoke from her continues to go up forever and ever."

⁴ Then the twenty-four elders and the four living creatures fell down and worshiped God who was seated on the throne, saying, "Amen! Praise the Lord!"

⁵ And there came a voice from the throne, saying, "Praise our God, all you slaves of His who fear Him, great and small."

⁶ Then I heard something like the shout of a great multitude and the roar of many waters and the peal of mighty thunders, saying:

"Praise the Lord! For the Lord, our Almighty God, has now begun to reign! ⁷ Let us be glad and shout for joy and give Him glory, because the marriage of the Lamb has come, and His bride has made herself ready. ⁸ Permission has been granted her to dress in clean, brilliant linen, for linen signifies the upright deeds of God's people."

⁹ Then he said to me, "Write, 'Blessed are they who are invited to the marriage supper of the Lamb.' These," he said to me, "are the true words of God."

¹⁰ Then I fell before his feet to worship him, but he said to me, "You must take care not to do [d] that. I am only a fellow-slave of yours and of your brothers who hold to the testimony borne by Jesus. Worship God. For the testimony borne by Jesus is the inspiring [d] spirit of prophecy."

¹¹ Then I saw heaven thrown open and a white horse appeared. His rider was called Faithful and True, and in justice He passes judgment and wages war. ¹² His eyes were like coals of fire. On His head were many diadems, and on Him a name was written which no one knew but Himself. ¹³ He wore a garment dipped in blood, and His name was the Word of God. ¹⁴ The armies of heaven, wearing pure white linen, followed Him on white horses. ¹⁵ From His mouth shot a sharp sword, so that He could smite

[a] In the art.
[b] Lit., *fornication.*
[c] An Ara. *and* used in sense of *for.*
[d] Implied.

the nations with it. He will rule them with a scepter of iron, and will tread the wine press of the raging wrath of the Almighty God. [16] On His garment and on His thigh He has this title written: King of kings and Lord of lords.

[17] Then I saw an angel standing on the sun, and in a loud voice shouting to all the birds that fly in mid-air: "Come! Gather for God's great banquet, [18] to feast on the flesh of kings, generals,[e] heroes,[e] of horses and their riders; yes, the flesh of all men, freemen and slaves, great and small."

[19] Then I saw the wild beast, the kings of the earth, and their armies gather to go to war with the Rider of the horse and His army. [20] Then the wild beast was captured and with him the false prophet who performed wonders in his presence, by which he led astray those who let the mark of the wild beast be put on them and worshiped his statue. Both of them were hurled alive into the fiery lake that burns with brimstone. [21] The rest were killed with the sword that shot from the mouth of the horse's Rider, and all the birds were gorged with their flesh.

20 THE DEVIL IS PUT INTO PRISON; THE MARTYRS ARE ENTHRONED IN A NEW LIFE; THEN THE DEVIL IS LET LOOSE A LITTLE WHILE; THE RESURRECTION AND THE JUDGMENT

Then I saw an angel coming down from heaven with the key of the abyss and a great chain in his hand. [2] He seized the dragon, the ancient serpent, who is the devil and Satan, and bound him for a thousand years. [3] Then he hurled him into the abyss, closed it, and sealed it over him, to keep him from leading the nations astray any more, until the thousand years are at an end; after that he must be let loose a little while.

[4] Then I saw thrones and those who were seated on them, and permission was granted them to pass judgment, even those who had been beheaded for bearing testimony to Jesus and for preaching the word of God, who refused [a] to worship the wild beast and his statue, and would not let his mark be stamped upon their foreheads and upon their hands. They lived and reigned with Christ a thousand years. [5] The rest of the dead did not live again [b]

---

[e] *Chiliarchs* (leaders of thousands), *great men.*
[a] *Did not worship*—refused to.
[b] Implied in the idea of resurrection.

until the thousand years had ended. This is the first resurrection.
⁶ Blessed and holy is the man who shares in the first resurrection! Over such the second death will have no power, but they will be priests of God and Christ, and reign with Him the thousand years.

⁷ When the thousand years have ended, Satan will be let loose from his prison. ⁸ He will go forth to lead astray the nations that are in the four corners of the earth, Gog and Magog, and to muster them for battle, and their number will be like the sands of the seashore. ⁹ They came up on the broad plain of the earth and surrounded the camp of God's people, and the beloved city. Then fire came down from heaven and consumed them. ¹⁰ Then the devil who led them astray was hurled into the fiery lake of burning brimstone, where the wild beast and false prophet were, and there they are to be tortured day and night forever and ever.

¹¹ Then I saw a great white throne and Him who was seated on it, from whose presence earth and sky fled away, no more to be found.ᶜ ¹² I saw the dead, great and small, standing before the throne, and books were opened. Then another book was opened; it was the book of life. And the dead were judged by what was written in the books in accordance with what they had done. ¹³ The sea gave up the dead that were in it, and death and the underworldᵈ gave up the dead that were in them, and they were all judged in accordance with what they had done. ¹⁴ Then death and the underworld were hurled into the fiery lake. This is the second death—the fiery lake. ¹⁵ If anyone's name was not found written in the book of life, he was hurled into the fiery lake.

21 HE SEES THE NEW JERUSALEM; THE EARTH BECOMES A NEW CREATION; THE SPLENDORS OF THE NEW JERUSALEM, ITS PRECIOUS STONES, ITS SANCTUARY, ITS SUN

Then I saw a new heaven and a new earth, for the first heaven and the first earth had passed away, and there was no longer any sea. ² And I saw the new Jerusalem, the holy city, coming down out of heaven from God, made ready like a bride to join her husband.

³ Then I heard a loud voice from the throne say: "See! God's

ᶜ Lit., *a place was not found for them.*
ᵈ *Hades,* the unseen world where all the dead are.

dwelling place is with men, and He will live with them, ⁴ and He will wipe every tear from their eyes. There will be no death any longer, no sorrow, no crying, no pain. The first order[a] of things has passed away."

⁵ Then He who was seated on the throne said, "See! I am making everything new." He continued, "Write this, for these words are trustworthy and true." ⁶ He further said to me: "They have come true. I am the Alpha and the Omega, the beginning and the end. I myself, without cost, will give to anyone who is thirsty water from the springs of living water. ⁷ Whoever conquers will come into possession of these things, and I will be his God and he will be my son. ⁸ But the cowards, the unfaithful, the polluted, the murderers, the sexually immoral, the practicers of magic, the worshipers of idols, and all liars will have their portion in the lake that keeps on burning with fire and brimstone. This is the second death."

⁹ Then one of the seven angels who had the seven bowls that were full of the seven plagues came and talked with me, and said, "Come; I will show you the bride, the wife of the Lamb."

¹⁰ So he carried me off under the power of the Spirit to a great, high mountain and showed me Jerusalem, the holy city, coming down out of heaven from God; ¹¹ and it continued to retain the glory of God. The luster of it was like a very precious stone, like jasper, clear as crystal. ¹² It had a great, high wall, with twelve huge gates, and twelve angels in charge of the gates, which had inscribed upon them the names of the twelve tribes of Israel. ¹³ There were three gates on the east, three gates on the north, three gates on the south, and three gates on the west. ¹⁴ The wall of the city had twelve foundation stones, and on them were the twelve names of the Lamb's twelve apostles. ¹⁵ The angel who was talking with me had a measuring rod of gold, to measure the city, its gates and wall. ¹⁶ The city lies in a square, its length the same as its breadth. He measured the city with his rod, and it was one thousand, five hundred miles.[b] Its length, breadth, and height were the same. ¹⁷ He measured its wall, two hundred and sixteen feet as a man measures, which is the way the angel measured.[c]

¹⁸ The material of its wall was jasper, but the city itself was pure

---

[a] Lit., *the first things*—order implied.
[b] *12,000 stadia* equal 1,500 miles.
[c] Lit., *the measure of a man—the measure of an angel.*

gold, as transparent as glass. ¹⁹ The foundation stones of the city's wall were ornamented with all sorts of precious stones. The first foundation stone was jasper, the second sapphire, the third chalcedony, the fourth emerald, ²⁰ the fifth sardonyx, the sixth sardius, the seventh chrysolite, the eighth beryl, the ninth topaz, the tenth chrysoprase, the eleventh jacinth, the twelfth amethyst. ²¹ The twelve gates were twelve pearls, each gate built of a single pearl. The Broadway ᵈ of the city was pure gold, as transparent as glass.

²² I saw no temple in it, for the Lord God Almighty Himself and the Lamb Himself are its temple.ᵉ ²³ The city does not need the sun or moon to shine in it, for the glory of God has lighted it, and the Lamb is its lamp. ²⁴ The nations will walk by its light; the kings of the earth will bring their splendor into it. ²⁵ Its gates will never be closed by day—for there will be no night there—²⁶ and they will bring the splendor and honor of the nations into it. ²⁷ Nothing unclean will ever enter it, nor anyone who practices abominable living and lying, but only those who are written in the Lamb's book of life.

22 HE SEES THE RIVER OF LIFE AND THE TREE OF LIFE; IS ASSURED THAT WHAT HE SEES WILL CERTAINLY COME TO PASS; THE LORD IS COMING SOON; HE MAKES A LAST, LOVING INVITATION; THAT BOOK NOT TO BE TAMPERED WITH

Then he showed me a river of living water, clear as crystal, which continued to flow from the throne of God and of the Lamb ² down the middle of the city's Broadway. On both sides of the river grew ᵃ the tree of life, which bore twelve kinds of fruit, yielding a different kind each month, and its leaves contained the remedy to cure the nations. ³ No longer will there be anything that has a curse on it. The throne of God and of the Lamb will be in the city, and His slaves will worship Him. ⁴ They will see His face, and His name will be on their foreheads. ⁵ There will be no night any longer; so they will need no lamplight nor sunlight, for the Lord God will give them light, and they will rule forever and ever.

⁶Then he said to me: "These words are trustworthy and true;

ᵈ Exact meaning of Grk. word.
ᵉ Everywhere is God's presence; so everywhere is opportunity to worship.
ᵃ Implied.

the Lord, the God of the spirits of the prophets, sent His angel to show His slaves what must soon take place. ⁷ See! I am coming soon! Blessed is he who practices the truths ᵇ of prophecy contained in this book."

⁸ It is I, John, who heard and saw these things. When I heard and saw them, I fell at the feet of the angel who was showing them to me, to worship him. ⁹ But he said to me:

"You must be careful not to do that; I am only a fellow-slave of yours, of your brothers the prophets, and of the people who practice the truths contained in this book. Worship God."

¹⁰ Then he said to me: "Do not seal up the words of prophecy contained in this book, for the time of their coming true is near. ¹¹ Let the person who is doing evil do evil still; let the filthy person be filthy still; let the upright person still do right; let the consecrated person still be consecrated.

¹² "See! I am coming soon, and my rewards ᶜ are with me, to repay each one just as his work has been. ¹³ I am the Alpha and the Omega, the first and the last, the beginning and the end. ¹⁴ Blessed are those who wash their robes, so as to have a right to the tree of life and to enter the gates of the city. ¹⁵ The dogs, that is,ᵃ those who practice magic and immorality, murderers, idolaters, and who love and practice lying, are on the outside.

¹⁶ "I, Jesus, sent my angel to bear this testimony to you for the churches. I belong to the line and family of David; I am the bright morning star."

¹⁷ The Spirit and the bride ᵈ say, "Come." Let everyone who hears this say, "Come." Let everyone who is thirsty come. Let everyone who wishes come and take the living water without any cost.

¹⁸ I warn everyone who hears the words of prophecy contained in this book that if anyone adds anything to it, God will add to him the plagues that are described in this book; ¹⁹ and if anyone subtracts from it some of the words of this prophetic book, God will subtract from him his share in the tree of life and the holy city which are described in this book.

²⁰ He who testifies to this says, "Yes, I am coming soon!" Amen! Come, Lord Jesus!

²¹ The spiritual blessing of the Lord Jesus ᵉ be with His people.ᵉ

ᵇ Lit., *who keeps the words,* etc.
ᶜ Pl. implied in context.
ᵈ The church, or Christians individually.
ᵉ Fol. WH.